KEY INDICATORS
FOR ASIA AND THE PACIFIC
2022
53RD EDITION

ADB

ASIAN DEVELOPMENT BANK

6 ADB Avenue, Mandaluyong City, 1550 Metro Manila, Philippines
Tel +63 2 8632 4444; Fax +63 2 8636 2444
www.adb.org

ISBN 978-92-9269-698-6 (print); 978-92-9269-699-3 (electronic); 978-92-9269-700-6 (ebook)
ISSN 0116-3000
Publication Stock No. FLS220346-3
DOI: http://dx.doi.org/10.22617/FLS220346-3

Corrigenda to ADB publications may be found at http://www.adb.org/publications/corrigenda.

Notes:
In this publication, "$" refers to US dollars.
ADB recognizes "Hong Kong" as Hong Kong, China; "China" as the People's Republic of China;
"Korea" as the Republic of Korea; and "East Timor" as Timor-Leste.
Photos: All photos by the Asian Development Bank unless otherwise indicated.

Cover design by Rhommell Rico.

Contents

Tables

Boxes

Sustainable Development Goals Tables

PART II: Regional Trends and Tables

Figures

Table

People

Globalization

Transport and Communication

Energy and Electricity

Environment

Government and Governance

PART III: Global Value Chains

Figures

Tables

PART IV: Harnessing Administrative Data for a More Resilient Data and Statistical System

Table

Figures

Definitions

Foreword

Key Indicators for Asia and the Pacific, now in its 53rd year, remains at the forefront of statistical knowledge for the region. This annual flagship statistical report of the Asian Development Bank serves as a vital source of data for policymakers, government officials, development professionals, researchers, and students around the world.

Almost 3 years after the emergence of the coronavirus disease (COVID-19) pandemic, some economies in Asia and the Pacific are gradually recovering from the severe socioeconomic setbacks. However, the recovery remains volatile. New variants and fresh waves of infections, along with shocks such as the Russian invasion of Ukraine, are hindering a return to swift and socially equitable growth. There is also an urgent need to regain momentum as we reach the halfway point for achieving the Sustainable Development Goals (SDGs).

High-quality and timely data will be critical for policymakers as they design appropriate platforms and programs to restore progress toward strong and lasting growth. This 2022 edition of *Key Indicators for Asia and the Pacific* provides the latest economic, financial, social, and environmental indicators for the Asian Development Bank's 49 members across Asia and the Pacific.

The main section of the report presents analysis of the direct and indirect effects of the COVID-19 pandemic and highlights key issues for charting a path forward. The report also reveals that socioeconomic deprivations have persisted or even widened across the region. Socioeconomic differences have the potential to be magnified in the longer term if setbacks in poverty reduction, gender equality, and educational equity are not addressed immediately. Data analyses suggest that promoting greater upward social mobility, supporting more resilient infrastructure, and fostering innovation can help the region maneuver its way back to a sustainable and inclusive path of development. However, a number of economies in Asia and the Pacific still lag global benchmarks for investment in research and development.

This report includes a special chapter on how data resilience can be achieved in the wake of pandemic disruptions to the operations of national statistical systems, especially the challenges for conducting the conventional surveys and censuses commonly used to compile development statistics, including SDG indicators. This year's special supplement demonstrates how harnessing social media text data can help policymakers understand the opinions, ideas, and expectations of the public.

We thank the statistical partners in our member economies for providing the most recently available data from their official sources. We are also grateful to the international agencies from which the data in many of the tables are sourced.

We hope the statistics and analysis from this report will help policymakers design strategies that overcome the impacts of the pandemic and minimize risks faced by the most vulnerable people in our region. With policies based on data and evidence, we can achieve a key aim of the SDGs to leave no one behind.

Masatsugu Asakawa
President
Asian Development Bank

Acknowledgments

This 53rd annual edition of *Key Indicators for Asia and the Pacific* was prepared by the Statistics and Data Innovation Unit (EROD-SDI) within the Economic Research and Regional Cooperation Department (ERCD) at the Asian Development Bank (ADB). The publication team was led by Arturo Martinez Jr, under the overall direction of Elaine S. Tan. Joseph Albert Nino Bulan, Rose Anne Dumayas, Anna Marie Fernando, Melissa Pascua, and Eric Suan provided technical and coordination support in preparing the publication.

The statistical tables presenting development indicators for ADB's regional member economies in Parts I and II of the printed publication (also available online via kidb.adb.org), as well as the 49 tables for individual economies available exclusively online, were prepared by EROD-SDI staff and consultants, under the supervision of Daniel Boller, Kaushal Joshi, Mahinthan Joseph Mariasingham, Arturo Martinez Jr, and Stefan Schipper. The research team included Mildred Addawe, Raymond Adofina, Maria Concordia Alfonso, Remedios Baes-Espineda, Nalwino Billones, Joseph Albert Nino Bulan, Criselda De Dios, Dennis Dizon, Madeline Dumaua-Cabauatan, Rose Anne Dumayas, Ron Lester Durante, Anna Marie Fernando, Pamela Lapitan, Rica Cynthia Maddawin, Jayzon Mag-Atas, Kristine Faith Maningding, Marymell Martillan, Melissa Pascua, Christian Flora Mae Soco, and Eric Suan. Proofreading of statistical tables was done by Ma. Roselia Babalo, Rose Anne Dumayas, and Aileen Gatson. The analyses of Sustainable Development Goal indicators in Part I were prepared by Nalwino Billones, Joseph Albert Nino Bulan, Madeline Dumaua-Cabauatan, Anna Marie Fernando, Rica Cynthia Maddawin, Kristine Faith Maningding, and Arturo Martinez Jr. Part II was written by Raymond Adofina, Maria Concordia Alfonso, Dennis Dizon, and Arturo Martinez Jr. Valuable research assistance was also received from Rose Anne Dumayas, Anna Marie Fernando, and Paolo Valdez. Gaurav Datt, Poullang Doung, Pamela Elmido, Anna Fink, Rana Hasan, Matthias Helbe, Jennet Hojanazarova, Cornie Huizenga, Anand Kumar, Matteo Lanzafame, Maria Lourdes Lopez, Joel Mangahas, Cholpon Mambetova, Ahmad Miraj, Shalini Mittal, Rhea Molato, Smita Luthra Nakhooda, Dave Pipon, Kenji Takamiya, Frank Thomas, and Michiel Van Der Auwera provided insightful feedback. We also thank Kunhyui Kim, Peter Morgan, and Long Trinh for sharing data from Asian Development Bank Institute surveys.

Mahinthan Joseph Mariasingham led the team that prepared the statistical tables for Part III. The multiregional input-output table was consolidated by Michael John Barsabal, John Arvin Bernabe, Julieta Magallanes, and Ana Francesca Rosales. Valuable contributions were made by Anurag Agarwal, Jenny de las Alas, Julian Thomas Alvarez, Gienneen Antonio, Ridhima Bahl, Faith Hyacinth Balisacan, Michael John Barsabal, John Arvin Bernabe, Veronica Castillo, Renz Marion Catapang, Ma. Charmaine Crisostomo, Jahm Mae Guinto-Alvarez, Arushi Gupta, Sameeksha Jain, Jessica Jola, Dale Maverenz Lim, Julieta Magallanes, Sarah Mae Manuel, Elyssa Mariel Mores, Danileen Parel-Cadag, Leila Rahnema-Badr, Ana Francesca Rosales, Anna Monina Sanchez, Maegan Saroca, Michelle Monique Sianghio, Irene Talam, Dean Joseph Villanueva, and Christian Marvin Zamora. Part III was written by Janine Elora Lazatin-de Leon as the lead writer, with data and visualization contributions from Julian Thomas Alvarez, Cherryl Chico, Christian Regie Jabagat, and Elyssa Mariel Mores, under the guidance of Mahinthan Joseph Mariasingham. The section was proofread by Janine Elora Lazatin-de Leon, Ma. Charmaine Crisostomo, and Christian Regie Jabagat. Eric Suan and Kijin Kim provided insightful comments and suggestions. Miro Frances Capili contributed to drafting the statements for Part III infographics.

Mildred Addawe, Joseph Albert Nino Bulan, Remedios Baes-Espineda, Marymell Martillan, Arturo Martinez Jr, Melissa Pascua, and Christian Flora Mae Soco summarized the key findings from the survey of national statistics offices that enabled the compilation of Part IV. We appreciate the feedback provided by Jose Ramon Albert, Margarita

Guerrero, and Kaushal Joshi as well as representatives of the national statistics offices, labor ministries, and social welfare and development ministries that responded to the survey on relevant administrative-data-related initiatives by their respective organizations. In particular, we acknowledge Lusine Kalantaryan and Karine Kuyumjyan of the Statistical Committee of the Republic of Armenia; Amalya Enokyan, Hrayr Hakobyan, Artak Karapetyan, Marat Sevoyan, and Marieta Sargsyan of the Ministry of Labour and Social Affairs of the Republic of Armenia; Gantuya Enkhtaivan and Bolorchimeg Nasanbayar of the National Statistics Office of Mongolia; H.E. Ariunzaya Ayush, Basan Batjargal, Bold Undral, Bor Altantulga, Zorigt Khuslen, Galbadrakh Munkhgerel, Magsarjav Batmagnai, Burged Batbaatar, Batbayar Davaa-Erdene, Ankhbayar Altangerel, Kobeikhan Sholpan, and Jargalsaikhan Tungalag of the Ministry of Labor and Social Protection of Mongolia; and for Singapore, the Department of Statistics; Ministry of Manpower; Accounting and Corporate Regulatory Authority; Enterprise Singapore; Immigration & Checkpoints Authority; Ministry of Health; Singapore Food Agency; Ministry of Education; Infocomm Media Development Authority; and all other technical staff and officials.

We are grateful for the support and guidance of Joseph E. Zveglich Jr and Chia-Hsin Hu; and feedback from ERCD colleagues throughout the process. The ADB Japanese Representative Office, Pacific Liaison and Coordination Office, Philippines Country Office, and Pacific Subregional Office also provided help in the data compilation.

We are very grateful for the contributions of ERCD's statistical partners—ADB regional members and international organizations who generously shared their data for the statistical tables on Sustainable Development Goal indicators (Part I), regional tables (Part II), global value chains (Part III), uses of administrative data (Part IV), and individual economy tables. ADB resident missions and/or support teams in Afghanistan, Armenia, Azerbaijan, Bangladesh, Bhutan, Cambodia, Georgia, India, Indonesia, Kazakhstan, the Kyrgyz Republic, the Lao People's Democratic Republic, Mongolia, Maldives, Myanmar, Nepal, Pakistan, Papua New Guinea, the People's Republic of China, the Philippines, Sri Lanka, Tajikistan, Thailand, Timor-Leste, Turkmenistan, Uzbekistan, and Viet Nam provided support in compiling the data for their respective economies. We greatly appreciate the continuing cooperation of the governments of ADB member economies and other international agencies.

Paul Dent edited *Key Indicators for Asia and the Pacific 2022*. The cover design and publication dividers were prepared by Rhommell Rico, who also led the typesetting process and provided technical support for the preparation of all promotional and awareness materials. Joseph Manglicmot and Rommel Marilla assisted with typesetting. Infographics were prepared by Mike Cortes. Staff from ADB's Information Technology Department provided database management and technology support in coordination with the Key Indicators Database team, comprising Ephraim Cuya, Karen Firshan, Pamela Lapitan, James Montecillo, Jeffrey Napoles, Le Kim Nguyen, and Lea Rotairo under the leadership of Stefan Schipper. The Logistics Management Unit of the Corporate Services Department facilitated the timely and smooth production of the publication. Terje Langeland and Lean Alfred Santos, with the assistance of ADB's Department of Communications staff, provided general guidance on production issues and organized promotional and awareness activities.

Albert Park
Chief Economist and Director General
Economic Research and Regional Cooperation Department
Asian Development Bank

Statistical Partners

The preparation and publication of *Key Indicators for Asia and the Pacific 2022* would not have been possible without the support, assistance, and cooperation of statistical partners in Asian Development Bank member economies[1] throughout the Asia and Pacific region, along with the invaluable contributions of international, private, and nongovernment organizations. These partners—who share their data, knowledge, expertise, and other information—help provide the Asian Development Bank, policymakers, and other data users with a better understanding of the performance of economies across the region, encouraging the design, formulation, and monitoring of better policies to improve the quality of life for people in this part of the world.

REGIONAL MEMBERS

Armenia	Central Bank of Armenia (https://www.cba.am) Ministry of Finance of the Republic of Armenia (https://www.minfin.am) Statistical Committee of the Republic of Armenia (https://www.armstat.am)
Australia	Australian Bureau of Statistics (http://www.abs.gov.au) Department of Industry, Science, Energy and Resources (https://www.industry.gov.au) Reserve Bank of Australia (https://www.rba.gov.au)
Azerbaijan	Central Bank of the Republic of Azerbaijan (https://www.cbar.az) Ministry of Finance (http://www.maliyye.gov.az) State Statistical Committee of the Republic of Azerbaijan (https://www.stat.gov.az)
Bangladesh	Bangladesh Bank (https://www.bb.org.bd) Bangladesh Bureau of Statistics (http://www.bbs.gov.bd) Ministry of Finance (https://mof.gov.bd)
Bhutan	Ministry of Finance (https://www.mof.gov.bt) Ministry of Labour and Human Resources (https://www.molhr.gov.bt) National Statistics Bureau (https://www.nsb.gov.bt) Royal Monetary Authority of Bhutan (https://www.rma.org.bt)
Brunei Darussalam	Brunei Darussalam Central Bank (https://www.bdcb.gov.bn) Department of Economic Planning and Statistics (https://deps.mofe.gov.bn) Ministry of Finance and Economy (https://www.mofe.gov.bn)
Cambodia	Electricity Authority of Cambodia (https://eac.gov.kh) Ministry of Economy and Finance (https://mef.gov.kh) National Bank of Cambodia (https://www.nbc.org.kh) National Institute of Statistics (https://nis.gov.kh)

[1] ADB placed on hold its assistance in Afghanistan effective 15 August 2021 (https://www.adb.org/news/adb-statement-afghanistan) and in Myanmar effective 1 February 2021 (https://www.adb.org/publications/myanmar-fact-sheet). ADB did not make any consultations with either Afghanistan or Myanmar for the data in this publication.

China, People's Republic of	National Bureau of Statistics of China (http://www.stats.gov.cn) The People's Bank of China (http://www.pbc.gov.cn) State Administration of Foreign Exchange (http://www.safe.gov.cn)
Cook Islands	Cook Islands Statistics Office under Ministry of Finance and Economic Management (http://www.mfem.gov.ck)
Fiji	Bureau of Statistics (http://www.statsfiji.gov.fj) Reserve Bank of Fiji (http://www.rbf.gov.fj) Ministry of Economy (http://www.economy.gov.fj)
Georgia	Ministry of Finance of Georgia (https://www.mof.ge) National Bank of Georgia (https://www.nbg.gov.ge) National Statistics Office of Georgia (https://www.geostat.ge)
Hong Kong, China	Census and Statistics Department (http://www.censtatd.gov.hk) Financial Services and the Treasury Bureau (https://www.fstb.gov.hk)
India	National Statistical Office under the Ministry of Statistics and Programme Implementation (https://www.mospi.gov.in) Department of Economic Affairs, Ministry of Finance (https://dea.gov.in/) Reserve Bank of India (http://www.rbi.org.in)
Indonesia	Bank Indonesia (https://www.bi.go.id) Badan Pusat Statistik-Statistics Indonesia (https://www.bps.go.id) Ministry of Energy and Mineral Resources (https://www.esdm.go.id) Ministry of Finance (https://www.kemenkeu.go.id) Pertamina (https://www.pertamina.com)
Japan	Bank of Japan (https://www.boj.or.jp) Economic and Social Research Institute (https://www.esri.cao.go.jp) Japan Customs (https://www.customs.go.jp) Japan Statistics Bureau (https://www.e-stat.go.jp) Ministry of Economy, Trade and Industry (https://www.meti.go.jp) Ministry of Finance (https://www.mof.go.jp) The Institute of Energy Economics, Japan (https://oil-info.ieej.or.jp)
Kazakhstan	Bureau of National Statistics, Agency for Strategic Planning and Reforms of the Republic of Kazakhstan (https://stat.gov.kz) Ministry of Finance of the Republic of Kazakhstan (https://www.gov.kz/memleket/entities/minfin?lang=kk) National Bank of Kazakhstan (https://nationalbank.kz)

Kiribati	Kiribati National Statistics Office (https://nso.gov.ki/)
Korea, Republic of	Bank of Korea (https://bok.or.kr) Statistics Korea (http://kostat.go.kr)
Kyrgyz Republic	National Bank of the Kyrgyz Republic (https://www.nbkr.kg) National Statistical Committee of the Kyrgyz Republic (http://www.stat.kg)
Lao People's Democratic Republic	Bank of the Lao PDR (https://www.bol.gov.la) Lao Statistics Bureau (https://www.lsb.gov.la) Ministry of Finance (https://www.mof.gov.la)
Malaysia	Bank Negara Malaysia (https://www.bnm.gov.my) Department of Statistics Malaysia (https://www.dosm.gov.my) Ministry of Finance Malaysia (https://www.mof.gov.my)
Maldives	National Bureau of Statistics (http://www.statisticsmaldives.gov.mv) Maldives Monetary Authority (http://www.mma.gov.mv) Ministry of Finance (https://www.finance.gov.mv)
Marshall Islands	Economic Policy, Planning and Statistics Office (https://www.rmieppso.org)
Micronesia, Federated States of	Division of Statistics (http://www.fsmstatistics.fm)
Mongolia	The Bank of Mongolia (https://www.mongolbank.mn) The Ministry of Finance Mongolia (https://mof.gov.mn) National Statistics Office of Mongolia (https://en.nso.mn/)
Nauru	Department of Finance (https://naurufinance.info/) Nauru Bureau of Statistics (https://nauru.prism.spc.int)
Nepal	Central Bureau of Statistics (https://cbs.gov.np) Ministry of Finance (https://www.mof.gov.np) Nepal Rastra Bank (https://www.nrb.org.np) Water and Energy Commission Secretariat (www.wecs.gov.np) Ministry of Energy, Water Resources and Irrigation (www.moewri.gov.np) Ministry of Industry, Commerce and Supplies (https://moics.gov.np) Ministry of Industry, Commerce and Supplies, Department of Mines and Geology (http://www.dmgnepal.gov.np)
New Zealand	Ministry of Business, Innovation and Employment (https://www.mbie.govt.nz) Reserve Bank of New Zealand (https://www.rbnz.govt.nz) Stats NZ Tatauranga Aotearoa (https://www.stats.govt.nz)

Niue	Statistics Niue Office (https://niue.prism.spc.int)
Pakistan	Ministry of Finance, Revenue and Economic Affairs - Finance Division (http://www.finance.gov.pk) Pakistan Bureau of Statistics (https://www.pbs.gov.pk) State Bank of Pakistan (https://www.sbp.org.pk)
Palau	Bureau of Budget and Planning, Ministry of Finance (https://www.palaugov.pw/mof)
Papua New Guinea	Bank of Papua New Guinea (https://www.bankpng.gov.pg) Department of Treasury (http://www.treasury.gov.pg) National Statistical Office (https://www.nso.gov.pg)
Philippines	Bangko Sentral ng Pilipinas (http://www.bsp.gov.ph) Bureau of Local Government Finance (https://blgf.gov.ph) Bureau of the Treasury (http://www.treasury.gov.ph) Department of Budget and Management (http://www.dbm.gov.ph) Department of Energy (https://www.doe.gov.ph) Philippine Statistics Authority (https://www.psa.gov.ph)
Samoa	Samoa Bureau of Statistics (https://www.sbs.gov.ws) Central Bank of Samoa (https://www.cbs.gov.ws)
Singapore	Department of Statistics Singapore (https://www.tablebuilder.singstat.gov.sg) Enterprise Singapore (https://www.enterprisesg.gov.sg) Ministry of Finance (https://www.mof.gov.sg) Ministry of Manpower (https://www.mom.gov.sg) Ministry of Trade and Industry (https://www.mti.gov.sg) Monetary Authority of Singapore (https://www.mas.gov.sg)
Solomon Islands	Central Bank of Solomon Islands (https://www.cbsi.com.sb) Solomon Islands National Statistics Office (https://www.statistics.gov.sb)
Sri Lanka	Central Bank of Sri Lanka (https://www.cbsl.gov.lk) Department of Census and Statistics (http://www.statistics.gov.lk)
Taipei,China	Central bank of Taipei,China (https://www.cbc.gov.tw) Directorate-General of Budget, Accounting and Statistics (https://eng.dgbas.gov.tw) Ministry of Finance (https://www.mof.gov.tw)
Tajikistan	National Bank of Tajikistan (https://www.nbt.tj) Agency on Statistics under President of the Republic of Tajikistan (https://www.stat.tj)

Thailand	Bank of Thailand (https://www.bot.or.th) Ministry of Finance (http://www2.mof.go.th) National Economic and Social Development Council (https://www.nesdc.go.th) National Statistical Office (http://www.nso.go.th) Ministry of Energy, Energy Policy and Planning Office (http://www.eppo.go.th)
Timor-Leste	Central Bank of Timor-Leste (https://www.bancocentral.tl) Ministry of Finance (https://www.mof.gov.tl) General Directorate of Statistics (https://www.statistics.gov.tl)
Tonga	Ministry of Finance (http://www.finance.gov.to) National Reserve Bank of Tonga (http://www.reservebank.to) Tonga Statistics Department (https://tongastats.gov.to)
Turkmenistan	Central Bank of Turkmenistan (https://www.cbt.tm) Ministry of Finance and Economy of Turkmenistan (https://fineconomic.gov.tm/) State Committee on Statistics of Turkmenistan (https://www.stat.gov.tm)
Tuvalu	Central Statistics Division (https://tuvalu.prism.spc.int)
Uzbekistan	Office of the Cabinet of Ministers (https://www.gov.uz) Central Bank of the Republic of Uzbekistan (https://www.cbu.uz) Ministry of Finance of the Republic of Uzbekistan (https://www.mf.uz) State Committee of the Republic of Uzbekistan on Statistics (https://www.stat.uz)
Vanuatu	Department of Finance and Treasury (https://doft.gov.vu) Reserve Bank of Vanuatu (https://www.rbv.gov.vu) Vanuatu National Statistics Office (http://www.vnso.gov.vu)
Viet Nam	General Statistics Office (https://www.gso.gov.vn) Ministry of Finance (https://www.mof.gov.vn) State Bank of Viet Nam (https://www.sbv.gov.vn)

INTERNATIONAL, PRIVATE, AND NONGOVERNMENT ORGANIZATIONS

Association of Southeast Asian Nations
Food and Agriculture Organization of the United Nations
International Labour Organization
International Monetary Fund
International Telecommunication Union
Interstate Statistical Committee of the Commonwealth of Independent States
Joint United Nations Programme on HIV/AIDS
Organisation for Economic Co-operation and Development
Secretariat of the Pacific Community
Transparency International
United Nations Children's Fund (UNICEF)
United Nations Conference on Trade and Development
United Nations Department of Economic and Social Affairs
United Nations Development Programme
United Nations Economic Commission for Europe
United Nations Economic and Social Commission for Asia and the Pacific
United Nations Educational, Scientific and Cultural Organization (UNESCO) Institute for Statistics
United Nations Environment Programme
United Nations Human Settlements Programme
United Nations Office on Drugs and Crime
United Nations Population Division
United Nations Statistics Division
United Nations World Tourism Organization
United States Agency for International Development
United States Census Bureau
United States Bureau of Economic Analysis
WHO/UNICEF Joint Monitoring Programme for Water Supply, Sanitation and Hygiene
World Bank
World Health Organization
World Trade Organization

Guide for Users

Key Indicators for Asia and the Pacific 2022 begins with a Highlights section that presents key messages from various parts of the publication.

Part I comprises data tables and data stories describing trends of selected indicators for the Sustainable Development Goals (SDGs) for which data were available. The indicators are presented according to the United Nations' SDG global indicator framework.

Part II presents specific indicators on social, economic, and environmental developments in member economies of the Asian Development Bank (ADB) located in Asia and the Pacific. The tables containing these indicators are grouped into eight themes: People; Economy and Output; Money, Finance, and Prices; Globalization; Transport and Communications; Energy and Electricity; Environment; and Government and Governance.

The SDGs in Part I and the themes in Part II are preceded by data stories, which are complemented by figures and charts describing the status of economies with respect to key trends of selected targets and indicators. The scales used in some figures and charts are adjusted to show very small numbers. In addition, figures and charts appearing in this publication are also provided with a digital object identifier to facilitate easier access to data.

The SDGs and regional tables presented in Part I and II cover 49 national economies across Asia and the Pacific, all of which are members of ADB. The term "country," used interchangeably with "economy", is not intended to make any judgment as to the legal or other status of any territory or area. The 49 economies have been broadly grouped into developing ADB member economies and developed ADB member economies. The term "developing Asia" refers to the 46 developing member economies of ADB. The developed economies refer to the economies of Australia, Japan, and New Zealand. Based on ADB's geographic operations, the 46 developing ADB member economies are divided into five subregions within the Asia and Pacific region. These subregions are Central and West Asia, East Asia, South Asia, Southeast Asia, and the Pacific. Economies are listed alphabetically within each subregion. The term "regional members", often used interchangeably with "Asia and the Pacific", refer to all 49 ADB members, both developing and developed. Indicators are shown for the most recent year (usually 2021) or period for which data were available and, in most tables, for a starting year or period (usually 2010). Depending on available data, the starting point may be a year nearest to 2010, and the most recent year (usually the year nearest to 2021). There may, however, be some exceptions to these general principles. In the tables, aggregates for regions include economies with available data and are shown if the indicator is available for more than half of the economies and if more than two-thirds of the reference population is represented.

Part III contains selected indicators for depicting participation by economies of Asia and the Pacific in global value chains, and the sector-specific comparative advantage of each economy in terms of exports. Typical indicators of international trade, which mainly refer to the value of exports and imports of goods and services, can be traced back to the traditional trading of final goods across borders. Today's globalization has made many economies more open to trade, providing opportunities for firms to scale up production and allocate their resources more efficiently by moving production chains across borders where there is comparative advantage. Analysis of global value chains provides detailed cross-border trading transactions of inputs used in different stages of production—from raw materials, to intermediate inputs, to the final products purchased by the end consumers.

Part IV provides stories behind the data and focuses on initiatives of the region's national statistics offices to provide data as the basis for actionable insights on development planning and policymaking.

This publication is also available on ADB's website at adb.org/ki-2022, along with individual statistical tables for each of the 49 ADB regional members.[1] The publication's vitally important data and time series are also accessible in digitized format via the Key Indicators Database (kidb.adb.org), which also presents longer data series (usually starting from 2000) for each indicator. Data for the SDG indicators, regional tables, and individual member tables were obtained mainly from two sources: (i) ADB's statistical partners linked to regional member economies, and (ii) international statistics agencies, particularly from the United Nations' SDG Global Database, a master set of data prepared by the Department of Economic and Social Affairs of the United Nations Secretariat. The term "economies' official sources", cited as a source in some tables, refers to data provided by the statistical partners linked to the ADB regional member economies.

The data presented for indicators in Part I were derived from either official economy sources, the SDG Global Database, or databases maintained by international agencies that, based on their areas of expertise, prepared one or more of the series of statistical indicators included in the SDG Global Database. The data presented in Part III were drawn mainly from the ADB Multiregional Input–Output Tables Database. The results of a survey conducted by ADB's Statistics and Data Innovation Unit informed the discussion presented in Part IV.
Data produced and disseminated by international agencies are generally based on data produced and disseminated by an individual economy (including data adjusted by the economy to meet international standards). However, it should be noted that national data may be compiled using national standards and practices and, as such, international agencies often adjust the data for international comparability. In such cases, data disseminated by the international agencies may differ from data available from national sources. In other cases, when data for a specific year, or set of years, are not available; or they are available from multiple national sources (surveys, administrative data sources, and other sources); or when there are data quality issues; the relevant international agency may estimate the data. Some indicators are regularly produced for the purpose of global monitoring by the designated agency, and there are no corresponding data at the national level (e.g., population living on less than $1.90 a day at 2011 purchasing power parity). In other cases, the differences between

[1] ADB placed on hold its assistance in Afghanistan effective 15 August 2021 (https://www.adb.org/news/adb-statement-afghanistan) and in Myanmar effective 1 February 2021 (https://www.adb.org/publications/myanmar-fact-sheet). ADB did not make any consultations with either Afghanistan or Myanmar for the data in this publication.

data from national and international agencies may be because the most recent and/or revised data available at the national level are not yet available with the relevant international agency. Some data gaps are filled by supplementing or deriving data collected through sample surveys financed and carried out by international agencies. For example, many of the health indicators are estimated using data from the Multiple Indicator Cluster Surveys and Demographic and Health Surveys. Data on money and interest rates, featured in several individual economy tables, are presented based on the International Monetary Fund's 2016 *Monetary and Financial Statistics Manual and Compilation Guide*, but there are a few economies that continue to present their data using the format applied in *Key Indicators for Asia and the Pacific 2020* and prior editions. *Key Indicators for Asia and the Pacific* now also features additional transport and communications indicators from ADB's Asian Transportation Outlook Database.

ADB exercises due care and caution in collecting data before publication. Nevertheless, data from international sources presented in this publication may differ from those available within individual member economies. Thus, for a detailed description of how the indicators are compiled by the international agencies, readers may refer to the metadata available from databases of the individual international agencies, or to the SDG Global Database website for metadata of SDG indicators. Modeled estimates as presented in the SDG Global Database are also identified. Comparable and standardized national data gathered through a robust data-reporting mechanism of the international agencies serve as the basis for all data in the global monitoring databases.

Data obtained from ADB member economies are comparable to the extent that the ADB members follow standard statistical concepts, definitions, and estimation methods recommended by the United Nations and other applicable international agencies. Nevertheless, member economies invariably develop and use their own concepts, definitions, and estimation methodologies to suit their individual circumstances, and these may not necessarily comply with recommended international standards. Therefore, even though attempts are made to present the data in a comparable and uniform format, the data are subject to variations in the statistical methods used by individual economies, so full comparability may not be possible. These variations are reflected in the footnotes of the statistical tables or noted in the Data Issues and Comparability sections. Information about changes in compilation methodology is also provided in the footnotes. In addition, some indicators are expressed as functions of two or more indicators (e.g., indicators expressed as a proportion of gross domestic product). Hence, a change in the compilation methodology of one component indicator might affect other indicators based upon it. Hence, readers are encouraged to refer to the footnotes before making comparisons between economies and/or over time.

Moreover, the aggregates shown in some tables for the developing ADB member economies and ADB regional members are treated as approximations of the actual total or average, or growth rates, due to missing data from the primary source. For a description of the regional aggregation method, readers may refer to the footnotes presented in the tables and/or the metadata in the Key Indicators Database (kidb.adb.org). Footnotes also provide information for earlier years (earlier than 2000), which are relevant for the longer data series presented in the Key Indicators Database. Aggregates for the World were sourced from international agencies, and readers may refer to the metadata available from databases of the individual international agencies.

The data published by ADB do not constitute any form of advice or recommendation. For answers to any questions on the data, users of this publication are requested to seek advice from the relevant data source or organization.

Fiscal Year

There are 25 regional members of the Asian Development Bank with fiscal years that do not coincide with the calendar year. Whenever statistical series (for example, national accounts or government finance) are compiled on the basis of a fiscal year, these series are presented in the column for the single-year during which most of the fiscal year occurred. The 25 fiscal year definitions for 2021 are outlined below.

Regional Member	Fiscal Year	Year Caption
Afghanistan[1] (fiscal year since 2012)	21 December 2020 to 20 December 2021	2021
Brunei Darussalam (fiscal year since 2002) Hong Kong, China India Japan New Zealand Singapore	1 April 2021 to 31 March 2022	2021
Fiji	1 August 2020 to 31 July 2021	2021
Australia Bangladesh Bhutan Cook Islands Kiribati Nauru Niue Pakistan Samoa Tonga	1 July 2020 to 30 June 2021	2021
Nepal	16 July 2020 to 15 July 2021	2021
Lao People's Democratic Republic Marshall Islands Micronesia, Federated States of Myanmar[2] Palau Thailand	1 October 2020 to 30 September 2021	2021

1 ADB placed on hold its assistance in Afghanistan effective 15 August 2021 (https://www.adb.org/news/adb-statement-afghanistan). ADB did not make any consultations with Afghanistan for the data in this publication.

2 ADB placed on hold its assistance in Myanmar effective 1 February 2021 (https://www.adb.org/publications/myanmar-fact-sheet). ADB did not make any consultations with Myanmar for the data in this publication.

Key Symbols

...	data not available
–	magnitude equals zero
(-/+) 0 or 0.0	magnitude is less than half of unit employed
*	provisional/preliminary/estimate/budget figure
|	marks break in series
>	greater than
<	less than
>	greater than or equal to
<	less than or equal to
n.a.	not applicable
%	percentage

Units of Measurement

GWh	gigawatt-hour
kg	kilogram
kl	kiloliter
kloe	kiloliter of oil equivalent
km	kilometer
km^2	square kilometer
kWh	kilowatt-hour
kt	kiloton
ktoe	kiloton of oil equivalent
L	liter
m^3	cubic meter
mj	megajoule
PM	particulate matter
teu	twenty-foot equivalent unit
t	metric ton
μg/m^3	micrograms per cubic meter

Abbreviations

ADB	Asian Development Bank
ADBI	Asian Development Bank Institute
BPM5	Balance of Payments Manual (Fifth Edition)
BPM6	Balance of Payments and International Investment Position Manual (Sixth Edition)
BPO	business process outsourcing
CIF	cost, insurance, and freight
CO_2	carbon dioxide
COICOP	Classification of Individual Consumption by Purpose
COVID-19	Coronavirus Disease 2019
CPI	consumer price index
CSO	Central Statistical Organization
Data4Now	Data For Now
DHS	Demographic and Health Survey
DOSM	Department of Statistics Malaysia
DVA_F	domestic value-added via forward linkages
EROD-SDI	Economic Research and Regional Cooperation Department, Statistics and Data Innovation Unit
FAO	Food and Agriculture Organization of the United Nations
FDI	foreign direct investment
FOB	free on board
FVA	foreign value-added
GDP	gross domestic product
GNI	gross national income
GPS	global positioning system
GVA	gross value-added
GVC	global value chain
HIV	human immunodeficiency virus
HHI	Hirschman Herfindahl Index
ICP	International Comparison Program
ICT	information and communication technology
ICP-APSS	International Comparison Program-Asia Pacific Software Suite
IEA	International Energy Agency
IDA	International Development Association
IHR	International Health Regulations
ILO	International Labour Organization
IMF	International Monetary Fund
IPCC	Intergovernmental Panel on Climate Change
ISIC	International Standard Industrial Classification
ITU	International Telecommunication Union
JRC	Joint Research Center
KIDB	Key Indicators Database
LFS	labor force survey

LGU	local government unit
MDG	Millennium Development Goal
MICS	Multiple Indicator Cluster Survey
MOF	Ministry of Finance
MRIOT	multiregional input-output table
MSMEs	micro, small, and medium-sized enterprises
NDC	nationally determined contribution
NO_2	nitrogen oxide
NPL	nonperforming loan
NRCA	new revealed comparative advantage
NSO	national statistics office; national statistical office
NSS	national statistical system
ODA	official development assistance
OECD	Organisation for Economic Co-operation and Development
PARIS21	Partnership in Statistics for Development in the 21st Century
PIP	Poverty and Inequality Platform
PLI	price level index
PPP	purchasing power parity
PRC	People's Republic of China
PSA	Philippine Statistics Authority
RCA	revealed comparative advantage
SCI	statistical capacity indicator
SDG	Sustainable Development Goal
SDMX	Statistical Data and Metadata Exchange
SNA	System of National Accounts
SPI	statistical performance indicator
TRCA	traditional revealed comparative advantage
UN	United Nations
UNAIDS	Joint United Nations Programme on HIV/AIDS
UNDESA	United Nations Department of Economic and Social Affairs
UNESCAP	United Nations Economic and Social Commission for Asia and the Pacific
UNFCC	UN Framework Convention on Climate Change
UNICEF	United Nations Children's Fund
UNSD	United Nations Statistics Division
UNWTO	United Nations World Tourism Organization
US	United States
WEF	World Economic Forum
WHO	World Health Organization
WVS	World Values Survey

Unless otherwise indicated, "$" refers to United States dollars.

SOCIAL MOBILITY IN ASIA AND THE PACIFIC

POLICYMAKERS NEED TO PROMOTE GREATER UPWARD SOCIAL MOBILITY

IF NO ONE IS TO BE LEFT BEHIND

HIGHER-INCOME ECONOMIES SCORE HIGHER IN METRICS OF SOCIAL MOBILITY ENABLERS

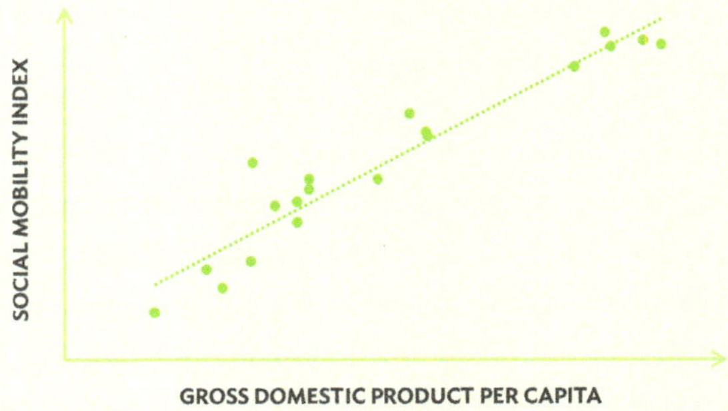

Economically unequal societies tend to have lower scores for enablers of social mobility.

Source: Box 1.1.

ASIANS EXPERIENCED VARYING DEGREES OF DOWNWARD AND UPWARD INCOME MOBILITY DURING THE PANDEMIC

40% of those who had financial difficulty in mid-2020 were encountering minor or no financial difficulty by early 2021. Conversely, one-third of those who did not experience financial difficulty in mid-2020 had fallen into such difficulty by early 2021.

Source: Figure 1.4.

EXTREME POVERTY CAN BE REDUCED TO LESS THAN 1% BY 2030 IF THE REGION REVERTS TO ITS PRE-PANDEMIC GROWTH PROSPECTS

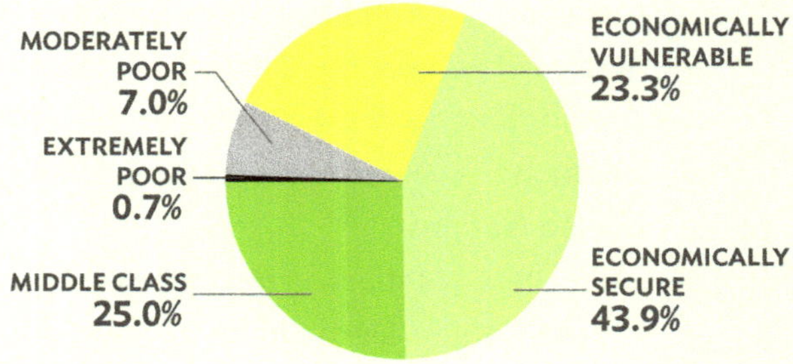

However, about 30% of the population may still remain moderately poor or economically vulnerable.

Source: Figure 1.6.

UNCERTAINTIES SUCH AS THE FULL IMPACT OF LEARNING LOSSES CHALLENGE THE POOR'S UPWARD SOCIAL MOBILITY PROSPECTS

Losses in future earnings are 47% higher for students in the poorest wealth quintile compared to those in the richest quintile.

Source: Figure 1.8.

TOWARDS BETTER SOCIAL MOBILITY PROSPECTS

POLICY FOCUS ON RESILIENCE, INNOVATION, AND INCLUSIVENESS CAN PROMOTE UPWARD SOCIAL MOBILITY FOR THE POOR

TO PROVIDE MORE BALANCED OPPORTUNITIES FOR UPWARD SOCIAL MOBILITY FOR EVERYONE

DEFICIENCIES IN ACCESS TO BASIC SERVICES NEED TO BE ADDRESSED

16% OF ASIA AND THE PACIFIC'S ECONOMIES HAVE ELECTRICITY PENETRATION RATES BELOW THE GLOBAL AVERAGE

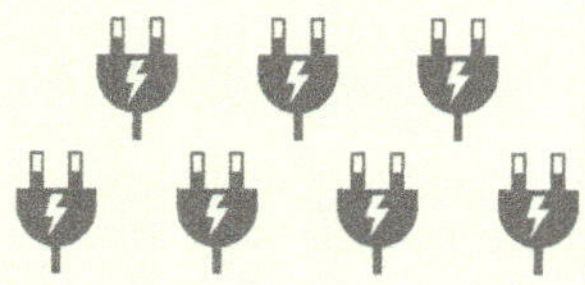

Source: Table 1.7.1.

IN TWO-FIFTHS OF THE REGION'S ECONOMIES, MORE THAN HALF OF THE POPULATION DOES NOT HAVE ACCESS TO SAFE DRINKING WATER OR SANITATION SERVICES

Source: Figure 1.16.

DURING THE PANDEMIC, MOST ECONOMIES OF ASIA AND THE PACIFIC INCREASED SOCIAL PROTECTION

Increased social protection coverage must extend beyond being a temporary response and target those who need it the most.

Source: Figure 1.14.

INNOVATION CAN HELP CREATE NEW ECONOMIC OPPORTUNITIES AND ENABLE UPWARD SOCIAL MOBILITY

R&D EXPENDITURE AS A SHARE OF GDP

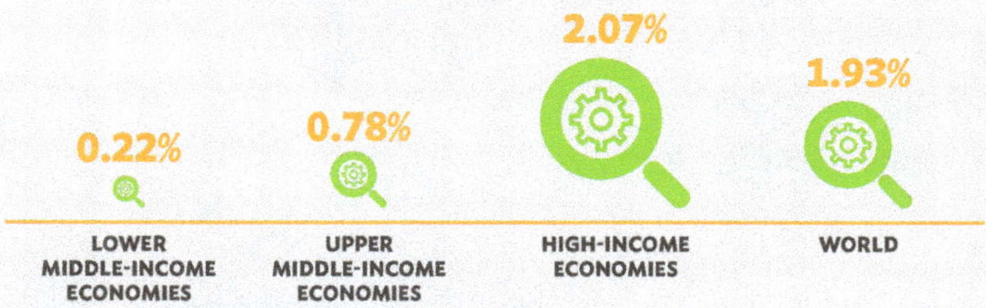

Middle-income economies in Asia and the Pacific lag behind in research and development investment, an important facilitator of innovation.

Source: Figure 1.18.

GLOBALLY, CLIMATE CHANGE THREATENS TO PUSH **MORE THAN 130 MILLION** PEOPLE INTO **POVERTY** OVER THE NEXT DECADE

Planetary health and climate resilience should be integrated into pandemic recovery efforts.

Source: Page 40.

PART II: REGIONAL TABLES

ECONOMIC RECOVERY AND UNCERTAINTIES

NEARLY ALL ECONOMIES REPORTED STRONGER ECONOMIC GROWTH IN 2021

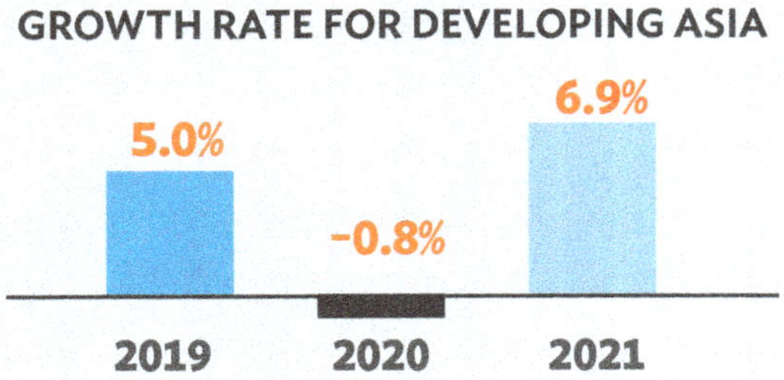

However, there are hints of divergent growth paths. Only about half of the region's economies have reverted to their pre-pandemic GDP levels.

Sources: Page 104 and Figure 2.2.

SOME ECONOMIES GREW MORE SLOWLY THAN ORIGINALLY FORECAST, WHILE OTHERS POSTED STRONGER ECONOMIC PERFORMANCE

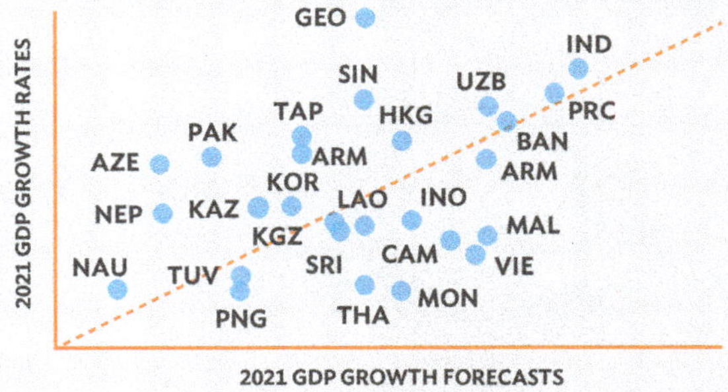

There are economic uncertainties that may hinder a return to swift and socially equitable growth.

Source: Figure 2.2.

ADDITIONAL WORK IS NEEDED TO REGAIN JOBS LOST DURING THE PANDEMIC

In 2021, the number of hours worked was still 3.6% lower than pre-pandemic levels.

Source: Table 2.1.

MOBILITY FLOWS WERE GREATLY AFFECTED IN 2020, BUT GRADUALLY MOVED CLOSER TO PRE-PANDEMIC PATTERNS DURING 2021

Nearly 1 in 3 economies saw a decline of at least 20% in their transport and storage gross value-added in 2020. In 2021, nearly 1 in 4 economies showed growth rates exceeding 10%.

ONE OF THE HARDEST HIT SECTORS AT THE PEAK OF THE PANDEMIC, TOURISM IS RECOVERING IN SEVERAL ECONOMIES

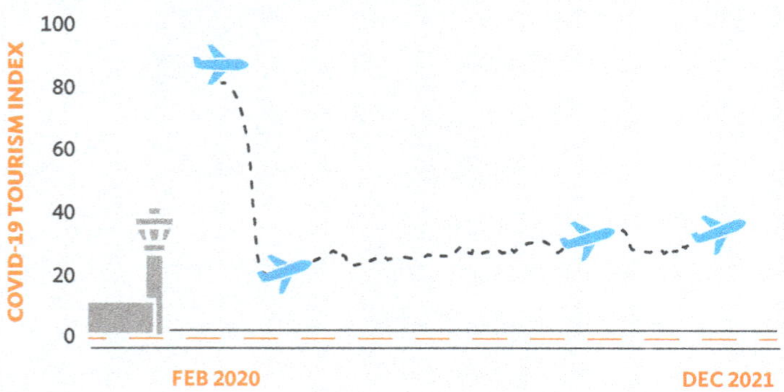

Source: Figure 2.5.

HIGHER-INCOME ECONOMIES GENERALLY SCORE HIGHER IN LOGISTICS PERFORMANCE

Economies that invest in robust digital capabilities to facilitate more efficient movement, storage, and flow of goods are likely to be more resilient to similar shocks in the future.

Sources: Figures 2.9 and 2.12.

PART II: REGIONAL TABLES

ECONOMIC RECOVERY AND UNCERTAINTIES

ICT-ENABLED INDUSTRIES ARE FUTURE GROWTH POWERHOUSES AS THE WORLD SHIFTS TOWARD MORE ICT-RELATED ECONOMIC ACTIVITIES

ICT's economic contribution of member economies grew, with its share of GDP between 1% and 7% in 2021.

Source: Figure 2.13.

BROADBAND INTERNET SUBSCRIPTIONS AMONG LOWER MIDDLE-INCOME ECONOMIES INCREASED BY 15% IN 2020

However, mobile data prices remained high for some developing economies and women were still less likely to use the internet.

Sources: Figures 2.14 and 2.16.

THE ENERGY SECTOR GREW IN 70% OF REPORTING ECONOMIES, WHICH POSTED GROWTH RATES BETWEEN 3% AND 44% IN 2021

This compared to energy sector contractions in more than half of all reporting economies in 2020. However, the pandemic continues to provide opportunities to redraw strategies for cleaner energy systems in the future.

Source: Figure 2.18.

GASOLINE RETAIL PRICES GREW 21% ON AVERAGE IN 2021 FOR 16 REPORTING ECONOMIES VERSUS AN AVERAGE DECLINE OF 10% IN 2020

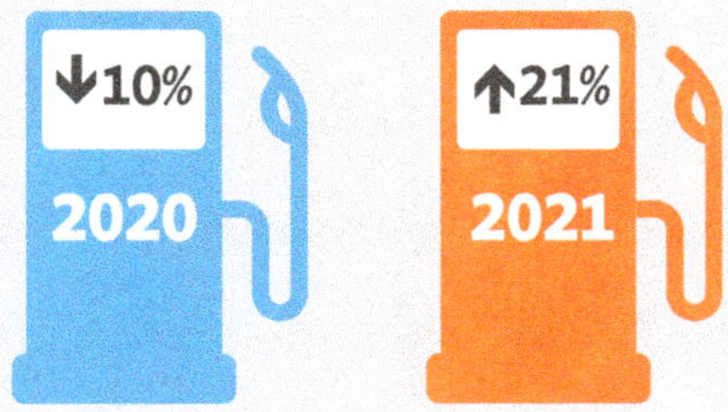

Increases in fuel prices were due to rising demand for energy as economies open up, compounded by supply disruptions.

Source: Figure 2.19.

IN THE DECADE PRIOR TO THE PANDEMIC, GROWTH IN ELECTRICITY FROM ALTERNATIVE SOURCES WAS 4.6 TIMES FASTER FOR SMALL ISLAND DEVELOPING STATES.

Source: Figure 2.21.

PART III: GLOBAL VALUE CHAINS

IMPACTS OF THE GLOBAL CHIP SHORTAGE

ASIA AND THE PACIFIC'S ECONOMIES PLAY A LEADING ROLE IN EXPORTING INTEGRATED CIRCUITS AND ELECTRICAL AND OPTICAL EQUIPMENT

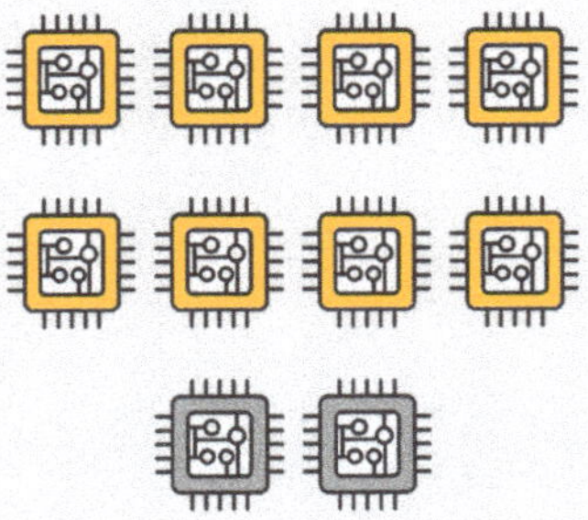

26 economies from the region contributed 83.7% of total world integrated circuit exports in 2016–2020 and 61.5% of total world electrical and optical equipment exports in 2021.

Sources: Pages 242–243 and Figure 3.1.

THE REGION LEADS IN GVCS FOR ELECTRICAL AND OPTICAL EQUIPMENT

56.3% of value-added from GVC intermediates in the sector originated from 26 economies of Asia and the Pacific.

Source: Figure 3.3.

SOME ECONOMIES MAY BENEFIT

A price rise caused by the chip shortage could favor economies with a large proportion of integrated circuits in total exports, high forward GVC participation, and revealed comparative advantage.

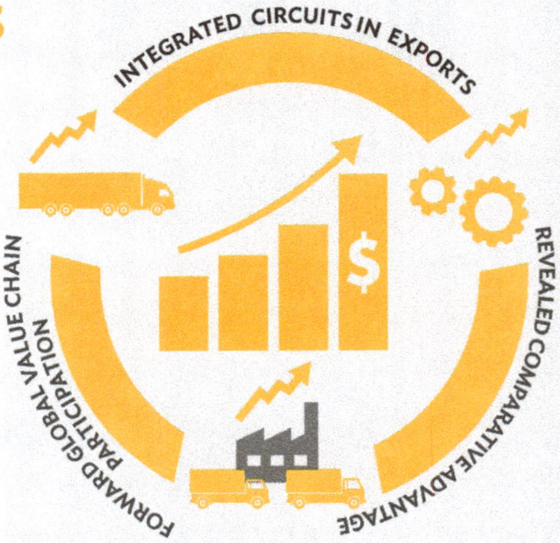

Source: Pages 247–253 and Figures 3.6–3.8.

PART IV: STORIES BEHIND DATA

DATA INITIATIVES IN THE COVID-19 ERA

HARNESSING DATA FROM ADMINISTRATIVE RECORDS CAN HELP WHEN CONVENTIONAL MODES OF COLLECTING DATA ARE DISRUPTED

A survey conducted by ADB statisticians showed that 25% of responding government agencies relied on administrative data to meet the data demands of policymakers when the pandemic struck.

Source: Pages 302–303.

THERE IS A NEED TO SCALE UP ONGOING INITIATIVES THAT PROMOTE THE USE OF ADMINISTRATIVE DATA

Only 47.2% of survey respondents had plans to expand collection of administrative data. Suitability of administrative data for compilation of statistical outputs was a major concern among respondents.

Source: Figure 4.5.

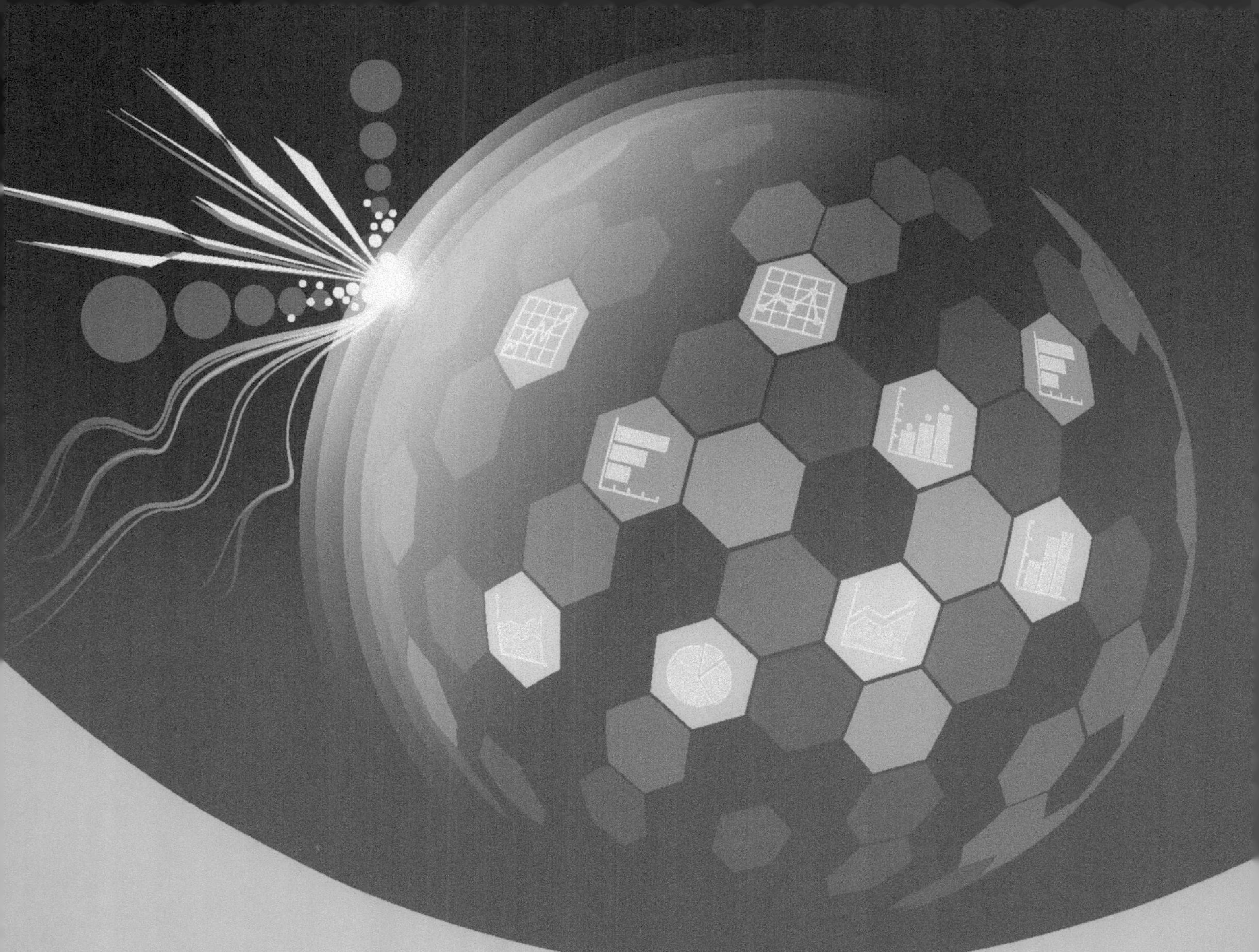

Introduction

Introduction

Having endured the COVID-19 pandemic for more than 2 years, the people of Asia and the Pacific are still weighing its impact on their societies and economies. Beginning as a health crisis, the pandemic has quickly sprawled into almost all aspects of daily life and has developed into a wider crisis engulfing economic well-being, food and housing supply, the social mobility of individuals, and longer-term political management (ADB 2020).

Evidence continues to mount of substantial losses in socioeconomic progress and the rise of more intractable development challenges in the wake of the pandemic. Mainly driven by significant job losses and limited access to social safety nets, the impacts of the crisis have weighed most heavily on the poorest and most vulnerable populations across Asia and the Pacific. The region has already posted a marked slowdown in achieving many of its Sustainable Development Goals, meaning unavoidable delays in reaching targets for reducing poverty and social inequality and improving social mobility, among many other notable goals.

Indeed, forecasts suggest that economic growth in 2022 will only reduce the prevalence of extreme poverty in Asia and the Pacific to what it would have been in 2020 had the pandemic not occurred (ADB 2021a; ADB 2021b). Furthermore, preexisting shortcomings in health and social protection systems, digital capacity, and trade and transportation linkages have magnified the economic shock caused by pandemic restrictions (UNESCAP 2021).

Despite these setbacks and challenges, signs of economic recovery abound. This can be attributed to the global effort to accelerate vaccine rollouts, which, for the most part, have dramatically decreased the rate of COVID-19 infection and allowed many economies to reopen. The world economy grew by 6.1% in 2021 and is projected to grow by 3.6% in 2022 (IMF 2022). Meanwhile, growth in developing Asia was estimated at 6.9% in 2021 and is expected to be 4.6% in 2022 and 5.2% in 2023 (ADB 2022a).

However, as time unfolds, it is apparent that the recovery process may not be linear for many economies of Asia and the Pacific. The unprecedented socioeconomic impacts of the COVID-19 pandemic require a long-term perspective as Asia and the Pacific navigates its way forward. Pandemic responses must pivot away from short-term solutions to transitory problems. Policy paradigms should embrace ongoing resilience, innovation, and inclusiveness to deliver frameworks that improve the lives of society's most vulnerable and provide more balanced opportunities for upward social mobility for everyone.

Part I of *Key Indicators for Asia and the Pacific 2022* revisits how developing Asia has fared with respect to the metrics of poverty and inequality since the COVID-19 pandemic began. By examining how prevailing social mobility regimes might have contributed to this performance, featured data stories provide a glimpse into the potential consequences of the pandemic for future generations. These data stories also explore resilient infrastructures and innovative systems to combat global threats such as climate change. Part II presents the latest economic data as compiled by national statistical systems, accompanied by commentaries on the status of hard-hit sectors such as tourism and transport. These data stories also provide insights into the opportunities for resilient recovery enabled by green growth, sustainable energy, and increased digitalization. Part III provides insights into the impact of the global chip shortage on developing Asia, as well as the region's vulnerability to reshoring of chip manufacturing by trade. Part IV seeks to establish good practices in using administrative data as source of information for a wide range of development indicators, particularly workforce and employment statistics. Administrative records offer rich data that can play a significant part in delivering integrated insights for informed policymaking. This year's edition of *Key Indicators for Asia and the Pacific* also features a special supplement that focuses on natural language processing of social media text data. This process enables continuous and granular mapping of topics and sentiments in society and allows researchers to track societal trends and detect anomalies over time, contributing to better policy formulation.

As Asia and the Pacific begins on the long path to full and sustainable recovery from the COVID-19 pandemic, it is important to generate actionable measures that accurately reflect the region's socioeconomic and development needs. *Key Indicators for Asia and the Pacific 2022* intends to make a valid contribution to this process by providing high-quality and timely data that can be used at the forefront of policymaking.

PART I
Sustainable Development Goals Trends and Tables

Regaining Momentum Toward the Sustainable Development Goals

The Decade of Action (2020–2030) is a call to galvanize efforts toward achieving the Sustainable Development Goals (SDGs). Its beginning, however, was marked by the emergence of the coronavirus disease (COVID-19) pandemic and the imposition of restrictions that have devastated economies the world over.

Appropriately, the 2021 edition of *Key Indicators for Asia and the Pacific* showed the immediate effect of the pandemic on attaining a number of SDGs in the region. Economies with less advanced health systems faced obstacles in delivering appropriate care to poor and isolated communities in rural and remote areas. In places where food insecurity and undernourishment were already a concern, millions had to reduce food consumption due to financial difficulties. School-aged children in poorer households were disadvantaged as they were less likely to be enrolled at schools with distance-learning programs and/or were deprived of remote learning resources due to lack of internet connectivity (ADB 2021a).

Encouragingly, estimates for a number of socioeconomic indicators presented in *Key Indicators for Asia and the Pacific 2022* suggest that the region has rebounded by varying degrees. There is, however, cause to remain on guard about the pace and sustainability of recovery. The potential for stagflation, ongoing conflict involving key global actors, looming threats to food security, and energy price shocks may yet inhibit the return to economic prosperity (UN 2022).

As we approach the halfway point of the 15-year period for achieving the 2030 Agenda for Sustainable Development, it is critical to note that inequitable distribution of socioeconomic opportunities could undermine the intergenerational prospects of the poor and vulnerable segments of society (UN 2020; UNESCAP, ADB, and UNDP 2022). This section therefore focuses on describing key trends involving SDG 1 (no poverty), SDG 4 (quality education), SDG 5 (gender equality), and SDG 10 (reduced inequalities) in the context of social mobility. Additionally, Part I discusses the importance of strengthening long-term resilience by examining trends for selected indicators of SDG 9 (industry, innovation, and infrastructure) and SDG 13 (climate action).

Opportunities for generational change. A mother plays with her children at Tanjung Aan Beach on Lombok island, Indonesia (photo by Achmad Ibrahim/ADB).

Social Mobility Before, During, and After the COVID-19 Pandemic

The concept of social mobility provides a framework to understand how socioeconomic disadvantage can entrench poverty and inequalities.

While available data and statistics point only to the immediate impacts of the COVID-19 crisis, there are hints that the pandemic may have longer-term consequences for the socioeconomic prospects of the poor and vulnerable (UNESCAP, ADB, and UNDP 2022). Under the immediate impacts, poorer households in many parts of Asia and the Pacific were more likely to have reduced consumption due to financial hardship caused by the pandemic (ADB 2021a). Moreover, for the first time in roughly 2 decades, global poverty reduction was interrupted in 2020 (Gopalakrishnan et al. 2021). Likewise, the pandemic derailed several decades of Asia and the Pacific's vibrant economic development (ADB 2020a) and poverty reduction (ADB 2021a). Taking the latest economic growth forecasts into account, it appears that progress on reducing extreme (income) poverty in developing Asia has been set back at least 2 years. The situation may even be bleaker when other dimensions of poverty are taken into account, with estimates suggesting that the pandemic's influence on multidimensional poverty could be much more severe (UNESCAP, ADB, and UNDP 2022).

In general, monitoring changes in aggregate poverty numbers helps assess progress toward the goal of poverty eradication. However, such changes do not provide a complete appraisal of the full poverty spectrum. Whereas some people are either consistently advantaged or disadvantaged, others move in and out of poverty and up and down other rungs of the socioeconomic ladder over time (Figure 1.1).

It is important to examine the concept of social mobility (movements from one socioeconomic status to another) to gain a more nuanced view of the long-term inequalities between rich and poor.[1] It also provides insights for policymaking. For instance, temporary increases in the prevalence of poverty due to economic shocks may merit less policy or structural intervention in places that enjoy high social mobility (where the poor may have good chances of getting out of poverty eventually). On the other hand, increased poverty levels in places with low social mobility (where poverty may be generational and due to factors beyond a person's control) could be more problematic and require strong policy intervention.

Figure 1.1: Poverty Status in Selected Economies of Developing Asia

(% of population)

Some people move into and out of poverty over time.

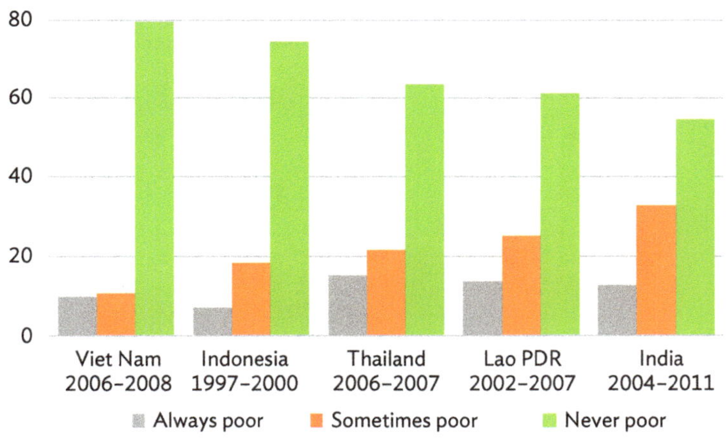

Lao PDR = Lao People's Democratic Republic.

Notes: As periods covered and duration are different, the figure is not intended to compare across economies. For instance, a longer panel may capture more movements than a shorter one. Hence, the figure is simply meant to highlight that some people remain poor for extended periods while others move in and out of poverty. Furthermore, some studies also suggest that, due to potential measurement errors, estimates of prevalence of chronic poverty may be regarded as lower bound estimates (Garces-Urzainqui, Lanjouw and Rongen 2021; Martinez et al. 2013).

Estimates for India, the Lao PDR, and Viet Nam are based on national poverty lines. Estimates for Thailand are based on weighted average poverty lines per region and area while estimates for Indonesia are based on the Törnqvist poverty line and on the Indonesian Family Life Survey.

Source: Based on data presented in Table 6.1 of V. Iversen, A. Krishna, and K. Sen (eds.). 2021. *Social Mobility in Developing Countries: Concepts, Methods, and Determinants* (oup.com). United Nations University, World Institute for Development Economics.

Click here for figure data

1 In addition to social mobility, a study conducted by Datt (unpublished) identifies inequality of opportunities and multidimensional poverty as emerging research frontiers which may also serve as alternative frameworks when examining socioeconomic inequalities in Asia and the Pacific.

Figure 1.2 illustrates the concept of social mobility, while Box 1.1 provides an overview of how it is measured empirically. There are two main factors which contribute to, and influence, a person's socioeconomic standing: initial socioeconomic status and policies of institutions. Parents pass on genetic and cultural endowments (Ermisch et al. 2012) and continuously make decisions on the quality and quantity of resources allocated to ensuring their children's futures (Haveman and Wolfe 1995). Institutions also play a critical role in transmitting advantage within and across generations. Society's wealth, history, cultural norms, and government policies are powerful forces affecting social mobility (Solon 2004; Corak 2013). For example, if governments provide progressive public investments, social mobility is more likely to be driven by differences in inherited nonfinancial characteristics rather than transference of financial advantage (Solon 2004). Additionally, a person's choices and efforts, given the opportunities available to them, are pivotal and integral to social mobility outcomes (Ermisch et al. 2012).

During crises such as a pandemic, however, all drivers of upward social mobility may be severely disrupted. While the better-off may be able to mitigate these disruptions, the less well-off are unable to do so, making it more difficult for poor and socioeconomically vulnerable people to exit the cycle of disadvantage.

Figure 1.2: What Factors Affect Social Mobility?

Both parental and institutional decisions can contribute to a person's social mobility.

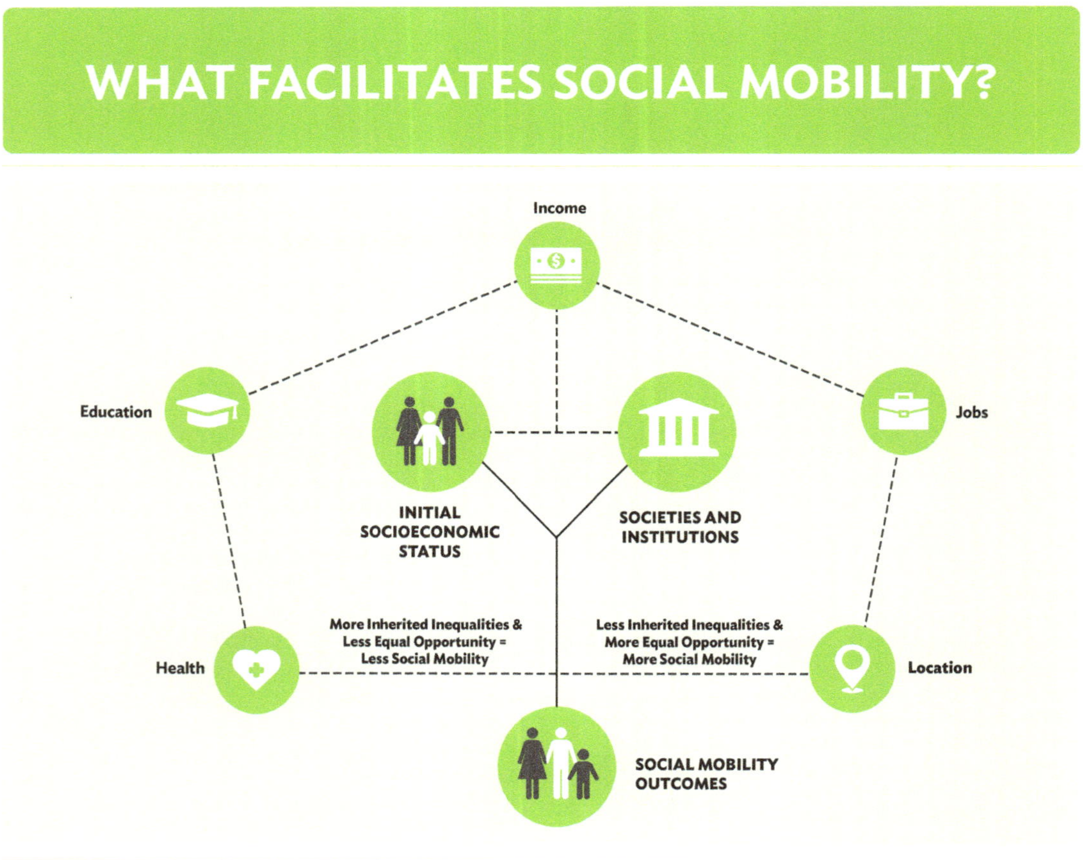

Source: Asian Development Bank visualization adopted from Figure 5 of the World Economic Forum's *The Global Social Mobility Report 2022.*

Box 1.1: How is Social Mobility Measured?

The concept of social mobility can be defined as the transitions between two socioeconomic status levels over time. Intragenerational mobility measures how a person's socioeconomic status changes over his or her lifetime, while intergenerational mobility compares an adult's status with that of his or her parents. Social mobility may also be characterized as either "relative" or "absolute" movements between socioeconomic status levels. Relative social mobility refers to a person's ranking with respect to a specific socioeconomic hierarchy (such as income deciles), so that a person ranking higher over time means that another person has ranked lower. Absolute social mobility ignores rankings and simply assesses whether a person has changed socioeconomic status over time, compared to a predefined level.

The figure below gauges intergenerational absolute social mobility in Asia and the Pacific. Here, adult respondents of a World Values Survey, conducted between 2017 and 2021, were asked to compare their standard of living with that of their parents at the same age. The results suggest that, while a majority felt their standard of living had improved relative to their parents, a considerable number felt that it had not changed or had even deteriorated. Lower-income individuals were less likely to feel that they experienced upward intergenerational social mobility (WVS n.d.).

Standard of Living Compared with That of Parents, by Household Income Grouping
(%)

Note: The figure represents 19 Asian Development Bank member economies with available data and includes: Australia; Bangladesh; Hong Kong, China; Indonesia; Japan; Kazakhstan; the Kyrgyz Republic; Myanmar; Malaysia; New Zealand; Pakistan; the People's Republic of China; the Philippines; the Republic of Korea; Singapore; Thailand; Tajikistan; Taipei,China; and Viet Nam.

Source: Asian Development Bank estimates using data from round seven (pooled datafile version) of the World Values Survey (accessed 15 February 2022).

The academic literature on social mobility probes beyond subjective assessments as in the example above. For instance, a well-used measure of relative income mobility is the intergenerational elasticity of income or earnings (IGE), which is estimated by regressing the (log of) parents' income on (log of) adult children's income when both groups are at similar ages (Iversen, Krishna, and Sen 2021). In general, higher elasticity, which indicates that parents' earning power is a strong driver of the child's earning power, suggests lower intergenerational social mobility. In addition to IGE, intergenerational regression (IGRC) or correlation coefficients (IGC) may also be used to measure educational or occupational mobility (Iversen, Krishna, and Sen 2021). Due to stringent data requirements, such as availability of longitudinal or reliable retrospective data, most income and occupational mobility studies have focused on highly industrialized economies.

To address knowledge gaps on social mobility in developing economies, a World Bank Group (WBG) study compiled the Global Database of Intergenerational Mobility. In particular, the WBG study ranked economies based on the relationship between parents' and children's highest educational attainment. The left panel in the figure below presents the proportion of respondents who obtained higher levels of education than their parents, contingent on the parents not having tertiary education—a measure of absolute mobility in education. Estimates of absolute education mobility generally show an increasing trend from 1940 to 1980 (with the exception of the 1970s cohort). Absolute education mobility was also higher in high-income economies than in developing economies. The right panel of the figure shows relative intergenerational mobility in education (WBG 2018). It depicts a decreasing trend in relative intergenerational persistence in education from 1950 to 1980 in developing economies, but an upward trend in high-income economies.

(continued on next page)

Box 1.1: How is Social Mobility Measured? *(continued)*

Changes in Absolute and Relative Mobility in Education, by Economy Status

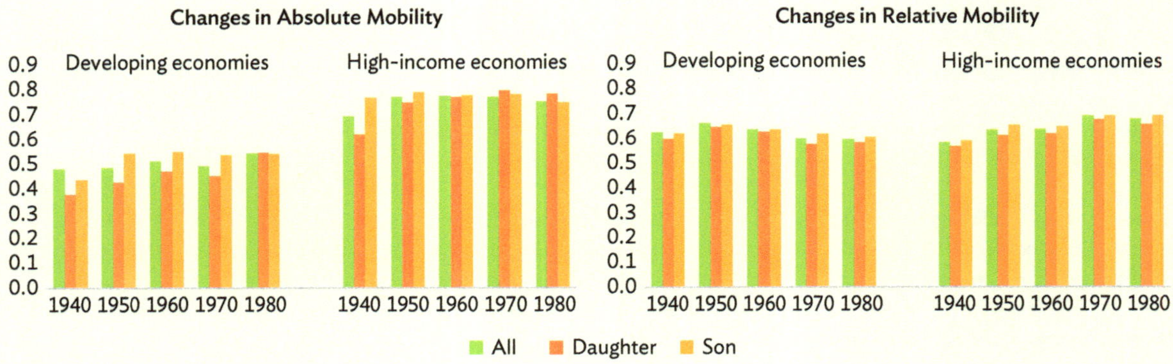

Notes: The figure represents 38 Asian Development Bank member economies with available data and includes: Afghanistan; Armenia; Australia; Azerbaijan; Bangladesh; Bhutan; Cambodia; Fiji; Georgia; Indonesia; India; Japan; Kazakhstan; Kiribati; the Kyrgyz Republic; the Lao People's Democratic Republic; Maldives; Myanmar; Mongolia; Malaysia; Nepal; New Zealand; Pakistan; the People's Republic of China; the Philippines; Papua New Guinea; the Republic of Korea; Solomon Islands; Sri Lanka; Tajikistan; Thailand; Timor-Leste; Tonga; Tuvalu; Tapei,China; Uzbekistan; Viet Nam; and Vanuatu. Values are calculated as the simple averages of economy-level estimates.

Source: Asian Development Bank estimates using data from World Bank's Global Database of Intergenerational Mobility (accessed 1 February 2022).

The figure below is based on individuals from the WBG study's 1980s cohort who were born to parents in the bottom half of the population in education, then assesses what proportion of those individuals have reached the top quartile in education. The results suggest that education mobility among people from lower socioeconomic classes was low in most economies. In fact, only few economies had at least 20% of the 1980s cohort coming from the bottom half in education to reach the top quartile.

Education Mobility of Those Born into the Bottom Half in Education, by Economy

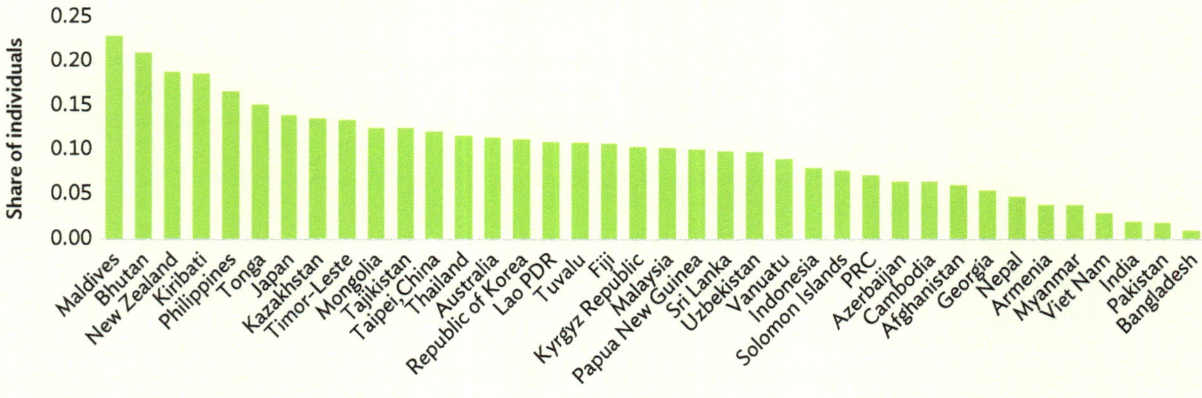

Lao PDR = Lao People's Democratic Republic, PRC = People's Republic of China.

Notes: The figure represents 38 Asian Development Bank member economies with available data. Educational attainment refers to the highest educational level completed among the following five categories based on the International Standard Classification of Education (ISCED): less than primary (ISCED 0), primary (ISCED 1), lower secondary (ISCED 2), upper secondary or postsecondary nontertiary (ISCED 3–4), and tertiary (ISCED 5–8).

Source: Asian Development Bank estimates using data from World Bank's Global Database of Intergenerational Mobility (accessed 1 February 2022).

(continued on next page)

Box 1.1: How is Social Mobility Measured? *(continued)*

It is important to note that findings from social mobility studies may be sensitive to the type of metric used—income, occupational, or educational mobility—and how the concept is applied using available data (Fields 2008; Iversen, Krishna, and Sen 2021). For instance, some measures of occupational mobility commonly used in developed economies may not work well in settings where agriculture and the informal economy absorb most of the workforce (Iversen, Krishna, and Sen 2009). There is also evidence that, in some economies, considerable increases in educational mobility have not translated into equivalent occupational progress (Iversen, Krishna, and Sen 2009).

A World Economic Forum (WEF) study generalized the concept of social mobility having multiple important facets: (i) the ability for an individual to move between socioeconomic classes within their own lifetime; (ii) the ability for a family group to move up or down the socioeconomic ladder across one or more generations; (iii) the ability for an individual to earn, in real terms, as much as or more than their parents at the same age; (iv) the ability for an individual to attain higher education than their parents; and (v) relative income mobility, which describes how much of an individual's income is determined by their parents' income (WEF 2020).

To capture different dimensions of social mobility, the WEF 2020 study constructed an index based on 10 enablers or pillars: (i) health, (ii) education access, (iii) education quality and equity, (iv) lifelong learning, (v) social protection, (vi) technology access, (vii) work opportunities, (viii) fair wages, (ix) working conditions, and (x) inclusive institutions. Raw values of each indicator are rescaled into a progress score whose value ranges from 0 to 100, with 100 representing the ideal situation. At each aggregation level, indicators within each pillar are assigned equal weights. The overall index is calculated as the simple average of the scores across the 10 pillars (WEF 2020). The figure below shows that higher-income economies generally fare better with respect to this metric.

Note: Readers who are interested to go through a more detailed literature review of social mobility may refer to the work of Fields (2019).

Scores on the World Economic Forum Social Mobility Index, by Economy

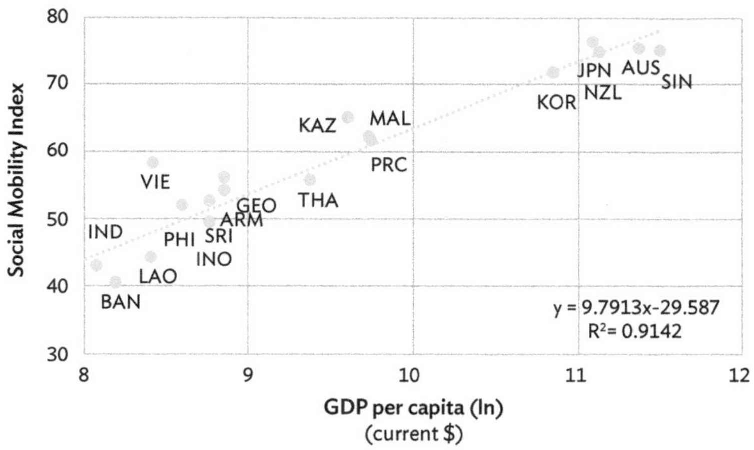

ARM = Armenia, AUS = Australia, BAN = Bangladesh, GEO = Georgia, IND = India, INO = Indonesia, JPN = Japan, KAZ = Kazakhstan, KOR = Republic of Korea, LAO = Lao People's Democratic Republic, MAL = Malaysia, NZL = New Zealand, PAK = Pakistan, PHI = Philippines, PRC = People's Republic of China, SIN = Singapore, SRI = Sri Lanka, THA = Thailand, VIE = Viet Nam.

Sources: World Economic Forum. 2020. *The Global Social Mobility Report 2020*; and Table 2.2.5 of *Key Indicators for Asia and the Pacific 2022*.

References:

G. Fields. 2008. Income Mobility. In L. Blume and S. Durlauf (eds), *The New Palgrave Dictionary of Economics*. New York, NY: Palgrave Macmillan.

G. Fields. 2019. Concepts of Social Mobility. https://ideas.repec.org/p/unu/wpaper/wp-2019-106.html.

V. Iversen, A. Krishna, and K. Sen. 2019. Beyond Poverty Escapes: Social Mobility in Developing Countries: A Review Article. *The World Bank Research Observer*. 34. pp. 239–272.

V. Iversen, A. Krishna, and K. Sen (eds). 2021. *Social Mobility in Developing Countries: Concepts, Methods, and Determinants*. United Nations University World Institute for Development Economics Research.

World Bank Group (WBG). 2018. *Fair Progress? Economic Mobility Across Generations Around the World*. https://openknowledge.worldbank.org/handle/10986/28428.

World Economic Forum (WEF). 2020. *The Global Social Mobility Report 2020: Equality, Opportunity, and a New Economic Imperative*. https://www3.weforum.org/docs/Global_Social_Mobility_Report.pdf.

World Values Survey (WVS). Round Seven, Pooled Datafile Version. Online Database. https://www.worldvaluessurvey.org/WVSDocumentationWV7.jsp.

Education drives upward social mobility. Elementary students from the Nazarbayev Intellectual School of Astana (photo by Ariel Javellana/ADB).

Policymakers Need to Promote Greater Social Mobility if No One is to be Left Behind

The left panel of Figure 1.3 illustrates the negative relationship (depicted by the downward slope) between income inequality as measured by the Gini coefficient and social mobility based on the index created by the World Economic Forum as part of its 2020 study (WEF 2020). Broadly speaking, more economically unequal societies had lower scores for social mobility enablers during 2015–2019. This corroborates the theory that greater economic inequality can potentially undermine social mobility, contributing to the hardening of socioeconomic stratification within educational systems and labor markets (WBG 2018a). With more equitable distribution of economic opportunities, those born into lower social classes can more easily reach higher status as their prospects are not strongly anchored on their initial socioeconomic status.

Among developing Asian economies with available data (green dots in Figure 1.3), about 69% had less equitable distribution of economic prospects than what the level of income inequality prior to the COVID-19 pandemic implied. This suggests that, even before the pandemic, the magnitude of long-term disparities between the poor and nonpoor were greater than what the level of income inequality showed in many parts of the region.

The right panel of Figure 1.3 illustrates the correlation between scores for social mobility enablers and extreme poverty[2] reduction based on the pre-pandemic experiences of selected developing Asian economies. The figure shows that areas with higher scores for social mobility enablers also experienced generally faster reductions of extreme poverty.[3]

Figure 1.3: Correlation Between Economic Inequality, Enablers of Social Mobility, and Poverty Reduction

Economically unequal societies tend to have lower scores for social mobility enablers, while there seems to be a positive correlation between scores for social mobility enablers and the pace of poverty reduction.

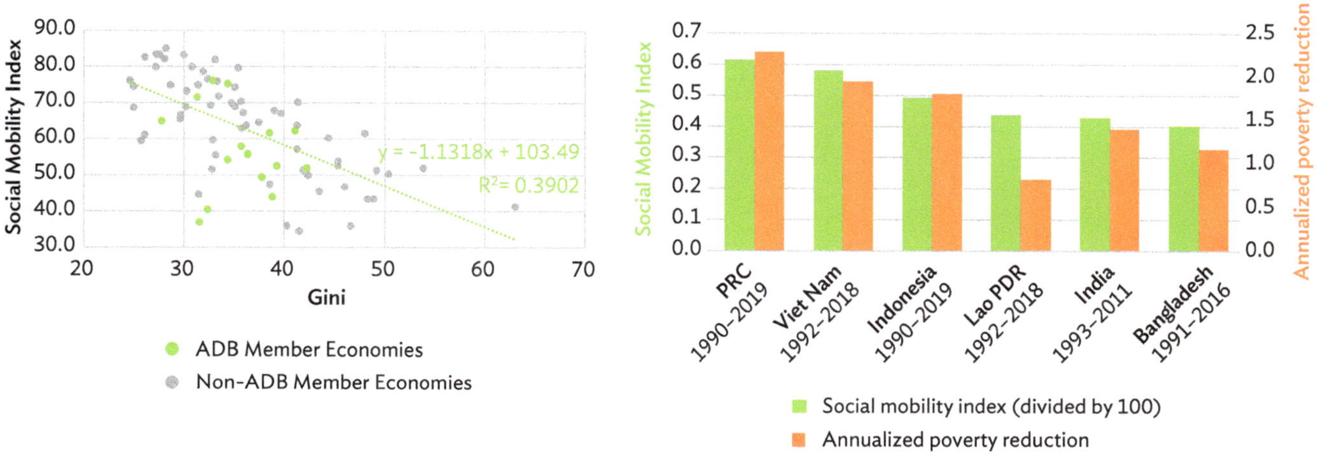

ADB = Asian Development Bank, Lao PDR = Lao People's Democratic Republic, PRC = People's Republic of China.

Notes: The data used by the World Economic Forum to calculate the Global Social Mobility Index 2020 are based on data from 2015 to 2019. Details are found in Appendix B of the World Economic Forum's *The Global Social Mobility Report 2020*. The annualized poverty reduction is calculated using $1.90 poverty estimates from 1990 to 2019. The years covered for annualized poverty reduction are as follows: Bangladesh (1991–2016), India (1993–2011), Indonesia (1990–2019), the Lao PDR (1992–2018), the PRC (1990–2019), and Viet Nam (1992–2018).

Sources: Asian Development Bank estimates using data from the World Economic Forum's Global Social Mobility Index and the World Bank Group's World Development Indicators Database and Poverty and Inequality Platform.

Click here for figure data

2 From the third quarter of 2022, the World Bank Group, which serves as data custodian for international poverty estimates, is expected to shift from using 2011 purchasing power parity (PPP) to 2017 PPP-based international poverty lines. As a result, the extreme poverty line will change from $1.90 (2011 PPP) to $2.15 (2017 PPP). Likewise, $3.20 (2011 PPP), which is the typical poverty line in lower middle-income economies, will be adjusted to $3.65 (2017 PPP) (Filmer, Haishan, and Sanchez-Paramo 2022; Joliffe et al. 2022).

3 Of course, there may be exemptions as some economies with high levels of social mobility have lower initial poverty levels and, therefore, poverty reduction may be slower. Furthermore, the positive association depicted in the second panel of Figure 1.3 does not point to a specific direction of causation.

Enduring the pandemic. Commuters using protective masks inside a Tokyo train in early 2020 (photo by Richard Atrero de Guzman/ADB).

Due to lack of available data, it is challenging to predict how the COVID-19 pandemic may have reshaped social mobility. However, simulations show that societies with lower levels of social mobility before the pandemic may experience longer-lasting setbacks.

Data from surveys conducted by the Asian Development Bank Institute (ADBI) show that many Asians experienced varying degrees of social mobility in the first 12 months of the pandemic (Figure 1.4).[4] Some people who reported reducing consumption expenditure by a substantial amount in mid-2020 reported increased expenditure by early 2021, while others saw little improvement. About 40% of those who reported having financial difficulty in mid-2020 were encountering just minor financial difficulty or no financial difficulty by early 2021. Conversely, one-third of those who did not experience financial difficulty in mid-2020 had fallen into such difficulty by early 2021.

4 The surveys conducted by ADBI were carried out using computer-assisted telephone interviews, covering eight ADB member economies: Cambodia, Indonesia, the Lao People's Democratic Republic, Malaysia, Myanmar, the Philippines, Thailand, and Viet Nam. The first round was conducted from May to July 2020 where a sample size of approximately 1,000 households were surveyed to provide nationally representative samples in each economy (Morgan and Trinh 2021). The second round was conducted from the end of January through February 2021 in Cambodia, Indonesia, the Lao People's Democratic Republic, Malaysia, the Philippines, Thailand, and Viet Nam with approximately the same sample size, but only half of the respondents were covered in both periods (Morgan, Trinh, and Kim 2022).

As vaccination programs rolled out and more economies opened up in 2021, there were expectations of greater upward social mobility. However, due to lack of available relevant data, it cannot be confirmed that such expectations have been fulfilled.

Figure 1.4: Income Mobility in Select Asian Economies During the COVID-19 Pandemic

Asians experienced varying degrees of downward and upward social mobility during pandemic.

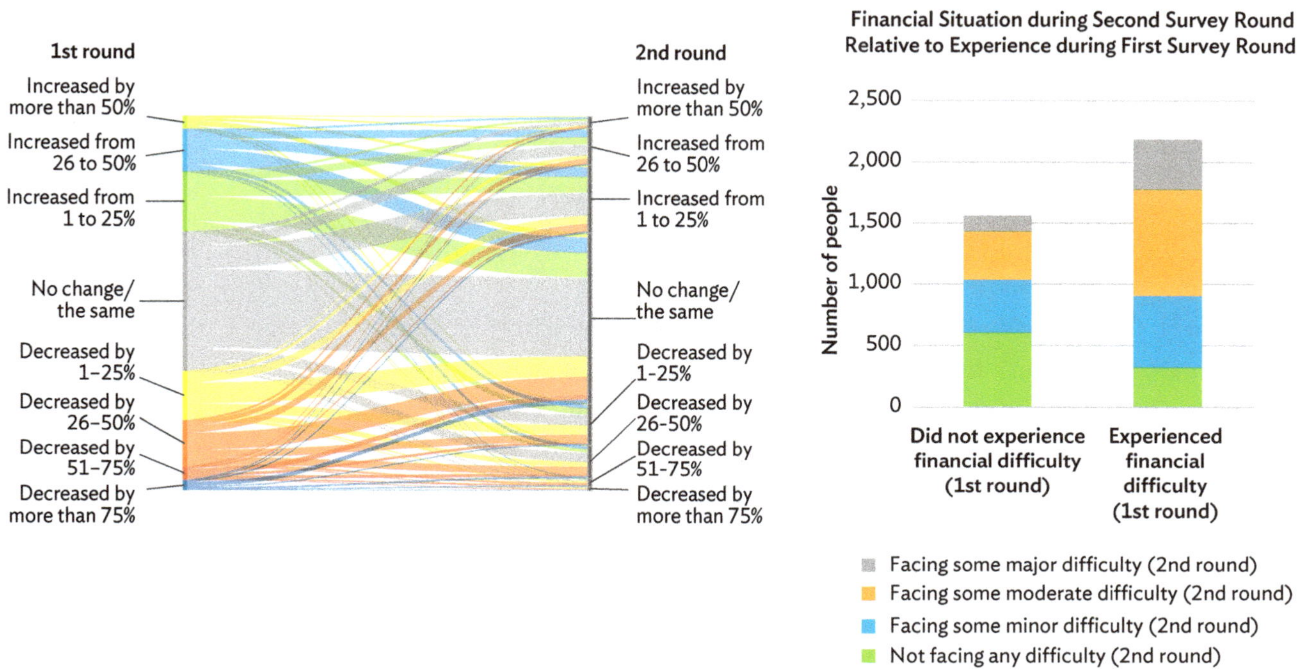

COVID-19 = coronavirus disease.

Note: The first survey round was conducted from May to July 2020 while the second round was conducted from January to February 2021.

Source: Asian Development Bank estimates using panel data from the Asian Development Bank Institute's Survey on the Impacts of COVID-19 and Related Policies on Households in 7 Developing Association of Southeast Asian Nations (ASEAN) Economies.

Click here for figure data

Instead, the relationship between pre-pandemic social mobility levels and changes in aggregate measures of poverty in 2020 and 2021 can be examined. Presumably, economies that enjoyed better social mobility before the pandemic were more likely to fare better in terms of managing poverty levels during the pandemic. Figure 1.5 provides insights into this hypothesis. The values on the vertical axis correspond to the impact of the pandemic on poverty rates (Box 1.2 provides technical details on how these numbers were calculated). Values exceeding 1 imply that poverty rates were higher than what they would have been had the pandemic not occurred. The figure shows that all economies in 2020 (left panel) had values of 1 or higher, while more than half of the economies in 2021 (right panel) had dropped to or below 1. This implies that economies were generally better able to manage poverty reduction during the second year of the pandemic.

Figure 1.5: Correlation Between Social Mobility Enablers and the COVID-19 Pandemic's Impact on Poverty

Simulated estimates of the pandemic's impact on poverty may not have adequately captured its impacts on income distribution.

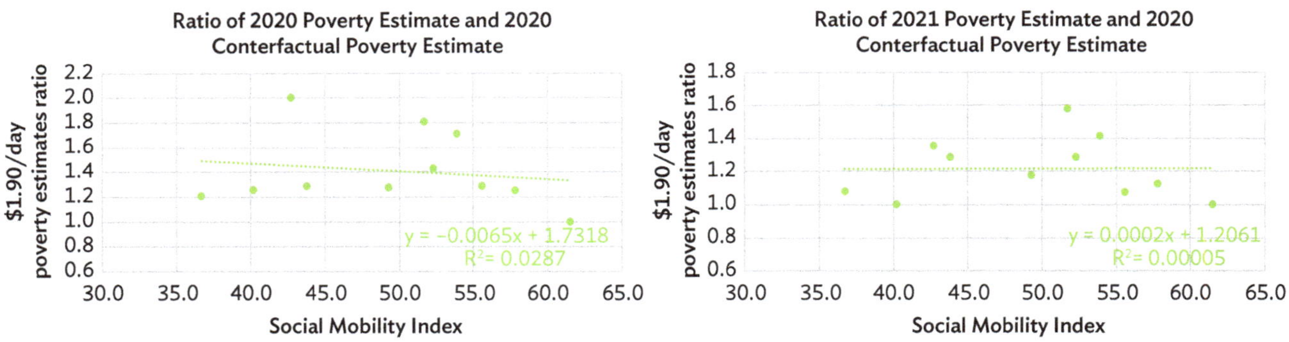

$ = United States dollars, COVID-19 = coronavirus disease.

Note: The y-axis is calculated by dividing the simulated $1.90 poverty rates under a "with COVID-19" scenario for 2020 and 2021 by counterfactual "no COVID-19"-based poverty estimates for 2020.

Sources: Asian Development Bank estimates using the World Economic Forum's Global Social Mobility Index and growth forecasts from the Asian Development Bank's *Asian Development Outlook 2022*.

Click here for figure data

Interestingly, there is no strong evidence of better performance in controlling poverty in economies with higher scores for enablers of social mobility (as depicted by the low R^2 value in Figure 1.5). However, there are important caveats worth noting. Simulated poverty rates were calculated under the assumption that the pandemic had no impact on inequality. Under such an assumption, Figure 1.5 suggests that there is no statistically significant relationship between the value of the index on social mobility enablers and the increase (or decrease) in poverty due to the pandemic.

Table 1.1: Relative Changes in Household Consumption Per Capita, by Income Decile

In some more populous Asian economies, low-income households experienced more severe impacts on consumption than did higher income deciles.

Economy	Overall	Bottom 10%	D2	D3	D4	D5	D6	D7	D8	D9	Top 10%
Armenia	-0.9	-0.3	1.7	5.7	4.2	-1.5	1.4	14.4	-2.5	7.9	-14.9
Georgia	-12.0	-8.5	-5.3	-12.1	-7.6	-14.9	-7.3	-6.6	-9.6	-15.2	-12.5
Indonesia	4.0	3.3	3.7	4.1	4.0	3.7	3.0	2.0	2.0	3.2	6.3
Kyrgyz Republic	-9.0	-11.2	-11.2	-9.6	-9.0	-7.4	-6.4	-5.2	-4.6	-4.2	-15.3
Philippines	-13.6	-21.1	-13.3	-12.1	-11.3	-10.9	-12.4	-12.5	-13.2	-14.3	-14.8
Thailand	1.1	-1.9	-0.7	0.6	1.4	1.6	1.7	1.7	1.7	2.3	0.5

Notes: The reference periods are: 2019–2020 (Armenia, Georgia, the Kyrgyz Republic, and Thailand) and 2018–2021 (Indonesia and the Philippines). Cells are highlighted green when the corresponding change is higher than the change in the specific economy's overall mean household consumption per capita and yellow if the change is lower. For Indonesia and the Kyrgyz Republic, the numbers are expressed as growth rates in real terms based on the World Bank's Poverty and Inequality Platform. For Armenia, Georgia, the Philippines and Thailand, the numbers were originally expressed as nominal growth rates based on data provided by statistical partners, and converted to real terms using relevant data from the consumer price index.

Sources: Asian Development Bank estimates using survey reports, data from the World Bank Group's Poverty and Inequality Platform (accessed 06 June 2022), and data provided by statistical partners. The poverty estimate in 2021 for the Philippines is based on first semester data from the Family Income and Expenditure Survey.

Table 1.1 hints at the potential shortcomings of the assumption that the pandemic had no impact on inequality. It shows relative changes in household consumption per capita from before the COVID-19 crisis compared to a period since the pandemic began. The second column shows the change in overall mean household consumption per capita, while the succeeding columns show the relative changes by income decile. In some economies, such as Armenia and Georgia, it appears that higher-income households experienced higher proportional reductions in their consumption. On the other hand, in economies such as the Philippines and Thailand, lower-income households experienced greater reductions in consumption relative to higher income deciles.

Box 1.2: Nowcasting and Forecasting of Poverty

Poverty statistics are commonly compiled using household income and expenditure surveys or living standards surveys. In developing Asia, these surveys are typically conducted every 3 to 5 years (Fiedler et al. 2012). Although several such surveys have been conducted since the coronavirus disease (COVID-19) pandemic struck in 2020, available data are not sufficient to provide a detailed regional assessment of the pandemic's impact on poverty.

In lieu of survey-based estimates, Asian Development Bank (ADB) statisticians have compiled poverty nowcasts and forecasts. The methodology entails compiling the latest mean household expenditures and/or income levels reported in the World Bank's PovcalNet database and Poverty and Inequality Platform. ADB's statisticians then extrapolated these to 2020, using the growth in mean household expenditures per capita imputed from the estimated relationship between household consumption expenditure per capita and gross domestic product (GDP) per capita.

For 2020 (without COVID-19 scenario), the statisticians used forecasts of GDP (and GDP per capita) reported in ADB's *Asian Development Outlook Supplement 2019* (ADB 2019). Released in December 2019, these forecasts do not take into account any pandemic-related effects and can be treated as the basis of estimating GDP per capita and, in turn, mean household expenditure per capita in a 2020 without COVID-19.

For 2020 and 2021 (with COVID-19 scenario), the statisticians used published GDP (and GDP per capita) growth rates. For 2022 and 2023, they used the latest growth forecasts from *Asian Development Outlook 2022 Supplement* (ADB 2022). For 2024 to 2030, they used the United States Department of Agriculture Economic Research Service's growth forecasts (USDA ERS 2022).

In most of these simulations, a key simplifying assumption made in the analysis was that all households within an economy experience the same percentage decline in their per capita consumption expenditure and/or income as predicted based on GDP per capita growth numbers. Nonetheless, the ADB statisticians also considered varying pro-poor growth scenarios by fixing the growth of overall mean based on predictions from GDP forecasts, but forced the bottom 10% to grow 0.6, 0.8, 1.2, and 1.4 times the growth in the overall mean. If growth of the overall mean is negative, which was the case for a number of economies in 2020, the statisticians used the adjustment factors as shown in the figure below. Focus is given to the bottom 10% to cover the poorest segments.

Adjustment Factors for Growth of Bottom 10%

← Less Pro-poor		More Pro-poor →		
0.6	0.8	1.2	1.4	if growth of overall mean is positive
1.4	1.2	0.8	0.6	if growth of overall mean is negative

References:

Asian Development Bank (ADB). 2019. *Asian Development Outlook Supplement 2019*. Manila.

ADB. 2022. *Asian Development Outlook (ADO) 2022: Mobilizing Taxes for Development*. Manila.

J. Fiedler, K. Lividini, O. Bermudez, and M. Smitz. 2012. Household Consumption and Expenditures Surveys (HCES): A Primer for Food and Nutrition Analysts in Low- and Middle-Income Countries. *Food and Nutrition Bulletin*. The United Nations University. https://journals.sagepub.com/doi/pdf/10.1177/15648265120333S205.

United States Department of Agriculture, Economic Research Service (USDA ERS). 2022. International Macroeconomic Data Set. https://www.ers.usda.gov/data-products/international-macroeconomic-data-set.aspx

Despite the COVID-19 pandemic, rates of extreme and moderate poverty in developing Asia might be reduced to less than 1% and 7%, respectively, by 2030. However, such outcomes are not guaranteed because of risks to economic growth paths and social mobility prospects.

Figure 1.6 and Table 1.2 provide insights into developing Asia's social mobility prospects by anticipating how the region's income distribution may look in 2030.

Figure 1.6 uses an assumption of neutral income distribution and it can be seen that, while the COVID-19 pandemic caused an uptick in the prevalence of extreme and moderate poverty in 2020, the prevalence of extreme poverty in developing Asia is anticipated to fall to less than 1% of the population by 2030. Meanwhile, about 7% of the region's residents are forecast to be moderately poor and about 25% may be regarded as economically vulnerable at the same milestone. On the other hand, forecasts suggest that about 43% may be economically secure and 25% classified as middle class by 2030.[5]

Figure 1.6: Forecasting of Income Groupings in Developing Asia by 2030

At least 20% of developing Asia's population were either extremely or moderately poor in 2021, but the proportion of people who are at least economically secure may reach nearly 70% by 2030.

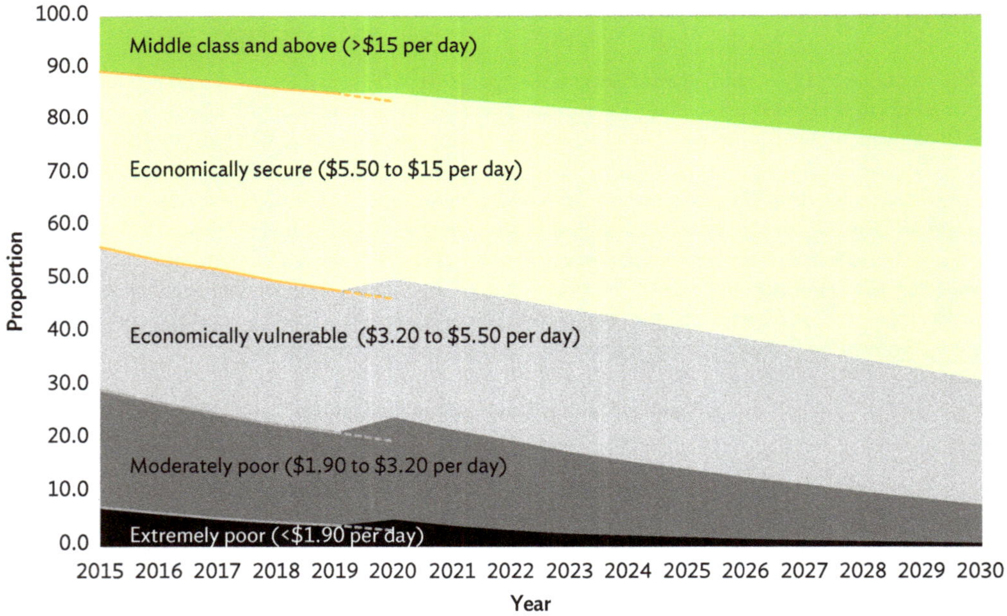

$ = United States dollars.

Notes: Each income grouping is calculated as the percentage of people in developing Asia. These are based on 29 developing Asian Development Bank member economies with available data required for calculations. Income thresholds are expressed in 2011 purchasing power parities. Estimates may be sensitive to assumptions employed for populous economies, which account for a significant portion of poverty in the region but have quite dated official poverty numbers (e.g., see Roy and van der Weide 2022). The dotted lines represent counterfactual estimates under the scenario that the coronavirus disease (COVID-19) pandemic did not happen.

Sources: Asian Development Bank estimates using data presented in Table 1.1.1 of *Key Indicators for Asia and the Pacific 2022* and simulated data derived from the World Bank's PovcalNet database and Poverty and Inequality Platform (accessed 30 May 2022).

[5] A number of studies use $15 (in 2011 purchasing power parities) per day as the threshold for middle class. On the other hand, those living on $3.10 to $5.50 per day are considered economically vulnerable, while those with $5.50 to $15 per day are considered economically secure (WB 2018b, WB 2019).

Table 1.2 presents poverty estimates derived when departing from the assumption of neutral income distribution. It shows the impacts on socioeconomic status of less pro-poor growth (growth of bottom 10% is 0.6 times or 0.8 times growth of overall mean) versus more pro-poor-growth (growth of bottom 10% is 1.2 times or 1.4 times growth of overall mean). The results suggest that almost 1.5% of the population of developing Asia could avoid extreme poverty by 2030 under the highest pro-poor growth scenario (compared to the lowest pro-poor growth scenario).

Table 1.2: Impact of Varying Pro-Poor Growth Scenarios on Socioeconomic Status in 2030

(% of population)

Poverty reduction may be more pronounced by 2030 if growth is more pro-poor.

Socioeconomic Status in 2030	Less Pro-Poor Growth		More Pro-Poor Growth	
	Growth of bottom 10% is 0.6 times growth of overall mean	Growth of bottom 10% is 0.8 times growth of overall mean	Growth of bottom 10% is 1.2 times growth of overall mean	Growth of bottom 10% is 1.4 times growth of overall mean
Extremely poor	1.77	1.10	0.43	0.27
Moderately poor	6.48	7.06	6.00	4.73
Economically vulnerable	24.32	23.65	24.38	25.64
Economically secure	42.45	43.31	44.44	44.69
Middle class and above	24.99	24.89	24.75	24.68

Notes: Each figure is calculated as the percentage of people in developing Asia. These are based on 29 developing Asian Development Bank member economies with available data required for calculations. Income thresholds are expressed in 2011 purchasing power parities. Estimates may be sensitive to assumptions employed for populous economies, which account for a significant portion of poverty in the region but have quite dated official poverty numbers (e.g., see Roy and van der Weide 2022).

Sources: Asian Development Bank estimates using data presented in Table 1.1.1 of *Key Indicators for Asia and the Pacific 2022* and simulated data derived from the World Bank's PovcalNet database and Poverty and Inequality Platform (accessed 30 May 2022).

It is important to note that, even if the nonneutral distribution assumption is made, there are a number of uncertainties surrounding these projections. First, economic growth may be affected by looming threats of stagflation, food insecurity, energy price shocks, debt burden, geopolitical tensions, and other risk factors. Second, assuming that societies with higher levels of social mobility prior to the COVID-19 pandemic can more easily revert to their former poverty reduction paths, the pandemic may have longer-term consequences that are yet unknown. For instance, the full implications of learning losses caused by school closures on future lifetime earnings and social mobility prospects may not be known for some decades.

Although education completion rates are improving across developing Asia, pandemic impacts on future lifetime earnings may be significant for today's students.

Data presented in Table 1.4.2 and in the left panel of Figure 1.7 suggest that most economies in Asia and the Pacific with available data showed progress in completion rates in lower secondary education from 2010 to 2020, however, gaps across wealth quintiles persist. Furthermore, even before the pandemic, there were serious concerns about whether children were actually learning (UNICEF 2022). Data presented in the right panel of Figure 1.7 suggest that the proportion of children and young people at the end of lower secondary school achieving at least a minimum proficiency level in reading and mathematics was below 70% in 11 economies.

Figure 1.7: Completion Rates in Lower Secondary Education (by Wealth Quintile for 2020 or Latest Year) and Proportion of Students at the End of Lower Secondary School Achieving the Minimum Proficiency Level

(%)

Completion rates have improved but learning is still low in many economies.

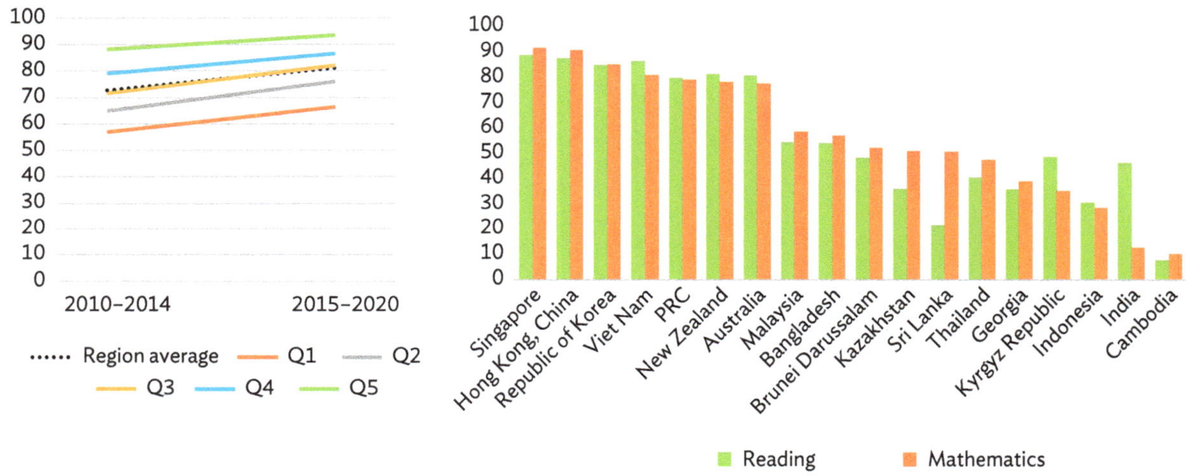

PRC = People's Republic of China, Q = quintile.
Source: Asian Development Bank estimates using data presented in Tables 1.4.1 and 1.4.2 of *Key Indicators for Asia and the Pacific 2022*.

Click here for figure data

The pandemic has further exacerbated the learning crisis for today's student cohort. Globally, estimates suggest that 70% of 10-year-olds are unable to read and understand a simple text, and this contributes to a loss in potential lifetime earnings by today's generation of students equivalent to 17% of current gross domestic product (GDP) levels (WBG et al. 2022). Similarly, in a study conducted by ADB (2022), estimates suggest that the lifetime earning losses of developing Asia's students may range from 3.9% to as much as 8.8% of pre-pandemic earnings. The upper panel of Figure 1.8 also shows that areas with lower scores for social mobility enablers are more likely to experience higher relative lifetime earning losses. Within each economy, inequality may also further expand due to differences in access to remote learning tools. Under a medium-efficacy scenario of remote learning, estimates show that students from the poorest wealth quintile are expected to have losses in future earnings that are 47% higher than those of the richest students in their economy, while girls may lose about 28% more in future earnings (ADB 2022). The disparities between rich and poor may be larger under a high-efficacy scenario of learning as shown in the lower panel of Figure 1.8.

Figure 1.8: Projected Lifetime Earning Losses due to Learning Losses in Developing Asia

The social mobility prospects of Asian students, as measured by expected lifetime earnings, are significantly lower than pre-pandemic levels due to learning losses.

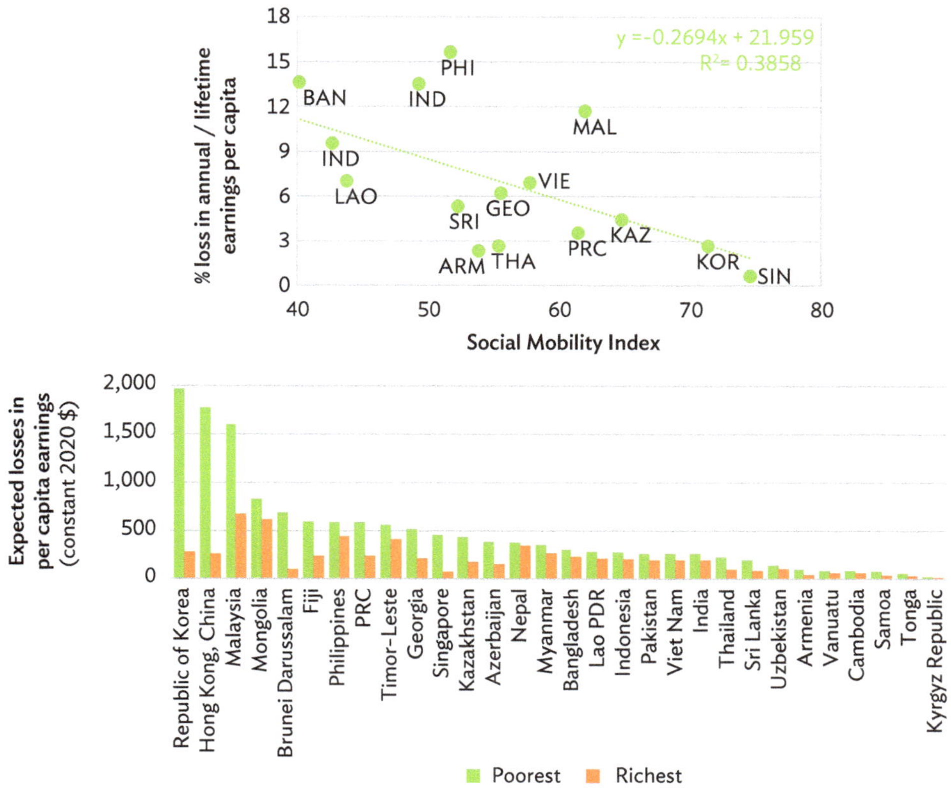

$ = United States dollar, ARM = Armenia, BAN = Bangladesh, GEO = Georgia, IND = India, INO = Indonesia, KAZ = Kazakhstan, KOR = Republic of Korea, Lao PDR = Lao People's Democratic Republic, MAL = Malaysia, PAK = Pakistan, PHI = Philippines, PRC = People's Republic of China, SIN = Singapore, SRI = Sri Lanka, THA = Thailand, VIE = Viet Nam.

Notes: Losses in earnings are calculated under the high-efficacy scenario of remote learning. Information on estimates under alternative scenarios are presented in a report by the Asian Development Bank (2022). The analysis considers three scenarios—high, medium, and low—for the efficacy of remote education relative to classroom instruction. Each scenario estimates the effectiveness of remote education in each economy by applying an adjustment factor to online-learning effectiveness in high-income economies. Online learning in high-income economies is assumed to be 88% as effective as in-person classes in the high-efficacy scenario, 66% in the medium-efficacy scenario, and 37% in the low-efficacy scenario. The adjustment factor includes measures of internet access, television access, effectiveness of television relative to online education, and the relative shares of television and online forms of remote instruction (ADB 2022).

Sources: Asian Development Bank estimates using data from the bank's *Asian Development Outlook 2022* and the World Economic Forum's Global Social Mobility Index.

Click here for figure data

To recover learning losses caused by COVID-19 school closures, an initial step may be to assess how much knowledge has been lost or forgone. This information would be useful in determining the level at which to restart instruction and how monitoring systems can be calibrated to ensure progress of learning is properly tracked. Additionally, it is important for learning recovery to focus on enhancing foundational skills, finding ways to extend instruction time, and encouraging the re-enrollment of dropouts (Molato-Gayares et al. 2022). These initiatives are particularly relevant for poor people in developing economies, which are more likely to reduce investment in education during income shocks (Morgan and Trinh 2021; Nestour, Carvalho, and Minardi 2020), in turn jeopardizing social mobility prospects.

Pandemic restrictions may have affected people's motivation levels and behaviors toward study and work, which can in turn limit social mobility.

Prolonged school closures and financial issues during the pandemic had impacts on student motivation. In an ADB survey conducted in Bangladesh, which asked parents about their child's desire or motivation to study, 20% were found to have either low or very low motivation levels as of August 2021 (compared to 5% in December 2019). In addition, about 13% of those enrolled before school closures began in March 2020 planned to drop out, and about two-thirds of those students had no plans of returning to a school (Li and Sharma 2022).

In terms of attitudes to work, many Asians had mixed opinions on the pathways to success even before COVID-19 struck. Respondents to a World Values Survey were asked whether hard work or luck is more important to success on a scale of 1 (all hard work) to 10 (all luck). The results, as shown in Figure 1.9, suggest that a majority of Asians from middle-income quintiles tended to have relatively neutral feelings (median score of 4), while those from the lowest and highest income classes had a slightly stronger belief that hard work is more important.

Figure 1.9: Perception of Whether Hard Work or Luck is More Important

Even before the COVID-19 pandemic, a significant number of Asians did not strongly believe that hard work is more important in society's reward systems.

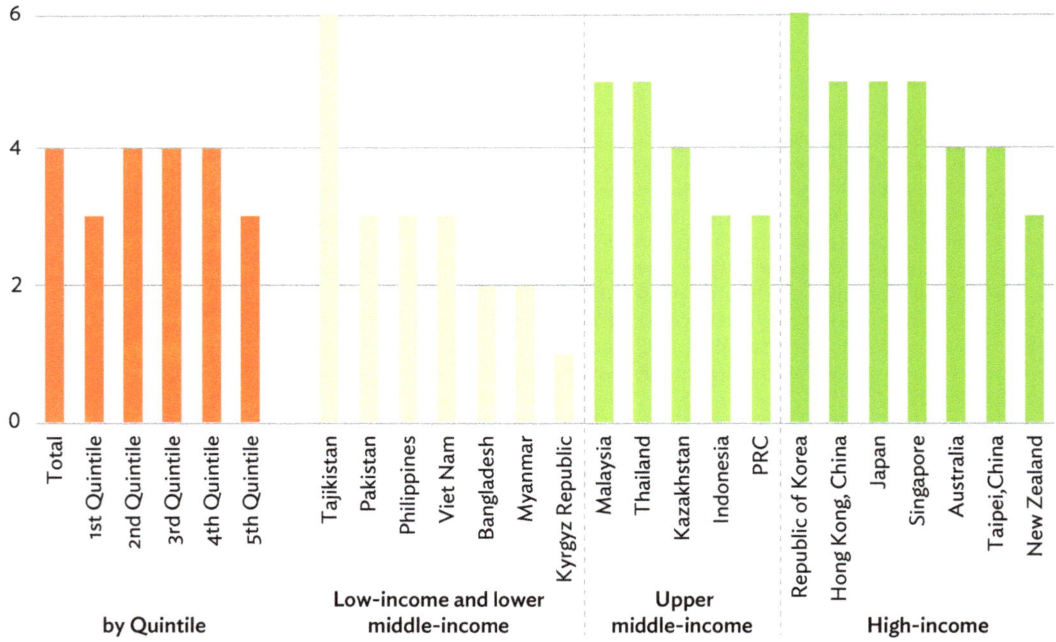

COVID-19 = coronavirus disease, PRC = People's Republic of China.

Notes: Lower median values indicate greater perceived importance of hard work while higher values indicate greater perceived importance of luck. These are based on World Values Survey data for the following economies: Australia; Bangladesh; Hong Kong, China; Indonesia; Japan; Kazakhstan; the Kyrgyz Republic; Myanmar; Malaysia; New Zealand; Pakistan; the People's Republic of China; the Philippines; the Republic of Korea; Singapore; Thailand; Tajikistan; Taipei,China; and Viet Nam. Income groupings follow the World Bank Group's 2019 classification as reported in the World Values Survey data. Income groupings follow the World Bank Group's 2019 classification as reported in the World Values Survey data.

Source: Asian Development Bank estimates using data from round seven (pooled datafile version) of the World Values Survey (accessed 15 February 2022).

Click here for figure data

There are some greater variations between lower middle-income, upper middle-income, and high-income economies.

The pandemic may have further eroded confidence in the expectation that hard work leads to success. Estimates suggest that Asia and the Pacific lost about 3.6% of its work hours in 2021, compared to the fourth quarter of 2019 (the pre-pandemic benchmark). This equates to 76.7 million full-time jobs as people became underemployed or unemployed in 2020 and 2021, based on data from the International Labour Organization (ILO)'s COVID-19 Monitor database (ILO 2022). Figure 1.10 suggests that many people in Asia and the Pacific may have given up on finding work, with labor force participation rates not bouncing back to pre-pandemic levels. There are studies showing that long periods out of employment may lead to discouraged jobseekers, outdated skillsets, and adverse effects on mental health (Krueger, Cramer and Cho 2014). Studies also suggest that the region's youth may bear higher longer-term economic and social costs, with nearly half of all young workers employed in sectors that were hit hardest by the pandemic (ILO and ADB 2020).

Figure 1.10: Labor Force Participation Rates in Asia and the Pacific

In Asia and the Pacific, workforce participation has not bounced back to pre-pandemic levels.

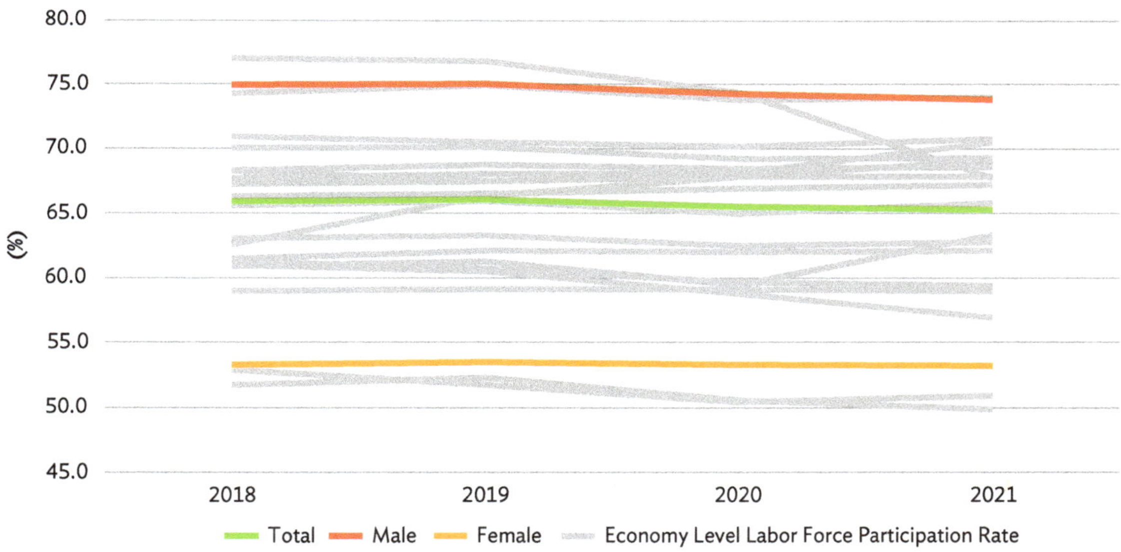

Note: Light shaded lines represent economy-level data while colored lines represent regional-level data.
Source: Asian Development Bank estimates using data from economies' official sources.

Click here for figure data

There are other social inequalities against vulnerable groups, including women, which may lead to lower social mobility prospects if left unaddressed.

Even before the pandemic, the incidence of domestic violence was pronounced in a number of Asia and the Pacific economies (as shown in the first panel of Figure 1.11), with estimates suggesting that about 10.6% of ever-partnered women and girls aged 15 years and over had experienced such incidents.

Figure 1.11: Incidence of Domestic Abuse and Child Marriage in Select Economies

The risk of gender-based violence and/or premature marriage remains alarmingly high in many economies of Asia and the Pacific.

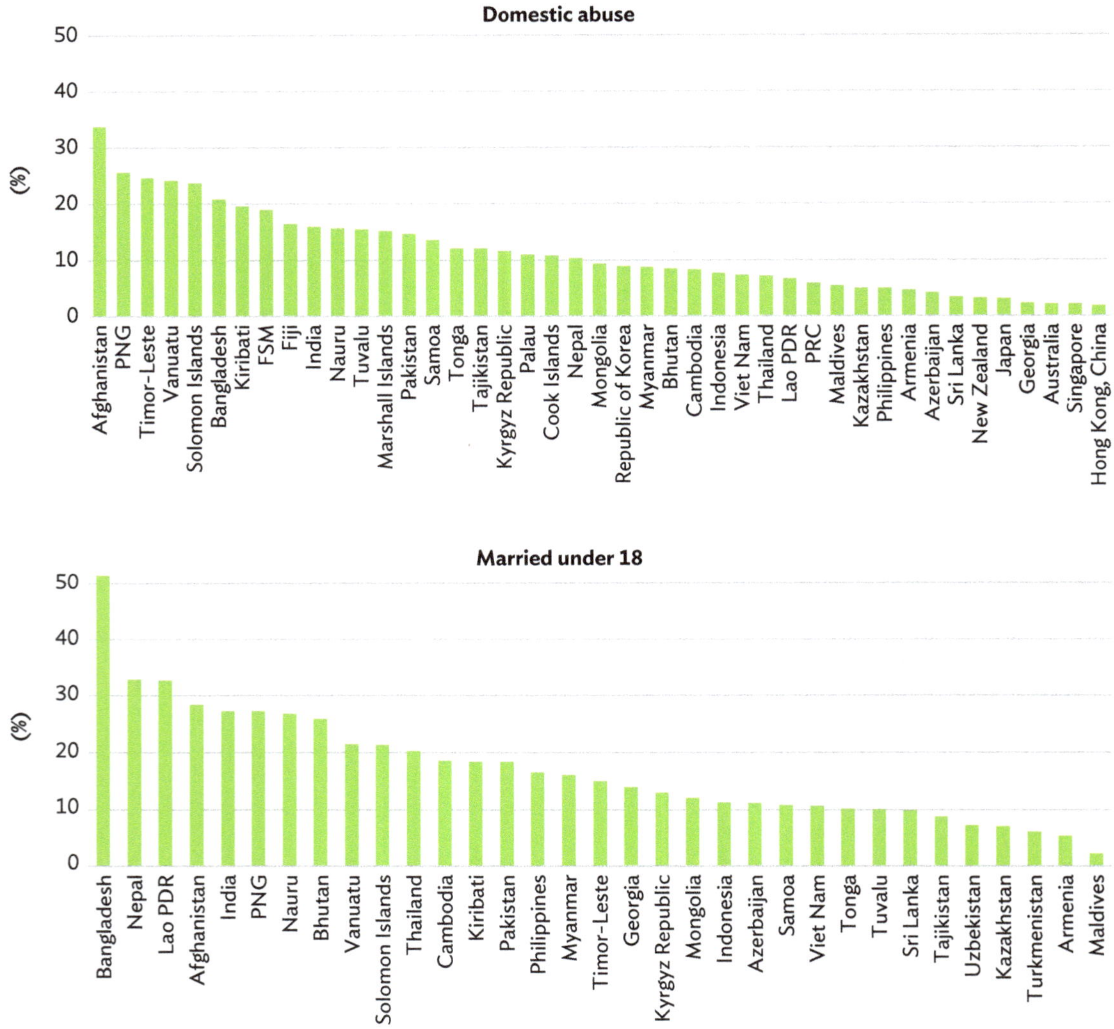

FSM = Federated States of Micronesia, Lao PDR = Lao People's Democratic Republic, PNG = Papua New Guinea, PRC = People's Republic of China.

Note: The figure for child marriage includes economies with latest data available from 2006 to 2019.

Source: United Nations SDG Global Database. https://unstats.un.org/sdgs/indicators/database/ (accessed 20 July 2022).

Click here for figure data

Additionally, pre-pandemic trends on child marriage, also considered to be another form of gender-based violence, showed that such marriage was commonly practiced in several parts of the region (UN 2013), as shown in the second panel of Figure 1.11. Worryingly, financial distress and mobility restrictions caused by the pandemic may exacerbate these forms of social inequalities. As people were confined to their homes at height of pandemic lockdowns, the incidence of domestic violence against women and children may have increased, based on a study conducted by United Nations Women (UN Women 2020). Victims of domestic violence also had reduced options for support and counseling due to lockdowns and social distancing measures (UN Women 2020).

Uncertain economic recovery beyond the pandemic may have adverse consequences on social mobility and cohesion.

A World Bank Group (2022) report on the global economic outlook hints at a protracted period of slow economic growth and elevated inflation in the medium term. This may have a profound impact on social mobility prospects, particularly for low- and middle-income economies. The 2022 Global Risk Report, published by the World Economic Forum, identified erosion of social cohesion as one of the risks that has worsened the most since the start of the COVID-19 pandemic (rated highest by 27.8% of respondents as shown in Figure 1.12). Additionally, 25.5% of respondents identified livelihood crises as worsening the most (WEF 2022).

Figure 1.12: Top 10 Risks that Have Worsened since the COVID-19 Pandemic Began

Adverse impacts on social cohesion, livelihoods, and mental health are among the greatest concerns in the wake of the COVID-19 crisis.

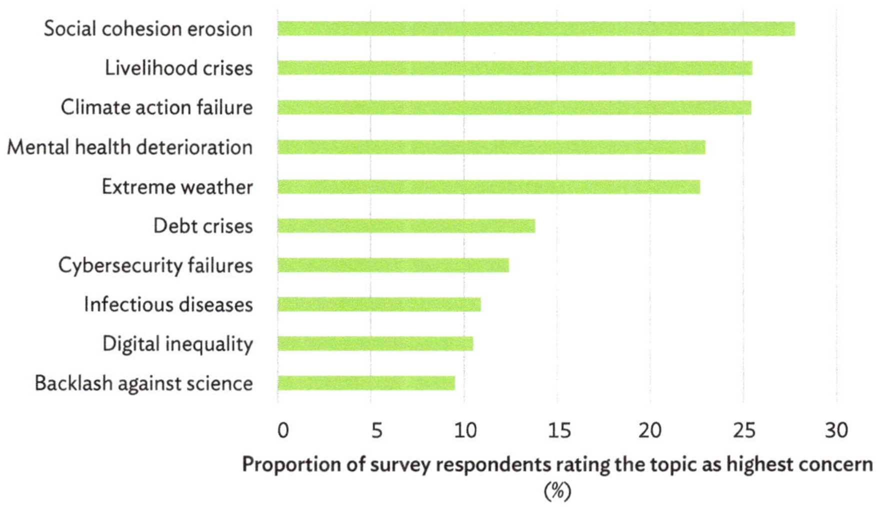

COVID-19 = coronavirus disease.
Source: Asian Development Bank visualization using data from Figure 1 of the World Economic Forum's *The Global Risks Report 2022*.

Click here for figure data

Providing adequate social protection minimizes downward social mobility and promotes greater upward social mobility through skills development, especially for the poor and vulnerable.

Having a wide social safety net, where people's livelihoods and well-being are protected against socioeconomic shocks, may prevent many from falling deeper into poverty. Those who have access to adequate social protection may be able to invest more resources in skills training and personal development, thereby boosting their social mobility prospects. In fact, the World Bank Group estimates suggest that, before the COVID-19 pandemic, more than one-third of the world's very poor managed to escape extreme poverty because of social safety nets (WBG 2018c). Figure 1.13 indicates that adequate social protection systems may have contributed to improved social mobility (as depicted by the upward slope in Figure 1.13).

Figure 1.13: Correlation between Social Protection Coverage and Enablers of Social Mobility

Greater social protection coverage is associated with better socioeconomic mobility prospects.

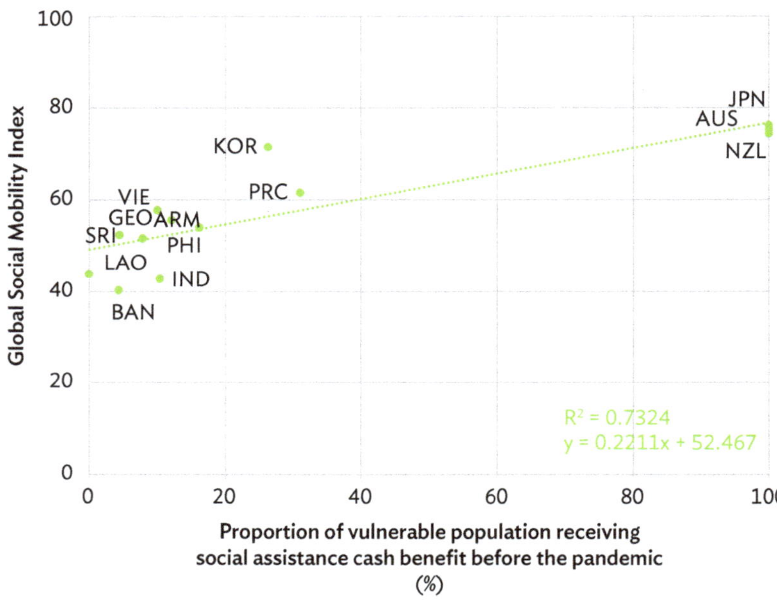

ARM = Armenia, AUS = Australia, BAN = Bangladesh, GEO = Georgia, IND = India, JPN = Japan, KOR = Republic of Korea, LAO = Lao People's Democratic Republic, NZL = New Zealand, PHI = Philippines, PRC = People's Republic of China, SRI = Sri Lanka, VIE = Viet Nam.

Sources: Table 1.1.2 of *Key Indicators for Asia and the Pacific 2022*; and the World Economic Forum's *The Global Social Mobility Report 2020*.

Click here for figure data

The latest available data from before the pandemic show that about 72% of ADB's member economies in Asia and the Pacific had less than half of their population covered by at least one social protection benefit. Nevertheless, as the COVID-19 pandemic unfolded, governments ramped up social protection coverage to help poor and vulnerable groups cope with disruptions that threatened their livelihoods and well-being. These measures came in the form of new or modified cash transfers, new unemployment programs, unemployment insurance, food subsidies, and sickness benefits. The ILO's Social Protection Monitor has recorded more than 400 social protection measures taken by 36 economies in Asia and the Pacific (ILO 2022).

Altogether, these initiatives have contributed to a substantial increase in social protection coverage for a number of the region's developing economies (Figure 1.14).

Figure 1.14: Social Protection Coverage in Selected Economies of Asia and the Pacific

Most economies increased social protection coverage during pandemic.

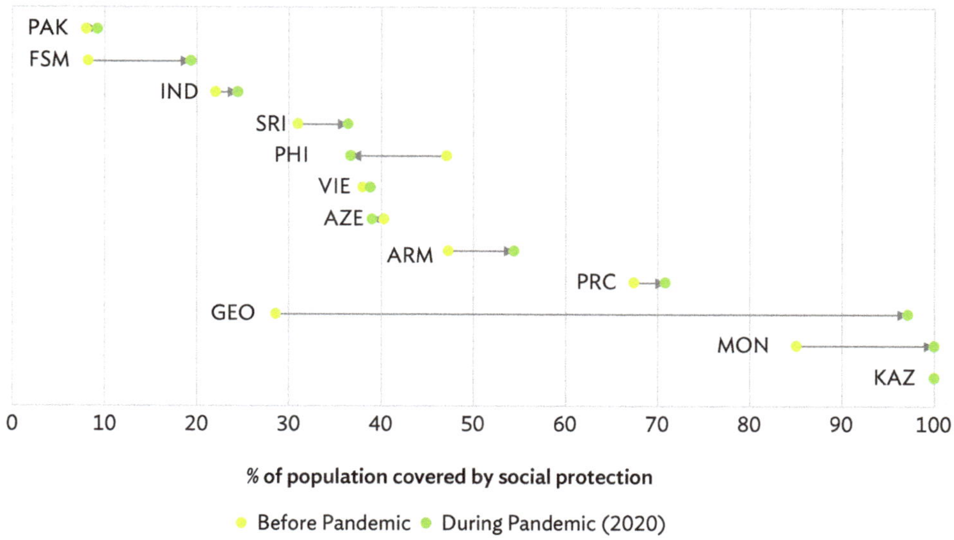

ARM = Armenia, AZE = Azerbaijan, FSM = Federated States of Micronesia, GEO = Georgia, IND = India, KAZ = Kazakhstan, MON = Mongolia, PAK = Pakistan, PHI = Philippines, PRC = People's Republic of China, SRI = Sri Lanka, VIE = Viet Nam.

Note: The data correspond to Sustainable Development Goal Indicator 1.3.1.a – Proportion of Population Covered by at Least One Social Protection Benefit.

Source: Table 1.1.2 of *Key Indicators for Asia and the Pacific 2022*.

Click here for figure data

Increased social protection coverage must extend beyond being a temporary pandemic response and target those who need it most.

It is important to sustain targeted social protection coverage as Asia and the Pacific moves towards post-pandemic recovery. There are a number of risks that threaten the region's social mobility prospects and those most vulnerable to such risks require ongoing access to appropriate assistance.

A working paper commissioned by ADB in 2021 characterized the nature of required social protection packages in three stages: (i) emergency (2020), (ii) recovery and/or transition (2021–2023), and (iii) progress toward relevant SDG targets (2024–2030) (Auwera, Meerendonk, and Kumar 2021). In the context of developing economies, which typically encounter constraints in mobilizing financial resources, it is important to gauge the cost associated with the social protection packages needed for each stage. Using the Social Protection Reform Simulation (SPRS20) model, it is estimated that the emergency phase amounted to 3% of GDP in 2020, while the recovery and/or transition stage is estimated to have required approximately 3.4% of GDP in 2021 and will gradually decrease to 3.2% in 2023. The costs estimated during these two phases are assumed to be in addition to existing social protection expenditures. Social protection for the third stage is estimated at 4.1% of GDP in 2024, increasing to 5.9% in 2030. The costs represent the sum of all social protection programs in an economy for the remaining period toward the SDG targets.

In 2020, while the proportion of vulnerable people receiving social assistance cash benefits increased relative to pre-pandemic levels, total social protection coverage among vulnerable populations remained low. Results from surveys conducted by ADBI suggest that almost 60% of respondents who did not receive assistance during the first year of pandemic were not aware of the various assistance programs (Figure 1.15).

Figure 1.15: Proportion of the Vulnerable Population Receiving Social Assistance Benefits and Reasons for Not Applying for Government Assistance, 2020

Increasing awareness of social protection programs, particularly among those who need them most, may help drive greater poverty reduction.

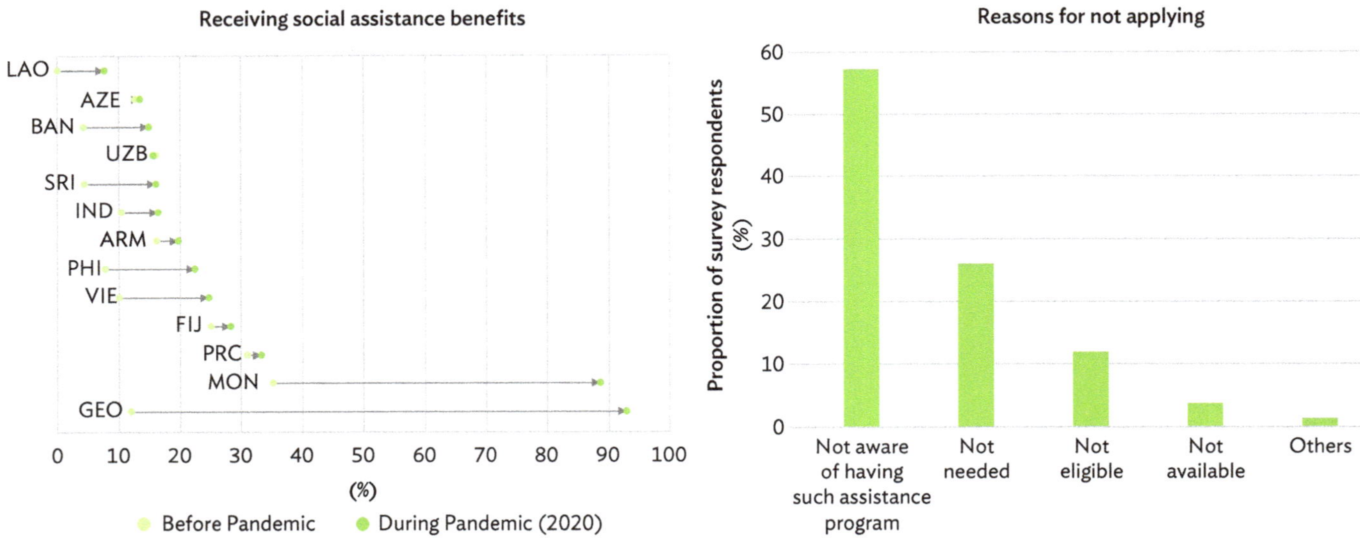

ARM = Armenia, AZE = Azerbaijan, BAN = Bangladesh, FIJ = Fiji, IND = India, GEO = Georgia, LAO = Lao People's Democratic Republic, MON = Mongolia, PHI = Philippines, PRC = People's Republic of China, SRI = Sri Lanka, UZB = Uzbekistan, VIE = Viet Nam.

Sources: Table 1.1.2 of *Key Indicators for Asia and the Pacific 2022*; and Asian Development Bank estimates using data from the second round of the Asian Development Bank Institute's Survey on the Impacts of COVID-19 and Related Policies on Households in Select Developing Association of Southeast Asian Nations (ASEAN) Economies.

Click here for figure data

Enhancing the efficiency and effectiveness of social protection systems requires continuous capacity building through various stages of such systems. This includes targeting, identification, registration, payment, and other delivery mechanisms as well as grievance redressal and system monitoring and evaluation. The COVID-19 pandemic has highlighted critical gaps in social protection systems, including a lack of up-to-date and relevant socioeconomic data for effective targeting and identification. Such gaps can cripple a system's ability to reach the most vulnerable people, who are often the intended recipients of social protection benefits. The pandemic has highlighted the need for innovative and cost-effective approaches to strengthen social protection systems, including in data collection and data management, to improve their overall efficiency and effectiveness and their ability to safeguard society's most vulnerable. Notably, advancements in information and communication technologies (ICT) have been a critical driving factor in reshaping the social protection landscape. For example, reports commissioned by ADB and Deutsche Gesellschaft für Internationale Zusammenarbeit (GIZ) provide insights for thinking about how digital tools, big data, and even artificial intelligence can enhance the functioning of social protection programs (ADB 2022b; Handayani et al. 2017; Ohlenburg 2022). In terms of targeting, there are studies showing how the combination of geospatial data (e.g., satellite images) with survey data on household income and expenditure could offer a cost-effective approach to collecting granular poverty data (ADB 2020b). There are also an increasing number of social protection initiatives that use biometric-technology data, e.g., fingerprint and/or iris recognition (Carmona 2018). For enhanced service delivery, some examples include the use of digital or other alternative payment solutions (e.g., use of electronic or mobile phone payments and cash-cards) that make it easier for beneficiaries to receive payments, instead of traveling to government offices and navigating paper-based administrative processes. Nonetheless, it is important to note that, while innovations in digital technology and big data offer opportunities to enhance management of social protection programs, mechanisms to protect privacy, narrow the digital divide, and address deficiencies in literacy on using such tools also remain important considerations (Carmona 2018; ADB 2020b).

Fostering Resilient and Innovative Infrastructure and Services

This section considers drivers of social mobility by examining trends with respect to selected indicators under SDG 9 (industry, innovation, and infrastructure).

Across Asia and the Pacific, disparities in access to infrastructure and services still exist.

The region's development path since the turn of the millennium chronicles improved transportation networks, enhanced electricity generation capacity, and greater access to telecommunications and water infrastructure (ADB 2020a). Collectively, such improvements contributed to faster economic growth and poverty reduction prior to the COVID-19 crisis and may help expedite post-pandemic recovery.

Despite this progress, disparities in access to key infrastructure and basic services still exist between Asia and the Pacific and the rest of the world. The latest estimates suggest that nearly 73.8% of the region's economies with available data had estimated road traffic death rates below the global average of 16.7 per 100,000 population (Table 1.3.3). On the other hand, some 16% of ADB's regional

Delivering sustainable infrastructure. Investment in Nuku'alofa, Tonga will improve access to safe water supply, solid waste, and sanitation (photo by Eric Sales/ADB).

members had electricity penetration rates falling below the global average of 90.5%, based on the latest available data in 2020 (Table 1.7.1). Likewise, in two-fifths of ADB's regional members with available data, more than half of the population were not using safely managed drinking water services, while the same proportion of economies had 50% or less of their populations using safely managed sanitation services (ADB 2021a) as shown in Figure 1.16.

Estimates made before the COVID-19 pandemic suggest that developing Asia needed approximately $1.7 trillion to be invested annually in infrastructure until 2030, to maintain the region's growth momentum, tackle poverty, and respond to climate change (ADB 2017). Such a figure is approximately 13.3% higher than a baseline estimate of $1.5 trillion per year, which does not include climate change mitigation and adaptation costs (ADB 2017).

Figure 1.16: Proportion of Population Using Safely Managed Drinking Water Services, by Economy Income Grouping

In 11 ADB regional member economies (mostly low and middle-income), more than half the population were not using safely managed drinking water services.

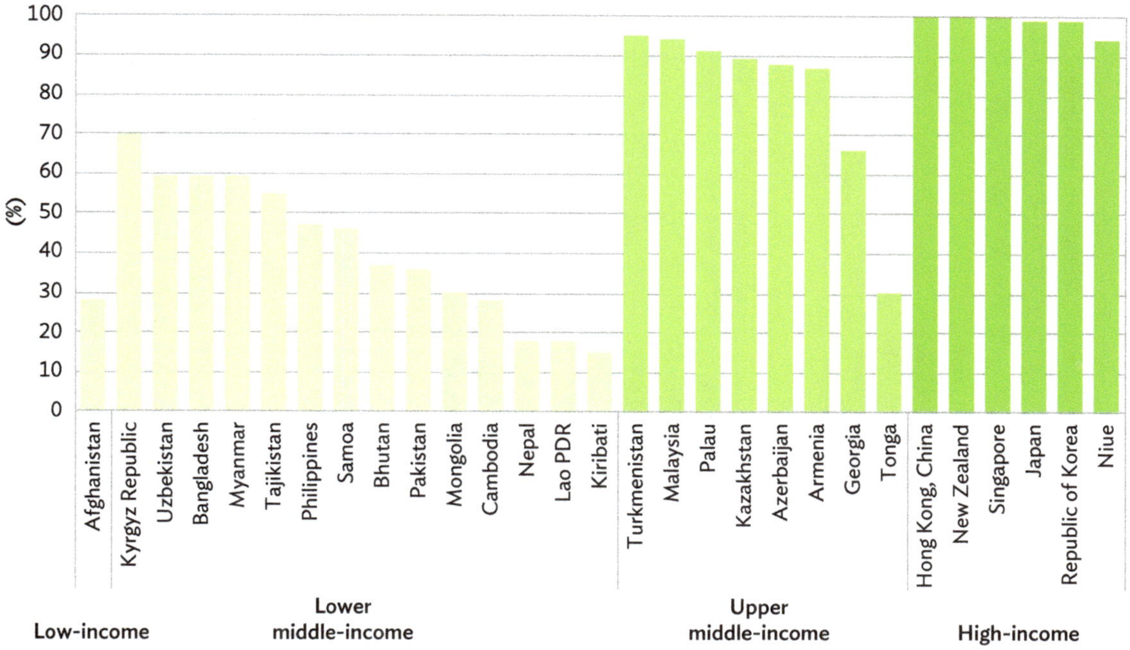

Lao PDR = Lao People's Democratic Republic.

Notes: Income groupings follow the World Bank Group's classification as of July 2022. For Niue, the "high-income" classification is based on 2019 gross national income per capita (Atlas method) of $16,247. Graphics are based on available data for the most recent year ranging from 2017 to 2020.

Source: Table 1.6.1 of *Key Indicators for Asia and the Pacific 2022*.

Click here for figure data

Sustainable innovation is important in driving economic growth and enhancing the region's social mobility prospects.

The COVID-19 pandemic has underscored the relevance of SDG 9, which aims to build resilient infrastructure, promote sustainable industrialization, and foster innovation. As millions of people were pushed into poverty due to disruptions caused by the pandemic, they require new economic opportunities and productive jobs, which sustainable development and innovation can help create.

Figure 1.17 illustrates a metric compiled by the World Intellectual Property Organization, which integrates around 80 indicators on political environment, education, infrastructure, and knowledge creation to provide a composite measure of innovation (WIPO 2021). It is apparent that higher-income economies generally scored higher for innovation in 2021. Among the lower middle-income economies, Viet Nam, India, and the Philippines scored highest.

Figure 1.17: Scores on the Global Innovation Index for Selected Economies, by Economy Income Grouping

High-income economies give high priority to innovation, while a number of fast-growing economies also score relatively highly.

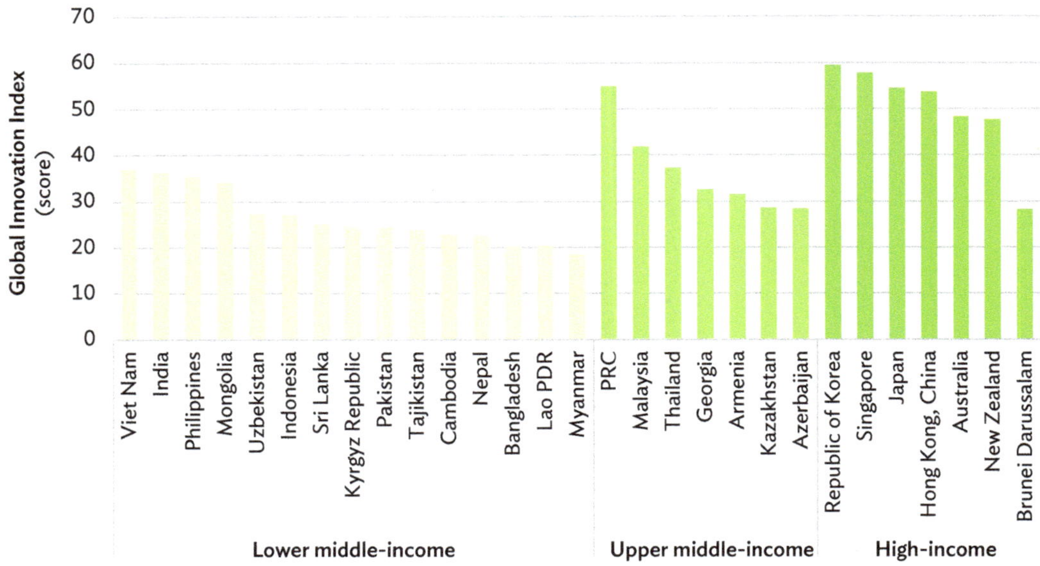

Lao PDR = Lao People's Democratic Republic, PRC = People's Republic of China.

Note: Income groupings follow the World Bank Group's classification as of July 2022.

Source: Global Innovation Index. 2021 Report. https://www.globalinnovationindex.org/gii-2021-report.

Click here for figure data

A number of economies in Asia and the Pacific lag behind in investments for the research and development that is critical to sustainable innovation.

Research and development (R&D) is an intrinsic component of innovation. In many ways, the COVID-19 pandemic has magnified the importance of R&D investments as it helped illuminate new frontiers in vaccine development, quarantine protocols, integration of digital technology for business continuity, and other aspects of pandemic management (UIS 2020).

In Asia and the Pacific, investment in R&D reached $870.5 billion (purchasing power parity) in 2018, up by 75.9% from 2010 (UIS Database). The average number of researchers per million inhabitants also increased, from 1,480 in 2010 to 2,013 in 2020. There are, however, notable disparities between economies in the region, as Figure 1.18 suggests. While allocations for R&D as a portion of GDP exceeds the world average in high-income economies such as Japan and the Republic of Korea (as well as the upper middle-income economy of the People's Republic of China), all lower middle-income economies and a majority of upper middle-income economies with available data had R&D allocations less than half the global average.

An eye on the future. Researchers are pioneering new technologies for Asia and the Pacific (photo by Lu Guang/ADB).

Figure 1.18: Research and Development Expenditure as a Proportion of Gross Domestic Product, by Economy Income Grouping

Several high-income economies invested more than the global average in R&D, but spending remains low in most developing economies.

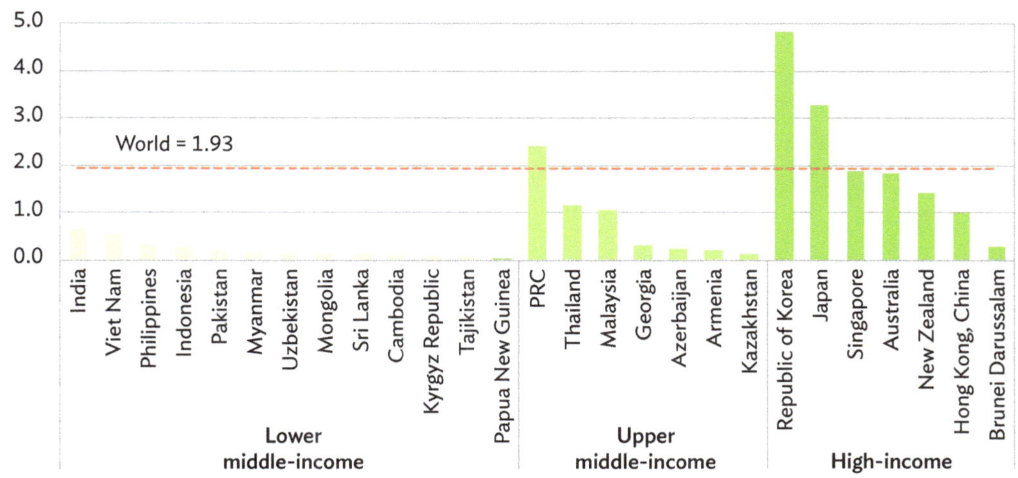

PRC = People's Republic of China, R&D = research and development.

Notes: The figure includes economies with the latest data available from 2015 to 2020. Income groupings follow the World Bank Group's classification as of July 2022.

Source: Table 1.9.4 of *Key Indicators for Asia and the Pacific 2022*.

Click here for figure data

All high-income economies and all but one upper middle-income economy (Kazakhstan) exceeded the global average of 1,342 researchers per million inhabitants in 2020 or the most recent year with available data (Figure 1.19). The Republic of Korea recorded the highest figure of 8,714 researchers per million inhabitants, followed by Singapore (7,287), New Zealand (5,854), and Japan (5,455). However, the number of researchers per million inhabitants recorded in lower middle-income economies reached as low as 30 and only as high as 757.

Figure 1.19: Number of Researchers per Million Inhabitants, by Economy Income Grouping

(full-time equivalent)

High-income economies vastly exceeded the global average for proportion of researchers by population, but several lower-income economies were substantially below this average.

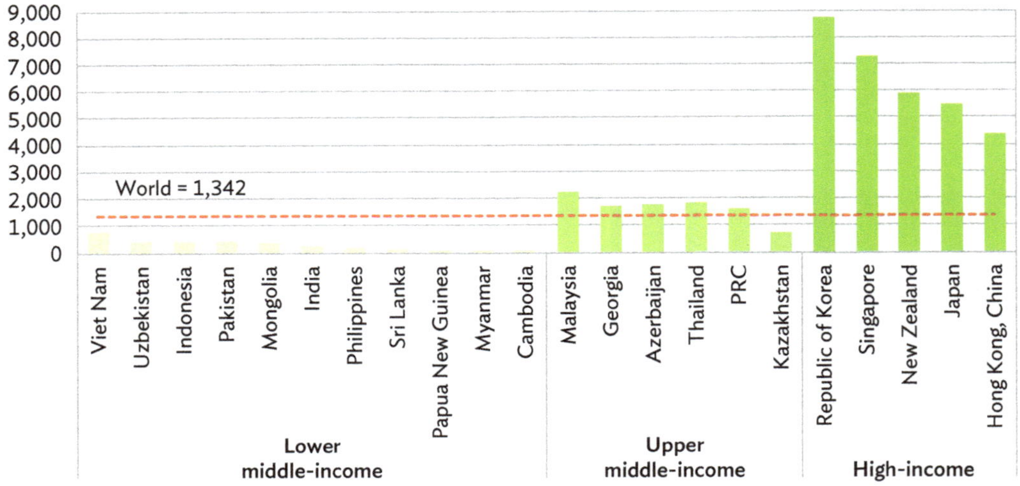

PRC = People's Republic of China.

Notes: The figure includes economies with the latest data available from 2015 to 2020. Income groupings follow the World Bank Group's classification as of July 2022.

Source: Table 1.9.4 of *Key Indicators for Asia and the Pacific 2022*.

Click here for figure data

Across Asia and the Pacific, there are ongoing disparities in the SDG 9 scorecard for sustainable industrialization as high-income economies continue to invest more in their manufacturing sectors.

Figure 1.20 illustrates the performance of economies in Asia and the Pacific with respect to expanding medium- and high-tech industries prior to the COVID-19 pandemic. On the one hand, the region included two economies with the world's most modern manufacturing sectors: Singapore (85.1%) and Taipei,China (68.4%). However, the region also included several economies in which the share of medium- and high-tech industries in manufacturing gross value-added was consistently below 5% from 2010. Most of these were lower and upper middle-income economies such as Cambodia, the Lao People's Democratic Republic, Maldives, Tajikistan, and Tonga.

Figure 1.20: Medium- and High-Tech Industry Output in Total Value-Added, by Economy Income Grouping

15 regional economies (mostly lower and upper middle-income) had medium- and high-tech industries that failed to contribute more than 10% of value-added in the manufacturing sector.

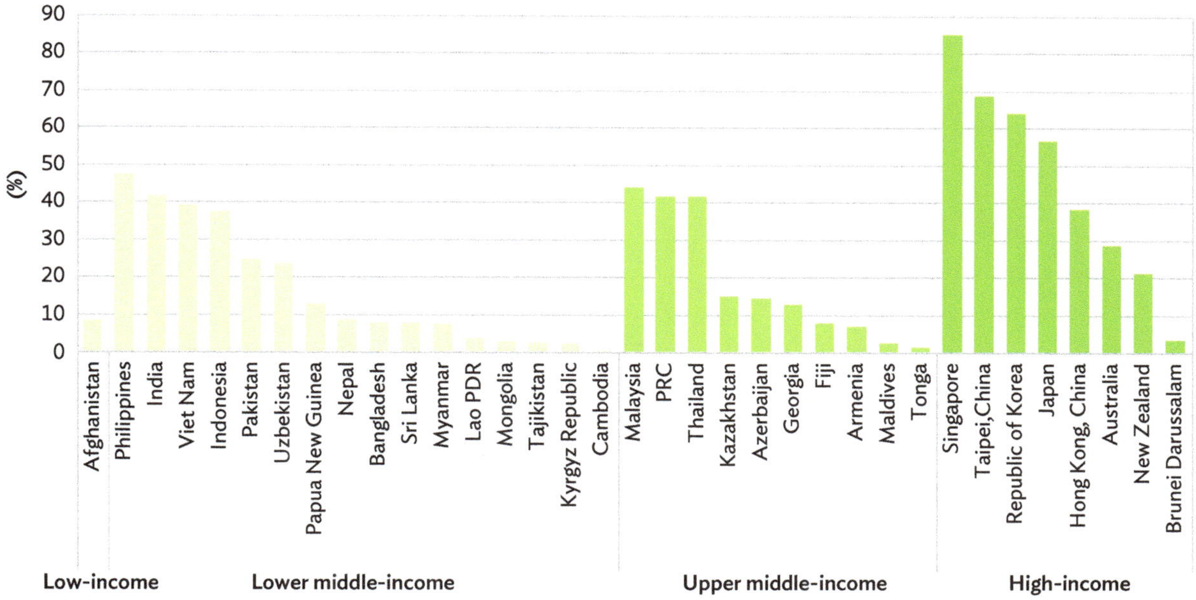

Lao PDR = Lao People's Democratic Republic, PRC = People's Republic of China.

Notes: Income groupings follow World Bank's classifications as of July 2022. Graphics are based on available data for the most recent year (2019).

Source: Table 1.9.5 of *Key Indicators for Asia and the Pacific 2022*.

Click here for figure data

From 2010 to 2019, only 17 of the 35 economies with available data managed to increase their share of the medium- and high-tech industries in manufacturing sector gross value-added. Azerbaijan, Mongolia, and Viet Nam were among those that experienced the fastest growth from 2010 to 2019.

The COVID-19 pandemic has greatly disrupted global production, demand, and supply chains, which underpin manufacturing processes. The Asia and Pacific region has been no exception as it took a deep dive from 2019 to 2020, both in terms of the manufacturing sector's economic output (upper panel) and employment (lower panel) as shown in Figure 1.21. There was some degree of recovery in economic output from 2020 to 2021, with the manufacturing sector of Uzbekistan increasing by at least 20%. Manufacturing employment plummeted in most economies from 2019 to 2020 and only Azerbaijan, Indonesia, the Philippines, and Uzbekistan showed signs of recovery from 2020 to 2021, each registering growth in manufacturing employment of at least 4%.

Figure 1.21: Changes in Economic Output and Number Employed in the Manufacturing Sector

The COVID-19 pandemic has had a significant economic impact on the manufacturing sector of Asia and the Pacific.

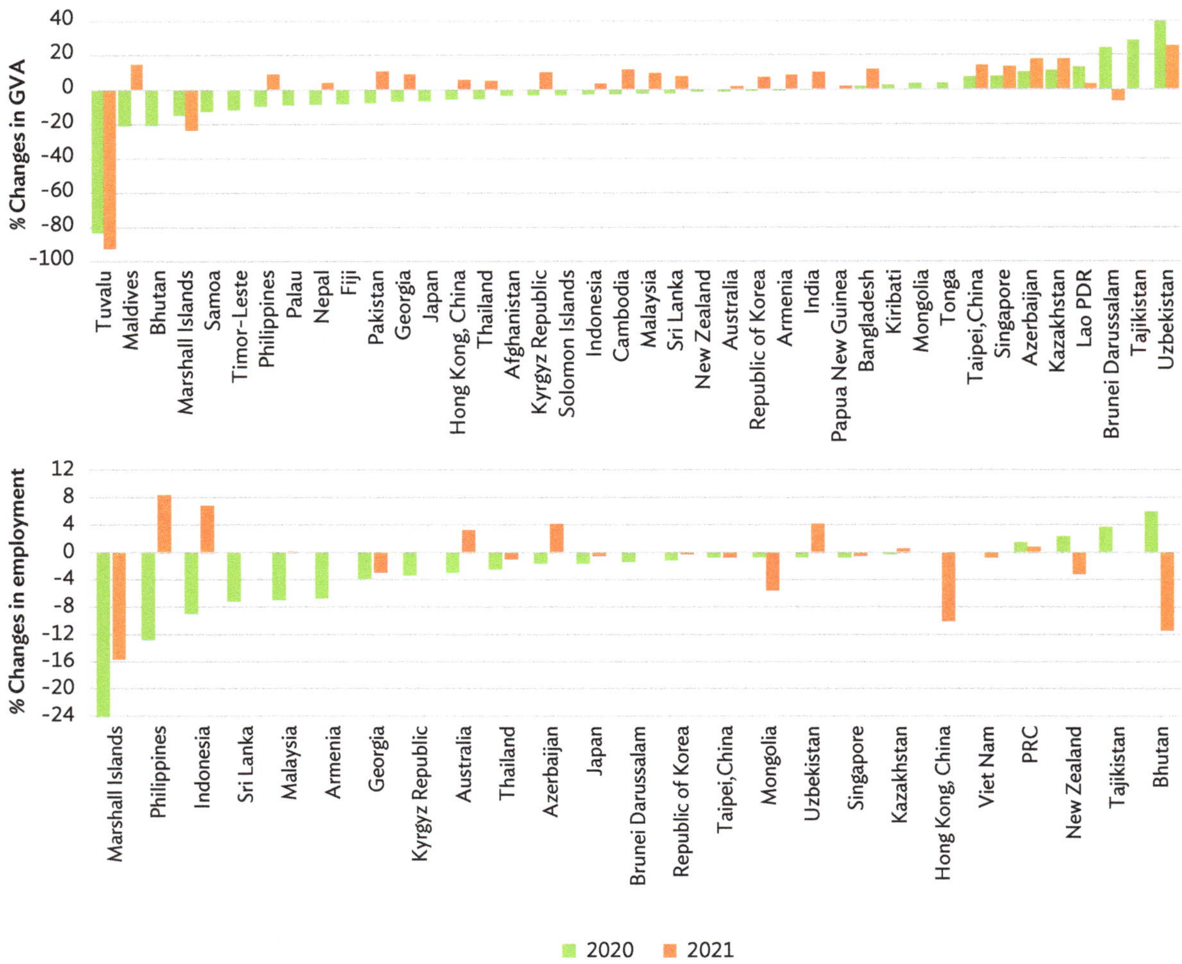

COVID-19 = coronavirus disease, GVA = gross value-added.
Lao PDR = Lao People's Democratic Republic, PRC = People's Republic of China.
Note: Additional information about underlying data are provided in individual economy tables.
Source: Asian Development Bank estimates using data in individual economy tables available at https://kidb.adb.org/.

Click here for figure data

As manufacturing begins to recover in more economies, it is important to retrofit the sector through greater adoption of clean and environmentally sound technologies and industrial processes. However, trends prior to the COVID-19 pandemic suggest there may be mixed commitment to this objective. Examining data on carbon dioxide (CO_2) emissions per unit of manufacturing value-added (MVA) since 2010, Figure 1.22 shows that, although emissions decreased at least marginally in most of the ADB member economies with available data, there are multiple economies in which emissions barely changed or even increased.

Figure 1.22: Carbon Dioxide Emissions Per Unit of Manufacturing Value-Added, by Economy Income Grouping

Most ADB member economies showed declines in their CO_2 emissions from 2010 to 2019, but several reported levels that had either barely changed or increased alarmingly.

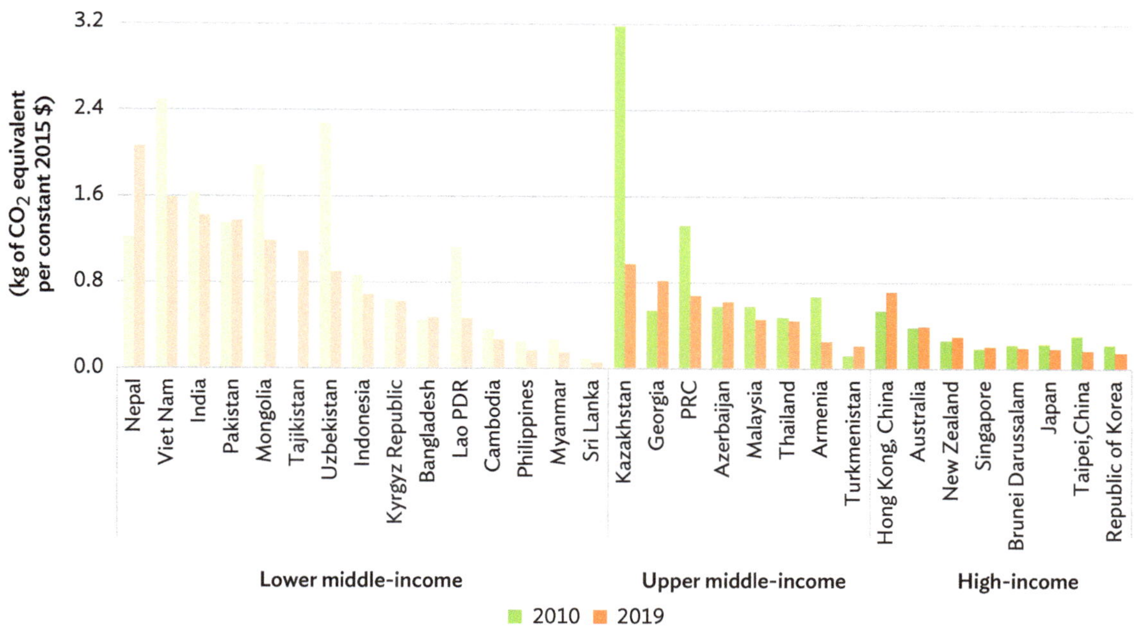

ADB = Asian Development Bank, CO_2 = carbon dioxide, kg = kilogram, Lao PDR = Lao People's Democratic Republic, PRC = People's Republic of China.

Notes: For this indicator, the SDG Global Database sources its data from the International Energy Agency and the United Nations Industrial Development Organization. An alternative source of data on CO_2 emissions is the Global Carbon Atlas. Income groupings follow the World Bank Group's classification as of July 2022.

Source: Table 1.9.3 of *Key Indicators for Asia and the Pacific 2022*.

Click here for figure data

Opportunities for More Sustainable Recovery through Greener Development

This section considers drivers of social mobility by examining trends with respect to selected indicators under SDG 13, which aims to galvanize efforts towards climate action.

SDG 13 enumerates five targets: (i) strengthen resilience and adaptive capacity to climate-related disasters, (ii) integrate climate change measures into policies and planning, (iii) build knowledge and capacity to meet climate change, (iv) implement the United Nations Framework Convention on Climate Change, and (v) promote mechanisms to raise capacity for planning and management.

However, the United Nations Economic and Social Commission for Asia and the Pacific's latest SDG Progress Report reveals that, for Asia and the Pacific, data are inadequate for the majority of SDG 13's targets, making it difficult to assess the region's performance. Where information is available, data suggest that the region should either accelerate progress to achieve targets by 2030 (SDG 13.1) or reverse (deteriorating) trends (SDG 13.2) (UNESCAP 2022).

Impacts of climate change. Locals prepare to tackle overflowing water caused by Typhoon Ulysses in the Philippines (photo by Veejay Villafranca/ADB).

Globally, climate change threatens to push more than 130 million people into poverty over the next decade.

Every year, climatic changes contribute to over 150,000 deaths around the world and this number is expected to double by 2030 (Kasotia n.d.). By destroying wealth and employment, climate change may also hold back social mobility prospects for the vast population of Asia and the Pacific and, if left unchecked, has the potential to push 132 million people around the world into poverty over the next 10 years (WBG 2022). Furthermore, economists forecast that climate change could lead to a 10% loss of the global economy's total value by 2050 if the upward trend in temperature stays on course and Paris Agreement and net-zero emission targets are not met (Marchant 2021).

Addressing climate change and promoting environmental sustainability are important development priorities, especially for a region such Asia and the Pacific, which relies heavily on natural resources and has large segments of its population living in coastal areas.

Planetary health and climate resilience should be integrated into pandemic recovery efforts.

As climate change is a pandemic-enabler and crisis-multiplier, as some studies suggest (Cadham 2020; UN 2022), there are compelling reasons to promote greener economic growth, aim for low-carbon development, and employ climate mitigation and adaptation strategies to strengthen resilience against the potentially catastrophic impacts of climate change.

For perspective on the potential benefits of minimizing the effects of climate change on public health, the loss of human life due to COVID-19 is significantly higher than mortality rates recorded due to natural disasters since 2005 (WHO Coronavirus Dashboard; Pandey 2021). The global death toll due to COVID-19 breached 5 million for 2021 (WHO Coronavirus Dashboard). This compares to just over 1 million deaths globally from natural disasters since 2005. Asia and the Pacific also suffered a substantial human toll due to the pandemic, with a number of its subregions noting considerably higher pandemic-related loss of life than due to natural disasters since 2005 (Figure 1.23). The exceptions were the Pacific, Central and West Asia, and developed ADB member economies.

Figure 1.23: Cumulative Deaths due to Natural Disasters versus Deaths in 2021 due to COVID-19

Asia and the Pacific lost more lives due to COVID-19 in 2021 than due to natural disasters since 2005. However, whereas the region accounted for one-fifth of global COVID-19 deaths, it has accounted for half of global deaths due to natural disasters.

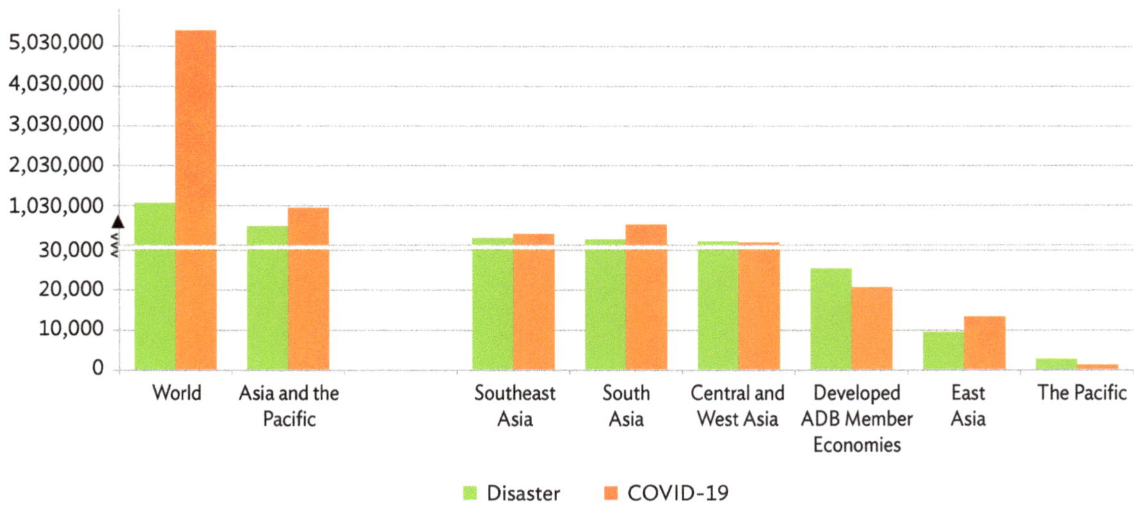

COVID-19 = coronavirus disease.

Sources: World Health Organization. WHO Coronavirus (COVID-19) Dashboard. https://covid19.who.int/idata (accessed 16 July 2022); Asian Development Bank estimates using data presented in Tables 1.13.1 of *Key Indicators for Asia and the Pacific 2022*.

Click here for figure data

The trajectory of greenhouse gas emissions is contributing to temperature increases that could lead to extra deaths greater than the COVID-19 total.

On an annualized basis, the COVID-19 toll in 2021 is equivalent to a death rate of 69 per 100,000. Some forecasts suggest that, if emissions growth stays high, global temperature increases may raise the mortality rate by almost 14 deaths per 100,000 by 2050 and could even reach 73 extra deaths per 100,000 people by the end of the century (Gates 2020). In Asia and the Pacific, available data point to worrying trends, particularly in vulnerable lower-income economies. Based on Global Carbon Atlas data, in 2020, Asia and the Pacific's developing economies accounted for about 49% of global CO_2 emissions, up from 41% in 2010.

The upper panel of Figure 1.24 shows the number of persons affected by natural disasters per 100,000 people from 2010 to the most recent year for which data were available. The Pacific subregion's small island developing states, such as the Cook Islands, Fiji, the Marshall Islands, Tonga, and Vanuatu, saw the highest number of people per 100,000 people affected by natural disasters during this period. This is not surprising as Pacific island economies have high exposure and are vulnerable to frequent natural disasters, including cyclones, floods, storm surges, earthquakes, volcanic eruptions, and tsunamis (WBG 2019). The lower panel of Figure 1.24 compares the average number of deaths due to natural disasters during 2005–2009, with the corresponding average recorded from 2010 to the latest year for which data were available. While the trend has declined for most economies, there are significant increases among some of the small island developing states from the Pacific as well as lower middle-income economies.

Figure 1.24: Number of Persons Affected by Natural Disasters and Number of Deaths due to Natural Disasters

(per 100,000 people)

In some Pacific and lower middle-income economies, the impact of natural disasters has become even more pronounced.

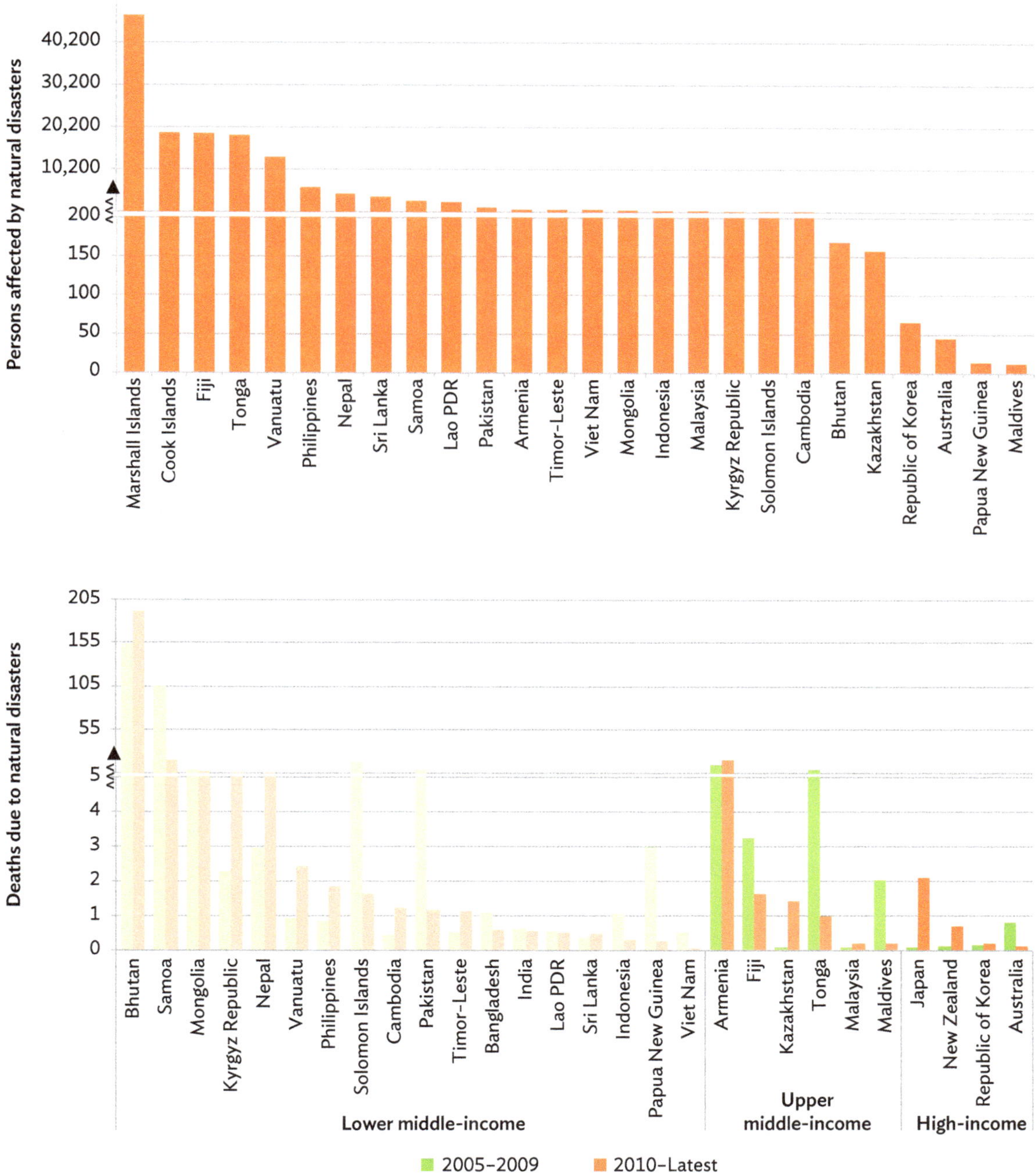

Lao PDR = Lao People's Democratic Republic.

Notes: The average number of persons affected by natural disasters per 100,000 people is calculated using data from 2010 to the most recent year for which data were available. The average number of deaths due to natural disasters per 100,000 people is calculated using data for 2005–2009 versus 2010 to the most recent year for which data were available. Income groupings follow the World Bank Group's classification as of July 2022.

Source: Asian Development Bank estimates using data presented in Tables 1.13.1 of *Key Indicators for Asia and the Pacific 2022*.

Click here for figure data

In the context of the impacts of natural disasters caused by rising temperatures, high levels of greenhouse gas emissions are a particular concern for the economies of Asia and the Pacific. Based on data from Global Carbon Atlas, the region's share of global CO_2 emissions increased from 46% in 2010 to 54% in 2020. As shown in the Figure 1.25, among the 49 ADB member economies with available data, 26 economies recorded a positive average annual change in CO_2 emissions for 2010 to 2019. This indicates that many of the economies sustained an increase in CO_2 emissions over the past decade. Meanwhile, high-income economies such as Australia, Brunei Darussalam, and Japan recorded a negative average annual change in their CO_2 emissions implying that their CO_2 emissions decreased during same period.

Figure 1.25: Changes in Carbon Dioxide Emissions in Selected Economies of Asia and the Pacific, 2010–2019

A majority of the economies in the region recorded an increase in CO_2 emissions.

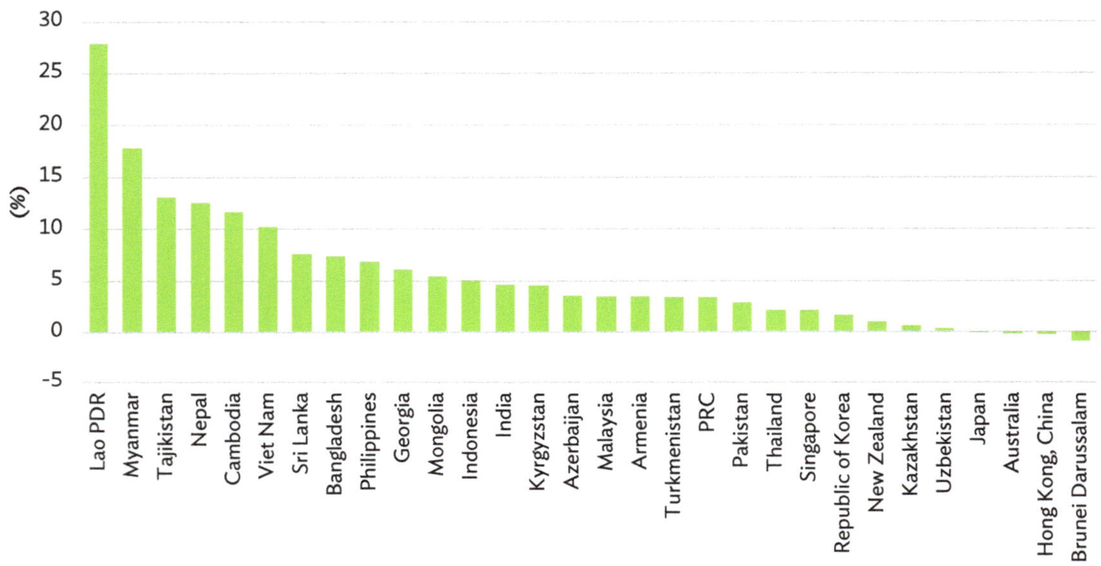

CO_2 = carbon dioxide, Lao PDR = Lao People's Democratic Republic, PRC = People's Republic of China.

Notes: Data refer to the average annual percent change of CO_2 emissions from fuel combustion (millions of metric tons) for 2010-2019. Total CO_2 emissions for an economy are estimated based on energy consumption data for all sectors. CO_2 emissions from manufacturing are based on energy data collected across subsectors (energy used for transport by industry is not included here, but is reported under transport).

Source: Asian Development Bank estimates based on the United Nations SDG Global Database (accessed 17 July 2022).

Click here for figure data

At the onset of the COVID-19 pandemic, lockdowns and containment measures contributed to lower greenhouse emissions, as Figure 1.26 illustrates for select metropolitan areas within Asia and the Pacific. However, according to a United Nations report, it was a temporary decline and, as economies started reopening, greenhouse gas emissions went back to pre-pandemic levels later in 2020 and began to exceed those levels in 2021 (UNEP 2021). According to the latest Global Energy Review (IEA 2022), global CO_2 emissions increased by 6% in 2021, after pandemic restrictions on human movement (notably vehicular travel) reduced global CO_2 emissions by 5.2% in 2020. It is therefore not surprising that the world remains well shy of the target of limiting global warming to below 2°C, preferably 1.5°C, compared to pre-industrial levels as set forth in the Paris Agreement.

Figure 1.26: Pre-Pandemic and Pandemic Levels of Tropospheric Nitrogen Dioxide in Selected Asian Cities

Greenhouse gas emissions reduced during lockdowns in a number of Asia's megacities.
However, there is evidence suggesting that such reductions were only temporary.

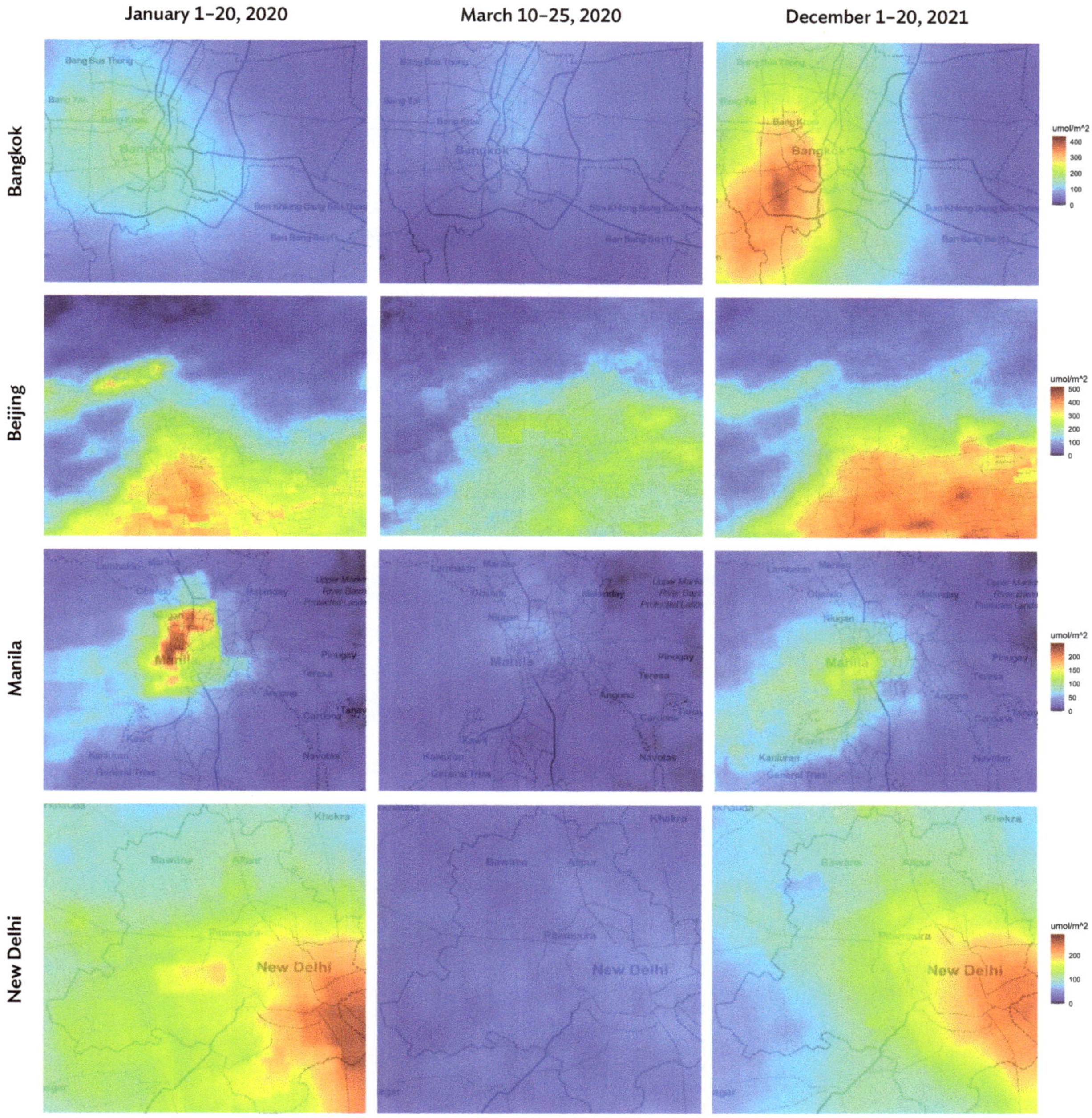

umol/m^2 = micromole per square meter area.

Notes: The maps show the concentration of nitrogen dioxide (NO_2) present in the troposphere as detected by the European Space Agency's Sentinel-5 Precursor satellite. This is one of the nitrogen oxide compounds that enters the atmosphere as a result of human activities (i.e. burning of biomass, fossil fuel combustion, etc.) and natural process (i.e. microbial activities, wildfires, etc.) (http://www.tropomi.eu/data-products/nitrogen-dioxide, accessed 02 June 2022).

Source: Sentinel-5P OFFL NO2. https://developers.google.com/earth-engine/datasets/catalog/COPERNICUS_S5P_OFFL_L3_NO2 (accessed 18 March 2022).

There are several important lessons that can be drawn from the pandemic and could be incorporated into climate change mitigation plans. First, there is an urgent need to strengthen resilience and adaptive capacity to respond to future threats, including natural disasters. The Sendai Framework for Disaster Risk Reduction provides specific actionable insights that can potentially minimize risks to lives and livelihoods. Figure 1.27 summarizes the self-assessment of economies in Asia and the Pacific for the alignment of their national disaster risk reduction strategies with the Sendai Framework, with higher scores representing more comprehensive alignment. Of the 31 economies with available data in 2020, 18 scored more than 0.75 (substantial alignment) and 7 economies across all income groupings were assessed to have scored 1.0 (comprehensive alignment). However, perhaps of even greater concern, a number of economies, including those more vulnerable to natural disasters, have no alignment to the framework or do not even have adequate data that can facilitate assessments.

Combating climate change also requires collective effort. There is cause for optimism in this regard as economies have started making voluntary efforts to reduce greenhouse gas emissions and adapt to climate change, as articulated in their nationally determined contributions (NDCs) under the Paris Agreement. According to the NDC Registry of the United Nations Climate Change Convention, 47 of the ADB regional member economies had already submitted their first rounds and updates of NDCs to the United Nations Framework Convention on Climate Change Secretariat by 2021. Parties to the Paris Agreement and to the convention were requested to submit first round of NDCs by 2020 and every 5 years thereafter. In the submitted NDCs as of December of 2020, economies articulated more on quantified targets and indicators for adaptation and identifying links between adaptation with SDGs and other frameworks (UNSD 2021). Among the NDCs submitted, priority areas in the adaptation components were identified as follows: (i) food security and production, (ii) terrestrial and wetland ecosystems, (iii) freshwater resources, (iv) human health, and (v) key economic sectors and services. Ocean ecosystems, urban areas and other human habitats, disaster risk management, and coastal and low-lying areas were also identified as adaptation components (UNSD 2021).

Figure 1.27: Alignment of Natural Disaster Risk Strategy with the Sendai Framework, 2020

More than half of the economies with available data scored at least substantial alignment of their national risk reduction strategies with the international framework.

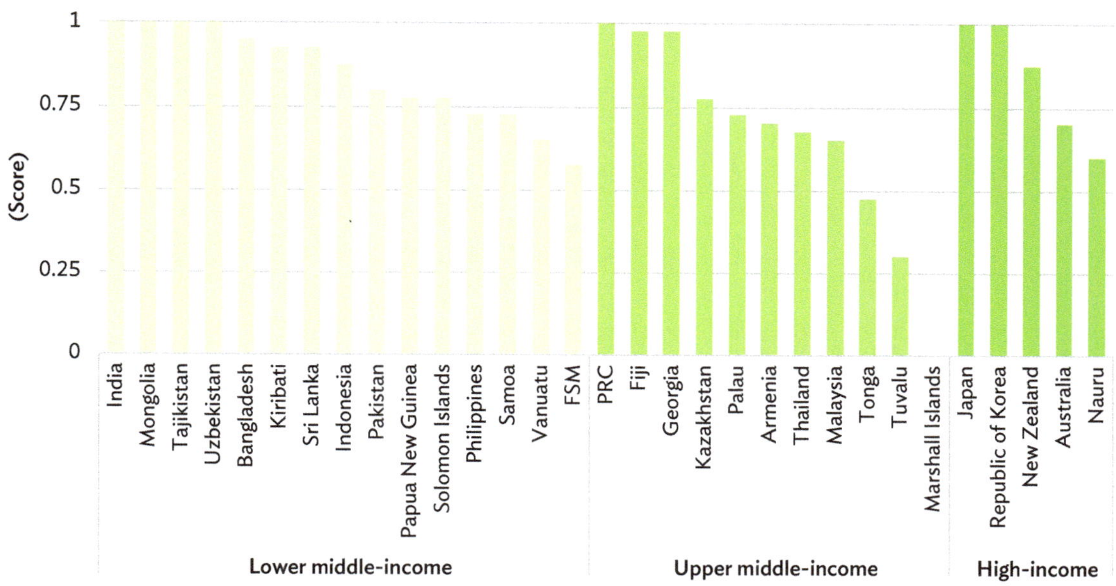

FSM = Federated States of Micronesia, PRC = People's Republic of China.

Notes: Economies displaying data have adopted and implemented national disaster risk reduction strategies. Data refer to the score for adoption and implementation of national disaster risk reduction strategies in line with the Sendai Framework. The scores indicate the compliance of alignment of national strategies with the Sendai Framework, based on self-assessments of the economy using 10 criteria for monitoring the progress of national disaster risk reduction strategies. The score ranges are as follows: 1 = comprehensive alignment, 0.75 = substantial alignment, 0.50 = moderate alignment, 0.25 = limited alignment, 0 = no alignment. Income groupings follow the World Bank Group's classification as of July 2022.

Source: Table 1.13.1 of *Key Indicators for Asia and the Pacific 2022*.

Click here for figure data

References

Asian Development Bank (ADB). 2017. *Meeting Asia's Infrastructure Needs.* Manila. https://www.adb.org/publications/asia-infrastructure-needs.

ADB. 2020a. *Asia's Journey to Prosperity. Policy, Market, and Technology Over 50 Years.* Manila. https://www.adb.org/publications/asias-journey-to-prosperity.

ADB. 2020b. *Mapping Poverty through Data Integration and Artificial Intelligence: A Special Supplement of the Key Indicators for Asia and the Pacific.* Manila. https://www.adb.org/publications/mapping-poverty-data-integration-ai.

ADB. 2021a. *Key Indicators for Asia and the Pacific 2021.* Manila. https://www.adb.org/publications/key-indicators-asia-and-pacific-2021.

ADB. 2021b. *Asian Development Outlook Update 2021.* Manila. https://www.adb.org/publications/asian-development-outlook-2021-update.

ADB. 2022a. *Asian Development Outlook (ADO) 2022 Supplement: Recovery Faces Diverse Challenges.* Manila. https://www.adb.org/publications/ado-supplement-july-2022.

ADB. 2022b. *Harnessing the Potential of Big Data in Post-Pandemic Southeast Asia.* Manila. https://www.adb.org/publications/big-data-post-pandemic-southeast-asia.

M. Auwera, A. Meerendonk, and A. Kumar. 2021. COVID-19 and Social Protection in Asia and the Pacific: Projected Costs for 2020–2030. *ADB Sustainable Development Working Paper.* No. 80. Manila. ADB.

J. Cadham. 2020. COVID-19 and Climate Change. *Centre for International Governance Innovation.* 24 August. https://www.cigionline.org/articles/covid-19-and-climate-change/.

M. Carmona. 2018. Is Biometric Technology in Social Protection Programmes Illegal or Arbitrary? An Analysis of Privacy and Data Protection. *ILO Extension of Social Security Working Paper.* No. 59. Geneva. International Labour Organization.

M. Corak. 2013. Income Inequality, Equality of Opportunity, and Intergenerational Mobility. *The Journal of Economic Perspectives.* 27. 3 (2013): pp. 79–102. http://www.jstor.org/stable/41955546.

G. Datt. Poverty-Inequality Research Frontiers for Asia and the Pacific. Unpublished.

J. Ermisch, M. Jäntti, and T. Smeeding. 2012. *From Parents to Children: The Intergenerational Transmission of Advantage.* Russell Sage Foundation. https://www.jstor.org/stable/10.7758/9781610447805.

J. Fiedler, K. Lividini, O. Bermudez, and M. Smitz. 2012. Household Consumption and Expenditures Surveys (HCES): A Primer for Food and Nutrition Analysts in Low- and Middle-Income Countries. https://journals.sagepub.com/doi/pdf/10.1177/15648265120333S205.

G. Fields. 2008. Income Mobility. In L. Blume and S. Durlauf (eds), *The New Palgrave Dictionary of Economics.* New York, NY: Palgrave Macmillan.

G. Fields. 2019. Concepts of Social Mobility. https://ideas.repec.org/p/unu/wpaper/wp-2019-106.html.

D. Filmer, H. Fu, and C. Sanchez-Paramo. 2022. An Adjustment to Global Poverty Lines. *World Bank Blogs*. May 2. https://blogs.worldbank.org/voices/adjustment-global-poverty-lines.

B. Gates. 2020. COVID-19 is Awful. Climate Change Could be Worse. *GatesNotes*. 4 August. https://www.gatesnotes.com/Energy/Climate-and-COVID-19.

D. Garces-Urzainqui, P. Lanjouw, and G. Rongen. Constructing Synthetic Panels for the Purpose of Studying Poverty Dynamics: A Primer. *Review of Development Economics*. 25. 4. pp. 1,803-1,815.

Global Carbon Atlas. 2021. Carbon Dioxide (CO_2) Emissions Data. http://www.globalcarbonatlas.org/en/CO2-emissions (accessed 23 July 2022).

V. Gopalakrishnan, D. Wadhwa, S. Haddad, and P. Blake. 2021. 2021 Year in Review in 11 Charts: The Inequality Pandemic. *World Bank News*. 21 December. https://www.worldbank.org/en/news/feature/2021/12/20/year-2021-in-review-the-inequality-pandemic.

R. Haveman and B. Wolfe. 1995. The Determinants of Children's Attainments: A Review of Methods and Findings. *Journal of Economic Literature*. 33. 4 (1995). pp. 1,829–1,878. http://www.jstor.org/stable/2729315.

V. Iversen, A. Krishna, and K. Sen. 2019. Beyond Poverty Escapes - Social Mobility in Developing Countries: A Review Article. *The World Bank Research Observer*. 34. pp. 239–272.

V. Iversen, A. Krishna, and K. Sen (eds). 2021. *Social Mobility in Developing Countries: Concepts, Methods, and Determinants*. United Nations University, World Institute for Development Economics Research.

D. Jolliffe, D. Mahler, C. Lakner, A. Atamanov, and S. Tetteh-Baah. 2022. Assessing the Impact of the 2017 PPPs on the International Poverty Line and Global Poverty. *World Bank Group Policy Research Working Paper*. No. 9941. https://documents1.worldbank.org/curated/en/353811645450974574/pdf/Assessing-the-Impact-of-the-2017-PPPs-on-the-International-Poverty-Line-and-Global-Poverty.pdf.

P. Kasotia. (no date). The Health Effects Of Global Warming: Developing Countries Are The Most Vulnerable. *United Nations Chronicle*. https://www.un.org/en/chronicle/article/health-effects-global-warming-developing-countries-are-most-vulnerable.

A. Krueger, J. Cramer, and D. Cho. 2014. Are the Long-term Unemployed on the Margins of the Labor Market? *Brookings Paper on Economic Activity*. Spring 2014. pp. 229–280.

S. Handayani, M. Domingo-Palacpac, C. Burkley, and P. Lovelock. 2017. Improving the Delivery of Social Protection Through ICT – Case Studies in Mongolia, Nepal, and Viet Nam. *ADB Sustainable Development Working Paper Series*. No. 50. Manila. ADB.

International Energy Agency (IEA). 2022. *Global Energy Review: CO2 Emissions in 2021*. https://www.iea.org/reports/global-energy-review-co2-emissions-in-2021-2.

International Labour Organization (ILO). 2022. Social Protection Monitor. https://www.social-protection.org/gimi/ShowWiki.action?id=3426.

International Monetary Fund (IMF). 2021. *World Economic Outlook: Recovery During a Pandemic*. https://www.imf.org/-/media/Files/Publications/WEO/2021/October/English/text.ashx.

IMF. 2022. *World Economic Outlook: War Sets Back the Global Recovery*. https://www.imf.org/en/Publications/WEO/Issues/2022/04/19/world-economic-outlook-april-2022.

A. Manstead. 2018. The Psychology of Social Class: How Socioeconomic Status Impacts Thoughts, Feelings, and Behaviour. *Social Psychology*. 57 (2). pp. 267–291.

N. Marchant. 2021. This is How Climate Change Could Impact the Global Economy. *World Economic Forum*. 28 June. https://www.weforum.org/agenda/2021/06/impact-climate-change-global-gdp/.

A. Martinez, M. Western, M. Haynes, and W. Tomaszewski. 2013. Measuring Income Mobility using Pseudo-Panel Data. *The Philippine Statistician*. 62. 2. pp. 71-99.

A. Martinez and J. Bulan. 2021. We are Just Now Discovering How Devastating COVID-19 Has Been for the Very Poor. *Asian Development Blog*. 27 August. https://blogs.adb.org/blog/we-are-just-now-discovering-how-devastating-covid-19-has-been-for-the-very-poor.

R. Molato-Gayares, A. Park, D. Raitzer, D. Suryadarma, M. Thomas, and P. Vandenberg. 2022. How to Recover Learning Losses from COVID-19 School Closures in Asia and the Pacific. *ADB Briefs*. No. 217. Manila. ADB.

P. Morgan and L. Trinh. 2021. Impacts of COVID-19 on Households in ASEAN Countries and Their Implications for Human Capital Development. *ADBI Working Paper 1226*. Tokyo: Asian Development Bank Institute.

A.Nestour, S. Carvalho, and A. Minardi. 2020. Unequal Burdens: The Impact of Shocks on Household Education Spending. *Center for Global Development Blog*. 3 December. https://www.cgdev.org/blog/unequal-burdens-impact-shocks-household-education-spending

T. Ohlenburg. 2022. Social Protection in a Pandemic – Trends, Challenges, and Technology. https://www.adb.org/publications/social-protection-pandemic-trends-challenges-technology.

K. Pandey. 2021. COVID-19 Killed More People in 16 Months than Natural Disasters in 20 Years. *Down to Earth*. 18 April. https://www.downtoearth.org.in/news/health/covid-19-killed-more-people-in-16-months-than-natural-disasters-in-20-years-76551.

S. Roy and R. van der Weide. 2022. Poverty in India Has Declined over the Last Decade But Not As Much As Previously Thought. *World Bank Group Policy Research Working Paper*. No. 9994.

G. Solon. 2004. A Model of Intergenerational Mobility Variation Over Time and Place. In *Generational Income Mobility in North America and Europe (Ed.)*. Cambridge University Press, Cambridge. pp. 38–47.

N. Vandycke, J. Viegas, and J. Morales Sarriera. 2020. A Wake-Up Call: Building Back Better to Achieve Sustainable Mobility for All. *World Bank Blogs*. 29 September. https://blogs.worldbank.org/transport/wake-call-building-back-better-achieve-sustainable-mobility-all.

United Nations (UN). 2022. *The Sustainable Development Goals Report 2022*. New York.

United Nations Economic and Social Commission for Asia and the Pacific (UNESCAP). 2021. Beyond the Pandemic: Building Back Better from Crises in Asia and the Pacific. 26 March. https://www.unescap.org/kp/2021/beyond-pandemic-building-back-better-crises-asia-and-pacific.

UNESCAP. 2022. *Asia and the Pacific SDG Progress Report 2022: Widening disparities amid COVID-19*. New York.

UNESCAP, ADB, and United Nations Development Programme (UNDP). 2022. *Building Forward Together: Towards an Inclusive and Resilient Asia and the Pacific*. Bangkok.

UNESCO Institute for Statistics (UIS). 2020. New UIS Data for SDG 9.5 on Research and Development (R&D). News. 29 June. http://uis.unesco.org/en/news/new-uis-data-sdg-9-5-research-and-development-rd.

UIS. UIS.Stat Database. http://data.uis.unesco.org/ (accessed 18 May 2022).

United Nations Children's Fund (UNICEF). 2022. Are Children Really Learning? Exploring Foundational Skills in the Midst of a Learning Crisis.

United Nations Entity for Gender Equality and the Empowerment of Women. 2013. *The Cost of Violence*. https://asiapacific.unwomen.org/sites/default/files/Field%20Office%20ESEAsia/Docs/Publications/2014/9/UNW%20The%20Costs%20of%20Violence%20final.pdf.

United Nations Environment Programme (UNEP). 2021. COVID-19 Caused Only a Temporary Reduction in Carbon Emissions – UN Report. UNEP Press Release. 16 September. https://www.unep.org/news-and-stories/press-release/covid-19-caused-only-temporary-reduction-carbon-emissions-un-report.

United Nations Women (UN Women). 2020. *COVID-19 and Ending Violence Against Women and Girls*. https://www.unwomen.org/sites/default/files/Headquarters/Attachments/Sections/Library/Publications/2020/Issue-brief-COVID-19-and-ending-violence-against-women-and-girls-en.pdf.

United Nations Statistics Division (UNSD). 2021. Take Urgent Action to Combat Climate Change and its Impacts. https://unstats.un.org/sdgs/report/2021/goal-13/.

United States Department of Agriculture, Economic Research Service (USDA ERS). 2022. International Macroeconomic Data Set. https://www.ers.usda.gov/data-products/international-macroeconomic-data-set.aspx (accessed 30 May 2022).

World Bank Group (WBG). 2018a. *Fair Progress? Economic Mobility Across Generations Around the World*. https://openknowledge.worldbank.org/handle/10986/28428.

WBG. 2018b. *Riding the Wave. An East Asian Miracle for the 21st Century*. https://openknowledge.worldbank.org/bitstream/handle/10986/28878/9781464811456.pdf?sequence=9&isAllowed=y.

WBG. 2018c. *The State of Social Safety Nets 2018*. https://openknowledge.worldbank.org/handle/10986/29115?show=full.

WBG. 2019. *World Bank East Asia and Pacific Economic Update April 2019*. Washington DC.

WBG. 2022. *Global Economic Prospects*. https://www.worldbank.org/en/publication/global-economic-prospects.

World Bank Group; United Nations Educational, Scientific and Cultural Organization; United Nations Children's Fund (UNICEF); Foreign, Commonwealth, and Development Office of the United Kingdom; United States Agency for International Development (USAID); and the Bill & Melinda Gates Foundation. 2022. *The State of Global Learning Poverty: 2022 Update*.

World Economic Forum (WEF). 2020. *The Global Social Mobility Report 2020: Equality, Opportunity, and a New Economic Imperative*. https://www3.weforum.org/docs/Global_Social_Mobility_Report.pdf.

WEF. 2022. *The Global Risks Report 2022*. https://www3.weforum.org/docs/WEF_The_Global_Risks_Report_2022.pdf.

World Health Organization (WHO). WHO Coronavirus (COVID-19) Dashboard. https://covid19.who.int/data (accessed 16 July 2022).

World Intellectual Property Organization (WIPO). 2021. *Global Innovation Index 2021: Tracking Innovation through the COVID-19 Crisis*. https://www.wipo.int/global_innovation_index/en/.

World Institute for Development Economic Research (UNU-WIDER). 2019. *Working Paper Series 2019-106*. https://ideas.repec.org/s/unu/wpaper.html.

World Values Survey (WVS). Round Seven, Pooled Datafile Version. Online Database. https://www.worldvaluessurvey.org/WVSDocumentationWV7.jsp.

L. Zhigang and U. Sharma. 2022. How Can We Help Kids from Poor Families Hit Hard by Pandemic School Closures? *Asian Development Blog*. 3 March. https://blogs.adb.org/blog/how-can-we-help-kids-from-poor-families-hit-hard-by-pandemic-school-closures.

Goal 1. End poverty in all its forms everywhere

Table 1.1.1: Selected Indicators for Sustainable Development Goal 1—No Poverty

ADB Regional Member	Target 1.1: By 2030, eradicate extreme poverty for all people everywhere, measured as people living below the international poverty line of $1.90 a day (2011 PPP)						
	1.1.1.a: Proportion of Population Living below the $1.90 a Day (2011 PPP) Poverty Line[a,b] (%)		1.1.1.b: Proportion of Employed Population Living below the International Poverty Line, by Age Group and Sex[b,c] (%)				
			2019				
			Age Group				
			15+			15–24	25+
	2010	2020	Total (2021)	Female	Male		
Developing ADB Member Economies							
Central and West Asia							
Afghanistan	...	...	...	...	...	...	...
Armenia	1.0	0.4	0.4	0.4	0.3	0.5	0.3
Azerbaijan[d]	0.0 (2005)	...	0.1	0.1	0.1	0.1	0.1
Georgia	12.0	4.2	2.5	2.4	3.3	3.5	2.8
Kazakhstan	0.1	0.0 (2018)	0.1	0.0	0.0	0.0	0.0
Kyrgyz Republic	2.8	1.1	0.3	0.1	0.2	0.2	0.2
Pakistan	7.4	3.6 (2018)	3.7	4.0	3.3	3.8	3.3
Tajikistan	4.0 (2009)	4.1 (2015)	1.4	2.5	1.6	2.2	1.9
Turkmenistan	...	...	0.5	0.7	0.5	0.8	0.5
Uzbekistan[d]	61.6 (2003)	...	6.5	4.8	9.3	8.2	7.4
East Asia							
China, People's Republic of	11.2	0.1 (2019)	0.2	0.2	0.2	0.3	0.2
Hong Kong, China[f]	...	...	...	...	...	...	...
Korea, Republic of[f]	0.5	0.2 (2016)	0.0	0.0	0.0	0.0	0.0
Mongolia	0.7	0.5 (2018)	0.1	0.1	0.1	0.1	0.1
Taipei,China	0.0	0.0 (2016)	...	...	...	...	...
South Asia							
Bangladesh	19.2	14.3 (2016)	4.0	6.2	5.3	6.5	5.4
Bhutan	2.2 (2012)	1.5 (2017)	0.8	0.9	0.7	1.3	0.7
India	22.5 (2011)	...	7.6	9.5	8.3	11.4	8.2
Maldives	3.5 (2009)	0.0 (2019)	0.1	0.1	0.1	0.1	0.1
Nepal	15.0	...	3.4	3.8	3.8	3.9	3.8
Sri Lanka	2.8 (2009)	0.9 (2016)	0.2	0.2	0.3	0.3	0.2
Southeast Asia							
Brunei Darussalam	...	...	...	...	...	...	...
Cambodia[i]	...	...	9.2	9.6	10.5	12.3	9.4
Indonesia	13.3	2.2 (2021)	2.9	3.2	3.1	3.4	3.2
Lao People's Democratic Republic	14.5 (2012)	10.0 (2018)	9.3	9.1	10.3	13.8	8.7
Malaysia	0.1 (2011)	0.0 (2015)	0.1	0.0	0.0	0.0	0.0
Myanmar	...	1.4 (2017)	1.3	1.1	1.0	1.3	1.0
Philippines	10.7 (2009)	4.7 (2018)	2.8	1.6	2.2	2.6	1.9
Singapore	...	...	...	...	...	...	...
Thailand	0.1	0.0	0.1	0.0	0.1	0.2	0.0
Timor-Leste	37.4 (2007)	22.0 (2014)	22.6	16.1	18.4	21.3	16.4
Viet Nam	4.0	1.8 (2018)	1.2	1.7	1.5	2.9	1.4
The Pacific							
Cook Islands	...	...	...	...	...	...	...
Fiji	1.6 (2008)	1.8 (2019)	0.2	0.1	0.1	0.1	0.1
Kiribati	12.9 (2006)	1.3 (2019)	...	...	...	...	...
Marshall Islands	...	...	...	...	...	...	...
Micronesia, Federated States of	15.4 (2013)	...	...	...	...	...	...
Nauru	0.9 (2012)	...	...	...	...	...	...
Niue	...	...	...	...	...	...	...
Palau	...	...	...	...	...	...	...
Papua New Guinea	38.0 (2009)	...	24.0	23.6	22.2	25.9	22.0
Samoa	0.6 (2008)	...	...	...	...	...	...
Solomon Islands	24.7 (2012)	...	23.5	19.0	21.5	26.7	18.0
Tonga	1.1 (2009)	1.0 (2015)	...	...	...	...	...
Tuvalu	3.3	...	...	...	...	...	...
Vanuatu	13.1	8.6 (2019)	...	...	...	...	...
Developed ADB Member Economies							
Australia	...	...	...	...	...	...	...
Japan	...	...	...	...	...	...	...
New Zealand	...	...	...	...	...	...	...

Table 1.1.1: Selected Indicators for Sustainable Development Goal 1—No Poverty *(continued)*

ADB Regional Member	Target 1.2: By 2030, reduce at least by half the proportion of men, women, and children of all ages living in poverty in all its dimensions according to national definitions 1.2.1: Proportion of Population Living below the National Poverty Line, by Urban–Rural Location[a] (%)					
	2010			2020		
	Total	Urban	Rural	Total	Urban	Rural
Developing ADB Member Economies						
Central and West Asia						
Afghanistan	38.3 (2011)	...	...	47.3	46.9	46.7
Armenia	35.8	35.7	36.0	27.0	22.5	33.6
Azerbaijan[d]	9.1	...	...	5.9 (2021)	...	...
Georgia	37.3 [e]	32.7 [e]	43.3 [e]	17.5 (2021)	15.0 (2021)	21.3 (2021)
Kazakhstan	6.5	3.7	10.1	5.2 (2021)	3.8 (2021)	7.2 (2021)
Kyrgyz Republic	33.7	23.6	39.5	25.3	29.3 (2015)	33.6 (2015)
Pakistan	36.8	18.2 (2013)	35.6 (2013)	21.9 (2018)	12.5 (2015)	30.7 (2015)
Tajikistan	34.3 (2013)	...	...	26.3 (2019)	...	...
Turkmenistan	...	...	...	...	...	...
Uzbekistan[d]	17.7	...	...	17.0 (2021)	...	...
East Asia						
China, People's Republic of	...	...	17.2	...	...	–
Hong Kong, China[f]	15.7	...	...	17.3	...	...
Korea, Republic of[f]	18.6 (2011)	...	...	15.3	...	...
Mongolia	38.8	33.2	49.0	27.8	27.2 (2018)	30.8 (2018)
Taipei,China	1.2 [g]	...	...	1.3	...	...
South Asia						
Bangladesh	31.5	21.3	35.2	20.5 (2019)	...	...
Bhutan	12.0 (2012)	1.8 (2012)	16.7 (2012)	8.2 (2017)	0.8 (2017)	11.9 (2017)
India	21.9 [h] (2011)	13.7 [h] (2011)	25.7 [h] (2011)	...	...	...
Maldives	...	...	...	8.2 (2016)	...	...
Nepal	25.2	15.5	27.4	...	...	...
Sri Lanka	6.7 (2012)	2.1 (2012)	7.6 (2012)	14.3 (2019)	1.9 (2016)	4.3 (2016)
Southeast Asia						
Brunei Darussalam	...	...	...	...	...	...
Cambodia[i]	21.1	17.0	22.7	17.8 (2019)	12.6 (2019)	22.8 (2019)
Indonesia	13.3	9.9	16.6	10.1 [j] (2021)	7.9 [j] (2021)	13.1 [j] (2021)
Lao People's Democratic Republic	24.6 (2013)	7.9 (2013)	31.4 (2013)	18.3 (2019)	7.0 (2019)	23.8 (2019)
Malaysia	1.7 (2011)	1.0 (2012)	...	8.4	0.2 (2016)	1.0 (2016)
Myanmar	42.4	...	...	24.8 (2017)	11.3 (2017)	30.2 (2017)
Philippines	25.2 (2012)	13.0 (2012)	...	23.7 [j] (2021)	9.3 (2018)	24.5 (2018)
Singapore	...	...	...	...	...	...
Thailand	16.4	...	...	6.8	...	...
Timor-Leste	41.8 (2014)	28.3 (2014)	47.1 (2014)	...	...	...
Viet Nam	14.2	6.9	17.4	4.8	1.1	7.1
The Pacific						
Cook Islands	...	...	...	...	...	...
Fiji	28.1 [k] (2013)	19.8 [k] (2013)	36.7 [k] (2013)	24.1 (2019)	14.0 (2019)	36.5 (2019)
Kiribati	...	...	...	21.9 (2019)	...	...
Marshall Islands	...	...	...	...	...	...
Micronesia, Federated States of	41.2 [k] (2013)	...	...	...	...	...
Nauru	24.0 [k] (2013)	...	...	...	...	...
Niue	...	...	...	...	...	...
Palau	...	...	...	...	...	...
Papua New Guinea	...	...	...	37.5 (2017)	...	...
Samoa	18.8 [k] (2013)	...	...	22.7 (2018)	...	...
Solomon Islands	12.7 [l] (2012)	9.1 [l] (2012)	13.6 [l] (2012)	...	...	...
Tonga	...	...	...	27.0 (2015)	...	...
Tuvalu	19.7 [k]	24.8 [k]	27.5 [k]	...	...	...
Vanuatu	12.7 [k]	...	10.0 [k]	...	...	...
Developed ADB Member Economies						
Australia	...	...	...	...	...	...
Japan	...	...	...	...	...	...
New Zealand	...	...	...	...	...	...

... = data not available, -= magnitude equals zero, 0.0 = magnitude is less than half of unit employed or true zero, $ = United States dollars, ADB = Asian Development Bank, PPP = purchasing power parity.

a For indicator 1.1.1.a and indicator 1.2.1, the year indicated in the table refers to the year when the household survey data were collected. For economies in which the household survey data collection period bridged 2 calendar years, the table reports the first year.
b For indicator 1.1.1.a, data are consumption-based, except for Malaysia; the Republic of Korea; and Taipei,China, whose estimates are income-based. For indicator 1.1.1.a and indicator 1.1.1.b, the estimates are based on the international poverty line of $1.90 a day (2011 PPP).
c Data are taken from estimates and projections modeled by the International Labour Organization. These modeled estimates present an internationally comparable series, which consists of economy-sourced estimates and imputations for missing data. Global and regional estimates are updated annually by the International Labour Organization.
d For indicator 1.1.1.a, the latest available estimate for Azerbaijan is for 2005: 0.0%; for Uzbekistan, the latest available estimate is for 2003: 61.6%.
e Refers to absolute poverty or the share of the population under the absolute poverty line.
f For indicator 1.2.1 for Hong Kong, China, data refer to the poverty rate after policy intervention (recurrent cash); for the Republic of Korea, data refer to the relative poverty rate.
g Refers to the percentage of the low-income population to the total population.
h Based on the Tendulkar methodology, using mixed reference period.
i The urban and rural poverty estimates refer to other areas excluding Phnom Penh.
j Sourced from first-semester poverty estimates.
k Data refer to the percentage of the population living below the basic-needs poverty line.
l Refers to the poverty headcount ratio using the upper poverty line, which serves as spatial deflator with respect to Honiara (the Solomon Islands capital).

Sources: For indicator 1.1.1.a: World Bank. World Development Indicators. http://data.worldbank.org/data-catalog/world-development-indicators (accessed 15 July 2022); World Bank. Poverty and Inequality Platform. https://pip.worldbank.org/ (accessed 30 May 2022); and United Nations. SDG Global Database. http://unstats.un.org/sdgs/indicators/database/ (accessed 27 July 2022).For indicator 1.1.1.b: International Labour Organization. ILOSTAT Database. http://www.ilo.org/ilostat (accessed 28 July 2022). For indicator 1.2.1: Economies' official sources; United Nations. SDG Global Database. http://unstats.un.org/sdgs/indicators/database/ (accessed 27 July 2022); and Secretariat of the Pacific Community. National Minimum Development Indicators. https://www.spc.int/nmdi/ (accessed 07 July 2022).

Click on the indicator name in the table header to access the time series in the Key Indicators Database.

Goal 1. End poverty in all its forms everywhere

Table 1.1.2: Selected Indicators for Sustainable Development Goal 1—Social Protection

ADB Regional Member	Target 1.3: Implement nationally appropriate social protection systems and measures for all, including floors, and by 2030 achieve substantial coverage of the poor and the vulnerable				
	1.3.1.a: Proportion of Population Covered by at least One Social Protection Benefit (%)		1.3.1.b: Proportion of Population above Statutory Pensionable Age Receiving a Pension (%)		
	2015	2020	2010	2015	2020
Developing ADB Member Economies					
Central and West Asia					
Afghanistan	...	7.5	10.7	...	24.7
Armenia	47.3 (2016)	54.4	87.0 (2000)	68.5 (2016)	65.2
Azerbaijan	40.3 (2016)	39.0	97.0 (2000)	81.1 (2016)	72.8
Georgia	28.6 (2016)	97.1	80.0 (2000)	91.9 (2016)	90.9
Kazakhstan	100.0 (2016)	100.0	100.0 (2000)	82.6 (2016)	99.6
Kyrgyz Republic	...	41.7	86.0 (2000)	100.0 (2016)	100.0
Pakistan	...	9.2	2.3	...	5.8
Tajikistan	...	26.6	88.0 (2005)	92.8 (2016)	93.7
Turkmenistan	...	...	...	...	...
Uzbekistan	...	42.7	98.1	100.0 (2017)	100.0
East Asia					
China, People's Republic of	63.0 (2016)	70.8	24.0 (2000)	100.0 (2016)	100.0
Hong Kong, China	...	59.7	76.0 (2000)	72.9 (2016)	73.2
Korea, Republic of	65.7 (2016)	82.9 (2018)	...	100.0 (2014)	100.0 (2018)
Mongolia	72.4 (2016)	100.0	80.0 (2000)	100.0 (2016)	100.0
Taipei,China	...	...	...	...	...
South Asia					
Bangladesh	28.4 (2016)	...	6.0 (2002)	33.4 (2016)	39.0
Bhutan	...	8.8	3.2 (2012)	...	18.8 (2019)
India	22.0 (2016)	24.4	7.0 (2000)	25.2 (2016)	42.5
Maldives	...	21.2	99.7 (2012)	...	100.0
Nepal	...	17.0	62.5	...	84.2
Sri Lanka	30.4 (2016)	36.4	19.0 (2000)	25.2 (2016)	35.7
Southeast Asia					
Brunei Darussalam	...	34.1	81.7 (2011)	...	100.0
Cambodia	...	6.2	1.0 (2000)	3.2 (2016)	6.6 (2018)
Indonesia	...	27.8	6.0 (2002)	14.0 (2016)	14.8
Lao People's Democratic Republic	...	12.1	5.6	...	6.3
Malaysia	...	27.3	19.8	...	18.6
Myanmar	...	6.3	...	0.9 (2016)	14.9
Philippines	47.1 (2016)	36.7	20.0 (2000)	39.8 (2016)	20.5
Singapore	...	100.0	...	...	33.1
Thailand	...	68.0	5.0 (2000)	83.0 (2016)	89.1
Timor-Leste	...	30.6	...	89.7 (2016)	100.0
Viet Nam	37.9 (2016)	38.8	16.0 (2000)	39.9 (2016)	40.9
The Pacific					
Cook Islands	...	86.3 (2019)	...	...	100.0
Fiji	...	58.9	9.0 (2000)	10.6	92.1
Kiribati	...	21.0	...	...	93.8
Marshall Islands	...	25.2	64.2	...	62.7
Micronesia, Federated States of	...	19.4	...	...	100.0
Nauru	...	45.4 (2019)	56.5	...	95.7
Niue	...	...	...	...	...
Palau	...	35.8 (2019)	48.0	...	100.0
Papua New Guinea	...	9.6	0.9	...	22.3
Samoa	...	21.1	49.5 (2011)	...	91.4
Solomon Islands	...	1.1 (2019)	13.1	...	20.5 (2019)
Tonga	...	22.2	...	...	90.0
Tuvalu	...	...	15.0 (2000)	...	...
Vanuatu	...	57.4	3.5 (2011)	...	8.5 (2019)
Developed ADB Member Economies					
Australia	82.0 (2016)	100.0 (2018)	80.0 (2000)	74.3 (2016)	100.0 (2018)
Japan	75.4 (2016)	92.5 (2018)	74.0 (2000)	100.0 (2014)	100.0 (2018)
New Zealand	66.6 (2016)	100.0 (2018)	100.0 (2000)	100.0 (2016)	100.0 (2018)

Click on the indicator name in the table header to access the time series in the Key Indicators Database

Table 1.1.2: Selected Indicators for Sustainable Development Goal 1—Social Protection *(continued)*

ADB Regional Member	Target 1.3: Implement nationally appropriate social protection systems and measures for all, including floors, and by 2030 achieve substantial coverage of the poor and the vulnerable					
	1.3.1.c: Proportion of Poor Population Receiving Social Assistance Cash Benefit (%)		1.3.1.d: Proportion of Vulnerable Population Receiving Social Assistance Cash Benefit (%)		1.3.1.e: Proportion of Children/ Households Receiving Child/ Family Cash Benefit (%)	
	2015	2020	2015	2020	2015	2020
Developing ADB Member Economies						
Central and West Asia						
Afghanistan	...	...	...	5.9	...	0.4
Armenia	38.2 (2016)	100.0 (2018)	16.2 (2016)	19.6	21.4 (2016)	30.2
Azerbaijan	100.0 (2016)	100.0 (2018)	12.6 (2016)	13.4	...	16.9
Georgia	100.0 (2016)	100.0 (2018)	12.0 (2016)	92.9	...	48.1
Kazakhstan	28.9 (2016)	...	...	74.2	100.0 (2016)	57.4
Kyrgyz Republic	...	89.4 (2018)	...	14.1	17.8 (2016)	16.9
Pakistan	...	69.2 (2018)	...	5.0	...	5.4
Tajikistan	...	28.1 (2018)	...	7.5	6.4 (2016)	14.0
Turkmenistan	...	...	...	...	...	...
Uzbekistan	68.0 (2017)	82.5 (2018)	16.0 (2017)	15.6	22.0 (2017)	29.2
East Asia						
China, People's Republic of	51.6 (2016)	100.0	31.0 (2017)	33.2	2.2 (2016)	3.0
Hong Kong, China	...	...	...	28.3	...	...
Korea, Republic of	21.4 (2016)	...	...	26.3 (2018)	...	22.9 (2019)
Mongolia	94.9 (2016)	100.0 (2018)	35.1 (2016)	88.5	100.0 (2016)	85.0
Taipei,China	...	...	...	...	...	...
South Asia						
Bangladesh	11.0 (2016)	61.0 (2018)	4.3 (2016)	14.9	29.4 (2016)	24.0 (2019)
Bhutan	...	60.2 (2018)	...	5.0	...	13.5
India	...	...	10.4 (2016)	16.4	...	24.1
Maldives	...	100.0 (2018)	...	8.1	...	8.2
Nepal	...	70.1 (2018)	...	14.8	...	22.9
Sri Lanka	51.5 (2016)	100.0 (2018)	4.4 (2016)	16.0	...	32.0
Southeast Asia						
Brunei Darussalam	...	...	...	14.7	...	...
Cambodia	...	48.4 (2018)	...	4.3	...	4.5
Indonesia	...	100.0 (2018)	...	16.5	...	25.6
Lao People's Democratic Republic	...	0.1 (2018)	...	7.7	...	...
Malaysia	...	100.0 (2018)	...	2.1	...	2.8
Myanmar	...	0.8 (2018)	...	1.1	...	2.1
Philippines	...	100.0 (2018)	7.8 (2016)	22.4	13.6 (2016)	31.1
Singapore	...	...	...	100.0	...	...
Thailand	...	100.0 (2019)	...	54.3	18.9 (2016)	21.0
Timor-Leste	...	94.9 (2018)	...	26.5	30.7 (2016)	38.2
Viet Nam	...	100.0 (2018)	10.0 (2016)	24.6	...	1.0 (2019)
The Pacific						
Cook Islands	...	...	...	85.8	...	100.0
Fiji	...	68.0 (2018)	...	28.2	...	2.6
Kiribati	...	15.9 (2018)	...	5.1	...	1.3 (2018)
Marshall Islands	...	...	...	1.7	...	...
Micronesia, Federated States of	...	...	...	2.2 (2019)	...	6.8
Nauru	...	...	...	45.4	...	...
Niue	...	...	...	...	...	...
Palau	...	56.0 (2018)	...	17.8	...	60.0 (2019)
Papua New Guinea	...	...	...	...	...	...
Samoa	...	69.2 (2018)	...	5.3	...	– (2018)
Solomon Islands	...	2.9 (2018)	...	0.4 (2019)	...	...
Tonga	...	16.7 (2018)	...	6.2	...	3.3
Tuvalu	...	...	...	...	...	...
Vanuatu	...	100.0 (2018)	...	53.3	...	12.9 (2019)
Developed ADB Member Economies						
Australia	100.0 (2016)	...	53.0 (2016)	100.0 (2018)	100.0 (2016)	100.0 (2018)
Japan	...	...	...	100.0 (2018)	...	85.4 (2018)
New Zealand	37.4 (2016)	...	9.7 (2016)	100.0 (2018)	...	67.1 (2018)

... = data not available, – = magnitude equals zero, ADB = Asian Development Bank.

Note: The population covered by at least one social protection benefit (effective coverage) refers to the proportion of the total population receiving at least one contributory or noncontributory cash benefit, or actively contributing to at least one social security scheme. For children, older persons, and the poor and vulnerable, effective coverage is expressed as a share of the respective population.

Source: United Nations. SDG Global Database. https://unstats.un.org/sdgs/dataportal (accessed 14 July 2022).

Goal 2. End hunger, achieve food security and improved nutrition, and promote sustainable agriculture

Table 1.2.1: Selected Indicators for Sustainable Development Goal 2—Zero Hunger

ADB Regional Member	Target 2.1: By 2030, end hunger and ensure access by all people, in particular the poor and people in vulnerable situations, including infants, to safe, nutritious, and sufficient food all year round		Target 2.2: By 2030, end all forms of malnutrition, including achieving, by 2025, the internationally agreed targets on stunting and wasting in children under 5 years of age, and address the nutritional needs of adolescent girls, pregnant and lactating women, and older persons					
	2.1.1: Prevalence of Undernourishment (%)		2.2.1: Prevalence of Stunting among Children under 5 Years of Age[a] (%)		2.2.2.c: Prevalence of Malnutrition (Overweight) among Children under 5 Years of Age[a] (%)		2.2.2.d: Prevalence of Malnutrition (Wasting) among Children under 5 Years of Age (%)	
	2010[b]	2020[c]	2010	2020	2010	2020	2010	2019
Developing ADB Member Economies								
Central and West Asia[d]	...	...	**39.2**	**30.8**	**6.0**	**4.1**	...	...
Afghanistan	21.2	29.8	47.2	35.1	5.6	3.9	8.6 (2004)	5.1 (2018)
Armenia	3.7	3.5	15.6	9.1	15.9	10.8	4.1	4.4 (2016)
Azerbaijan	<2.5	<2.5	18.4	16.3	11.3	9.4	6.6 (2011)	3.2 (2013)
Georgia	6.7	7.6	10.3	5.7	16.0	7.6	1.3 (2009)	0.6 (2018)
Kazakhstan	3.2	<2.5	12.3	6.7	12.0	8.8	4.1	3.1 (2015)
Kyrgyz Republic	7.3	5.3	17.7	11.4	8.4	5.8	1.3 (2009)	2.0 (2018)
Pakistan	15.4	16.9	44.2	36.7	4.9	3.4	14.9 (2011)	7.1 (2018)
Tajikistan	26.5	8.6	29.5	15.3	6.4	3.5	4.3 (2009)	5.6 (2017)
Turkmenistan	4.3	3.5	14.7	7.6	5.4	3.8	7.2 (2006)	4.1
Uzbekistan	5.4	<2.5	15.8	9.9	10.1	5.0	4.4 (2006)	1.8 (2017)
East Asia[d]	...	...	**8.6**	**4.7**	**7.0**	**8.3**	...	...
China, People's Republic of	<2.5	<2.5	8.7	4.7	7.0	8.3	2.3	1.9 (2017)
Hong Kong, China	<2.5	<2.5	...	...	...	...	...	...
Korea, Republic of	<2.5	<2.5	2.3	2.2	7.4	8.8	1.2 (2009)	...
Mongolia	16.5	3.6	15.2	7.1	10.1	10.1	1.6	0.9 (2018)
Taipei,China	4.5	3.5	...	...	...	...	...	...
South Asia[d]	...	...	**43.7**	**30.6**	**2.4**	**1.9**	...	...
Bangladesh	15.2	11.4	40.2	30.2	1.5	2.1	15.7 (2011)	9.8
Bhutan	...	...	33.0	22.4	6.0	5.2	5.9	...
India	15.9	16.3	44.5	30.9	2.6	1.9	20.0 (2006)	17.3 (2017)
Maldives	...	...	18.3	14.2	5.9	4.6	10.6 (2009)	9.1 (2017)
Nepal	9.9	5.5	42.8	30.4	1.3	1.8	11.2 (2011)	12.0
Sri Lanka	9.6	3.4	17.2	16.0	1.2	1.3	11.8 (2009)	15.1 (2016)
Southeast Asia[d]	...	...	**31.6**	**27.4**	**5.3**	**7.4**	...	...
Brunei Darussalam	11.4	5.9	18.4	12.7	8.1	9.3	2.9 (2009)	...
Cambodia	11.2	6.3	37.5	29.9	2.3	2.1	11.0	9.7 (2014)
Indonesia	13.0	6.5	35.7	31.8	7.2	11.1	12.3	10.2 (2018)
Lao People's Democratic Republic	14.1	5.1	43.2	30.2	2.2	3.0	5.9 (2011)	9.0 (2017)
Malaysia	3.4	<2.5	17.9	20.9	6.0	6.1	13.2 (2006)	9.7
Myanmar	10.2	3.1	33.2	25.2	2.6	1.5	7.9 (2009)	6.7 (2018)
Philippines	12.2	5.2	32.7	28.7	3.1	4.2	7.0 (2011)	5.8
Singapore	...	...	3.3	2.8	3.8	4.8	3.6 (2000)	...
Thailand	9.9	8.8	14.9	12.3	8.4	9.2	6.7 (2012)	7.7
Timor-Leste	31.2	26.2	54.4	48.8	3.1	2.6	18.9 (2009)	8.3 (2020)
Viet Nam	10.9	5.7	27.6	22.3	3.7	6.0	4.1	5.2
The Pacific[d]	...	...	**40.7**	**42.4**	**7.1**	**8.1**	...	...
Cook Islands	...	...	...	...	...	...	...	...
Fiji	5.6	5.7	8.5	7.5	4.7	5.2	6.3 (2004)	...
Kiribati	4.4	4.2	16.3	14.9	2.4	2.4	...	3.5 (2018)
Marshall Islands	...	...	37.6	32.2	4.0	4.2	...	3.5 (2017)
Micronesia, Federated States of	...	...	...	...	...	...	...	...
Nauru	...	...	21.6	15.0	3.1	3.7	1.0 (2007)	...
Niue	...	...	...	...	...	...	...	...
Palau	...	...	...	...	...	...	...	...
Papua New Guinea	26.2	21.6	46.6	48.4	7.7	8.9	14.1	...
Samoa	4.2	4.4	5.6	6.8	6.6	7.1	...	3.1
Solomon Islands	13.7	18.1	33.0	29.3	3.4	4.0	4.3 (2007)	8.5 (2015)
Tonga	...	...	7.8	2.6	13.0	12.6	5.2 (2012)	1.1
Tuvalu	...	...	10.1	9.7	6.1	6.4	3.3 (2007)	2.8
Vanuatu	6.3	11.9	27.0	28.7	4.8	4.9	5.9 (2008)	4.7 (2013)
Developed ADB Member Economies[d]	...	...	**5.9**	**4.6**	**4.2**	**6.5**	...	...
Australia	<2.5	<2.5	2.0	2.1	13.0	18.5	– (2007)	...
Japan	2.7	3.2	6.9	5.5	1.9	2.4	2.3	...
New Zealand	<2.5	<2.5	...	...	...	...	...	...
DEVELOPING ADB MEMBER ECONOMIES[d]	...	...	**31.9**	**23.4**	**4.6**	**4.9**	...	...
ALL ADB REGIONAL MEMBERS[d]	...	...	**31.4**	**23.0**	**4.6**	**4.9**	...	...
WORLD	**8.6**	**9.8 (2021)**	**27.7**	**22.0**	**5.6**	**5.7**	...	**6.7 (2020)**

... = data not available, < = less than, – = magnitude equals zero, ADB = Asian Development Bank.

a Refers to modeled estimates from the Joint Child Malnutrition Estimates Database. The estimates for 2020 do not account for the full impact of coronavirus disease 2019 (COVID-19). Household survey data on child height and age were not collected in 2020 due to physical-distancing policies. One of the covariates used in the model takes the impact of COVID-19 partially into account.

b Economy level data refer to the 3-year average for 2009–2011. World estimate refers to annual value.

c Economy level data refer to the 3-year average for 2019–2021. World estimate refers to annual value.

d For indicators 2.2.1 and 2.2.2.c, estimated as weighted averages using total population of children aged 0–5 years from the United Nations' World Population Prospects 2022 as weightings.

Source: For Indicator 2.1.1: Food and Agriculture Organization of the United Nations. FAOSTAT Database. http://www.fao.org/faostat/en/#data/FS (accessed 23 July 2022). For Indicator 2.2.1, Indicator 2.2.2.c, and Indicator 2.2.2.d: United Nations. SDG Global Database. https://unstats.un.org/sdgs/dataportal (accessed 23 July 2022); and United Nations Children's Fund (UNICEF). Malnutrition Data. https://data.unicef.org/resources/dataset/malnutrition-data/ (accessed 23 July 2022). For total population of children 0–5 years old used as weightings: United Nations. World Population Prospects 2022. https://population.un.org/wpp/Download/Standard/Interpolated/ (accessed 23 July 2022).

Table 1.2.2: Selected Indicators for Sustainable Development Goal 2—Improved Agricultural Investment

ADB Regional Member	Target 2.a: Increase investment, including through enhanced international cooperation, in rural infrastructure, agricultural research and extension services, technology development, and plant and livestock gene banks in order to enhance agricultural productive capacity in developing countries, in particular least developed countries					
	2.a.1: The Agriculture Orientation Index for Government Expenditures			2.a.2: Total Official Flows to the Agriculture Sector[a] (constant 2020 $ million)		
	2010	2015	2020	2010	2015	2020
Developing ADB Member Economies						
Central and West Asia	**...**	**...**	**...**	**1,182.2**	**1,007.8**	**1,011.7**
Afghanistan	0.2	0.2	...	725.8	351.2	234.5
Armenia	0.3	0.1	0.1	89.1	39.4	21.7
Azerbaijan	0.5	0.5	0.5	17.2	54.8	8.9
Georgia	0.1	0.3	0.4	17.3	44.6	51.5
Kazakhstan	0.9	0.9	1.1 (2019)	56.5	69.3	20.0
Kyrgyz Republic	0.1	0.1	0.1	23.5	26.1	9.4
Pakistan	0.1	0.1	0.1	166.9	313.8	198.1
Tajikistan	...	0.0	0.0 (2019)	52.3	35.1	29.3
Turkmenistan	...	...	...	1.1	0.1	2.6
Uzbekistan	0.2 (2011)	0.2	0.2 (2019)	32.6	73.3	435.8
East Asia	**...**	**...**	**...**	**372.6**	**427.0**	**529.8**
China, People's Republic of	0.9	1.1	1.3 (2019)	330.5	408.4	500.6
Hong Kong, China	2.7	1.8	2.4 (2019)	...	...	...
Korea, Republic of	2.1	2.1	2.1 (2019)	...	...	...
Mongolia	0.4	0.1	0.1	42.1	18.6	29.2
Taipei,China	...	...	...	...	...	...
South Asia	**...**	**...**	**...**	**1,087.3**	**1,541.6**	**1,204.0**
Bangladesh	0.5	0.5	...	189.0	265.6	352.9
Bhutan	0.8	0.8	0.7	6.4	7.6	10.5
India	0.5	0.4	0.5 (2019)	752.5	1,124.1	641.9
Maldives	0.2	0.0	0.1 (2018)	0.0	0.7	59.0
Nepal	0.3	0.3	0.2	103.8	107.7	81.9
Sri Lanka	0.6	0.8	0.6 (2019)	35.7	36.0	57.8
Southeast Asia	**...**	**...**	**...**	**1,614.9**	**979.8**	**1,716.3**
Brunei Darussalam	...	...	...	...	...	...
Cambodia	...	...	...	77.5	119.5	134.0
Indonesia	0.1	0.2	0.3	991.8	232.5	324.1
Lao People's Democratic Republic	...	0.1 (2017)	0.1 (2019)	54.0	70.7	97.3
Malaysia	0.3	0.4	0.2	2.3	4.9	1.4
Myanmar	0.1 (2012)	0.2	0.3 (2019)	39.0	147.5	253.9
Philippines	0.5	0.4	0.3	134.7	118.4	649.6
Singapore	6.8	7.7	4.6	...	...	...
Thailand	0.4	0.8	0.8 (2019)	12.2	7.8	7.5
Timor-Leste	0.1	0.1	0.1 (2019)	26.5	25.4	22.7
Viet Nam	0.3	0.3	0.3	276.9	253.1	225.6
The Pacific[b]	**...**	**...**	**...**	**55.5**	**85.2**	**132.4**
Cook Islands	0.9	0.9	0.6 (2019)	1.2	0.3	0.7 (2019)
Fiji	0.3	0.6	0.3	3.2	21.4	17.1
Kiribati	...	...	...	3.0	2.6	6.6
Marshall Islands	0.2	0.2	0.3 (2018)	3.9	1.5	2.4
Micronesia, Federated States of	0.1	0.1	0.2 (2019)	1.1	2.0	2.7
Nauru	...	...	...	0.5	0.4	2.4
Niue	...	...	...	0.2	0.1	0.4
Palau	0.1	0.2	0.2 (2018)	0.6	0.8	1.0
Papua New Guinea	0.1	0.1	0.1 (2019)	20.9	31.3	55.2
Samoa	0.2	0.4	0.7	1.5	4.1	3.4
Solomon Islands	0.2 (2011)	0.1	0.1	10.7	12.8	9.3
Tonga	...	...	...	2.2	1.8	1.7
Tuvalu	...	...	...	0.9	2.2	3.5
Vanuatu	0.1	0.1	0.1 (2019)	5.6	3.9	26.7
Developed ADB Member Economies	**...**	**...**	**...**	**...**	**...**	**...**
Australia	0.5	0.3	0.3	...	...	...
Japan	2.1	2.0	1.9 (2019)	...	...	...
New Zealand	0.2	0.1	0.1	...	...	...
DEVELOPING ADB MEMBER ECONOMIES	...	...	...	**4,312.6**	**4,041.4**	**4,594.3**

... = data not available, 0.0 = magnitude is less than half of unit employed, $ = United States dollars, ADB = Asian Development Bank.

a Total official flows refer to official development assistance plus other official flows. Data refer to gross disbursements.

b Includes only reporting economies with data corresponding to the year heading.

Source: United Nations. SDG Global Database. https://unstats.un.org/sdgs/dataportal (accessed 12 July 2022).

Goal 3. Ensure healthy lives and promote well-being for all at all ages

Table 1.3.1: Selected Indicators for Sustainable Development Goal 3—Maternal and Child Health

ADB Regional Member	Target 3.1: By 2030, reduce the global maternal mortality ratio to less than 70 per 100,000 live births				Target 3.2: By 2030, end preventable deaths of newborns and children under 5 years of age, with all countries aiming to reduce neonatal mortality to at least as low as 12 per 1,000 live births and under-5 mortality to at least as low as 25 per 1,000 live births			
	3.1.1: Maternal Mortality Ratio[a,b] (per 100,000 live births)		3.1.2: Proportion of Births Attended by Skilled Health Personnel[c] (%)		3.2.1: Under-5 Mortality Rate[a,b] (per 1,000 live births)		3.2.2: Neonatal Mortality Rate[a,b] (per 1,000 live births)	
	2010	2017	2010	2020	2010	2020	2010	2020
Developing ADB Member Economies								
Central and West Asia	**264**	**182**	...	...	**75**	**55**	**42**	**33**
Afghanistan	954	638	34.3 [d]	61.8 [d]	88	58	47	35
Armenia	32	26	99.5 [d]	99.8 [e] (2016)	18	11	10	6
Azerbaijan	31	26	99.4 [f]	99.9 [f]	37	19	20	10
Georgia	32	25	99.6 [d]	99.8 [f]	14	9	10	5
Kazakhstan	22	10	99.4 [f]	99.9 [g] (2018)	20	10	12	5
Kyrgyz Republic	79	60	98.3 [f]	99.8 [d] (2018)	30	18	17	12
Pakistan	191	140	43.0 [d] (2011)	68.0 [e]	87	65	50	40
Tajikistan	23	17	87.7 [f]	94.8 [d] (2017)	43	32	20	14
Turkmenistan	10	7	99.5 [d] (2006)	100.0 [e] (2019)	43	42	23	24
Uzbekistan	31	29	100.0 [f]	100.0 [d]	29	14	16	8
East Asia	**35**	**29**	...	...	**16**	**7**	**8**	**3**
China, People's Republic of	36	29	99.6 [f]	99.9 [f] (2016)	16	7	8	4
Hong Kong, China	1	–* (2020)	...	...	...	...	1	1*
Korea, Republic of	15	11	99.9 [g] (2009)	100.0 [g] (2015)	4	3	2	2
Mongolia	66	45	98.8 [d]	99.3 [e] (2018)	26	15	11	8
Taipei,China	4	13 (2020)	...	...	...	...	3	2
South Asia	**215**	**148**	...	...	**56**	**32**	**31**	**20**
Bangladesh	258	173	26.5 [e]	59.0 [e] (2019)	49	29	29	18
Bhutan	247	183	64.5 [e]	96.3 [f] (2019)	42	28	23	15
India	210	145	52.3 [f] (2008)	89.4 [e] (2021)	58	33	32	20
Maldives	67	53	98.2 [d]	99.5 [d] (2017)	14	7	8	4
Nepal	305	186	36.0 [d] (2011)	77.2 [e] (2019)	46	28	27	17
Sri Lanka	38	36	98.6 [d] (2007)	99.5 [d] (2016)	11	7	6	4
Southeast Asia	**172**	**137**	...	...	**33**	**24**	**16**	**12**
Brunei Darussalam	28	31	99.8 [f]	99.8 [f] (2017)	10	12	5	6
Cambodia	248	160	71.0 [d] (2011)	...	44	26	21	13
Indonesia	228	177	83.1 [e] (2012)	94.7 [d] (2019)	34	23	18	12
Lao People's Democratic Republic	292	185	40.1 [d] (2012)	64.4 [d] (2017)	68	44	29	22
Malaysia	30	29	98.6 [f]	99.6 [e] (2019)	8	9	4	5
Myanmar	265	250	70.6 [e]	60.2 [e] (2016)	64	44	29	22
Philippines	144	121	72.2 [d] (2011)	84.4 [d] (2017)	32	26	15	13
Singapore	10	8	99.7 [g]	99.6 [e]	3	2	1	1
Thailand	42	37	99.4 [d] (2009)	99.1 [e] (2019)	14	9	8	5
Timor-Leste	219	142	29.3 [d]	56.7 [e] (2016)	62	42	25	19
Viet Nam	47	43	91.9 [d] (2011)	96.1 [f] (2021)	23	21	12	10
The Pacific	**151**	**130**	...	...	**51**	**40**	**23**	**19**
Cook Islands	...	...	100.0 [f] (2009)	...	11	7	6	4
Fiji	39	34	99.7 [f]	99.8 [f] (2021)	24	27	9	12
Kiribati	112	92	98.3 [f]	91.9 [e] (2019)	64	50	25	21
Marshall Islands	...	...	90.0 [d]	92.4 [d] (2017)	39	31	18	14
Micronesia, Federated States of	110	88	100.0 [f] (2009)	...	33	25	18	13
Nauru	...	...	97.4 [e] (2007)	...	38	29	24	18
Niue	...	...	100.0 [f]	...	33	25	18	13
Palau	...	...	99.6 [d]	97.2 [d]	23	17	12	9
Papua New Guinea	168	145	53.0 [d] (2006)	56.4 [e] (2018)	58	44	26	22
Samoa	58	43	80.8 [e] (2009)	88.9 [d]	19	17	8	7
Solomon Islands	141	104	85.5 [e] (2007)	86.2 [e] (2015)	26	19	11	8
Tonga	57	52	99.0 [f]	98.3 [e] (2019)	13	11	6	5
Tuvalu	...	...	93.1 [d] (2007)	99.5 [e]	31	22	16	10
Vanuatu	92	72	89.4 [e] (2013)	...	29	25	12	11
Developed ADB Member Economies	**6**	**6**	...	...	**4**	**3**	**2**	**1**
Australia	5	6	99.1 [g]	98.8 [g] (2019)	5	4	3	2
Japan	6	5	99.8 [g]	99.9 [g]	3	3	1	1
New Zealand	11	9	96.8 [g]	96.4 [g] (2018)	6	5	3	3
DEVELOPING ADB MEMBER ECONOMIES	**166**	**119**	...	...	**44**	**27**	**24**	**16**
ALL ADB REGIONAL MEMBERS	**163**	**117**	...	...	**43**	**27**	**23**	**16**
WORLD	**253**	**218**	**76.9 (2011)**	**83.6 (2021)**	**51**	**37**	**22**	**17**

... = data not available, – = magnitude equals zero, * = provisional, preliminary, ADB = Asian Development Bank.

a Regional aggregates are weighted averages estimated using population of annual live births for the respective year headings. The data for maternal, under-5, and neonatal deaths are from United Nations databases. For Taipei,China, maternal and neonatal deaths data are from the Government of Taipei,China's Ministry of Health and Welfare. Aggregates are derived for reporting economies only. Aggregates for East Asia exclude Hong Kong, China. For under-5 mortality rate, aggregates also exclude Taipei,China.

b Data are estimates as published on the United Nations' SDG Global Database.

c Based on data from national-level household surveys and routine service statistics.

d Estimates are aligned with the standard definition of doctor, nurse, and/or midwife.

e Includes other health personnel not in alignment with the standard definition.

f Estimate provided with no clear definition of health personnel.

g Refers to institutional births, including all deliveries that occurred at a health facility.

Sources: For Indicators 3.1.1, 3.2.1, 3.2.1, and 3.2.2: United Nations. SDG Global Database. https://unstats.un.org/sdgs/dataportal (accessed 16 July 2022). For Indicators 3.1.1 and 3.2.2 for Taipei,China: Government of Taipei,China, Ministry of Health and Welfare. 2020 Cause of Death Statistics. https://www.mohw.gov.tw/np-128-2.html (accessed 16 July 2022). For Indicator 3.1.1 for Hong Kong, China: Government of the Hong Kong Special Administrative Region of the People's Republic of China. Centre for Health Protection Statistics. https://www.chp.gov.hk/en/statistics/data/10/27/110.html (accessed 16 July 2022). For Indicator 3.2.2 for Hong Kong, China: Government of the Hong Kong Special Administrative Region of the People's Republic of China, Department of Health. Health Facts of Hong Kong 2021 Edition; past editions. https://www.dh.gov.hk/english/statistics/statistics_hs/files/2021.pdf (accessed 16 July 2022).

Table 1.3.2: Selected Indicators for Sustainable Development Goal 3—Incidence of Communicable Diseases

ADB Regional Member	Target 3.3: By 2030, end the epidemics of AIDS, tuberculosis, malaria, and neglected tropical diseases; and combat hepatitis, water-borne diseases, and other communicable diseases					
	3.3.1: Number of New HIV Infections[a] (per 1,000 uninfected population)		3.3.2: Tuberculosis Incidence[b] (per 100,000 population)		3.3.3: Malaria Incidence[c] (per 1,000 population)	
	2010	2020	2010	2020	2010	2020
Developing ADB Member Economies						
Central and West Asia						
Afghanistan	0.03	0.04	189.0	193.0	13.0	8.4
Armenia	0.10	0.11	61.0	23.0	–	–
Azerbaijan	0.08	0.04	104.0	58.0	0.2	–
Georgia	0.13	0.17	127.0	70.0	–	–
Kazakhstan	0.13	0.19	144.0	69.0	–	–
Kyrgyz Republic	0.12	0.11	120.0	105.0	0.0	–
Pakistan	0.08	0.12	276.0	259.0	8.2	2.5
Tajikistan	0.19	0.09	128.0	84.0	0.0	–
Turkmenistan	...	...	79.0	47.0	–	–
Uzbekistan	0.17	0.08	97.0	66.0	0.1	–
East Asia						
China, People's Republic of	...	...	76.0	59.0	0.0	–
Hong Kong, China	...	...	81.0	56.0	...	...
Korea, Republic of	...	...	95.0	49.0	0.4	0.1
Mongolia	0.02	0.01	428.0	437.0	...	...
Taipei,China	...	...	...	...	...	...
South Asia						
Bangladesh	...	...	221.0	218.0	4.4	0.4
Bhutan	0.15	0.09	239.0	165.0	0.9	0.0
India	0.08	0.04	247.0	188.0	17.5	3.2
Maldives	...	...	32.0	37.0	...	...
Nepal	0.08	0.03	311.0	235.0	3.9	0.0
Sri Lanka	0.01	<0.01	66.0	64.0	0.1	–
Southeast Asia						
Brunei Darussalam	...	...	70.0	83.0	...	...
Cambodia	0.14	0.07	438.0	274.0	34.9	5.8
Indonesia	0.20	0.10	342.0	301.0	8.9	2.9
Lao People's Democratic Republic	0.17	0.13	221.0	149.0	13.5	1.5
Malaysia	0.18	0.19	75.0	92.0	4.6	–
Myanmar	...	...	500.0	308.0	67.0	2.5
Philippines	0.05	0.15	531.0	539.0	1.0	0.7
Singapore	0.12	<0.01	35.0	46.0	...	...
Thailand	0.23	0.10	181.0	150.0	2.5	0.2
Timor-Leste	0.07	0.10	498.0	508.0	99.7	0.0
Viet Nam	0.16	0.06	231.0	176.0	0.4	0.0
The Pacific						
Cook Islands	...	...	–	13.0	...	...
Fiji	0.08	0.16	27.0	66.0	...	...
Kiribati	...	...	347.0	425.0	...	...
Marshall Islands	...	...	428.0	483.0	...	...
Micronesia, Federated States of	...	...	199.0	75.0	...	...
Nauru	...	...	34.0	180.0	...	...
Niue	...	...	–	48.0	...	...
Palau	...	...	122.0	64.0	...	...
Papua New Guinea	0.36	0.39	432.0	441.0	147.6	164.3
Samoa	...	...	8.7	6.1	...	...
Solomon Islands	...	...	80.0	65.0	174.9	167.7
Tonga	...	...	12.0	10.0	...	...
Tuvalu	...	...	153.0	296.0	...	...
Vanuatu	...	...	69.0	38.0	88.8	3.0
Developed ADB Member Economies						
Australia	0.05	0.03	6.5	7.3	...	...
Japan	<0.01	<0.01	20.0	12.0	...	...
New Zealand	0.04	0.02	7.9	7.5	...	...

... = data not available, < = less than, – = magnitude equals zero, 0.0 = magnitude is less than half of unit employed, ADB = Asian Development Bank.

a Figures are based on modeled HIV estimates. For more information on the HIV estimates methodology, please see https://www.unaids.org.

b Estimates of tuberculosis incidence are produced through a consultative and analytical process led by the World Health Organization and are published annually. These estimates are based on annual case notifications, assessments of the quality and coverage of tuberculosis notification data, national surveys of the prevalence of tuberculosis disease, and information from death (vital) registration systems.
Estimates of incidence for each economy are derived, using one or more of the following approaches, depending on available data: (i) incidence = case notifications and/or estimated proportion of cases detected; (ii) capture-recapture modelling, (iii) incidence = prevalence and/or duration of condition.

c Malaria incidence is expressed as the number of new cases per 100,000 population per year, with the population of each economy derived from projections made by the United Nations Population Division and the total proportion at risk estimated by an economy's national malaria control program. More specifically, the economy estimates the total proportion of the population at risk of malaria and then, for each year, the total population at risk is estimated as the United Nations population figure for that year times the proportion of the population at risk.

Sources: For Indicator 3.3.1: The Joint United Nations Programme on HIV/AIDS. AIDSinfo. https://aidsinfo.unaids.org/ (accessed 16 July 2022). For Indicators 3.3.2 and 3.3.3: United Nations. SDG Global Database. https://unstats.un.org/sdgs/dataportal (accessed 16 July 2022).

Goal 3. Ensure healthy lives and promote well-being for all at all ages

Table 1.3.3: Selected Indicators for Sustainable Development Goal 3—Mortality Rates, Reproductive Health

ADB Regional Member	Target 3.4: By 2030, reduce by one-third premature mortality from noncommunicable diseases through prevention and treatment, and promote mental health and well-being					Target 3.6: By 2020, halve the number of global deaths and injuries from road traffic accidents	
	3.4.1: Mortality Rate Attributed to Cardiovascular Disease, Cancer, Diabetes, or Chronic Respiratory Disease[a] (%)		3.4.2: Suicide Mortality Rate[a] (per 100,000 population)			3.6.1: Death Rate Due to Road Traffic Injuries[a] (per 100,000 population)	
	2010	2019	2019			2010	2019
			Total	Female	Male		
Developing ADB Member Economies							
Central and West Asia							
Afghanistan	37.8	35.3	4.1	3.6	4.6	14.4	15.9
Armenia	25.0	19.9	3.3	1.3	5.6	18.0	20.0
Azerbaijan	29.8	27.2	4.1	1.6	6.6	11.4	6.7
Georgia	27.1	24.9	9.2	3.0	16.0	17.2	12.4
Kazakhstan	31.4	22.4	17.6	6.8	29.0	25.9	12.7
Kyrgyz Republic	27.9	20.3	7.4	3.2	11.7	18.0	12.7
Pakistan	31.8	29.4	8.9	4.3	13.3	14.7	13.0
Tajikistan	30.5	28.3	4.3	2.8	5.7	18.7	15.7
Turkmenistan	33.1	27.7	5.7	2.6	8.8	16.9	13.5
Uzbekistan	28.9	25.3	8.0	4.8	11.3	11.3	11.7
East Asia							
China, People's Republic of	19.0	15.9	8.1	6.2	9.8	20.3	17.4
Hong Kong, China	...	...	...	...	...	1.7	1.3 (2020)
Korea, Republic of	10.6	7.3	28.6	16.9	40.2	13.7	8.6
Mongolia	41.6	35.0	17.9	5.4	30.7	18.6	21.0
Taipei,China	...	...	15.5 (2020)	...	...	...	...
South Asia							
Bangladesh	21.5	18.9	3.7	1.7	5.7	16.9	15.3
Bhutan	19.4	18.5	4.6	2.7	6.3	13.6	16.2
India	23.7	21.9	12.7	11.1	14.1	17.2	15.6
Maldives	16.5	11.6	2.7	0.8	3.9	3.0	1.6
Nepal	20.2	21.5	9.0	2.7	16.4	15.8	16.3
Sri Lanka	17.0	13.2	14.0	6.2	22.3	14.2	19.7
Southeast Asia							
Brunei Darussalam	19.9	18.5	2.7	0.8	4.4	7.7	7.5
Cambodia	23.7	22.5	4.9	2.8	7.0	18.1	19.6
Indonesia	26.1	24.8	2.4	1.1	3.7	13.7	11.3
Lao People's Democratic Republic	28.3	26.8	5.4	3.2	7.6	14.3	17.9
Malaysia	18.9	18.4	5.7	2.3	8.9	25.1	22.5
Myanmar	28.3	24.9	2.9	1.1	4.9	19.1	20.4
Philippines	24.4	24.5	2.2	1.2	3.1	11.5	12.0
Singapore	11.0	9.5	11.2	7.1	15.0	5.1	2.1
Thailand	14.9	13.7	8.8	2.9	15.0	38.3	32.2
Timor-Leste	19.9	19.9	3.7	2.0	5.3	15.3	11.9
Viet Nam	22.4	21.2	7.5	4.7	10.4	25.6	30.6
The Pacific							
Cook Islands	...	...	...	...	...	...	...
Fiji	39.6	37.7	9.0	5.7	12.2	9.8	13.5
Kiribati	53.0	50.8	28.3	8.6	48.6	5.8	1.9
Marshall Islands	...	...	...	...	...	...	...
Micronesia, Federated States of	44.6	46.3	28.2	12.7	43.2	2.9	0.2
Nauru	...	30.0 (2017)	...	...	...	...	...
Niue	...	18.5 (2016)	...	...	...	...	...
Palau	...	...	...	...	...	...	...
Papua New Guinea	35.4	36.0	2.9	1.6	4.2	17.1	12.6
Samoa	32.4	31.2	12.6	6.7	18.0	12.9	13.0
Solomon Islands	40.4	39.2	14.7	1.9	27.0	17.8	16.5
Tonga	26.3	24.8	3.8	2.6	5.0	5.8	33.0
Tuvalu	...	...	...	...	...	...	...
Vanuatu	40.4	39.7	18.0	7.6	28.1	13.5	14.9
Developed ADB Member Economies							
Australia	9.9	8.6	12.5	6.4	18.6	6.5	4.9
Japan	9.5	8.3	15.3	9.2	21.8	5.3	3.6
New Zealand	11.8	10.3	11.0	5.8	16.5	9.3	9.6

Table 1.3.3: Selected Indicators for Sustainable Development Goal 3—Mortality Rates, Reproductive Health *(continued)*

ADB Regional Member	Target 3.7: By 2030, ensure universal access to sexual and reproductive health-care services, including for family planning, information, and education, and the integration of reproductive health into natural strategies and programs				Target 3.8: Achieve universal health coverage, including financial risk protection; access to quality essential health-care services; and access to safe, effective, quality, and affordable essential medicines and vaccines for all	Target 3.9: By 2030, substantially reduce the number of deaths and illnesses from hazardous chemicals and air, water, and soil pollution and contamination	
	3.7.1: Proportion of Women of Reproductive Age (Aged 15–49 Years) Who Have Their Need for Family Planning Satisfied with Modern Methods		3.7.2: Adolescent Birth Rate (Aged 15–19 Years) per 1,000 Women in That Age Group		3.8.1: Coverage of Essential Health Services[b] (index in a unitless scale of 0 to 100)	3.9.1: Mortality Rate Attributed to Household and Ambient Air Pollution (per 100,000 population)	3.9.2: Mortality Rate Attributed to Unsafe Water, Unsafe Sanitation, and Lack of Hygiene (per 100,000 population)
	2010	2018	2010	2019	2019	2019	2019
Developing ADB Member Economies							
Central and West Asia							
Afghanistan	...	42.2 [c] (2016)	80.0 (2009)	62.0 (2017)	37.0	269.0	16.6
Armenia	39.4	40.2 [c] (2016)	27.1	18.9 (2018)	69.0	73.0	5.8
Azerbaijan	21.5 [c] (2006)	...	60.0	42.2 (2020)	65.0	124.0	3.6
Georgia	52.8 [c]	50.5 [c]	48.5	27.3 (2020)	65.0	92.0	3.3
Kazakhstan	79.1 [c] (2011)	73.2 [c]	28.3	24.6 (2020)	76.0	85.0	3.2
Kyrgyz Republic	62.1 (2012)	64.6	34.1	34.0 (2020)	70.0	125.0	2.3
Pakistan	47.0 [c] (2013)	48.6 [c]	48.1	54.0 (2017)	45.0	194.0	38.8
Tajikistan	50.9 [c] (2012)	52.1 [c] (2017)	47.0	45.6	66.0	204.0	9.0
Turkmenistan	67.5 (2000)	79.6 [c] (2019)	25.4 (2009)	22.4 (2018)	73.0	88.0	5.7
Uzbekistan	...	...	24.3 (2011)	18.9 (2017)	71.0	152.0	2.9
East Asia							
China, People's Republic of	96.6 [c] (2001)	...	5.9	6.1 (2020)	82.0	95.0	2.2
Hong Kong, China	...	...	3.0	1.7 (2020)	...	...	...
Korea, Republic of	...	...	1.8	0.9	87.0	19.0	5.2
Mongolia	65.0 [c]	63.6	18.9	26.9 (2020)	63.0	215.0	3.2
Taipei,China	...	...	...	...	...	...	...
South Asia							
Bangladesh	69.7 [c] (2011)	77.4 [c] (2019)	118.3	74.0	51.0	146.0	18.2
Bhutan	84.6 [c]	...	91.2 (2003)	8.0	62.0	99.0	15.7
India	64.0 [c] (2008)	72.8 (2016)	37.2	12.2 (2018)	61.0	143.0	36.4
Maldives	42.6 [c] (2009)	29.2 (2017)	15.4	5.9	69.0	32.0	2.3
Nepal	56.2 (2011)	61.9 [c] (2019)	90.0	63.0 (2018)	53.0	183.0	17.8
Sri Lanka	69.4 [c] (2007)	74.3 [c] (2016)	24.5	21.0 (2015)	67.0	93.0	4.8
Southeast Asia							
Brunei Darussalam	...	...	14.5 (2011)	9.9 (2018)	77.0	19.0	1.7
Cambodia	51.6 (2011)	...	53.8	...	61.0	167.0	17.1
Indonesia	79.0 (2012)	77.0 (2017)	48.0	36.0 (2016)	59.0	96.0	15.8
Lao People's Democratic Republic	60.5 (2012)	72.3 (2017)	94.4	83.4 (2016)	50.0	195.0	20.5
Malaysia	...	...	14.0	8.6	76.0	76.0	14.4
Myanmar	56.0 [c] (2001)	74.9 (2016)	16.7 (2007)	21.3 (2018)	61.0	186.0	12.9
Philippines	54.1 [c] (2011)	56.0 (2017)	0.8	35.6	55.0	203.0	16.9
Singapore	...	...	4.8	2.1	86.0	23.0	8.5
Thailand	89.2 [c] (2012)	88.2 (2019)	50.1	31.7 (2018)	83.0	46.0	11.8
Timor-Leste	38.4	45.9 (2016)	50.0	41.9 (2015)	53.0	185.0	20.4
Viet Nam	72.8 [c] (2011)	...	38.0	29.0 (2020)	70.0	105.0	6.9
The Pacific							
Cook Islands	...	76.2 (2015)	43.2 (2009)	41.9 (2017)	53.8	...	...
Fiji	...	51.3 (2021)	32.5 (2011)	23.1 (2016)	61.0	121.0	10.8
Kiribati	35.8 [c] (2009)	53.1 [d] (2019)	49.0	50.6 (2017)	51.0	247.0	37.4
Marshall Islands	80.5 [c] (2007)	...	82.2	...	61.8	...	...
Micronesia, Federated States of	66.0 (2002)	...	44.0 (2009)	...	48.0	255.0	14.0
Nauru	42.5 [c] (2007)	...	60.5	94.0 (2015)	53.9	...	...
Niue	...	...	20.0 (2011)	...	55.0	...	...
Palau	...	39.4 (2015)	26.0	33.8 (2017)	58.8	...	...
Papua New Guinea	40.6 [c] (2007)	49.2	88.2 (2013)	68.0 (2016)	33.0	188.0	24.9
Samoa	34.9 (2009)	29.0 (2019)	39.2 (2011)	54.9 (2018)	53.0	150.0	8.2
Solomon Islands	60.0 [c] (2007)	38.0 [c] (2015)	61.6 (2009)	...	50.0	281.0	32.7
Tonga	47.9 [c] (2012)	49.9 [e] (2019)	24.0	...	56.0	53.0	7.1
Tuvalu	41.0 (2007)	44.9 (2020)	44.2 (2009)	43.8 (2018)	51.6	...	...
Vanuatu	50.7 [c] (2013)	...	78.0 (2011)	...	52.0	259.0	25.0
Developed ADB Member Economies							
Australia	...	...	16.7	8.7	87.0	10.0	1.9
Japan	...	...	4.5	2.8	85.0	12.0	8.4
New Zealand	...	...	29.0	12.6 (2020)	86.0	12.0	2.1

... = data not available, ADB = Asian Development Bank.

a For detailed information regarding the nature of the data, please refer to the United Nations' SDG Global Database at https://unstats.un.org/sdgs/dataportal.

b The universal health coverage service coverage index is calculated as the geometric mean of 14 tracer indicators of health service coverage. The index is reported on a unitless scale of 0 to 100, with 100 being the optimal value. The reported values do not directly translate to the percentage of the population covered by universal health coverage services, but they can be viewed as performance scores.

c The global indicator represents all women of reproductive age: this survey estimate represents women who are married or in a union.

d Figures by method do not sum to the total: answers about specific contraceptive methods used were not defined as either modern or traditional.

e Unmet need estimated from microdata by the United Nations Population Division as not reported for all women.

Sources: For Indicators 3.4.1, 3.4.2, 3.6.1, 3.7.1, 3.7.2, 3.8.1, 3.9.1, and 3.9.2: United Nations. SDG Global Database. https://unstats.un.org/sdgs/dataportal (accessed 12 July 2022). For Indicator 3.4.1 for Nauru and Niue: Pacific Data Hub. Explorer. https://stats.pacificdata.org/ (accessed 12 July 2022). For Indicator 3.4.2 for Taipei,China: Government of Taipei,China, Ministry of Health and Welfare. 2020 Cause of Death Statistics. https://www.mohw.gov.tw/np-128-2.html (accessed 12 July 2022). For Indicator 3.6.1 for Hong Kong, China: Government of the Hong Kong Special Administrative Region of the People's Republic of China. Road Traffic Accident Statistics. https://www.td.gov.hk/en/road_safety/road_traffic_accident_statistics/accident_trend_since_1953/index.html (accessed 12 July 2022). For Indicator 3.7.1 for Fiji, Samoa, and Tuvalu: Pacific Data Hub. Explorer. https://stats.pacificdata.org/ (accessed 12 July 2022). For Indicator 3.8.1 for Cook Islands, Marshall Islands, Nauru, Niue, Palau, and Tuvalu: World Health Organization. The Global Health Observatory. https://www.who.int/data/gho (accessed 12 July 2022).

Goal 3. Ensure healthy lives and promote well-being for all at all ages

Table 1.3.4: Selected Indicators for Sustainable Development Goal 3—Health Workforce and National and Global Health Risks

ADB Regional Member	Target 3.c: Substantially increase health financing and the recruitment, development, training, and retention of the health workforce in developing countries, especially in least developed countries and small island developing states						Target 3.d: Strengthen the capacity of all countries, in particular developing countries, for early warning, risk reduction, and management of national and global health risks
	3.c.1: Health Worker Density, by Type of Occupation[a,b] (per 10,000 population)						3.d.1: International Health Regulations Capacity and Health Emergency Preparedness[b,c,d] (%)
	Density of Medical Doctors			Density of Nursing and Midwifery Personnel			Average of 13 International Health Regulations Core Capacity Scores
	2010	2015	2020	2010	2015	2020	2021
Developing ADB Member Economies							
Central and West Asia	**13.4**	**13.7**	**...**	**26.1**	**23.9**	**...**	**66**
Afghanistan	2.4	2.9	2.5	6.1 (2009)	1.3	4.5 (2018)	41
Armenia	28.4	29.1	...	52.4	49.5	...	84
Azerbaijan	36.6	33.7	31.7 (2019)	73.5	64.3 (2014)	...	84
Georgia	44.5	50.1	51.1	39.5	40.2	55.5	63
Kazakhstan	39.3	39.7	40.7	77.2	72.9	...	88
Kyrgyz Republic	23.4	22.1 (2014)	...	56.5	59.5 (2014)	56.0 (2019)	42
Pakistan	8.1	9.3	11.2 (2019)	5.6	4.8	4.8 (2019)	52
Tajikistan	17.0	17.2 (2014)	...	39.5	47.5 (2014)	...	57
Turkmenistan	22.7	22.3 (2014)	...	45.1	44.3 (2014)	...	81
Uzbekistan	25.4	23.7 (2014)	...	113.8	112.8 (2014)	...	65
East Asia	**14.6**	**17.9**	**...**	**14.9**	**22.9**	**...**	**89**
China, People's Republic of	14.3	17.7	22.3 (2019)	14.9	22.9	30.8 (2019)	94
Hong Kong, China	...	...	...	...	...	...	...
Korea, Republic of	19.8	22.5	24.8 (2019)	46.4	59.8	81.8 (2019)	95
Mongolia	27.6	32.2	38.5 (2018)	36.3	40.9	42.1 (2018)	78
Taipei,China	...	...	...	...	...	...	...
South Asia	**...**	**...**	**7.4**	**...**	**19.2**	**16.6**	**60**
Bangladesh	3.6	4.9	6.7	1.8	2.8	4.9	68
Bhutan	2.8 (2012)	3.5	5.0	10.5 (2012)	14.7	20.8	52
India	...	...	7.4	...	21.1 (2017)	17.5	84
Maldives	14.4	17.7 (2014)	20.5 (2019)	51.1	65.7	46.6	50
Nepal	5.2 (2012)	9.1 (2017)	8.5	16.0 (2012)	21.4 (2014)	33.4	44
Sri Lanka	7.2	8.6	12.3	17.5	19.6	25.0	64
Southeast Asia	**5.3**	**5.3**	**8.2**	**27.0**	**22.3**	**...**	**68**
Brunei Darussalam	14.5	17.8	...	74.8	66.4	59.0 (2018)	...
Cambodia	2.3	1.9 (2014)	...	8.6	5.9	10.1 (2019)	57
Indonesia	1.4	2.7	6.2	...	13.0	39.5	64
Lao People's Democratic Republic	2.0 (2009)	5.0 (2014)	3.5	8.6	12.2	11.9	51
Malaysia	11.7	15.4	22.9	32.0	41.8	34.8 (2019)	85
Myanmar	5.2	6.2 (2016)	7.4 (2019)	8.9	10.3 (2016)	10.8 (2019)	57
Philippines	12.7	6.0 (2017)	7.7	56.5 (2009)	52.7 (2017)	54.4 (2019)	63
Singapore	17.6	22.3	24.6 (2019)	57.2	60.1	...	94
Thailand	3.9	4.7	9.5	20.6	23.7	31.5 (2019)	88
Timor-Leste	...	7.0	7.6	11.5	14.8	17.5	60
Viet Nam	7.1	8.0	...	12.3	14.2	...	64
The Pacific	**1.2**	**...**	**...**	**9.1**	**...**	**...**	**56**
Cook Islands	12.9 (2009)	14.1 (2014)	...	62.4 (2009)	68.2	80.0 (2019)	59
Fiji	4.4 (2009)	8.6	...	22.9 (2009)	30.2	39.6 (2019)	54
Kiribati	4.0	2.0 (2013)	...	39.3	57.5 (2013)	38.3 (2018)	64
Marshall Islands	5.7	...	...	22.5	...	33.4 (2018)	49 (2020)
Micronesia, Federated States of	1.9 (2009)	...	9.4	...	...	21.5 (2019)	43
Nauru	11.0	13.5	...	69.3 (2011)	67.3	78.5 (2018)	34 (2018)
Niue	18.8 (2008)	...	...	100.0 (2008)	...	125.0 (2018)	67 (2019)
Palau	16.1	14.2 (2014)	17.7	66.1	63.1 (2014)	64.6	47
Papua New Guinea	0.5	...	0.7 (2019)	5.0	...	4.5 (2019)	21 (2019)
Samoa	3.4	3.5 (2016)	6.0	15.4	18.6 (2014)	32.7	49
Solomon Islands	2.0 (2011)	1.9 (2016)	...	17.9 (2011)	19.9 (2013)	21.6 (2018)	51
Tonga	5.6	5.4 (2013)	9.5	38.5	40.1 (2013)	45.4	55
Tuvalu	11.5 (2009)	9.1 (2014)	11.9	62.1 (2008)	37.3 (2014)	34.8	61
Vanuatu	1.8 (2012)	1.7 (2016)	...	18.4 (2012)	...	14.2 (2019)	74
Developed ADB Member Economies	**23.8**	**26.0**	**27.8**	**103.0**	**116.0**	**...**	**90**
Australia	33.4	34.9	41.3	104.0	122.0	131.4 (2019)	88
Japan	22.1	24.1 (2016)	24.8 (2018)	102.7	115.2 (2016)	119.5 (2018)	98
New Zealand	26.1	30.3	36.2	105.8	107.8	117.8	85
DEVELOPING ADB MEMBER ECONOMIES	**...**	**...**	**...**	**...**	**21.5**	**...**	**65**
ALL ADB REGIONAL MEMBERS	**...**	**...**	**...**	**...**	**25.1**	**...**	**67**
WORLD	**...**	**...**	**16.4**	**...**	**...**	**39.5**	**64**

... = data not available, ADB = Asian Development Bank.

a Regional aggregates are population weighted averages of the densities of the economies calculated by ADB. The data for number of doctors and nurses and midwifery personnel are from the World Health Organization's Global Health Workforce Database.

b Aggregates are derived for reporting economies only.

c The scores are based on based on self-assessment and self-reporting by the economy. In 2018, the World Health Organization introduced a new State Parties Self-Assessment Annual Reporting Tool, which has been in use since. The tool's questionnaire is different from that used during 2010–2017, and thus the scores are not comparable for these two periods.

d Regional aggregates are averages of the scores of the economies calculated by ADB.

Sources: For Indicator 3.c.1: United Nations. SDG Global Database. https://unstats.un.org/sdgs/dataportal (accessed 22 July 2022). For Indicator 3.d.1: World Health Organization. Electronic State Parties Self-Assessment Annual Reporting Tool (e-SPAR). https://extranet.who.int/e-spar/ (accessed 22 July 2022).

Table 1.4.1: Selected Indicators for Sustainable Development Goal 4—Proficiency in Reading and Mathematics

ADB Regional Member	Target 4.1: By 2030, ensure that all girls and boys complete free, equitable, and quality primary and secondary education leading to relevant and effective learning outcomes					
	4.1.1.a: Proportion of Children and Young People in Grades 2 or 3 Achieving at Least a Minimum Proficiency Level (%)		4.1.1.b: Proportion of Children and Young People at the End of Primary School Achieving at Least a Minimum Proficiency Level (%)		4.1.1.c: Proportion of Children and Young People at the End of Lower Secondary School Achieving at Least a Minimum Proficiency Level (%)	
	Reading 2019	Mathematics 2019	Reading 2019	Mathematics 2019	Reading 2019	Mathematics 2019
Developing ADB Member Economies						
Central and West Asia						
Afghanistan	22.0 (2016)	24.5 (2016)	13.0 (2013)	11.0 (2013)	...	...
Armenia	...	...	...	64.3	...	50.4 (2015)
Azerbaijan	...	...	80.8 (2016)	73.4	...	...
Georgia	...	...	86.5 (2016)	55.8	35.6 (2018)	39.0 (2018)
Kazakhstan	...	...	98.1 (2016)	70.8	35.8 (2018)	50.9 (2018)
Kyrgyz Republic	38.7 (2018)	30.1 (2018)	40.3 (2017)	39.8 (2017)	48.5 (2017)	35.1 (2017)
Pakistan	23.4 (2017)	2.8 (2017)	52.1 (2016)	7.6	...	...
Tajikistan	...	...	...	...	...	...
Turkmenistan	71.3	53.2	...	...	...	...
Uzbekistan	...	...	...	...	...	...
East Asia						
China, People's Republic of	81.8 (2016)	84.6 (2015)	...	...	79.6 (2016)	78.9 (2015)
Hong Kong, China	...	...	98.6 (2016)	95.6	87.4 (2018)	90.8 (2018)
Korea, Republic of	...	...	...	95.2	84.9 (2018)	85.0 (2018)
Mongolia	44.4 (2018)	33.6 (2018)	...	...	...	...
Taipei,China	...	...	...	...	...	...
South Asia						
Bangladesh	77.8 (2017)	67.4 (2017)	52.6 (2017)	47.3 (2017)	54.0 (2015)	57.0 (2015)
Bhutan	...	...	...	...	56.0 (2015)	...
India	60.6 (2017)	36.5 (2017)	36.5 (2017)	38.8 (2017)	46.1 (2017)	12.3 (2017)
Maldives	...	...	...	...	...	...
Nepal	19.9	19.7	3.4 (2018)	46.6 (2018)	...	...
Sri Lanka	...	...	55.5 (2015)	73.4 (2015)	21.3 (2016)	50.6 (2016)
Southeast Asia						
Brunei Darussalam	...	...	...	...	48.2 (2018)	52.1 (2018)
Cambodia	...	...	11.0	19.0	7.5 (2017)	9.9 (2017)
Indonesia	...	...	66.2 (2011)	17.5 (2015)	30.1 (2018)	28.1 (2018)
Lao People's Democratic Republic	24.0 (2011)	46.4 (2011)	2.0	8.0	...	...
Malaysia	...	...	58.0	64.0	54.2 (2018)	58.5 (2018)
Myanmar	...	...	11.0	12.0	...	...
Philippines	...	...	10.0	17.0	19.4 (2018)	...
Singapore	...	...	97.3 (2016)	95.5	88.8 (2018)	91.8
Thailand	57.1	51.2	...	43.4 (2011)	40.5 (2018)	47.3 (2018)
Timor-Leste	...	...	...	...	...	...
Viet Nam	...	...	82.0	92.0	86.2 (2015)	80.9 (2015)
The Pacific						
Cook Islands	...	...	...	...	...	...
Fiji	...	...	...	...	...	...
Kiribati	29.0 (2018)	12.0 (2018)	...	...	...	...
Marshall Islands	...	...	...	...	...	...
Micronesia, Federated States of	...	...	...	...	...	...
Nauru	...	...	...	...	...	...
Niue	...	...	...	...	...	...
Palau	...	...	...	...	...	...
Papua New Guinea	...	...	...	...	...	...
Samoa	11.7	21.6	...	...	...	...
Solomon Islands	71.4 (2015)	76.3 (2015)	57.8 (2015)	90.5 (2015)	...	...
Tonga	46.9	25.4	...	...	...	...
Tuvalu	...	...	...	...	...	...
Vanuatu	...	...	...	...	...	...
Developed ADB Member Economies						
Australia	94.5 (2016)	69.6	...	68.0	80.4 (2018)	77.6 (2018)
Japan	...	...	...	...	...	...
New Zealand	...	...	90.0 (2016)	55.9	81.0 (2018)	78.2 (2018)

... = data not available, ADB = Asian Development Bank.

Source: United Nations. SDG Global Database. https://unstats.un.org/sdgs/dataportal (accessed 15 July 2022).

Table 1.4.2: Selected Indicators for Sustainable Development Goal 4—Education Completion

ADB Regional Member	Target 4.1: By 2030, ensure that all girls and boys complete free, equitable, and quality primary and secondary education leading to relevant and effective learning outcomes											
	4.1.2: Completion Rate (Primary Education, Lower Secondary Education, Upper Secondary Education)[a] (%)											
	Primary											
	2010						2020					
	Total		Q1		Q2		Total		Q1		Q2	
Developing ADB Member Economies												
Central and West Asia												
Afghanistan	41.20		20.70	(2011)	26.24	(2011)	65.40		44.81	(2015)	46.31	(2015)
Armenia	99.82		99.26		100.00		99.60		98.63	(2018)	99.39	(2018)
Azerbaijan	98.00		94.76	(2006)	98.60	(2006)	98.70		...		...	
Georgia	98.70		...		...		99.10		100.00	(2018)	100.00	(2018)
Kazakhstan	99.78		99.36		100.00		100.00		100.00	(2015)	99.86	(2015)
Kyrgyz Republic	99.00		99.91	(2012)	99.05	(2012)	99.50		100.00	(2018)	99.60	(2018)
Pakistan	49.80		24.13	(2012)	49.84	(2012)	59.20		28.44	(2018)	47.98	(2018)
Tajikistan	97.80		97.47	(2012)	96.57	(2012)	98.60		97.86	(2017)	99.41	(2017)
Turkmenistan	99.80		99.67	(2006)	100.00	(2006)	99.90		98.78	(2019)	99.88	(2019)
Uzbekistan	100.00		100.00	(2006)	100.00	(2006)	100.00		...		...	
East Asia												
China, People's Republic of	96.69		93.16		94.76		95.60		93.44	(2016)	97.62	(2016)
Hong Kong, China	...		...		...		...		...		...	
Korea, Republic of	100.00	(2012)	100.00	(2012)	100.00	(2012)	...		...		...	
Mongolia	96.52		89.50		95.19		99.00		96.80	(2018)	99.16	(2018)
Taipei,China	...		...		...		...		...		...	
South Asia												
Bangladesh	72.30		47.34	(2011)	68.82	(2011)	80.60		70.44	(2019)	79.88	(2019)
Bhutan	67.86		42.27		54.78		88.20		...		...	
India	86.90		84.02	(2011)	85.24	(2011)	93.60		80.48	(2016)	91.19	(2016)
Maldives	97.10		93.97	(2008)	95.87	(2008)	99.80		96.61	(2017)	95.97	(2017)
Nepal	65.00		58.41	(2011)	66.78	(2011)	81.20		73.84	(2019)	75.46	(2019)
Sri Lanka	98.38	(2006)	96.44	(2006)	98.83	(2006)	...		...		...	
Southeast Asia												
Brunei Darussalam	...		...		...		...		...		...	
Cambodia	71.07		43.38		60.83		75.40		...		...	
Indonesia	93.60		87.09	(2012)	94.86	(2012)	96.90		90.56	(2017)	97.09	(2017)
Lao People's Democratic Republic	63.90		27.65	(2011)	54.02	(2011)	86.10		63.15	(2017)	81.93	(2017)
Malaysia	98.30		...		...		99.60		...		...	
Myanmar	63.80		...		...		83.20		64.70	(2016)	83.14	(2016)
Philippines	86.77		60.13	(2008)	82.94	(2008)	89.70		79.27	(2018)	92.14	(2018)
Singapore	...		...		...		...		...		...	
Thailand	97.70		98.17	(2012)	98.17	(2012)	99.40		97.37	(2019)	97.42	(2019)
Timor-Leste	60.06	(2009)	39.43	(2009)	47.89	(2009)	80.48	(2016)	59.68	(2016)	70.98	(2016)
Viet Nam	95.53		88.77		94.66		97.80		...		...	
The Pacific												
Cook Islands	...		...		...		...		...		...	
Fiji	98.00		...		...		97.60		...		...	
Kiribati	...		...		...		94.09	(2019)	88.40	(2019)	93.22	(2019)
Marshall Islands	...		...		...		...		...		...	
Micronesia, Federated States of	...		...		...		...		...		...	
Nauru	...		...		...		...		...		...	
Niue	...		...		...		...		...		...	
Palau	...		...		...		...		...		...	
Papua New Guinea	49.60		...		...		56.30		38.56	(2018)	49.45	(2018)
Samoa	...		...		...		97.43	(2019)	96.84	(2019)	97.47	(2019)
Solomon Islands	...		...		...		...		...		...	
Tonga	...		...		...		98.21	(2019)	96.91	(2019)	98.31	(2019)
Tuvalu	...		...		...		99.15		100.00		100.00	
Vanuatu	78.20		63.88	(2007)	81.40	(2007)	82.60		...		...	
Developed ADB Member Economies												
Australia	99.02	(2014)	98.05	(2014)	99.10	(2014)	...		...		...	
Japan	...		...		...		...		...		...	
New Zealand	...		...		...		...		...		...	

Table 1.4.2: Selected Indicators for Sustainable Development Goal 4—Education Completion *(continued)*

ADB Regional Member	Target 4.1: By 2030, ensure that all girls and boys complete free, equitable, and quality primary and secondary education leading to relevant and effective learning outcomes — 4.1.2: Completion Rate (Primary Education, Lower Secondary Education, Upper Secondary Education) (%) — Lower Secondary											
	2010						2020					
	Total		Q1		Q2		Total		Q1		Q2	
Developing ADB Member Economies												
Central and West Asia												
Afghanistan	23.40		7.83	(2011)	12.41	(2011)	50.40		24.71	(2015)	29.32	(2015)
Armenia	94.28		94.30		88.27		98.00		95.92	(2018)	96.24	(2018)
Azerbaijan	93.50		84.28	(2006)	85.89	(2006)	95.60		...		...	
Georgia	96.00		97.84	(2013)	96.82	(2013)	97.10		93.17	(2018)	97.25	(2018)
Kazakhstan	99.10		98.25		98.45		100.00		99.33	(2015)	99.87	(2015)
Kyrgyz Republic	96.60		98.14	(2012)	97.04	(2012)	98.80		96.12	(2018)	99.67	(2018)
Pakistan	41.50		11.30	(2012)	30.61	(2012)	53.30		13.35	(2018)	34.38	(2018)
Tajikistan	86.60		82.85	(2012)	85.54	(2012)	92.40		94.69	(2017)	91.69	(2017)
Turkmenistan	99.40		97.15	(2006)	98.38	(2006)	99.80		97.34	(2019)	99.38	(2019)
Uzbekistan	97.70		95.39	(2006)	96.32	(2006)	98.70		...		...	
East Asia												
China, People's Republic of	84.94		66.41		85.47		86.50		84.49	(2016)	90.73	(2016)
Hong Kong, China	...		...		...		...		...		...	
Korea, Republic of	100.00	(2012)	100.00	(2012)	100.00	(2012)	...		...		...	
Mongolia	85.13		49.46		80.10		94.30		83.34	(2018)	93.32	(2018)
Taipei,China	...		...		...		...		...		...	
South Asia												
Bangladesh	50.40		16.27	(2011)	36.43	(2011)	64.20		43.27	(2019)	57.70	(2019)
Bhutan	38.78		16.01		19.20		61.90		...		...	
India	72.80		69.65	(2011)	71.21	(2011)	86.40		59.14	(2016)	75.27	(2016)
Maldives	79.60		63.50	(2008)	69.93	(2008)	96.80		81.76	(2017)	89.98	(2017)
Nepal	52.40		35.61	(2011)	48.82	(2011)	71.10		59.79	(2019)	67.77	(2019)
Sri Lanka	88.11	(2006)	77.02	(2006)	85.92	(2006)	...		...		...	
Southeast Asia												
Brunei Darussalam	...		...		...		...		...		...	
Cambodia	36.68		11.73		17.82		48.10		...		...	
Indonesia	74.90		51.01	(2012)	66.84	(2012)	88.30		66.41	(2017)	82.51	(2017)
Lao People's Democratic Republic	41.40		4.21	(2011)	15.84	(2011)	64.80		16.56	(2017)	39.30	(2017)
Malaysia	91.80		...		...		97.20		...		...	
Myanmar	40.30		...		...		53.10		13.31	(2016)	24.25	(2016)
Philippines	71.10		26.77	(2008)	57.36	(2008)	75.10		51.86	(2018)	76.24	(2018)
Singapore	...		...		...		...		...		...	
Thailand	83.80		76.53	(2012)	79.68	(2012)	91.10		67.63	(2019)	86.47	(2019)
Timor-Leste	43.87	(2009)	23.83	(2009)	28.70	(2009)	66.04	(2016)	33.55	(2016)	46.46	(2016)
Viet Nam	80.54		67.01		73.19		87.60		...		...	
The Pacific												
Cook Islands	...		...		...		...		...		...	
Fiji	88.20		...		...		93.40		...		...	
Kiribati	...		...		...		78.36	(2019)	62.15	(2019)	71.91	(2019)
Marshall Islands	...		...		...		...		...		...	
Micronesia, Federated States of	...		...		...		...		...		...	
Nauru	...		...		...		...		...		...	
Niue	...		...		...		...		...		...	
Palau	...		...		...		...		...		...	
Papua New Guinea	...		...		...		50.21	(2018)	25.73	(2018)	37.45	(2018)
Samoa	...		...		...		96.74	(2019)	94.87	(2019)	96.74	(2019)
Solomon Islands	...		...		...		...		...		...	
Tonga	...		...		...		92.43	(2019)	87.12	(2019)	88.33	(2019)
Tuvalu	...		...		...		85.19		75.56		83.42	
Vanuatu	37.50		11.16	(2007)	18.49	(2007)	45.70		...		...	
Developed ADB Member Economies												
Australia	99.15		96.56		99.25		...		...		...	
Japan	...		...		...		...		...		...	
New Zealand	...		...		...		...		...		...	

Table 1.4.2: Selected Indicators for Sustainable Development Goal 4—Education Completion *(continued)*

ADB Regional Member	Target 4.1: By 2030, ensure that all girls and boys complete free, equitable, and quality primary and secondary education leading to relevant and effective learning outcomes											
	4.1.2: Completion Rate (Primary Education, Lower Secondary Education, Upper Secondary Education) (%)											
	Upper Secondary											
	2010						2020					
	Total		Q1		Q2		Total		Q1		Q2	
Developing ADB Member Economies												
Central and West Asia												
Afghanistan	13.90		2.92	(2011)	4.49	(2011)	28.60		13.12	(2015)	15.07	(2015)
Armenia	60.19		31.47		42.73		77.99	(2018)	75.40	(2018)	73.88	(2018)
Azerbaijan	81.50		53.89	(2006)	71.18	(2006)	90.20		...		...	
Georgia	96.01	(2013)	89.14	(2013)	92.75	(2013)	77.27	(2018)	53.50	(2018)	68.68	(2018)
Kazakhstan	91.17		85.38		87.89		95.50		88.06	(2015)	92.17	(2015)
Kyrgyz Republic	83.40		88.86	(2012)	84.88	(2012)	84.90		77.61	(2018)	83.89	(2018)
Pakistan	18.50		3.33	(2012)	8.70	(2012)	28.00		1.62	(2018)	8.14	(2018)
Tajikistan	60.80		50.86	(2012)	52.27	(2012)	71.30		66.11	(2017)	67.83	(2017)
Turkmenistan	92.40		10.29	(2006)	10.09	(2006)	93.90		90.71	(2016)	97.69	(2016)
Uzbekistan	85.00		64.66	(2006)	68.05	(2006)	91.50		...		...	
East Asia												
China, People's Republic of	43.97		26.51		34.93		59.30		50.94	(2016)	60.82	(2016)
Hong Kong, China	...		...		...		...		...		...	
Korea, Republic of	98.57	(2012)	95.16	(2012)	98.79	(2012)	...		...		...	
Mongolia	62.62		26.43		49.69		81.30		50.50	(2018)	62.30	(2018)
Taipei,China	...		...		...		...		...		...	
South Asia												
Bangladesh	15.70		0.24	(2011)	3.49	(2011)	27.10		12.10	(2019)	20.36	(2019)
Bhutan	20.98		6.12		8.19		35.70		...		...	
India	41.00		24.02	(2011)	24.12	(2011)	61.00		13.48	(2016)	24.79	(2016)
Maldives	15.50		4.84	(2008)	4.49	(2008)	26.20		19.07	(2017)	27.91	(2017)
Nepal	7.20		0.65	(2007)	1.80	(2007)	8.00		9.61	(2019)	14.03	(2019)
Sri Lanka	25.03	(2006)	8.29	(2006)	12.68	(2006)	...		...		...	
Southeast Asia												
Brunei Darussalam	...		...		...		...		...		...	
Cambodia	16.98		0.67		3.56		23.20		...		...	
Indonesia	48.40		21.76	(2012)	34.51	(2012)	60.20		31.61	(2017)	46.39	(2017)
Lao People's Democratic Republic	25.00		1.14	(2011)	5.51	(2011)	40.70		4.57	(2017)	15.49	(2017)
Malaysia	48.10		...		...		63.10		...		...	
Myanmar	15.60		...		...		22.10		1.73	(2016)	5.64	(2016)
Philippines	66.12		21.30	(2008)	48.96	(2008)	71.00		47.69	(2018)	71.01	(2018)
Singapore	...		...		...		...		...		...	
Thailand	55.77	(2012)	30.79	(2012)	42.65	(2012)	66.41	(2019)	39.68	(2019)	60.61	(2019)
Timor-Leste	50.82	(2009)	27.12	(2009)	33.00	(2009)	51.89	(2016)	18.98	(2016)	28.40	(2016)
Viet Nam	48.39		20.09		32.54		57.00		...		...	
The Pacific												
Cook Islands	...		...		...		...		...		...	
Fiji	79.30		...		...		85.90		...		...	
Kiribati	...		...		...		16.73	(2019)	–	(2019)	–	(2019)
Marshall Islands	...		...		...		...		...		...	
Micronesia, Federated States of	...		...		...		...		...		...	
Nauru	...		...		...		...		...		...	
Niue	...		...		...		...		...		...	
Palau	...		...		...		...		...		...	
Papua New Guinea	6.70		...		...		8.20		–	(2018)	–	(2018)
Samoa	...		...		...		56.76	(2019)	38.51	(2019)	43.71	(2019)
Solomon Islands	...		...		...		...		...		...	
Tonga	...		...		...		35.84	(2019)	13.55	(2019)	16.07	(2019)
Tuvalu	...		...		...		55.18		30.50		47.34	
Vanuatu	8.80		–	(2007)	0.84	(2007)	11.90		...		...	
Developed ADB Member Economies												
Australia	85.02		73.48		77.22		...		...		...	
Japan	...		...		...		...		...		...	
New Zealand	...		...		...		...		...		...	

... = data not available, – = magnitude equals zero, ADB = Asian Development Bank, Q = wealth quintile.

a Refers to the "percentage of a cohort of children or young people aged 3–5 years above the intended age for the last grade of each level of education who have completed that grade" as defined by the United Nations Educational, Scientific and Cultural Organization (UNESCO) Institute for Statistics.

Source: United Nations. SDG Global Database. https://unstats.un.org/sdgs/dataportal (accessed 13 July 2022).

Table 1.4.3: Selected Indicators for Sustainable Development Goal 4—Early Childhood Education

ADB Regional Member	Target 4.2: By 2030, ensure that all girls and boys have access to quality early childhood development, care, and preprimary education, so that they are ready for primary education — 4.2.2: Participation Rate in Organized Learning (1 Year before the Official Primary Entry Age)[a,b] (%)					
	2010			2019		
	Total	Female	Male	Total	Female	Male
Developing ADB Member Economies						
Central and West Asia						
Afghanistan	…	…	…	…	…	…
Armenia	…	…	…	62.9	62.1	63.7
Azerbaijan	30.4	29.7	30.9	83.2	82.7	83.7
Georgia	47.8 (2007)	50.5 (2007)	45.5 (2007)	…	…	…
Kazakhstan	99.2 (2011)	100.0 (2011)	98.4 (2011)	77.7	77.5	78.0
Kyrgyz Republic	54.0	55.5	52.5	87.1	87.7	86.5
Pakistan	…	…	…	94.3 (2019)	88.1 (2019)	100.0 (2019)
Tajikistan	8.0	7.4	8.6	12.5 (2017)	11.6 (2017)	13.4 (2017)
Turkmenistan	…	…	…	…	…	…
Uzbekistan	33.8	34.3	33.3	62.8	62.3	63.3
East Asia						
China, People's Republic of	…	…	…	…	…	…
Hong Kong, China	98.2 (2012)	100.0 (2012)	96.5 (2012)	97.0	100.0	94.4
Korea, Republic of	…	…	…	89.3 (2019)	89.6 (2019)	89.1 (2019)
Mongolia	98.0	99.1	96.8	96.1 (2019)	95.1 (2019)	97.1 (2019)
Taipei,China	…	…	…	…	…	…
South Asia						
Bangladesh	36.6	36.7	36.6	77.5 (2019)	…	…
Bhutan	4.3 (2000)	4.2 (2000)	4.4 (2000)	41.4	41.3	41.5
India	…	…	…	85.2	85.7	84.8
Maldives	82.9 (2011)	83.8 (2011)	82.1 (2011)	93.2 (2019)	94.6 (2019)	92.0 (2019)
Nepal	82.2 (2011)	86.9 (2011)	77.8 (2011)	89.4	85.0	93.8
Sri Lanka	…	…	…	…	…	…
Southeast Asia						
Brunei Darussalam	99.3	98.5	100.0	94.3	94.1	94.6
Cambodia	36.8	37.0	36.5	70.5	70.6	70.4
Indonesia	86.5	88.6	84.6	95.8 (2018)	100.0 (2018)	91.8 (2018)
Lao People's Democratic Republic	35.6	35.9	35.3	70.5	71.0	70.1
Malaysia	85.9	88.4	83.6	90.3	90.9	89.8
Myanmar	8.8	9.0	8.5	11.8 (2018)	11.8 (2018)	11.7 (2018)
Philippines	41.5 (2009)	42.1 (2009)	40.9 (2009)	65.6	66.9	64.4
Singapore	…	…	…	97.1 (2019)	…	…
Thailand	98.5	100.0	97.1	99.7	99.8	99.7
Timor-Leste	…	…	…	50.2 (2019)	51.8 (2019)	48.7 (2019)
Viet Nam	90.4	…	…	99.9 (2018)	99.8 (2018)	100.0 (2018)
The Pacific						
Cook Islands	…	…	…	92.7	100.0	85.9
Fiji	49.6 (2006)	50.6 (2006)	48.7 (2006)	87.0	84.7	89.3
Kiribati	…	…	…	97.7	100.0	95.6
Marshall Islands	69.5 (2002)	69.7 (2002)	69.3 (2002)	60.5	58.8	62.1
Micronesia, Federated States of	…	…	…	68.0 (2019)	65.6 (2019)	70.3 (2019)
Nauru	88.1 (2012)	76.0 (2012)	100.0 (2012)	96.0	100.0	92.0
Niue	…	…	…	80.2	61.9	100.0
Palau	…	…	…	89.3	100.0	80.0
Papua New Guinea	…	…	…	71.4 (2018)	71.2 (2018)	71.6 (2018)
Samoa	25.6	28.5	22.8	35.1 (2019)	35.3 (2019)	34.8 (2019)
Solomon Islands	66.7	…	…	65.6 (2019)	67.0 (2019)	64.3 (2019)
Tonga	…	…	…	94.6	88.9	100.0
Tuvalu	…	…	…	95.0 (2019)	100.0 (2019)	90.2 (2019)
Vanuatu	66.7 (2011)	…	…	98.0	100.0	96.2
Developed ADB Member Economies						
Australia	52.6	52.1	53.0	82.0	81.8	82.2
Japan	…	…	…	…	…	…
New Zealand	…	…	…	91.5 (2019)	90.8 (2019)	92.2 (2019)

… = data not available, ADB = Asian Development Bank.

a According to the United Nations Educational, Scientific and Cultural Organization (UNESCO), this is the percentage of children who participate in one or more organized learning programs, including programs that offer a combination of education and care, 1 year before the official age for entry to primary education (varies by economy). An organized learning program is one that consists of a coherent set or sequence of educational activities designed with the intention of achieving predetermined learning outcomes or the accomplishment of a specific set of educational tasks.

b The figures for the following economies and years are estimates by the UNESCO Institute for Statistics (UIS) as published on the Global SDG Indicators Database: Azerbaijan (2000–2005); Bangladesh (2010); Cambodia (2015); Hong Kong, China (2012–2020); Indonesia (2014, 2018); Nepal (2013); Pakistan (2014–2019); Samoa (2001); Tuvalu (2018); Viet Nam (2013–2014). For the purposes of estimating participation rates by age, the UIS may make one or more of the following: (i) an adjustment to account for over- or under-reporting in enrolments; (ii) an estimate of the number of enrolments in a given age group; (iii) a redistribution of enrolments of unknown age (across known ages); or (iv) for small economies, an estimate of the population in the official age group. In all cases, estimates are based on evidence from the economy itself.

Source: United Nations. SDG Global Database. https://unstats.un.org/sdgs/dataportal (accessed 11 July 2022).

Goal 4. Ensure inclusive and equitable quality education and promote lifelong learning opportunities for all

Table 1.4.4: Selected Indicators for Sustainable Development Goal 4—Teacher Training and Supply

ADB Regional Member	Target 4.c: By 2030, substantially increase the supply of qualified teachers, including through international cooperation for teacher training in developing countries, especially least developed countries and small island developing states. Proportion of Teachers Who Have Received at Least the Minimum Organized Teacher Training, by Education Level (% of total teachers)															
	4.c.1.a: Preprimary				4.c.1.b: Primary				4.c.1.c: Lower Secondary				4.c.1.d: Upper Secondary			
	2010		2020		2010		2020		2010		2020		2010		2020	
Developing ADB Member Economies																
Central and West Asia																
Afghanistan	...		...		...		...		...		...		...		...	
Armenia	87.8		82.0	(2017)	77.5	(2005)	75.1		...		75.1		...		77.1	
Azerbaijan[a]	90.9		91.2		100.0		99.9		...		99.7		...		72.0	
Georgia	96.6	(2003)	...		94.6	(2009)	...		94.6	(2009)	...		94.8	(2009)	...	
Kazakhstan[b]	...		100.0	(2014)	...		100.0		...		...		...		...	
Kyrgyz Republic	42.7		...		68.4		95.4	(2017)	...		...		...		...	
Pakistan[a]	...		...		84.2		77.3	(2019)	...		58.6	(2019)	88.1	(2011)	84.7	(2017)
Tajikistan	85.2		100.0	(2016)	92.9		100.0	(2017)	94.0	(2003)	...		94.3	(2003)	...	
Turkmenistan	...		...		...		99.9		...		...		...		...	
Uzbekistan	100.0		99.9		100.0		99.2		...		99.0	(2017)	...		93.4	(2017)
East Asia																
China, People's Republic of	...		...		...		...		...		...		...		...	
Hong Kong, China	95.1		97.1		95.6		95.7		...		...		...		...	
Korea, Republic of	...		...		...		...		...		...		...		...	
Mongolia	89.9		95.7	(2019)	97.6		88.9	(2019)	100.0	(2007)	...		100.0	(2006)	...	
Taipei,China	...		...		...		...		...		...		...		...	
South Asia																
Bangladesh	...		...		57.7	(2011)	50.4	(2017)	58.5		62.2		40.7		61.3	
Bhutan	93.8	(2000)	100.0		91.5	(2008)	100.0		90.2	(2008)	100.0		72.2	(2008)	100.0	(2018)
India[a,b,c]	...		...		...		77.7		...		78.9		...		81.7	
Maldives	39.0		88.7	(2018)	77.0		88.8	(2019)	97.6		94.1	(2019)	94.5		91.3	(2019)
Nepal	81.5		82.4		73.7		97.2		57.2		86.0		72.3		81.1	
Sri Lanka[a,c]	83.1		81.5		82.1		82.6		...		83.7		...		78.9	
Southeast Asia																
Brunei Darussalam[a,c]	73.0		58.1		87.1		85.2		...		89.5	(2019)	...		90.6	(2019)
Cambodia	98.3		100.0		99.1		100.0		99.8		100.0		99.8	(2007)	...	
Indonesia	...		...		...		...		...		...		...		...	
Lao People's Democratic Republic	97.5		94.1		95.4		98.8		99.3		99.5		99.4		99.5	
Malaysia	...		38.8		95.4		96.6		...		...		...		...	
Myanmar	58.5		81.4	(2018)	99.9		95.3	(2018)	98.3		89.5	(2018)	100.0		87.7	(2018)
Philippines[a,b,c,d]	...		100.0		...		100.0		...		100.0		...		100.0	
Singapore	...		100.0	(2019)	98.6	(2009)	97.8	(2019)	...		...		...		...	
Thailand[a,b,c]	...		...		...		100.0		...		100.0		...		100.0	
Timor-Leste	...		...		...		...		...		...		...		...	
Viet Nam	98.5	(2011)	99.7		98.3		99.7		99.1		99.9		...		...	
The Pacific																
Cook Islands	69.7	(2011)	95.5		96.6	(2011)	98.3		...		...		...		...	
Fiji	...		93.5		100.0	(2011)	87.6		100.0	(2012)	...		100.0	(2012)	...	
Kiribati	...		93.6		94.1		90.5		79.2	(2008)	85.9		33.6	(2008)	47.0	(2016)
Marshall Islands	100.0	(2002)	...		...		...		...		46.9		...		66.9	
Micronesia, Federated States of	...		99.3	(2016)	...		100.0	(2016)	...		100.0	(2016)	...		31.5	(2018)
Nauru	82.1	(2007)	100.0	(2016)	74.2	(2007)	100.0	(2016)	...		100.0	(2016)	...		100.0	(2016)
Niue[a,b,d]	...		25.0		...		92.3	(2016)	...		80.0	(2016)	...		100.0	(2015)
Palau	...		...		...		...		...		...		...		...	
Papua New Guinea	...		...		...		...		100.0	(2012)	...		100.0	(2012)	...	
Samoa[d]	...		100.0	(2018)	93.5	(2012)	93.9	(2014)	...		...		71.9	(2009)	54.7	
Solomon Islands	61.3	(2011)	...		58.0		82.4	(2019)	70.8		93.9	(2019)	70.9		63.0	(2015)
Tonga[b]	100.0	(2012)	52.7		...		94.1		...		...		...		...	
Tuvalu[a,b,c,d]	100.0	(2012)	96.3		...		78.3	(2019)	...		67.1	(2018)	...		62.0	(2018)
Vanuatu	100.0	(2007)	60.0	(2019)	100.0	(2007)	36.0	(2019)	...		21.5	(2015)	...		...	
Developed ADB Member Economies																
Australia	...		...		...		...		...		...		...		...	
Japan	...		...		...		...		...		...		...		...	
New Zealand	...		...		...		...		...		...		...		...	

... = data not available, ADB = Asian Development Bank.

a For Indicator 4.c.1.c, the earliest available estimate for Azerbaijan is for 2016: 91.6%. For Pakistan, the earliest available estimate is for 2015: 61.2%. For India, the earliest available estimate is for 2016: 77.0%. For Sri Lanka, the earliest available estimate is for 2013: 72.1%. For Brunei Darussalam, the earliest available estimate is for 2014: 94.0%. For the Philippines, the earliest available estimate is for 2016: 100%. For Thailand, the earliest available estimate is for 2015: 100%. For Niue, the earliest available estimate is for 2015: 100%. For Tuvalu, the earliest available estimate is for 2016: 52.4%.

b For Indicator 4.c.1.b, the earliest available estimate for Kazakhstan is for 2014: 100%. For India, the earliest available estimate is for 2017: 69.8%. For the Philippines, the earliest available estimate is for 2014: 100%. For Thailand, the earliest available estimate is for 2014: 100%. For Niue, the earliest available estimate is for 2015: 100%. For Tonga, the earliest available estimate is for 2013: 99.6%. For Tuvalu, the earliest available estimate is for 2016: 76.6%.

c For Indicator 4.c.1.d, the earliest available estimate for India is for 2017: 76.4%. For Sri Lanka, the earliest available estimate is for 2016: 77.3%. For Brunei Darussalam, the earliest available estimate is for 2014: 90.4%. For the Philippines, the earliest available estimate is for 2016: 100%. For Thailand, the earliest available estimate is for 2015: 100%. For Tuvalu, the earliest available estimate is for 2016: 34.6%.

d For Indicator 4.c.1.a, the latest available estimate for the Philippines is for 2015: 100%. For Niue, the earliest available estimate is for 2015: 100%. For Samoa, the earliest available estimate is for 2014: 100%. For Tuvalu, the earliest available estimate is for 2012: 100%.

Source: United Nations. SDG Global Database. https://unstats.un.org/sdgs/dataportal (accessed 13 July 2022).

Table 1.5.1: Selected Indicators for Sustainable Development Goal 5—Early Marriage and Women in Leadership

ADB Regional Member	Target 5.3: Eliminate all harmful practices such as child, early, and forced marriage, and female genital mutilation — 5.3.1: Proportion of Women Aged 20–24 Years Who Were Married or in a Union (%)				Target 5.5: Ensure women's full and effective participation in, and equal opportunities for leadership at, all levels of decision-making in political, economic, and public life — 5.5.1.a: Proportion of Seats Held by Women in National Parliaments (%)		5.5.2: Proportion of Women in Managerial Positions (%)
	Before Age 15		Before Age 18				
	2010	2018	2010	2018	2010	2021	2020
Developing ADB Member Economies							
Central and West Asia[a]					**18.7**	**24.2**	
Afghanistan	...	4.2 (2017)	...	28.3 (2017)	27.3	27.0	4.9
Armenia	...	0.0 (2016)	...	5.3 (2016)	9.2	22.7	28.1
Azerbaijan	1.9 (2011)	...	11.0 (2011)	...	11.4	18.2	35.5
Georgia	1.1	0.3	14.0	13.9	5.1	20.7	36.1
Kazakhstan	...	0.2 (2015)	...	7.0 (2015)	17.8	27.1	41.1
Kyrgyz Republic	0.9 (2014)	0.3	11.6 (2014)	12.9	25.6	17.1	47.4
Pakistan	2.8 (2013)	3.6	21.0 (2013)	18.3	22.2	20.2	5.7 (2021)
Tajikistan	...	0.1 (2017)	...	8.7 (2017)	17.5	23.8	...
Turkmenistan	...	0.2 (2019)	...	6.1 (2019)	16.8	25.0	...
Uzbekistan	0.3 (2006)	...	7.2 (2006)	...	22.0	32.7	...
East Asia[a]					**20.3**	**24.2**	
China, People's Republic of	...	...	...	...	21.3	24.9	...
Hong Kong, China	...	...	...	...	...	...	33.1 (2015)
Korea, Republic of	...	...	...	...	14.7	19.0	16.3 (2021)
Mongolia	0.1 (2013)	0.9	5.2 (2013)	12.0	4.0	17.3	49.8
Taipei,China	...	...	...	...	...	...	30.5
South Asia[a]					**18.7**	**17.3**	
Bangladesh	22.4 (2014)	15.5 (2019)	58.6 (2014)	51.4 (2019)	18.6	20.9	10.7 (2017)
Bhutan	6.2	...	25.8	...	8.5	14.9	32.7
India	...	6.8 (2016)	...	27.3 (2016)	10.8	14.4	17.6
Maldives	0.3 (2009)	0.0 (2017)	3.9 (2009)	2.2 (2017)	6.5	4.6	18.7 (2019)
Nepal	...	7.9 (2019)	...	32.8 (2019)	33.2	32.7	13.2 (2017)
Sri Lanka	...	0.9 (2016)	...	9.8 (2016)	5.8	5.4	27.2 (2019)
Southeast Asia[a]					**19.3**	**21.2**	
Brunei Darussalam	...	...	...	...	...	9.1	36.5
Cambodia	1.9 (2014)	...	18.5 (2014)	...	21.1	21.6	31.0 (2019)
Indonesia	...	0.6	...	11.2	18.0	21.0	32.4 (2021)
Lao People's Democratic Republic	...	7.1 (2017)	...	32.7 (2017)	25.2	27.5	59.0 (2017)
Malaysia	...	...	...	...	9.9	14.9	24.9
Myanmar	...	1.9 (2015)	...	16.0 (2015)	4.3 (2011)	15.3	27.8
Philippines	...	2.2 (2017)	...	16.5 (2017)	21.0	28.0	53.0
Singapore	...	0.0 (2020)	...	0.1 (2020)	23.4	29.5	38.1 (2021)
Thailand	...	3.0 (2019)	...	20.2 (2019)	13.3	15.8	39.2
Timor-Leste	...	2.6 (2016)	...	14.9 (2016)	29.2	38.5	24.5 (2016)
Viet Nam	0.9 (2014)	...	10.6 (2014)	...	25.8	26.7	24.9 (2021)
The Pacific[a]					**2.5**	**6.4**	**...**
Cook Islands	...	...	...	...	...	...	59.8 (2019)
Fiji	...	...	...	...	8.5 (2006)	21.6	38.9 (2016)
Kiribati	2.8 (2009)	2.4 (2019)	20.3 (2009)	18.4 (2019)	4.4	6.7	37.2 (2015)
Marshall Islands	5.5 (2007)	...	26.3 (2007)	...	3.0	6.1	...
Micronesia, Federated States of	...	...	...	...	–	–	20.3 (2014)
Nauru	1.9 (2007)	...	26.8 (2007)	...	–	10.5	36.1 (2013)
Niue	...	...	...	...	...	...	...
Palau	...	...	...	...	–	6.3	29.9 (2014)
Papua New Guinea	2.1 (2006)	8.0	21.3 (2006)	27.3	0.9	–	18.1 (2010)
Samoa	0.7 (2014)	0.9 (2020)	10.8 (2014)	7.4 (2020)	8.2	10.0	43.0 (2017)
Solomon Islands	...	5.6 (2015)	...	21.3 (2015)	–	8.0	25.7 (2013)
Tonga	0.3 (2012)	0.4 (2019)	5.6 (2012)	10.1 (2019)	3.1	7.4	41.6 (2018)
Tuvalu	– (2007)	...	9.9 (2007)	...	–	6.3	35.9 (2016)
Vanuatu	2.5 (2013)	...	21.4 (2013)	...	3.9	–	37.1 (2019)
Developed ADB Member Economies[a]					**18.1**	**20.5**	**...**
Australia	...	...	...	...	27.3	31.1	40.0
Japan	...	...	...	...	11.3	9.9	13.2 (2021)
New Zealand	...	...	...	...	33.6	48.3	...
DEVELOPING ADB MEMBER ECONOMIES[a]					**18.7**	**21.4**	**...**
ALL ADB REGIONAL MEMBERS[a]					**18.6**	**21.3**	**...**

... = data not available, 0.0 = magnitude is less than half of unit employed, – = magnitude equals zero, ADB = Asian Development Bank.

a For proportion of seats held by women in national parliaments, regional aggregates are estimated as weighted averages based on the number of parliament seats in reporting economies.

Sources: United Nations. SDG Global Database. https://unstats.un.org/sdgs/dataportal (accessed 20 July 2022). For Afghanistan, Bangladesh, and Nepal for indicator 5.5.1.a: Inter-Parliamentary Union. Women in National Parliaments. http://archive.ipu.org/wmn-e/classif-arc.htm (accessed 20 July 2022). For indicator 5.5.2: International Labour Organization. ILOSTAT Database. https://ilostat.ilo.org/data (accessed 20 July 2022).

Click on the indicator name in the table header to access the time series in the Key Indicators Database

Goal 6. Ensure availability and sustainable management of water and sanitation for all

Table 1.6.1: Selected Indicators for Sustainable Development Goal 6—Clean Water and Sanitation

ADB Regional Member	Target 6.1: By 2030, achieve universal and equitable access to safe and affordable drinking water for all 6.1.1: Proportion of Population Using Safely Managed Drinking Water Services (%)					
	2010			2020		
	Total	Urban	Rural	Total	Urban	Rural
Developing ADB Member Economies						
Central and West Asia						
Afghanistan	19.0	28.0	16.0	28.0	36.0	24.0
Armenia	81.0	...	...	87.0	...	...
Azerbaijan	77.0	93.0	58.0	88.0	96.0	78.0
Georgia	64.0	84.0	39.0	66.0	84.0	40.0
Kazakhstan	78.0	...	...	89.0	...	...
Kyrgyz Republic	58.0	88.0	41.0	70.0	92.0	57.0
Pakistan	37.0	46.0	32.0	36.0	40.0	33.0
Tajikistan	47.0	...	...	55.0	...	...
Turkmenistan	82.0	92.0	73.0	95.0	97.0	92.0
Uzbekistan	58.0	85.0	30.0	59.0	86.0	31.0
East Asia						
China, People's Republic of	...	89.0	...	...	95.0	...
Hong Kong, China	97.2	97.2	...	100.0 (2017)	100.0 (2017)	...
Korea, Republic of	98.0	...	...	99.0	...	...
Mongolia	27.0	37.0	5.0	30.0	39.0	11.0
Taipei,China	...	...	...	...	...	...
South Asia						
Bangladesh	55.0	42.0	60.0	59.0	53.0	62.0
Bhutan	34.0	49.0	25.0	37.0	49.0	28.0
India	...	...	43.0	...	...	56.0
Maldives	...	...	...	...	...	...
Nepal	29.0	38.0	28.0	18.0	25.0	16.0
Sri Lanka	...	88.0	...	...	93.0	...
Southeast Asia						
Brunei Darussalam	...	...	...	...	...	...
Cambodia	22.0	51.0	15.0	28.0	57.0	18.0
Indonesia	...	...	...	...	...	...
Lao People's Democratic Republic	14.0	24.0	9.0	18.0	27.0	12.0
Malaysia	93.0	...	...	94.0	...	...
Myanmar	44.0	68.0	34.0	59.0	74.0	52.0
Philippines	45.0	61.0	32.0	47.0	62.0	35.0
Singapore	100.0	100.0	...	100.0	100.0	...
Thailand	...	...	...	...	...	...
Timor-Leste	...	...	...	...	...	...
Viet Nam	...	...	...	...	...	...
The Pacific						
Cook Islands	...	...	...	...	...	...
Fiji	...	...	...	...	...	...
Kiribati	12.0	19.0	6.0	15.0	21.0	7.0
Marshall Islands	...	...	...	...	...	...
Micronesia, Federated States of	...	...	...	...	...	...
Nauru	...	...	...	...	...	...
Niue	97.0	...	...	...	...	...
Palau	79.0	85.0	63.0	...	...	...
Papua New Guinea	...	...	...	...	...	...
Samoa	45.0	...	...	...	...	...
Solomon Islands	...	...	...	...	...	...
Tonga	29.0	50.0	23.0	...	...	...
Tuvalu	...	50.0	...	...	...	...
Vanuatu	41.8	55.0	...	...	...	...
Developed ADB Member Economies						
Australia	...	99.0	...	...	...	...
Japan	98.0	...	...	...	...	...
New Zealand	89.0	...	...	...	...	...

Table 1.6.1: Selected Indicators for Sustainable Development Goal 6—Clean Water and Sanitation *(continued)*

ADB Regional Member	Target 6.2: By 2030, achieve access to adequate and equitable sanitation and hygiene for all and end open defecation, paying special attention to the needs of women and girls and those in vulnerable situations. 6.2.1a: Proportion of Population Using Safely Managed Sanitation Services (%)					
	2010			2020		
	Total	Urban	Rural	Total	Urban	Rural
Developing ADB Member Economies						
Central and West Asia						
Afghanistan	...	...	...	...	...	...
Armenia	54.0	53.0	...	69.0	71.0	...
Azerbaijan	25.0	14.0	...	21.0 (2019)	9.0	...
Georgia	41.0	33.0	51.0	34.0	28.0	44.0
Kazakhstan	...	92.0	...	...	91.0	...
Kyrgyz Republic	89.0	82.0	93.0	92.0	86.0	96.0
Pakistan	...	...	...	...	...	...
Tajikistan	...	...	57.0	...	...	59.0
Turkmenistan	...	...	...	...	...	...
Uzbekistan	...	...	...	...	...	...
East Asia						
China, People's Republic of	35.0	54.0	17.0	70.0	86.0	44.0
Hong Kong, China	91.9	91.9	...	91.8 (2017)	91.8 (2017)	...
Korea, Republic of	89.0	...	...	100.0	...	...
Mongolia	41.0	45.0	34.0	56.0	59.0	49.0
Taipei,China	...	...	...	...	...	...
South Asia						
Bangladesh	28.0	31.0	27.0	39.0	34.0	42.0
Bhutan	65.0	69.0	62.0	65.0	63.0	67.0
India	25.0	29.0	24.0	46.0	37.0	51.0
Maldives	...	...	...	...	...	...
Nepal	27.0	28.0	27.0	49.0	42.0	50.0
Sri Lanka	...	...	...	...	...	...
Southeast Asia						
Brunei Darussalam	...	...	...	...	...	...
Cambodia	...	...	...	...	...	...
Indonesia	...	...	...	...	...	...
Lao People's Democratic Republic	44.0	56.0	39.0	61.0	63.0	60.0
Malaysia	69.0	...	...	77.0 (2018)	...	...
Myanmar	61.0	61.0	61.0	61.0	53.0	64.0
Philippines	49.0	48.0	50.0	61.0	55.0	66.0
Singapore	100.0	100.0	...	100.0	100.0	...
Thailand	23.0	26.0	20.0	26.0	30.0	22.0
Timor-Leste	...	...	...	...	...	...
Viet Nam	...	...	...	...	...	...
The Pacific						
Cook Islands	...	...	...	...	...	...
Fiji	...	...	...	...	...	...
Kiribati	23.0	26.0	20.0	27.0	26.0	27.0
Marshall Islands	...	...	...	...	...	...
Micronesia, Federated States of	...	...	...	...	...	...
Nauru	...	...	...	...	...	...
Niue	...	...	...	...	...	...
Palau	...	...	...	...	...	...
Papua New Guinea	...	30.0	...	...	...	...
Samoa	48.0	38.0	51.0	...	...	...
Solomon Islands	...	...	...	...	...	...
Tonga	36.0	29.0	39.0	...	...	...
Tuvalu	6.0	5.0	7.0	...	...	...
Vanuatu	...	...	...	...	...	...
Developed ADB Member Economies						
Australia	65.0	...	...	...	...	...
Japan	77.0	...	...	...	...	...
New Zealand	80.0	...	...	...	...	...

Goal 6: Ensure availability and sustainable management of water and sanitation for all

Table 1.6.1: Selected Indicators for Sustainable Development Goal 6—Clean Water and Sanitation *(continued)*

	Target 6.4: By 2030, substantially increase water-use efficiency across all sectors and ensure sustainable withdrawals and supply of freshwater to address water scarcity and substantially reduce the number of people suffering from water scarcity			Target 6.a: By 2030, expand international cooperation and capacity-building support to developing countries in water- and sanitation-related activities and programmes, including water harvesting, desalination, water efficiency, wastewater treatment, and recycling and reuse technologies		
ADB Regional Member	6.4.2: Level of Water Stress, Freshwater Withdrawal as a Proportion of Available Freshwater Resources (%)			6.a.1: Amount of Water- and Sanitation-Related Official Development Assistance as Part of a Government-Coordinated Spending Plan ($ million)		
	2010	2015	2019	2010	2015	2020
Developing ADB Member Economies						
Central and West Asia						
Afghanistan	54.8	54.8	54.8	107.7	77.2	140.3
Armenia	42.9	66.0	57.8	83.5	40.2	15.3
Azerbaijan	48.4	51.6	55.6	17.8	72.7	48.6
Georgia	5.7	5.3	5.1	53.1	46.1	35.3
Kazakhstan	33.0	30.0	32.7	21.7	0.2	0.6
Kyrgyz Republic	50.0	50.0	50.0	11.4	23.1	24.4
Pakistan	113.7	120.8	108.6	81.3	293.0	164.8
Tajikistan	71.6	68.7	69.9	22.3	43.4	93.7
Turkmenistan	143.6	143.6	143.6	0.0	...	0.0
Uzbekistan	143.1	158.1	168.9	31.7	110.1	126.6
East Asia						
China, People's Republic of	42.9	43.2	43.2	292.8	210.9	103.6
Hong Kong, China	...	...	...	...	...	...
Korea, Republic of	85.2	85.2	85.2	...	...	...
Mongolia	3.9	3.2	3.4	25.1	7.9	32.8
Taipei,China	...	...	...	...	...	...
South Asia						
Bangladesh	5.7	5.7	5.7	179.5	207.3	273.9
Bhutan	1.4	1.4	1.4	2.6	7.3	12.4
India	66.5	66.5	66.5	465.0	480.5	305.5
Maldives	3.4	15.7	15.7	2.1	7.8	13.7
Nepal	8.3	8.3	8.3	76.2	110.8	152.5
Sri Lanka	90.8	90.8	90.8	168.8	157.9	132.0
Southeast Asia						
Brunei Darussalam	3.5	3.5	3.5	...	...	...
Cambodia	1.0	1.0	1.0	41.1	82.0	197.7
Indonesia	24.2	28.8	29.7	278.7	131.9	185.3
Lao People's Democratic Republic	3.8	5.1	4.8	27.1	110.8	74.0
Malaysia	3.1	3.2	3.4	60.4	73.5	0.6
Myanmar	5.8	5.8	5.8	20.0	85.0	97.2
Philippines	25.5	26.4	26.3	45.0	28.7	27.1
Singapore	219.9	84.6	82.2	...	...	...
Thailand	23.0	23.0	23.0	7.4	8.4	1.5
Timor-Leste	28.3	28.3	28.3	17.5	16.9	3.9
Viet Nam	18.1	18.1	18.1	382.1	575.3	428.1
The Pacific						
Cook Islands	...	...	...	0.5	4.2	1.8 (2019)
Fiji	0.3	0.3	0.3	1.9	3.3	2.6
Kiribati	...	...	...	0.1	6.7	5.0
Marshall Islands	...	...	...	0.2	1.0	3.7
Micronesia, Federated States of	...	...	...	0.1	1.9	1.7
Nauru	...	...	...	0.2	4.9	0.2 (2019)
Niue	...	...	...	0.3	0.0 (2016)	0.0 (2019)
Palau	...	...	...	0.2	1.4	7.1 (2019)
Papua New Guinea	0.1	0.1	0.1 (2018)	13.4	6.2	26.9 (2019)
Samoa	...	...	...	14.8	19.8	7.8 (2019)
Solomon Islands	...	...	...	5.6	7.7	16.2 (2019)
Tonga	...	...	...	1.0	1.6	...
Tuvalu	...	...	...	0.0	3.0	...
Vanuatu	...	...	...	0.8	3.0	...
Developed ADB Member Economies						
Australia	5.3	6.7	...	...	...	...
Japan	37.3	36.7	...	...	...	...
New Zealand	4.2	8.1	...	...	...	...

... = data not available, 0.0 = magnitude is less than half of unit employed, ADB = Asian Development Bank.

Source: United Nations. SDG Global Database. https://unstats.un.org/sdgs/dataportal (accessed 25 July 2022).

Table 1.7.1: Selected Indicators for Sustainable Development Goal 7—Affordable and Clean Energy

ADB Regional Member	Target 7.1: By 2030, ensure universal access to affordable, reliable, and modern energy services								Target 7.2: By 2030, increase substantially the share of renewable energy in the global energy mix		Target 7.3: By 2030, double the global rate of improvement in energy efficiency	
	7.1.1: Proportion of Population with Access to Electricity (%)						7.1.2: Proportion of Population with Primary Reliance on Clean Fuels and Technology (%)		7.2.1: Renewable Energy Share in Total Final Energy Consumption (%)		7.3.1: Energy Intensity Measured in Terms of Primary Energy and GDP (MJ/$ 2011 PPP GDP)	
	Total		Urban		Rural							
	2010	2020	2010	2020	2010	2020	2010	2020	2010	2019	2010	2019
Developing ADB Member Economies												
Central and West Asia												
Afghanistan	42.7	97.7	82.8	99.5	30.2	97.1	20.0	33.0	15.2	18.5	2.5	2.4
Armenia	99.8	100.0	99.7	100.0	100.0	100.0	>95	>95	9.4	10.3	3.9	3.5
Azerbaijan	99.9	100.0	100.0	100.0	99.9	100.0	93.0	>95	4.5	1.6	3.8	4.6
Georgia	100.0	100.0	100.0	100.0	100.0	100.0	66.0	89.0	39.2	25.2	3.6	3.8
Kazakhstan	100.0	100.0	100.0	100.0	100.0	100.0	92.0	93.0	1.4	1.7	8.6	6.3
Kyrgyz Republic	99.0	100.0	99.1	99.5	98.9	100.0	72.0	77.0	25.6	27.9	5.1	5.0
Pakistan	70.8	75.4	97.1	100.0	56.6	60.8	36.0	49.0	47.4	43.4	5.1	4.6
Tajikistan	98.7	99.8	99.4	99.1	98.4	100.0	70.0	82.0	61.8	38.6	5.1	4.8
Turkmenistan	100.0	100.0	100.0	100.0	100.0	100.0	>95	>95	0.1	0.1	21.7	12.9
Uzbekistan	99.9	100.0	100.0	100.0	99.8	100.0	86.0	84.0	1.4	1.6	14.2	8.4
East Asia												
China, People's Republic of	99.7	100.0	100.0	100.0	99.4	100.0	56.0	79.0	12.3	14.5	8.9	6.3
Hong Kong, China	100.0	100.0	100.0	100.0	100.0	100.0	...	...	0.2	0.2	1.6	1.3
Korea, Republic of	100.0	100.0	100.0	100.0	100.0	100.0	>95	>95	1.3	3.4	6.1	5.3
Mongolia	78.5	98.1	96.1	99.7	41.9	94.6	35.0	52.0	4.5	3.3	8.1	7.0
Taipei,China	...	...	...	...	...	...	...	...	1.6	2.1 (2015)	...	...
South Asia												
Bangladesh	55.3	96.2	90.1	97.8	40.0	95.2	13.0	25.0	40.3	24.8	2.9	2.4
Bhutan	73.3	100.0	99.3	100.0	59.4	100.0	64.0	80.0	90.8	82.3	10.1	7.9
India	76.3	99.0	94.0	100.0	68.4	98.5	35.0	68.0	36.2	32.9	5.3	4.3
Maldives	99.2	100.0	99.6	100.0	98.9	100.0	93.0	>95	1.4	1.1	2.3	2.7
Nepal	68.6	89.9	95.5	94.2	63.2	88.8	22.0	35.0	87.3	77.4	5.9	5.2
Sri Lanka	85.3	100.0	95.6	100.0	83.0	100.0	22.0	32.0	61.9	49.9	2.2	1.8
Southeast Asia												
Brunei Darussalam	100.0	100.0	100.0	100.0	100.0	100.0	>95	>95	–	0.0	5.2	6.4
Cambodia	31.1	86.4	91.3	97.3	15.8	82.9	12.0	37.0	64.8	53.4	5.1	4.7
Indonesia	94.2	97.0	99.0	99.6	89.4	93.5	41.0	84.0	34.8	19.1	4.2	3.2
Lao People's Democratic Republic	70.1	100.0	97.2	100.0	58.5	100.0	<5	8.0	64.9	48.4	3.3	4.4
Malaysia	99.4	100.0	99.7	100.0	98.6	100.0	>95	>95	2.0	5.1	5.2	4.3
Myanmar	48.8	70.4	89.0	93.0	32.5	60.2	10.0	31.0	84.9	57.9	3.7	3.6
Philippines	85.4	96.8	93.9	98.2	78.3	95.6	41.0	48.0	32.6	26.7	3.1	2.7
Singapore	100.0	100.0	100.0	100.0	100.0	100.0	>95	>95	0.5	0.8	2.5	2.6
Thailand	99.7	100.0	100.0	100.0	99.5	100.0	74.0	84.0	22.8	24.0	5.1	4.5
Timor-Leste	38.0	96.1	83.4	100.0	20.6	94.4	<5	14.0	34.8	11.7	1.4	2.1
Viet Nam	97.4	100.0	99.9	100.0	96.4	100.0	49.0	65.0	34.6	18.7	5.5	4.9
The Pacific												
Cook Islands	99.0	100.0	99.0	100.0	...	...	81.0	76.0	–	3.7	...	...
Fiji	89.2	100.0	96.1	100.0	81.8	100.0	32.0	51.0	26.5	26.5	2.3	2.2
Kiribati	63.2	92.0	89.5	88.4	39.4	96.4	<5	10.0	48.4	41.0	6.8	5.9
Marshall Islands	89.2	99.2	92.4	96.0	80.4	100.0	53.0	64.0	13.3	11.7	10.5	9.7
Micronesia, Federated States of	64.5	82.9	84.6	96.7	58.8	78.8	12.0	13.0	2.0	1.8	4.1	5.5
Nauru	99.2	100.0	98.4	100.0	100.0 (2015)	100.0	>95	>95	0.0	0.6	8.7	5.1
Niue	99.4	99.7	99.6	100.0	...	...	93.0	>95	26.7	22.4	...	...
Palau	98.7	100.0	99.4	100.0	96.5	100.0	>95	>95	–	0.3	10.7	9.6
Papua New Guinea	19.5	60.4	71.2	83.6	11.8	56.8	8.0	9.0	55.3	53.1	5.7	5.3
Samoa	96.4	100.0	98.9	100.0	95.7	100.0	27.0	36.0	41.3	34.2	3.8	4.4
Solomon Islands	34.8	73.3	65.3	77.3	27.1	72.0	8.0	9.0	45.1	48.4	6.2	4.3
Tonga	92.7	100.0	97.9	100.0	91.1	100.0	60.0	84.0	1.0	1.8	3.1	3.4
Tuvalu	96.6	99.7	98.1	100.0	94.8	99.1	49.0	71.0	0.3	8.2	3.9	2.6
Vanuatu	44.1	67.3	82.3	95.6	31.7	57.7	12.0	8.0	38.4	31.9	3.7	3.5
Developed ADB Member Economies												
Australia	100.0	100.0	100.0	100.0	100.0	100.0	>95	>95	8.2	10.1	5.3	4.3
Japan	100.0	100.0	100.0	100.0	100.0	100.0	>95	>95	4.7	7.7	4.4	3.3
New Zealand	100.0	100.0	100.0	100.0	100.0	100.0	>95	>95	31.7	29.7	4.6	4.0
WORLD	**83.2**	**90.5**	**95.7**	**97.3**	**71.9**	**82.6**	**57.0**	**69.0**	**16.1**	**17.7**	**5.6**	**4.7**

... = data not available, – = magnitude equals zero, 0.0 = magnitude is less than half of unit employed, < = less than, > = greater than, $ = United States dollars, ADB = Asian Development Bank, GDP = gross domestic product, MJ = megajoule, PPP = purchasing power parity.

Sources: United Nations. SDG Global Database. https://unstats.un.org/sdgs/dataportal (accessed 12 July 2022). For Indicator 7.2.1 of Taipei,China: World Bank. DataBank: Sustainable Energy for All. https://databank.worldbank.org/source/sustainable-energy-for-all# (accessed 15 July 2022).

Goal 8. Promote sustained, inclusive, and sustainable economic growth; full and productive employment; and decent work for all

Table 1.8.1: Selected Indicators for Sustainable Development Goal 8—Decent Work and Economic Growth

ADB Regional Member	Target 8.1: Sustain per capita economic growth in accordance with national circumstances and, in particular, at least 7% gross domestic product per annum in the least developed countries 8.1.1: Annual Growth Rate of Real GDP per Capita at Constant 2015 $ (%)			Target 8.2: Achieve higher levels of economic productivity through diversification, technological upgrading, and innovation, including through a focus on high-value-added and labor-intensive sectors 8.2.1: Annual Growth Rate of Real GDP per Employed Person at Constant 2010 $[a] (%)		
	2010	2015	2020	2010	2015	2021
Developing ADB Member Economies						
Central and West Asia						
Afghanistan	2.4	-4.4	-4.2	11.2	-3.2	6.0
Armenia	2.6	2.8	-7.6	-1.6	5.2	4.5
Azerbaijan	3.5	-0.2	-5.2	3.2	-0.7	0.5
Georgia	6.8	3.3	-6.0	4.6	0.9	-0.8
Kazakhstan	5.9	-0.4	-3.7	4.7	0.2	2.4
Kyrgyz Republic	-2.1	1.9	-10.1	-2.3	1.8	-0.3
Pakistan	-0.6	2.6	-1.4	-2.1	1.9	1.2
Tajikistan	4.2	6.2	2.1	2.8	2.9	3.4
Turkmenistan	12.8	-0.3	-4.8	8.0	5.3	3.5
Uzbekistan	6.8	5.7	0.2	6.2	6.5	4.6
East Asia						
China, People's Republic of	10.0	6.5	2.0	10.5	6.6	7.6
Hong Kong, China	6.1	1.7	-6.9	6.7	1.7	6.5
Korea, Republic of	6.4	2.4	-0.9	5.5	2.0	3.3
Mongolia	4.6	0.4	-6.9	3.7	1.6	3.7
Taipei,China	...	...	...	8.0	0.4	5.7
South Asia						
Bangladesh	4.4	5.4	4.2	2.3	4.9	2.3
Bhutan	10.8	5.3	-1.9	11.3	3.3	-3.8
India	7.0	6.8	-8.2	8.1	7.4	4.1
Maldives	3.6	-1.6	-34.7	0.3	-4.6	17.2
Nepal	5.7	3.6	-3.9	3.6	2.8	-3.6
Sri Lanka	7.3	4.4	-4.0	6.5	3.5	2.1
Southeast Asia						
Brunei Darussalam	1.3	-1.6	0.1	1.5	-0.3	0.9
Cambodia	4.3	5.3	-4.5	0.3	5.7	0.3
Indonesia	4.8	3.6	-3.1	3.3	3.7	1.3
Lao People's Democratic Republic	6.4	5.7	1.8	5.7	5.1	0.5
Malaysia	5.6	3.7	-6.8	4.7	3.0	2.4
Myanmar	7.0	5.6	-18.5	8.9	5.8	-15.0
Philippines	5.6	4.7	-10.8	4.2	4.8	-1.3
Singapore	10.9	1.8	-6.1	7.0	0.4	5.7
Thailand	7.0	2.7	-6.3	7.9	3.3	1.2
Timor-Leste	7.4	0.9	9.1	6.9	0.3	-0.3
Viet Nam	5.4	5.6	2.0	3.6	6.0	3.1
The Pacific						
Cook Islands	-3.8	6.4	-25.4	...	...	...
Fiji	2.3	4.4	-16.3	–	5.9	-4.0
Kiribati	-3.0	8.3	-2.1	...	...	...
Marshall Islands	6.2	1.2	-2.9	...	...	...
Micronesia, Federated States of	2.3	3.2	-2.8	...	...	...
Nauru	12.8	35.3	0.4	...	...	...
Niue	...	...	...	...	...	...
Palau	2.0	4.8	-10.1	...	...	...
Papua New Guinea	7.6	4.5	-5.7	12.8	4.4	-0.9
Samoa	1.6	6.0	-9.8	-0.6	4.2	-7.3
Solomon Islands	7.1	-1.3	-6.7	5.6	-1.4	-1.5
Tonga	0.7	1.4	-0.5	1.5	2.4	-3.0
Tuvalu	-4.3	9.2	-0.2	...	...	...
Vanuatu	-0.9	-2.5	-11.4	-1.5	-1.8	-1.8
Developed ADB Member Economies						
Australia	0.6	1.3	0.3	-0.2	0.3	-0.1
Japan	4.1	1.7	-4.3	4.6	0.7	2.7
New Zealand	-0.2	3.4	-1.1	1.1	2.3	3.8

... = data not available, – = magnitude equals zero, $ = United States dollars, ADB = Asian Development Bank, GDP = gross domestic product.

a Modeled data based on GDP per person engaged, at constant 2010 United States dollars.

Sources: United Nations. SDG Global Database. https://unstats.un.org/sdgs/dataportal (accessed 18 July 2022). For Taipei,China: International Labour Organization. ILOSTAT Database. https://ilostat.ilo.org/data/ (accessed 18 July 2022).

Goal 8. Promote sustained, inclusive, and sustainable economic growth; full and productive employment; and decent work for all

Table 1.8.2: Selected Indicators for Sustainable Development Goal 8—Unemployment

ADB Regional Member	Target 8.5: By 2030, achieve full and productive employment and decent work for all women and men, including for young people and persons with disabilities, and equal pay for work of equal value 8.5.2.a: Unemployment Rate for Age Group 15+ Years, by Sex (%)					
	2010			2020		
	Total	Female	Male	Total	Female	Male
Developing ADB Member Economies						
Central and West Asia						
Afghanistan	1.7 (2012)	3.3 (2012)	1.4 (2012)	5.6 (2021)	5.5 (2021)	5.6 (2021)
Armenia	19.0	21.2	17.0	12.2	9.6	14.9
Azerbaijan	5.6	6.9	4.4	7.2	8.4	6.0
Georgia	20.2	17.6	22.5	11.7	10.2	13.1
Kazakhstan	5.8	6.6	4.9	4.9	5.4	4.4
Kyrgyz Republic	8.6	9.9	7.7	4.6	5.0	4.4
Pakistan	0.7	0.6	0.7	6.3 (2021)	9.2 (2021)	5.5 (2021)
Tajikistan	11.5 (2009)	10.5 (2009)	12.3 (2009)	6.9 (2016)	5.5 (2016)	7.9 (2016)
Turkmenistan	4.0	2.3	5.3	...	...	...
Uzbekistan[a]	5.4	6.3	4.6	5.3	3.9	7.7
East Asia						
China, People's Republic of	4.1	...	...	5.2 (2019)	...	...
Hong Kong, China	4.3	3.5	5.1	5.2 (2021)	4.2 (2021)	6.1 (2021)
Korea, Republic of	3.3	2.8	3.7	3.6 (2021)	3.7 (2021)	3.6 (2021)
Mongolia	6.6	5.9	7.1	6.6	6.3	6.8
Taipei,China	5.2	4.5	5.8	3.8	3.8	3.9
South Asia						
Bangladesh	3.4	4.4	3.0	4.4 (2017)	6.7 (2017)	3.3 (2017)
Bhutan	3.3	4.0	2.7	5.0	6.0	4.1
India	2.4	3.3	2.2	4.7	4.4	4.8
Maldives[b]	11.7 (2009)	13.8 (2009)	10.4 (2009)	4.6 (2019)	3.9 (2019)	5.0 (2019)
Nepal	1.3 (2008)	1.1 (2008)	1.6 (2008)	10.7 (2017)	12.0 (2017)	9.8 (2017)
Sri Lanka	4.8	7.4	3.4	5.2	7.5	4.1
Southeast Asia						
Brunei Darussalam	6.9 (2014)	7.8 (2014)	6.1 (2014)	7.4	8.9	6.4
Cambodia	0.8	0.8	0.8	0.5 (2019)	0.5 (2019)	0.5 (2019)
Indonesia	5.6	6.4	5.1	3.8 (2021)	3.2 (2021)	4.3 (2021)
Lao People's Democratic Republic	0.7	0.7	0.8	3.3 (2017)	2.8 (2017)	3.7 (2017)
Malaysia	3.4	3.3 (2011)	2.9 (2011)	4.5	4.7	4.5
Myanmar	...	...	...	1.5	2.1	1.0
Philippines	3.6	3.8	3.5	2.5	2.7	2.4
Singapore	4.1	4.4	3.9	3.5 (2021)	3.8 (2021)	3.3 (2021)
Thailand	0.6	0.6	0.6	1.1	1.1	1.1
Timor-Leste	3.3	4.3	2.9	4.7 (2016)	6.3 (2016)	3.3 (2016)
Viet Nam	1.1	1.1	1.2	2.4 (2021)	2.3 (2021)	2.5 (2021)
The Pacific						
Cook Islands	8.2 (2011)	8.1 (2011)	8.2 (2011)	1.3 (2019)	0.9 (2019)	1.6 (2019)
Fiji	8.9	4.6 (2011)	4.3 (2011)	4.3 (2016)	5.5 (2016)	3.7 (2016)
Kiribati	30.6	34.1	27.6	...	...	...
Marshall Islands	4.7 (2011)	4.5 (2011)	4.9 (2011)	...	...	...
Micronesia, Federated States of	8.9 (2014)	13.9 (2014)	5.4 (2014)	...	...	...
Nauru	23.0 (2011)	25.5 (2011)	21.4 (2011)	...	...	...
Niue	2.2 (2001)	2.1 (2001)	2.3 (2001)	...	...	...
Palau	1.4 (2014)	1.8 (2014)	1.1 (2014)	...	...	...
Papua New Guinea	2.0	1.3	2.7	...	...	...
Samoa	5.7 (2011)	6.8 (2011)	5.2 (2011)	9.4 (2017)	14.5 (2017)	6.3 (2017)
Solomon Islands	2.0 (2009)	1.8 (2009)	2.3 (2009)	...	...	...
Tonga	1.1 (2006)	7.4 (2003)	3.8 (2003)	2.3 (2018)	3.1 (2018)	1.6 (2018)
Tuvalu	6.5 (2002)	8.6 (2002)	5.0 (2002)	8.5 (2016)	16.2 (2016)	4.6 (2016)
Vanuatu	1.9	1.6	2.1	5.4 (2019)	6.8 (2019)	4.3 (2019)
Developed ADB Member Economies						
Australia	5.2	5.4	5.1	5.1 (2021)	5.0 (2021)	5.2 (2021)
Japan	5.1	4.6	5.5	2.8 (2021)	2.5 (2021)	3.1 (2021)
New Zealand	6.6	6.9	6.2	3.8 (2021)	3.9 (2021)	3.7 (2021)

Click on the indicator name in the table header to access the time series in the Key Indicators Database

Goal 8. Promote sustained, inclusive and sustainable economic growth; full and productive employment; and decent work for all

Table 1.8.2: Selected Indicators for Sustainable Development Goal 8—Unemployment *(continued)*

ADB Regional Member	Target 8.5: By 2030, achieve full and productive employment and decent work for all women and men, including for young people and persons with disabilities, and equal pay for work of equal value 8.5.2.b: Unemployment Rate for Age Group 15–24 Years, by Sex (%)					
	2010			2020		
	Total	Female	Male	Total	Female	Male
Developing ADB Member Economies						
Central and West Asia						
Afghanistan	2.9 (2012)	4.5 (2012)	2.6 (2012)	8.7 (2021)	9.4 (2021)	8.5 (2021)
Armenia	38.9	48.0	31.9	24.0	22.1	25.4
Azerbaijan	14.9	13.4	17.3	12.4 (2019)	14.2 (2019)	10.9 (2019)
Georgia	41.5	45.7	39.1	31.3	32.7	30.5
Kazakhstan	5.2	5.7	4.8	3.8	4.2	3.4
Kyrgyz Republic	16.7	20.3	14.5	8.5	10.0	7.6
Pakistan	1.3	1.1	1.3	11.1 (2021)	14.4 (2021)	10.0 (2021)
Tajikistan	5.9 (2007)	2.9 (2007)	8.4 (2007)	...	...	...
Turkmenistan	...	...	...	...	...	...
Uzbekistan[a]	...	...	...	13.2	8.3	21.5
East Asia						
China, People's Republic of	...	...	...	...	...	...
Hong Kong, China	12.2	10.3	14.1	12.8 (2021)	10.4 (2021)	15.2 (2021)
Korea, Republic of	8.7	7.8	10.2	8.1 (2021)	7.5 (2021)	9.1 (2021)
Mongolia	14.8	14.2	15.2	16.2	17.4	15.4
Taipei,China	13.1	12.7	13.6	11.6	12.1	11.3
South Asia						
Bangladesh	6.4	7.0	6.0	12.8 (2017)	16.8 (2017)	10.8 (2017)
Bhutan	9.2	11.0	7.1	22.6	25.4	19.2
India	9.0	10.4	8.6	19.8	21.0	19.5
Maldives[b]	25.4 (2009)	21.4 (2009)	29.1 (2009)	13.9 (2019)	9.7 (2019)	17.2 (2019)
Nepal	2.2 (2008)	1.6 (2008)	2.9 (2008)	20.5 (2017)	22.5 (2017)	19.2 (2017)
Sri Lanka	19.0	23.8	16.1	21.0 (2019)	28.1 (2019)	17.1 (2019)
Southeast Asia						
Brunei Darussalam	25.3 (2014)	27.9 (2014)	23.4 (2014)	26.4	32.4	22.7
Cambodia	1.0	0.9	1.0	1.7 (2019)	1.6 (2019)	1.8 (2019)
Indonesia	17.6	18.8	16.7	13.9 (2021)	12.7 (2021)	14.7 (2021)
Lao People's Democratic Republic	1.8	1.7	1.9	5.9 (2017)	5.4 (2017)	6.5 (2017)
Malaysia	9.7 (2011)	10.7 (2011)	9.1 (2011)	12.0	13.0	11.4
Myanmar	...	...	...	4.9	5.8	4.1
Philippines	9.9	12.0	8.7	7.0	8.5	6.1
Singapore	9.9	12.5	7.6	7.5 (2021)	10.2 (2021)	5.0 (2021)
Thailand	2.5	3.1	2.2	5.2	5.9	4.6
Timor-Leste	12.4	19.1	8.7	13.2 (2016)	15.9 (2016)	10.9 (2016)
Viet Nam	3.6	3.5	3.6	7.0 (2021)	7.0 (2021)	7.0 (2021)
The Pacific						
Cook Islands	15.5 (2011)	15.3 (2011)	15.6 (2011)	3.5 (2019)	1.7 (2019)	4.6 (2019)
Fiji	14.2 (2011)	18.4 (2011)	12.1 (2011)	15.4 (2016)	22.4 (2016)	11.9 (2016)
Kiribati	54.0	61.8	47.6	...	...	...
Marshall Islands	...	...	...	...	...	...
Micronesia, Federated States of	18.9 (2014)	29.9 (2014)	10.4 (2014)	...	...	...
Nauru	26.6 (2013)	37.5 (2013)	20.9 (2013)	...	...	...
Niue	9.0 (2001)	7.6 (2001)	10.3 (2001)	...	...	...
Palau	5.6 (2014)	- (2014)	- (2014)	...	...	...
Papua New Guinea	3.6	3.0	4.3	...	...	...
Samoa	16.1 (2011)	22.2 (2011)	13.8 (2011)	19.7 (2017)	30.0 (2017)	13.3 (2017)
Solomon Islands	1.3 (2013)	1.6 (2013)	1.1 (2013)	...	...	...
Tonga	...	...	...	6.7 (2018)	11.7 (2018)	3.4 (2018)
Tuvalu	...	...	...	20.6 (2016)	45.9 (2016)	9.8 (2016)
Vanuatu	4.8	4.8	4.8	12.3 (2019)	14.4 (2019)	10.3 (2019)
Developed ADB Member Economies						
Australia	11.6	11.1	12.0	11.3 (2021)	9.8 (2021)	12.6 (2021)
Japan	9.4	8.1	10.8	4.6 (2021)	4.2 (2021)	5.1 (2021)
New Zealand	17.4	17.8	17.1	10.5 (2021)	10.2 (2021)	10.8 (2021)

Goal 8. Promote sustained, inclusive, and sustainable economic growth; full and productive employment; and decent work for all

Table 1.8.2: Selected Indicators for Sustainable Development Goal 8—Unemployment *(continued)*

ADB Regional Member	Target 8.5: By 2030, achieve full and productive employment and decent work for all women and men, including for young people and persons with disabilities, and equal pay for work of equal value — 8.5.2.c: Unemployment Rate for Age Group 25+ Years, by Sex (%)					
	2010			2020		
	Total	Female	Male	Total	Female	Male
Developing ADB Member Economies						
Central and West Asia						
Afghanistan	1.2 (2012)	2.7 (2012)	0.9 (2012)	4.4 (2021)	3.8 (2021)	4.6 (2021)
Armenia	15.9	17.5	14.5	11.1	8.6	13.8
Azerbaijan	4.2	5.6	3.0	3.8 (2019)	4.6 (2019)	3.1 (2019)
Georgia	17.6	14.9	20.1	10.1	8.7	11.2
Kazakhstan	5.9	6.8	5.0	5.0	5.5	4.6
Kyrgyz Republic	6.3	7.3	5.5	3.9	4.1	3.7
Pakistan	0.4	0.5	0.4	4.7 (2021)	7.2 (2021)	3.9 (2021)
Tajikistan	1.9 (2007)	0.9 (2007)	2.5 (2007)	...	...	...
Turkmenistan	...	...	...	...	...	...
Uzbekistan[a]	...	...	...	4.2	3.3	5.6
East Asia						
China, People's Republic of	...	...	...	...	...	...
Hong Kong, China	3.6	2.8	4.3	4.8 (2021)	3.9 (2021)	5.6 (2021)
Korea, Republic of	3.0	2.4	3.4	3.4 (2021)	3.5 (2021)	3.4 (2021)
Mongolia	5.1	4.6	5.6	5.5	5.3	5.7
Taipei,China	4.5	3.5	5.3	3.2	3.0	3.3
South Asia						
Bangladesh	2.5	3.3	2.2	2.6 (2017)	4.4 (2017)	1.8 (2017)
Bhutan	2.1	2.4	1.9	3.2	3.7	2.8
India	1.0	1.8	0.7	2.2	2.2	2.2
Maldives[b]	6.6 (2009)	9.9 (2009)	4.7 (2009)	2.8 (2019)	2.8 (2019)	2.8 (2019)
Nepal	1.0 (2008)	0.9 (2008)	1.1 (2008)	8.2 (2017)	9.3 (2017)	7.5 (2017)
Sri Lanka	2.6	4.6	1.5	2.7 (2019)	4.7 (2019)	1.6 (2019)
Southeast Asia						
Brunei Darussalam	4.1 (2014)	4.9 (2014)	3.4 (2014)	4.5	5.4	3.9
Cambodia	0.7	0.7	0.6	0.2 (2019)	0.3 (2019)	0.2 (2019)
Indonesia	3.1	3.7	2.7	2.1 (2021)	1.4 (2021)	2.6 (2021)
Lao People's Democratic Republic	0.4	0.3	0.4	2.5 (2017)	1.9 (2017)	3.0 (2017)
Malaysia	1.5 (2011)	1.4 (2011)	1.5 (2011)	3.0	3.0	3.1
Myanmar	...	...	...	0.8	1.2	0.4
Philippines	2.0	1.8	2.1	1.7	1.7	1.7
Singapore	3.5	3.5	3.5	3.3 (2021)	3.3 (2021)	3.2 (2021)
Thailand	0.3	0.3	0.4	0.7	0.6	0.7
Timor-Leste	2.3	2.4	2.2	2.5 (2016)	3.8 (2016)	1.5 (2016)
Viet Nam	0.6	0.6	0.6	1.9 (2021)	1.8 (2021)	1.9 (2021)
The Pacific						
Cook Islands	6.5 (2011)	6.5 (2011)	6.4 (2011)	0.8 (2019)	0.8 (2019)	0.8 (2019)
Fiji	2.7 (2011)	2.4 (2011)	2.8 (2011)	2.2 (2016)	2.4 (2016)	2.2 (2016)
Kiribati	20.9	22.8	19.2	...	...	...
Marshall Islands	...	...	...	...	...	...
Micronesia, Federated States of	6.1 (2014)	9.0 (2014)	4.0 (2014)	...	...	...
Nauru	9.1 (2013)	13.1 (2013)	6.1 (2013)	...	...	...
Niue	1.0 (2001)	1.2 (2001)	0.8 (2001)	...	...	...
Palau	1.0 (2014)	1.4 (2014)	0.7 (2014)	...	...	...
Papua New Guinea	1.5	0.7	2.2	...	...	...
Samoa	3.0 (2011)	2.8 (2011)	3.0 (2011)	6.5 (2017)	10.1 (2017)	4.4 (2017)
Solomon Islands	0.5 (2013)	0.4 (2013)	0.6 (2013)	...	...	...
Tonga	...	...	...	1.4 (2018)	1.7 (2018)	1.3 (2018)
Tuvalu	...	...	...	5.5 (2016)	9.7 (2016)	3.3 (2016)
Vanuatu	1.1	0.7	1.5	3.9 (2019)	5.0 (2019)	2.9 (2019)
Developed ADB Member Economies						
Australia	3.8	4.0	3.7	4.0 (2021)	4.1 (2021)	3.9 (2021)
Japan	4.7	4.2	5.1	2.7 (2021)	2.4 (2021)	2.9 (2021)
New Zealand	4.5	4.8	4.2	2.7 (2021)	2.8 (2021)	2.5 (2021)

... = data not available, - = magnitude equals zero, ADB = Asian Development Bank.

a For 2020, data were derived using the International Labour Organization's ILOSTAT microdata processing.

b For 2009 and 2019, data were derived using the International Labour Organization's ILOSTAT microdata processing.

Source: International Labour Organization. ILOSTAT Database. https://ilostat.ilo.org/data (accessed 18 July 2022).

Goal 8. Promote sustained, inclusive and sustainable economic growth; full and productive employment; and decent work for all

Table 1.8.3: Selected Indicators for Sustainable Development Goal 8—Youth Participation in Education and Work, Child Labor

ADB Regional Member	Target 8.6: By 2020, substantially reduce the proportion of youth not in employment, education, or training — 8.6.1: Proportion of Youth (Aged 15–24 Years) not in Education, Employment, or Training (%)		Target 8.7: Take immediate and effective measures to eradicate forced labor, end modern slavery and human trafficking, and secure the prohibition and elimination of the worst forms of child labor, including recruitment and use of child soldiers; and, by 2025, end child labor in all its forms — 8.7.1: Proportion of Children (Aged 5–17 Years) Engaged in Child Labor (%)		
	2010	2020	Total 2020	Female 2020	Male 2020
Developing ADB Member Economies					
Central and West Asia					
Afghanistan	...	53.8	9.0	5.1	12.6
Armenia	44.6 (2011)	27.7	3.9 (2015)	2.7 (2015)	4.9 (2015)
Azerbaijan	...	...	...	...	...
Georgia	32.6 (2012)	28.5	1.5 (2015)	0.9 (2015)	2.1 (2015)
Kazakhstan	8.2	9.5 (2016)	...	...	...
Kyrgyz Republic	18.5	21.7	20.1 (2018)	15.6 (2018)	24.2 (2018)
Pakistan	31.1	29.7 (2019)	9.0 (2018)	5.1 (2018)	12.4 (2018)
Tajikistan	42.2 (2009)	...	...	...	...
Turkmenistan	...	...	0.3 (2016)	0.1 (2016)	0.4 (2016)
Uzbekistan	...	...	...	...	...
East Asia					
China, People's Republic of	...	...	...	...	...
Hong Kong, China	7.0	9.1	...	...	...
Korea, Republic of	...	...	...	...	...
Mongolia	17.6	19.7	7.9 (2018)	6.5 (2018)	9.1 (2018)
Taipei,China	...	...	...	...	...
South Asia					
Bangladesh	30.1	27.4 (2017)	5.9 (2019)	3.0 (2019)	8.7 (2019)
Bhutan	...	...	1.7 (2010)	1.7 (2010)	1.6 (2010)
India	27.9	28.2	4.3 (2012)	3.1 (2012)	5.3 (2012)
Maldives	32.5 (2009)	27.6 (2019)	...	...	...
Nepal	23.1 (2008)	35.4 (2017)	19.0 (2014)	19.3 (2014)	19.2 (2014)
Sri Lanka	26.7	21.2 (2019)	0.8 (2016)	0.6 (2016)	0.9 (2016)
Southeast Asia					
Brunei Darussalam	17.2 (2014)	8.8	...	...	...
Cambodia	0.2	12.7 (2019)	11.5 (2012)	12.2 (2012)	10.8 (2012)
Indonesia	26.7	21.8	...	...	...
Lao People's Democratic Republic	5.1	42.1 (2017)	26.3 (2017)	26.2 (2017)	26.3 (2017)
Malaysia	14.4 (2011)	13.6	...	...	...
Myanmar	...	14.9 (2019)	8.1 (2015)	7.6 (2015)	8.7 (2015)
Philippines	25.3	18.6	1.0	0.7	1.2
Singapore	3.7 (2013)	4.5	...	...	...
Thailand	12.5	15.1	...	...	...
Timor-Leste	19.0	21.0 (2016)	7.2 (2016)	6.9 (2016)	7.6 (2016)
Viet Nam	8.2	15.4	5.4 (2021)	...	...
The Pacific					
Cook Islands	...	12.6 (2019)	...	...	...
Fiji	18.4 (2011)	20.1 (2016)	...	...	...
Kiribati	...	49.8 (2019)	7.1 (2019)	5.5 (2019)	8.6 (2019)
Marshall Islands	...	41.2 (2019)	...	...	...
Micronesia, Federated States of	23.7 (2014)	...	...	...	...
Nauru	36.4 (2013)	...	...	...	...
Niue	...	...	...	...	...
Palau	12.9 (2014)	...	...	...	...
Papua New Guinea	27.7	...	...	...	...
Samoa	38.9 (2012)	37.9 (2017)	13.0	10.8	14.9
Solomon Islands	7.0 (2013)	...	13.8 (2015)	13.8 (2015)	13.8 (2015)
Tonga	...	30.3 (2018)	25.9 (2019)	18.5 (2019)	32.9 (2019)
Tuvalu	...	29.0 (2016)	3.7	4.0	3.4
Vanuatu	31.0	43.2 (2019)	15.0 (2013)	15.8 (2013)	14.2 (2013)
Developed ADB Member Economies					
Australia	11.3	8.9 (2017)	...	...	...
Japan	4.3	3.1 (2019)	...	...	...
New Zealand	13.6	13.0	...	...	...

... = data not available, ADB = Asian Development Bank.

Source: United Nations. SDG Global Database. https://unstats.un.org/sdgs/dataportal (accessed 17 July 2022).

Table 1.8.4: Access to Banking, Insurance and Financial Services, and Trade

ADB Regional Member	Target 8.10: Strengthen the capacity of domestic financial institutions to encourage and expand access to banking, insurance, and financial services for all					
	8.10.1: Number of Commercial Bank Branches and ATMs per 100,000 Adults				8.10.2: Proportion of Adults (15 Years and Older) with an Account at a Bank or Other Financial Institution or with a Mobile-Money Service Provider (%)	
	Commercial Bank Branches		ATMs			
	2010	2020	2010	2020	2011	2021
Developing ADB Member Economies						
Central and West Asia						
Afghanistan	2.4	1.9 (2019)	0.5	1.6 (2019)	9.0	9.7
Armenia	18.6	24.6	34.0	65.5	17.5	55.4
Azerbaijan	9.9	6.2	27.1	35.1	14.9	28.6 (2017)
Georgia	21.2	31.7	48.3	90.9	33.0	70.5
Kazakhstan	3.3	2.4	61.4	95.8	42.1	81.1
Kyrgyz Republic	6.1	7.5	7.3	41.8	3.8	45.1
Pakistan	8.4	10.3	4.3	11.1	10.3	21.0
Tajikistan	7.0	26.7	4.5	21.4	2.5	39.5
Turkmenistan	...	...	...	...	0.4	40.6 (2017)
Uzbekistan	39.2	42.4	4.0	48.4	22.5	44.1
East Asia						
China, People's Republic of	7.8 (2012)	8.8	24.9	87.9	63.8	88.7
Hong Kong, China	23.8	20.2	46.9	52.0	88.7	97.8
Korea, Republic of	18.2	14.4	265.4	264.6 (2019)	93.1	98.7
Mongolia	54.6	62.6	18.5	48.0	77.7	98.5
Taipei,China	17.2 (2011)	16.4 (2021)	134.9 (2015)	154.3 (2021)	87.3	94.7
South Asia						
Bangladesh	7.7	9.0	2.1	10.5	31.7	52.8
Bhutan	15.3	19.3 (2019)	8.9	48.1 (2019)	33.7 (2014)	...
India	10.0	14.7	7.2	21.5	35.2	77.5
Maldives	11.7	13.8	16.5	38.0	...	79.6 (2017)
Nepal	5.1	21.5	7.4 (2011)	19.8	25.3	54.0
Sri Lanka	15.9	...	13.4	...	68.5	89.3
Southeast Asia						
Brunei Darussalam	23.3	17.6 (2019)	82.0	74.0 (2019)	...	...
Cambodia	4.1	11.6	5.3	26.3	3.7	33.4
Indonesia	8.1	15.2	13.0	51.7	19.6	51.8
Lao People's Democratic Republic	2.5	3.2	8.7	27.4	26.8	37.3
Malaysia	10.9	9.0	51.3	55.6	66.2	88.4
Myanmar	1.5	5.6 (2019)	0.1 (2012)	6.9 (2019)	22.8 (2014)	47.8
Philippines	7.5	9.2	15.1	29.7	26.6	51.4
Singapore	9.8	7.0	59.1	54.0	98.2	97.6
Thailand	11.0	10.6	81.9	111.8	72.7	95.6
Timor-Leste	1.8	5.6	2.4	13.4	...	...
Viet Nam	3.2	4.0	17.0	26.3	21.4	30.8 (2017)
The Pacific						
Cook Islands	...	...	...	...	...	...
Fiji	11.1	10.7	33.1	53.0	...	...
Kiribati	6.0 (2011)	...	10.5 (2011)	...	...	...
Marshall Islands	17.6	13.4	2.9	5.7	...	...
Micronesia, Federated States of	15.1	12.6	9.1	12.6	...	...
Nauru	...	...	...	...	...	...
Niue	...	...	...	...	...	...
Palau	...	...	36.5	45.8 (2017)	...	...
Papua New Guinea	1.6	1.6	5.3	8.2	...	...
Samoa	25.3	24.1	25.3	59.4	...	...
Solomon Islands	4.5	3.9	11.2	15.1	...	...
Tonga	21.5	33.0 (2018)	27.7	40.5 (2018)	...	...
Tuvalu	...	...	...	...	...	...
Vanuatu	20.6	21.1	28.1	47.6	...	...
Developed ADB Member Economies						
Australia	30.8	25.4	168.7	129.7	99.1	99.3
Japan	33.8	33.9	130.9	121.7	96.4	98.5
New Zealand	34.5	21.4	72.2	54.1	99.4	98.8

Goal 8. Promote sustained, inclusive, and sustainable economic growth; full and productive employment; and decent work for all

Table 1.8.4: Access to Banking, Insurance and Financial Services, and Trade *(continued)*

ADB Regional Member	Target 8.10: Strengthen the capacity of domestic financial institutions to encourage and expand access to banking, insurance, and financial services for all 8.a.1: Aid for Trade (millions of constant 2020 USD)			
	Commitments		Disbursement	
	2010	2020	2010	2020
Developing ADB Member Economies				
Central and West Asia				
Afghanistan	1,845.7	679.8	2,032.5	750.3
Armenia	153.7	112.7	168.0	94.7
Azerbaijan	93.6	12.2	58.8	128.4
Georgia	323.7	187.7	256.5	307.6
Kazakhstan	190.5	4.9	59.4	10.2
Kyrgyz Republic	...	...	...	...
Pakistan	803.2	1,495.4	345.4	1,205.4
Tajikistan	240.1	563.1	169.0	222.1
Turkmenistan	18.4	10.9	3.1	13.0
Uzbekistan	450.4	509.3	86.8	695.2
East Asia				
China, People's Republic of	597.1	896.0	482.3	354.6
Hong Kong, China	...	...	...	...
Korea, Republic of	...	...	...	...
Mongolia	301.9	227.5	133.3	133.5
Taipei,China	...	...	...	...
South Asia				
Bangladesh	1,120.8	3,784.7	454.2	2,491.9
Bhutan	53.9	76.9	82.5	83.5
India	2,895.6	4,367.9	2,100.5	2,747.7
Maldives	14.5	59.8	30.4	79.7
Nepal	461.9	1,373.5	241.2	472.6
Sri Lanka	315.7	132.7	326.0	352.1
Southeast Asia				
Brunei Darussalam	...	...	...	...
Cambodia	435.7	717.1	205.6	415.9
Indonesia	712.1	955.8	981.7	850.4
Lao People's Democratic Republic	...	...	...	...
Malaysia	14.9	3.3	33.1	6.1
Myanmar	33.5	2,426.9	42.0	1,032.9
Philippines	120.6	1,650.1	342.0	608.2
Singapore	...	...	...	...
Thailand	318.5	20.1	172.4	219.6
Timor-Leste	87.3	30.4	42.5	61.0
Viet Nam	...	...	...	...
The Pacific				
Cook Islands	...	...	...	...
Fiji	18.8	41.7	9.4	47.3
Kiribati	4.3	74.0	3.6	10.2
Marshall Islands	0.9	10.8	9.8	15.5
Micronesia, Federated States of	...	...	...	...
Nauru	0.3	8.3	0.9	8.0
Niue	...	...	...	...
Palau	1.5	13.4	7.0	23.8
Papua New Guinea	228.2	267.4	115.3	268.9
Samoa	23.5	44.5	30.7	18.7
Solomon Islands	39.6	22.2	23.9	47.3
Tonga	27.9	18.9	30.2	31.2
Tuvalu	1.3	12.8	1.5	11.2
Vanuatu	18.1	70.2	37.0	44.4
Developed ADB Member Economies				
Australia	...	...	...	...
Japan	...	...	...	...
New Zealand	...	...	...	...

... = data not available, $ = United States dollars, ADB = Asian Development Bank.

Sources: For indicator 8.10.1: Commercial bank branches for Taipei,China: Central bank of Taipei,China. https://www.cbc.gov.tw/en/cp-535-1059-E918E-2.html (accessed 18 July 2022); and ATMs for Taipei,China: Financial Supervisory Commission, Banking Bureau. https://www.banking.gov.tw/en/home.jsp?id=124&parentpath=0,100,122 (accessed 18 July 2022). For Indicator 8.10.2: World Bank. World Development Indicators. https://data.worldbank.org/indicator (accessed 18 July 2022). For indicator 8.a.1: United Nations. SDG Global Database. https://unstats.un.org/sdgs/dataportal (accessed 18 July 2022).

Table 1.9.1: Selected Indicators for Sustainable Development Goal 9—Road and Rail Transport, Passenger and Freight Volume

	Target 9.1: Develop quality, reliable, sustainable, and resilient infrastructure, including regional and transborder infrastructure, to support economic development and human well-being, with a focus on affordable and equitable access for all			
ADB Regional Member	9.1.2: Passenger Volume, by Road Transport[a] (p-km million)	9.1.2: Freight Volume, by Road Transport[b] (t-km million)	9.1.2: Passenger Volume, by Rail Transport[a] (p-km million)	9.1.2: Freight Volume, by Rail Transport[b] (t-km million)
	2020	2020	2020	2020
Developing ADB Member Economies				
Central and West Asia	**730,173.0**	**884,061.0**	**176,540.0**	**262,601.0**
Afghanistan	31,611.0	7,077.0	308.0	...
Armenia	7,461.0	5,766.0	4,706.0	1,473.0
Azerbaijan	24,099.0	24,107.0	17,534.0	14,481.0
Georgia	8,325.0	7,304.0	6,797.0	6,290.0
Kazakhstan	31,848.0	315,256.0	16,505.0	162,675.0
Kyrgyz Republic	9,142.0	7,378.0	3,392.0	130.0
Pakistan	519,409.0	446,358.0	79,241.0	53,505.0
Tajikistan	12,581.0	2,580.0	5,384.0	240.0
Turkmenistan	14,078.0	17,051.0	13,694.0	4,674.0
Uzbekistan	71,619.0	51,184.0	28,979.0	19,133.0
East Asia[c]	**4,279,711.0**	**7,271,050.0**	**1,245,948.0**	**3,666,098.0**
China, People's Republic of	4,001,853.0	7,098,480.0	1,151,463.0	3,616,630.0
Hong Kong, China	23,060.0	5,369.0	7,139.0	12,312.0
Korea, Republic of	243,168.0	88,526.0	82,346.0	23,930.0
Mongolia	11,630.0	78,675.0	5,000.0	13,226.0
Taipei,China	...	...	...	...
South Asia[c]	**4,699,823.0**	**2,113,842.0**	**2,748,830.0**	**452,323.0**
Bangladesh	775,032.0	45,798.0	62,906.0	31,876.0
Bhutan	3,875.0	326.0	596.0	...
India	3,787,862.0	2,045,566.0	2,621,553.0	417,072.0
Maldives	2,359.0	13.0	96.0	...
Nepal	36,129.0	1,442.0	4,249.0	...
Sri Lanka	94,566.0	20,697.0	59,430.0	3,375.0
Southeast Asia[c]	**2,335,582.0**	**1,049,570.0**	**153,156.0**	**81,977.0**
Brunei Darussalam	6,149.0	524.0	375.0	...
Cambodia	38,411.0	23,040.0	2,491.0	4,014.0
Indonesia	983,697.0	472,412.0	35,975.0	11,728.0
Lao People's Democratic Republic	21,337.0	15,114.0	1,125.0	...
Malaysia	209,279.0	119,512.0	22,221.0	22,375.0
Myanmar	68,414.0	11,361.0	3,895.0	4,180.0
Philippines	356,802.0	73,542.0	30,161.0	722.0
Singapore	80,742.0	1,679.0	10,406.0	8,933.0
Thailand	274,826.0	179,558.0	31,513.0	22,714.0
Timor-Leste	207.0	...	...	...
Viet Nam	295,718.0	152,828.0	14,994.0	7,311.0
The Pacific[c]	**18,045.0**	**1,347.0**	**473.0**	**...**
Cook Islands	39.0	...	1.0	...
Fiji	1,862.0	158.0	48.0	...
Kiribati	187.0	7.0	7.0	...
Marshall Islands	524.0	...	5.0	...
Micronesia, Federated States of	280.0	10.0	10.0	...
Nauru	18.0	...	1.0	...
Niue	2.0	...	–	...
Palau	217.0	5.0	10.0	...
Papua New Guinea	11,473.0	1,147.0	282.0	...
Samoa	649.0	–	24.0	...
Solomon Islands	1,448.0	–	37.0	...
Tonga	394.0	19.0	14.0	...
Tuvalu	28.0	1.0	1.0	...
Vanuatu	924.0	–	33.0	...
Developed ADB Member Economies	**957,694.0**	**1,403,695.0**	**191,669.0**	**293,690.0**
Australia	272,278.0	1,118,087.0	8,008.0	210,249.0
Japan	646,363.0	269,007.0	182,689.0	68,645.0
New Zealand	39,053.0	16,601.0	972.0	14,796.0
DEVELOPING ADB MEMBER ECONOMIES[c]	**12,063,334.0**	**11,319,870.0**	**4,324,947.0**	**4,462,999.0**
ALL ADB REGIONAL MEMBERS[c]	**13,021,028.0**	**12,723,565.0**	**4,516,616.0**	**4,756,689.0**
WORLD	**31,400,105.0**	**26,778,363.0**	**6,131,895.0**	**10,836,936.0**

... = data not available, – = magnitude equals zero, ADB = Asian Development Bank, p-km = passenger-kilometer, t-km = ton-kilometer.
Note: The numbers shown in the table are modeled estimates as published on the United Nations' SDG Global Database.

a A passenger-kilometer, abbreviated as p-km, is a unit of measurement representing the transport of 1 passenger by a defined mode of transport over 1 kilometer.
b A ton-kilometer, abbreviated as t-km, is a unit of measurement of freight transport representing the transport of 1 metric ton of goods (including packaging and tare weights of intermodal transport units) by a defined mode of transport over 1 kilometer.
c For reporting economies only.

Source: United Nations. SDG Global Database. https://unstats.un.org/sdgs/dataportal (accessed 18 July 2022).

Click on the indicator name in the table header to access the time series in the Key Indicators Database

Goal 9. Build resilient infrastructure, promote inclusive and sustainable industrialization, and foster innovation

Table 1.9.2: Selected Indicators for Sustainable Development Goal 9—Growth in Manufacturing

ADB Regional Member	Target 9.2: Promote inclusive and sustainable industrialization; and, by 2030, significantly raise industry's share of employment and GDP, in line with national circumstances, and double its share in least developed countries					
	9.2.1: Manufacturing Value-Added[a]				9.2.2: Manufacturing Employment as a Proportion of Total Employment (%)	
	As a Proportion of GDP (%)		Per Capita (at constant 2015 $)			
	2010	2021	2010	2021	2010	2020
Developing ADB Member Economies						
Central and West Asia						
Afghanistan	7.0	5.9	35.3	28.1	6.8 (2012)	8.2
Armenia	9.0	11.9	267.4	504.3	5.7	10.1
Azerbaijan	4.5	6.4	239.4	336.6	4.8	5.3
Georgia	8.8	9.2	252.9	423.7	5.3	8.1
Kazakhstan	11.2	11.4	1,005.1	1,286.6	7.0	6.8 (2017)
Kyrgyz Republic	17.6	15.3	170.9	173.2	7.6 (2012)	11.6
Pakistan	12.9	11.7	158.1	175.6	13.5	15.1 (2019)
Tajikistan	20.2	15.4	157.5	200.2	5.5 (2009)	5.4 (2018)
Turkmenistan	46.4	35.6	2,541.6	1,906.0	...	...
Uzbekistan	13.1	14.6	262.1	474.7	11.5	11.9 (2019)
East Asia						
China, People's Republic of	27.5	28.1	1,517.0	3,076.1	...	...
Hong Kong, China	1.3	1.0	504.3	428.8	3.8	2.8
Korea, Republic of	26.8	26.6	6,820.4	8,745.0	16.8	15.9 (2021)
Mongolia	9.0	10.3	238.6	420.8	6.3	7.7
Taipei,China	27.8	35.5	5,557.8	9,773.6	27.3	27.4 (2021)
South Asia						
Bangladesh	14.3	20.6	138.2	356.1	12.4	14.4 (2017)
Bhutan	8.7	7.6	193.8	228.9	3.9	6.5 (2015)
India	15.3	16.6	194.7	331.0	11.1	11.3
Maldives	2.0	2.2	167.4	196.1	9.1 (2009)	10.4 (2019)
Nepal	5.3	4.8	37.2	48.0	0.2 (2008)	15.1 (2017)
Sri Lanka	18.7	16.1	550.4	688.3	17.1	18.4 (2019)
Southeast Asia						
Brunei Darussalam	14.7	19.8	4,924.7	5,977.5	3.7 (2014)	4.3
Cambodia	14.3	16.6	127.2	230.4	10.7	16.7 (2019)
Indonesia	21.5	20.1	584.2	775.9	12.5	13.9 (2021)
Lao People's Democratic Republic	8.0	8.8	126.5	232.4	5.1	7.9 (2017)
Malaysia	22.8	22.7	1,881.2	2,459.0	16.8	16.7
Myanmar	19.3	20.8	171.2	201.9	10.9 (2015)	10.5 (2019)
Philippines	20.6	19.2	500.7	655.7	8.3 (2012)	8.1
Singapore	21.1	22.0	10,136.4	13,276.0	14.6 (2011)	9.6
Thailand	30.1	25.8	1,553.5	1,623.2	14.1	15.9
Timor-Leste	0.9	1.5	10.9	23.5	3.2	7.2 (2016)
Viet Nam	11.5	18.0	189.9	487.0	14.3	23.1 (2021)
The Pacific						
Cook Islands	2.5	2.1	359.2	328.2	3.9 (2011)	3.8 (2019)
Fiji	11.1	12.0	501.7	558.3	9.3 (2011)	5.6 (2016)
Kiribati	5.1	4.1	69.8	60.6	13.2	5.2 (2019)
Marshall Islands	7.5	2.2	238.7	74.0	0.7	3.2 (2019)
Micronesia, Federated States of	0.4	0.8	13.7	20.8	2.4 (2014)	2.4 (2014)
Nauru	25.6	21.6	1,075.6	2,243.9	0.5 (2013)	...
Niue	...	...	...	...	...	...
Palau	0.7	1.1	94.1	132.1	3.2 (2008)	0.5 (2014)
Papua New Guinea	2.6	1.6	57.8	42.8	1.8	...
Samoa	10.4	5.6	412.7	196.7	6.8 (2012)	6.8 (2017)
Solomon Islands	11.7	11.5	244.1	239.9	5.5 (2013)	...
Tonga	6.1	5.8	211.4	242.2	...	20.2 (2018)
Tuvalu	1.1	1.6	29.5	62.7	...	3.7 (2016)
Vanuatu	5.0	3.4	148.5	86.8	2.3	4.5 (2019)
Developed ADB Member Economies						
Australia	7.5	5.3	3,661.8	2,932.3	8.9	6.9 (2021)
Japan	20.8	23.0	6,828.9	8,110.4	16.8	15.6 (2021)
New Zealand	12.4	10.3	4,325.3	4,572.7	11.6	9.2

... = data not available, $ = United States dollars, ADB = Asian Development Bank, GDP = gross domestic product.

a United Nations figures calculated from GDP, manufacturing value-added, and population data.

Source: Sources: United Nations. SDG Global Database. https://unstats.un.org/sdgs/dataportal (accessed 14 July 2022); For Taipei,China: United Nations Industrial Development Organization. Statistics Data Portal. https://stat.unido.org/SDG (accessed 14 July 2022).

Goal 9. Build resilient infrastructure, promote inclusive and sustainable industrialization, and foster innovation

Table 1.9.3: Selected Indicators for Sustainable Development Goal 9—Carbon Dioxide Emissions

ADB Regional Member	Target 9.4: By 2030, upgrade infrastructure and retrofit industries to make them sustainable, with increased resource-use efficiency and greater adoption of clean and environmentally sound technologies and industrial processes, with all countries taking action in accordance with their respective capabilities			
	9.4.1: Carbon Dioxide Emissions[a]			
	Per Unit of GDP (PPP) (kg of CO_2 equivalent per constant 2017 $)		Per Unit of Manufacturing Value-Added (kg of CO_2 equivalent per constant 2015 $)	
	2010	2019	2010	2019
Developing ADB Member Economies				
Central and West Asia				
Afghanistan	...	...	...	...
Armenia	0.15	0.15	0.7	0.3
Azerbaijan	0.18	0.24	0.6	0.6
Georgia	0.14	0.17	0.5	0.8
Kazakhstan	0.65	0.42	3.2	1.0
Kyrgyz Republic	0.27	0.27	0.6	0.6
Pakistan	0.18	0.17	1.3	1.4
Tajikistan	0.13	0.23	–	1.1
Turkmenistan	1.30	0.75	0.1	0.2
Uzbekistan	0.90	0.48	2.3	0.9
East Asia				
China, People's Republic of	0.66	0.44	1.3	0.7
Hong Kong, China	0.12	0.10	0.5	0.7
Korea, Republic of	0.32	0.27	0.2	0.1
Mongolia	0.70	0.57	1.9	1.2
Taipei,China	...	...	0.3	0.2
South Asia				
Bangladesh	0.12	0.12	0.5	0.5
Bhutan	...	...	...	...
India	0.30	0.25	1.6	1.4
Maldives	...	...	...	...
Nepal	0.06	0.09	1.2	2.1
Sri Lanka	0.07	0.08	0.1	0.1
Southeast Asia				
Brunei Darussalam	0.26	0.25	0.2	0.2
Cambodia	0.12	0.18	0.4	0.3
Indonesia	0.20	0.18	0.9	0.7
Lao People's Democratic Republic	0.08	0.30	1.1	0.5
Malaysia	0.33	0.26	0.6	0.5
Myanmar	0.05	0.13	0.3	0.2
Philippines	0.14	0.14	0.3	0.2
Singapore	0.11	0.08	0.2	0.2
Thailand	0.23	0.20	0.5	0.4
Timor-Leste	...	...	...	...
Viet Nam	0.28	0.36	2.5	1.6
The Pacific				
Cook Islands	...	...	...	...
Fiji	...	...	...	...
Kiribati	...	...	...	...
Marshall Islands	...	...	...	...
Micronesia, Federated States of	...	...	...	...
Nauru	...	...	...	...
Niue	...	...	...	...
Palau	...	...	...	...
Papua New Guinea	...	...	...	...
Samoa	...	...	...	...
Solomon Islands	...	...	...	...
Tonga	...	...	...	...
Tuvalu	...	...	...	...
Vanuatu	...	...	...	...
Developed ADB Member Economies				
Australia	0.39	0.30	0.4	0.4
Japan	0.24	0.20	0.2	0.2
New Zealand	0.19	0.16	0.3	0.3

... = data not available, – = magnitude equals zero, $ = United States dollars, ADB = Asian Development Bank, CO_2 = carbon dioxide, GDP = gross domestic product, kg = kilogram, PPP = purchasing power parity.

a Refers to carbon dioxide emissions from fuel combustion.

Sources: United Nations. SDG Global Database. https://unstats.un.org/sdgs/dataportal/database (accessed 16 July 2022); For CO_2 per unit of manufacturing value-added for Taipei,China: United Nations Industrial Development Organization. UNIDO Statistics Data Portal. https://stat.unido.org/SDG (accessed 16 July 2022).

Goal 9. Build resilient infrastructure, promote inclusive and sustainable industrialization, and foster innovation

Table 1.9.4: Selected Indicators for Sustainable Development Goal 9—Research and Development

ADB Regional Member	Target 9.5: Enhance scientific research, upgrade the technological capabilities of industrial sectors in all countries, in particular developing countries, including, by 2030, encouraging innovation and substantially increasing the number of research and development workers per 1 million people and public and private research and development spending			
	9.5.1: Research and Development Expenditure as a Proportion of GDP (%)		9.5.2: Researchers (Full-Time Equivalent) (per million inhabitants)	
	2010	2020	2010	2020
Developing ADB Member Economies				
Central and West Asia				
Afghanistan	...	...	...	...
Armenia	0.24	0.21	...	...
Azerbaijan	0.22	0.22	...	1,735
Georgia	0.08 (2013)	0.30	566 (2013)	1,712
Kazakhstan	0.15	0.13 (2021)	371	630 (2021)
Kyrgyz Republic	0.16	0.09	...	...
Pakistan	0.33 (2011)	0.20 (2019)	143 (2011)	383 (2019)
Tajikistan	0.09	0.09	...	...
Turkmenistan	...	...	...	...
Uzbekistan	0.15	0.14	545	424
East Asia				
China, People's Republic of	1.71	2.40	885	1,585
Hong Kong, China	0.75	0.99	3,115	4,352
Korea, Republic of	3.32	4.81	5,331	8,714
Mongolia	0.24	0.13	...	331
Taipei,China	...	...	...	...
South Asia				
Bangladesh	...	...	...	...
Bhutan	...	...	...	...
India	0.79	0.66 (2018)	156	253 (2018)
Maldives	...	...	...	...
Nepal	0.30	...	61 (2002)	...
Sri Lanka	0.14	0.13 (2018)	106	106 (2018)
Southeast Asia				
Brunei Darussalam	0.04 (2004)	0.28 (2018)	284 (2004)	...
Cambodia	0.05 (2002)	0.12 (2015)	18 (2002)	30 (2015)
Indonesia	0.08 (2009)	0.28	89 (2009)	396
Lao People's Democratic Republic	0.04 (2002)	...	16 (2002)	...
Malaysia	1.04	1.04 (2018)	1,462	2,185 (2018)
Myanmar	0.20 (2002)	0.15	18 (2002)	32
Philippines	0.11 (2011)	0.32 (2018)	84 (2011)	174 (2018)
Singapore	1.93	1.89 (2019)	6,242	7,287 (2019)
Thailand	0.36 (2011)	1.14 (2019)	539 (2011)	1,790 (2019)
Timor-Leste	...	...	...	...
Viet Nam	0.19 (2011)	0.53 (2019)	679 (2013)	757 (2019)
The Pacific				
Cook Islands	...	...	...	...
Fiji	...	...	...	...
Kiribati	...	...	...	...
Marshall Islands	...	...	...	...
Micronesia, Federated States of	...	...	...	...
Nauru	...	...	...	...
Niue	...	...	...	...
Palau	...	...	...	...
Papua New Guinea	...	0.03 (2016)	...	35 (2016)
Samoa	...	...	...	...
Solomon Islands	...	...	...	...
Tonga	...	...	...	...
Tuvalu	...	...	...	...
Vanuatu	...	...	...	...
Developed ADB Member Economies				
Australia	2.37	1.83 (2019)	4,532	...
Japan	3.10	3.26	5,104	5,455
New Zealand	1.23 (2011)	1.41 (2019)	3,689 (2011)	5,854 (2019)

... = data not available, ADB = Asian Development Bank, GDP = gross domestic product.

Source: United Nations Educational, Scientific and Cultural Organization (UNESCO) Institute for Statistics. UIS.Stat Database. http://data.uis.unesco.org/# (accessed 14 July 2022).

Goal 9. Build resilient infrastructure, promote inclusive and sustainable industrialization, and foster innovation

Table 1.9.5: Selected Indicators for Sustainable Development Goal 9—Official International Support and Industry Value-Added

ADB Regional Member	Target 9.a: Faciltate sustainable and resilient infrastructure development in developing countries through enhanced financial, technological, and technical support to African countries, least developed countries, landlocked developing countries and small island developing States — 9.a.1: Total Official International Support to Infrastructure[a] (constant 2020 $ million)		Target 9.b: Support domestic technology development, research, and innovation in developing countries, including by ensuring a conducive policy environment for, *inter alia*, industrial diversification and value addition to commodities — 9.b.1: Proportion of Medium and High-Tech Industry Value-Added in Total Value-Added (%)	
	2010	2020	2010	2019
Developing ADB Member Economies				
Central and West Asia	**4,065.1**	**5,215.1**		
Afghanistan	1,313.5	506.6	9.5	8.5
Armenia	234.0	259.4	4.5	7.1
Azerbaijan	216.5	414.9	10.1	14.2
Georgia	350.1	766.0	17.2	12.8
Kazakhstan	1,171.9	476.6	12.8	15.0
Kyrgyz Republic	67.1	110.2	3.5	2.4
Pakistan	494.0	1,287.2	24.6	24.6
Tajikistan	127.5	235.0	3.7	2.7
Turkmenistan	1.6	90.0	...	...
Uzbekistan	88.9	1,069.1	19.7	23.3
East Asia[b]	**2,539.8**	**1,939.7**		
China, People's Republic of	2,445.3	1,733.1	41.4	41.5
Hong Kong, China	...	...	38.1	38.1
Korea, Republic of	...	...	61.2	63.8
Mongolia	94.5	206.7	2.1	3.0
Taipei,China	...	...	67.9	68.4
South Asia	**6,894.4**	**10,312.2**		
Bangladesh	446.0	2,822.9	9.1	7.8
Bhutan	94.3	84.5	...	...
India	5,685.3	6,190.7	39.2	41.3
Maldives	30.2	76.8	2.6	2.6
Nepal	185.9	396.9	8.2	8.6
Sri Lanka	452.7	740.4	11.8	7.7
Southeast Asia[b]	**3,681.9**	**7,303.8**		
Brunei Darussalam	...	...	3.3	3.3
Cambodia	130.2	368.0	0.3	0.3
Indonesia	1,164.1	1,899.0	39.7	37.3
Lao People's Democratic Republic	106.3	96.9	3.8	3.8
Malaysia	26.3	6.8	42.6	44.0
Myanmar	5.4	1,193.8	27.6	23.7
Philippines	270.2	1,793.2	45.7	47.3
Singapore	...	...	85.2	85.1
Thailand	153.7	433.7	43.8	41.4
Timor-Leste	24.4	53.2	...	...
Viet Nam	1,801.4	1,459.2	25.4	39.0
The Pacific[c]	**241.4**	**905.1**		
Cook Islands	1.6	9.4 (2019)	...	...
Fiji	12.2	164.8	7.9	7.8
Kiribati	1.3	3.1	...	...
Marshall Islands	5.8	13.1	...	...
Micronesia, Federated States of	11.4	13.1	...	...
Nauru	0.2	6.6	...	...
Niue	3.3	3.0	...	...
Palau	6.2	23.3	...	...
Papua New Guinea	98.1	573.3	12.6	12.6
Samoa	24.3	13.8	...	...
Solomon Islands	14.3	37.4	...	...
Tonga	27.2	18.9	1.6	1.6
Tuvalu	0.8	7.6	...	...
Vanuatu	34.7	17.7	...	...
Developed ADB Member Economies	**...**	**...**		
Australia	...	...	27.8	28.5
Japan	...	...	55.6	56.6
New Zealand	...	...	17.6	21.3
DEVELOPING ADB MEMBER ECONOMIES[c]	**17,422.7**	**25,675.9**		

... = data not available, $ = United States dollars, ADB = Asian Development Bank.

a Gross disbursements of total official development assistance and other official flows from all donors in support of infrastructure.
b Includes only reporting economies with data corresponding to the year heading.
c For estimating aggregates, imputation was done for economies with missing data by substituting available data from the nearest years.

Sources: United Nations. SDG Global Database. https://unstats.un.org/sdgs/dataportal (accessed 14 July 2022); For Taipei,China: United Nations Industrial Development Organization. Statistics Data Portal. https://stat.unido.org/SDG (accessed 14 July 2022).

Click on the indicator name in the table header to access the time series in the Key Indicators Database

Goal 9. Build resilient infrastructure, promote inclusive and sustainable industrialization, and foster innovation

Table 1.9.6: Selected Indicators for Sustainable Development Goal 9—Coverage by Mobile Networks

ADB Regional Member	Target 9.c: Significantly increase access to information and communications technology and strive to provide universal and affordable access to the internet in least developed countries by 2020					
	9.c.1.a: Proportion of Population Covered by 2G Mobile Networks (%)		9.c.1.b: Proportion of Population Covered by 3G Mobile Networks (%)		9.c.1.c: Proportion of Population Covered by LTE Mobile Networks (%)	
	2010	2020	2010	2020	2012	2020
Developing ADB Member Economies						
Central and West Asia						
Afghanistan	80.0	90.0	28.0 (2013)	57.0	– (2014)	26.0
Armenia	98.9	100.0	93.0	100.0	17.5	100.0
Azerbaijan	100.0	100.0	69.2	97.6	6.7	93.0
Georgia	99.0	100.0	74.4 (2012)	100.0	8.9 (2013)	99.7
Kazakhstan	95.0	98.0	45.7 (2012)	93.4	2.7	81.3
Kyrgyz Republic	96.0	99.3	32.0 (2011)	91.0	0.5 (2014)	85.0
Pakistan	75.0 (2012)	88.8	– (2012)	76.7	–	68.8
Tajikistan	60.0 (2015)	90.0	60.0 (2014)	90.0	8.4	80.0
Turkmenistan	60.0 (2015)	95.8	28.5 (2012)	75.8	6.0 (2013)	67.0
Uzbekistan	92.0 (2012)	99.3	40.0 (2012)	90.0	1.0 (2014)	65.9
East Asia						
China, People's Republic of	99.5	99.9	43.6 (2014)	99.9	10.0 (2013)	99.9
Hong Kong, China	100.0	100.0	99.0	99.0	91.7	99.0
Korea, Republic of	99.9	99.9	99.0	99.9	99.0 (2014)	99.9
Mongolia	85.0	100.0	49.8	100.0	6.9 (2016)	73.0
Taipei,China	...	...	...	...	...	...
South Asia						
Bangladesh	96.0	99.6	1.0 (2012)	97.8	59.0 (2014)	97.8
Bhutan	98.0	98.0	15.0	95.0	5.0 (2013)	80.0
India	93.5 (2013)	99.1	36.5 (2012)	98.6	2.0 (2014)	98.5
Maldives	100.0	100.0	57.1	100.0	11.4 (2013)	100.0
Nepal	35.1	93.0	30.0 (2014)	54.1	– (2014)	45.0
Sri Lanka	98.0	99.0	72.0 (2012)	96.0	5.0	96.0
Southeast Asia						
Brunei Darussalam	97.0 (2015)	99.0	80.8 (2012)	96.0	5.0 (2013)	95.3
Cambodia	99.0	99.0	60.0 (2014)	88.6	9.0 (2014)	91.5
Indonesia	100.0 (2011)	97.9	60.0 (2014)	96.3	5.0 (2013)	96.1
Lao People's Democratic Republic	59.0	95.0	17.0	82.0	2.0 (2014)	43.0
Malaysia	95.0	96.7	81.1	95.3	15.0 (2013)	93.5
Myanmar	73.0 (2014)	96.7	9.7 (2012)	90.9	– (2014)	93.9
Philippines	99.0	99.0	69.0	96.0	6.0	80.0
Singapore	100.0	100.0	100.0	100.0	99.0 (2014)	100.0
Thailand	100.0 (2011)	98.8	80.0 (2013)	98.8	– (2014)	98.0
Timor-Leste	86.0	96.5	96.0 (2014)	96.5	– (2015)	45.0
Viet Nam	94.0 (2015)	99.8	31.0 (2012)	99.8	– (2014)	99.5
The Pacific						
Cook Islands	...	100.0	20.2 (2014)	55.0	55.0 (2017)	55.0
Fiji	88.0 (2015)	98.0	30.0 (2013)	96.0	15.0 (2014)	80.0
Kiribati	70.0 (2015)	73.4	15.0 (2013)	72.1	10.0 (2013)	53.3
Marshall Islands	65.0 (2015)	65.0	...	...	...	...
Micronesia, Federated States of	80.0 (2015)	80.0	– (2014)	15.0	– (2015)	– (2017)
Nauru	98.0	98.0	98.0	98.0	– (2014)	30.0
Niue	...	...	– (2014)	– (2015)	...	...
Palau	95.0	98.0 (2015)	88.0 (2015)	88.0	...	...
Papua New Guinea	89.0 (2015)	89.0	60.0 (2014)	64.4	7.0 (2014)	50.0
Samoa	97.0 (2015)	97.0	31.4 (2012)	91.0	– (2015)	49.0
Solomon Islands	91.0 (2015)	95.0	27.1 (2012)	45.0	11.5 (2015)	25.0
Tonga	92.0 (2015)	99.0	15.0 (2013)	99.0	– (2014)	96.0
Tuvalu	19.0 (2015)	50.0	19.0 (2015)	48.0	– (2015)	– (2017)
Vanuatu	87.0	90.0	23.0 (2011)	70.0	18.0 (2015)	70.0
Developed ADB Member Economies						
Australia	99.0	99.5	99.0	99.5	52.2	99.5
Japan	99.9	99.9	99.9 (2012)	99.9	84.0	99.9
New Zealand	97.0	98.5	97.0	98.5	50.0 (2014)	97.5

... = data not available, – = magnitude equals zero, 2G = second generation, 3G = third generation, ADB = Asian Development Bank, LTE = Long-Term Evolution.

Source: United Nations. SDG Global Database. https://unstats.un.org/sdgs/dataportal (accessed 22 July 2022).

Table 1.10.1: Selected Indicators for Sustainable Development Goal 10—Household Expenditure or Income Growth

ADB Regional Member	Target 10.1: By 2030, progressively achieve and sustain income growth of the bottom 40% of the population at a rate higher than the national average			
	10.1.1.a: Growth Rates of Household Expenditure or Income per Capita among the Bottom 40% of the Population[a,b] (%)		10.1.1.b: Growth Rates of Household Expenditure or Income per Capita[a,b] (%)	
Developing ADB Member Economies				
Central and West Asia				
Afghanistan	...		...	
Armenia[c]	1.3	(2013–2018)	2.4	(2013–2018)
Azerbaijan	...		...	
Georgia[c]	-0.6	(2015–2020)	-1.5	(2015–2020)
Kazakhstan[c]	-0.3	(2013–2018)	-0.2	(2013–2018)
Kyrgyz Republic[c]	0.8	(2015–2020)	1.1	(2015–2020)
Pakistan[c]	1.3	(2013–2018)	1.3	(2013–2018)
Tajikistan[c]	1.3	(2009–2015)	2.7	(2009–2015)
Turkmenistan	...		...	
Uzbekistan	...		...	
East Asia				
China, People's Republic of[c]	7.2	(2014–2019)	6.3	(2014–2019)
Hong Kong, China	...		...	
Korea, Republic of[d]	2.5	(2012–2016)	2.3	(2012–2016)
Mongolia[c]	-3.7	(2014–2018)	-3.2	(2014–2018)
Taipei,China	...		...	
South Asia				
Bangladesh[c]	1.4	(2010–2016)	1.5	(2010–2016)
Bhutan[c]	1.6	(2012–2017)	1.7	(2012–2017)
India[c]	3.2	(2004–2011)	3.7	(2004–2011)
Maldives	...		...	
Nepal[c]	8.3	(2003–2010)	4.7	(2003–2010)
Sri Lanka[c]	3.7	(2012–2016)	4.1	(2012–2016)
Southeast Asia				
Brunei Darussalam	...		...	
Cambodia	...		...	
Indonesia[c]	4.6	(2015–2019)	3.8	(2015–2019)
Lao People's Democratic Republic[c]	1.9	(2012–2018)	3.1	(2012–2018)
Malaysia[d]	7.0	(2011–2015)	5.0	(2011–2015)
Myanmar[c]	9.5	(2015–2017)	1.3	(2015–2017)
Philippines[d]	6.1	(2015–2018)	3.4	(2015–2018)
Singapore	...		...	
Thailand[c]	0.7	(2015–2019)	0.1	(2015–2019)
Timor-Leste	...		...	
Viet Nam[c]	5.8	(2014–2018)	6.5	(2014–2018)
The Pacific				
Cook Islands	...		...	
Fiji[c]	1.2	(2008–2013)	-0.5	(2008–2013)
Kiribati	...		...	
Marshall Islands	...		...	
Micronesia, Federated States of	...		...	
Nauru	...		...	
Niue	...		...	
Palau	...		...	
Papua New Guinea	...		...	
Samoa	...		...	
Solomon Islands	...		...	
Tonga[c]	1.0	(2009–2015)	0.6	(2009–2015)
Tuvalu	...		...	
Vanuatu	...		...	
Developed ADB Member Economies				
Australia[d]	4.3	(2003–2010)	4.6	(2003–2010)
Japan	...		...	
New Zealand	...		...	

... = data not available, – = magnitude equals zero, ADB = Asian Development Bank.

a Based on real mean per capita consumption or income measured at 2011 purchasing power parity using the World Bank's Poverty and Inequality Platform (https://www.pip.worldbank.org). Data reported are based on consumption, except for Australia, Malaysia, the Philippines, and the Republic of Korea, which are based on income.

b For the data collection periods in brackets, the initial year refers to the most recently conducted survey prior to the latest survey (only surveys conducted between 3 and 7 years before the latest survey are considered). The final year refers to the latest survey (those available between 2010 and 2020).

c Estimated from individual consumption data.

d Estimated from individual income data.

Source: United Nations. SDG Global Database. https://unstats.un.org/sdgs/dataportal (accessed 17 July 2022).

Goal 11. Make cities and human settlements inclusive, safe, resilient, and sustainable

Table 1.11.1: Selected Indicators for Sustainable Development Goal 11—Sustainable Cities and Environment

ADB Regional Member	Target 11.1: By 2030, ensure access for all to adequate, safe, and affordable housing and basic services, and upgrade slums. 11.1.1: Proportion of Urban Population Living in Slums, Informal Settlements, or Inadequate Housing (%)		Target 11.5: By 2030, significantly reduce the number of deaths and the number of people affected, and substantially decrease the direct economic losses relative to global gross domestic product caused by disasters, including water-related disasters, with a focus on protecting the poor and people in vulnerable situations. 11.5.2: Direct Economic Loss Attributed to Disasters[a] ($ million)		Target 11.6: By 2030, reduce the adverse per capita environmental impact of cities, including by paying special attention to air quality and municipal and other waste management. 11.6.2: Annual Mean Levels (μg/m³) of Fine Particulate Matter (e.g., PM2.5 and PM10) in Cities[b] (population weighted)	
	2010	2020	2010	2020	Total 2019	Urban 2019
Developing ADB Member Economies						
Central and West Asia						
Afghanistan	64.8	73.3	...	25,125.5 (2019)	69.4	80.3
Armenia	10.4	8.4	7.0	7.9	32.5	34.5
Azerbaijan	26.9	...	...	– (2017)	23.5	25.1
Georgia	10.9	7.1	...	0.0	18.6	20.3
Kazakhstan	10.5	0.8	–	19.1	27.9	37.3
Kyrgyz Republic	24.8	2.4	1.4 (2012)	7.0	38.1	40.2
Pakistan	63.6	56.0	– (2009)	...	54.3	55.4
Tajikistan	37.5	17.1	...	5.1	53.2	56.1
Turkmenistan	9.8	8.5	...	– (2019)	26.6	26.0
Uzbekistan	...	...	...	4.3	41.8	44.9
East Asia						
China, People's Republic of	...	...	...	...	37.7	39.6
Hong Kong, China	...	...	...	...	...	...
Korea, Republic of	...	...	– (2013)	68.3	23.7	24.0
Mongolia	37.7	17.9	...	154.2	40.9	49.9
Taipei,China	...	...	...	...	...	...
South Asia						
Bangladesh	55.1	51.9	– (2008)	...	52.9	53.5
Bhutan	...	...	...	269.4 (2018)	32.7	19.7
India	51.8	49.0	...	– (2019)	58.5	62.4
Maldives	39.9	34.8	– (2008)	– (2019)	13.3	13.2
Nepal	51.9	40.3	–	–	46.2	47.1
Sri Lanka	...	...	– (2009)	115.4	26.7	27.3
Southeast Asia						
Brunei Darussalam	...	...	...	...	6.7	6.6
Cambodia	56.6	39.7	34.9	– (2018)	22.1	23.3
Indonesia	26.9	19.4	–	–	19.2	19.7
Lao People's Democratic Republic	37.3	21.8	–	...	21.1	24.2
Malaysia	...	...	7.1	112.8	21.5	23.6
Myanmar	45.4	58.3	2,518.8	–	30.3	30.8
Philippines	42.9	36.6	...	–	22.4	24.1
Singapore	...	...	...	...	12.8	12.8
Thailand	12.0	6.8	...	...	24.6	25.3
Timor-Leste	50.0	33.9	–	– (2017)	19.2	20.1
Viet Nam	20.6	5.8	–	...	23.2	24.4
The Pacific						
Cook Islands	...	...	–	–	8.2	8.2
Fiji	12.5	9.4	–	24.3	7.9	8.6
Kiribati	...	...	...	–	7.7	8.0
Marshall Islands	...	...	– (2011)	–	7.3	7.6
Micronesia, Federated States of	...	...	– (2009)	–	7.9	8.3
Nauru	...	...	– (2012)	–	7.7	7.7
Niue	...	...	...	...	7.3	...
Palau	...	...	–	–	7.6	7.7
Papua New Guinea	...	...	...	...	8.4	9.0
Samoa	...	...	– (2009)	–	9.1	9.4
Solomon Islands	...	...	–	–	8.6	9.3
Tonga	...	...	– (2011)	–	7.9	8.1
Tuvalu	...	...	– (2011)	–	7.4	...
Vanuatu	...	...	–	–	8.3	8.8
Developed ADB Member Economies						
Australia	...	...	– (2013)	–	9.1	9.3
Japan	...	...	...	2,960.7	10.8	11.1
New Zealand	...	...	...	857.3	8.8	8.9

... = data not available, – = magnitude equals zero, 0.0 = magnitude is less than half of unit employed, $ = United States dollars, ADB = Asian Development Bank, m^3 = cubic meter, PM = particulate matter, μg = microgram.

a The data are submitted to the United Nation's SDG Global Database by the United Nations Office for Disaster Risk Reduction and have been extracted from two sources: (i) the Sendai Framework Monitoring System as provided by designated national focal points; and (ii) Desinventar disaster loss databases. Some of the data have not undergone an official validation process and may be subject to revision at a later date.

b Data are estimates as published on the United Nations' SDG Global Database.

Source: United Nations. SDG Global Database. https://unstats.un.org/sdgs/indicators/dataportal (accessed 20 July 2022).

Table 1.12.1: Selected Indicators for Sustainable Development Goal 12—Responsible Consumption and Production

ADB Regional Member	Target 12.2: By 2030, achieve the sustainable management and efficient use of natural resources							
	12.2.1: Material Footprint				12.2.2: Domestic Material Consumption			
	All (t million)		Per Capita (t)		All (t million)		Per Capita (t)	
	2010	2019	2010	2019	2010	2019	2010	2019
Developing ADB Member Economies								
Central and West Asia	**1,412.7**	**1,987.6**	**...**	**...**	**1,486.7**	**2,164.5**	**...**	**...**
Afghanistan	51.7	52.6	1.8	1.4	46.6	46.5	1.5	1.2
Armenia	18.6	17.6	6.5	6.0	30.0	49.2	10.0	15.9
Azerbaijan	86.5	106.1	9.6	10.6	68.2	84.1	7.6	8.2
Georgia	37.8	41.4	9.2	10.3	24.9	45.1	5.5	10.0
Kazakhstan	478.2	638.3	29.4	34.4	431.7	561.5	26.6	30.3
Kyrgyz Republic	36.6	50.2	6.8	7.8	33.5	55.5	5.8	8.4
Pakistan	500.7	747.8	2.8	3.5	555.9	852.5	3.1	3.9
Tajikistan	22.1	53.6	2.9	5.7	17.8	59.2	2.3	6.3
Turkmenistan	29.0	78.0	5.7	13.1	48.7	80.2	10.1	13.9
Uzbekistan	151.6	202.0	5.3	6.1	229.5	330.7	8.1	9.9
East Asia[a]	**25,157.0**	**33,479.1**	**...**	**...**	**...**	**...**	**...**	**...**
China, People's Republic of	23,584.8	31,480.2	17.2	22.0	26,277.8	32,531.7	19.3	22.9
Hong Kong, China	488.2	837.2	70.1	112.6	70.1	131.9	5.5	12.9
Korea, Republic of	1,056.7	1,127.5	21.3	22.0	769.9	904.9	17.0	19.9
Mongolia	27.3	34.2	10.0	10.6	82.1	161.4	29.9	48.5
Taipei,China[b]	...	...	...	...	307.5	276.7	13.3	11.6
South Asia	**6,112.0**	**7,887.6**	**...**	**...**	**6,143.1**	**8,125.1**	**...**	**...**
Bangladesh	357.1	470.2	2.4	2.9	372.0	414.4	2.4	2.4
Bhutan	17.6	24.7	25.7	32.4	13.0	21.1	18.9	26.2
India	5,577.6	7,140.1	4.5	5.2	5,587.9	7,443.4	4.6	5.5
Maldives	5.2	...	14.2	...	2.2	5.8	4.0	8.2
Nepal	67.0	159.7	2.5	5.6	89.4	160.7	3.1	5.3
Sri Lanka	87.6	92.9	4.3	4.4	78.6	79.8	3.5	3.0
Southeast Asia[a]	**4,118.2**	**5,650.2**	**...**	**...**	**4,354.0**	**5,695.3**	**...**	**...**
Brunei Darussalam	25.1	37.1	64.7	85.7	7.6	4.4	18.2	9.1
Cambodia	92.2	94.0	6.4	5.7	123.0	124.0	8.3	6.8
Indonesia	1,259.6	1,831.4	5.2	6.8	1,218.6	1,814.2	4.9	6.5
Lao People's Democratic Republic	41.5	69.1	6.6	9.6	52.0	104.7	8.0	14.3
Malaysia	443.1	625.8	15.7	19.6	491.5	676.8	17.8	21.8
Myanmar	105.8	111.5	2.1	2.1	229.3	229.1	4.4	3.9
Philippines	451.2	948.3	4.8	8.8	433.3	886.3	4.5	7.8
Singapore	261.8	292.7	51.0	50.4	114.3	119.7	19.8	17.6
Thailand	676.3	817.9	10.1	11.7	720.1	834.3	11.3	12.5
Timor-Leste	...	...	...	...	2.6	6.1	2.3	4.2
Viet Nam	761.5	822.3	8.7	8.5	961.7	895.8	10.7	9.3
The Pacific[a]			**...**	**...**	**113.7**	**97.4**	**...**	**...**
Cook Islands	...	...	...	...	0.1	0.1	1.8	1.4
Fiji	5.1	...	6.0	...	8.7	5.1	8.8	4.6
Kiribati	...	...	...	...	0.5	0.6	4.9	5.2
Marshall Islands	...	...	...	...	0.1	0.1	1.1	1.0
Micronesia, Federated States of	...	...	...	...	0.4	0.4	2.8	2.7
Nauru	...	...	...	...	0.4	0.1	41.6	6.9
Niue	...	...	...	...	...	...	...	...
Palau	...	...	...	...	0.1	0.2	0.3	3.1
Papua New Guinea	34.2	45.9	4.7	5.2	94.7	74.6	12.6	8.0
Samoa	1.3	...	7.2	...	1.2	1.6	5.8	6.8
Solomon Islands	...	...	...	...	3.5	8.3	4.2	9.3
Tonga	...	...	...	...	1.4	3.8	12.0	35.6
Tuvalu	...	...	...	...	0.0	0.0	0.1	0.5
Vanuatu	1.9	...	7.9	...	2.5	2.5	10.2	7.9
Developed ADB Member Economies	**3,668.5**	**3,633.3**	**...**	**...**	**2,336.7**	**2,585.3**	**...**	**...**
Australia	1,005.9	1,180.1	45.4	46.8	847.5	1,082.4	36.4	40.6
Japan	2,530.3	2,306.3	19.7	18.2	1,344.3	1,342.4	10.9	10.9
New Zealand	132.3	146.8	30.3	30.7	144.9	160.5	31.6	30.8

... = data not available, 0.0 = magnitude is less than half of unit employed, ADB = Asian Development Bank, t = metric ton.

a Regional aggregates include reporting economies only.
b For 2000–2019, data were based on data from the Organisation for Economic Co-operation and Development.

Source: For Indicator 12.2.1: Organisation for Economic Co-operation and Development. OECD.Stat Database. https://stats.oecd.org/ (accessed 21 July 2022). For Indicator 12.2.2: United Nations. SDG Global Database. https://unstats.un.org/sdgs/dataportal/database/ (accessed 21 July 2022); and for Taipei,China: Organisation for Economic Co-operation and Development. OECD.Stat Database. https://stats.oecd.org/viewhtml.aspx?datasetcode=MATERIAL_RESOURCES&lang=en (accessed 21 July 2022).

Click on the indicator name in the table header to access the time series in the Key Indicators Database

Goal 13. Take urgent action to combat climate change and its impacts

Table 1.13.1: Selected Indicators for Sustainable Development Goal 13—Impact of Disasters and Risk Reduction Strategies

ADB Regional Member	Target 13.1: Strengthen resilience and adaptive capacity to climate-related hazards and natural disasters in all countries				
	13.1.1.a: Number of Persons Affected by Disaster[a]		13.1.1.b: Number of Deaths Due to Disaster[a]		13.1.2: Countries that Adopt and Implement National Disaster Risk Reduction Strategies in Line with the Sendai Framework for Disaster Risk Reduction 2015–2030[b,c]
	2010	2020	2010	2020	2020
Developing ADB Member Economies					
Central and West Asia					
Afghanistan	...	372,261 (2019)	...	368 (2019)	0.73 (2019)
Armenia	7,641	169,952	155	3,284	0.70
Azerbaijan	...	– (2017)	...	– (2017)	– (2017)
Georgia	...	227,492	...	2,516	0.98
Kazakhstan	–	154,115	9	2,793	0.78
Kyrgyz Republic	–	81,771	158	3,957	0.90 (2019)
Pakistan	2,963	404	2,199	10,599	0.80
Tajikistan	...	2,085	...	8	1.00
Turkmenistan	...	– (2019)	...	– (2019)	0.75 (2019)
Uzbekistan	...	99,640	...	1	1.00
East Asia					
China, People's Republic of	...	7,300,250	...	522	1.00
Hong Kong, China	...	...	...	...	...
Korea, Republic of	93,032	131,737	28	1,070	1.00
Mongolia	9,086	6,222	226	255	1.00
Taipei,China	...	...	...	...	...
South Asia					
Bangladesh	–	–	96	7,840	– (2021)
Bhutan	1,711	– (2019)	2,763	21 (2019)	0.50 (2018)
India	–	–	7,489	6,347	1.00
Maldives	132 (2008)	– (2019)	4 (2008)	1 (2019)	– (2017)
Nepal	182,678	78,543	1,002	558	0.75 (2019)
Sri Lanka	1,193,504	64,507	50	40	0.93
Southeast Asia					
Brunei Darussalam	...	...	...	...	...
Cambodia	27,264	20	91	–	0.65 (2019)
Indonesia	333,235	4,972,765	1,630	22,514	0.88
Lao People's Democratic Republic	44,425	...	50	...	...
Malaysia	9,882	207,819	4	479	0.65
Myanmar	545,156	1,830	55	21	0.70 (2017)
Philippines	1,489,711	3,327,096	192	13,610	0.73
Singapore	...	...	...	...	...
Thailand	...	142,780 (2018)	...	81 (2018)	0.68
Timor-Leste	26,207	– (2017)	10	...	...
Viet Nam	639,292	...	60	...	...
The Pacific					
Cook Islands	4,443	–	3	–	...
Fiji	7,640	237,073	3	16	0.98
Kiribati	85 (2008)	15	...	–	0.93
Marshall Islands	– (2011)	56,718	– (2011)	1	–
Micronesia, Federated States of	– (2011)	–	2 (2011)	–	0.58
Nauru	...	...	...	...	0.60
Niue	– (2012)	–	– (2012)	–	...
Palau	– (2011)	...	– (2011)	...	0.73
Papua New Guinea	–	3,297	16	40	0.78
Samoa	10,433 (2009)	195	369 (2009)	–	0.73
Solomon Islands	1,456	2,339	4	35	0.03 (2021)
Tonga	–	68	– (2011)	–	0.48
Tuvalu	– (2011)	4,548	– (2011)	–	0.30
Vanuatu	500	246,802	–	3	0.65
Developed ADB Member Economies					
Australia	15,419	13,973	38 (2011)	92	0.70
Japan	–	–	89	155 (2019)	1.00
New Zealand	–	745	–	25	0.88

... = data not available, – = magnitude equals zero, ADB = Asian Development Bank.

a The data are submitted to the SDG Global Database by the United Nations Office for Disaster Risk Reduction and have been extracted from two sources: (i) the Sendai Framework Monitoring System as provided by designated national focal points; and (ii) Desinventar disaster loss databases. Some of the data have not undergone an official validation process and may be subject to revision at a later date.

b Economies displaying data in this column have adopted and implemented national disaster risk reduction strategies. Data refer to the score for adoption and implementation of national disaster risk reduction strategies in line with the Sendai Framework. The scores indicate the compliance of alignment of national strategies with the Sendai Framework, based on self-assessments of the economy using 10 criteria for monitoring the progress of national national disaster risk reduction strategies. The score ranges are as follows: 1 = comprehensive alignment, 0.75 = substantial alignment, 0.50 = moderate alignment, 0.25 = limited alignment, 0 = no alignment.

c Some of the data have not undergone an official validation process and may be subject to revision at a later date.

Source: United Nations. SDG Global Database. https://unstats.un.org/sdgs/dataportal/database (accessed 16 July 2022).

Goal 14. Conserve and sustainably use the oceans, seas, and marine resources for sustainable development

Table 1.14.1: Selected Indicators for Sustainable Development Goal 14—Life Below Water

ADB Regional Member	Target 14.5: By 2020, conserve at least 10% of coastal and marine areas, consistent with national and international law and based on the best available scientific information			
	14.5.1.a: Average Proportion of Marine Key Biodiversity Areas Covered by Protected Areas (%)		14.5.1.b: Coverage of Protected Areas in Relation to Marine Areas (Exclusive Economic Zones)[a] (%)	14.5.1.c: Protected Marine Areas (Exclusive Economic Zones)[a] (km^2)
	2010	2021	2021	2021
Developing ADB Member Economies				
Central and West Asia				
Afghanistan	...	...	–	–
Armenia	...	...	–	–
Azerbaijan	...	...	0.0	37.2
Georgia	35.6	35.6	0.7	153.0
Kazakhstan	...	...	48.5	57,768.7
Kyrgyz Republic	...	...	–	–
Pakistan	14.6	14.6	0.3	567.5
Tajikistan	...	...	–	–
Turkmenistan	...	...	2.5	1,956.8
Uzbekistan	...	...	–	–
East Asia				
China, People's Republic of	6.8	7.1	0.7	5,876.9
Hong Kong, China	32.5	32.5	–	–
Korea, Republic of	32.7	38.7	2.4	7,951.5
Mongolia	...	...	–	–
Taipei,China	...	...	1.1 (2015)	3,846.0 (2015)
South Asia				
Bangladesh	34.4	34.5	5.3	4,454.3
Bhutan	...	...	–	–
India	4.2	4.2	0.0	128.1
Maldives	–	–	0.1	825.5
Nepal	...	...	–	–
Sri Lanka	46.3	50.0	0.1	320.9
Southeast Asia				
Brunei Darussalam	5.4	5.4	0.6	149.7
Cambodia	41.2	51.0	1.4	691.5
Indonesia	15.4	25.7	2.9	174,732.9
Lao People's Democratic Republic	...	...	–	–
Malaysia	16.1	19.7	5.4	24,414.4
Myanmar	9.3	19.2	0.5	2,488.7
Philippines	32.5	46.6	3.6	66,645.2
Singapore	3.3	3.3	0.0	0.1
Thailand	36.3	44.0	4.3	13,319.7
Timor-Leste	18.7	19.6	1.4	581.2
Viet Nam	18.0	23.9	0.5	3,362.9
The Pacific				
Cook Islands	17.8	50.1	99.9	1,970,508.3
Fiji	16.5	16.5	0.9	11,847.0
Kiribati	32.9	32.9	11.9	412,755.0
Marshall Islands	6.7	7.8	0.3	5,221.7
Micronesia, Federated States of	1.6	1.6	0.0	478.7
Nauru	–	–	–	–
Niue	...	...	40.2	128,042.0
Palau	52.2	72.3	100.0	608,158.4
Papua New Guinea	1.9	1.9	0.1	3,343.7
Samoa	54.2	54.2	0.1	95.2
Solomon Islands	3.1	3.2	0.1	1,539.8
Tonga	19.2	19.2	0.1	334.2
Tuvalu	...	...	...	...
Vanuatu	3.3	3.3	0.1	544.2
Developed ADB Member Economies				
Australia	54.4	65.5	40.9	3,036,805.3
Japan	45.4	66.0	8.0	322,999.0
New Zealand	46.5	47.1	29.8	1,224,140.2

... = data not available, – = magnitude equals zero, 0.0 = magnitude is less than half of unit employed, ADB = Asian Development Bank, km^2 = square kilometer.

a An Exclusive Economic Zone comprises an area that extends either from the coast, or, in federal systems, from the seaward boundaries of the constituent states (3 to 12 nautical miles, in most cases) to 200 nautical miles (370 kilometres) off the coast.

Sources: United Nations. SDG Global Database. https://unstats.un.org/sdgs/indicators/database/ (accessed 12 July 2022). For Taipei,China: United Nations Environment Programme World Conservation Monitoring Centre. Protected Area Profile: World Database 2022. https://www.protectedplanet.net (accessed 27 July 2022).

Click on the indicator name in the table header to access the time series in the Key Indicators Database

Goal 15. Protect, restore, and promote sustainable use of terrestrial ecosystems; sustainably manage forests; combat desertification and halt and reverse land degradation; and halt biodiversity loss

Table 1.15.1: Selected Indicators for Sustainable Development Goal 15—Protection of Ecosystems and Biodiversity

ADB Regional Member	Target 15.1: By 2020, ensure the conservation, restoration, and sustainable use of terrestrial and inland freshwater ecosystems and their services, in particular forests, wetlands, mountains, and drylands, in line with obligations under international agreements					
	15.1.1: Forest Area as a Proportion of Total Land Area[a] (%)		15.1.2: Proportion of Important Sites for Terrestrial and Freshwater Biodiversity that are Covered by Protected Areas (%)			
			Terrestrial		Freshwater	
	2010	2020	2010	2021	2010	2021
Developing ADB Member Economies						
Central and West Asia	**3.9**	**4.0**	...	...	...	...
Afghanistan	1.9	1.9	5.8	46.4	–	60.9
Armenia	11.6	11.5	21.6	22.6	26.8	30.5
Azerbaijan	12.5	13.7	36.1	36.6	12.7	14.5
Georgia	40.6	40.6	34.4	40.3	22.5	38.9
Kazakhstan	1.1	1.3	26.2	28.5	19.7	20.5
Kyrgyz Republic	6.4	6.9	23.6	23.6	35.4	35.4
Pakistan	5.3	4.8	34.8	34.8	35.9	35.9
Tajikistan	2.9	3.1	15.8	16.8	27.9	30.5
Turkmenistan	8.8	8.8	14.0	14.0	12.7	12.7
Uzbekistan	7.7	8.4	15.4	17.7	13.4	13.4
East Asia	**20.1**	**21.8**	...	...	...	...
China, People's Republic of	21.3	23.3	8.6	10.1	6.9	9.6
Hong Kong, China	...	...	48.9	48.9	16.6	16.6
Korea, Republic of	65.7	64.4	33.8	37.6	36.8	36.8
Mongolia	9.1	9.1	40.4	45.0	35.7	41.4
Taipei,China	58.1	60.7	...	...	...	...
South Asia	**24.5**	**25.3**	...	...	...	...
Bangladesh	14.5	14.5	41.5	41.5	–	–
Bhutan	71.0	71.4	45.4	47.0	30.5	34.8
India	23.4	24.3	1.4	6.2	2.6	8.2
Maldives	2.7	2.7	–	–	–	–
Nepal	41.6	41.6	51.7	51.7	35.1	35.1
Sri Lanka	33.5	34.2	41.4	43.7	40.2	43.9
Southeast Asia	**49.7**	**47.1**	...	...	...	...
Brunei Darussalam	72.1	72.1	41.7	41.7	50.0	50.0
Cambodia	60.0	45.7	24.7	54.5	12.9	45.0
Indonesia	53.1	49.1	19.4	25.9	36.3	39.0
Lao People's Democratic Republic	73.4	71.9	36.2	49.7	17.3	30.1
Malaysia	57.7	58.2	31.6	37.0	31.7	32.5
Myanmar	48.1	43.7	18.8	22.3	27.1	27.1
Philippines	22.9	24.1	24.8	42.8	35.4	56.1
Singapore	25.3	21.7	21.1	21.1	–	–
Thailand	39.3	38.9	66.7	68.0	36.3	36.3
Timor-Leste	62.9	61.9	40.7	45.6	–	–
Viet Nam	42.7	46.7	31.1	40.0	29.2	38.2
The Pacific	**78.3**	**77.8**	...	...	...	...
Cook Islands	65.0	65.0	24.4	30.9	–	–
Fiji	58.7	62.4	11.2	11.2	0.1	0.1
Kiribati	1.5	1.5	40.0	40.0	–	–
Marshall Islands	52.2	52.2	8.4	10.1	–	–
Micronesia, Federated States of	91.6	92.0	0.0	0.0	–	–
Nauru	–	–	–	–	–	–
Niue	72.2	72.6	95.3	95.3	–	–
Palau	88.2	90.0	42.7	48.1	–	–
Papua New Guinea	79.9	79.2	7.2	7.3	–	–
Samoa	58.8	57.1	47.0	47.1	–	–
Solomon Islands	90.4	90.1	4.5	4.6	–	–
Tonga	12.4	12.4	26.1	26.1	–	–
Tuvalu	33.3	33.3	...	...	...	...
Vanuatu	36.3	36.3	2.8	2.8	–	–
Developed ADB Member Economies	**19.8**	**20.3**	...	...	...	...
Australia	16.9	17.4	46.0	57.2	29.7	37.4
Japan	68.5	68.4	50.0	64.8	46.7	63.5
New Zealand	37.4	37.6	45.4	46.2	22.9	24.2
DEVELOPING ADB MEMBER ECONOMIES	**23.5**	**24.0**	...	...	...	...
ALL ADB REGIONAL MEMBERS	**22.6**	**23.0**	...	...	...	...

Goal 15. Protect, restore, and promote sustainable use of terrestrial ecosystems; sustainably manage forests; combat desertification and halt and reverse land degradation; and halt biodiversity loss

Table 1.15.1: Selected Indicators for Sustainable Development Goal 15—Protection of Ecosystems and Biodiversity *(continued)*

ADB Regional Member	Target 15.4: By 2030, ensure the conservation of mountain ecosystems, including their biodiversity, in order to enhance their capacity to provide benefits that are essential for sustainable development		Target 15.5: Take urgent and significant action to reduce the degradation of natural habitats, halt the loss of biodiversity and, by 2020, protect and prevent the extinction of threatened species	
	15.4.1: Coverage by Protected Areas of Important Sites for Mountain Biodiversity (%)		15.5.1: Red List Index[b]	
	2010	2021	2010	2021
Developing ADB Member Economies				
Central and West Asia	...	...	...	...
Afghanistan	7.6	45.8	0.84	0.84
Armenia	22.3	23.4	0.83	0.83
Azerbaijan	55.5	55.5	0.91	0.91
Georgia	34.8	40.9	0.89	0.89
Kazakhstan	38.1	45.3	0.87	0.87
Kyrgyz Republic	31.5	31.5	0.99	0.98
Pakistan	35.2	35.2	0.90	0.85
Tajikistan	15.8	16.8	0.99	0.99
Turkmenistan	15.2	15.2	0.98	0.98
Uzbekistan	30.6	35.6	0.98	0.97
East Asia	...	...	...	...
China, People's Republic of	10.2	11.8	0.77	0.73
Hong Kong, China	57.0	57.0	0.84	0.84
Korea, Republic of	20.2	20.2	0.73	0.70
Mongolia	45.0	49.3	0.96	0.96
Taipei,China	...	...	...	...
South Asia	...	...	...	...
Bangladesh	–	–	0.79	0.75
Bhutan	45.4	47.0	0.80	0.80
India	1.1	10.0	0.71	0.67
Maldives	–	–	0.89	0.84
Nepal	62.1	62.1	0.83	0.83
Sri Lanka	29.9	30.4	0.61	0.56
Southeast Asia	...	...	...	...
Brunei Darussalam	69.5	69.5	0.86	0.85
Cambodia	60.8	93.8	0.81	0.78
Indonesia	21.4	27.5	0.80	0.76
Lao People's Democratic Republic	42.4	57.0	0.82	0.82
Malaysia	39.8	48.3	0.75	0.70
Myanmar	33.1	37.1	0.83	0.79
Philippines	21.4	43.3	0.71	0.67
Singapore	–	–	0.89	0.85
Thailand	85.7	85.7	0.81	0.78
Timor-Leste	45.4	50.8	0.88	0.85
Viet Nam	34.1	44.3	0.76	0.71
The Pacific	...	...	...	...
Cook Islands	–	–	0.80	0.77
Fiji	5.5	5.5	0.72	0.70
Kiribati	–	–	0.81	0.77
Marshall Islands	–	–	0.87	0.84
Micronesia, Federated States of	–	–	0.69	0.64
Nauru	–	–	0.81	0.76
Niue	–	–	0.84	0.81
Palau	–	–	0.79	0.69
Papua New Guinea	7.3	7.4	0.87	0.83
Samoa	35.6	35.7	0.77	0.76
Solomon Islands	0.0	0.1	0.79	0.76
Tonga	–	–	0.74	0.72
Tuvalu	...	...	0.87	0.83
Vanuatu	3.8	3.8	0.70	0.66
Developed ADB Member Economies	...	...	...	...
Australia	48.0	68.5	0.85	0.82
Japan	60.1	67.8	0.80	0.76
New Zealand	32.8	34.0	0.67	0.62
DEVELOPING ADB MEMBER ECONOMIES	...	...	...	...
ALL ADB REGIONAL MEMBERS	...	...	...	...

... = data not available, 0.0 = magnitude is less than half of unit employed, – = magnitude equals zero, ADB = Asian Development Bank.

a The regional aggregates are calculated by averaging the combined estimates for each economy. The aggregates for East Asia exclude Hong Kong, China.

b The Red List Index value ranges from 1, which means all species are categorized as "Least Concern" (no species expected to become extinct in the near future), to 0, meaning that all species are categorized as "Extinct". The index therefore indicates how far the set of species has moved overall towards extinction.

Sources: United Nations. SDG Global Database. https://unstats.un.org/sdgs/dataportal (accessed 12 July 2022). For Taipei,China: Government of Taipei,China, Directorate-General of Budget, Accounting and Statistics. https://eng.dgbas.gov.tw/mp.asp (accessed 12 July 2022).

Goal 16. Promote peaceful and inclusive societies for sustainable development; provide access to justice for all; and build effective, accountable, and inclusive institutions at all levels

Table 1.16.1: Selected Indicators for Sustainable Development Goal 16—Peace, Justice, and Strong Institutions

ADB Regional Member	Target 16.1: Significantly reduce all forms of violence and related death rates everywhere		Target 16.3: Promote the rule of law at the national and international levels and ensure equal access to justice for all		Target 16.5: Substantially reduce corruption and bribery in all their forms	Target 16.9: By 2030, provide legal identity for all, including birth registration
	16.1.1: Number of Victims of Intentional Homicide (per 100,000 population)		16.3.2: Unsentenced Detainees as a Proportion of Overall Prison Population (%)		16.5.2: Proportion of Firms Experiencing at least One Bribe Payment Request (%)	16.9.1: Proportion of Children Under 5 Years of Age Whose Births have been Registered with a Civil Authority[a] (%)
	2010	2019	2015	2019	2019	2019
Developing ADB Member Economies						
Central and West Asia						
Afghanistan	3.4	6.7 (2018)	29.5	27.7 (2018)	46.8 (2014)	42.3 (2015)
Armenia	2.0	2.5	28.8	45.8	1.5 (2020)	98.7 (2016)
Azerbaijan	2.3	1.7	16.9	15.9	12.1	93.6 (2006)
Georgia	4.6	1.9	13.5	18.5	1.3	98.5 (2017)
Kazakhstan	8.5	3.2 (2020)	13.8	18.3 (2020)	11.6	99.7 (2015)
Kyrgyz Republic	16.8	2.2	18.0	14.5 (2018)	31.4	98.9 (2018)
Pakistan	7.4	3.8	69.1	66.1 (2018)	30.8 (2013)	42.2 (2018)
Tajikistan	2.4	0.9 (2020)	...	...	11.1	95.8 (2017)
Turkmenistan	4.2 (2006)	...	...	...	...	99.9
Uzbekistan	3.0 (2008)	1.2	...	...	5.9	99.9 (2006)
East Asia						
China, People's Republic of	1.0	0.5 (2018)	...	...	11.6 (2012)	...
Hong Kong, China	0.5	0.3	18.8	18.8	...	...
Korea, Republic of	1.0	0.6	43.9	35.9	...	...
Mongolia	8.8	6.2 (2018)	17.6	25.2	24.7	99.6 (2018)
Taipei,China	0.8	0.8 (2015)	5.5	5.2 (2018)	...	...
South Asia						
Bangladesh	2.7	2.4 (2018)	73.8	81.3	47.7 (2013)	56.0
Bhutan	2.3	2.5 (2020)	26.9 (2017)	14.2	0.9 (2015)	99.9 (2010)
India	3.8	3.0	67.2	69.1	22.7 (2014)	79.7 (2016)
Maldives	1.6	0.6	...	...	...	98.8 (2017)
Nepal	3.0	2.2 (2016)	...	...	14.5 (2013)	77.2
Sri Lanka	3.8	3.5	52.8	57.8 (2018)	10.0 (2011)	97.2 (2007)
Southeast Asia						
Brunei Darussalam	0.3	...	7.1	7.1 (2018)	...	...
Cambodia	2.3	...	49.3	28.7 (2018)	64.7 (2016)	73.3 (2014)
Indonesia	0.4	0.4 (2017)	33.2	30.7 (2018)	30.6 (2015)	77.0 (2021)
Lao People's Democratic Republic	...	...	...	...	40.3 (2018)	73.0 (2017)
Malaysia	1.9	...	25.8	27.5	28.2 (2015)	...
Myanmar	1.6	0.0 (2020)	...	...	29.3 (2016)	81.3 (2016)
Philippines	9.2	4.4	69.1	59.2	17.2 (2015)	91.8 (2017)
Singapore	0.4	0.2	10.6	10.5	...	99.9 (2020)
Thailand	5.4	2.6 (2017)	18.6	9.9	9.9 (2016)	99.8
Timor-Leste	3.6	4.1 (2015)	78.3	23.2 (2018)	44.2 (2015)	60.4 (2016)
Viet Nam	1.5	...	...	12.4 (2018)	26.1 (2015)	96.1 (2014)
The Pacific						
Cook Islands	3.5 (2012)	...	21.6	14.6 (2018)	...	100.0 (2017)
Fiji	2.3	2.2 (2020)	22.7	25.9 (2018)	10.5 (2009)	86.6 (2021)
Kiribati	3.9	...	9.8	5.4 (2018)	...	91.6
Marshall Islands	...	...	...	...	...	83.8 (2017)
Micronesia, Federated States of	...	0.9	...	...	4.6 (2009)	...
Nauru	...	...	...	...	...	95.9 (2013)
Niue	...	...	...	...	...	...
Palau	...	11.2 (2018)	...	...	...	...
Papua New Guinea	9.8	...	37.9	37.8 (2018)	26.4 (2015)	13.4 (2018)
Samoa	8.6	6.6 (2018)	5.2	6.5 (2018)	30.5 (2009)	66.9 (2020)
Solomon Islands	3.8 (2008)	...	61.3	50.4 (2018)	43.8 (2015)	88.0 (2015)
Tonga	1.0	2.9	7.4	7.4 (2018)	24.9 (2009)	97.7
Tuvalu	9.5	–	...	...	...	87.2 (2020)
Vanuatu	...	0.7	12.1	22.4 (2018)	11.9 (2009)	43.4 (2013)
Developed ADB Member Economies						
Australia	1.0	0.9	26.4	32.3	...	100.0 (2017)
Japan	0.4	0.3	11.3	12.4	...	100.0 (2017)
New Zealand	1.0	2.6	25.0	36.3	...	100.0 (2017)

... = data not available, – = magnitude equals zero, 0.0 = magnitude is less than half of unit employed, ADB = Asian Development Bank.

a Changes in the definition of birth registration were made from the second and third rounds of Multiple Indicator Cluster Surveys (MICS2 and MICS3) to the fourth round (MICS4). In order to allow for comparability with the latter round, data from MICS2 and MICS3 on birth registration were recalculated according to the MICS4 indicator definition. Therefore, the recalculated data presented here may differ from estimates included in MICS2 and MICS3 national reports.

Sources: For Indicator 16.1.1: United Nations Office on Drugs and Crime. dataUNODC. https://dataunodc.un.org/ (accessed 15 July 2022). For Indicator 16.3.2: United Nations. SDG Global Database. https://unstats.un.org/sdgs/dataportal (accessed 15 July 2022). For Indicator 16.5.2: World Bank. World Development Indicators. https://data.worldbank.org/indicator (accessed 15 July 2022). For Indicator 16.9.1: United Nations Children's Fund (UNICEF). UNICEF Data Warehouse. https://data.unicef.org/dv_index/ (accessed 15 July 2022).

Click on the indicator name in the table header to access the time series in the Key Indicators Database

Goal 17. Strengthen the means of implementation and revitalize the Global Partnership for Sustainable Development

Table 1.17.1: Selected Indicators for Sustainable Development Goal 17—Financial Sustainability of Developing Economies

ADB Regional Member	Target 17.4: Assist developing economies in attaining long-term debt sustainability through coordinated policies aimed at fostering debt financing, debt relief, and debt restructuring, as appropriate, and address the external debt of highly indebted poor economies to reduce debt distress. 17.4.1: Debt Service as a Proportion of Exports of Goods and Services (%)		Target 17.9: Enhance international support for implementing effective and targeted capacity-building in developing economies to support national plans to implement all the Sustainable Development Goals, including through North-South, South-South, and triangular cooperation. 17.9.1: Dollar Value of Financial and Technical Assistance Committed to Developing Economies[a] (constant 2020 $ million)	
	2010	2020	Average, 2000–2010	Average, 2011–2020
Developing ADB Member Economies				
Central and West Asia	...	...	**1,631.0**	**3,609.1**
Afghanistan	0.3	2.2	810.5	1,257.6
Armenia	2.7	13.3	68.3	105.3
Azerbaijan	1.1	7.9	36.3	114.5
Georgia	6.3	13.6	86.3	237.3
Kazakhstan	0.5	3.9	95.2	265.8
Kyrgyz Republic	3.7	8.4	53.7	99.3
Pakistan	11.5	26.6	403.3	1,150.2
Tajikistan	2.7	6.4	33.5	50.9
Turkmenistan	...	...	6.2	6.4
Uzbekistan	3.3	5.6	37.6	321.8
East Asia[b]	...	...	**421.1**	**1,021.3**
China, People's Republic of	0.8	1.1	376.9	808.6
Hong Kong, China	...	...	...	...
Korea, Republic of	...	...	...	...
Mongolia	4.3	9.6	44.2	212.7
Taipei,China	...	...	...	...
South Asia	...	...	**1,113.7**	**1,693.1**
Bangladesh	4.5	5.0	246.0	600.5
Bhutan	14.4	5.7	16.9	30.4
India	1.7	5.1	636.3	709.9
Maldives	3.0	15.2	4.7	11.5
Nepal	10.4	11.6	92.7	221.7
Sri Lanka	10.7	33.0	117.1	119.1
Southeast Asia[b]	...	...	**1,706.2**	**3,262.0**
Brunei Darussalam	...	...	...	...
Cambodia	1.0	1.7	94.4	142.2
Indonesia	6.6	15.2	867.8	1,365.1
Lao People's Democratic Republic	4.0	15.1	55.4	88.3
Malaysia	...	...	19.5	11.7
Myanmar	3.1	3.2	15.5	259.0
Philippines	16.0	6.1	158.8	589.4
Singapore	...	...	...	...
Thailand	0.4	0.5	46.5	81.6
Timor-Leste	–	1.1	54.2	45.0
Viet Nam	2.1	1.6	394.0	679.7
The Pacific	...	...	**333.1**	**396.8**
Cook Islands	...	...	2.6	4.2
Fiji	1.3	19.8	17.3	29.6
Kiribati	...	...	7.7	10.3
Marshall Islands	...	...	18.6	9.0
Micronesia, Federated States of	...	...	40.2	16.7
Nauru	...	...	10.1	6.3
Niue	...	...	2.0	6.8
Palau	...	...	1.8	4.0
Papua New Guinea	1.4	10.8	101.4	186.4
Samoa	5.0	18.7	17.4	37.3
Solomon Islands	3.1	1.4	91.3	42.4
Tonga	9.3	3.9	10.9	18.6
Tuvalu	...	...	2.9	5.2
Vanuatu	1.4	7.1	14.5	20.2
Developed ADB Member Economies	...	...	...	...
Australia	...	...	...	...
Japan	...	...	...	...
New Zealand	...	...	...	...
DEVELOPING ADB MEMBER ECONOMIES[b]	...	...	**5,205.1**	**9,982.3**
DEVELOPING ECONOMIES WORLDWIDE[c]	...	...	**21,825.7**	**33,475.2**

... = data not available, – = magnitude equals zero, $ = United States dollars, ADB = Asian Development Bank.

a Technical assistance includes assistance through North-South, South-South, and triangular cooperation. The United Nations dataset and metadata refer to this indicator as total official development assistance (gross disbursements) for technical cooperation.

b For reporting economies only.

c The figures provided refer to aggregates for all developing economies as reported in the United Nations' SDG Global Database.

Source: United Nations. SDG Global Database. https://unstats.un.org/sdgs/dataportal (accessed 20 July 2022).

Goal 17. Strengthen the means of implementation and revitalize the Global Partnership for Sustainable Development

Table 1.17.2: Selected Indicators for Sustainable Development Goal 17—Statistical Capacity Building

ADB Regional Member	Target 17.18: By 2020, enhance capacity-building support to developing countries, including for least developed countries and small island developing states, to increase significantly the availability of high-quality, timely, and reliable data disaggregated by income, gender, age, race, ethnicity, migratory status, disability, geographic location, and other characteristics relevant in national contexts	Target 17.19: By 2030, build on existing initiatives to develop measurements of progress on sustainable development that complement gross domestic product and support statistical capacity-building in developing countries	
	Availability of National Statistical Plan[a]	Value of All Resources Made Available to Strengthen Statistical Capacity in Developing Countries (current $)	Countries that Have Conducted at Least One Population and Housing Census in the Past 10 Years[b]
	2021	2019	2020
Developing ADB Member Economies			
Central and West Asia			
Afghanistan	B	12,479,706.8	...
Armenia	A, B, C, D	542,641.8	2011
Azerbaijan	B	905,399.2	2019
Georgia	B	390,208.8	2014
Kazakhstan	A, B, C	126,269.7	...
Kyrgyz Republic	A, B, C, D	72,580.0	...
Pakistan	A, B, C	24,181,798.7	2017
Tajikistan	C, D, E (2019)	323,965.5	2010
Turkmenistan	...	145,899.6	2012
Uzbekistan	A, B, C, D, E	606,311.5	...
East Asia			
China, People's Republic of	A, B, C	733,619.2	2010
Hong Kong, China	A, B, C	33,428.6 (2016)	2016
Korea, Republic of	B, C	...	2015
Mongolia	A, B, C, D	265,029.4	2010
Taipei,China	...	...	2010
South Asia			
Bangladesh	A, B, C, D	3,694,202.0	2011
Bhutan	A, B, C, D	89,315.7	2017
India	B, C	5,104,537.5	2011
Maldives	B, C	202,105.0	2014
Nepal	B, C	5,998,413.3	2011
Sri Lanka	B	1,305,751.2	2012
Southeast Asia			
Brunei Darussalam	A, C (2019)	43,925.0	2011
Cambodia	B	1,348,437.5	2019
Indonesia	B	4,281,350.7	2010
Lao People's Democratic Republic	B	8,052,217.4	2015
Malaysia	B	392,697.4	2010
Myanmar	B	1,004,588.0	2014
Philippines	B	335,267.1	2015
Singapore	A, B, C	20,291.5 (2018)	2010
Thailand	A, B, C	208,076.7	2010
Timor-Leste	B (2019)	1,112,740.6	2015
Viet Nam	B	1,803,155.1	2019
The Pacific		...	
Cook Islands	B, C (2019)	153,515.9	2016
Fiji	...	425,489.1	2017
Kiribati	...	160,876.6	2015
Marshall Islands	...	214,205.7	2011
Micronesia, Federated States of	...	5,771.0	2010
Nauru	C (2019)	213,145.0	2011
Niue	...	85,449.7	2017
Palau	A, C (2019)	93,695.0	2015
Papua New Guinea	B	289,398.6	2011
Samoa	A, B, C, D	406,377.2	2016
Solomon Islands	B	55,152.4	2019
Tonga	A, B, C, D, E	259,025.0	2016
Tuvalu	B	143,467.0	2012
Vanuatu	C (2019)	91,966.8	2016
Developed ADB Member Economies			
Australia	A, B, C	...	2016
Japan	A, B, C	...	2015
New Zealand	A, B, C, E	46,404.3 (2018)	2018

... = data not available, $ = United States dollars, ADB = Asian Development Bank.

a A = a national statistical plan fully funded, B = a national statistical plan under implementation, C = a national statistical plan with funding from government, D = a national statistical plan with funding from donors, E = a national statistical plan with funding from others.

b Refers to the most recent year in which a population and housing census was conducted.

Sources: United Nations. SDG Global Database. https://unstats.un.org/sdgs/dataportal (accessed 17 July 2022). For Taipei,China: Government of Taipei,China, Directorate-General of Budget, Accounting and Statistics. https://eng.stat.gov.tw/lp.asp?ctNode=1629&CtUnit=779&BaseDSD=7&mp=5 (accessed 18 July 2022).

Data Gaps and Other Data-Related Issues

New and huge data demands. The approved global framework for monitoring the SDGs consists of 231 unique indicators with greater disaggregation and across a wider spectrum of topics than the Millennium Development Goals. With international development support, governments are strengthening their national statistical systems to address data demands across all SDG indicators.

Limited data availability for Sustainable Development Goal indicators. While there have been many improvements to data availability and timeliness since the launch of the SDGs in 2015, there is more to be done. While only 50% of SDG indicators of internationally comparable data for monitoring are available in 2016, sufficient data availability had increased to 93% of indicators by 2022, but significant data gaps still exist in terms of geographic coverage, timeliness, and level of disaggregation.

Differing priorities among national statistics offices with regard to economic data production result in disparities in data availability. Most national statistics offices across Asia and the Pacific conduct population and housing censuses every decade. Such sources provide baseline socioeconomic data that overlap SDG indicators with economic and social dimensions. Depending on the frequency of data collection, administrative reporting systems and household surveys—such as labor force surveys, household income and expenditure surveys, demographic and health surveys, establishment surveys, and agriculture surveys—can be other good sources of data for SDG indicators.

Gaps in data granularity. Many SDG indicators require disaggregation by location, sex, gender, age, income, ethnicity, migration status, disability status, and other relevant dimensions. Granular data can illustrate disparities within and across economies.

However, the extent to which specific groups are disproportionately at risk is difficult to decipher given the lack of data disaggregation and interlinkages across indicators. Sex disaggregations, even for basic indicators such as extreme poverty rates based on the $1.90 a day (at 2011 purchasing power parity) level, are not currently available. Similarly, poverty numbers are currently unavailable for vulnerable groups, such as people with disabilities or indigenous peoples, since the sample surveys these poverty calculations are based on are designed to obtain an overview of welfare conditions. Investments are needed (e.g., in special surveys) to obtain poverty data for vulnerable groups that make up only a small proportion of the total population.

Innovative data sources, such as big data and crowdsourced data, can potentially address these data gaps and strengthen the monitoring of SDG indicators. However, some types of big data may not represent the underlying groups of interest. Therefore, it is necessary to ensure that reliable statistical inferences can be made when complementing surveys and other conventional data sources with big data (Cox, Kartsonaki, and Keogh 2018).

Lack of data comparability. Differences in definitions mean that SDG indicators, such as the proportion of the population with access to safely managed drinking water services, rely on data related to housing conditions, which may not be fully comparable across economies. Likewise, comparisons of SDG indicators across economies are difficult for urban–rural disaggregation due to various definitions of "urban" and "rural" across time and economies.

Sparse data and irregular frequency. Some indicators that provide a useful description of income inequality—such as the growth in household expenditure among those in an economy's bottom 40th percentile of income distribution in relation to national averages are only currently available for a few economies. In another example, data on progress made toward addressing climate change are sparse.

Frequency is also of concern as some indicators, such as the coverage of protected areas in relation to marine areas, are not regularly collected. Indicators on material footprint and domestic material consumption, which are widely accepted as strategic sustainability indicators of production and consumption, are not produced annually.

Further, some protected areas are not assigned management categories. While access to remote sensing data has improved in recent years, forest regrowth cannot easily be detected with remote-sensing techniques.

Data limitations. The indicators included in the framework for monitoring the SDGs, while carefully chosen, may have some limitations. For example, the labor share in GDP does not include the income of the self-employed, even though a sizeable proportion of the employed population in developing Asia comprises people who are self-employed. Current measures of poverty used by economies are largely based on income or consumption data, while the SDG indicators include a multidimensional poverty measure that has yet to be tested on a wider scale.

The many challenges facing cities—pollution, traffic congestion, and inadequate housing for the poor—can be exacerbated by migration and population growth, changes in family structures, inequality of opportunity for excluded groups, and rising insecurity. Currently available data do not allow for a simple assessment of these issues.

The Red List Index is a composite index aggregated across multiple taxonomic groups. While it can be updated annually, the index does not adequately capture the deteriorating status of common species that are abundant and widespread yet declining gradually. Data on other indicators for monitoring many targets under SDG 15 are also sparsely available. The absence of a framework for monitoring terrestrial ecosystems, low data availability, and the lack of good-quality data must be carefully addressed.

Measurement errors. The quality of data for all SDG indicators needs to be considered when identifying trends and drawing inferences. For example, self-reporting of land area and production by farmers is known to have significant biases (Dillon and Rao 2018). The calculation of under-5 mortality rates requires complete counts of live births and child deaths by a precise age, which are not always available in economies of Asia and the Pacific that lack civil registration systems. Maternal deaths are likewise not always accounted for, given incomplete or inaccurate records on causes of death. The measurement of quality education across economies is hampered by the lack of standard definitions for minimum competency. Anthropometric measures of malnutrition (including stunted heights) are subject to measurement errors and issues around reference standards (i.e., local versus international standards). Access to safely managed drinking water and sanitation services, and information on hygiene all depend on more and better data, particularly administrative data sources (WHO and UNICEF 2017).

A complete stocktaking of all statistical capacity development programs cannot be guaranteed in the data compiled by PARIS21 for measuring the dollar-value support for statistics development. Double counting of projects can occur, or the data may also be inflated by the inaccurate inclusion of multisector projects. Further, donor commitments do not always lead to actual disbursements to recipient economies.

Ultimately, the reliability of data on SDG indicators depends on the quality of the underlying data sources. Governments across Asia and the Pacific need to increase investment, look for innovative data sources, and form strategic partnerships with a range of stakeholders to enhance data quality, comparability, measurement, and timeliness. Reliable and comprehensive data supports evidence-based policymaking that leads to better development outcomes.

PART II

Regional Trends and Tables

Regional Trends and Tables

The resilience of the Asia and Pacific region over the years showcases its ability to learn from previous experiences and rebound after global and regional crises and other socioeconomic hardships.

Most recently, the region has faced multiple vulnerabilities that threaten its long-term development. These include geopolitical tensions that have the potential to undermine regional stability, mounting natural disasters that are increasing in intensity and frequency as a result of climate change (IPCC 2012), and, of course, the impacts of the coronavirus disease (COVID-19) pandemic. Indeed, the pandemic provides a compelling opportunity to reflect on the factors that shape economies' resilience and capacity to innovate.

For this reason, Part II of *Key Indicators for Asia and the Pacific 2022* examines data on the performance of selected sectors that were severely disrupted by the pandemic. These include the tourism, transport, information and communication technology, and energy sectors. The analyses here draw on the latest 2021 estimates for nominated economic indicators, as compiled by national and international statistical systems.

The data from 2021 presented here show different growth trajectories for different economies: some are recovering faster and more robustly than initially forecast, while others are still navigating heavy socioeconomic setbacks. These observations highlight the risk of increased inequality between economies in the region.

As Asia and the Pacific maneuvers its way out of the pandemic, it is important for governments and their development partners to identify factors that may have contributed to the diverse impacts of the pandemic across sectors and economies and establish how policies can be calibrated to ensure these drivers do not contribute to a further diverging of recovery paths and worsening of socioeconomic scarring effects. It is also vital to accelerate efforts in addressing other systemic problems, such as climate change, by creating new and greener economic opportunities for more sustainable and resilient development.

Pandemic productivity. A woman works from home due to the COVID-19 lockdown in Tbilisi, Georgia, while a man works at his office in Dhaka, Bangladesh (photo by Khatia Jijeishvili (left) and Abir Abdullah (right)/ADB).

Economic Growth and Uncertainties for Recovery

As Asia and the Pacific's economic recovery gathers pace, there are hints of divergent growth paths.

As overall COVID-19 infections across Asia and the Pacific decreased consistently from the last quarter of 2020 to the first quarter of 2021, economic recovery in many parts of the region was also evident. Regional inflation started to taper off, while exports and remittances of a number of economies had either reverted back or drew closer to pre-pandemic levels (ADB 2021a). Unemployment rates also declined in certain economies such as Indonesia, Malaysia, the People's Republic of China (PRC), and the Philippines during the first half of 2021 (ADB 2021a).

However, from the second quarter of 2021 onward, the situation was more challenging, with the emergence of the COVID-19 Delta variant. Cases in the region rose sharply (Figure 2.1) and economic activity in the manufacturing and services sectors, along with export volumes, fell correspondingly. Protracted capital outflows extended to July and August 2021 (ADB 2021a).

Fortunately, vaccination programs managed to contain the number of COVID-19 cases. By the end of December 2021, only 5 of the 49 economies in Asia and the Pacific had positive growth in average daily COVID-19 cases per month. This stabilization in the transmission of the disease enabled economies to reopen. Collectively, developing Asia's economy grew by 6.9% in 2021 (ADB 2022a). Almost all economies in the region reported stronger growth rates for the year, compared to 2020. In a number of economies, the rebound was stronger than initially forecast (Figure 2.2). Some economies suffered substantial economic losses in 2020 but managed to grow in 2021. However, in most economies, the pace of growth was not sufficient to undo the economic contractions of 2020. Figure 2.2 also shows that there were significant variations in economic performance across the region. Studies suggest that differences in the stringency of COVID-19 containment measures used by governments may be one reason for these variations (Bajra et al. 2022). Furthermore, it is also important to note that economic performance during the COVID-19 pandemic may not necessarily be indicative of economic performance in future crises due to the distinctive features of pandemic-induced disruptions.

Figure 2.1: Number of New Daily COVID-19 Cases and Vaccination Rates in Asia and the Pacific

The number of new COVID-19 infections surged between the second and third quarter of 2021, before declining toward the end of the year.

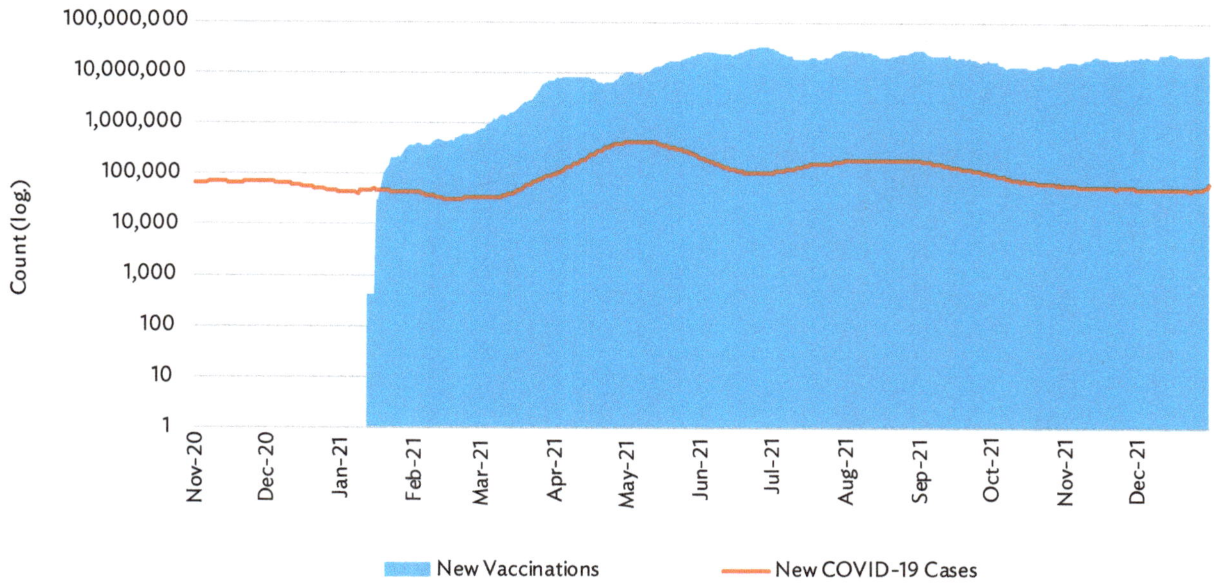

COVID-19 = coronavirus disease.

Note: The figures plotted on the graph represent the number of new COVID-19 cases recorded and new vaccinations administered per day, i.e., not cumulative cases and vaccinations. Graphs are smoothed based on a 7-day rolling average.

Source: Our World in Data. Coronavirus Pandemic (COVID-19). https://ourworldindata.org/coronavirus (accessed 4 January 2022).

Click here for figure data

Figure 2.2: Latest Economic Growth Estimates versus Initial Growth Forecasts and Comparison of Growth Estimates in 2020 and 2021

Economies of Asia and the Pacific reported various growth paths as the COVID-19 pandemic progressed. Some economies grew more slowly than originally forecast, while others posted stronger economic performance.

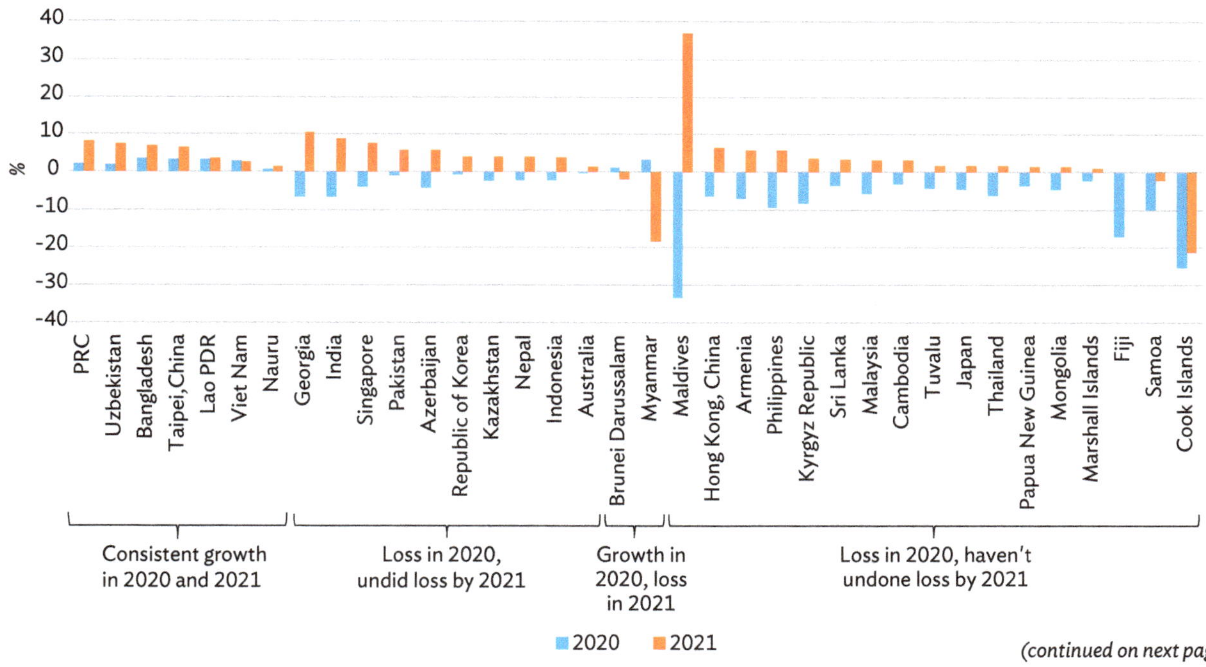

(continued on next page)

Click here for figure data

Figure 2.2: Latest Economic Growth Estimates versus Initial Growth Forecasts and Comparison of Growth Estimates in 2020 and 2021 *(continued)*

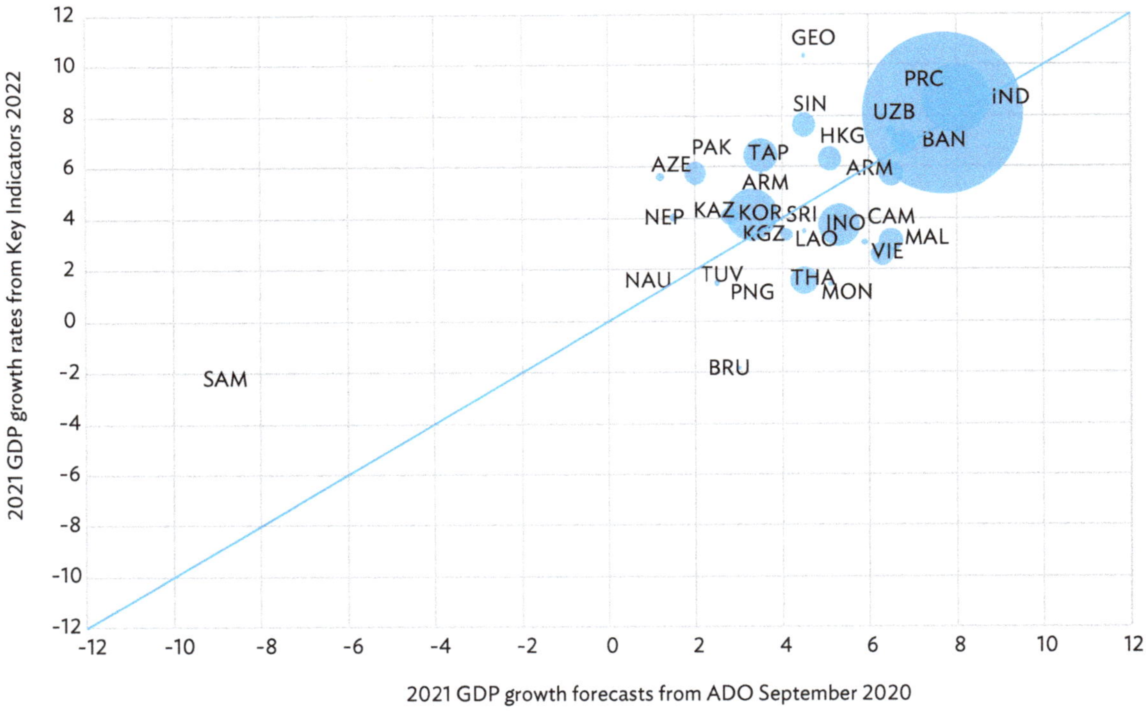

$ = United States dollars; ADO = Asian Development Outlook; ARM = Armenia; AZE = Azerbaijan; BAN = Bangladesh; BRU = Brunei Darussalam; CAM = Cambodia; COVID-19 = coronavirus disease; GDP = gross domestic product; GEO = Georgia; HKG = Hong Kong, China; IND = India; INO = Indonesia; KAZ = Kazakhstan; KGZ = Kyrgyz Republic; KOR = Republic of Korea; LAO PDR = Lao People's Democratic Republic; MAL = Malaysia; MON = Mongolia; NAU = Nauru; NEP = Nepal; PAK = Pakistan; PNG = Papua New Guinea; PHI = Philippines; PRC = People's Republic of China; SAM = Samoa; SIN = Singapore; SRI = Sri Lanka; TAP = Taipei,China; THA = Thailand; TUV = Tuvalu; UZB = Uzbekistan, VIE = Viet Nam.

Note: "Key Indicators" is a shortened form of the Asian Development Bank's *Key Indicators for Asia and the Pacific*. The first graphic shows only economies with complete data for 2020 and 2021.

Sources: Asian Development Bank (ADB) estimates using data presented in Tables 2.2.2 and 2.2.11 of *Key Indicators for Asia and the Pacific 2022*; ADB. Key Indicators Database. https://kidb.adb.org/ (accessed 16 July 2022) and ADB. 2020. *Asian Development Outlook Update 2020.* Manila.

Click here for figure data

Additional effort is needed to regain jobs lost during pandemic.

Estimates of employment data compiled by the International Labour Organization (ILO) suggest that, in 2021, the number of hours worked in Asia and the Pacific remained lower than pre-pandemic levels. The region, which lost 8.0% of working hours in 2020 in comparison to the fourth quarter of 2019, saw working hours lower by 3.6% in 2021 with respect to the same baseline period. In 2020, the subregion of South Asia registered the highest loss of work hours at 13.8%. For 2021, the subregion of Southeast Asia recorded the highest loss of work hours at 6.8%, while the loss recorded in the Pacific was higher than the estimate a year earlier.[1]

Aside from decreases in employment, changes in the overall sectoral employment profile during the first year of the pandemic are also evident. As shown in Figure 2.3, a shift in employment share away from the industry and services sectors and toward agriculture can be noted from 2019 to 2020 for the whole of Asia and the Pacific, as well as within the

1 Individual economy tables available at https://kidb.adb.org provide additional information on how employment in some subregions was more affected than in others.

region's developing economies. This sectoral shift in employment is mirrored in certain subregions, particularly in South Asia. In a span of just 1 year through the pandemic, South Asia posted a combined reduction of 2.9 percentage points in the industry and services sectors' employment share and this fall was displaced to the subregion's agriculture sector. Similar shifts can be observed in the agriculture and services sectors of Central and West Asia, in the agriculture sector of East Asia, as well as in the industry and services sectors of Southeast Asia, which adds to the fact that these subregions also experienced overall declines in employment in the sectors assessed.

Table 2.1: Work Hours Lost, by Subregion of Asia and the Pacific

Across all ADB regional member economies, the number of hours worked in 2021 was still 3.6% lower than pre-pandemic levels.

		Central and West Asia	East Asia	South Asia	Southeast Asia	The Pacific	Developed ADB Member Economies	ADB Regional Member Economies
2020	Work hours lost as expressed in number of FTE jobs (Total)	11,598,960	37,631,669	91,404,043	24,734,983	128,640	3,767,660	169,265,955
	Work Hours Lost (%)	-9.2	-4.1	-13.8	-7.4	-3.3	-4.9	-8.0
2021	Work hours lost as expressed in number of FTE jobs (Total)	6,460,224	8,718,126	35,483,198	22,751,748	205,446	3,109,999	76,728,741
	Work Hours Lost (%)	-5.1	-0.9	-5.4	-6.8	-5.3	-4.0	-3.6

ADB = Asian Development Bank, FTE = full-time employment.

Note: Work hours lost are expressed as full-time equivalent employment losses. The estimates of working hours lost (%) are expressed as percentage of hours lost compared to the baseline (4th quarter of 2019, seasonally adjusted), as modeled by the International Labour Organization. For further information about these projections, including their limitations, readers may refer to the corresponding source below.

Source: Asian Development Bank estimates using data from the International Labour Organization. ILOSTAT Database. https://ilostat.ilo.org/ (accessed 5 June 2022).

Figure 2.3: Broad Sectoral Employment Shares in Asia and the Pacific, 2019–2020

In 2020, there were shifts in employment in most subregions and sectors.

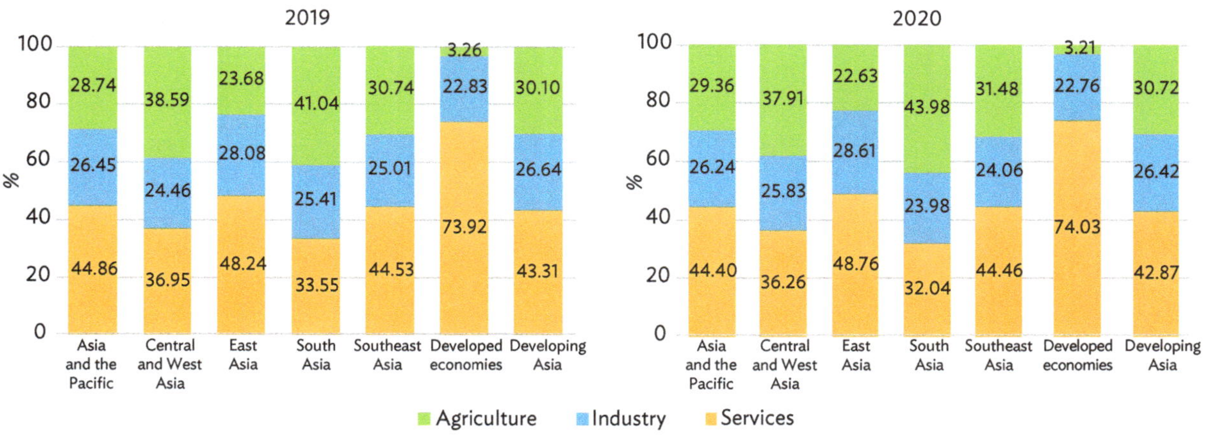

Notes: The charts represent 29 economies with complete broad-sector employment data for both 2019 and 2020 from either the Asian Development Bank's Key Indicators Database or the International Labour Organization's ILOSTAT database. Central and West Asia comprises Afghanistan; Armenia; Azerbaijan; Georgia; Kazakhstan; the Kyrgyz Republic; Pakistan; Tajikistan; and Uzbekistan. South Asia comprises Bhutan; India; and Sri Lanka. Southeast Asia comprises Brunei Darussalam; Indonesia; Malaysia; Myanmar; the Philippines; Singapore; Thailand; and Viet Nam. East Asia comprises Hong Kong, China; Mongolia; the People's Republic of China; the Republic of Korea; and Taipei,China. The developed economies are Australia, Japan, and New Zealand, while developing Asia includes all economies mentioned, except for Australia, Japan, and New Zealand. In the absence of 2020 figures, 2021 figures were used if available, e.g., in the case of Pakistan. Subregions that are not represented here did not have adequate available data.

Sources: Asian Development Bank estimates using data presented in individual economy tables available at https://kidb.adb.org; and International Labour Organization. ILOSTAT Database. https://ilostat.ilo.org/ (accessed 20 June 2022). Economy-level estimates for more recent years, including 2021, are presented in Table 2.1.5 of *Key Indicators for Asia and the Pacific 2022*.

Click here for figure data

A restricted view. Due to COVID-19, flights over the mountains of Nepal operated only once a week in 2021 (photo by Narendra Shretha/ADB).

Tourism and the Options for Greater Inclusion and Sustainability

In recent years, tourism has been a critical driver of economic growth in Asia and the Pacific. This is largely because of improved financial means for individuals to travel, the emergence of low-cost airlines, and more relaxed visa requirements among the region's economies (ADB 2020b). Within the region, the top 10 economies with the highest estimated gross domestic product (GDP) contributions from tourism are presented in Figure 2.4.

Figure 2.4: Top 10 Economies of Asia and the Pacific with the Highest Estimated Tourism Contribution to Gross Domestic Product in 2019 and Percentage Loss in Tourism Receipts in 2020

The region is home to several economies that had tourism accounting for at least 8% of GDP before the COVID-19 pandemic. In 2020, these economies incurred substantial losses in tourism receipts.

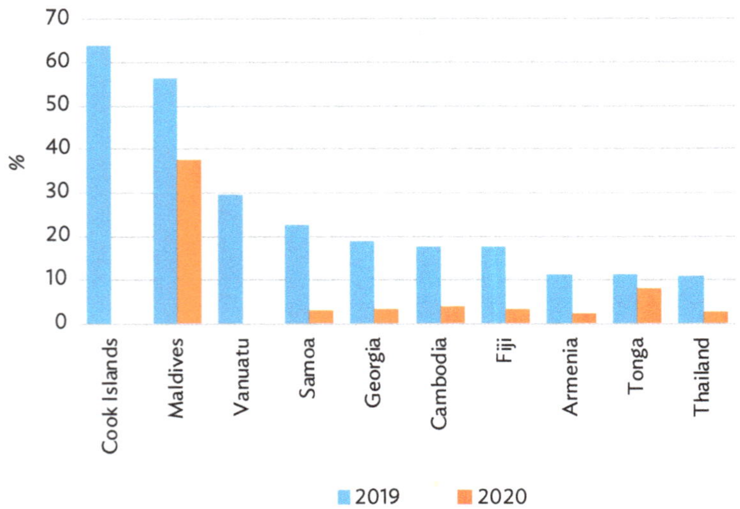

Economy	% loss in tourism receipts in 2020
Cook Islands	...
Maldives	-55.72
Vanuatu	-77.70
Samoa	-88.41
Georgia	-83.42
Cambodia	-78.72
Fiji	-84.01
Armenia	- 80.82
Tonga	-29.82
Thailand	-77.39

... = data not available, COVID-19 = coronavirus disease, GDP = gross domestic product.

Note: Tourism's contribution to the economy is estimated based on international tourist receipts over GDP. No 2020 figures are available on the Cook Islands' international tourist receipts and Vanuatu's GDP from the sources specified below.

Source: Asian Development Bank estimates using data presented in Tables 2.2.2 and 2.4.25 of *Key Indicators of Asia and the Pacific 2022*.

Click here for figure data

At the peak of the pandemic, tourism was one of Asia and the Pacific's hardest-hit sectors.

Reliance on tourism across Asia and the Pacific caused serious economic challenges when the pandemic halted international travel. Figure 2.4 illustrates drastic declines in GDP contributions by tourism from 2019 to 2020, as arrivals into many economies dipped to record lows and remained very low or negligible for many months. By December 2021, or nearly 2 years after the pandemic began, international tourist arrivals were still low and had not yet fully recovered to pre-pandemic levels as can be seen in Figure 2.5.

Figure 2.5: International Tourism Arrivals and COVID-19 Tourism Index in Asia and the Pacific, 2020–2021

Since plummeting to its lowest level in April 2020, tourism had not reverted to pre-pandemic levels by the end of 2021.

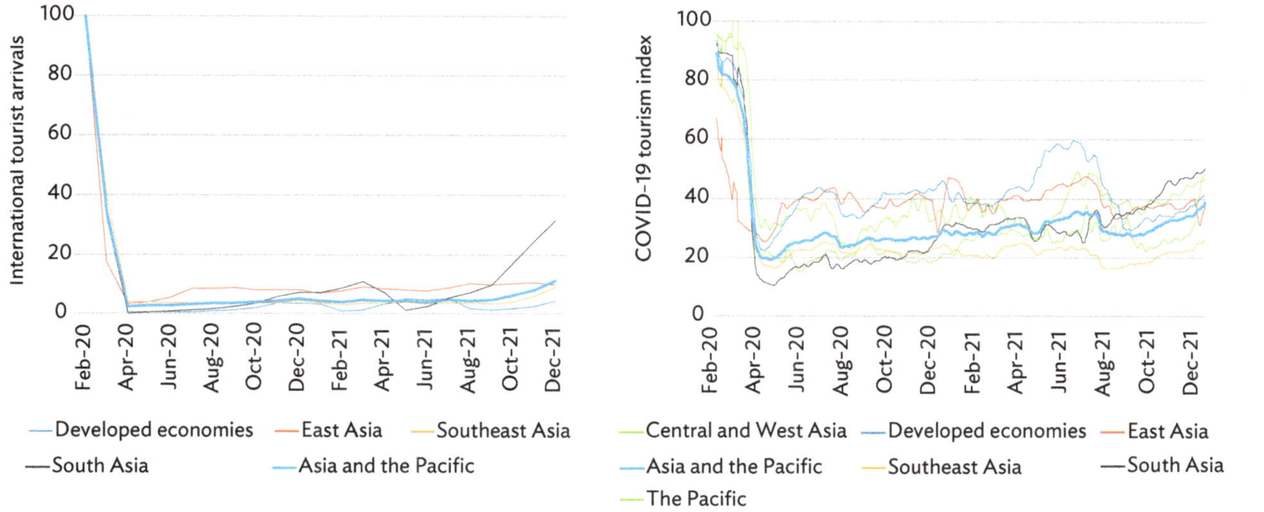

COVID-19 = coronavirus disease.

Notes: For the chart on the left, figures for actual monthly international tourist arrivals are standardized, such that February 2020 = 100. For annual estimates on international tourist arrivals, refer to Regional Table 2.4.24. Only economies with complete data are represented. East Asia comprises Hong Kong, China; the Republic of Korea; and Taipei,China. Southeast Asia comprises Indonesia; the Philippines; Singapore; Thailand; and Viet Nam. South Asia comprises India; Nepal; and Sri Lanka. The developed economies are Australia, Japan, and New Zealand. For the chart on the right, actual daily COVID-19 tourism index values are averaged among economies per subregion and smoothed based on a 7-day rolling average. Only economies with complete data are represented. East Asia comprises Mongolia; the People's Republic of China; and the Republic of Korea. Southeast Asia comprises Cambodia; Indonesia; the Lao People's Democratic Republic; Myanmar; Malaysia; the Philippines; Singapore; Thailand; and Viet Nam. South Asia comprises Bangladesh; India; Maldives; and Sri Lanka. Central and West Asia comprises Armenia; Azerbaijan; Georgia; and Kazakhstan. The developed economies are Australia, Japan, and New Zealand.

Sources: Asian Development Bank calculations based on the CEIC database. https://www.ceicdata.com/en (accessed 8 March 2022); and COVID-19 Tourism Index. www.covid19tourism.com (accessed 25 February 2022).

Click here for figure data

Tourism has been heavily impacted in both developed and developing economies, especially in Southeast Asia and the Pacific.

The loss of tourism revenue was felt across the entire Asia and Pacific region and among both developed and developing economies. Japan lost at least $35.3 billion in international tourism receipts in 2020, compared to its figure in 2019 (Figure 2.6). Thailand incurred the biggest decrease, at least $46.3 billion, or about 16% of the total estimated loss in international travel receipts for the whole region.

Figure 2.6: Top 10 Economies of Asia and the Pacific with the Highest Estimated Losses in Tourism, 2019–2020

A number of economies recorded substantial losses in international travel receipts and tourist arrivals.

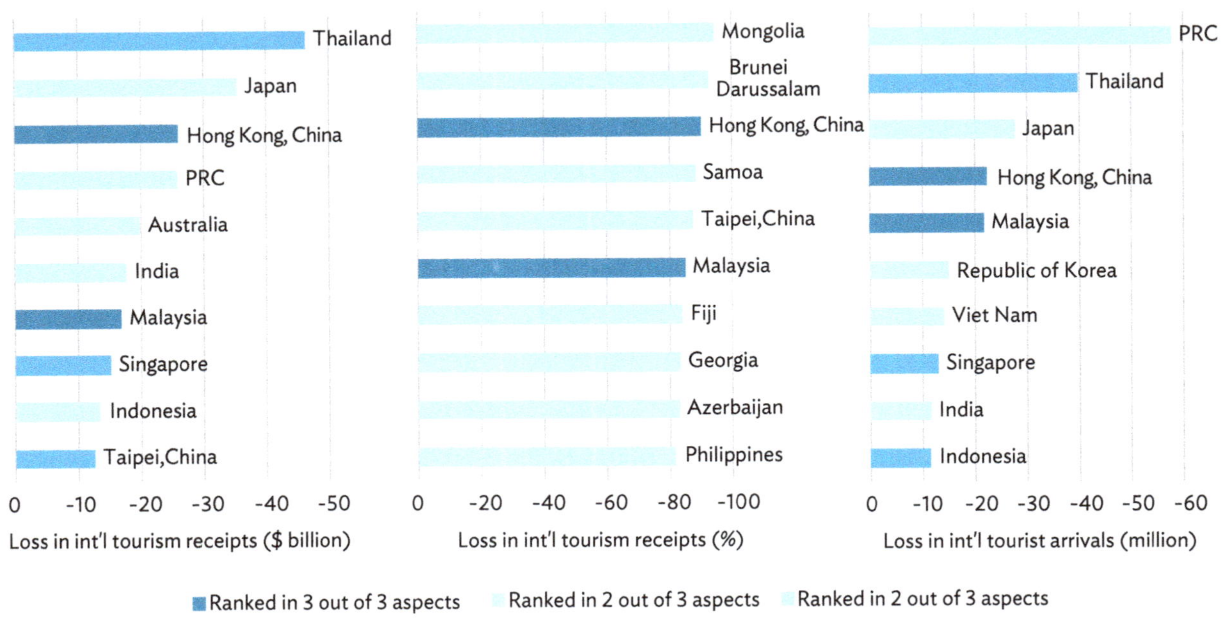

$ = United States dollars, PRC = People's Republic of China.

Note: Economies listed in the graphics represent the top 10 economies with the highest losses in tourism in terms of three aspects: (i) international tourism receipts (in United States dollars); (ii) international tourism receipts (as a percentage); and (iii) international tourist arrivals. Losses are estimated by calculating the difference between 2019 and 2020 figures.

Sources: Asian Development Bank estimates using data presented in Tables 2.4.24 and 2.4.25 of *Key Indicators for Asia and the Pacific 2022*; and Asian Development Bank. Key Indicators Database. http://kidb.adb.org (accessed 17 June 2022).

Click here for figure data

At the subregional level, Southeast Asia, which can be considered the region's tourism hub in terms of international tourism receipts and tourist arrivals, was also the most impacted by the pandemic. Its total losses in international tourism receipts compared to 2019 are estimated at $113.8 billion, with at least four of its 11 economies listed in the top 10 economies with the biggest losses in international tourism receipts (Indonesia, Malaysia, Singapore, and Thailand) and in international tourist arrivals (Indonesia, Malaysia, Singapore, Thailand, and Viet Nam), and two of its economies listed in the 10 biggest losses in tourism-related sector output (the Lao People's Democratic Republic [Lao PDR] and the Philippines).

Tourism-related sectors, such as accommodation, food service, and transport and storage, were also hit badly. Based on gross value-added from 2019 to 2020, Fiji, Maldives, and the Cook Islands recorded the highest losses for these sectors, at least halving their production output (Figure 2.7). Four economies in the Pacific (the Cook Islands, Fiji, Palau, and Samoa) were in the top 10 for losses in these tourism-related sectors, with falls ranging from 45.5% to as much as 77.7%. Despite the losses, some economies in the region were already showing signs of recovery by 2021.

Figure 2.7: Top 10 Economies of Asia and the Pacific with the Highest Falls in Tourism-Related Industry Sectors

Multiple economies, particularly those from the Pacific, recorded high losses in tourism-related sectors from 2019 to 2020.

Lao PDR = Lao People's Democratic Republic.

Note: Figures for 2020 and 2021 represent losses from 2019 to 2020 and 2020 to 2021, respectively. Losses were estimated by calculating the difference in total gross value-added between 2019 and 2020 for the following sectors: (i) accommodation and food services, and (ii) transportation and storage.

Source: Asian Development Bank estimates using data presented in individual economy tables available at https://kidb.adb.org.

Click here for figure data

As a result of revenue losses, many tourism-related jobs were lost. Based on 24 regional economies[2] with available employment data, about 334,000 jobs were lost in the accommodation and food services sector in 2020 compared to 2019, and about 1.4 million jobs were lost in the transportation and storage sector over the same period. This equals almost 1.7 million jobs lost in these two tourism-related sectors in just the first year of the pandemic.

In summary, the COVID-19 pandemic exposed many challenges confronting the tourism sector in Asia and the Pacific. These include an overdependence on international arrivals, limited control over sector growth, external costs, and labor market challenges (ADB 2021c). Although the tourism sector is expected to recover further as more travel restrictions are eased, support should be targeted to encourage the sector's sustainable development instead of focusing solely on revenue growth. An ADB (2021c) report outlines several steps to do this. There is a need to establish more inclusive and sustainability-oriented governance frameworks. It is equally important to include the voices of marginalized groups in tourism development. Having clear accountability frameworks and other mechanisms to monitor progress is also essential. In developing all of these, enhancing the timeliness and granularity of tourism data and information systems is vital.

---

2 Armenia; Australia; Azerbaijan; Bhutan; Brunei Darussalam; Georgia; Hong Kong, China; Indonesia; Japan; Kazakhstan; the Kyrgyz Republic; Malaysia; the Marshall Islands; Mongolia; New Zealand; the Philippines; the Republic of Korea; Singapore; Sri Lanka; Taipei,China; Tajikistan; Thailand; Uzbekistan; and Viet Nam.

Keeping international trade open. The Port of Nuku'alofa is the leading port serving Tonga's global cargo interests (photo by Eric Sales/ADB).

The Transport Sector's Decline and Rebound During the Pandemic

Where travel restrictions, border closures, shifts to work-from-home arrangements, and other social distancing protocols were imposed, these impacted all modes of transportation. In the aviation industry alone, estimates for economies of Asia and the Pacific with available data suggest that passenger movements (measured in person-kilometers) and freight movements (measured in metric ton-kilometers) declined, on average, by 51.9% and 6.4%, respectively, in 2020 (Regional Table 2.5.6). Significant reductions were also noted for land and marine transport, particularly in the first half of 2020. While there were pockets of the transport sector, such as urban freight and logistics, that might have benefited due to the surge in online shopping and food deliveries, for the most part, there were also disruptions in container port traffic.

Mobility flows were greatly affected at the height of pandemic, but gradually moved closer to pre-pandemic patterns during 2021.

Mobility data compiled by Google show stark changes in the commuting behavior of Asians from the time lockdowns started in the first quarter of 2020 until restrictions were gradually eased during 2021. In particular, the solid lines presented in Figure 2.8 represent increases or decreases in median time spent in different localities relative to time spent in the same localities during the baseline period (3 January to 6 February 2020). The blue and red dotted lines represent the proportion of ADB regional member economies imposing public transport and domestic travel restrictions, respectively.

In April 2020, when approximately half the ADB regional member economies imposed some form of domestic travel restrictions, people stayed 20% longer in residential areas while time spent in transit stations dropped by nearly 60%. As mobility restrictions gradually eased, time spent in nonresidential areas increased. By the end of 2021, general mobility patterns had reverted to pre-pandemic levels and, perhaps unsurprisingly, time spent in groceries and pharmacies greatly exceeded those levels. Progress in vaccination coverage, reducing the severity of COVID-19 infections, and helping people to cope better with life during the pandemic may have contributed to more normalized mobility patterns. This recovery was despite half the region's economies having public transport restrictions and 40% retaining some domestic travel restrictions through until the end of December 2021.

Figure 2.8: Mobility Patterns in Asia and the Pacific

Despite some restrictions still being in place, mobility patterns had largely normalized by the end of 2021.

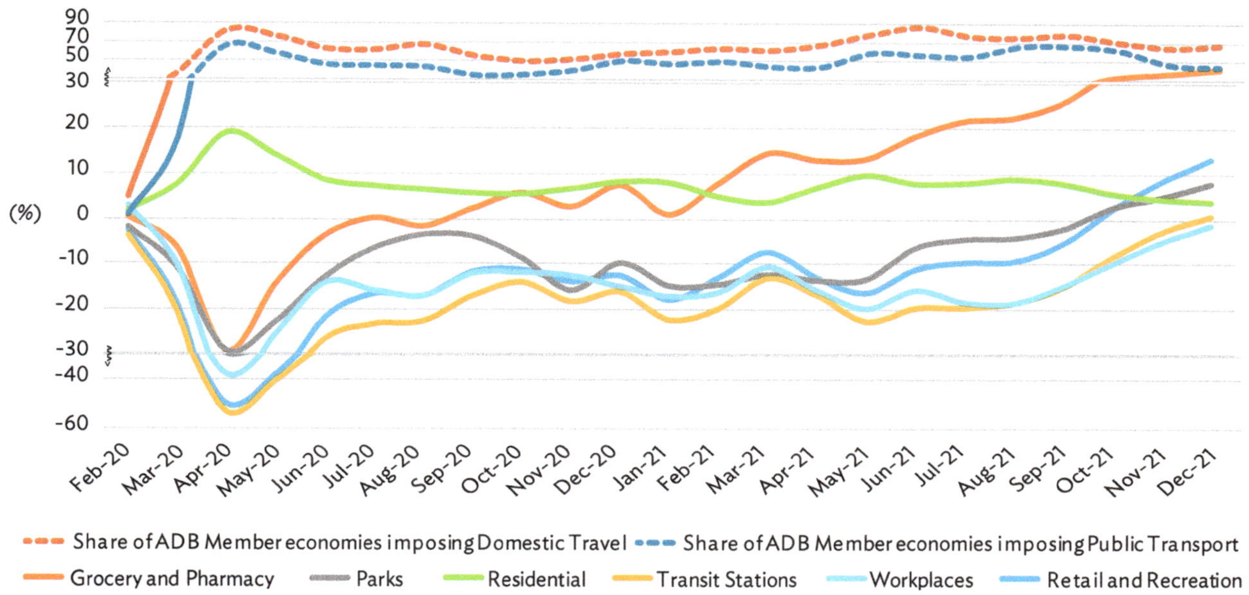

ADB = Asian Development Bank.

Note: Solid lines refer to increase/decrease in time spent on different place categories relative to the baseline numbers. The baseline is the median value, for the corresponding day of the week, during the 5-week period Jan 3–Feb 6, 2020. Public transport restrictions and domestic travel restrictions refer to recommended or required restrictions. Economies included in the aggregation are Afghanistan; Australia; Bangladesh; Cambodia; Fiji; Georgia; Hong Kong, China; India; Indonesia; Japan; Kazakhstan; the Republic of Korea; the Kyrgyz Republic; the Lao People's Democratic Republic; Malaysia; Mongolia; Nepal; New Zealand; Pakistan; Papua New Guinea; the Philippines; Singapore; Sri Lanka; Taipei,China; Tajikistan; Thailand; and Viet Nam.

Source: Google Covid-19 Mobility Report. https://www.google.com/covid19/mobility/ (accessed 4 January 2022); and Oxford University COVID-19 Government Response Tracker. https://www.bsg.ox.ac.uk/research/research-projects/covid-19-government-response-tracker (accessed 4 January 2022).

Click here for figure data

Figure 2.9 illustrates how the transport and storage sector fared during the pandemic. With the exception of Azerbaijan, Bangladesh, and Uzbekistan, all economies with available data saw their transport and storage sectors contract in 2020. The hardest hit were Armenia; the Cook Islands; Georgia; Hong Kong, China; the Kyrgyz Republic; Malaysia; Maldives; the Philippines; Samoa; Singapore; and Thailand, registering declines in gross value-added that exceeded 20%. In 2021, signs of recovery were notable, especially in the Cook Islands, Georgia, the Kyrgyz Republic, Maldives, and Uzbekistan, with growth rates exceeding 20%. Similar trends were noted using employment data.

Figure 2.9: Changes in Economic Output and Employment in the Transport and Storage Sector

In 2020, nearly one in three regional economies saw their transport and storage sectors decline in gross value-added by at least 20%.

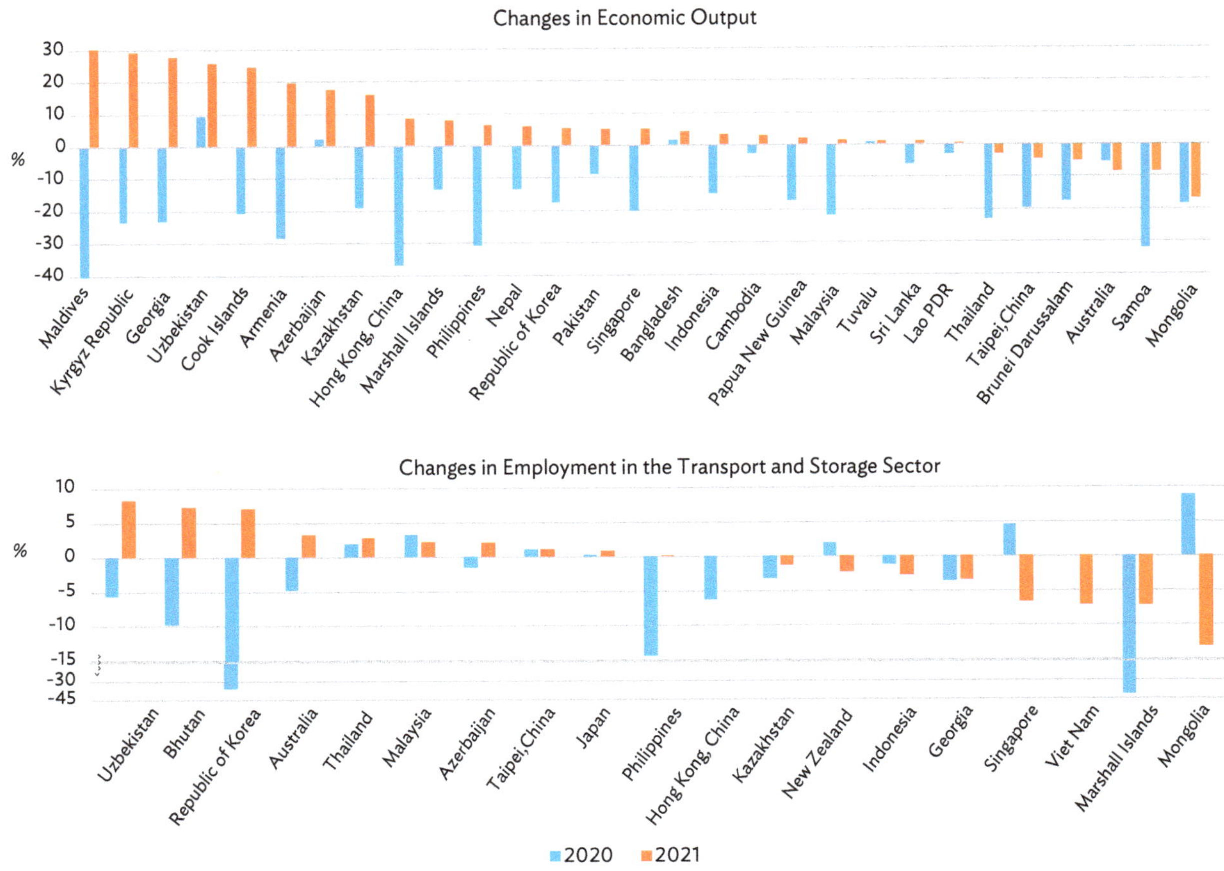

Lao PDR = Lao People's Democratic Republic.

Notes: Additional information about underlying data are provided in individual economy tables.

Source: Asian Development Bank estimates using data presented in individual economy tables available at https://kidb.adb.org.

Click here for figure data

Aviation transport suffered huge declines in terms of passengers and freight.

Figure 2.10 shows economy-level data depicting changes in passengers and goods carried by airlines. Generally, those economies that imposed total travel bans longer than 3 months saw higher declines (by an average of 19 percentage points) from 2019 to 2020. Likewise, the average decline in airline goods carried was 22 percentage points higher among areas that imposed longer travel bans.

The first year of the pandemic also led to substantial disruptions in transport and trade connectivity. Factors such as reduced production and consumption along with disruptions to shipping routes contributed to substantial reductions in container port traffic all over the globe in 2020 (UNESCAP and UNCTAD 2020). Subregions such South Asia and Southeast Asia saw port traffic drop by 5.3% and 3.2%, respectively, while Asia and the Pacific as a whole saw a lower decline of 0.8%. Despite this, as seen in Figure 2.11, there were economies within Asia and the Pacific, such as Bangladesh and the Philippines, that experienced container port traffic declines of at least 10% in 2020.

Figure 2.10: Changes in Airline Passengers and Goods Carried, 2019 to 2020

The volume of airline passengers and goods carried plummeted by at least 50% in a number of economies with available data.

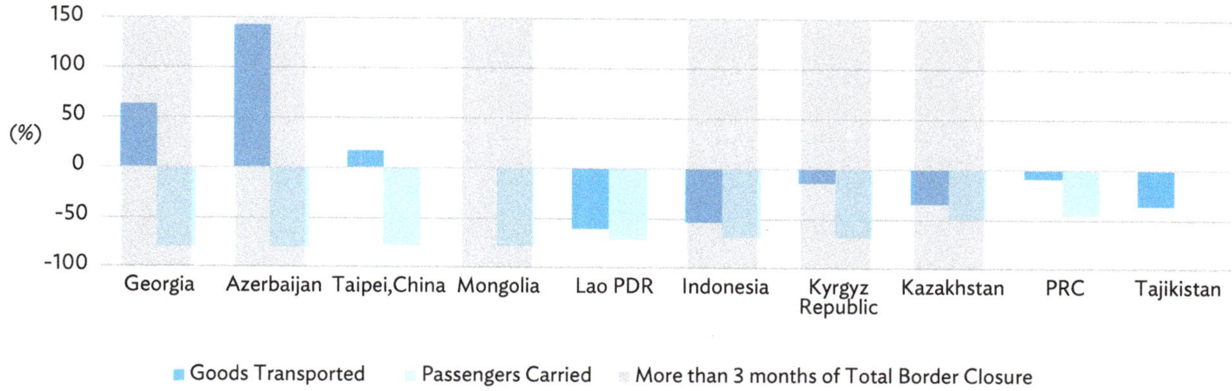

Lao PDR =Lao People's Democratic Republic, PRC = People's Republic of China.
Note: Legends refer to 2020 international travel restrictions, which cover land and air.
Source: Table 2.5.6 of *Key Indicators for Asia and the Pacific 2022*.

Click here for figure data

Figure 2.11: Changes in Container Port Traffic, 2019 to 2020

In more than one-third of reporting economies, container port traffic dropped by at least 5% from 2019 to 2020.

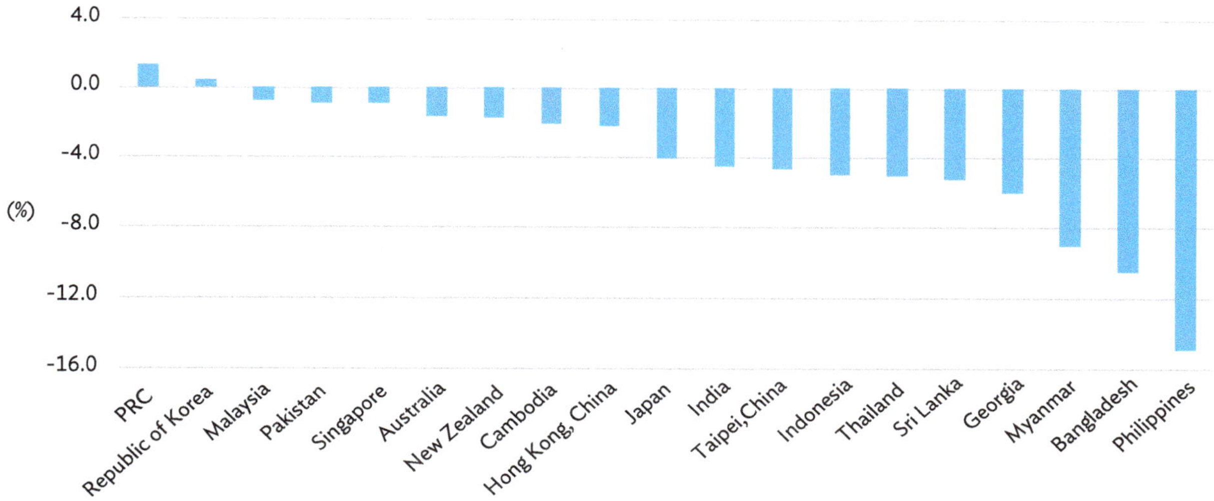

PRC = People's Republic of China.
Source: Table 2.5.7 of *Key Indicators for Asia and the Pacific 2022*.

Click here for figure data

As economies recover from the COVID-19 pandemic, there are several factors that may affect future logistics performance. These include investments in digital technology and reconfiguration of global value chains (IFC 2020a). As the pandemic ushered in tech-driven innovations, those economies that invest in robust digital capabilities to facilitate more efficient movement, storage, and flow of goods are more likely to be more resilient to future shocks or other disruptions. Economies that experienced severe supply disruptions during the pandemic may also decide to diversify by nearshoring or reshoring value chains.

Figure 2.12: Correlation Between Logistics Performance and Gross Domestic Product per Capita

Higher-income economies generally score higher in logistics performance.

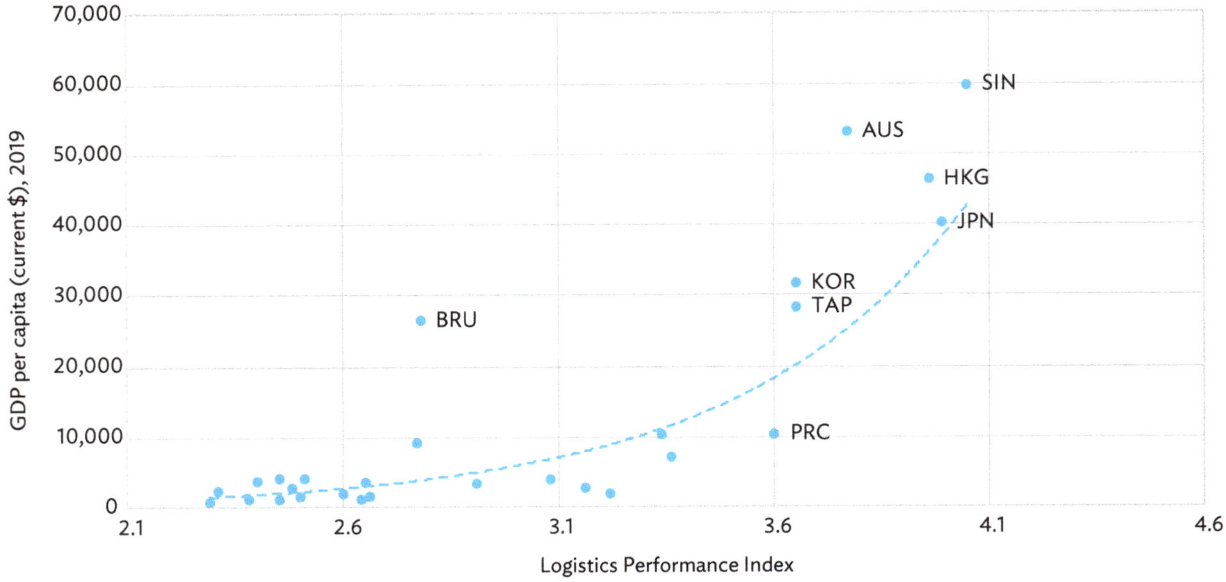

$ = United States dollar; AUS = Australia; BRU = Brunei Darussalam; GDP = gross domestic product; HKG = Hong Kong, China; JPN = Japan; KOR = Republic of Korea; PRC = People's Republic of China; SIN = Singapore; TAP = Taipei,China.

Note: The Logistics Performance Index is based on six components, including (i) customs performance, (ii) infrastructure quality, (iii) ease of arranging shipments, (iv) competence and quality of logistics services, (v) ability to track and trace consignments, and (vi) timeliness of shipments. Each component is scored a value ranging from 1 to 5, with 5 representing highest quality or performance and principal component analysis used to derive an aggregate score.

Source: Table 2.5.7 of *Key Indicators for Asia and the Pacific 2022.*

Click here for figure data

Information and Communication Technology Steps Forward

Parts of the information and communication technology (ICT) sector expanded significantly during the COVID-19 pandemic. The increased prevalence of work-from-home arrangements boosted demand for reliable and cost-effective internet connection while construction of data centers occurred at an accelerated pace.

Even before the COVID-19 pandemic, the ICT sector's economic contribution had gradually expanded.

Despite the diminutive size of the sector, Figure 2.13 illustrates the increasing role of ICT in many economies of Asia and the Pacific in the decade prior to the pandemic. This partly reflects how the ICT sector and ICT-enabled industries are regarded as potential growth powerhouses for the future, permeating many sectors such as health, education, and social protection, among others, as the world witnesses a transformational shift into more technology-related economic activities.

Figure 2.13: Economic Contribution and Employment Share of the Information and Communication Sector

Since 2010, the information and communication sector has made a gradually expanding contribution to GDP and job creation.

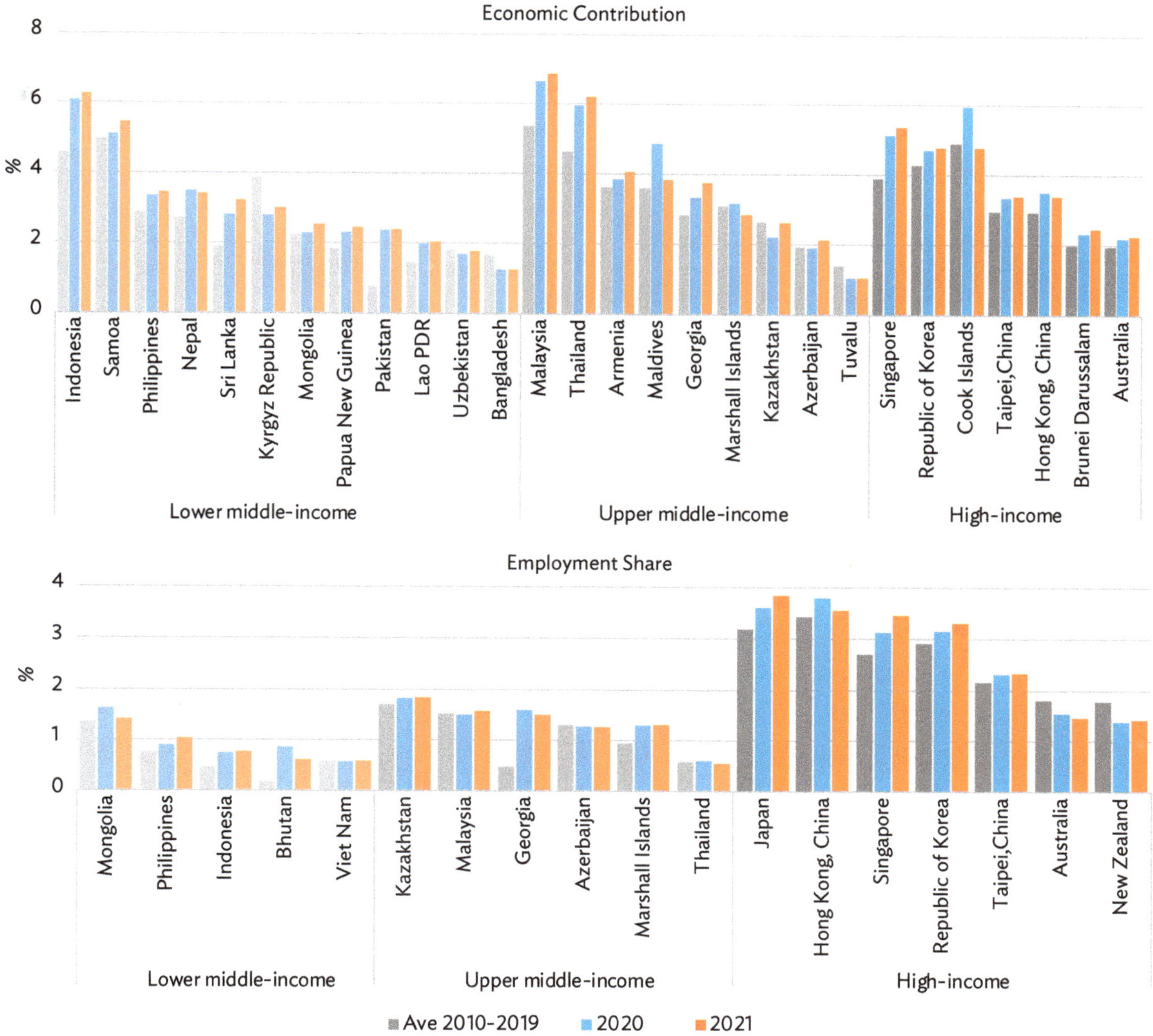

GDP = gross domestic product, Lao PDR = Lao People's Democratic Republic.

Note: The "Ave 2010–2019" bar shows the simple average of all the calculated individual percentage shares for each year from 2010 to 2019. Income groupings follow the World Bank Group's classification as of July 2022.

Source: Asian Development Bank estimates using data presented in individual economy tables available at https://kidb.adb.org.

Click here for figure data

The ICT sector helped economies navigate the pandemic by providing efficient tools for remote work and other business continuity arrangements.

In the midst of the COVID-19 pandemic, the ICT sector played a critical role in keeping society linked, ensuring business continuity, and steering pandemic response.[3] As lockdowns and social distancing measures were implemented, telecommuting tools such as video conferencing proved useful for maintaining social contact and working remotely (Jinjarak et al. 2021). Digital technology also served as an important mechanism

3 Digital infrastructure (such as fiber, telecommunications towers, active networks, and data centers), operators (mobile and fixed broadband, data centers, and cloud computing), and applications (broadband connections, telephony, video, e-commerce, and others) make up the telecommunications services industry (IFC 2020b).

Business as usual. An online meeting takes place in the People's Republic of China (photo by Deng Jia/ADB).

to deliver health care and education and facilitate trade and other important financial services. In fact, while total GDP contracted in many parts of Asia and the Pacific, a number of economies saw the economic output of their ICT sectors grow in 2020. There are, however, notable variations across the region, as seen in Figure 2.14. In a number of lower middle-income economies, the rate of growth in the ICT sector remained low. This may lead to greater divergence in this sector and, to the extent that the ICT sector enables growth in other sectors, could point to broader economic divergence between economies.

Although access to the internet is expanding, prices remain prohibitively expensive for some low-income societies.

With the pandemic amplifying the need for reliable internet connections, Asia and the Pacific posted substantial increases in mobile and fixed broadband subscriptions during 2020. Estimates suggest that the region's lower middle-income economies exhibited the fastest growth, at an average of 15.0% from 2019 to 2020 (Figure 2.14). This increase could be attributed to lower prices of services coupled with increasing demand (ITU 2020). Figure 2.14 shows the affordability of broadband data prices as a percentage of gross national income (GNI) from the International Telecommunication Union (ITU). Across the globe, mobile data prices became more affordable in 2020 as compared to 2019. The world's 2020 mobile data average price was below the UN Broadband Commission's target of 2% of GNI for 2025. However, several economies in the Asia and Pacific region still reported prices way beyond the 2% target. This could pose challenges for a region where roughly 55% of the population still do not have access to the internet (ITU 2021). Tables 2.5.8 and 2.5.9 present economy-level estimates of indicators such as each economy's number of internet users, among other related indicators.

Figure 2.14: Changes in Broadband Subscription Rates and Mobile Data Prices

Broadband internet subscriptions among lower middle-income economies increased by 15% in 2020, but prices remained expensive for a number of developing ADB member economies.

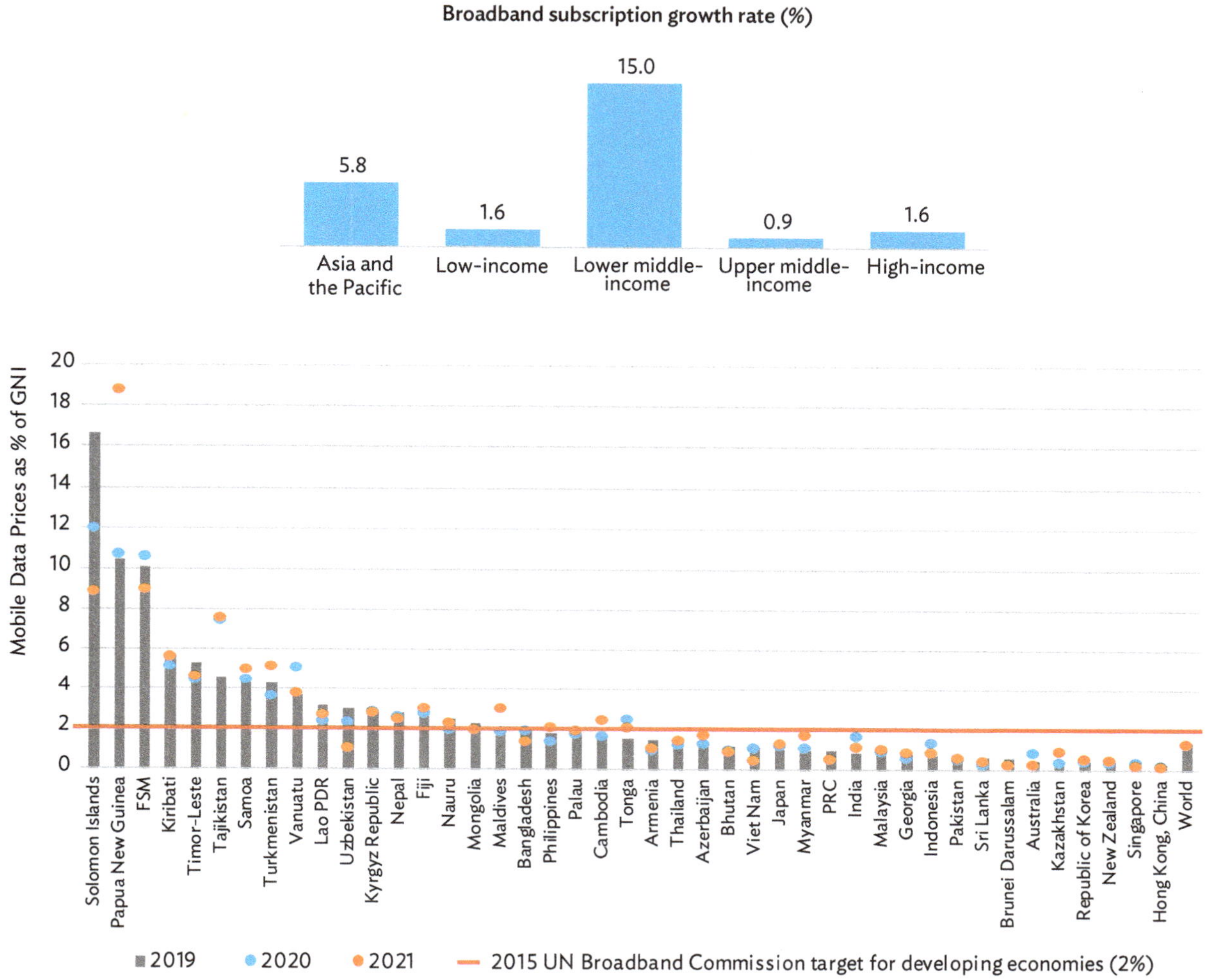

ADB = Asian Development Bank, FSM = Federated States of Micronesia, GNI = gross national income, Lao PDR = Lao People's Democratic Republic, PRC = People's Republic of China.

Note: Figure on broadband subscription rates refers to the growth rate between 2019 and 2020 and include only economies with data for 2019 and 2020.

Sources: Asian Development Bank estimates using broadband subscription data from the International Telecommunications Union. https://www.itu.int/ (accessed on 16 May 2022); and mobile prices data from the International Telecommunications Union website (accessed on 14 May 2022).

Click here for figure data

Figure 2.15 illustrates the correlation between an economy's epidemic risk (vulnerabilities to epidemic-prone diseases as well as epidemic prevention and preparedness tactics) and its level of access to internet connection. There is a negative correlation between epidemic risk and broadband subscriptions perhaps because, in economies with wider internet access, societies can facilitate timely flow of the information necessary to respond efficiently to fast-evolving situations (Jiang and Ryan 2020). In addition to expanding internet access, it is also important to strengthen the security of the data centers that house computer systems and associated components. As seen during the pandemic, reliable internet connections facilitate effective work and study at home when lockdowns are essential to contain infection rates (Jiang and Ryan 2020).

Figure 2.15: Correlation Between Epidemic Risk and Internet Broadband Subscriptions

There is a negative correlation between epidemic risk and depth of internet connection.

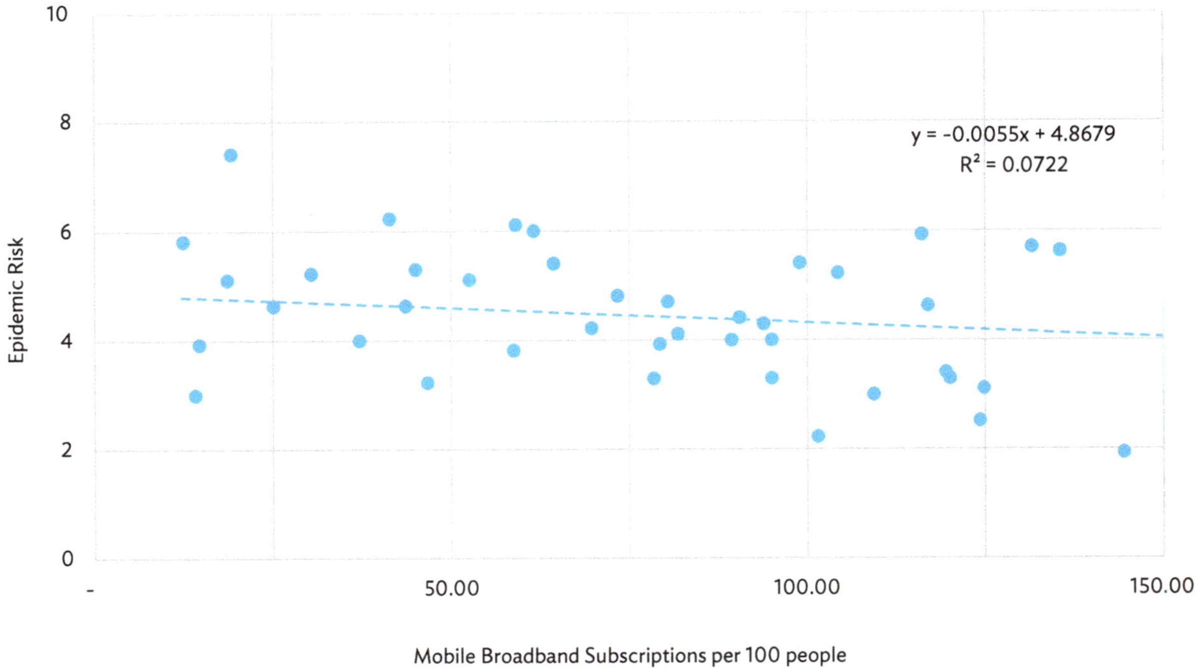

Note: Data on epidemic risk were compiled in 2018 under the technical lead of the European Commission's Joint Research Center and in close collaboration with the World Health Organization for the epidemic components. The Epidemic Risk Index uses a data-driven model to assess national and subnational vulnerabilities and risks to epidemic-prone diseases, as well as a simulation platform to test epidemic prevention and preparedness tactics. The risk score ranges from 0 to 10, where 10 is the highest risk.

Sources: International Telecommunications Union. https://www.itu.int/ (accessed on 16 May 2022); and European Union- Joint Research Center. INFORM Epidemic Risk Index. https://drmkc.jrc.ec.europa.eu/inform-index/Other-INFORM-Products/INFORM-Epidemic-Risk-Index (accessed 22 June 2022).

Click here for figure data

There is a further need to narrow the digital divide across genders. Figure 2.16 shows that, in general, women in Asia and the Pacific are less likely to use the internet than their male counterparts are. In fact, in some economies, women are nearly half as likely as men to use the internet. Figure 2.17 also shows that women's share of employment in ICT is lower than for men in most economies, regardless of the economy's income level. Furthermore, there are studies suggesting that gender disparities in internet use (and the digital divide in general) may also vary across economic sectors (Okuda, Cappelle, and Bell 2022). Providing women and girls with greater ICT access and use of digital technologies, particularly in economies and sectors where gender disparities are more pronounced, can help improve their social mobility prospects by giving them more opportunities to be entrepreneurial and sell products to wider markets, find better-paid work, and access important services for education, health, and financial advice.

Figure 2.16: Proportion of Individuals Using the Internet (by Gender) and Gender Parity Score in Internet Use

Men were more likely than women to use the internet in most economies of Asia and the Pacific. However, the gender parity scores of regional economies were, in general, better than the world average. In 2020, there were hints of better gender parity in internet use.

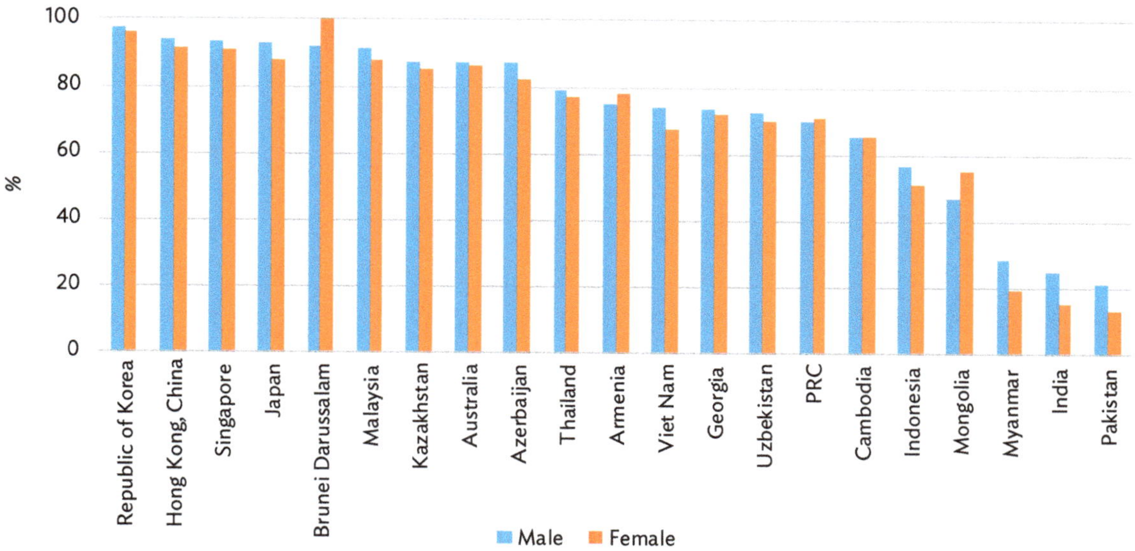

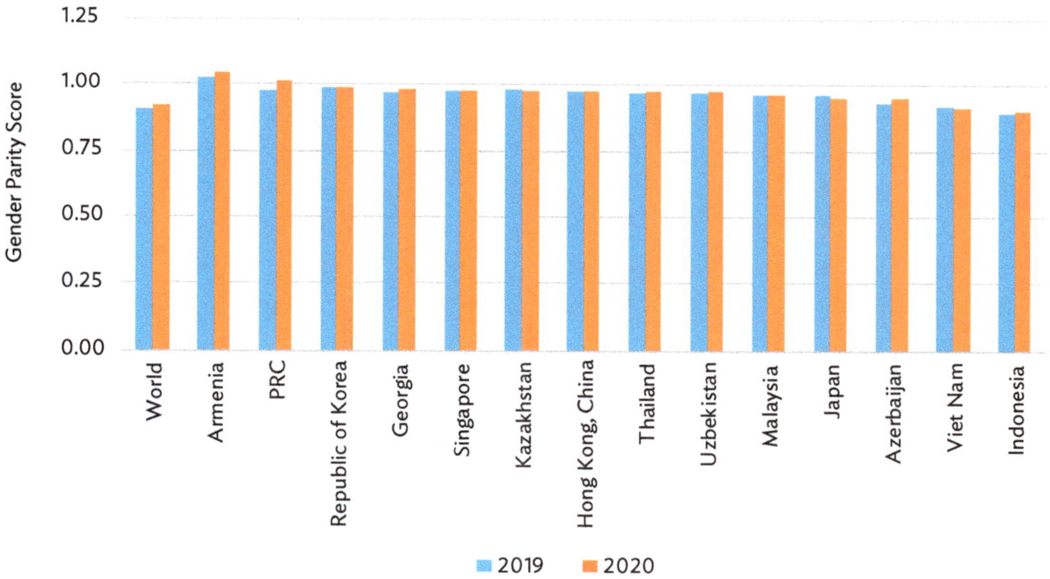

PRC = People's Republic of China.

Note: The gender parity scores are calculated as the proportion of women who use the internet, divided by the proportion of men who use the internet. A value lower than 1 indicates that men are more likely than women to use the internet, while a value greater than 1 indicates that women are more likely than men to use the internet.

Sources: For gender disaggregated data on internet use: International Telecommunications Union. ICT Statistics by Gender. https://www.itu.int/ITU-D/ict/statistics/Gender/index.html (accessed 3 May 2022). For the gender parity index: Asian Development Bank estimates using data from official communication with the International Telecommunications Union, 8 June 2022.

Click here for figure data

Figure 2.17: Women's Share of Employment in Information and Communication Technology

In general, the proportion of women working in the ICT sector is lower throughout the region.

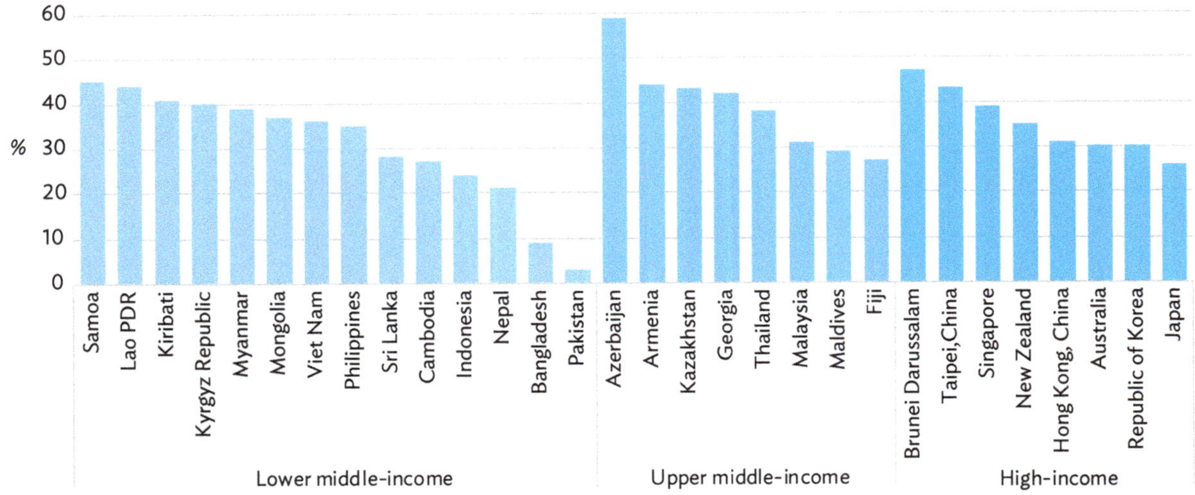

ICT = information and communication technology, Lao PDR = Lao People's Democratic Republic.

Note: Income groupings follow the World Bank Group's classification as of July 2022.

Source: International Labor Organization. 2019. Tech's Persistent Gender Gap. November 12. https://ilostat.ilo.org/techs-persistent-gender-gap/.

Click here for figure data

Energy and a Glimpse at a Greener Future

The pandemic has presented opportunities to rethink the future of the energy sector across Asia and the Pacific. At the onset of the COVID-19 pandemic, the International Energy Agency estimated that global energy demand dropped by 4.0% due to constrained economic activities (IEA 2021), accompanied by a (temporary) reduction in greenhouse gas (GHG) emissions in 2020. While reduced GHG emissions came at an economic cost, the pandemic brings into focus the need for low-carbon energy systems to facilitate a greener and resilient recovery.

The pandemic delivered sharp reductions in energy demand and fuel prices.

Figure 2.18 shows how the energy sector in each of the region's economies has fared since the COVID-19 pandemic began. In 2020, half of the economies with available data saw their energy sector's economic output contract by approximately 1% to 8%.

Reductions in energy demand presumably impacted fuel prices. In 2020, retail prices of fuel energy declined by at least 0.6% (relative to 2019 prices) as a result of reduced economic activity in several economies (Figure 2.19). However, more recent data show fuel prices increasing again due to increased demand for energy as economies reopen, compounded by supply disruptions caused by tensions between major oil-producing economies.

The pandemic has provided the opportunity to redraw strategies for cleaner energy systems in the future.

Figure 2.18: Changes in the Economic Output of the Energy Sector

In 2020, the economic output of the energy sector contracted in a number of Asia and the Pacific economies, albeit at a slower rate than what was seen in other economic sectors. In 2021, most economies managed to rebound and posted positive growth.

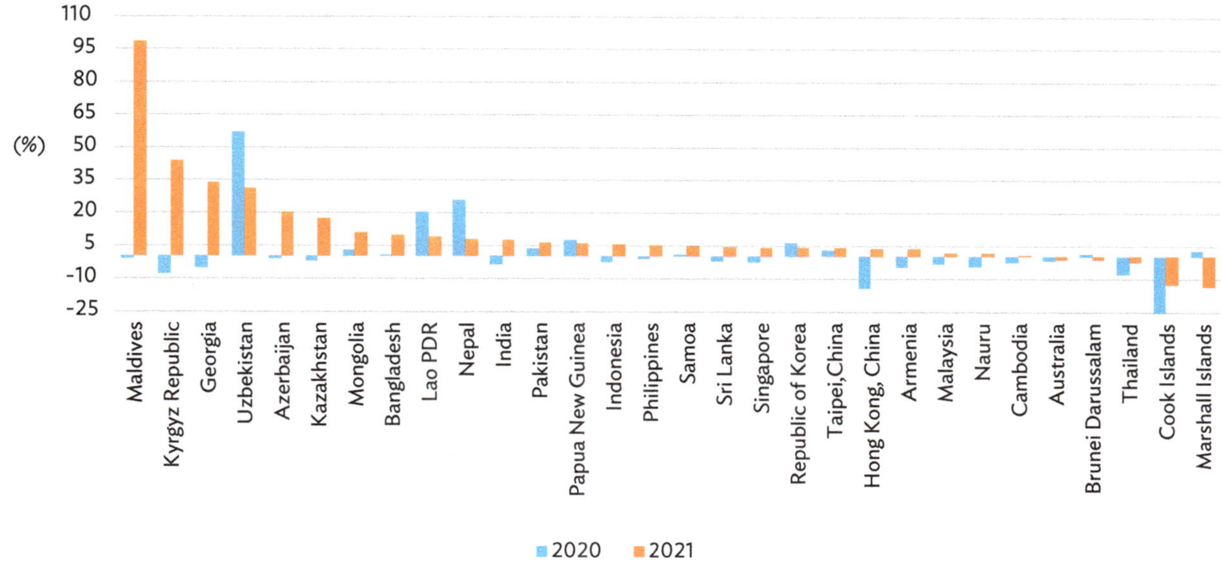

Lao PDR = Lao People's Democratic Republic.

Note: In general, the energy sector includes electricity, gas, steam, and air-conditioning supply; water supply; and sewerage, waste management, and remediation activities. Additional information about underlying data is provided in individual economy tables available at https://kidb.adb.org. The 2020 and 2021 figures refer to the growth rates for 2019–2020 and 2020–2021, respectively.

Source: Asian Development Bank estimates using data from the Key Indicators Database. https://kidb.adb.org (accessed 29 July 2022).

Click here for figure data

Figure 2.19: Changes in Gasoline and Diesel Retail Prices, 2020 and 2021

Reductions in energy prices in 2020 were countered by larger increases during 2021.

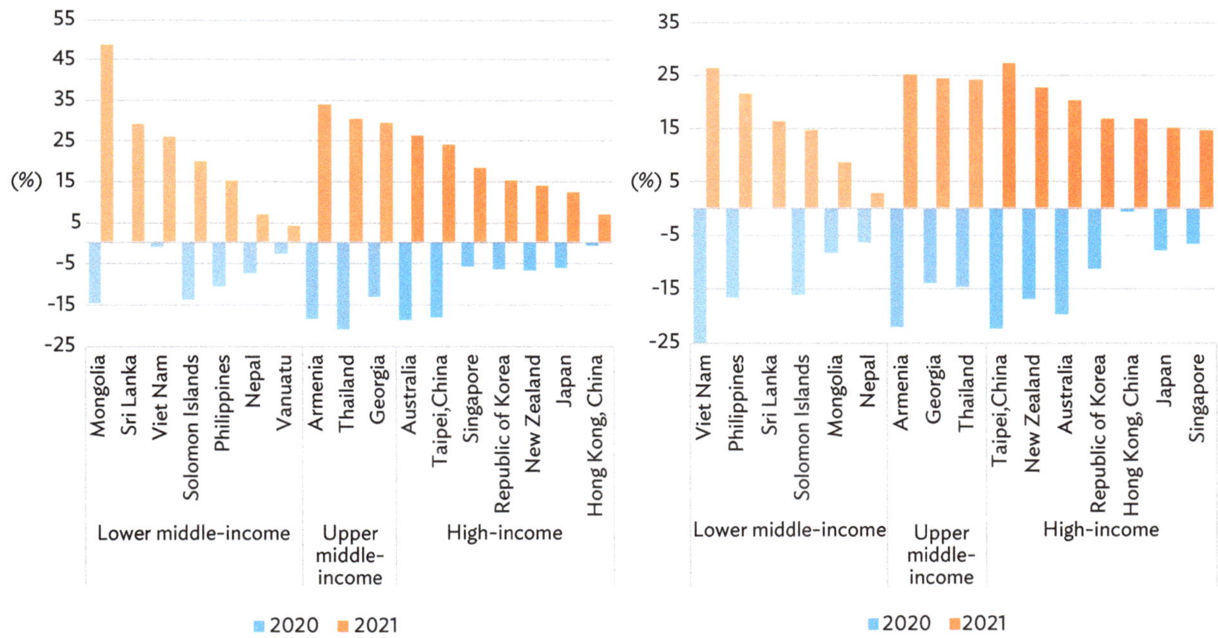

Note: The 2020 and 2021 figures refer to the growth rates for 2019–2020 and 2020–2021, respectively. Income groupings follow the World Bank Group's classification as of July 2022.

Source: Asian Development Bank estimates using data presented in individual economy tables available at https://kidb.adb.org.

Click here for figure data

Changing views on energy. A motorcyclist passes the Burgos Wind Farm in the Philippines (photo by Al Benavente/ADB).

During the COVID-19 pandemic, a reliable energy sector could help meet the needs of hospitals and other health care facilities in providing advanced medical services (ADB 2021b). It could also help sustain economic activity by supplying continuous and reliable electricity for people working from home and in other remote locations. Figure 2.20 shows electricity sufficiency for a range of economies in Asia and the Pacific. This is a measure of energy reliability calculated by dividing electricity production per capita by electricity consumption per capita (multiplied by 100). Prior to the pandemic, most economies with available data were electricity sufficient and half of the reporting economies further improved their sufficiency ratios in 2020.

The pandemic has also provided a glimpse of what it would look like if economies moved away from using fossil fuels as source of energy. Data from the International Energy Agency shows that global carbon dioxide emissions declined by more than 5.8% in 2020 (IEA 2021), primarily due to restrictions on human movements and the associated reduction in vehicular use. Yet, as economies reopen, GHG emissions have started increasing again.

It is therefore important to accelerate efforts toward greener sources of energy. Part I of this publication hinted that, prior to the pandemic, most regional economies with available data showed declines in carbon dioxide emissions per unit of manufacturing value-added, but several economies needed to improve their performance on this important measure. As well as declines in emissions, many upper middle-income and high-income economies also saw faster growth in the amount of electricity produced from alternative sources prior to the pandemic (Figure 2.21). Interestingly, the rate of increase is above average among small island developing states, perhaps because of their strong desire to introduce greener, more financially viable power generation solutions to limit the impacts of climate change (Dornan and Jotzo 2015).

Figure 2.20: Electricity Sufficiency in Selected Economies of Asia and the Pacific

Economies of Asia and the Pacific are generally electricity sufficient, making the region better able to cope in times of crisis.

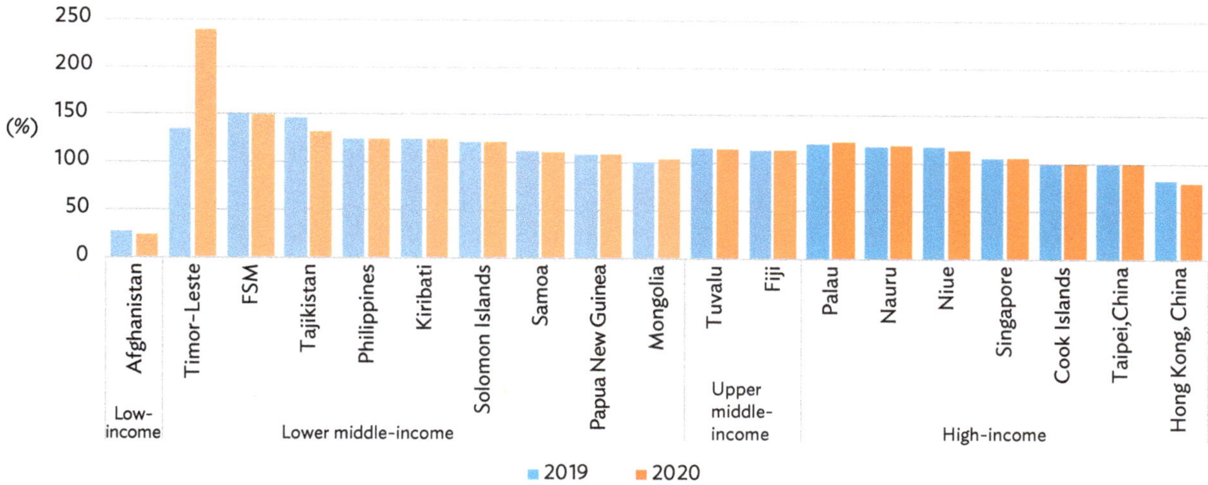

FSM = Federated States of Micronesia.

Notes: An electricity sufficiency greater than 100% indicates that electricity production is greater than electricity consumption. Income groupings follow the World Bank Group's classification as of July 2022. For Cook Islands and Niue, the "high-income" classification is based on 2019 gross national income per capita (Atlas method) of $18,761 and $16,247, respectively.

Source: Asian Development Bank estimates using data from Table 2.6.1 and Table 2.6.2 of *Key Indicators for Asia and the Pacific 2022* and the United Nations' World Population Prospects 2019.

Click here for figure data

Figure 2.21: Average Annual Growth Rate of Electricity from Alternative Sources

Growth in electricity from alternative sources is generally faster in upper middle-income and high-income economies, but small island developing states are also ramping their efforts in green energy solutions.

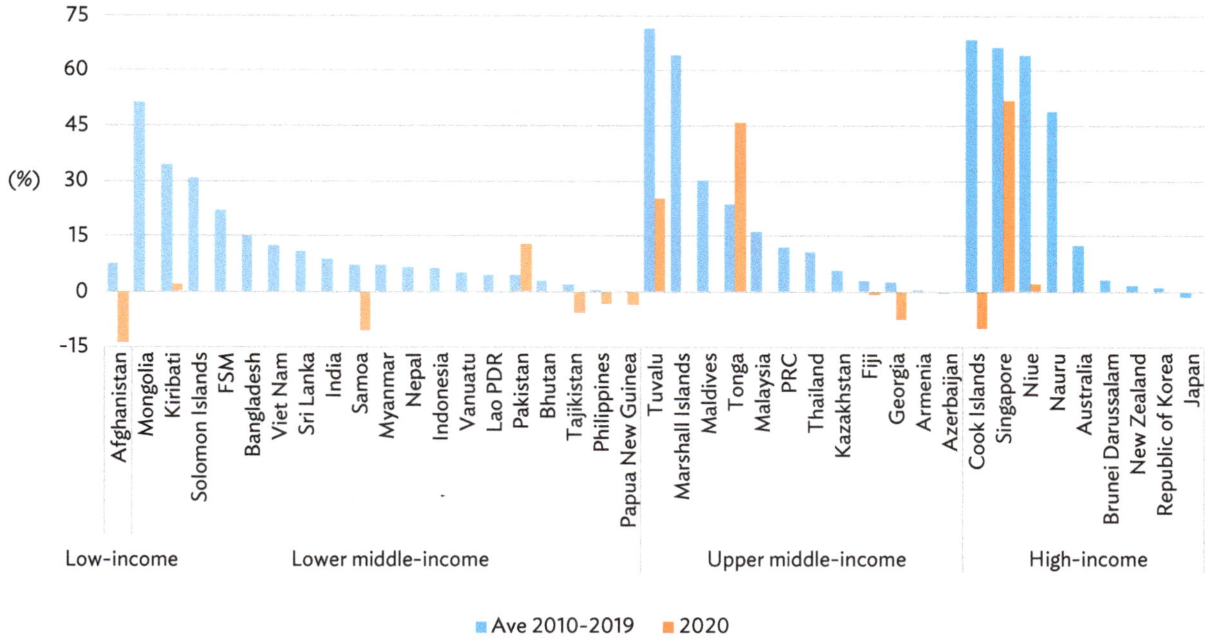

FSM = Federated States of Micronesia, Lao PDR = Lao People's Democratic Republic, PRC = People's Republic of China.

Notes: "Alternative sources" refers to hydropower, solar, chemical heat, geothermal, nuclear, tide, other marine electricity, wind, wave, and other sources of energy. The "Ave 2010–2019" bar shows the simple average of all the calculated individual percentage shares for each year from 2010 to 2019. The 2020 data refer to the growth rate from 2019 to 2020. Income groupings follow the World Bank Group's classification as of July 2022. For Cook Islands and Niue, the "high-income" classification is based on 2019 gross national income per capita (Atlas method) of $18,761 and $16,247, respectively.

Source: Asian Development Bank estimates using data from Table 2.6.1 of *Key Indicators for Asia and the Pacific 2022* and individual economy tables available at https://kidb.adb.org.

Click here for figure data

References

Asian Development Bank (ADB). 2020a. *Asia's Journey to Prosperity: Policy, Market, and Technology over 50 Years*. http://dx.doi.org/10.22617/TCS190290.

ADB. 2020b. *Reviving Tourism amid the COVID-19 Pandemic*. https://www.adb.org/sites/default/files/publication/633726/reviving-tourism-amid-covid-19-pandemic.pdf.

ADB. 2021a. *Asian Development Outlook Update*. Manila.

ADB. 2021b. *COVID-19 and Energy Sector Development in Asia and the Pacific*. Manila.

ADB 2021c. *Sustainable Tourism After COVID-19 – Insights and Recommendations for Asia and the Pacific*. https://www.adb.org/sites/default/files/publication/761511/sustainable-tourism-after-covid-19.pdf.

ADB. 2022a. *Asian Development Outlook 2022 Supplement*. Manila.

ADB. 2022b. *Reimagining the Future of Transport across Asia and the Pacific*. Manila.

U. Bajra, F. Aliu, B. Aver, and S. Cadez. 2022. COVID-19 Pandemic-Related Stringency and Economic Decline: Was it Really Inevitable? *Economic Research-Ekonomska Istraživanja*. DOI: 10.1080/1331677X.2022.2077792.

M. Dornan, and F. Jotzo. 2015. Renewable Technologies and Risk Mitigation in Small Island Developing States: Fiji's Electricity Sector. *Renewable and Sustainable Energy Reviews*. 48. pp. 35-48. https://www.sciencedirect.com/science/article/abs/pii/S1364032115002129.

International Energy Agency (IEA). 2021. Global Energy Review 2021: CO_2 Emissions https://www.iea.org/reports/global-energy-review-2021/co2-emissions.

International Finance Corporation (IFC). 2020a. The Impact of COVID-19 on Logistics. https://www.ifc.org/wps/wcm/connect/2d6ec419-41df-46c9-8b7b-96384cd36ab3/IFC-Covid19-Logistics-final_web.pdf?MOD=AJPERES&CVID=naqOED5.

IFC. 2020b. COVID-19's Impact on the Global Telecommunications Industry. https://www.ifc.org/wps/wcm/connect/1d490aec-4d57-4cbf-82b3-d6842eecd9b2/IFC-Covid19-Telecommunications_final_web_2.pdf?MOD=AJPERES&CVID=n9nxogP.

International Labour Organization (ILO). 2021. *ILO Monitor: COVID-19 and the World of Work: Eighth edition. Updated Estimates and Analysis*. https://www.ilo.org/wcmsp5/groups/public/---dgreports/---dcomm/documents/briefingnote/wcms_824092.pdf.

ILO. 2022. ILOSTAT Database. https://ilostat.ilo.org/data/ (accessed 5 June 2022).

ILO. 2019. Tech's Persistent Gender Gap. November 12. https://ilostat.ilo.org/techs-persistent-gender-gap/.

Intergovernmental Panel on Climate Change (IPCC). 2012. *Managing the Risks of Extreme Events and Disasters to Advance Climate Change Adaptation*. https://www.ipcc.ch/site/assets/uploads/2018/03/SREX_Full_Report-1.pdf.

International Telecommunication Union (ITU). 2020. *The Economic Impact of Broadband and Digitization through the COVID-19 Pandemic: Econometric Modelling*.

ITU. 2021. *Telecommunication Industry in the Post-COVID-19 World: Report of the 7th ITU Economic Experts Roundtable*.

N. Jiang and J. Ryan. 2020. How Does Digital Technology Help in the Fight Against COVID-19? *World Bank Blogs.* 29 May. https://blogs.worldbank.org/developmenttalk/how-does-digital-technology-help-fight-against-covid-19.

Y. Jinjarak, J. Kim, D. Park, and S. Tian. 2021. Did Internet Access Improve Economic Resilience During COVID-19? *Asian Development Blog.* 24 September. https://blogs.adb.org/blog/did-internet-access-improve-economic-resilience-during-covid-19.

Okuda, F. van Cappelle, and J. Bell. 2022. Tackling the Digital Gender Divide in Asia. https://www.itu.int/hub/2022/05/digital-gender-divide-asia-unicef-rosa/.

Organisation for Economic Co-operation and Development (OECD). 2020. Rebuilding Tourism for the Future: COVID-19 Policy Responses and Recovery. 14 December. https://www.oecd.org/coronavirus/policy-responses/rebuilding-tourism-for-the-future-covid-19-policy-responses-and-recovery-bced9859/.

United Nations Economic and Social Commission for Asia and the Pacific (UNESCAP) and United Nations Conference on Trade and Development (UNCTAD). 2020. *Covid-19 and its Impact on Shipping and Port Sector in Asia and the Pacific.* Technical Note. 30 September. https://www.unescap.org/sites/default/d8files/knowledge-products/ShippingPoliyBrief-16Oct2020-FINAL.pdf.

Table 2.1.1: Midyear Population

ADB Regional Member	Population (million)					Population Growth Rates[a] (%)				
	2010	2015	2019	2020	2021	2010	2015	2019	2020	2021
Developing ADB Member Economies										
Central and West Asia[b]	**276.6**	**303.9**	**337.1**	**343.5**	**349.4***	**2.0**	**1.9**	**1.9**	**1.9**	**1.9***
Afghanistan[c]	24.5	27.1	30.7	31.4	...	2.1	2.1	2.2	2.2	...
Armenia	3.1	3.0	3.0	3.0	3.0	-0.7	-0.2	-0.2	-0.2	0.1
Azerbaijan	9.1	9.6	10.0	10.1	10.1	1.2	1.2	0.9	0.7	0.4
Georgia	3.8	3.7	3.7	3.7	3.7	-0.7	0.2	-0.2	0.1	-0.4
Kazakhstan	16.1	17.5	18.5	18.8	19.0	1.7	1.5	1.3	1.4	1.3
Kyrgyz Republic[c]	5.4	5.9	6.4	6.5	6.6	1.3	2.1	2.1	2.1	1.7
Pakistan	173.5	191.7	216.1	220.4	224.8	2.1	2.0	2.0	2.0	2.0
Tajikistan	7.5	8.5	9.2	9.4	9.8*	2.5	2.4	2.2	2.0	1.7*
Turkmenistan	5.1	5.6	5.9	6.0	6.1	1.6	1.8	1.6	1.5	1.4
Uzbekistan	28.6	31.3	33.6	34.2	34.9	2.9	1.8	1.9	1.9	2.0
East Asia[b]	**1,423.3**	**1,468.0**	**1,496.2**	**1,498.4**	**1,498.6**	**0.5**	**0.5**	**0.3**	**0.1**	**0.0**
China, People's Republic of[c]	1,340.9	1,383.3	1,410.1	1,412.1	1,412.6	0.5	0.5	0.3	0.1	0.0
Hong Kong, China	7.0	7.3	7.5	7.5	7.4	0.7	0.9	0.7	-0.4	-0.9
Korea, Republic of	49.6	51.0	51.8	51.8	51.7	0.5	0.5	0.3	0.1	-0.2
Mongolia	2.7	3.0	3.3	3.4	3.4	1.6	2.1	1.8	1.8	1.6
Taipei,China	23.1	23.5	23.6	23.6	23.5	0.3	0.2	0.1	-0.0	-0.4
South Asia[b]	**1,382.6**	**1,492.6**	**1,561.2**	**1,577.4**	**1,594.4**	**1.4**	**1.2**	**1.1**	**1.1**	**1.0**
Bangladesh	148.6	158.9	166.5	168.2	171.7	1.4	1.4	1.4	1.4	1.4
Bhutan	0.7	0.8	0.7	0.7	0.8	1.8	1.6	1.0	0.9	1.0
India[c]	1,186.0	1,284.0	1,343.0	1,357.0	1,370.0	1.4	1.2	1.1	1.1	1.0
Maldives	0.4	0.5	0.5	0.6	0.6	2.3	3.9	4.3	4.4	2.0
Nepal	26.3	27.5	28.6	28.9	29.2	1.4	1.0	1.0	1.0	0.9
Sri Lanka	20.7	21.0	21.8	21.9	22.2	1.0	0.9	0.6	0.5	1.1
Southeast Asia[b]	**589.2**	**630.7**	**657.2**	**664.3**	**669.9***	**1.2**	**1.3**	**1.0**	**1.1**	**0.8***
Brunei Darussalam	0.4	0.4	0.5	0.5	0.4*	1.8	1.2	3.9	-1.3	-5.2*
Cambodia	14.1	15.1	16.0	16.2	16.6	1.3	1.4	1.4	1.4	1.5
Indonesia	237.6	255.6	266.9	270.2	272.7	1.4	1.4	1.0	1.2	1.0
Lao People's Democratic Republic	6.0	6.5	6.9	7.0	7.1	1.5	1.4	1.4	1.4	1.4
Malaysia	28.6	31.2	32.5	32.6	32.7	1.8	1.6	0.4	0.2	0.2
Myanmar[c]	50.2	52.5	54.3	54.8	55.3	0.7	0.9	0.9	0.9	0.9
Philippines	93.1	100.8	107.3	109.0	110.2	1.0	1.7 (2016)	1.5	1.6	1.1
Singapore	5.1	5.5	5.7	5.7	5.5	1.8	1.2	1.2	-0.3	-4.1
Thailand	65.9	68.0	69.3	69.5	69.7	0.6	0.6	0.3	0.3	0.3
Timor-Leste	1.1	1.2	1.3	1.3	1.3	1.8	1.9	2.0	2.0	1.9
Viet Nam	87.1	92.2	96.5	97.6	98.5	1.2	1.1	1.2	1.1	0.9
The Pacific[b,d]	**9.3**	**10.6***	**11.8***	**12.1***	**12.4***	**2.7**	**2.7***	**2.7***	**2.7***	**2.7***
Cook Islands	23.7	18.4*	20.2*	17.9*	18.2*	1.1	–*	1.6	-2.3	0.3
Fiji	850.7	869.5	889.3	891.4	893.5	0.6	0.4	0.6	0.6	0.6
Kiribati[c]	103.1	110.1	117.5	119.4	124.0	2.2	1.3	1.6	1.6	3.8
Marshall Islands	52.9	54.0	54.8*	55.0*	...	1.1	0.4	0.4*	0.4*	...
Micronesia, Federated States of[c]	102.8	103.7	104.5*	104.6*	104.8*	-0.5	0.2	0.2*	0.2*	0.2*
Nauru	9.7	10.8	11.6	11.7*	11.9*	1.9	1.7	1.6	1.6	1.6*
Niue	1.6 (2011)	1.5	1.9*	1.9*	...	1.4 (2013)	1.5	4.4	1.4*	...
Palau	18.3	17.7	17.5	17.6*	17.5*	-1.9	1.8	-0.5*	0.8	-0.6
Papua New Guinea	7,055.4	8,225.6	9,300.0	9,589.9	9,888.8	3.1	3.1	3.1	3.1	3.1
Samoa	185.9	193.8	200.3	201.9	203.6	0.8	0.8	0.8	0.8	0.8
Solomon Islands	555.5	625.6	680.8	694.6	708.5	2.6 (2011)	2.3	2.1	2.0	2.0
Tonga	102.8	101.7	99.6	99.0	98.5	0.2	-0.5	-0.5	-0.5	-0.5
Tuvalu	11.1	10.7	10.6	10.6	10.5	0.5	-0.3	-0.3	-0.3	-0.3
Vanuatu	239.7	268.6	291.7	297.2	304.0	2.4	2.3	2.3	1.9	2.3
Developed ADB Member Economies[b]	**154.5**	**155.6**	**156.6**	**156.6**	**156.5**	**0.3**	**0.2**	**0.1**	**0.0**	**-0.1**
Australia	22.0	23.8	25.4	25.7	25.7	1.5	1.4	1.5	1.3	0.2
Japan	128.1	127.1	126.3	125.8	125.7	0.0	-0.1	-0.2	-0.3	-0.1
New Zealand	4.4	4.6	5.0	5.1	5.1	1.1	2.1	1.6	2.2	0.4
DEVELOPING ADB MEMBER ECONOMIES[b]	**3,681.1**	**3,905.9***	**4,063.6***	**4,095.8***	**4,124.8***	**1.0**	**1.0***	**0.9***	**0.8***	**0.7***
ALL ADB REGIONAL MEMBERS[b]	**3,835.6**	**4,061.5***	**4,220.2***	**4,252.4***	**4,281.3***	**1.0**	**1.0***	**0.9***	**0.8***	**0.7***
WORLD	**6,956.8**	**7,379.8**	**7,713.5**	**7,794.8**	**7,875.0**	**1.2**	**1.2**	**1.1**	**1.1**	**1.0**

... = data not available; * = provisional, preliminary, estimate; – = magnitude equals zero; 0.0 = magnitude is less than half of unit employed; ADB = Asian Development Bank.

a The annual population growth rate is calculated as the percentage change in population when comparing the reference year with the year prior. For example, the population growth rates under the column heading "2020" refer to population growth from 2019 to 2020.

b Regional population totals include only reporting economies with data corresponding to the year heading, while regional population growth rates are estimated as a weighted average of the annual population growth rates of the reporting economies. Weights are based on the total population of the region for the years in which the reporting economies have published the annual growth rates.

c Estimates of population size are as of: 1 January for the Kyrgyz Republic; 10 June for Afghanistan; 30 September for the Federated States of Micronesia; 1 October for India and Myanmar; 7 November for Kiribati; and 31 December for the People's Republic of China.

d The total population for the Pacific subregion is expressed in millions, while estimates of population size for ADB developing member economies in the Pacific are expressed in thousands.

Sources: Economies' official sources. For Lao PDR (2000–2004), Nauru (2020 and 2021), Nepal (2012–2020), Papua New Guinea, Uzbekistan: Asian Development Bank estimates using data from the economies' official sources. For Korea (2021): Asian Development Bank estimates using data from the bank's Basic Statistics 2022 publication. For Myanmar (2010): World Bank. World Development Indicators. http://databank.worldbank.org/data/reports.aspx?source=world-development-indicators# (accessed 1 July 2017). For Nauru (2000-2012): Secretariat of the Pacific Community. http://www.spc.int/sdd/ (accessed 14 May 2016). For Nauru (2012–2013): International Monetary Fund. Staff Country Reports. Republic of Nauru: 2017 Article IV. http://www.imf.org/en/Publications/CR/Issues/2017/04/03/Republic-of-Nauru-2017-Article-IV-Consultation-Press-Release-Staff-Report-and-Statement-by-44794 (accessed 9 May 2021). For Turkmenistan and World: United Nations. World Population Prospects 2019. https://population.un.org/wpp/Download/Standard/Population/ (accessed 05 April 2022).

Table 2.1.2: Migration and Urbanization

ADB Regional Member	Net International Migration Rate[a] (per 1,000 population)		Urban Population[b] (% of total population)						
	2010–2015	2016–2021	2010	2016	2017	2018	2019	2020	2021
Developing ADB Member Economies									
Central and West Asia	...	...	**39.2**	**42.4**	**39.0**	**39.0**	**39.1**	**39.2**	**39.3***
Afghanistan[c]	3.3	-1.5	23.2	25.0	25.3	25.0	25.3	25.6	...
Armenia	-2.1	-1.7	63.4	63.1	63.1	63.1	63.2	63.3	63.4
Azerbaijan	0.2	–	53.0	53.0	53.0	52.9	52.8	53.0	52.9
Georgia	-4.7	-2.5	56.5	57.9	58.2	58.5	58.9	59.2	59.5
Kazakhstan	1.9	–	53.8	57.1	57.3	57.6	58.3	58.8	59.2
Kyrgyz Republic	-3.3	-1.5	34.1	33.7	33.8	33.9	34.0	34.2	34.4
Pakistan	-1.1	-0.9	36.9	41.7	36.5	36.6	36.7	36.8	36.8
Tajikistan	-3.4	-2.0	26.4	26.9	26.3	26.4	26.3	26.3	26.3*
Turkmenistan[d]	-1.9	-0.6	48.5	50.7	51.2	51.6	52.0	52.5	53.0
Uzbekistan	-0.4	-0.3	51.5	50.6	50.6	50.6	50.5	50.6	50.7
East Asia	...	...	**51.5**	**59.9**	**61.2**	**62.4**	**63.5**	**64.6**	**65.4**
China, People's Republic of	-0.2	-0.3	50.0	58.8	60.2	61.5	62.7	63.9	64.7
Hong Kong, China	2.1	3.1	100.0	100.0	100.0	100.0	100.0	100.0	100.0
Korea, Republic of[d]	1.6	0.4	81.9	81.6	81.5	81.5	81.4	81.4	81.4
Mongolia	-0.3	-0.3	69.2	68.3	67.6	67.9	68.5	69.0	69.4
Taipei,China[e]	1.5	1.0	59.3	61.0	61.1	60.9	61.0	61.1	61.1
South Asia	...	...	**29.1**	**32.8**	**33.1**	**33.6**	**33.9**	**35.0**	**35.4**
Bangladesh[d]	-3.0	-2.1	25.9	35.1	35.9	36.6	37.4	38.2	38.9
Bhutan[d]	0.1	0.4	34.8	39.4	37.8	40.9	40.9	42.3	43.0
India	-0.4	-0.3	29.9	33.0	33.3	33.7	34.0	34.3	34.6
Maldives[d]	28.4	-16.3	36.4	39.0	39.4	39.8	40.2	40.7	41.3
Nepal[f]	-15.1	5.1	16.6	19.6	20.1	20.8	21.4	62.4	63.2
Sri Lanka[d]	-4.7	-4.0	18.2	18.3	18.4	18.5	18.6	18.7	18.9
Southeast Asia	...	...	**44.2**	**47.8**	**48.3**	**48.8**	**49.4**	**50.2**	**50.8**
Brunei Darussalam[d]	-0.4	–	75.0	77.0	77.3	77.6	77.9	78.3	78.6
Cambodia[d]	-2.0	-1.7	20.3	22.6	23.0	23.4	23.8	24.2	24.7
Indonesia[d]	-0.4	-0.4	49.9	54.0	54.7	55.3	56.0	56.6	57.3
Lao People's Democratic Republic[d]	-3.5	-2.0	30.1	33.7	34.4	35.0	35.6	36.3	36.9
Malaysia	1.7	1.5	71.0	74.8	75.2	75.6	76.2	76.7	77.3
Myanmar[d]	-2.0	-0.7	28.9	29.4	29.5	30.0	30.0	31.1	31.4
Philippines[d]	-1.7	-0.6	45.3	46.5	46.7	46.9	47.1	47.4	47.7
Singapore	11.8	4.5	100.0	100.0	100.0	100.0	100.0	100.0	100.0
Thailand[g]	0.5	0.3	42.0	50.0	51.0	52.3	53.6	54.8	56.0
Timor-Leste	-4.9	-3.6	27.7	29.8	30.2	30.6	30.9	31.3	31.7
Viet Nam	-0.9	-0.9	30.4	33.7	33.9	34.2	35.0	36.8	37.1
The Pacific	...	...	**18.6**	**18.8**	**18.9**	**18.9**	**19.0**	**19.1***	**19.2**
Cook Islands[d]	...	...	73.3	74.6	74.8	75.1	75.3	75.5	75.7
Fiji	-12.0	-3.7	52.2	55.2	55.9	56.2	56.8	57.2	57.6
Kiribati	-7.7	-3.2	47.4	52.4	53.3	54.1	54.8	55.6	56.3
Marshall Islands[d]	...	...	73.6	76.2	76.6	77.0	77.4	77.8	78.2
Micronesia, Federated States of[d]	-5.7	-5.1	22.3	22.5	22.6	22.7	22.8	22.9	23.1
Nauru[d]	...	...	100.0	100.0	100.0	100.0	100.0	100.0	100.0
Niue[d]	...	...	38.7	43.3	44.1	44.8	45.5	46.2	46.9
Palau	...	...	77.0	78.7 (2015)	...	...	...	78.9*	...
Papua New Guinea[d]	-0.1	-0.1	13.0	13.1	13.1	13.2	13.3	13.3	13.5
Samoa	-12.8	-7.5	19.9	19.1	19.0	18.9	18.8	18.8	18.7
Solomon Islands[d]	-2.8	-2.2	20.0	22.8	23.3	23.7	24.2	24.7	25.1
Tonga	-25.4	-7.4	23.4	23.1	23.0	22.8	22.6	22.5	23.1
Tuvalu[d]	...	...	54.8	60.6	61.5	62.4	63.2	64.0	64.8
Vanuatu	1.4	–	24.4	24.9	24.9	25.0	25.1	25.2	25.3
Developed ADB Member Economies	...	...	**89.9**	**90.5**	**90.5**	**90.6**	**90.7**	**90.7**	**90.8**
Australia	8.6	5.2	85.7	86.5	86.7	86.8	86.9	87.0	86.9
Japan[d]	0.6	0.5	90.8	91.5	91.5	91.6	91.7	91.8	91.9
New Zealand	4.0	2.5	83.9	84.0	84.1	84.1	84.1	84.0	83.9
DEVELOPING ADB MEMBER ECONOMIES	...	...	**40.9**	**46.1**	**46.5**	**47.1**	**47.7**	**48.6***	**49.1***
ALL ADB REGIONAL MEMBERS	...	...	**42.9**	**47.8**	**48.1**	**48.7**	**49.3**	**50.2***	**50.6***
WORLD	...	...	**51.6**	**54.4**	**54.8**	**55.3**	**55.7**	**56.2**	**56.6**

... = data not available; * = provisional, preliminary, estimate; – = magnitude equals zero; ADB = Asian Development Bank.

a Refers to annual average migration over the period shown. United Nations population estimates and projections are based on all available sources of data on population size and levels of fertility, mortality, and international migration. Statistics on international migration are sourced from population registers and other administrative sources. These estimates and projections are made for 235 distinct national economies or areas comprising the total population of the world.

b In estimating the aggregates for Asia and the Pacific, imputation was done for economies with missing data by substituting available data from the nearest years. The aggregates were derived using data on total population and percentage of urban population from economies' official sources and the United Nations' World Urbanization Prospects 2018 and World Population Prospects 2019.

c For urban population, refers to the share of urban population to total resident population, i.e., excluding the nomadic population.

d For urban population, refers to data from World Urbanization Prospects 2018 for: 2014–2021 for Bangladesh; 2016, 2018, 2020, and 2021 for Bhutan; 2000–2020 for Maldives; 2000–2013, 2020, and 2021 for Myanmar; and the whole data series for Brunei Darussalam, Cambodia, the Cook Islands, the Federated States of Micronesia, Indonesia, Japan, the Lao People's Democratic Republic, the Marshall Islands, Nauru, Niue, Papua New Guinea, the Philippines, the Republic of Korea, Solomon Islands, Sri Lanka, Turkmenistan, and Tuvalu.

e For urban population, refers to localities of 100,000 or more inhabitants.

f For 2000, the figure is an estimate based on the 2001 census. For 2002–2010 and 2012 onward, the figures are estimates based on the 2011 census and refer to 58 urban municipalities. For 2020 onward, data refer to 293 urban municipalities.

g For urban population, data for 2010 onward include non-Thai citizens who are listed in the civil registration.

Sources: For net international migration rate: United Nations. World Population Prospects 2019. https://population.un.org/wpp/Download/Standard/Migration/ (accessed 08 July 2022). For urban population: economies' official sources; and United Nations. World Urbanization Prospects 2018. https://population.un.org/wup/Download/ (accessed 30 June 2022).

Table 2.1.3: Proportion of Total Population by Age Bracket, and Age Dependency Ratio

ADB Regional Member	Population Aged 0–14 Years (% of total population)				Population Aged 15–64 Years (% of total population)			
	2010	2015	2020	2021	2010	2015	2020	2021
Developing ADB Member Economies								
Central and West Asia	**35.9**	**34.7**	**34.1**	**33.9**	**59.7**	**60.9**	**61.3**	**61.4**
Afghanistan	48.2	44.9	41.8	41.2	49.5	52.6	55.5	56.1
Armenia	19.5	20.1	20.8	20.8	69.5	69.0	67.4	66.9
Azerbaijan	22.8	22.9	23.5	23.4	71.3	71.4	69.7	69.5
Georgia	18.0	19.0	20.2	20.3	67.8	66.7	64.5	64.2
Kazakhstan	24.1	26.7	29.1	29.2	69.1	66.5	63.0	62.7
Kyrgyz Republic	29.9	31.5	32.6	32.6	65.6	64.2	62.6	62.5
Pakistan	37.7	35.9	34.8	34.6	58.1	59.8	60.8	61.0
Tajikistan	35.7	35.8	37.3	37.4	61.0	61.2	59.6	59.3
Turkmenistan	29.5	30.4	30.8	30.6	66.3	65.5	64.4	64.4
Uzbekistan	29.1	28.4	28.8	28.7	66.4	67.6	66.4	66.2
East Asia	**18.5**	**17.8**	**17.5**	**17.3**	**73.3**	**72.7**	**70.4**	**70.0**
China, People's Republic of	18.7	18.1	17.7	17.6	73.3	72.6	70.3	70.0
Hong Kong, China	11.9	11.2	12.7	13.0	75.1	73.6	69.1	68.1
Korea, Republic of	16.1	13.8	12.5	12.3	73.2	73.4	71.7	71.2
Mongolia	27.0	28.9	31.1	31.2	69.2	67.3	64.6	64.3
Taipei,China	15.9	13.6	12.7	12.6	73.4	73.9	71.4	70.8
South Asia	**31.0**	**28.6**	**26.2**	**25.8**	**64.0**	**65.8**	**67.3**	**67.5**
Bangladesh	32.0	29.3	26.8	26.3	63.2	65.6	68.0	68.4
Bhutan	31.2	27.4	24.9	24.6	63.7	66.9	68.9	69.1
India	30.8	28.4	26.2	25.8	64.1	65.9	67.3	67.4
Maldives	25.3	21.2	19.6	19.8	70.2	74.8	76.8	76.4
Nepal	36.3	33.4	28.8	28.1	58.7	61.1	65.4	66.0
Sri Lanka	25.4	24.8	23.7	23.4	67.2	65.8	65.1	64.9
Southeast Asia	**27.9**	**26.5**	**25.2**	**24.9**	**66.6**	**67.5**	**67.7**	**67.7**
Brunei Darussalam	26.0	24.1	22.3	21.9	70.7	71.8	72.1	72.1
Cambodia	33.3	31.6	30.9	30.7	62.9	64.3	64.2	64.3
Indonesia	28.8	27.5	25.9	25.6	66.2	67.2	67.8	67.9
Lao People's Democratic Republic	36.4	33.6	31.9	31.6	59.9	62.6	63.8	64.0
Malaysia	28.0	25.1	23.4	23.3	67.1	68.9	69.4	69.3
Myanmar	30.0	27.8	25.5	25.1	65.1	67.0	68.3	68.4
Philippines	34.0	32.3	30.0	29.5	61.9	63.1	64.4	64.7
Singapore	14.0	12.6	12.3	12.4	78.7	78.3	74.3	73.3
Thailand	19.2	18.0	16.6	16.3	71.9	71.4	70.5	70.2
Timor-Leste	42.5	39.5	36.8	36.6	53.4	56.1	58.9	59.1
Viet Nam	23.6	23.0	23.2	23.2	69.9	70.3	68.9	68.6
The Pacific	**37.5**	**36.4**	**35.0**	**34.8**	**59.0**	**60.1**	**61.1**	**61.3**
Cook Islands	27.9	27.8	25.1	24.6	63.8	62.6	63.7	63.9
Fiji	29.0	29.8	29.0	28.9	66.2	65.2	65.2	65.1
Kiribati	36.1	35.0	35.9	35.8	60.3	61.4	59.9	59.8
Marshall Islands	41.8	39.8	37.5	37.0	55.9	57.5	58.7	59.1
Micronesia, Federated States of	35.7	32.8	31.2	31.0	61.1	63.8	64.4	64.4
Nauru	35.6	39.5	37.5	37.8	63.1	58.8	60.3	59.9
Niue	24.8	24.2	27.0	26.5	63.0	63.0	58.0	58.4
Palau	20.3	19.3	19.7	19.6	73.2	70.6	70.6	70.2
Papua New Guinea	38.3	36.8	35.1	34.8	58.4	60.0	61.3	61.5
Samoa	38.3	38.8	37.2	37.1	56.7	56.7	57.7	57.7
Solomon Islands	40.8	40.4	40.0	39.9	55.9	56.0	56.3	56.4
Tonga	37.4	36.4	34.8	34.4	56.9	57.6	59.3	59.7
Tuvalu	32.0	32.7	32.1	32.3	62.7	61.7	61.4	60.9
Vanuatu	38.2	39.1	38.4	38.2	57.9	57.2	58.0	58.2
Developed ADB Member Economies	**14.4**	**14.1**	**13.8**	**13.7**	**64.7**	**61.9**	**60.2**	**60.0**
Australia	19.0	18.9	19.3	19.3	67.6	66.3	64.5	64.2
Japan	13.4	13.0	12.4	12.3	64.1	61.0	59.2	59.0
New Zealand	20.5	20.0	19.4	19.3	66.4	65.4	64.2	64.0
DEVELOPING ADB MEMBER ECONOMIES	**26.1**	**24.7**	**23.5**	**23.3**	**67.6**	**68.2**	**68.0**	**67.9**
ALL ADB REGIONAL MEMBERS	**25.6**	**24.3**	**23.2**	**22.9**	**67.5**	**68.0**	**67.7**	**67.6**
WORLD	**27.0**	**26.2**	**25.4**	**25.4**	**65.5**	**65.6**	**65.2**	**65.2**

continued on next page

Table 2.1.3: Proportion of Total Population by Age Bracket, and Age Dependency Ratio *(continued)*

ADB Regional Member	Population Aged 65 Years and Older (% of total population)				Age Dependency Ratio for Total Population			
	2010	2015	2020	2021	2010	2015	2020	2021
Developing ADB Member Economies								
Central and West Asia	**4.5**	**4.4**	**4.6**	**4.7**	**67.6**	**64.3**	**63.1**	**62.9**
Afghanistan	2.3	2.5	2.6	2.7	102.0	90.0	80.1	78.2
Armenia	11.0	10.9	11.8	12.3	43.8	44.8	48.4	49.4
Azerbaijan	5.9	5.7	6.7	7.1	40.3	40.1	43.4	44.0
Georgia	14.2	14.3	15.3	15.6	47.5	50.0	55.0	55.8
Kazakhstan	6.8	6.8	7.9	8.2	44.6	50.3	58.8	59.6
Kyrgyz Republic	4.5	4.3	4.7	4.9	52.5	55.8	59.7	60.0
Pakistan	4.2	4.3	4.3	4.4	72.2	67.4	64.4	64.0
Tajikistan	3.3	2.9	3.2	3.3	63.9	63.4	67.9	68.6
Turkmenistan	4.1	4.1	4.8	5.0	50.7	52.7	55.2	55.3
Uzbekistan	4.5	4.1	4.8	5.0	50.7	48.0	50.6	51.0
East Asia	**8.2**	**9.5**	**12.2**	**12.6**	**36.5**	**37.6**	**42.1**	**42.8**
China, People's Republic of	8.1	9.3	12.0	12.4	36.5	37.7	42.2	42.9
Hong Kong, China	12.9	15.2	18.2	18.9	33.1	35.8	44.7	46.9
Korea, Republic of	10.7	12.9	15.8	16.6	36.6	36.3	39.5	40.5
Mongolia	3.8	3.9	4.3	4.5	44.6	48.6	54.8	55.5
Taipei,China	10.7	12.5	15.8	16.6	36.2	35.4	40.0	41.3
South Asia	**5.1**	**5.6**	**6.5**	**6.7**	**56.3**	**51.9**	**48.6**	**48.2**
Bangladesh	4.8	5.1	5.2	5.3	58.1	52.4	47.0	46.3
Bhutan	5.1	5.7	6.2	6.3	57.0	49.5	45.1	44.7
India	5.1	5.6	6.6	6.8	56.0	51.6	48.7	48.3
Maldives	4.6	3.9	3.6	3.8	42.5	33.6	30.2	30.9
Nepal	5.0	5.5	5.8	5.9	70.4	63.6	53.0	51.5
Sri Lanka	7.4	9.4	11.2	11.6	48.8	51.9	53.7	54.0
Southeast Asia	**5.5**	**6.0**	**7.1**	**7.4**	**50.1**	**48.2**	**47.7**	**47.7**
Brunei Darussalam	3.4	4.1	5.6	6.0	41.5	39.2	38.7	38.7
Cambodia	3.7	4.1	4.9	5.0	58.9	55.6	55.7	55.5
Indonesia	5.0	5.4	6.3	6.5	51.0	48.9	47.5	47.3
Lao People's Democratic Republic	3.7	3.8	4.3	4.4	67.0	59.9	56.8	56.2
Malaysia	4.9	6.0	7.2	7.4	49.0	45.1	44.2	44.3
Myanmar	4.8	5.2	6.2	6.5	53.5	49.2	46.5	46.2
Philippines	4.1	4.6	5.5	5.7	61.6	58.4	55.2	54.4
Singapore	7.3	9.0	13.4	14.3	27.0	27.7	34.5	36.4
Thailand	8.9	10.6	13.0	13.5	39.0	40.0	41.9	42.5
Timor-Leste	4.0	4.4	4.3	4.3	87.2	78.2	69.8	69.3
Viet Nam	6.5	6.7	7.9	8.2	43.1	42.2	45.1	45.7
The Pacific	**3.5**	**3.5**	**3.8**	**3.9**	**69.6**	**66.5**	**63.6**	**63.1**
Cook Islands	8.2	9.6	11.2	11.5	56.7	59.8	57.1	56.4
Fiji	4.8	5.0	5.8	6.0	51.1	53.4	53.4	53.7
Kiribati	3.6	3.5	4.2	4.3	65.8	62.7	67.0	67.2
Marshall Islands	2.3	2.7	3.8	4.0	78.8	74.0	70.5	69.3
Micronesia, Federated States of	3.2	3.4	4.4	4.6	63.7	56.9	55.2	55.2
Nauru	1.3	1.7	2.2	2.3	58.5	70.0	65.9	67.0
Niue	12.1	12.8	15.0	15.1	58.7	58.8	72.4	71.2
Palau	6.5	10.1	9.7	10.2	36.7	41.7	41.7	42.4
Papua New Guinea	3.3	3.2	3.6	3.7	71.3	66.8	63.2	62.6
Samoa	5.0	4.5	5.1	5.2	76.3	76.5	73.3	73.3
Solomon Islands	3.3	3.5	3.7	3.7	78.9	78.4	77.6	77.3
Tonga	5.7	6.0	5.9	6.0	75.8	73.6	68.6	67.6
Tuvalu	5.3	5.6	6.6	6.8	59.5	61.9	63.0	64.1
Vanuatu	3.9	3.7	3.6	3.6	72.8	74.8	72.5	71.8
Developed ADB Member Economies	**20.9**	**24.0**	**26.0**	**26.3**	**54.5**	**61.5**	**66.2**	**66.6**
Australia	13.4	14.9	16.2	16.5	47.9	50.9	55.1	55.8
Japan	22.5	26.0	28.4	28.7	55.9	64.0	69.0	69.5
New Zealand	13.1	14.6	16.4	16.7	50.5	52.9	55.8	56.3
DEVELOPING ADB MEMBER ECONOMIES	**6.3**	**7.0**	**8.5**	**8.8**	**47.9**	**46.5**	**47.1**	**47.3**
ALL ADB REGIONAL MEMBERS	**6.9**	**7.7**	**9.1**	**9.4**	**48.1**	**47.1**	**47.8**	**47.9**
WORLD	**7.6**	**8.2**	**9.3**	**9.3**	**52.8**	**52.4**	**53.3**	**53.3**

ADB = Asian Development Bank.

Notes:

1 All figures presented in this table are ADB estimates using data from the United Nations' World Population Prospects 2019 and/or official communications from The Pacific Community's Statistics for Development Division.

2 United Nations population estimates are based on all available sources of data on population size and levels of fertility, mortality, and international migration for 235 distinct economies or areas comprising the total population of the world.

Sources: United Nations. World Population Prospects 2019. https://population.un.org/wpp/ (accessed 04 April 2022). For the Cook Islands, the Marshall Islands, Nauru, Niue, Palau, and Tuvalu: The Pacific Community, Statistics for Development Division. Official communication, 15 April 2022; past communication.

Table 2.1.4: Labor Force Participation Rates
(%)

ADB Regional Member	2010	2015	2016	2017	2018	2019	2020	2021
Developing ADB Member Economies								
Central and West Asia								
Afghanistan[a,b]	49.8 (2011)	55.4 (2013)	...	53.9	...	...	41.9	...
Armenia[c]	61.2	62.5	61.0	60.9	58.9	59.9	58.5	...
Azerbaijan[c]	64.8	65.4	66.0	66.2	66.3	66.5	66.9	67.2
Georgia[c]	51.5	55.5	55.0	54.5	52.9	51.8	50.5	50.9
Kazakhstan	71.2	69.7	70.0	69.7	70.0	70.1	69.2	69.3
Kyrgyz Republic	64.2	62.4	61.5	60.1	59.8	60.2	60.1	...
Pakistan	45.9	45.2	...	...	44.3	44.8	...	44.9
Tajikistan	50.3	47.7	46.7	46.2	45.7	45.5	45.5	...
Turkmenistan[d]	48.9	47.1	46.9	46.8	46.6	46.5	46.0	45.8
Uzbekistan[c]	70.7	71.9	72.5	73.5	74.3	74.9	73.8	74.1
East Asia								
China, People's Republic of[d]	71.0	70.3	70.1	69.8	69.4	69.1	68.3	68.1
Hong Kong, China	59.6	61.1	61.1	61.1	61.3	60.7	59.7	59.4
Korea, Republic of	61.1	62.8	62.9	63.2	63.1	63.3	62.5	62.8
Mongolia[c]	61.6	61.5	60.5	61.1	61.0	60.5	58.8	56.9
Taipei,China	58.1	58.7	58.7	58.8	59.0	59.2	59.1	59.0
South Asia								
Bangladesh	59.3	57.1 (2013)	58.5	58.2	...	...	...	...
Bhutan[e]	68.6	63.1	62.2	63.3	62.6	66.4	67.8	69.1
India	40.0	...	...	...	36.9	37.5	40.1	41.6
Maldives[f]	52.1	63.8 (2014)	57.6	...	...	60.2	...	...
Nepal[c]	74.3 (2012)	72.2 (2014)	...	...	38.5	...	...	...
Sri Lanka	48.6	53.8	53.8	54.1	51.8	52.3	50.6	49.9
Southeast Asia								
Brunei Darussalam[c]	68.9 (2011)	65.6 (2014)	...	62.7	65.4	64.3	65.2	...
Cambodia	87.0	82.7	84.0	86.6	...	69.3	...	...
Indonesia	67.7	65.8	66.3	66.7	67.3	67.5	67.8	67.8
Lao People's Democratic Republic[c]	79.2	...	...	40.8	...	...	...	...
Malaysia[c]	63.7	67.9	67.7	68.0	68.3	68.7	68.4	68.6
Myanmar	67.0	64.7	...	61.2	61.5	63.2	...	...
Philippines	64.1	63.7	63.5	61.2	60.9	61.3	59.5	63.3
Singapore[g]	66.2	68.3	68.0	67.7	67.7	68.0	68.1	70.5
Thailand[h]	72.3	69.8	68.8	68.1	68.3	67.5	67.8	67.8
Timor-Leste[c]	24.0	30.6 (2013)	46.9	...	...	...	...	...
Viet Nam	76.7	77.4	77.3	76.9	77.0	76.8	74.4	67.7
The Pacific								
Cook Islands	71.0 (2011)	...	71.9	...	...	70.4	...	...
Fiji[i]	...	55.2 (2014)	58.3	57.1	...	64.1	...	...
Kiribati	59.3	66.0	...	...	...	...	53.0	...
Marshall Islands	41.7 (2011)	...	...	...	...	...	...	...
Micronesia, Federated States of	57.3	49.3 (2013)	...	...	...	...	...	...
Nauru[b]	64.0 (2011)	68.7 (2013)	...	...	...	...	...	...
Niue	68.9 (2011)	...	...	68.6	...	...	...	...
Palau	68.1 (2012)	77.4	...	...	...	...	...	...
Papua New Guinea[d]	48.3	47.8	47.8	47.7	47.8	47.7	47.3	47.2
Samoa[b]	41.3 (2011)	...	47.4	43.3	...	...	...	...
Solomon Islands	62.9 (2009)	73.8 (2013)	...	...	...	...	...	...
Tonga	94.8 (2003)	...	63.7	...	46.7	...	...	...
Tuvalu	59.4 (2012)	...	52.3	...	...	...	...	...
Vanuatu[d]	69.2	69.4	69.4	69.3	69.3	69.3	68.6	68.9
Developed ADB Member Economies								
Australia	65.4	65.0	64.9	65.2	65.6	66.0	65.0	65.8
Japan	59.6	59.6	60.0	60.5	61.5	62.1	62.0	62.1
New Zealand	67.6	68.8	70.0	70.9	70.9	70.5	70.2	70.8

... = data not available, * = provisional or preliminary, ADB = Asian Development Bank.

Note: Based on varying concepts and definitions of "labor force" across economies.

a For 2017, data cover the period from April 2016 to April 2017. For 2020, data cover the period from October 2019 to September 2020.
b Figures for different years may not be directly comparable with each other due to changes in methodology and labor concepts adopted.
c Recommendations from the 19th International Conference of Labour Statisticians were adopted by: Armenia, beginning 2018; Azerbaijan, beginning 2015; Brunei Darussalam, beginning 2017; Georgia, beginning 2010; the Lao People's Democratic Republic, for 2017; Malaysia, beginning 2019; Mongolia, beginning 2019; Nepal, for 2018; Timor-Leste, beginning 2010; and Uzbekistan, beginning 2017. Hence, data for these years may not be directly comparable with data in other years. The 19th conference provided the statistical concept of work for reference purposes; and the operational concepts, definitions, and guidelines for (i) three distinct subsets of work activities, referred to as forms of work, which include own-use production work, employment work, and volunteer work; (ii) related classifications of the population according to their labor force status and main work status; and (iii) measures of labor underutilization. The concept of employment has also been refined to refer to work for pay or profit.
d Data refer to estimates modeled by the International Labour Organization.
e For 2017, data are from the census of population. For all other years, data are from labor force surveys. Thus, data prior to and after the census year may not be directly comparable with 2017 data.
f Includes local population only.
g Refers to Singapore residents only.
h Includes the seasonally inactive labor force.
i For 2017, the reported number of employed people excludes those who are engaged in unpaid employment as of end of June. Hence, data for 2014 and 2016 are not comparable with data for 2017 because the former years include unpaid employment.

Sources: Economies' official sources. For Papua New Guinea, the People's Republic of China, Turkmenistan, and Vanuatu: International Labour Organization. ILOSTAT Database. http://www.ilo.org/ilostat/ (accessed 15 July 2022). For the Federated States of Micronesia (2013), Solomon Islands (2013), and Tuvalu: Pacific Data Hub. Explorer: National Minimum Development Indicators. https://stats.pacificdata.org/vis?lc=en&df[ds]=SPC2&df[id]=DF_NMDI&df[ag]=SPC&df[vs]=1.0&dq=A..NMDI0014%2BOTH._T._T._T..&pd=2010%2C2020&ly[rw]=GEO_PICT&ly[cl]=TIME_PERIOD&fs[0]=Development%20indicators%2C0%7CNational%20Minimum%20Development%20Indicators%23NMDI%23&pg=0&fc=Development%20indicators&lo=1 (accessed 15 July 2022).

Table 2.1.5: Employment in Agriculture, Industry, and Services
(% of total employment)

ADB Regional Member	Agriculture				
	2010	2015	2019	2020	2021
Developing ADB Member Economies					
Central and West Asia					
Afghanistan[a]	69.6 (2004)	43.6 (2017)	...	44.5	...
Armenia[b]	38.6	35.3	21.9	21.8	...
Azerbaijan[b]	38.2	36.4	36.0	36.3	36.3
Georgia[b,c]	26.2	23.0	19.1	19.8	18.9
Kazakhstan	28.3	16.2	13.5	13.5	13.4
Kyrgyz Republic	31.2	29.3	18.1	18.3	...
Pakistan	45.0	42.3	39.2	...	37.5
Tajikistan	65.9	64.9	61.2	60.9	...
Turkmenistan	29.4	24.6	20.7	...	...
Uzbekistan[b]	26.8	27.6	26.2	26.4	26.5
East Asia					
China, People's Republic of[d]	36.7	28.1	24.7	23.6	22.9
Hong Kong, China[e]	–	–	–	–	–
Korea, Republic of	6.6	5.1	5.1	5.4	5.3
Mongolia[b]	33.5	28.5	25.3	23.8	25.9
Taipei,China	5.2	5.0	4.9	4.8	4.7
South Asia					
Bangladesh	47.5	42.7 (2016)	...	...	...
Bhutan	59.4	58.0	51.1	49.9	49.2
India	53.2	...	...	...	...
Maldives[f]	4.3	9.0 (2016)	7.4	...	...
Nepal[b]	64.0 (2011)	...	21.5 (2018)	...	...
Sri Lanka[g]	32.5	28.7	25.3	27.1	...
Southeast Asia					
Brunei Darussalam[b]	1.3 (2011)	0.5 (2014)	2.0	1.3	...
Cambodia	72.3	64.3 (2014)	33.1	...	...
Indonesia	38.3	32.9	27.5	29.8	28.3
Lao People's Democratic Republic[b]	72.2	31.3 (2017)	...	...	...
Malaysia[b]	13.6	12.5	10.2	10.5	10.3
Myanmar	...	51.7	45.3	...	...
Philippines	33.2	29.2	22.2	24.8	24.2
Singapore[h]	0.2	0.1	0.1	0.1	0.1
Thailand	38.2	32.3	31.4	31.3	31.9
Timor-Leste[b]	26.3	31.6 (2016)	...	...	...
Viet Nam[i]	48.7	43.5	34.4	33.0	28.9
The Pacific					
Cook Islands[j]	4.3 (2011)	5.3 (2016)	2.5	...	...
Fiji[k]	1.7	19.2 (2016)	3.2	...	...
Kiribati[l]	22.1	24.3	...	23.2	...
Marshall Islands	1.0	1.1	1.0	0.8	0.7
Micronesia, Federated States of	52.2 (2000)	1.7	2.0 (2018)	...	...
Nauru	...	...	...	...	...
Niue	10.4 (2011)	8.7 (2017)	...	...	...
Palau[m]	7.8 (2005)	6.4	...	...	...
Papua New Guinea	65.3	59.0	55.4	...	...
Samoa	37.0 (2011)	41.9 (2016)	...	...	...
Solomon Islands[n]	25.2 (2009)	...	...	...	...
Tonga	27.9 (2006)	24.1 (2016)	20.0 (2018)	...	...
Tuvalu	...	...	...	...	...
Vanuatu	...	...	...	...	...
Developed ADB Member Economies					
Australia	3.2	2.6	2.5	2.8	2.4
Japan	4.0	3.6	3.3	3.2	3.1
New Zealand	6.7	6.2	5.8	6.0	6.1

continued on next page

Table 2.1.5: Employment in Agriculture, Industry, and Services *(continued)*
(% of total employment)

ADB Regional Member	Industry				
	2010	2015	2019	2020	2021
Developing ADB Member Economies					
Central and West Asia					
Afghanistan[a]	6.2 (2004)	17.8 (2017)	...	18.1	...
Armenia[b]	17.4	15.9	22.8	21.0	...
Azerbaijan[b]	13.7	14.1	14.8	14.6	14.9
Georgia[b,c]	10.5	10.1	19.2	18.2	19.0
Kazakhstan	18.7	21.0	19.7	19.7	19.7
Kyrgyz Republic	21.1	20.9	26.7	25.9	...
Pakistan	20.9	23.6	24.0	...	25.4
Tajikistan	7.9	6.7	8.6	8.6	...
Turkmenistan	35.2	37.7	39.9	...	...
Uzbekistan[b]	22.7	22.9	23.2	23.5	23.5
East Asia					
China, People's Republic of[d]	28.7	29.7	28.1	28.7	29.1
Hong Kong, China[e]	11.2	11.4	11.4	11.1	11.4
Korea, Republic of	25.0	25.4	24.6	24.7	24.6
Mongolia[b]	16.2	20.3	21.6	20.7	22.1
Taipei,China	35.9	36.0	35.6	35.4	35.5
South Asia					
Bangladesh	17.6	20.5 (2016)	...	...	...
Bhutan	6.6	9.6	15.5	14.9	15.4
India	21.5	...	...	...	...
Maldives[f]	9.4	18.4 (2016)	18.0	...	...
Nepal[b]	9.5 (2011)	...	30.8 (2018)	...	...
Sri Lanka[g]	24.6	25.8	27.6	26.9	...
Southeast Asia					
Brunei Darussalam[b]	19.6 (2011)	17.9 (2014)	20.7	23.7	...
Cambodia	9.2	9.0 (2014)	27.0	...	...
Indonesia	19.3	22.2	23.4	21.6	22.3
Lao People's Democratic Republic[b]	8.1	14.1 (2017)	...	...	...
Malaysia[b]	28.3	27.5	27.9	26.2	25.9
Myanmar	...	15.8	15.7	...	...
Philippines	15.0	16.2	19.3	18.3	18.4
Singapore[h]	21.8	17.2	14.8	14.8	14.4
Thailand	20.8	23.7	22.8	22.6	22.2
Timor-Leste[b]	14.3	17.5 (2016)	...	...	...
Viet Nam[i]	22.0	23.2	30.2	30.8	33.2
The Pacific					
Cook Islands[j]	11.7 (2011)	10.1 (2016)	11.3	...	...
Fiji[k]	23.9	14.4 (2016)	24.0	...	...
Kiribati[l]	16.1	18.2	...	5.6	...
Marshall Islands	22.0	14.4	15.1	13.5	12.8
Micronesia, Federated States of	...	9.1	9.6 (2018)	...	...
Nauru	...	...	...	...	...
Niue	14.2 (2011)	14.2 (2017)	...	...	...
Palau[m]	2.6 (2005)	11.7	...	...	...
Papua New Guinea	7.9	11.0	13.0	...	...
Samoa	12.2 (2011)	9.1 (2016)	...	...	...
Solomon Islands[n]	7.9 (2009)	...	...	...	...
Tonga	27.8 (2006)	25.6 (2016)	29.7 (2018)	...	...
Tuvalu	...	...	...	...	...
Vanuatu	...	...	...	...	...
Developed ADB Member Economies					
Australia	21.0	19.4	19.1	19.2	18.7
Japan	25.4	24.6	23.7	23.5	23.3
New Zealand	20.7	21.7	19.5	20.4	20.0

continued on next page

Table 2.1.5: Employment in Agriculture, Industry, and Services *(continued)*
(% of total employment)

ADB Regional Member	Services				
	2010	2015	2019	2020	2021
Developing ADB Member Economies					
Central and West Asia					
Afghanistan[a]	24.2 (2004)	38.6 (2017)	...	36.7	...
Armenia[b]	44.0	48.8	55.3	57.2	...
Azerbaijan[b]	48.1	49.6	49.2	49.0	48.8
Georgia[b,c]	63.3	66.8	61.7	61.9	62.1
Kazakhstan	53.0	62.8	66.8	66.8	66.9
Kyrgyz Republic	47.7	49.8	55.2	55.9	...
Pakistan	34.2	34.2	36.8	...	37.2
Tajikistan	26.3	28.4	30.2	30.5	...
Turkmenistan	35.4	37.7	39.3	...	...
Uzbekistan[b]	50.5	49.5	50.6	50.0	50.0
East Asia					
China, People's Republic of[d]	34.6	42.3	47.1	47.7	48.0
Hong Kong, China[e]	88.9	88.5	88.6	88.6	88.6
Korea, Republic of	68.4	69.5	70.3	70.0	70.1
Mongolia[b]	50.2	51.3	53.1	55.5	52.0
Taipei,China	58.8	59.0	59.6	59.8	59.8
South Asia					
Bangladesh	35.3	36.9 (2016)	...	...	...
Bhutan	33.7	32.4	33.4	35.2	35.4
India	25.3	...	...	...	...
Maldives[f]	86.3	72.6 (2016)	74.6	...	...
Nepal[b]	25.7 (2011)	...	47.7 (2018)	...	...
Sri Lanka[g]	42.9	45.6	47.1	46.0	...
Southeast Asia					
Brunei Darussalam[b]	79.1 (2011)	81.6 (2014)	77.4	74.9	...
Cambodia	18.6	26.6 (2014)	39.8	...	...
Indonesia	42.3	44.9	49.0	48.7	49.3
Lao People's Democratic Republic[b]	19.7	54.6 (2017)	...	...	...
Malaysia[b]	58.1	60.0	61.9	63.4	63.8
Myanmar	...	32.5	39.0	...	...
Philippines	51.8	54.6	58.4	56.9	57.4
Singapore[h]	77.9	82.7	84.9	85.1	85.4
Thailand	41.0	44.0	45.7	46.1	45.9
Timor-Leste[b]	59.4	50.9 (2016)	...	...	...
Viet Nam[i]	29.7	33.3	35.3	36.2	38.0
The Pacific					
Cook Islands[j]	84.0 (2011)	84.6 (2016)	86.3	...	...
Fiji[k]	74.4	66.4 (2016)	72.8	...	...
Kiribati[l]	61.8	57.5	...	71.2	...
Marshall Islands	77.1	84.5	83.0	84.8	85.7
Micronesia, Federated States of	...	89.2	88.4 (2018)	...	...
Nauru	...	...	...	...	...
Niue	75.4 (2011)	77.1 (2017)	...	...	...
Palau[m]	89.6 (2005)	82.0	...	...	...
Papua New Guinea	26.7	28.7	30.2	...	...
Samoa	50.9 (2011)	48.5 (2016)	...	...	...
Solomon Islands[n]	66.9 (2009)	...	...	...	...
Tonga	44.3 (2006)	50.3 (2016)	50.3 (2018)	...	...
Tuvalu	...	...	...	...	...
Vanuatu	...	...	...	...	...
Developed ADB Member Economies					
Australia	75.9	78.0	78.4	78.0	78.9
Japan	70.5	71.8	73.0	73.3	73.6
New Zealand	72.6	72.1	74.7	73.6	73.9

... = data not available, – = magnitude equals zero, ADB = Asian Development Bank.

Note: Data are based on varying labor force concepts and definitions adopted by different economies. Some values may not add up to 100% due to limitations on data availability.

a For 2017, data cover the period from April 2016 to April 2017. For 2020, data cover the period from October 2019 to September 2020. For 2011 onward, different methodologies were used in surveys for labor force estimation, therefore, data are not directly comparable overtime.
b Recommendations from the 19th International Conference of Labour Statisticians have been adopted by: Armenia, beginning 2018; Azerbaijan, beginning 2015; Brunei Darussalam, beginning 2017; Georgia, beginning 2010; the Lao People's Democratic Republic, for 2017; Malaysia, beginning 2019; Mongolia, beginning 2019; Nepal, for 2018; Timor-Leste, beginning 2010; and Uzbekistan, beginning 2017. Hence, data for these years may not be directly comparable with data for other years. The 19th conference provided the statistical concept of work for reference purposes; and the operational concepts, definitions, and guidelines for (i) three distinct subsets of work activities, referred to as forms of work, which include own-use production work, employment work, and volunteer work; (ii) related classifications of the population according to their labor force status and main work status; and (iii) measures of labor underutilization. The concept of employment has also been refined to refer to work for pay or profit.
c Prior to 2017, employment in services includes people who were engaged in construction industries.
d Refers to persons engaged in social labor and receiving remuneration or earning business income.
e Employment in services includes people who are engaged in electricity and gas supply; water supply; and sewerage, waste management, and remediation activities.
f Figures include local population only. For 2010, employment in services includes people who were engaged in industries other than agriculture, forestry, and fishing; mining and quarrying; or manufacturing.
g Some data may not add up because data for 2010 exclude the northern and eastern provinces.
h Refers to Singapore residents only.
i Refers to total number of persons engaged in any activity regardless of age.
j Covers all wage and salary earners from all islands.
k For 2010 and 2018, the reported number of employed people excludes those who are engaged in unpaid employment as of end of June. For 2016, figures are not comparable with other years because they include unpaid employment.
l Refers to cash work and unpaid village work. For 2010, employment in agriculture includes people who were engaged in mining and quarrying.
m For 2005, employment in services includes people who were engaged in electricity, gas, water, and construction industries.
n For 2009, the figure refers to paid employment.

Source: Asian Development Bank estimates using data from economies' official sources.

Table 2.1.6: Poverty and Inequality

ADB Regional Member	Proportion of Population Living on Less Than $1.90 a Day (2011 PPP)[a] (%)			Proportion of Population Living on Less Than $3.20 a Day (2011 PPP)[a] (%)			Income Ratio of Highest 20% to Lowest 20%[b]			Gini Coefficient[c]		
	2010	2015	2020	2010	2015	2020	2010	2015	2019	2010	2015	2020
Developing ADB Member Economies												
Central and West Asia												
Afghanistan	...	...	...	...	...	...	...	...	...	...	...	...
Armenia	1.0	1.3	0.4	14.1	9.5	6.9	4.3	5.0	4.3	0.300	0.324	0.252
Azerbaijan[d]	0.0(2005)	...	...	0.0(2005)	...	...	3.5(2005)	...	...	0.266(2005)	...	...
Georgia	12.0	3.7	4.2	30.6	15.7	17.0	8.0	6.5	6.3	0.395	0.365	0.345
Kazakhstan	0.1	0.0	0.0(2018)	1.5	0.3	0.2(2018)	4.0	3.7	3.9(2018)	0.280	0.268	0.278(2018)
Kyrgyz Republic	2.8	1.8	1.1	19.0	18.4	16.2	4.5	4.1	4.1	0.301	0.290	0.290
Pakistan[e]	7.4	3.8	3.6(2018)	47.1	35.5	34.5(2018)	4.1	4.7	4.5(2018)	0.288	0.313	0.296(2018)
Tajikistan	4.0(2009)	4.1	...	22.5(2009)	17.8	...	4.7(2009)	5.6	...	0.308(2009)	0.340	...
Turkmenistan	...	...	...	...	...	...	...	...	...	...	...	...
Uzbekistan[f]	61.6(2003)	...	...	86.2(2003)	...	...	5.9(2003)	...	...	0.353(2003)	...	...
East Asia												
China, People's Republic of	11.2	0.7	0.1(2019)	28.6	7.0	1.7(2019)	9.6	7.1	7.0(2016)	0.437	0.386	0.382(2019)
Hong Kong, China	...	...	...	...	...	...	...	...	...	...	...	...
Korea, Republic of	0.5	0.2(2014)	0.2(2016)	0.7	0.5(2014)	0.2(2016)	5.4	5.2(2014)	5.2(2016)	0.320	0.312(2014)	0.314(2016)
Mongolia	0.7	0.2(2014)	0.5(2018)	9.6	3.0(2014)	5.0(2018)	5.3	5.0(2014)	5.2(2018)	0.331	0.320(2014)	0.327(2018)
Taipei,China[g]	0.0	0.0(2013)	0.0(2016)	0.2	0.2(2013)	0.0(2016)	4.3	3.9	3.8(2020)	0.296	0.279	0.274
South Asia												
Bangladesh	19.2	...	14.3(2016)	60.0	...	52.3(2016)	4.7	...	4.8(2016)	0.321	...	0.324(2016)
Bhutan	8.2(2007)	2.2(2012)	1.5(2017)	30.6(2007)	14.7(2012)	12.2(2017)	6.7(2007)	6.9(2012)	6.6(2017)	0.381(2007)	0.388(2012)	0.374(2017)
India[e]	22.5(2011)	...	...	61.7(2011)	...	...	5.5(2011)	...	...	0.357(2011)	...	...
Maldives[e]	3.5(2009)	...	0.0(2019)	16.6(2009)	...	0.0(2019)	7.0(2009)	...	4.8(2016)	0.384(2009)	...	0.293(2019)
Nepal[e]	15.0	...	...	50.9	...	...	5.0	...	...	0.328	...	...
Sri Lanka	2.8(2009)	1.9(2012)	0.9(2016)	19.9(2009)	16.2(2012)	11.0(2016)	5.7(2009)	6.4(2012)	6.6(2016)	0.361(2009)	0.387(2012)	0.393(2016)
Southeast Asia												
Brunei Darussalam	...	...	...	...	...	...	...	...	...	...	...	...
Cambodia	...	...	...	...	...	...	...	...	...	...	...	...
Indonesia	13.3	5.8	2.2(2021)	45.0	30.6	18.0(2021)	5.8	6.8	6.6	0.364	0.397	0.373(2021)
Lao People's Democratic Republic[e]	25.7(2007)	14.5(2012)	10.0(2018)	64.1(2007)	46.6(2012)	37.4(2018)	5.5(2007)	5.8(2012)	6.6(2018)	0.354(2007)	0.360(2012)	0.388(2018)
Malaysia	0.1(2011)	0.0	...	1.2(2011)	0.3	...	9.5(2011)	8.2	...	0.439(2011)	0.411	...
Myanmar	...	4.8	1.4(2017)	...	24.6	15.0(2017)	...	6.3	4.5(2017)	...	0.381	0.307(2017)
Philippines[h]	10.7(2009)	7.8	4.7(2018)	37.0(2009)	31.9	25.5(2018)	9.9(2009)	9.1	7.9(2018)	0.418(2009)	0.404	0.378(2018)
Singapore	...	...	...	...	...	...	...	...	...	...	...	...
Thailand	0.1	0.0	0.0	2.4	0.5	0.4	7.0	5.8	5.6	0.394	0.360	0.350
Timor-Leste	37.4(2007)	22.0(2014)	...	77.3(2007)	65.9(2014)	...	3.9(2007)	4.1(2014)	...	0.278(2007)	0.287(2014)	...
Viet Nam	4.0	2.6(2014)	1.8(2018)	16.8	11.0(2014)	6.6(2018)	7.1	5.9(2014)	6.4(2018)	0.393	0.348(2014)	0.357(2018)
The Pacific												
Cook Islands	...	...	...	...	...	...	...	...	...	...	...	...
Fiji[e]	1.6(2008)	0.5(2013)	1.8(2019)	10.9(2008)	7.5(2013)	14.5(2019)	7.2(2008)	6.0(2013)	...	0.404(2008)	0.367(2013)	0.307(2019)
Kiribati	12.9(2006)	...	1.3(2019)	34.6(2006)	...	16.2(2019)	6.7(2006)	...	...	0.370(2006)	...	0.278(2019)
Marshall Islands	...	...	...	...	...	...	...	...	...	...	...	...
Micronesia, Federated States of	8.1(2005)	15.4(2013)	...	24.6(2005)	38.7(2013)	...	8.7(2005)	8.4(2013)	...	0.424(2005)	0.401(2013)	...
Nauru	...	0.9(2012)	...	...	13.3(2012)	...	...	5.7(2012)	...	...	0.348(2012)	...
Niue	...	...	...	...	...	...	...	...	...	...	...	...
Palau	...	...	...	...	...	...	...	...	...	...	...	...
Papua New Guinea[e]	38.0(2009)	...	...	65.6(2009)	...	...	9.3(2009)	...	...	0.419(2009)	...	...
Samoa[e]	0.6(2008)	1.1(2013)	...	9.6(2008)	9.6(2013)	...	7.7(2008)	6.8(2013)	...	0.420(2008)	0.387(2013)	...
Solomon Islands	48.6(2005)	24.7(2012)	...	73.0(2005)	58.1(2012)	...	10.4(2005)	6.4(2012)	...	0.461(2005)	0.371(2012)	...
Tonga	1.1(2009)	1.0	...	8.9(2009)	7.5	...	6.7(2009)	6.7	...	0.375(2009)	0.376	...
Tuvalu	3.3	...	...	17.6	...	...	7.0	...	...	0.391	...	...
Vanuatu	13.1	...	8.6(2019)	39.4	...	32.3(2019)	6.7	...	...	0.374	...	0.323(2019)
Developed ADB Member Economies												
Australia	...	...	...	...	...	...	5.8	5.7(2014)	...	0.347	0.344(2014)	0.343(2018)
Japan	...	...	...	...	...	...	4.9	5.3(2013)	...	0.321	0.329(2013)	...
New Zealand[i]	...	...	...	...	...	...	...	...	...	0.335	0.325	0.320

... = Data not available, 0.0 = magnitude is less than half the unit employed or true zero value, $ = United States dollars, ADB = Asian Development Bank, PPP = purchasing power parity.

a Poverty estimates are consumption-based, except for Malaysia; the Republic of Korea; and Taipei,China, whose estimates are income-based.
b Derived from the income or expenditure share of the highest 20% and lowest 20% groups by income.
c Inequality estimates are consumption-based, except for Malaysia; the Republic of Korea; and Taipei,China, whose estimates are income-based.
d The most recent year data are for 2005: 0.0% for proportion of population below $1.90 a day (2011 PPP); 0.0% for proportion of population below $3.20 a day (2011 PPP); 3.5 for income ratio of highest 20% to lowest 20%; and 0.266 for Gini coefficient.
e Household income and expenditure surveys for these economies were conducted in overlapping years. The table adopts the approach of the World Bank's World Development Indicators, i.e., using the initial year of the survey as the reference period for the poverty estimates.
f The most recent year data are for 2003: 61.6% for proportion of population below $1.90 a day (2011 PPP); 86.2% for proportion of population below $3.20 a day (2011 PPP); 5.9 for income ratio of highest 20% to lowest 20%; and 0.353 for Gini coefficient.
g The Gini coefficient reflected in the table refers to the coefficient using per capita disposable income published by the Government of Taipei,China's Directorate-General of Budget, Accounting and Statistics. The estimates using disposable income of households are 0.326 for 2000 and 0.340 for 2020. Alternative estimates for the Gini coefficient are available in the World Bank's Poverty and Inequality Platform.
h Consumption-based poverty estimates were used. However, income-based estimates are also available for the $1.90 poverty line, 10.7% (2009), 6.1% (2015), and 2.7% (2018); and for the $3.20 poverty line 38.2% (2009), 25.7% (2015), and 17.0% (2018).
i The Gini coefficient data are based on disposable income post taxes and transfers, using the new definition.

Sources: World Bank. World Development Indicators. http://data.worldbank.org/data-catalog/world-development-indicators (accessed 15 July 2022); and World Bank. Poverty and Inequality Platform. https://pip.worldbank.org/ (accessed 30 May 2022). For New Zealand's Gini coefficient: Organisation for Economic Co-operation and Development. Income Distribution and Poverty. https://stats.oecd.org/index.aspx?queryid=66670# (accessed 24 July 2022). For Taipei,China's income ratio and Gini coefficient: Government of Taipei,China, Directorate-General of Budget, Accounting and Statistics. http://eng.dgbas.gov.tw/mp.asp?mp=2 (accessed 24 July 2022).

Table 2.1.7: Human Development Index

ADB Regional Member	2010	2013	2015	2016	2017	2018	2019	Rank in 2019[a]
Developing ADB Member Economies								
Central and West Asia	**0.661**	**0.679**	**0.688**	**0.691**	**0.696**	**0.699**	**0.704**	...
Afghanistan	0.472	0.496	0.500	0.502	0.506	0.509	0.511	169
Armenia	0.747	0.762	0.768	0.766	0.769	0.771	0.776	81
Azerbaijan	0.726	0.735	0.744	0.751	0.754	0.754	0.756	88
Georgia	0.751	0.775	0.790	0.792	0.799	0.805	0.812	61
Kazakhstan	0.764	0.791	0.806	0.808	0.815	0.819	0.825	51
Kyrgyz Republic	0.662	0.680	0.690	0.691	0.694	0.696	0.697	120
Pakistan	0.512	0.523	0.536	0.542	0.550	0.552	0.557	154
Tajikistan	0.638	0.653	0.652	0.653	0.657	0.661	0.668	125
Turkmenistan	0.666	0.685	0.694	0.699	0.701	0.710	0.715	111
Uzbekistan	0.669	0.692	0.701	0.705	0.713	0.717	0.720	106
East Asia	**0.812**	**0.830**	**0.839**	**0.845**	**0.848**	**0.852**	**0.856**	...
China, People's Republic of	0.699	0.724	0.739	0.746	0.750	0.755	0.761	85
Hong Kong, China	0.904	0.918	0.930	0.936	0.941	0.946	0.949	4
Korea, Republic of	0.889	0.901	0.907	0.910	0.912	0.914	0.916	23
Mongolia	0.696	0.727	0.735	0.729	0.728	0.735	0.737	99
Taipei,China	0.873	0.882	0.885	0.903	0.907	0.911	0.916	...
South Asia	**0.614**	**0.640**	**0.655**	**0.660**	**0.666**	**0.671**	**0.676**	...
Bangladesh	0.557	0.579	0.595	0.606	0.616	0.625	0.632	133
Bhutan	0.574	0.610	0.628	0.637	0.646	0.649	0.654	129
India	0.579	0.604	0.624	0.630	0.640	0.642	0.645	131
Maldives	0.685	0.709	0.724	0.728	0.731	0.734	0.740	95
Nepal	0.537	0.568	0.583	0.586	0.588	0.596	0.602	142
Sri Lanka	0.754	0.769	0.776	0.773	0.775	0.779	0.782	72
Southeast Asia	**0.678**	**0.696**	**0.703**	**0.707**	**0.710**	**0.713**	**0.718**	...
Brunei Darussalam	0.827	0.839	0.838	0.839	0.838	0.836	0.838	47
Cambodia	0.539	0.559	0.570	0.576	0.582	0.585	0.594	144
Indonesia	0.665	0.687	0.695	0.703	0.707	0.712	0.718	107
Lao People's Democratic Republic	0.552	0.582	0.598	0.605	0.608	0.609	0.613	137
Malaysia	0.772	0.785	0.796	0.800	0.805	0.805	0.810	62
Myanmar	0.515	0.543	0.557	0.563	0.572	0.579	0.583	147
Philippines	0.671	0.691	0.701	0.704	0.708	0.711	0.718	107
Singapore	0.909	0.921	0.931	0.935	0.933	0.936	0.938	11
Thailand	0.724	0.734	0.749	0.756	0.765	0.772	0.777	79
Timor-Leste	0.628	0.630	0.610	0.598	0.599	0.599	0.606	141
Viet Nam	0.661	0.681	0.688	0.693	0.696	0.700	0.704	117
The Pacific	**0.638**	**0.651**	**0.659**	**0.660**	**0.665**	**0.666**	**0.669**	...
Cook Islands	...	...	...	...	...	...	...	...
Fiji	0.715	0.728	0.737	0.738	0.740	0.742	0.743	93
Kiribati	0.593	0.608	0.625	0.622	0.627	0.628	0.630	134
Marshall Islands	...	...	...	...	0.699	0.702	0.704	117
Micronesia, Federated States of	0.601	0.605	0.612	0.614	0.616	0.618	0.620	136
Nauru	...	...	...	...	...	...	...	...
Niue	...	...	...	...	...	...	...	...
Palau	0.786	0.821	0.820	0.822	0.822	0.822	0.826	50
Papua New Guinea	0.522	0.537	0.548	0.549	0.549	0.549	0.555	155
Samoa	0.698	0.700	0.707	0.710	0.710	0.709	0.715	111
Solomon Islands	0.537	0.558	0.563	0.561	0.562	0.564	0.567	151
Tonga	0.699	0.708	0.720	0.722	0.723	0.723	0.725	104
Tuvalu	...	...	...	...	...	...	...	...
Vanuatu	0.590	0.593	0.598	0.598	0.601	0.603	0.609	140
Developed ADB Member Economies	**0.908**	**0.916**	**0.922**	**0.925**	**0.927**	**0.929**	**0.931**	...
Australia	0.930	0.931	0.938	0.939	0.941	0.943	0.944	8
Japan	0.887	0.902	0.908	0.912	0.915	0.917	0.919	19
New Zealand	0.906	0.914	0.921	0.924	0.926	0.928	0.931	14
DEVELOPING ADB MEMBER ECONOMIES	**0.672**	**0.690**	**0.699**	**0.702**	**0.706**	**0.709**	**0.713**	
ALL ADB REGIONAL MEMBERS	**0.688**	**0.705**	**0.714**	**0.718**	**0.721**	**0.724**	**0.728**	
WORLD[b]	**0.697**	**0.713**	**0.722**	**0.727**	**0.729**	**0.731**	**0.737**	

... = data not available, ADB = Asian Development Bank.

Notes:

1 Regional indexes are calculated as an arithmetic average of the indexes of reporting economies with data corresponding to the year heading.

2 The Human Development Index (HDI) is calculated by the Human Development Report Office of the United Nations Development Programme (UNDP) using the most recently revised historical data from national and international agencies, which continually improve their data series. Hence, the HDI values and ranks presented in this table are not comparable to those published in previous editions. For this 2022 edition, HDI data presented depict the state of human development before the COVID-19 pandemic, based on available data for 2019 and previous years. More information is available from the UNDP website at http://hdr.undp.org/en/content/human-development-report-2020-readers-guide.

a Rank in 2019 among the 189 national economies presented in the Human Development Report 2020 of the UNDP.

b Calculated by the UNDP Human Development Report Office by applying the human development index formula to the weighted group averages of component indicators. Missing values are estimated using cross-economy regression models.

Sources: United Nations Development Programme. Human Development Data (1990–2019). http://hdr.undp.org/en/data# (accessed 04 July 2022). For Taipei,China: Government of Taipei,China, Directorate-General of Budget, Accounting and Statistics. https://eng.stat.gov.tw/ct.asp?xItem=25280&ctNode=6032&mp=5 (accessed 04 July 2022).

Table 2.1.8: Life Expectancy at Birth
(years)

ADB Regional Member	Both Sexes		Female		Male	
	2010	2020	2010	2020	2010	2020
Developing ADB Member Economies						
Central and West Asia[a]	**66.0**	**68.3**	**67.8**	**70.0**	**64.3**	**66.8**
Afghanistan	61.0	65.2	62.5	66.7	59.7	63.7
Armenia	73.3	75.2	76.4	78.7	70.0	71.5
Azerbaijan	70.9	73.1	74.1	75.6	67.8	70.6
Georgia	71.5	73.9	76.0	78.3	66.9	69.5
Kazakhstan	68.5	71.4	73.4	75.5	63.6	67.1
Kyrgyz Republic	69.3	71.8	73.5	76.0	65.3	67.8
Pakistan	65.3	67.4	66.2	68.5	64.4	66.5
Tajikistan	68.7	71.3	71.2	73.6	66.5	69.1
Turkmenistan	66.7	68.3	70.2	71.9	63.2	64.8
Uzbekistan	69.7	71.8	72.5	74.0	66.9	69.7
East Asia[a]	**74.7**	**76.1**	**76.9**	**78.4**	**72.7**	**74.0**
China, People's Republic of	74.4	77.1	76.6	79.4	72.5	75.0
Hong Kong, China	83.0	85.4	86.0	88.0	80.1	82.9
Korea, Republic of	80.1	83.4	83.6	86.5	76.8	80.5
Mongolia	67.4	70.1	71.6	74.3	63.5	66.0
Taipei,China	79.2	81.3	82.5	84.7	76.1	78.1
South Asia[a]	**67.2**	**70.3**	**68.3**	**71.8**	**66.1**	**69.0**
Bangladesh	69.9	72.9	71.3	74.9	68.7	71.1
Bhutan	68.4	72.1	68.6	72.5	68.2	71.7
India	66.7	69.9	67.7	71.2	65.7	68.7
Maldives	75.9	79.2	77.4	81.0	74.7	77.8
Nepal	67.6	71.1	69.0	72.5	66.3	69.5
Sri Lanka	75.4	77.1	78.9	80.4	72.0	73.8
Southeast Asia[a]	**70.5**	**72.8**	**73.4**	**75.8**	**67.6**	**69.8**
Brunei Darussalam	74.7	76.0	75.9	77.3	73.7	74.9
Cambodia	66.6	70.1	68.6	72.2	64.3	67.7
Indonesia	69.2	71.9	71.3	74.2	67.2	69.8
Lao People's Democratic Republic	64.3	68.2	66.1	70.1	62.5	66.4
Malaysia	74.5	76.3	76.7	78.5	72.5	74.4
Myanmar	63.5	67.4	66.9	70.3	60.1	64.3
Philippines	69.8	71.4	74.0	75.6	66.0	67.4
Singapore	81.5	83.7	84.0	86.1	79.2	81.5
Thailand	74.2	77.3	77.7	81.1	70.7	73.7
Timor-Leste	67.2	69.7	68.8	71.9	65.6	67.7
Viet Nam	74.8	75.5	78.9	79.6	70.7	71.4
The Pacific[a,b]	**63.6**	**66.0**	**65.1**	**67.5**	**62.1**	**64.6**
Cook Islands	74.5	76.9 (2021)	77.4	79.9 (2021)	71.7	74.1 (2021)
Fiji	66.7	67.6	68.3	69.5	65.2	65.8
Kiribati	65.8	68.6	69.7	72.6	61.9	64.5
Marshall Islands	71.4	74.4 (2021)	73.5	76.8 (2021)	69.3	72.1 (2021)
Micronesia, Federated States of	66.5	68.0	68.2	69.7	64.9	66.3
Nauru	64.0	67.6 (2021)	67.6	71.3 (2021)	60.5	64.1 (2021)
Niue[c]	73.1[d] (2011)	73.6[e] (2016)	76.3[d] (2011)	75.7[e] (2016)	70.1[d] (2011)	71.8[e] (2016)
Palau	71.3	74.4 (2021)	74.6	77.8 (2021)	68.2	71.2 (2021)
Papua New Guinea	62.0	64.7	63.4	66.1	60.7	63.5
Samoa	71.7	73.5	74.0	75.6	69.5	71.4
Solomon Islands	70.7	73.1	72.5	75.0	69.1	71.4
Tonga	70.1	71.0	72.0	73.0	68.1	69.1
Tuvalu	64.5	68.1 (2021)	66.7	70.6 (2021)	62.3	65.7 (2021)
Vanuatu	69.1	70.6	70.8	72.3	67.6	69.1
Developed ADB Member Economies[a]	**82.6**	**84.3**	**85.9**	**87.2**	**79.5**	**81.5**
Australia	81.7	83.2	84.0	85.3	79.5	81.2
Japan	82.8	84.6	86.3	87.7	79.6	81.6
New Zealand	80.7	82.1	82.7	83.9	78.8	80.3
DEVELOPING ADB MEMBER ECONOMIES[a,b]	**70.5**	**72.7**	**72.4**	**74.7**	**68.7**	**70.8**
ALL ADB REGIONAL MEMBERS[a,b]	**71.0**	**73.1**	**73.0**	**75.2**	**69.1**	**71.2**
WORLD[f]	**70.6**	**72.7**	**72.8**	**75.1**	**68.4**	**70.6**

ADB = Asian Development Bank.

a Estimated as weighted averages using total population of appropriate sex(es) from the United Nations' World Population Prospects 2019 as weight. For the Cook Islands, Marshall Islands, Nauru, Niue, Palau, and Tuvalu, sex-disaggregated population figures were derived using total populations from World Population Prospects 2019 and the proportions of total population by sex for Pacific small island states from the World Bank's World Development Indicators.

b For estimating regional aggregates, imputation was done for economies with missing data by substituting available data from the nearest years.

c Calculated directly from recorded deaths, through 5-year periods.

d Covers 2007–2011.

e Covers 2012–2016.

f Estimated by the World Bank as weighted averages using total population of appropriate sex(es) as weight.

Sources: United Nations. World Population Prospects 2019. https://population.un.org/wpp/Download/Standard/Population/ (accessed 05 April 2022); and World Bank. World Development Indicators. https://databank.worldbank.org/source/world-development-indicators (accessed 23 May 2022). For the Cook Islands, the Marshall Islands, Nauru, Palau, and Tuvalu: United States Census Bureau. International Data Base. https://www.census.gov/programs-surveys/international-programs/data/tools/international-data-base.html (accessed 23 May 2022). For Niue: Statistics Niue. Vital Statistics Report 2012–2016. https://niue.prism.spc.int/ (accessed 23 May 2022). For Taipei,China: Government of Taipei,China, Directorate-General of Budget, Accounting and Statistics. https://eng.dgbas.gov.tw/mp.asp?mp=2 (accessed 23 May 2022).

Table 2.1.9: Births, Deaths, and Fertility Rates

ADB Regional Member	Crude Birth Rate (per 1,000 people)		Crude Death Rate (per 1,000 people)		Total Fertility Rate (births per woman)	
	2010	2020	2010	2020	2010	2020
Developing ADB Member Economies						
Central and West Asia[a]	**29.0**	**26.5**	**7.4**	**6.7**	**3.7**	**3.3**
Afghanistan	39.8	31.2	8.3	6.2	6.0	4.2
Armenia	15.3	13.3	9.7	9.8	1.7	1.8
Azerbaijan	18.3	12.5	5.9	7.5	1.9	1.7
Georgia	13.9	12.9	13.1	12.7	1.9	2.0
Kazakhstan	22.5	22.8	9.0	8.6	2.6	3.1
Kyrgyz Republic	26.8	24.0	6.6	6.1	3.1	3.0
Pakistan	30.1	27.4	7.6	6.8	4.0	3.4
Tajikistan	31.6	29.2	5.7	4.7	3.6	3.5
Turkmenistan	25.4	22.3	7.2	7.0	2.8	2.7
Uzbekistan	22.0	24.6	4.8	5.1	2.3	2.9
East Asia[a]	**11.8**	**8.4**	**7.0**	**7.0**	**1.6**	**1.7**
China, People's Republic of	11.9	8.5	7.1	7.1	1.6	1.7
Hong Kong, China	12.6	5.8	6.0	6.8	1.1	0.9
Korea, Republic of	9.4	5.3	5.1	5.9	1.2	0.8
Mongolia	24.7	22.6	6.6	6.4	2.6	2.8
Taipei,China	7.2	6.6 (2021)	6.3	7.8 (2021)	0.9	1.0
South Asia[a]	**21.1**	**17.5**	**7.3**	**7.1**	**2.5**	**2.2**
Bangladesh	21.1	17.5	5.7	5.5	2.3	2.0
Bhutan	19.4	16.7	6.4	6.3	2.3	1.9
India	21.1	17.4	7.5	7.3	2.6	2.2
Maldives	19.6	13.1	3.5	2.7	2.2	1.8
Nepal	22.7	19.3	6.8	6.3	2.5	1.8
Sri Lanka	17.8	15.3	6.0	6.9	2.2	2.2
Southeast Asia[a]	**19.8**	**16.9**	**6.5**	**6.6**	**2.4**	**2.2**
Brunei Darussalam	17.3	14.1	3.8	4.7	1.9	1.8
Cambodia	25.5	21.6	6.5	6.0	2.9	2.5
Indonesia	20.8	17.4	6.7	6.6	2.5	2.3
Lao People's Democratic Republic	26.9	22.7	7.4	6.3	3.1	2.6
Malaysia	17.3	16.4	4.6	5.3	2.1	2.0
Myanmar	19.8	17.2	8.9	8.3	2.4	2.1
Philippines	25.0	19.9	5.6	6.0	3.2	2.5
Singapore	9.3	8.5	4.4	5.2	1.2	1.1
Thailand	11.8	10.0	7.2	7.9	1.5	1.5
Timor-Leste	30.7	29.0	6.5	5.9	4.8	3.9
Viet Nam	17.3	16.1	5.8	6.4	1.9	2.0
The Pacific[a,b]	**29.4**	**26.2**	**7.9**	**7.1**	**3.9**	**3.5**
Cook Islands	15.4	12.9 (2021)	7.2	8.9 (2021)	2.4	2.1 (2021)
Fiji	22.3	20.6	8.0	8.3	2.8	2.7
Kiribati	29.6	27.0	7.0	6.3	3.8	3.5
Marshall Islands	29.9	22.4 (2021)	4.5	4.3 (2021)	3.5	2.8 (2021)
Micronesia, Federated States of	24.1	22.6	7.2	6.7	3.5	3.0
Nauru	28.2	21.5 (2021)	6.3	6.2 (2021)	3.1	2.6 (2021)
Niue	15.8[c]	8.8[e]	8.3[c]	4.7[e]	2.8[c]	2.7[d] (2016)
Palau	11.9	11.0	8.1	7.6	2.2 (2012)	2.2 (2015)
Papua New Guinea	30.0	26.5	8.3	7.3	4.0	3.5
Samoa	28.0	23.9	5.8	5.2	4.3	3.8
Solomon Islands	34.0	31.4	4.8	4.2	4.4	4.3
Tonga	27.4	23.8	7.2	7.0	3.9	3.5
Tuvalu	23.0	23.0 (2021)	9.3	8.0 (2021)	3.1	2.9 (2021)
Vanuatu	32.3	28.8	5.5	5.1	4.1	3.7
Developed ADB Member Economies[a]	**9.4**	**7.7**	**9.0**	**10.2**	**1.5**	**1.4**
Australia	13.7	11.5	6.5	6.3	1.9	1.6
Japan	8.5	6.8	9.5	11.1	1.4	1.3
New Zealand	14.7	11.3	6.5	6.4	2.2	1.6
DEVELOPING ADB MEMBER ECONOMIES[a,b]	**17.9**	**14.8**	**7.1**	**7.0**	**2.2**	**2.1**
ALL ADB REGIONAL MEMBERS[a,b]	**17.6**	**14.6**	**7.1**	**7.1**	**2.2**	**2.1**
WORLD[f]	**19.8**	**17.3**	**7.8**	**7.7**	**2.5**	**2.4**

ADB = Asian Development Bank.

a ADB estimates using (i) data on total population from the United Nations' World Population Prospects 2019; (ii) data on crude birth rates, crude death rates, and total fertility rates from the World Bank's World Development Indicators, the United States Census Bureau's international database, and each economy's official sources; and (iii) data on the population of women of reproductive age from the World Health Organization's data portal, World Population Prospects 2019, and official communication from The Pacific Community's Statistics for Development Division.

b For estimating aggregates, imputation was done for economies with missing data by substituting available data from the nearest years.

c Refers to a multiyear average for the intercensal years 2007–2011. Crude birth rate and crude death rate are calculated by dividing the average annual number of births and deaths of the intercensal period 2007–2011 by the midperiod population size of the intercensal period. For total fertility rate, the estimate is based on the average registered number of children born, by age of mother, of the intercensal period 2007–2011, and the estimated midperiod number of women of childbearing age.

d Refers to a multiyear average for the intercensal years 2012–2016. Total fertility rate is estimated based on the average registered number of children born, by age of mother, of the intercensal period 2012–2016, and the estimated midperiod number of women of childbearing age.

e Refers to July–December 2020.

f Estimated by the World Bank as weighted averages of the rates using the value of the denominator or, in some cases, another indicator as a weight. Aggregation is done after imputing values for missing data according to certain imputation rules by the World Bank, as described in their data compilation methodology.

Sources: The Pacific Community, Statistics for Development Division. Official communication, 15 April 2022; past communication; United Nations. World Population Prospects 2019. https://population.un.org/wpp/Download/Standard/Population/ (accessed 04 April 2022); World Bank. World Development Indicators. https://databank.worldbank.org/source/world-development-indicators (accessed 23 May 2022); and World Health Organization. Maternal, Newborn, Child & Adolescent Health. https://www.who.int/data/maternal-newborn-child-adolescent/indicator-explorer-new/mca/women-of-reproductive-age-(15-49-years)-population-(thousands) (accessed 24 May 2022). For the Cook Islands, the Marshall Islands, Nauru, and Tuvalu: United States Census Bureau. International Database. https://www.census.gov/programs-surveys/international-programs/data/tools/international-data-base.html (accessed 23 May 2022). For Niue: Statistics Niue, Department of Finance and Planning. https://niue.prism.spc.int (accessed 23 May 2022). For Taipei,China: Government of Taipei,China, Ministry of the Interior. https://www.moi.gov.tw/english/ (accessed 23 May 2022).

Table 2.1.10: Adult (15 Years and Older) Literacy Rate

(%)

ADB Regional Member	Both Sexes		Female		Male	
	2010	2019	2010	2019	2010	2019
Developing ADB Member Economies						
Central and West Asia						
Afghanistan	31.4 (2011)	37.3 (2021)	17.0 (2011)	22.6 (2021)	45.4 (2011)	52.1 (2021)
Armenia	99.7 (2011)	99.8 (2020)	99.7 (2011)	99.7 (2020)	99.8 (2011)	99.8 (2020)
Azerbaijan	99.8[a]	99.8	99.7[a]	99.7	99.9[a]	99.9
Georgia	99.7 (2002)	99.6	99.6 (2002)	99.5	99.8 (2002)	99.7
Kazakhstan	99.8[b]	99.8[b] (2018)	99.7[b]	99.7[b] (2018)	99.8[b]	99.8[b] (2018)
Kyrgyz Republic	99.2 (2009)	99.6[b] (2018)	99.0 (2009)	99.5[b] (2018)	99.5 (2009)	99.7[b] (2018)
Pakistan	55.4	58.0	41.0	46.5	68.9	69.3
Tajikistan	99.5 (2000)	99.8[b] (2014)	99.2 (2000)	99.7[b] (2014)	99.7 (2000)	99.8[b] (2014)
Turkmenistan	...	99.7[b] (2014)	...	99.6[b] (2014)	...	99.8[b] (2014)
Uzbekistan	98.6 (2000)	100.0	98.1 (2000)	100.0	99.2 (2000)	100.0
East Asia						
China, People's Republic of	95.1	96.8[b] (2018)	92.7	95.2[b] (2018)	97.5	98.5[b] (2018)
Hong Kong, China	...	...	...	...	...	...
Korea, Republic of	98.0 (2008)	...	97.6 (2008)	...	98.3 (2008)	...
Mongolia	98.3	99.2 (2020)	98.3	99.2 (2020)	98.2	99.1 (2020)
Taipei,China	...	...	...	...	...	...
South Asia						
Bangladesh	58.8 (2011)	74.9 (2020)	55.1 (2011)	72.0 (2020)	62.5 (2011)	77.8 (2020)
Bhutan	55.3 (2012)	66.6 (2017)	45.2 (2012)	57.1 (2017)	66.0 (2012)	75.0 (2017)
India	69.3 (2011)	74.4[b] (2018)	59.3 (2011)	65.8[b] (2018)	78.9 (2011)	82.4[b] (2018)
Maldives	98.4 (2006)	97.7 (2016)	98.4 (2006)	98.1 (2016)	98.4 (2006)	97.3 (2016)
Nepal	59.6 (2011)	67.9[b] (2018)	48.8 (2011)	59.7[b] (2018)	71.7 (2011)	78.6[b] (2018)
Sri Lanka	91.2	92.3	90.0	91.6	92.6	93.0
Southeast Asia						
Brunei Darussalam	96.1 (2011)	97.2[b] (2018)	94.7 (2011)	96.3[b] (2018)	97.4 (2011)	98.1[b] (2018)
Cambodia	76.1 (2009)	80.5 (2015)	69.1 (2009)	75.0 (2015)	83.9 (2009)	86.5 (2015)
Indonesia	92.8 (2011)	96.0 (2020)	90.1 (2011)	94.6 (2020)	95.6 (2011)	97.4 (2020)
Lao People's Democratic Republic	58.3[b] (2011)	84.7 (2015)	49.7[b] (2011)	79.4 (2015)	67.4[b] (2011)	90.0 (2015)
Malaysia	93.1	95.0	90.7	93.6	95.4	96.2
Myanmar	89.9 (2000)	89.1	86.4 (2000)	86.3	93.9 (2000)	92.4
Philippines	95.4 (2008)	96.3	95.8 (2008)	96.9	95.0 (2008)	95.7
Singapore	95.9	97.5	93.8	96.1	98.0	98.9
Thailand	96.4	93.8 (2018)	96.4	92.4 (2018)	96.4	95.2 (2018)
Timor-Leste	58.3	68.1[b] (2018)	53.0	64.2[b] (2018)	63.6	71.9[b] (2018)
Viet Nam	93.5 (2009)	95.8	91.4 (2009)	94.6	95.8 (2009)	97.0
The Pacific						
Cook Islands	...	...	...	...	...	...
Fiji	...	...	...	...	...	...
Kiribati	...	...	...	...	...	...
Marshall Islands	98.3 (2011)	...	98.2 (2011)	...	98.3 (2011)	...
Micronesia, Federated States of	...	...	...	...	...	...
Nauru	...	...	...	...	...	...
Niue	...	...	...	...	...	...
Palau	...	96.6 (2015)	...	96.3 (2015)	...	96.8 (2015)
Papua New Guinea	61.6[b]	...	57.9[b]	...	65.3[b]	...
Samoa	99.0 (2011)	99.1[b] (2018)	99.1 (2011)	99.2[b] (2018)	98.9 (2011)	99.0[b] (2018)
Solomon Islands	76.6[b] (2009)	...	69.0[b] (2009)	...	83.7[b] (2009)	...
Tonga	99.4 (2011)	99.4[b] (2018)	99.4 (2011)	99.5[b] (2018)	99.3 (2011)	99.4[b] (2018)
Tuvalu	...	...	...	...	...	...
Vanuatu	78.4[b] (2004)	87.5[b] (2018)	76.2[b] (2004)	86.7[b] (2018)	80.5[b] (2004)	88.3[b] (2018)
Developed ADB Member Economies						
Australia	...	...	...	...	...	...
Japan	...	...	...	...	...	...
New Zealand	...	...	...	...	...	...
WORLD	**84.0**	**86.7 (2020)**	**79.8**	**83.3 (2020)**	**88.3**	**90.1 (2020)**

... = data not available, ADB = Asian Development Bank.

a Based on national estimation.
b Refers to UNESCO Institute for Statistics estimates.

Source: United Nations Educational, Scientific and Cultural Organization (UNESCO) Institute for Statistics. UIS.Stat Database. http://data.uis.unesco.org/ (accessed 27 May 2022).

Table 2.1.11: Years of Schooling

ADB Regional Member	Expected[a]					
	Both Sexes		Female		Male	
	2010	2020	2010	2020	2010	2020
Developing ADB Member Economies						
Central and West Asia						
Afghanistan	9.3 (2011)	10.2[c] (2018)	7.2 (2011)	7.7[c] (2018)	11.2 (2011)	12.6[c] (2018)
Armenia	13.1[c]	13.1	13.4[c]	13.8	12.8[c]	12.5
Azerbaijan	...	13.5[d]	...	13.6[d]	...	13.4[d]
Georgia	13.5[c] (2009)	15.6	13.5[c] (2008)	15.9	12.8[c] (2008)	15.2
Kazakhstan	14.6	15.8	14.8	16.0	14.3	15.5
Kyrgyz Republic	12.4[d]	13.2	12.7[d]	13.4	12.2[d]	13.0
Pakistan	6.8[c] (2011)	8.7[c] (2019)	6.1[c] (2011)	8.1[c] (2019)	7.4[c] (2011)	9.2[c] (2019)
Tajikistan	11.2	11.4 (2013)	10.4	10.7 (2013)	12.0	12.1 (2013)
Turkmenistan	...	13.2[c]	...	13.0[c]	...	13.4[c]
Uzbekistan	11.5	12.5 (2019)	11.3	12.4 (2019)	11.6	12.6 (2019)
East Asia						
China, People's Republic of	12.4[c]	...	12.4[c]	...	12.4[c]	...
Hong Kong, China	15.9[c] (2012)	17.3[c]	15.7[c] (2012)	17.6[c]	15.6[c] (2012)	17.0[c]
Korea, Republic of	16.8	16.5 (2019)	16.0	16.1 (2019)	17.6	16.9 (2019)
Mongolia	14.6[c]	15.0 (2019)	15.3[c]	15.6 (2019)	13.9[c]	14.4 (2019)
Taipei,China	16.7 (2012)	16.8 (2021)	16.8 (2012)	17.0 (2021)	16.7 (2012)	16.6 (2021)
South Asia						
Bangladesh	9.2[d] (2009)	12.4[c]	9.3[d] (2009)	13.0[c]	9.1[d] (2009)	11.9[c]
Bhutan	11.7	13.1[c] (2018)	11.8	13.5[c] (2018)	11.6	12.8[c] (2018)
India	10.7[c]	11.9	10.5[c]	11.9	10.9[c]	11.8
Maldives	12.2 (2003)	12.6[c] (2019)	12.3 (2003)	14.2[c] (2019)	12.0 (2003)	11.9[c] (2019)
Nepal	11.9[c]	13.2 (2019)	12.0[c]	13.4 (2019)	11.9[c]	12.9 (2019)
SriLanka	13.6[c]	14.1 (2018)	13.8[c]	14.5 (2018)	13.4[c]	13.8 (2018)
Southeast Asia						
Brunei Darussalam	14.1[c]	14.0	14.3[c]	14.4	13.8[c]	13.5
Cambodia	10.6[c] (2008)	...	9.9[c] (2008)	...	11.2[c] (2008)	...
Indonesia	12.3	13.6 (2018)	12.4	13.7 (2018)	12.3	13.5 (2018)
Lao People's Democratic Republic	10.0	10.1	9.2	9.9	10.7	10.3
Malaysia	12.9	13.5 (2019)	13.2	14.0 (2019)	12.5	13.0 (2019)
Myanmar	8.2 (2007)	10.7 (2018)	...	10.9 (2018)	...	10.5 (2018)
Philippines	11.4 (2009)	13.1[c] (2017)	11.6 (2009)	13.5[c] (2017)	11.1 (2009)	12.8[c] (2017)
Singapore	...	16.5[d] (2019)	...	16.7[d] (2019)	...	16.4[d] (2019)
Thailand	13.3[c]	15.4[c] (2016)	13.7[c]	15.8[c] (2016)	12.8[c]	15.1[c] (2016)
Timor-Leste	12.4	...	12.0	...	12.9	...
Viet Nam	...	...	...	...	...	...
The Pacific						
Cook Islands	11.0	14.8 (2012)	11.1	14.2 (2012)	10.9	15.5 (2012)
Fiji	13.9 (2004)	...	14.1 (2004)	...	13.7 (2004)	...
Kiribati	11.8 (2008)	...	12.2 (2008)	...	11.4 (2008)	...
Marshall Islands	12.2[c] (2002)	10.2 (2019)	12.2[c] (2002)	10.4 (2019)	12.2[c] (2002)	10.1 (2019)
Micronesia, Federated States of	...	...	...	...	...	...
Nauru	9.6 (2008)	...	9.7 (2008)	...	9.5 (2008)	...
Niue	12.2 (2005)	...	12.4 (2005)	...	12.0 (2005)	...
Palau	14.1[c] (2000)	16.6 (2013)	14.8[c] (2000)	17.2 (2013)	13.4[c] (2000)	16.1 (2013)
Papua New Guinea	...	...	...	...	...	...
Samoa	12.0 (2000)	...	12.4[c] (2000)	...	11.7[c] (2000)	...
Solomon Islands	9.2 (2007)	...	8.8 (2007)	...	9.6 (2007)	...
Tonga	14.5[c] (2003)	16.0	13.9[c] (2002)	17.3	13.4[c] (2002)	14.8
Tuvalu	10.9 (2001)	...	11.0 (2001)	...	10.8 (2001)	...
Vanuatu	10.6[c] (2004)	...	10.2[c] (2004)	...	10.9[c] (2004)	...
Developed ADB Member Economies						
Australia	...	21.6 (2019)	...	22.2 (2019)	...	21.0 (2019)
Japan	...	15.2[c] (2018)	...	15.2[c] (2018)	...	15.2[c] (2018)
NewZealand	...	20.3 (2019)	...	20.8 (2019)	...	19.7 (2019)
WORLD	**11.5**	**12.5[c]**	**11.3**	**12.5[c]**	**11.6**	**12.5[c]**

continued on next page

Table 2.1.11: Years of Schooling *(continued)*

ADB Regional Member	Mean[b]					
	Both Sexes		Female		Male	
	2010	2020	2010	2020	2010	2020
Developing ADB Member Economies						
Central and West Asia						
Afghanistan		3.0 (2021)	...	2.3 (2021)	...	3.4 (2021)
Armenia	11.2 (2011)	11.2 (2017)	11.2 (2011)	11.2 (2017)	11.2 (2011)	11.2 (2017)
Azerbaijan	10.5	10.5 (2017)	10.2	10.2 (2017)	10.8	10.9 (2017)
Georgia	12.5 (2012)	12.8 (2019)	12.4 (2012)	12.9 (2019)	12.6 (2012)	12.8 (2019)
Kazakhstan	11.0 (2009)	12.2 (2018)	11.0 (2009)	12.2 (2018)	11.0 (2009)	12.2 (2018)
Kyrgyz Republic	10.9 (2009)	...	10.9 (2009)	...	10.8 (2009)	...
Pakistan	4.6	4.5 (2019)	2.9	3.9 (2019)	6.1	5.0 (2019)
Tajikistan	10.8 (2000)	11.4 (2017)	10.3 (2000)	10.8 (2017)	11.3 (2000)	12.0 (2017)
Turkmenistan	...	...	...	...	...	...
Uzbekistan	...	11.9 (2019)	...	11.7 (2019)	...	12.1 (2019)
East Asia						
China, People's Republic of	6.7	...	6.2	...	7.2	...
Hong Kong, China	11.4	12.2 (2019)	11.0	11.8 (2019)	11.9	12.7 (2019)
Korea, Republic of	11.6	12.1 (2015)	10.9	11.4 (2015)	12.5	12.9 (2015)
Mongolia	10.1	9.4	10.3	9.9	9.8	8.8
Taipei,China	...	...	...	...	...	...
South Asia						
Bangladesh	5.2 (2011)	6.5 (2019)	4.4 (2011)	6.0 (2019)	6.0 (2011)	7.1 (2019)
Bhutan	2.2 (2012)	4.1 (2017)	1.5 (2012)	3.2 (2017)	3.0 (2012)	4.8 (2017)
India	5.3 (2011)	5.3 (2011)	4.0 (2011)	4.0 (2011)	6.5 (2011)	6.5 (2011)
Maldives	...	...	...	...	...	...
Nepal	3.5 (2011)	3.5 (2011)	2.3 (2011)	2.3 (2011)	4.9 (2011)	4.9 (2011)
Sri Lanka	10.2 (2009)	11.0 (2018)	10.1 (2009)	11.1 (2018)	10.4 (2009)	11.0 (2018)
Southeast Asia						
Brunei Darussalam	11.6 (2011)	11.6 (2011)	11.3 (2011)	11.3 (2011)	11.8 (2011)	11.8 (2011)
Cambodia	3.9 (2009)	3.7 (2015)	3.1 (2009)	2.8 (2015)	5.0 (2009)	4.8 (2015)
Indonesia	7.5 (2011)	8.6	7.0 (2011)	8.2	8.0 (2011)	8.9
Lao People's Democratic Republic	...	...	...	...	...	...
Malaysia	9.7	10.6 (2019)	9.4	10.6 (2019)	10.0	10.7 (2019)
Myanmar	...	6.4 (2019)	...	6.1 (2019)	...	6.7 (2019)
Philippines	8.9	9.0 (2019)	9.0	9.2 (2019)	8.8	8.7 (2019)
Singapore	11.2	11.9 (2019)	10.8	11.5 (2019)	11.6	12.2 (2019)
Thailand	7.6	8.7 (2019)	7.4	8.6 (2019)	7.8	8.8 (2019)
Timor-Leste	...	...	...	...	...	...
Viet Nam	7.5 (2009)	8.4 (2019)	7.0 (2009)	8.0 (2019)	8.1 (2009)	8.7 (2019)
The Pacific						
Cook Islands	9.9 (2006)	...	9.8 (2006)	...	10.0 (2006)	...
Fiji	9.2 (2007)	10.6 (2017)	9.2 (2007)	10.7 (2017)	9.3 (2007)	10.6 (2017)
Kiribati	...	...	...	...	...	...
Marshall Islands	10.9 (2011)	10.9 (2011)	10.7 (2011)	10.7 (2011)	11.1 (2011)	11.1 (2011)
Micronesia, Federated States of	...	...	...	...	...	...
Nauru	...	...	...	...	...	...
Niue	...	...	...	...	...	...
Palau	...	12.8 (2013)	...	12.9 (2013)	...	12.8 (2013)
Papua New Guinea	...	...	...	...	...	...
Samoa	11.7 (2011)	11.7 (2011)	11.8 (2011)	11.8 (2011)	11.6 (2011)	11.6 (2011)
Solomon Islands	...	...	...	...	...	...
Tonga	10.9 (2011)	10.9 (2011)	10.9 (2011)	10.9 (2011)	10.9 (2011)	10.9 (2011)
Tuvalu	...	...	...	...	...	...
Vanuatu	...	...	...	...	...	...
Developed ADB Member Economies						
Australia	12.0	12.6 (2018)	12.0	12.6 (2018)	12.0	12.5 (2018)
Japan	12.5	...	12.2	...	12.9	...
New Zealand	13.4 (2011)	12.9	13.3 (2011)	12.9	13.5 (2011)	13.0
WORLD	...	...	...	...	...	...

... = data not available, ADB = Asian Development Bank.

a Refers to the expected number of years of schooling from primary to tertiary level of education.

b Refers to the average number of completed years of education among the population aged 25 years and older (excluding years spent repeating individual grades), by highest level of education attained.

c UNESCO Institute of Statistics estimate.

d National estimate.

Sources: United Nations Educational, Scientific and Cultural Organization (UNESCO) Institute for Statistics. UIS.Stat Database. http://data.uis.unesco.org/ (accessed 25 May 2022). For expected years of schooling for Taipei,China: Government of Taipei,China, Ministry of Education. Gender Statistics. https://english.moe.gov.tw/cp-87-14508-95005-1.html (accessed 25 May 2022).

Table 2.1.12: Education Resources

ADB Regional Member	Pupil/Trained Teacher Ratio[a]				Pupil/Qualified Teacher Ratio[b]			
	Primary		Secondary		Primary		Secondary	
	2010	2020	2010	2020	2010	2020	2010	2020
Developing ADB Member Economies								
Central and West Asia								
Afghanistan	...	...	...	...	...	60.4 (2019)	...	42.1 (2018)
Armenia	27.4 (2005)	25.6	...	14.1	...	19.2	...	10.7
Azerbaijan	11.0	16.2	...	...	...	16.2	...	8.1
Georgia	9.4[c] (2009)	...	8.0[c] (2009)	...	...	...	...	...
Kazakhstan	...	16.8	...	8.3	...	16.8	...	8.3
Kyrgyz Republic	35.5	26.1 (2017)	18.8	14.0 (2017)	48.8 (2002)	...	...	...
Pakistan	48.0	61.9 (2019)	30.6 (2011)	31.9 (2017)	82.2 (2011)	92.1 (2017)	37.0 (2011)	34.4 (2017)
Tajikistan	27.1	22.3 (2017)	17.0 (2004)	...	...	23.0 (2017)	...	...
Turkmenistan	...	26.0	...	9.6	...	25.9	...	9.6
Uzbekistan	17.8	20.7	13.0	11.0 (2019)	15.4 (2012)	20.6	13.1 (2012)	10.9 (2019)
East Asia								
China, People's Republic of	...	...	...	...	...	17.0	...	14.2
Hong Kong, China	15.9	13.4	17.7[d]	11.4	...	12.9	...	10.9
Korea, Republic of	...	...	...	...	...	...	...	...
Mongolia	31.0	34.2 (2019)	14.8	15.3 (2019)	...	32.3 (2019)	...	14.1 (2019)
Taipei,China	...	...	...	...	...	...	...	...
South Asia								
Bangladesh	78.3[c] (2009)	59.6[d] (2017)	57.4[c] (2012)	53.2	...	30.1[d] (2018)	...	32.8
Bhutan	32.7 (2008)	32.0	28.5 (2008)	10.8[d] (2018)	...	32.0	...	10.6
India	...	34.0	...	25.4	...	28.5	...	22.9
Maldives	15.2	10.9 (2019)	8.4	5.8 (2019)	...	21.9 (2019)	...	7.2 (2019)
Nepal	43.3	20.3 (2019)	49.1[d]	36.5	...	20.4 (2019)	...	34.2
Sri Lanka	29.1	26.1 (2019)	21.9	22.1 (2018)	...	26.0 (2019)	...	22.3 (2018)
Southeast Asia								
Brunei Darussalam	13.0	10.9	10.9 (2011)	8.3	...	9.3	...	7.8
Cambodia	48.9	42.1	25.4 (2011)	21.9 (2019)	...	42.1	...	...
Indonesia	...	...	...	...	37.2 (2012)	17.5	22.3 (2012)	16.8
Lao People's Democratic Republic	30.2	22.1	20.4[d]	17.1	...	24.8[d] (2018)	...	22.4[d] (2017)
Malaysia	13.2	12.3 (2019)	14.6	12.7 (2019)	...	12.2 (2019)	...	11.8 (2019)
Myanmar	28.3	25.6 (2018)	34.5	30.6 (2018)	...	26.7 (2018)	...	28.1 (2018)
Philippines	...	25.7 (2019)	...	25.2 (2019)	...	25.8 (2019)	...	25.2 (2019)
Singapore	18.5 (2009)	14.5 (2019)	16.3 (2009)	11.6 (2019)	18.2 (2009)	14.2 (2019)	16.2 (2009)	11.3 (2019)
Thailand	...	11.8	...	23.6	...	11.8	...	23.6
Timor-Leste	...	...	...	...	...	34.8 (2019)	...	32.3 (2019)
Viet Nam	20.2	23.1	...	...	...	...	...	...
The Pacific								
Cook Islands	16.5 (2011)	16.3	15.6 (2011)	15.2	...	16.7 (2019)	...	14.8 (2019)
Fiji	30.8 (2011)	21.2 (2019)	26.5 (2011)	19.3 (2012)	...	19.6 (2019)	...	...
Kiribati	26.1	28.9	26.0	25.8 (2013)	25.7	30.1	22.2	31.2 (2016)
Marshall Islands	...	...	...	11.8	...	...	...	9.9
Micronesia, Federated States of	...	22.6 (2016)	...	...	...	23.3	...	...
Nauru	26.8 (2007)	40.2 (2016)	57.4 (2007)	...	...	28.1 (2019)	...	60.2 (2019)
Niue	...	43.4 (2019)	...	39.8 (2019)	...	13.1	...	6.2 (2019)
Palau	...	...	...	...	...	...	...	...
Papua New Guinea	...	...	27.4 (2012)	27.4 (2012)	...	...	...	...
Samoa	21.9 (2012)	24.3 (2014)	...	...	...	30.1 (2019)	...	...
Solomon Islands	34.4	29.9 (2019)	39.6	37.1 (2012)	...	29.9 (2019)	16.1	27.6 (2017)
Tonga	...	23.3	...	24.8 (2015)	...	21.9	...	18.3 (2015)
Tuvalu	...	15.9 (2019)	...	25.7	...	12.5 (2019)	...	16.5
Vanuatu	23.8 (2007)	79.0 (2019)	36.1	23.3 (2017)	...	44.4 (2019)	...	26.1 (2015)
Developed ADB Member Economies								
Australia	...	...	...	...	...	...	...	...
Japan	...	...	...	...	...	...	...	...
New Zealand	...	...	...	...	...	...	...	...
WORLD	**...**	**27.3**[d]	**...**	**19.6**[d] **(2019)**	**...**	**24.6**[d]	**...**	**17.6**[d]

... = data not available, ADB = Asian Development Bank.

a The UNESCO Institute for Statistics (UIS) defines a trained teacher as one who has received at least the minimum organized pedagogical teacher training pre-service and in-service required for teaching at the relevant level in a given economy in a given academic year.
b The UIS defines a qualified teacher as one who has at least the minimum academic qualifications required for teaching their subjects at the relevant level in a given economy in a given academic year.
c National estimation.
d UIS estimation.

Source: United Nations Educational, Scientific and Cultural Organization (UNESCO) Institute for Statistics Database. UIS.Stat. http://data.uis.unesco.org/ (accessed 30 May 2022).

Table 2.1.13: Health Care Resources
(per 1,000 population)

ADB Regional Member	Physicians[a]		Hospital Beds[b]	
	2000	2019	2000	2017
Developing ADB Member Economies				
Central and West Asia				
Afghanistan	0.24	0.25	0.4	0.4 (2017)
Armenia	2.84	4.40 (2017)	3.7	4.2 (2015)
Azerbaijan	3.66	3.17 (2019)	5.1	4.8 (2014)
Georgia	4.45	5.11	3.0	2.9 (2014)
Kazakhstan	3.93	4.07	7.3	6.1 (2014)
Kyrgyz Republic	2.34	2.21 (2014)	4.8	4.4 (2014)
Pakistan	0.81	1.12 (2019)	0.6	0.6 (2017)
Tajikistan	1.70	1.72 (2014)	5.1	4.7 (2014)
Turkmenistan	2.27	2.22 (2014)	4.1	4.0 (2014)
Uzbekistan	2.54	2.37 (2014)	4.4	4.0 (2014)
East Asia				
China, People's Republic of	1.43	2.23 (2019)	2.5	4.3 (2017)
Hong Kong, China	...	...	...	...
Korea, Republic of	1.98	2.48 (2019)	8.7	12.4
Mongolia	2.76	3.85 (2018)	6.0	8.0 (2017)
Taipei,China[c]	1.91	2.48	6.9	7.2 (2020)
South Asia				
Bangladesh	0.36	0.67	0.3 (2005)	0.8 (2016)
Bhutan	0.25 (2008)	0.50	1.7 (2006)	1.7 (2012)
India	0.69	0.74	0.5	0.5 (2017)
Maldives	1.44	2.05 (2019)	4.3 (2009)	4.3 (2009)
Nepal	0.21 (2004)	0.85	5.0 (2006)	0.3 (2012)
Sri Lanka	0.72	1.23	3.5	4.2 (2017)
Southeast Asia				
Brunei Darussalam	1.45	1.61 (2017)	2.5	2.9 (2017)
Cambodia	0.23	0.19 (2014)	0.8	0.9 (2016)
Indonesia	0.14	0.62	0.6	1.0 (2017)
Lao People's Democratic Republic	0.20 (2009)	0.35	0.7	1.5 (2012)
Malaysia	1.17	2.29	1.8	1.9 (2017)
Myanmar	0.52	0.74 (2019)	0.6 (2006)	1.0 (2017)
Philippines	1.27	0.77	1.1	1.0 (2014)
Singapore	1.76	2.46 (2019)	3.1 (2008)	2.5 (2017)
Thailand	0.39	0.95	2.1	2.1 (2010)
Timor-Leste	0.08	0.76	5.9	5.9 (2010)
Viet Nam	0.71	0.83 (2016)	2.9	2.6 (2014)
The Pacific				
Cook Islands	1.29 (2009)	1.41 (2014)	...	...
Fiji	0.44 (2009)	0.86 (2015)	2.1 (2009)	2.0 (2016)
Kiribati	0.40	0.20 (2013)	1.4	1.9 (2016)
Marshall Islands	0.57	0.42 (2012)	2.7	2.7 (2010)
Micronesia, Federated States of	0.19 (2009)	...	3.2 (2009)	3.2 (2009)
Nauru	1.10	1.35 (2015)	5.0	5.0 (2010)
Niue	1.88 (2008)	...	...	...
Palau	1.61	1.77	4.8	4.8 (2010)
Papua New Guinea	0.05	0.07 (2019)	...	...
Samoa	0.34	0.60	1.0 (2007)	...
Solomon Islands	0.18 (2008)	0.19 (2016)	1.4 (2005)	1.4 (2012)
Tonga	0.56	0.95	2.6	2.6 (2010)
Tuvalu	1.15 (2009)	1.19	5.6 (2001)	...
Vanuatu	0.12 (2008)	0.17 (2016)	1.7 (2008)	1.7 (2008)
Developed ADB Member Economies				
Australia	3.34	4.13	3.8	3.8 (2016)
Japan	2.21	2.48 (2018)	13.5	13.0
New Zealand	2.61	3.62	2.8	2.6 (2019)
WORLD	**1.52**	**1.76 (2017)**	**2.6**	**2.9 (2017)**

... = data not available, ADB = Asian Development Bank.

a Main source of data is the United Nations Statistics Division's Global SDG Indicators database.
b Main source of data is the World Health Organization's Global Health Observatory.
c Physicians include doctors of Chinese medicine.

Sources: World Bank. World Development Indicators. https://databank.worldbank.org/source/world-development-indicators (accessed 4 May 2022); World Health Organization. Global Health Observatory. https://www.who.int/data/gho (accessed 4 May 2022); and United Nations Statistics Division. Global SDG Indicators Database. https://unstats.un.org/sdgs/indicators/database/ (accessed 4 May 2022). For Taipei,China: Government of Taipei,China, Directorate-General of Budget, Accounting and Statistics. https://eng.dgbas.gov.tw/mp.asp (accessed 4 May 2022).

Table 2.1.14: Adults Aged 15 Years and Older Living with HIV
('000)

ADB Regional Member	All Adults		Women	
	2010	2019	2010	2019
Developing ADB Member Economies				
Central and West Asia				
Afghanistan	4.3	11.0	1.2	3.3
Armenia	3.8	4.7	1.4	1.7
Azerbaijan	8.4	9.8	3.2	3.6
Georgia	3.0	8.3	1.0	2.6
Kazakhstan	15.0	35.0	4.6	11.0
Kyrgyz Republic	3.7	8.9	1.1	2.8
Pakistan	66.0	200.0	7.3	38.0
Tajikistan	5.0	13.0	1.9	5.3
Turkmenistan	...	...	...	...
Uzbekistan	22.0	53.0	7.9	20.0
East Asia				
China, People's Republic of	...	...	...	...
Hong Kong, China	...	...	...	...
Korea, Republic of	...	...	...	...
Mongolia	0.5	0.6	0.1	0.2
Taipei,China	...	...	...	...
South Asia				
Bangladesh	...	...	...	...
Bhutan	1.1	1.3	0.5	0.5
India	...	...	...	...
Maldives	...	...	...	...
Nepal	30.0	29.0	11.0	13.0
Sri Lanka	3.9	3.7	1.1	1.1
Southeast Asia				
Brunei Darussalam	...	...	...	...
Cambodia	76.0	72.0	40.0	38.0
Indonesia	390.0	520.0	120.0	190.0
Lao People's Democratic Republic	8.6	15.0	3.6	6.0
Malaysia	72.0	92.0	12.0	17.0
Myanmar	...	...	...	...
Philippines	17.0	110.0	1.1	7.1
Singapore	6.1	8.0	0.7	0.7
Thailand	610.0	470.0 (2019)	280.0	220.0
Timor-Leste	...	...	...	...
Viet Nam	210.0	240.0	60.0	80.0
The Pacific				
Cook Islands	...	...	...	...
Fiji	0.5	1.2	0.5	0.6
Kiribati	...	...	...	...
Marshall Islands	...	...	...	...
Micronesia, Federated States of	...	...	...	...
Nauru	...	...	...	...
Niue	...	...	...	...
Palau	...	...	...	...
Papua New Guinea	30.0	52.0	17.0	31.0
Samoa	...	...	...	...
Solomon Islands	...	...	...	...
Tonga	...	...	...	...
Tuvalu	...	...	...	...
Vanuatu	...	...	...	...
Developed ADB Member Economies				
Australia	21.0	30.0	2.6	4.1
Japan	22.0	30.0	2.3	3.0
New Zealand	2.4	3.6	0.5	0.6
WORLD	**28,600.0**	**36,000.0**	**14,900.0**	**19,300.0**

... = data not available, 0.0 = magnitude is less than half of unit employed, ADB = Asian Development Bank.

Note: Figures reported in this table are based on modelled HIV estimates. According to the Joint United Nations Programme on HIV/AIDS, modelled HIV estimates provide a scientifically appropriate way of describing HIV epidemic levels and trends, and are required because it is impossible to count the exact number of people living and newly infected with HIV, or people who have died from AIDS-related causes, in any given economy. Doing so would require regularly testing every person for HIV and investigating all deaths, which is logistically impossible and ethically problematic.

Source: Joint United Nations Programme on HIV/AIDS (UNAIDS). AIDSInfo. https://aidsinfo.unaids.org/ (accessed 5 April 2022).

Data Issues and Comparability

Demographic data are based on vital registration records, censuses, and surveys. Since vital registration records in many developing ADB member economies are incomplete, they cannot be used for statistical purposes. In most economies, population censuses, which are used to provide more accurate estimates of population sizes, are conducted every 10 years. Population numbers in between census years are products of imputation methods that use various population distributional assumptions.

The United Nations (UN) Department of Economics and Social Affairs' Population Division uses future trends on fertility, mortality, and international migration to project population numbers through to 2100. The medium-fertility variant included in the UN's World Population Prospects 2019 assumes, over the remainder of the century, a decline of fertility in economies where large families are still prevalent, a slight increase of fertility in several economies where women have fewer than two live births on average over a lifetime, and continued reductions in mortality at all ages.

Urban population statistics are compiled according to each economy's national definition, as there is no agreed international standard for defining an urban area, which poses constraints in comparability of urban and city indicators across economies. Data from World Urbanization Prospects were used when national estimates were not available.

Household surveys, which are the best source of labor force data, are not carried out in all economies on a regular basis. Some economies rely on census data supplemented by enterprise surveys and unemployment registration records, which are often incomplete and may refer only to formal employment. Furthermore, a breakdown by economic activities also may not be available. An initiative is underway to adopt new standards for work and employment statistics, following the recommendations of the 19th International Conference of Labour Statisticians in 2013. These recommendations were adopted by Armenia, beginning 2018; Azerbaijan, beginning 2015; Brunei Darussalam, beginning 2017; Georgia, beginning 2010; the Lao People's Democratic Republic, beginning 2017; Malaysia, beginning 2019; Mongolia, beginning 2019; Nepal, beginning 2018; Timor-Leste, beginning 2010; and Uzbekistan, beginning 2017. Hence, data for these years may not be directly comparable with data in other years. For all other economies, the conceptual definitions used are based on the old framework.

Table 2.2.1: Gross Domestic Product at Purchasing Power Parity
(current international dollars, million)

ADB Regional Member	2010	2015	2016	2017	2018	2019	2020	2021
Developing ADB Member Economies								
Central and West Asia	**1,486,906**	**1,909,014**	**...**	**...**	**...**	**...**	**...**	**...**
Afghanistan	51,348	74,020	70,098	74,712	77,407	81,873	80,912	...
Armenia	21,600	29,167	31,429	35,677	38,428	42,089	39,445	43,425
Azerbaijan	132,906	144,146	140,230	139,153	144,614	150,881	146,133	160,730
Georgia	28,646	45,036	47,930	50,663	54,385	58,116	54,840	63,036
Kazakhstan	313,824	407,416	423,833	448,473	478,013	508,459	501,722	549,751
Kyrgyz Republic	16,812	25,107	28,459	31,280	33,231	35,382	32,801	35,398
Pakistan	698,091	872,097	1,010,730	1,058,469	1,150,425	1,200,250	1,199,042	1,330,980
Tajikistan	17,529	26,634	26,986	28,887	31,825	34,791	36,760	41,810
Turkmenistan	49,914	76,309	...	...	...	...	...	...
Uzbekistan	156,236	209,082	216,467	221,561	239,002	257,167	265,176	296,689
East Asia	**15,208,508**	**21,275,594**	**22,304,501**	**23,611,726**	**25,665,102**	**27,438,274**	**28,411,513**	**31,754,075**
China, People's Republic of	12,380,166	17,796,747	18,712,097	19,887,033	21,736,535	23,441,909	24,255,796	27,312,548
Hong Kong, China	345,525	411,294	419,838	442,425	465,892	466,266	441,294	490,439
Korea, Republic of	1,572,680	1,933,589	2,026,968	2,103,651	2,220,442	2,225,804	2,353,522	2,444,559
Mongolia	20,623	31,928	32,818	35,392	39,044	41,969	40,539	42,824
Taipei,China	889,513	1,102,036	1,112,781	1,143,224	1,203,189	1,262,325	1,320,361	1,463,705
South Asia	**5,829,255**	**8,066,857**	**8,837,722**	**9,465,611**	**10,314,225**	**10,922,747**	**10,431,179**	**...**
Bangladesh	359,986	555,570	728,388	781,590	858,837	943,103	987,380	1,099,767
Bhutan	4,589	6,915	7,704	8,307	8,766	9,436	8,588	...
India	5,229,907	7,159,798	7,735,002	8,276,934	9,021,614	9,526,237	9,005,119	10,227,546
Maldives	4,650	7,628	8,279	8,964	9,924	10,796	7,266	...
Nepal	58,482	80,943	81,509	98,516	108,558	117,856	117,229	126,115
Sri Lanka	171,640	256,002	276,840	291,299	306,526	315,319	305,597	329,324
Southeast Asia	**5,057,617**	**6,618,127**	**6,936,482**	**7,363,886**	**7,933,658**	**8,446,600**	**...**	**...**
Brunei Darussalam	31,203	25,949	23,633	25,891	26,523	28,042	28,702	29,332
Cambodia	34,743	52,598	57,942	62,891	69,203	75,410	73,956	79,360
Indonesia	2,057,207	2,647,707	2,744,897	2,894,126	3,116,595	3,331,571	3,302,097	3,566,265
Lao People's Democratic Republic	22,603	41,583	46,850	50,464	54,898	58,929	60,256	64,849
Malaysia	578,575	750,777	783,874	829,297	890,232	946,384	903,704	970,742
Myanmar	161,769	227,959	213,835	225,517	245,694	266,971	...	...
Philippines	528,742	733,864	798,601	854,095	929,956	1,004,508	919,850	1,012,714
Singapore	382,734	481,405	501,496	534,906	567,737	584,224	566,769	635,267
Thailand	886,760	1,087,226	1,146,041	1,205,839	1,286,784	1,337,984	1,270,216	1,343,720
Timor-Leste[a]	2,120	3,484	3,817	3,950	4,017	4,889	6,247	...
Viet Nam	371,161	565,575	615,496	676,910	742,019	807,688	838,515	1,134,151
The Pacific[b]	**32,525**	**48,329**	**50,940**	**53,854**	**55,707**	**...**	**...**	**...**
Cook Islands	...	...	...	...	...	...	...	...
Fiji	6,805	10,782	11,020	11,784	12,525	12,659	10,664	...
Kiribati	175	231	232	236	255	258	259	...
Marshall Islands	183	201	204	215	228	248	245	255
Micronesia, Federated States of	336	365	372	389	399	...	...	...
Nauru	62	158	143	138	149	151	155	164
Niue	...	...	...	...	...	...	...	...
Palau	238	313	319	319	324	323	295	...
Papua New Guinea	21,316	32,167	34,273	36,158	36,918	39,262	38,345	40,537
Samoa	1,028	1,247	1,315	1,353	1,406	1,475	1,362	1,389
Solomon Islands	1,219	1,477	1,579	1,678	1,850	1,915	1,787	...
Tonga	479	582	626	660	677	695	708	...
Tuvalu	31	39	44	46	48	55	53	58
Vanuatu	651	768	812	880	927	974	...	...
Developed ADB Member Economies	**5,527,896**	**6,474,131**	**6,490,300**	**6,656,172**	**6,802,571**	**6,893,829**	**6,912,823**	**...**
Australia	866,656	1,101,457	1,143,149	1,190,694	1,253,361	1,312,637	1,369,885	1,436,442
Japan	4,525,401	5,199,915	5,158,900	5,262,255	5,340,832	5,354,366	5,315,621	5,396,820
New Zealand	135,840	172,759	188,251	203,223	208,377	226,827	227,317	...

... = data not available, ADB = Asian Development Bank.

Note: Gross domestic product figures in local currency units are obtained from the economies' official sources and converted into a common currency using the purchasing power parity (PPP) from the World Bank's World Development Indicators. For 2011 and 2017, PPP figures are based on results from the 2011 and 2017 benchmark cycles of the International Comparison Program (ICP). For 2010 (and years prior featured in the Key Indicators Database), the PPP figures are extrapolated from the revised 2011 ICP. For 2012–2016, PPP estimates are interpolated from the two ICP reference years 2011 and 2017. For 2017 onward, the PPP figures are extrapolated from the 2017 ICP PPPs or imputed based on a regression model. For Taipei,China, the PPP figures for 2010 and 2018–2021 are Asian Development Bank estimates using data from the economy's official sources and the World Bank, while the PPP conversion factor used for 2011–2017 was from the World Bank's ICP 2017 database.

a From September 2019, oil revenue from the Joint Petroleum Development Area is now included in GDP based on the new Timor-Leste Australia Maritime Boundary Treaty.
b For reporting economies only.

Source: Asian Development Bank estimates based on data from the economies' official sources.

Table 2.2.2: Gross Domestic Product
(current $ million)

ADB Regional Member	2010	2015	2016	2017	2018	2019	2020	2021
Developing ADB Member Economies								
Central and West Asia	**496,071**	**687,867**	**...**	**...**	**...**	**...**	**...**	**...**
Afghanistan	16,078	20,607	18,020	18,896	18,419	18,904	20,143	...
Armenia	9,260	10,553	10,546	11,527	12,458	13,619	12,642	13,861
Azerbaijan	52,906	53,076	37,867	40,867	47,112	48,174	42,693	54,622
Georgia	12,243	14,954	15,142	16,243	17,600	17,477	15,846	18,696
Kazakhstan	148,047	184,388	137,278	166,806	179,340	181,667	171,082	193,018
Kyrgyz Republic	4,794	6,678	6,813	7,703	8,271	8,871	7,781	8,543
Pakistan	174,508	267,035	312,354	337,137	321,692	291,919	293,752	342,501
Tajikistan	5,642	8,271	6,992	7,536	7,765	8,301	8,134	8,746
Turkmenistan	22,582	36,107	...	...	...	...	...	...
Uzbekistan	50,010	86,196	86,138	62,081	52,633	59,908	59,894	69,239
East Asia	**7,911,047**	**13,383,287**	**13,608,241**	**14,877,114**	**16,604,531**	**16,920,080**	**17,359,661**	**20,703,991**
China, People's Republic of	6,087,192	11,061,573	11,233,315	12,310,490	13,894,907	14,279,968	14,687,744	17,734,131
Hong Kong, China	228,639	309,386	320,860	341,271	361,731	363,052	344,930	369,174
Korea, Republic of	1,143,672	1,466,039	1,499,680	1,623,074	1,725,373	1,651,423	1,644,313	1,810,966
Mongolia	7,189	11,620	11,181	11,481	13,178	14,206	13,313	15,098
Taipei,China	444,354	534,670	543,205	590,798	609,342	611,431	669,362	774,622
South Asia	**1,863,181**	**2,456,146**	**2,673,969**	**3,044,311**	**3,213,709**	**3,331,619**	**3,170,251**	**...**
Bangladesh	114,508	194,466	264,543	288,958	316,206	349,474	373,562	414,907
Bhutan	1,548	2,004	2,159	2,450	2,447	2,536	2,315	...
India	1,669,620	2,146,759	2,290,587	2,624,329	2,763,535	2,850,718	2,672,204	3,201,471
Maldives	2,588	4,109	4,379	4,754	5,301	5,608	3,743	...
Nepal	16,281	23,667	24,288	29,443	31,726	34,268	33,079	36,114
Sri Lanka	58,636	85,141	88,012	94,376	94,494	89,015	85,349	88,361
Southeast Asia	**1,988,718**	**2,480,735**	**2,598,304**	**2,800,317**	**2,999,617**	**3,173,365**	**...**	**...**
Brunei Darussalam	13,707	12,930	11,400	12,128	13,567	13,469	12,006	13,967
Cambodia	11,242	18,050	20,017	22,177	24,572	27,089	25,873	26,961
Indonesia	755,094	860,854	931,877	1,015,619	1,042,272	1,119,100	1,058,689	1,186,093
Lao People's Democratic Republic	6,747	14,426	15,913	17,071	18,142	18,741	19,082	19,074
Malaysia	255,018	301,355	301,255	319,109	358,789	365,279	337,007	372,702
Myanmar	...	62,543	60,100	60,793	64,896	69,329	...	...
Philippines	208,369	306,446	318,627	328,481	346,842	376,823	361,751	394,086
Singapore	239,808	307,999	318,822	343,187	376,987	375,484	345,286	396,992
Thailand	341,105	401,296	413,366	456,357	506,754	544,081	499,682	505,982
Timor-Leste[a]	882	1,594	1,651	1,616	1,584	2,049	2,177	...
Viet Nam	115,932	193,241	205,276	223,780	245,214	261,921	271,158	362,638
The Pacific	**21,169**	**31,075**	**30,627**	**33,373**	**35,260**	**...**	**...**	**...**
Cook Islands	241	302	310	346	362	357	283	315
Fiji	3,140	4,682	4,930	5,353	5,581	5,482	4,476	...
Kiribati	155	170	179	188	196	178	181	...
Marshall Islands	162	185	201	213	221	240	244	254
Micronesia, Federated States of	297	316	332	367	402	...	...	...
Nauru	51	90	102	111	120	115	117	134
Niue	18	24	25	26	30	31	...	...
Palau	184	279	297	288	285	274	258	...
Papua New Guinea	14,251	21,723	20,759	22,743	24,110	24,751	24,667	26,595
Samoa	699	826	870	882	894	913	829	857
Solomon Islands	898	1,308	1,379	1,470	1,615	1,619	1,536	...
Tonga	371	403	421	461	480	508	491	...
Tuvalu	31	35	41	45	48	54	52	60
Vanuatu	671	731	781	880	915	937	...	...
Developed ADB Member Economies	**7,100,697**	**5,842,452**	**6,424,843**	**6,485,844**	**6,626,753**	**6,689,703**	**6,615,056**	**...**
Australia	1,195,108	1,219,457	1,232,327	1,348,383	1,376,964	1,352,950	1,363,214	1,552,714
Japan	5,759,072	4,444,931	5,003,678	4,930,837	5,037,835	5,123,318	5,040,108	4,937,423
New Zealand	146,518	178,064	188,838	206,624	211,953	213,435	211,735	...

... = data not available, $ = United States dollars, ADB = Asian Development Bank.

Note: Gross domestic product figures in local currency units are obtained from the economies' official sources and converted to United States dollars using the official exchange rates from the International Monetary Fund. The exchange rates used are expressed as the average rate for a period of time (average of period), calculated as annual averages based on the monthly averages (local currency units relative to the United States dollar). For Myanmar, the 2010 figure for gross domestic product in US dollars was converted from the domestic currency using the World Bank's alternative conversion factor to calculate the aggregate for Southeast Asia.

a From September 2019, oil revenue from the Joint Petroleum Development Area is now included in GDP based on the new Timor-Leste Australia Maritime Boundary Treaty.

Source: Asian Development Bank estimates based on data from the economies' official sources.

Table 2.2.3: Gross Domestic Product per Capita at Purchasing Power Parity
(current international dollars)

ADB Regional Member	2010	2015	2016	2017	2018	2019	2020	2021
Developing ADB Member Economies								
Central and West Asia	**5,375**	**6,398**	...	...	...	...	...	...
Afghanistan	2,097	2,787	2,535	2,647	2,574	2,665	2,578	...
Armenia	7,070	9,667	10,481	11,948	12,927	14,194	13,327	14,672
Azerbaijan	14,679	15,117	14,371	14,121	14,549	15,052	14,479	15,925
Georgia	7,565	12,108	12,858	13,590	14,594	15,622	14,731	16,933
Kazakhstan	19,433	23,571	23,814	24,868	26,160	27,472	26,744	29,304
Kyrgyz Republic	3,103	4,346	4,728	5,094	5,311	5,538	5,028	5,426
Pakistan	4,023	4,638	5,084	5,097	5,431	5,555	5,440	6,039
Tajikistan	2,331	3,226	3,121	3,269	3,531	3,777	3,907	4,444
Turkmenistan	9,812	13,960	...	...	...	...	...	...
Uzbekistan	5,470	6,798	6,797	6,841	7,252	7,658	7,746	8,667
East Asia	**10,685**	**14,564**	**15,096**	**15,895**	**17,211**	**18,338**	**18,961**	**21,192**
China, People's Republic of	9,233	12,929	13,440	14,204	15,466	16,625	17,177	19,342
Hong Kong, China	49,191	56,891	57,225	59,842	62,514	62,103	58,989	65,558
Korea, Republic of	31,737	38,103	39,575	40,957	43,044	42,998	45,403	47,159
Mongolia	7,638	10,643	10,586	11,417	12,201	12,718	11,923	12,595
Taipei,China	38,439	47,088	47,320	48,533	51,026	53,505	55,986	62,064
South Asia	**4,216**	**5,473**	**5,853**	**6,197**	**6,681**	**6,996**	**6,613**	...
Bangladesh	2,423	3,543	4,530	4,804	5,218	5,664	5,870	6,538
Bhutan	6,595	9,280	10,024	11,425	11,936	12,723	11,466	...
India	4,410	5,647	5,955	6,299	6,793	7,093	6,636	7,537
Maldives	11,814	17,435	17,525	18,235	19,381	20,220	13,035	...
Nepal	2,228	2,967	2,931	3,508	3,828	4,116	4,055	4,362
Sri Lanka	8,311	12,325	13,057	13,584	14,145	14,462	13,942	15,025
Southeast Asia	**8,583**	**10,643**	**10,903**	**11,442**	**12,196**	**12,853**	...	...
Brunei Darussalam	80,669	63,663	56,638	60,282	59,952	61,028	63,276	64,664
Cambodia	2,460	3,534	3,786	4,053	4,397	4,725	4,572	4,906
Indonesia	8,657	10,500	10,619	11,073	11,798	12,482	12,221	13,198
Lao People's Democratic Republic	3,741	6,498	7,113	7,552	8,099	8,569	8,637	9,295
Malaysia	20,238	24,449	24,780	25,897	27,491	29,099	27,735	29,792
Myanmar	3,225	4,385	4,041	4,224	4,562	4,913	...	...
Philippines	5,677	7,347	7,789	8,199	8,793	9,362	8,436	9,288
Singapore	75,390	88,013	89,437	95,310	100,686	102,431	99,681	111,728
Thailand	13,452	16,091	16,794	17,505	18,620	19,303	18,274	19,332
Timor-Leste[a]	1,939	2,967	3,131	3,177	3,168	3,781	4,739	...
Viet Nam	4,263	6,201	6,600	7,179	7,779	8,371	8,593	11,622
The Pacific[b]	**3,492**	**4,676**	**4,676**	**4,811**	**4,848**	...	...	...
Cook Islands	...	...	...	...	...	...	...	...
Fiji	8,000	12,454	12,620	13,317	14,134	14,234	11,964	...
Kiribati	1,701	2,127	2,076	2,076	2,202	2,193	2,172	...
Marshall Islands	3,454	3,739	3,764	3,958	4,182	4,533	4,466	4,633
Micronesia, Federated States of	3,268	3,522	3,577	3,736	3,827	...	...	...
Nauru	6,362	14,802	13,020	12,287	13,112	13,108	13,187	13,982
Niue	...	...	...	...	...	...	...	...
Palau	13,037	18,028	17,869	17,815	18,490	18,510	16,773	...
Papua New Guinea	3,021	4,032	4,041	4,134	4,093	4,222	3,998	4,227
Samoa	5,532	6,489	6,727	6,865	7,079	7,366	6,745	6,880
Solomon Islands	2,195	2,414	2,470	2,569	2,773	2,813	2,573	...
Tonga	4,665	5,695	6,194	6,556	6,768	6,976	7,144	...
Tuvalu	2,754	3,653	4,084	4,287	4,490	5,183	5,027	5,473
Vanuatu	2,716	2,925	2,981	3,156	3,251	3,339	...	...
Developed ADB Member Economies	**35,790**	**41,696**	**41,631**	**42,613**	**43,491**	**44,019**	**44,138**	...
Australia	39,337	46,919	47,255	48,399	50,169	51,748	53,317	55,907
Japan	35,335	40,855	40,623	41,505	42,210	42,406	42,242	42,888
New Zealand	31,222	38,251	39,934	42,219	42,521	45,555	44,658	...

... = data not available, ADB = Asian Development Bank.

Note: The figures in the table are calculated as gross domestic product (GDP) at purchasing power parity (PPP) divided by the midyear population. GDP figures in local currency units are obtained from the economies' official sources and converted into a common currency using the PPP from the World Bank's World Development Indicators. For 2011 and 2017, PPP figures are based on results from the 2011 and 2017 benchmark cycles of the International Comparison Program (ICP). For 2010 (and years prior featured in the Key Indicators Database), the PPP figures are extrapolated from the revised 2011 ICP. For 2012–2016, PPP estimates are interpolated from the two ICP reference years 2011 and 2017. For 2017 onward, the PPP figures are extrapolated from the 2017 ICP PPPs or imputed based on a regression model. For Taipei,China, the PPP figures for 2010 and 2018–2021 are Asian Development Bank estimates using data from the economy's official sources and the World Bank, while the PPP conversion factor used for 2011–2017 was from the World Bank's ICP 2017 database.

a From September 2019, oil revenue from the Joint Petroleum Development Area is now included in GDP based on the new Timor-Leste Australia Maritime Boundary Treaty.

b For reporting economies only.

Source: Asian Development Bank estimates based on data from the economies' official sources.

Table 2.2.4: Gross National Income per Capita, Atlas Method
(current $)

ADB Regional Member	2010	2015	2016	2017	2018	2019	2020	2021
Developing ADB Member Economies								
Central and West Asia[a]	**1,580**	**2,214**	**2,059**	**2,032**	**2,115**	**2,124**	**1,986**	**2,052**
Afghanistan	510	590	550	530	510	520	500	...
Armenia	3,470	4,010	3,760	3,950	4,240	4,660	4,220	4,560
Azerbaijan	5,410	6,610	4,790	4,110	4,080	4,510	4,480	4,880
Georgia	3,210	4,410	4,080	4,040	4,460	4,690	4,260	4,740
Kazakhstan	7,440	11,380	8,770	8,040	8,070	8,820	8,710	8,720
Kyrgyz Republic	850	1,180	1,110	1,110	1,220	1,240	1,180	1,180
Pakistan	970	1,260	1,360	1,490	1,670	1,620	1,460	1,500
Tajikistan	920	1,260	1,110	1,030	1,030	1,070	1,050	1,150
Turkmenistan	4,070	7,030	6,830	6,380	6,740	7,220	...	...
Uzbekistan	1,410	2,740	2,790	2,470	2,110	1,870	1,740	1,960
East Asia[b]	**5,358**	**9,017**	**9,347**	**9,847**	**10,801**	**11,583**	**11,766**	**13,195**
China, People's Republic of	4,340	7,890	8,210	8,670	9,540	10,310	10,530	11,890
Hong Kong, China	33,620	41,180	42,970	46,380	50,050	50,480	48,560	54,450
Korea, Republic of	22,290	28,720	29,330	30,300	32,750	33,830	32,930	34,980
Mongolia	2,000	3,800	3,490	3,240	3,690	3,850	3,740	3,760
Taipei,China	19,903	23,316	23,440	24,473	26,239	27,483	28,712	32,149
South Asia[a]	**1,182**	**1,582**	**1,672**	**1,823**	**2,025**	**2,132**	**1,971**	**2,226**
Bangladesh	800	1,220	1,430	1,670	2,040	2,250	2,340	2,620
Bhutan	2,040	2,520	2,650	2,800	2,970	3,150	2,840	...
India	1,220	1,600	1,680	1,820	2,010	2,100	1,910	2,170
Maldives	5,960	7,650	8,070	8,600	9,210	9,640	6,450	8,400
Nepal	540	890	880	990	1,120	1,230	1,190	1,230
Sri Lanka	2,410	3,760	3,810	3,870	4,040	4,010	3,720	3,820
Southeast Asia[a]	**2,996**	**4,068**	**4,060**	**4,169**	**4,499**	**4,765**	**4,557**	**4,796**
Brunei Darussalam	33,300	38,850	33,170	29,800	29,390	32,230	31,510	...
Cambodia	750	1,060	1,140	1,230	1,380	1,530	1,510	1,550
Indonesia	2,530	3,430	3,400	3,530	3,840	4,050	3,870	4,140
Lao People's Democratic Republic	1,000	1,980	2,130	2,260	2,490	2,540	2,490	2,520
Malaysia	8,260	10,680	10,150	9,950	10,650	11,260	10,570	10,930
Myanmar	620	1,170	1,200	1,180	1,220	1,270	1,340	1,140
Philippines	2,370	3,380	3,450	3,530	3,710	3,850	3,430	3,640
Singapore	44,930	53,160	53,250	54,590	56,670	58,060	55,010	64,010
Thailand	4,580	5,710	5,700	5,970	6,610	7,250	7,070	7,260
Timor-Leste	2,850	2,200	1,750	1,800	1,820	2,050	1,990	1,940
Viet Nam	1,360	2,460	2,570	2,700	3,030	3,280	3,390	3,560
The Pacific[a]	**2,043**	**3,124**	**3,011**	**2,928**	**3,008**	**3,115**	**3,007**	**...**
Cook Islands	9,349	17,157	18,347	17,360	19,709	18,761	15,695	...
Fiji	3,650	5,100	5,280	5,370	5,910	5,800	4,930	4,860
Kiribati	2,040	3,450	2,800	2,930	3,170	3,440	2,910	...
Marshall Islands	3,550	4,290	4,250	4,440	4,840	5,050	4,940	5,050
Micronesia, Federated States of	2,900	3,490	3,410	3,450	3,400	3,940	3,960	3,880
Nauru	8,870 (2012)	13,690	12,720	12,310	14,500	16,230	17,330	19,470
Niue	10,896 (2011)	16,820	16,211	14,016	15,990	16,247	...	...
Palau	11,400	15,860	16,720	16,540	17,380	16,710	14,390	...
Papua New Guinea	1,740	2,860	2,710	2,590	2,600	2,720	2,720	2,790
Samoa	3,450	3,960	4,110	4,070	4,050	4,230	4,050	3,860
Solomon Islands	1,470	2,130	2,140	2,220	2,360	2,370	2,300	2,300
Tonga	3,370	4,440	4,410	4,590	4,800	5,150	5,190	...
Tuvalu	4,520	5,580	5,300	5,070	5,820	6,240	6,340	6,760
Vanuatu	2,600	2,820	2,830	2,900	3,170	3,440	3,240	3,140
Developed ADB Member Economies[b]	**43,905**	**42,647**	**40,915**	**40,903**	**43,571**	**44,129**	**42,935**	**45,037**
Australia	46,690	60,490	54,090	51,480	53,070	54,910	53,680	56,760
Japan	43,910	39,380	38,460	38,930	41,770	42,010	40,810	42,620
New Zealand	29,680	40,660	39,440	38,870	41,650	43,050	41,480	45,340
DEVELOPING ADB MEMBER ECONOMIES[a]	**3,088**	**4,798**	**4,930**	**5,178**	**5,654**	**6,009**	**5,949**	**6,585**
ALL ADB REGIONAL MEMBERS[a]	**4,705**	**6,234**	**6,287**	**6,515**	**7,063**	**7,417**	**7,305**	**7,981**
WORLD	**9,478**	**10,664**	**10,408**	**10,489**	**11,179**	**11,577**	**11,099**	**12,070**

... = data not available, $ = United States dollars, ADB = Asian Development Bank.

Note: The Atlas method refers to a conversion factor that averages the exchange rate for a given year and the 2 preceding years, adjusted for differences in rates of inflation between the member economy and the G5 economies.

a Aggregates are weighted averages estimated using midyear population. For estimating aggregates, imputation was done for economies with missing data by substituting available data from the nearest years.

b Aggregates are weighted averages estimated using midyear population.

Sources: World Bank. World Development Indicators. https://databank.worldbank.org/source/world-development-indicators (accessed 4 July 2022). For the Cook Islands; Niue; and Taipei,China: Asian Development Bank estimates using the Atlas method based on the economies' official sources.

Table 2.2.5: Gross Domestic Product per Capita
(current $)

ADB Regional Member	2010	2015	2016	2017	2018	2019	2020	2021
Developing ADB Member Economies								
Central and West Asia	**1,793**	**2,305**	...	...	...	...	...	...
Afghanistan	657	776	652	670	612	615	642	...
Armenia	3,031	3,498	3,517	3,860	4,191	4,593	4,271	4,683
Azerbaijan	5,843	5,566	3,881	4,147	4,740	4,806	4,230	5,412
Georgia	3,233	4,020	4,062	4,357	4,723	4,698	4,257	5,022
Kazakhstan	9,168	10,668	7,713	9,249	9,815	9,816	9,119	10,289
Kyrgyz Republic	885	1,156	1,132	1,255	1,322	1,388	1,193	1,310
Pakistan	1,006	1,420	1,571	1,623	1,519	1,351	1,333	1,554
Tajikistan	750	1,002	809	853	862	901	864	930
Turkmenistan	4,439	6,605	...	...	...	...	...	...
Uzbekistan	1,751	2,802	2,705	1,917	1,597	1,784	1,750	2,023
East Asia	**5,558**	**9,161**	**9,210**	**10,015**	**11,135**	**11,308**	**11,585**	**13,817**
China, People's Republic of	4,540	8,036	8,068	8,793	9,887	10,127	10,401	12,559
Hong Kong, China	32,550	42,795	43,734	46,160	48,538	48,356	46,107	49,348
Korea, Republic of	23,079	28,889	29,280	31,601	33,447	31,902	31,721	34,936
Mongolia	2,663	3,873	3,607	3,703	4,118	4,305	3,916	4,441
Taipei,China	19,202	22,846	23,099	25,081	25,841	25,916	28,382	32,845
South Asia	**1,348**	**1,666**	**1,771**	**1,993**	**2,082**	**2,134**	**2,010**	...
Bangladesh	771	1,240	1,645	1,776	1,921	2,099	2,221	2,466
Bhutan	2,225	2,689	2,809	3,370	3,332	3,419	3,092	...
India	1,408	1,693	1,763	1,997	2,081	2,123	1,969	2,359
Maldives	6,576	9,392	9,269	9,671	10,353	10,503	6,714	...
Nepal	620	868	873	1,048	1,119	1,197	1,144	1,249
Sri Lanka	2,839	4,099	4,151	4,401	4,361	4,083	3,894	4,031
Southeast Asia	**3,375**	**3,989**	**4,084**	**4,351**	**4,611**	**4,829**	...	...
Brunei Darussalam	35,437	31,723	27,322	28,238	30,667	29,313	26,468	30,791
Cambodia	796	1,213	1,308	1,429	1,561	1,698	1,600	1,667
Indonesia	3,177	3,414	3,605	3,886	3,946	4,193	3,918	4,390
Lao People's Democratic Republic	1,117	2,254	2,416	2,555	2,676	2,725	2,735	2,734
Malaysia	8,920	9,813	9,523	9,965	11,080	11,231	10,343	11,438
Myanmar	...	1,203	1,136	1,139	1,205	1,276	...	...
Philippines	2,237	3,068	3,108	3,153	3,280	3,512	3,318	3,614
Singapore	47,237	56,310	56,859	61,150	66,857	65,833	60,728	69,822
Thailand	5,174	5,939	6,057	6,625	7,333	7,849	7,189	7,279
Timor-Leste[a]	806	1,358	1,354	1,299	1,249	1,584	1,651	...
Viet Nam	1,332	2,119	2,201	2,373	2,571	2,715	2,779	3,716
The Pacific	**2,730 (2011)**	**3,006**	**2,811**	**2,981**	**3,069**	...	...	...
Cook Islands	10,160	16,422	16,055	17,725	19,477	17,663	15,832	17,576
Fiji	3,691	5,409	5,646	6,050	6,298	6,164	5,021	...
Kiribati	1,507	1,567	1,595	1,654	1,697	1,514	1,515	...
Marshall Islands	3,064	3,434	3,704	3,917	4,056	4,376	4,448	4,621
Micronesia, Federated States of	2,887	3,056	3,197	3,522	3,854	...	...	...
Nauru	5,275	8,468	9,280	9,951	10,515	9,969	9,991	11,417
Niue	13,021 (2011)	15,575	15,656	14,644	16,885	16,548	...	...
Palau	10,044	16,065	16,601	16,062	16,265	15,704	14,640	...
Papua New Guinea	2,020	2,723	2,447	2,600	2,673	2,661	2,572	2,773
Samoa	3,759	4,297	4,453	4,475	4,500	4,556	4,106	4,245
Solomon Islands	1,617	2,138	2,157	2,250	2,422	2,378	2,211	...
Tonga	3,612	3,945	4,162	4,585	4,795	5,107	4,959	...
Tuvalu	2,816	3,266	3,869	4,253	4,522	5,110	4,899	5,698
Vanuatu	2,798	2,784	2,866	3,157	3,208	3,211	...	...
Developed ADB Member Economies	**45,973**	**37,628**	**41,211**	**41,522**	**42,367**	**42,716**	**42,236**	...
Australia	54,245	51,946	50,942	54,808	55,117	53,338	53,057	60,433
Japan	44,968	34,924	39,401	38,891	39,816	40,576	40,053	39,237
New Zealand	33,677	39,425	40,058	42,925	43,250	42,865	41,597	...

... = data not available, $ = United States dollars, ADB = Asian Development Bank.

Note: The figures in the table are calculated as gross domestic product (GDP) in current United States (US) dollars divided by the midyear population. GDP figures in local currency units are obtained from the economies' official sources and converted to US dollars using the official exchange rates from the International Monetary Fund. The exchange rates used are expressed as the average rate for a period of time (average of period), calculated as annual averages based on the monthly averages (local currency units relative to the US dollar). For Myanmar, the 2010 figure for GDP in US dollars was converted from the domestic currency using the World Bank's alternative conversion factor to calculate the aggregate for Southeast Asia.

a From September 2019, oil revenue from the Joint Petroleum Development Area is now included in GDP based on the new Timor-Leste Australia Maritime Boundary Treaty.

Source: Asian Development Bank estimates based on data from the economies' official sources.

Click on the indicator name in the table header to access the time series in the Key Indicators Database

Table 2.2.6: Agriculture, Industry, and Services Value-Added
(% of GDP)

ADB Regional Member	Agriculture Value-Added			Industry Value-Added			Services Value-Added		
	2010	2015	2021	2010	2015	2021	2010	2015	2021
Developing ADB Member Economies									
Central and West Asia									
Afghanistan	28.8	22.7	28.1 (2020)	21.3	22.7	14.7 (2020)	49.8	54.7	57.2 (2020)
Armenia	18.8	18.9	12.5	36.3	28.2	29.3	45.0	52.9	58.2
Azerbaijan	5.9	6.8	6.4	64.1	49.3	52.9	30.0	43.9	40.7
Georgia	9.6	8.8	7.0*	19.1	21.5	25.0*	71.4	69.7	68.0*
Kazakhstan	4.7	5.0	5.4*	41.9	32.5	37.6*	53.4	62.5	56.9*
Kyrgyz Republic	18.8	15.4	16.3*	28.2	27.5	29.7*	53.1	57.1	53.9*
Pakistan	24.3	25.1	24.2	20.6	20.1	20.1	55.1	54.9	55.7
Tajikistan	21.8	23.7	26.8*	27.9	33.2	29.1*	50.3	43.1	44.1*
Turkmenistan	11.5	9.3	...	60.0	56.9	...	28.5	33.8	...
Uzbekistan	30.6	32.1	26.9*	24.1	24.8	34.5*	45.3	43.1	38.5*
East Asia									
China, People's Republic of	9.3	8.4	7.3*	46.5	40.8	39.4*	44.2	50.8	53.3*
Hong Kong, China	0.1	0.1	0.1 (2020)	7.0	7.3	6.4 (2020)	93.0	92.7	93.4 (2020)
Korea, Republic of	2.4	2.2	2.0	37.5	37.2	35.6	60.1	60.6	62.5
Mongolia	11.6	14.0	13.1	36.1	34.1	40.5	52.4	52.0	46.4
Taipei,China	1.6	1.8	1.5	33.4	36.3	38.0	65.0	62.0	60.6
South Asia									
Bangladesh	17.8	15.5	12.1	26.1	28.2	34.6	56.0	56.4	53.3
Bhutan	14.8	14.4	19.2 (2020)	43.8	42.5	34.4 (2020)	41.4	43.1	46.4 (2020)
India	18.4	17.7	18.6*	33.1	30.0	28.7*	48.5	52.3	52.7*
Maldives	6.1	6.3	8.8 (2020)	10.2	12.1	13.1 (2020)	83.8	81.7	78.1 (2020)
Nepal	35.4	29.4	25.8	15.1	14.6	13.1	49.5	56.0	61.1
Sri Lanka	10.1	8.9	9.3	30.9	32.1	31.8	59.0	58.9	58.9
Southeast Asia									
Brunei Darussalam	0.7	1.1	1.2	67.4	60.2	61.9	31.9	38.7	36.9
Cambodia	36.0	28.2	24.3	23.3	29.4	39.2	40.7	42.3	36.4
Indonesia	14.3	13.9	13.8	43.9	41.4	41.5	41.8	44.7	44.6
Lao People's Democratic Republic	30.6	19.7	18.1	29.8	31.0	38.6	39.6	49.4	43.3
Malaysia	10.2	8.4	9.7	40.9	38.9	38.2	48.9	52.7	52.1
Myanmar	36.9	26.8	21.4 (2019)	26.5	34.5	38.0 (2019)	36.7	38.8	40.7 (2019)
Philippines	13.7	11.0	10.1	32.3	30.5	28.9	53.9	58.5	61.0
Singapore	0.0	0.0	0.0	28.2	25.8	26.4	71.8	74.2	73.6
Thailand[a]	10.5	8.9	8.5*	37.1	33.4	32.1*	52.4	57.7	59.4*
Timor-Leste[b]	24.7	17.8	13.8 (2020)	8.8	18.4	36.7 (2020)	66.5	63.8	49.5 (2020)
Viet Nam	21.0	18.9	12.4	36.7	37.0	37.9	42.2	44.2	40.9
The Pacific									
Cook Islands	3.4	3.2	2.8*	7.9	11.3	8.1*	88.7	85.4	79.6*
Fiji	11.0	10.0	17.1* (2020)	20.9	19.3	19.8* (2020)	68.1	70.6	63.1* (2020)
Kiribati	24.3	22.2	25.2* (2020)	12.0	15.7	9.4* (2020)	63.7	62.1	65.4* (2020)
Marshall Islands	11.2	12.5	23.5	14.5	12.9	10.4	76.8	77.3	66.8
Micronesia, Federated States of	26.7	27.8	23.9* (2018)	7.8	6.5	5.2* (2018)	65.5	65.7	70.9* (2018)
Nauru	6.3	4.0	4.7*	32.7	6.1	7.5*	61.0	89.9	73.3*
Niue	23.0	21.0	19.1* (2018)	4.0	1.6	3.7* (2018)	73.0	77.5	77.2* (2018)
Palau	4.2	3.3	3.7* (2020)	11.0	8.9	15.0* (2020)	84.8	87.8	82.8* (2020)
Papua New Guinea	20.2	18.3	20.2	34.2	36.4	35.8	45.5	45.3	44.0
Samoa	9.5	9.2	10.2	16.2	16.2	12.8	74.4	74.6	76.9
Solomon Islands	34.6	33.3	34.1 (2020)	13.8	15.6	17.2 (2020)	51.6	51.2	48.6 (2020)
Tonga	18.7	19.7	21.1 (2020)	20.5	18.1	17.6 (2020)	60.9	62.3	61.2 (2020)
Tuvalu	27.3	21.4	9.1	5.7	12.7	16.0	67.0	65.9	74.8
Vanuatu	20.8	24.0	22.8 (2019)	13.7	10.6	10.2 (2019)	65.6	65.4	67.0 (2019)
Developed ADB Member Economies									
Australia	2.4	2.5	2.4	27.1	25.4	27.3	70.6	72.1	70.3
Japan	1.1	1.0	1.0 (2020)	28.3	28.8	29.2 (2020)	70.6	70.2	69.8 (2020)
New Zealand	7.1	4.9	6.2 (2019)	23.0	23.1	22.3 (2019)	69.9	72.0	71.6 (2019)

... = data not available; 0.0 = magnitude is less than half of the unit employed; * = provisional, preliminary, estimate; ADB = Asian Development Bank; GDP = gross domestic product.

a Value-added for construction is included under services.
b From September 2019, oil revenue from the Joint Petroleum Development Area is now included in GDP based on the new Timor-Leste Australia Maritime Boundary Treaty.

Source: Economies' official sources.

Table 2.2.7: Household and Government Consumption Expenditure
(% of GDP)

ADB Regional Member	Household Consumption			Government Consumption		
	2010	2015	2021	2010	2015	2021
Developing ADB Member Economies						
Central and West Asia[a]	**60.2**	**65.0**	**66.4 (2019)**	**11.1**	**11.7**	**11.3 (2019)**
Afghanistan	97.4	82.9	91.8 (2020)	14.0	12.1	21.2 (2020)
Armenia[b]	82.0	77.9	71.8	13.1	13.1	15.8
Azerbaijan	38.9	56.3	60.5 (2020)	10.9	12.4	16.2 (2020)
Georgia	79.5	73.6	77.7*	15.3	14.3	14.0*
Kazakhstan[b]	45.4	53.7	51.6*	10.8	11.6	11.7*
Kyrgyz Republic[b]	84.6	90.5	75.2 (2020)	18.1	17.8	19.3 (2020)
Pakistan[b]	79.7	79.8	82.4	10.3	11.0	10.9
Tajikistan[b]	84.7	71.2	77.6 (2020)	11.3	11.6	11.6 (2020)
Turkmenistan[b]	5.0	9.3 (2013)	...	9.3	9.1 (2013)	...
Uzbekistan[b]	61.5	64.9	59.1*	12.5	13.6	16.7*
East Asia	**38.3**	**40.0**	**39.8 (2020)**	**14.4**	**15.8**	**16.0**
China, People's Republic of	34.3	37.8	38.4*	14.6	16.2	15.9*
Hong Kong, China[b]	61.4	66.4	65.0	8.9	9.6	12.5
Korea, Republic of	49.1	46.9	44.5	14.2	15.1	18.2
Mongolia[b]	55.2	61.9	51.0	12.7	14.9	14.2
Taipei,China[b]	53.2	51.5	48.5 (2020)	15.1	13.9	13.5
South Asia	**56.5**	**60.5**	**62.0 (2020)**	**10.5**	**10.0**	**11.3 (2020)**
Bangladesh	74.1	72.4	68.8	5.1	5.4	5.9
Bhutan[b]	45.3	55.3	62.0 (2020)	20.5	18.3	20.9 (2020)
India[b]	54.7	59.0	59.6*	11.0	10.4	11.1*
Maldives	...	41.1	50.8 (2020)	...	18.2	22.6 (2020)
Nepal[b]	78.6	85.8	88.0	10.0	9.0	8.9
Sri Lanka	68.5	67.4	70.3	8.5	9.0	9.6
Southeast Asia	**52.3**	**54.1**	**54.8 (2019)**	**10.5**	**11.1**	**10.6 (2019)**
Brunei Darussalam[b]	14.7	19.8	24.6	22.2	25.1	22.5
Cambodia[b]	81.3	76.8	65.2	6.3	5.4	7.6
Indonesia[b]	55.2	56.3	54.4	9.0	9.7	9.1
Lao People's Democratic Republic	...	...	...	...	...	...
Malaysia[b]	48.1	54.0	57.9	12.6	13.1	12.8
Myanmar[c]	67.3	74.0	70.4 (2019)	...	...	...
Philippines[b]	70.2	72.5	75.3	9.7	10.9	15.6
Singapore	36.3	37.2	31.0	9.7	10.2	11.5
Thailand	51.7	49.7	51.6*	16.0	16.9	18.3*
Timor-Leste[d]	68.7	55.2	48.3 (2020)	103.2	58.8	44.0 (2020)
Viet Nam	66.6	68.0	56.4	6.0	6.3	9.3
The Pacific	**...**	**...**	**...**	**...**	**...**	**...**
Cook Islands	...	...	...	...	...	...
Fiji[e]	72.3	57.2	63.7* (2020)	15.0	20.2	24.8* (2020)
Kiribati	87.9	84.2	83.3* (2020)	61.6	62.9	66.0* (2020)
Marshall Islands	75.2	75.9	67.4	56.1	55.4	57.6
Micronesia, Federated States of	...	...	...	...	...	...
Nauru	...	...	...	...	...	...
Niue	...	...	...	...	...	...
Palau	67.8	64.5	64.5* (2019)	37.4	28.7	33.4* (2019)
Papua New Guinea[b]	48.0 (2005)	...	...	16.1 (2005)	...	...
Samoa	66.9	63.2	80.5	13.9	14.4	19.4
Solomon Islands	61.6	60.5	59.6 (2020)	31.5	29.6	25.1 (2020)
Tonga	89.1	94.3	92.6 (2020)	18.7	21.3	23.8 (2020)
Tuvalu	...	...	...	...	...	...
Vanuatu	62.6	66.9	54.0 (2019)	18.3	16.5	20.6 (2019)
Developed ADB Member Economies	**55.8**	**55.0**	**52.5 (2020)**	**19.0**	**19.3**	**21.0 (2020)**
Australia	56.0	56.9	51.7	18.1	18.3	21.4
Japan[b]	56.9	55.8	53.9	19.2	19.6	21.4
New Zealand	56.5	56.3	56.7 (2020)	19.7	18.5	20.6 (2020)
DEVELOPING ADB MEMBER ECONOMIES[a]	**44.2**	**45.4**	**46.5 (2019)**	**13.0**	**14.3**	**14.8 (2019)**
ALL ADB REGIONAL MEMBERS[a]	**48.5**	**47.7**	**48.1 (2019)**	**15.2**	**15.5**	**15.9 (2019)**
WORLD	**57.1**	**56.7**	**55.3 (2020)**	**17.5**	**16.7**	**17.8 (2020)**

.... = data not available, * = provisional or preliminary, ADB = Asian Development Bank, GDP = gross domestic product.

Note: Figures in the table are calculated as a percentage of GDP at current prices.

a For estimating aggregates, GDP figures in domestic currencies were converted to United States dollars using official exchange rates, and imputation was done for economies with missing data by substituting available data from the nearest years.

b Data for household consumption includes nonprofit institutions serving households.

c Data refer to total final consumption expenditure.

d From September 2019, oil revenue from the Joint Petroleum Development Area is now included in GDP based on the new Timor-Leste Australia Maritime Boundary Treaty.

e For years prior to 2005 (as featured in the Key Indicators Database), data for household consumption includes nonprofit institutions serving households.

Sources: Economies' official sources. For "World": World Bank. World Development Indicators. https://databank.worldbank.org/source/world-development-indicators (accessed 22 July 2022).

Table 2.2.8: Gross Capital Formation and Changes in Inventories
(% of GDP)

ADB Regional Member	Gross Capital Formation			Changes in Inventories		
	2010	2015	2021	2010	2015	2021
Developing ADB Member Economies						
Central and West Asia[a]	**22.4**	**24.2**	**24.1 (2019)**	...	...	...
Afghanistan[b,c]	17.5	19.0	11.9 (2020)	5.3	28.1	...
Armenia	32.9	20.7	20.6	-0.6	0.1	2.3
Azerbaijan	18.1	27.9	23.7 (2020)	-0.1	0.1	1.0 (2020)
Georgia	20.5	26.3	21.9*	1.6	1.9	1.5*
Kazakhstan	25.4	27.9	26.7*	1.0	5.0	3.3*
Kyrgyz Republic[d]	28.1	33.0	27.7 (2020)	-0.7	1.7	-1.3 (2020)
Pakistan	15.8	15.7	14.6	1.6	1.6	1.6
Tajikistan	23.8	44.7	33.5 (2020)	-0.6	6.0	5.9 (2020)
Turkmenistan	51.9	50.3 (2013)	...	...	...	...
Uzbekistan	27.2	26.3	40.6*	4.6	4.3	5.4*
East Asia	**42.7**	**40.4**	**40.8**	...	...	...
China, People's Republic of	46.6	43.2	42.8*	2.6	1.1	1.0*
Hong Kong, China	23.9	21.5	17.6	2.1	-0.9	0.2
Korea, Republic of	32.6	29.5	32.1	2.3	0.5	0.5
Mongolia	42.1	24.5	35.2	7.6	6.2	9.4
Taipei,China	25.1	21.7	26.9	1.4	0.3	0.8
South Asia	**38.6**	**31.8**	**27.7 (2020)**	...	...	...
Bangladesh[b,e]	26.2	28.9	30.8	...	...	...
Bhutan	63.2	55.5	33.8 (2020)	0.5	-0.3	– (2020)
India[f]	39.8	32.1	27.3* (2020)	4.4	1.9	0.9*
Maldives	...	33.6	45.5 (2020)	...	0.5	3.8 (2020)
Nepal[g]	38.3	32.1	31.9	16.1	3.8	3.6
Sri Lanka	30.4	31.2	27.7	5.9	5.1	1.4
Southeast Asia	**28.1**	**27.7**	**27.7 (2019)**	...	...	...
Brunei Darussalam	23.7	35.2	30.8	0.2	0.2	0.2
Cambodia	17.4	22.5	26.6	1.2	1.0	0.8
Indonesia	32.9	34.1	31.5	1.9	1.3	0.7
Lao People's Democratic Republic	...	...	...	...	...	...
Malaysia[h]	23.4	25.4	22.3	1.0	-0.4	3.0
Myanmar	23.2	34.8	30.6 (2019)	0.3	0.2	0.7 (2019)
Philippines	20.4	21.3	21.2	0.0	-0.9	-1.1
Singapore	27.7	25.4	24.4	2.1	-1.9	1.2
Thailand	25.6	22.1	29.4*	1.4	-2.1	5.6*
Timor-Leste[i]	42.7	36.8	16.1 (2020)	0.0	1.3	1.7 (2020)
Viet Nam	35.7	27.7	33.4	3.0	3.0	1.8
The Pacific	...	...	...	...	...	...
Cook Islands	...	...	...	...	...	...
Fiji	15.9	18.6	12.0* (2020)	2.9	2.4	–* (2020)
Kiribati	14.4	41.8	17.8* (2020)	0.3	-0.9	-0.0* (2020)
Marshall Islands	41.1	17.8	19.9	-2.2	-0.8	0.1
Micronesia, Federated States of	...	...	...	...	...	...
Nauru	...	...	...	...	...	...
Niue	...	...	...	...	...	...
Palau	24.5	25.4	30.4* (2019)	0.7	-1.9	–* (2019)
Papua New Guinea	17.5 (2005)	...	...	1.0 (2005)	...	...
Samoa	39.1	34.9	34.4	1.1	0.4	1.5
Solomon Islands	17.9	16.0	18.8 (2020)	-1.4 (2012)	-0.0	-2.1 (2020)
Tonga	29.6	25.4	24.8 (2020)	0.5	2.0	1.3 (2020)
Tuvalu	...	...	...	...	...	...
Vanuatu	37.0	32.9	24.4 (2019)	1.6	0.8	0.5 (2019)
Developed ADB Member Economies	**23.3**	**25.3**	**24.7 (2020)**	...	...	...
Australia	26.8	26.3	22.7	-0.2	0.1	0.3
Japan	22.6	25.2	25.2	-0.0	0.2	-0.1
New Zealand	20.2	23.2	22.5 (2020)	0.4	0.3	-0.0 (2020)
DEVELOPING ADB MEMBER ECONOMIES[a]	**38.8**	**37.0**	**37.2 (2019)**	...	...	...
ALL ADB REGIONAL MEMBERS[a]	**33.1**	**34.2**	**34.6 (2019)**	...	...	...
WORLD	**24.4**	**25.8**	**26.2 (2020)**	...	...	...

.... = data not available, -0.0 or 0.0 = magnitude is less than half of unit employed, – = magnitude equals zero, * = provisional or preliminary, ADB = Asian Development Bank, GDP = gross domestic product.

Note: Figures in the table are calculated as a percentage of GDP at current prices.

a For estimating aggregates, GDP figures in domestic currencies were converted to United States dollars using official exchange rates, and imputation was done for economies with missing data by substituting available data from the nearest years.
b Refers to gross fixed capital formation.
c Changes in inventories include statistical discrepancy.
d Refers to gross fixed capital formation and acquisitions less disposals of valuables.
e Includes data on changes in inventories.
f Refers to gross capital formation, which refers to the sum of gross fixed capital formation, valuables, increases in stocks, and errors and omissions.
g Changes in inventories were derived residually; hence, statistical discrepancies or errors are included in this entry.
h Changes in inventories include valuables and statistical discrepancy.
i From September 2019, oil revenue from the Joint Petroleum Development Area is now included in GDP based on the new Timor-Leste Australia Maritime Boundary Treaty.

Sources: Economies' official sources. For "World": World Bank. World Development Indicators. https://databank.worldbank.org/source/world-development-indicators (accessed 22 July 2022).

Table 2.2.9: Exports and Imports of Goods and Services
(% of GDP)

ADB Regional Member	Exports of goods and services			Imports of goods and services		
	2010	2015	2021	2010	2015	2021
Developing ADB Member Economies						
Central and West Asia[a]	**32.0**	**22.7**	**24.1 (2019)**	**27.4**	**25.1**	**29.1 (2019)**
Afghanistan	9.8	6.9	7.3 (2020)	43.9	49.0	34.7 (2020)
Armenia	20.8	29.7	35.0	45.3	42.0	43.2
Azerbaijan	54.3	37.8	35.6 (2020)	20.7	34.8	36.4 (2020)
Georgia	33.0	40.9	43.1*	49.9	57.9	58.6*
Kazakhstan	44.2	28.5	34.2*	29.9	24.5	24.5*
Kyrgyz Republic	51.6	35.2	31.3 (2020)	81.7	75.8	52.2 (2020)
Pakistan	13.5	10.6	9.1	19.4	17.1	18.0
Tajikistan	26.8	9.8	17.3 (2020)	59.0	40.1	38.4 (2020)
Turkmenistan	76.3	74.8 (2013)	...	44.5	44.1 (2013)	...
Uzbekistan	24.3	13.8	23.7*	25.0	17.0	40.1*
East Asia	**38.4**	**29.7**	**27.0**	**34.7**	**25.7**	**23.8**
China, People's Republic of	27.2	21.4	20.0*	23.5	18.1	17.4*
Hong Kong, China[b]	205.3	195.9	203.5	199.4	193.5	198.7
Korea, Republic of	47.1	43.0	42.0	44.3	36.1	38.5
Mongolia	46.7	44.2	58.4	56.7	45.5	58.9
Taipei,China	79.6	71.3	66.3	73.0	58.4	51.4
South Asia	**21.8**	**19.7**	**17.6 (2020)**	**26.7**	**22.8**	**19.1 (2020)**
Bangladesh	16.0	17.3	10.7	21.8	24.8	17.1
Bhutan	43.5	34.4	29.8 (2020)	72.4	63.5	46.5 (2020)
India	22.4	19.8	21.4*	26.9	22.1	23.9*
Maldives	...	78.4	49.5 (2020)	...	71.2	68.4 (2020)
Nepal	9.6	10.5	5.3	36.4	37.4	34.1
Sri Lanka	19.6	21.0	17.7	26.8	28.5	25.3
Southeast Asia	**64.8**	**60.5**	**59.1 (2019)**	**58.1**	**55.2**	**54.6 (2019)**
Brunei Darussalam	67.4	52.2	79.5	28.0	37.7	64.3
Cambodia	54.1	61.7	64.6	59.5	66.1	67.6
Indonesia	24.3	21.2	21.6	22.4	20.8	18.9
Lao People's Democratic Republic	...	...	...	...	...	...
Malaysia	86.9	69.4	68.9	71.0	61.9	61.8
Myanmar	19.6	17.4	30.4 (2019)	15.1	27.9	30.3 (2019)
Philippines	32.9	27.2	25.7	33.2	31.9	37.8
Singapore	198.0	178.4	184.8	171.7	151.1	153.5
Thailand	67.1	66.8	58.8*	61.3	56.5	59.0*
Timor-Leste[c]	8.6	3.0	36.4 (2020)	125.8	56.9	46.3 (2020)
Viet Nam	72.0	89.8	93.8	80.2	89.0	93.5
The Pacific	**...**	**...**	**...**	**...**	**...**	**...**
Cook Islands	...	...	...	...	...	...
Fiji	57.4	48.8	27.5* (2020)	63.8	52.4	44.2* (2020)
Kiribati	12.3	15.7	12.7* (2020)	79.0	107.9	83.0* (2020)
Marshall Islands	38.4	45.5	29.8	108.3	93.1	71.0
Micronesia, Federated States of	...	...	...	...	...	...
Nauru	...	...	...	...	...	...
Niue	...	...	...	...	...	...
Palau	49.7	58.6	41.9* (2019)	77.0	76.0	78.8* (2019)
Papua New Guinea	74.5 (2005)	...	...	56.1 (2005)	...	...
Samoa	28.2	28.7	11.8	53.8	46.0	51.9
Solomon Islands	35.2	40.4	27.9 (2020)	61.0	47.8	32.3 (2020)
Tonga	12.5	17.0	19.0 (2020)	58.3	64.5	62.3 (2020)
Tuvalu	...	...	...	...	...	...
Vanuatu	48.7	46.0	50.3 (2019)	55.1	67.0	49.0 (2019)
Developed ADB Member Economies	**16.1**	**18.3**	**17.7 (2020)**	**15.1**	**19.0**	**17.0 (2020)**
Australia	19.8	20.1	22.2	20.7	21.6	17.8
Japan	14.9	17.4	18.4	13.6	18.0	19.0
New Zealand	30.3	27.9	21.9 (2020)	28.0	27.0	22.3 (2020)
DEVELOPING ADB MEMBER ECONOMIES[a]	**39.9**	**32.1**	**28.8 (2019)**	**36.9**	**29.1**	**27.7 (2019)**
ALL ADB REGIONAL MEMBERS[a]	**31.1**	**28.9**	**26.7 (2019)**	**28.9**	**26.7**	**25.8 (2019)**
WORLD	**28.9**	**28.3**	**29.1**	**28.0**	**27.6**	**28.1**

.... = data not available, * = provisional or preliminary, ADB = Asian Development Bank, GDP = gross domestic product.

Note: Figures in the table are calculated as a percentage of GDP at current prices.

a For estimating aggregates, imputation was done for economies with missing data by substituting available data from the nearest years.
b The statistics for trade in goods and services were compiled based on the change of ownership principle in recording goods sent abroad for processing and merchanting under the standards stipulated in the System of National Accounts 2008.
c From September 2019, oil revenue from the Joint Petroleum Development Area is now included in GDP based on the new Timor-Leste Australia Maritime Boundary Treaty.

Sources: Economies' official sources. For "World": World Bank. World Development Indicators. https://databank.worldbank.org/source/world-development-indicators (accessed 22 July 2022).

Table 2.2.10: Gross Domestic Saving
(% of GDP)

ADB Regional Member	2010	2015	2016	2017	2018	2019	2020	2021
Developing ADB Member Economies								
Central and West Asia[a]	**28.2**	...	...	...	...	...	...	...
Afghanistan	-11.4	5.0	-3.2	5.1	-8.4	-19.9	-20.4	...
Armenia	4.9	9.0	10.2	7.7	8.7	4.0	9.7	12.4
Azerbaijan	49.8	30.9	28.5	31.1	35.4	31.4	...	...
Georgia	3.5	9.3	14.9	16.3	17.5	16.3	4.6	...
Kazakhstan	43.8	34.6	33.8	36.9	39.6	38.6	34.3	...
Kyrgyz Republic	-2.7	-8.3	-0.2	0.8	0.3	7.2	5.5	...
Pakistan	10.0	9.3	8.7	7.3	6.6	5.4	6.7	5.7
Tajikistan	4.0	17.2	8.5	8.2	12.4	12.6	10.8	...
Turkmenistan	85.6	81.6 (2013)	...	...	...	...	...	...
Uzbekistan	26.0	21.5	19.6	23.2	24.7	24.5	25.2	24.2*
East Asia[a]	**47.1**	**44.0**	**43.1**	**43.3**	**43.1**	**42.1**	**43.0**	...
China, People's Republic of	51.1	46.0	45.0	45.1	44.9	44.0	44.7	...
Hong Kong, China	29.8	23.9	23.8	23.1	21.8	19.7	20.8	22.4
Korea, Republic of	35.4	36.4	36.8	37.0	35.9	34.3	35.6	35.7
Mongolia	32.1	23.2	23.3	29.8	29.4	29.6	23.7	33.1
Taipei,China	31.5	34.4	34.1	34.7	33.8	33.6	37.1	41.5
South Asia	...	...	...	...	...	...	...	...
Bangladesh	20.8	22.2	27.3	27.1	26.5	26.9	27.1	25.3
Bhutan	31.8	22.1	30.8	29.3	22.5	21.6	17.1	...
India	...	...	...	...	...	...	...	...
Maldives	...	...	...	...	...	...	...	...
Nepal	11.5	7.6	3.6	13.0	14.8	15.3	6.3	...
Sri Lanka	22.3	22.4	19.3	22.6	20.9	19.6	17.8	19.1
Southeast Asia	...	...	...	...	...	...	...	...
Brunei Darussalam	63.1	55.2	52.6	53.0	56.3	54.5	50.8	52.9
Cambodia	14.5	19.6	20.4	23.2	26.0	27.2	24.4	...
Indonesia	34.8	32.8	32.7	33.6	...	...	...	...
Lao People's Democratic Republic	...	...	...	...	...	...	...	...
Malaysia	39.3	33.0	32.6	32.4	30.6	28.6	26.2	29.3
Myanmar	32.7	23.4	22.6	22.3	24.2	28.3	...	...
Philippines	...	...	...	...	...	...	...	...
Singapore	54.0	52.7	52.7	53.7	53.7	53.4	54.2	55.7
Thailand	31.1	32.8	34.7	35.4	34.1	33.2	29.0	28.9*
Timor-Leste[b]	-74.5	-17.0	-14.1	-16.6	-21.4	-0.3	-6.3	...
Viet Nam	27.4	25.7	24.9	25.5	26.0	25.4	25.0	34.3
The Pacific	...	...	...	...	...	...	...	...
Cook Islands	...	...	...	...	...	...	...	...
Fiji	12.7	22.7	19.7	19.9	19.2	18.6	...	...
Kiribati	-52.1	-49.2	-54.2	-56.0	-52.3	-63.9	-51.4*	...
Marshall Islands	-30.9	-30.7	-28.0	-29.5	-29.9	-30.9	-16.0	-24.4
Micronesia, Federated States of	...	...	...	...	...	...	...	...
Nauru	...	...	...	...	...	...	...	...
Niue	...	...	...	...	...	...	...	...
Palau[c]	-7.5	5.0	4.7	0.9	-1.8	-0.9	...	...
Papua New Guinea	35.9 (2005)	...	...	...	...	...	...	...
Samoa	10.7	19.3	18.5	18.9	19.6	17.1	5.1	-2.2
Solomon Islands	...	...	...	...	...	...	...	...
Tonga	-15.1	-22.3	-17.1	-16.4	-20.3	-15.8	-22.9	...
Tuvalu	...	...	...	...	...	...	...	...
Vanuatu	28.2	25.3 (2014)	...	...	...	...	...	...
Developed ADB Member Economies[a]	**24.5**	**25.1**	**25.7**	**26.1**	**25.7**	**25.9**	**26.1**	...
Australia	21.8	22.6	20.7	21.8	21.7	22.5	24.1	25.8
Japan	25.1	25.9	27.0	27.3	26.9	26.8	26.8	26.4
New Zealand	22.5	24.1	23.9	24.6	23.9	24.0	21.7	...

.... = data not available, * = provisional or preliminary, ADB = Asian Development Bank, GDP = gross domestic product.

Note: Figures in the table are calculated as a percentage of GDP at current prices.

a For estimating aggregates, GDP figures in domestic currencies were converted to United States dollars using official exchange rates.
b From September 2019, oil revenue from the Joint Petroleum Development Area is now included in GDP based on the new Timor-Leste Australia Maritime Boundary Treaty.
c Estimated as the difference between GDP by industrial origin at producer's prices and final consumption expenditure.

Source: Economies' official sources.

Table 2.2.11: Growth Rates of Real Gross Domestic Product
(%)

ADB Regional Member	2010	2015	2016	2017	2018	2019	2020	2021
Developing ADB Member Economies								
Central and West Asia								
Afghanistan	3.2	-1.8	3.5	2.6	1.2	3.9	-2.4	...
Armenia	2.2	3.2	0.2	7.5	5.2	7.6	-7.2	5.7
Azerbaijan	5.0	1.1	-3.1	0.2	1.5	2.5	-4.2	5.6
Georgia	6.2	3.0	2.9	4.8	4.8	5.0	-6.8	10.4*
Kazakhstan	7.3	1.2	1.1	6.8	4.1	4.5	-2.5	4.1*
Kyrgyz Republic	-0.5	3.9	4.3	4.7	3.8	4.6	-8.4	3.6*
Pakistan	2.6	4.1	4.6	4.6	6.1	3.1	-0.9	5.7
Tajikistan	6.5	6.0	6.9	7.1	7.6	7.4	4.4	...
Turkmenistan	14.6	10.3 (2014)	...	...	...	...	...	5.0
Uzbekistan	7.1	7.2	5.9	4.4	5.4	5.7	1.9	7.4*
East Asia								
China, People's Republic of	10.6	7.0	6.8	6.9	6.7	6.0	2.2	8.1*
Hong Kong, China	6.8	2.4	2.2	3.8	2.8	-1.7	-6.5	6.3
Korea, Republic of	6.8	2.8	2.9	3.2	2.9	2.2	-0.7	4.1
Mongolia	17.3 (2011)	2.4	1.5	5.6	7.7	5.6	-4.6	1.4
Taipei,China	10.3	1.5	2.2	3.3	2.8	3.1	3.4	6.5
South Asia								
Bangladesh	5.6	6.6	7.1	6.6	7.3	7.9	3.5	6.9
Bhutan	11.9	6.6	8.1	4.7	3.1	5.8	-10.1	...
India	8.5	8.0	8.3	6.8	6.5*	3.7*	-6.6*	8.7*
Maldives	7.3	2.9	6.3	7.2	8.1	6.9	-33.5	37.0*
Nepal	4.8	4.0	0.4	9.0	7.6	6.7	-2.1	4.0
Sri Lanka	8.0	4.2	5.1	6.5	2.3	-0.2	-3.5	3.3
Southeast Asia								
Brunei Darussalam	3.7 (2011)	-0.4	-2.5	1.3	0.1	3.9	1.1	-1.9
Cambodia	6.0	7.0	7.0	7.0	7.5	6.8	-3.1	3.0
Indonesia	6.2	4.9	5.0	5.1	5.2	5.0	-2.1	3.7
Lao People's Democratic Republic	8.1	7.3	7.0	6.9	6.2	5.5	3.3	3.5
Malaysia	7.4	5.1	4.4	5.8	4.8	4.4	-5.6	3.1
Myanmar	9.6	7.0	5.9	5.8	6.4	6.8	3.2*	-18.4*
Philippines	7.3	6.3	7.1	6.9	6.3	6.1	-9.5	5.7
Singapore	14.5	3.0	3.6	4.7	3.7	1.1	-4.1	7.6
Thailand	7.5	3.1	3.4	4.2	4.2	2.2	-6.2	1.6*
Timor-Leste	9.3	2.8	3.4	-3.1	-0.7	2.1	-8.6	...
Viet Nam	6.4	6.7	6.2	6.8	7.1	7.0	2.9	2.6
The Pacific								
Cook Islands	-4.9	5.7	4.9	9.5	5.7	4.8	-25.4*	-21.3*
Fiji	3.0	4.5	2.4	5.4	3.8	-0.6	-17.2	...
Kiribati	-1.1	9.9	-0.5	-0.2	5.3	-0.5	-0.5*	...
Marshall Islands	7.6	1.6	1.3	4.1	3.6	5.3	-2.2	0.8
Micronesia, Federated States of	2.3	4.6	0.9	2.7	0.2	...	...	...
Nauru	13.6	2.8	3.0	-5.5	5.7	1.0	0.7*	1.5*
Niue	0.6	4.0	3.5	2.4	6.5*	...	...	...
Palau	0.1	5.0	-0.4	-2.0	5.8	-1.9*	-9.7*	...
Papua New Guinea	10.1	6.6	5.5	3.5	-0.3	4.5	-3.5	1.5
Samoa	3.1	6.1	4.5	-0.5	2.9	2.8	-10.1	-2.3
Solomon Islands	9.7	1.7	5.6	3.1	2.7	1.7	-3.4	...
Tonga	0.8	1.2	6.6	3.3	0.3	0.7	0.7	...
Tuvalu	-3.3	9.2	...	3.3	1.4	13.8	-4.3	1.8
Vanuatu	1.3	0.4	4.7	6.3	2.9	3.2	...	...
Developed ADB Member Economies								
Australia	2.2	2.2	2.7	2.3	2.9	2.1	-0.0	1.5
Japan	4.1	1.6	0.8	1.7	0.6	-0.2	-4.5	1.6
New Zealand	1.5	3.7	3.8	3.6	3.4	2.2	-1.4	...

... = data not available, * = provisional or preliminary, ADB = Asian Development Bank.

Source: Economies' official sources.

Table 2.2.12: Growth Rates of Real Gross Domestic Product per Capita
(%)

ADB Regional Member	2010	2015	2016	2017	2018	2019	2020	2021
Developing ADB Member Economies								
Central and West Asia								
Afghanistan	1.2	-3.8	1.5	0.6	-5.0	1.7	-4.5	...
Armenia	2.9	3.5	0.6	8.0	5.7	7.9	-7.0	5.6
Azerbaijan	3.8	-0.1	-4.2	-0.8	0.6	1.6	-4.9	5.2
Georgia	7.0	2.9	2.8	4.8	4.9	5.2	-6.8	10.8
Kazakhstan	5.5	-0.3	-0.4	5.4	2.7	3.2	-3.8	2.7
Kyrgyz Republic	-1.8	1.8	2.2	2.7	1.8	2.4	-10.3	1.8
Pakistan	0.5	2.1	2.4	2.2	4.0	1.1	-2.9	3.7
Tajikistan	3.9	3.5	4.5	4.8	5.3	5.1	2.3	...
Turkmenistan	12.8	8.3 (2014)	...	...	...	...	...	3.5
Uzbekistan	4.1	5.4	4.1	2.7	3.5	3.7	-0.1	5.3
East Asia								
China, People's Republic of	10.1	6.5	6.1	6.3	6.3	5.6	2.1	8.1
Hong Kong, China	6.0	1.5	1.6	3.0	2.0	-2.4	-6.1	7.3
Korea, Republic of	6.3	2.3	2.5	2.9	2.5	1.8	-0.8	4.3
Mongolia	15.2 (2011)	0.3	-0.5	3.7	5.7	3.7	-6.2	-0.2
Taipei,China	10.0	1.3	1.9	3.1	2.7	3.0	3.4	6.9
South Asia								
Bangladesh	4.2	5.1	5.7	5.1	5.9	6.4	2.1	5.5
Bhutan	9.9	5.0	6.5	3.3	2.0	4.7	-10.9	...
India	7.0	6.7	7.0	5.6	5.3	2.6	-7.6	7.6
Maldives	4.9	-0.9	2.3	3.0	3.8	2.5	-36.3	34.3
Nepal	3.4	3.0	-0.5	7.9	6.6	5.6	-3.0	3.1
Sri Lanka	7.0	3.2	3.9	5.3	1.2	-0.8	-4.0	2.2
Southeast Asia								
Brunei Darussalam	2.0 (2011)	-1.6	-3.6	-1.6	-2.9	0.0	2.4	3.5
Cambodia	4.6	5.6	5.5	5.5	6.0	5.4	-4.4	1.5
Indonesia	4.8	3.5	3.9	3.9	4.1	3.9	-3.3	2.7
Lao People's Democratic Republic	6.6	5.7	5.5	5.4	4.7	4.0	1.8	2.0
Malaysia	5.5	3.5	3.0	4.5	3.7	4.0	-5.8	2.9
Myanmar	8.9	6.1	4.9	4.8	5.5	5.8	2.3	-19.1
Philippines	6.3	4.6 (2014)	5.4	5.2	4.7	4.6	-10.9	4.6
Singapore	12.5	1.8	2.2	4.6	3.1	-0.1	-3.9	12.2
Thailand	6.9	2.5	3.0	3.2	3.9	1.8	-6.5	1.3
Timor-Leste	7.4	0.9	1.4	-4.9	-2.6	0.1	-10.3	...
Viet Nam	5.1	5.5	5.0	5.6	5.8	5.8	1.7	1.6
The Pacific								
Cook Islands	-6.0	5.7	4.0	9.3	6.6	3.1	-23.6	-21.5
Fiji	2.3	4.1	2.0	4.8	3.2	-1.2	-17.6	...
Kiribati	-3.2	8.4	-2.1	-1.8	3.6	-2.1	-2.1	...
Marshall Islands	6.3	1.2	0.9	3.7	3.2	4.9	-2.6	...
Micronesia, Federated States of	2.8	4.4	0.7	2.5	0.0	...	...	...
Nauru	11.4	1.1	1.3	-7.0	4.0	-0.6	-0.9	-0.1
Niue	...	2.4	1.7	...	6.5	...	...	...
Palau	2.0	3.2	-1.6	-2.1	8.0	-1.4	-10.5	...
Papua New Guinea	6.8	3.4	2.3	0.4	-3.3	1.3	-6.4	-1.6
Samoa	2.3	5.2	3.6	-1.3	2.1	2.0	-10.8	-3.1
Solomon Islands	4.8 (2011)	-0.6	3.3	0.9	0.6	-0.3	-5.3	...
Tonga	0.6	1.7	7.1	3.9	0.8	1.3	1.2	...
Tuvalu	-3.8	9.5	...	3.5	1.6	14.1	-4.0	2.1
Vanuatu	-1.2	-1.9	3.2	3.9	0.6	0.9	...	...
Developed ADB Member Economies								
Australia	0.6	0.7	1.2	0.6	1.3	0.6	-1.3	1.3
Japan	4.1	1.7	0.9	1.8	0.8	-0.0	-4.2	1.7
New Zealand	0.4	1.6	1.4	1.4	1.5	0.6	-3.5	...

... = data not available, ADB = Asian Development Bank.

Source: Asian Development Bank estimates based on data from the economies' official sources.

Table 2.2.13: Growth Rates of Agriculture Real Value-Added
(%)

ADB Regional Member	2010	2015	2016	2017	2018	2019	2020	2021
Developing ADB Member Economies								
Central and West Asia								
Afghanistan	-18.0	-16.9	12.4	6.4	-4.4	17.5	5.9	...
Armenia	-16.0	13.2	-5.0	-5.1	-6.9	-5.8	-3.7	-0.6
Azerbaijan	-4.7	6.6	2.6	4.2	4.6	7.3	1.9	3.4
Georgia	-4.2	-0.1	-2.8	-7.7	13.8	0.7	8.1	-1.4
Kazakhstan	-12.9	3.5	5.4	6.9	3.8	-0.1	5.9	-2.4*
Kyrgyz Republic	-2.6	6.2	2.9	2.2	2.6	2.5	0.9	-5.0*
Pakistan	0.2	2.1	0.2	2.2	3.9	0.9	3.9	3.5
Tajikistan	6.8	3.4	5.2	7.6	7.0	7.0	7.9	...
Turkmenistan	23.6	1.7 (2014)	...	...	...	...	...	...
Uzbekistan	6.1	6.1	6.2	1.2	0.3	3.1	2.9	4.0*
East Asia								
China, People's Republic of	4.3	3.9	3.3	4.0	3.5	3.1	3.1	7.1*
Hong Kong, China[a]	3.9	-6.8	-2.0	-5.2	-1.8	-0.8	3.8	-2.8
Korea, Republic of	-3.6	-0.2	-5.6	2.3	0.2	3.9	-5.8	3.8
Mongolia	-0.3 (2011)	10.7	5.4	-0.3	6.5	5.2	5.8	-5.5
Taipei,China	2.1	-7.7	-9.7	8.3	4.5	-0.9	-1.6	-4.2
South Asia								
Bangladesh	6.2	3.3	2.8	3.2	3.5	3.3	3.4	3.2
Bhutan	0.8	4.7	4.2	2.9	4.2	1.3	4.6	...
India	8.8	0.6	6.8	6.6	2.1*	5.5*	3.3*	3.0*
Maldives	-3.5	-0.4	1.5	8.3	4.8	-7.6	7.0	14.8*
Nepal	2.0	1.2	-0.1	5.2	2.6	5.2	2.2	2.6
Sri Lanka	7.0	5.4	-4.7	-1.8	6.3	0.5	-1.4	2.5
Southeast Asia								
Brunei Darussalam	-2.6 (2011)	6.4	-3.6	-1.6	-1.6	-1.4	14.4	16.9
Cambodia	4.0	0.2	1.3	1.7	1.2	-0.7	0.6	1.1
Indonesia	3.0	3.8	3.4	3.9	3.9	3.6	1.8	1.8
Lao People's Democratic Republic	3.2	3.6	2.8	2.9	1.3	1.2	1.2	2.5
Malaysia	2.4	1.4	-3.7	5.9	0.1	2.0	-2.2	-0.2
Myanmar	4.7	3.4	-0.5	-1.5	0.1	1.6	1.7*	0.8*
Philippines	1.3	0.7	-1.0	4.2	1.1	1.2	-0.2	-0.3
Singapore[a]	2.8	-0.4	-0.4	2.9	3.3	6.6	-4.2	10.8
Thailand	-0.5	-6.5	-1.2	4.8	6.1	-0.9	-3.5	1.4*
Timor-Leste	4.4	-4.4	-1.3	-3.0	2.9	2.5	5.1	...
Viet Nam	0.5	2.4	1.4	2.9	3.8	2.0	2.7	2.9
The Pacific								
Cook Islands	0.4	-2.2	-3.1	3.2	-2.5	-3.0	-5.7*	-8.7*
Fiji	-2.6	2.9	-10.9	10.8	3.7	4.5	3.3	...
Kiribati	-3.9	-4.8	11.1	13.1	-2.6	2.5	-1.0*	...
Marshall Islands	11.1	6.1	-1.6	1.8	4.2	32.9	0.6	14.3
Micronesia, Federated States of	-3.1	9.5	-4.8	-0.9	0.1	...	...	...
Nauru	3.7	5.2	10.6	43.4	-8.7	24.9	0.7*	1.5*
Niue	-0.4	2.0	1.2	3.5	1.7*	...	...	...
Palau	-5.0	-3.7	7.7	8.4	-5.2	-5.5*	-13.1*	...
Papua New Guinea	2.8	-2.6	2.7	2.4	4.6	2.3	0.1	3.9
Samoa	-9.0	1.9	7.2	7.1	-12.4	2.3	-5.8	-0.1
Solomon Islands	13.0	3.2	3.4	3.6	0.4	0.1	-3.8	...
Tonga	4.7	-1.7	-1.3	-2.5	0.4	3.6	0.8	...
Tuvalu	12.8	-1.8	...	0.0	1.2	-5.9	-4.8	3.2
Vanuatu	4.6	-5.7	5.9	0.2	0.9	6.2	...	...
Developed ADB Member Economies								
Australia	-0.7	1.5	-7.1	9.4	-2.8	-10.5	-10.1	21.5
Japan	-5.2	-4.2	-8.1	0.7	-6.7	4.0	-6.2	...
New Zealand	-7.9	2.2	0.5	-3.8	7.0	-2.6	3.3	...

... = data not available; * = provisional, preliminary, estimate; ADB = Asian Development Bank.

a Refers to other goods industries comprising agriculture, forestry, and fishing; and mining and quarrying.

Source: Economies' official sources.

Table 2.2.14: Growth Rates of Industry Real Value-Added
(%)

ADB Regional Member	2010	2015	2016	2017	2018	2019	2020	2021
Developing ADB Member Economies								
Central and West Asia								
Afghanistan	6.3	4.5	-1.8	9.2	11.1	4.8	-4.6	...
Armenia	5.7	2.8	-0.3	9.0	3.7	10.5	-2.5	3.4
Azerbaijan	3.7	-1.9	-5.7	-3.1	-0.7	1.0	-5.0	3.0
Georgia[a]	8.2	2.6	6.7	4.4	-0.5	2.7	-6.8	2.6
Kazakhstan	9.5	-0.4	1.1	7.7	4.4	5.5	1.5	4.5*
Kyrgyz Republic	2.5	2.9	7.1	8.6	5.9	8.0	-9.9	3.1*
Pakistan	3.4	5.2	5.7	4.6	9.2	0.3	-5.8	7.8
Tajikistan	2.8	16.3	22.2	7.3	17.0	10.3	17.3	...
Turkmenistan	11.2	11.6 (2014)	...	...	...	...	...	...
Uzbekistan	5.5	8.3	5.9	5.4	11.5	8.3	2.5	8.4*
East Asia								
China, People's Republic of	12.7	5.9	6.0	5.9	5.8	4.9	2.5	8.2*
Hong Kong, China[a,b]	7.7	2.4	3.0	-0.7	2.5	-6.4	-11.7	2.1
Korea, Republic of[a]	...	...	...	...	...	...	...	...
Mongolia	8.8 (2011)	9.9	-2.4	1.4	8.5	3.1	-4.4	-2.8
Taipei,China[a]	21.5	0.9	3.7	4.8	2.6	1.4	7.0	12.8
South Asia								
Bangladesh	7.0	9.7	11.1	8.3	10.2	11.6	3.6	10.3
Bhutan	12.5	8.2	6.9	2.5	-5.0	2.0	-13.1	...
India	7.9	9.6	7.7	5.9	5.3*	-1.4*	-3.3*	10.3*
Maldives	7.3	18.1	8.9	13.0	15.5	1.9	-25.4	6.6*
Nepal	4.0	2.0	-4.1	17.1	10.4	7.4	-3.7	5.0
Sri Lanka	8.4	1.1	7.4	13.0	-1.1	-4.1	-5.3	5.6
Southeast Asia								
Brunei Darussalam	3.2 (2011)	-0.0	-2.9	1.5	-0.4	4.2	2.9	-4.2
Cambodia	13.6	11.7	10.9	9.8	11.6	10.7	-1.4	8.6
Indonesia	4.9	3.0	3.8	4.1	4.3	3.8	-2.8	3.4
Lao People's Democratic Republic	17.5	7.0	12.0	11.6	7.8	5.6	9.2	6.1
Malaysia	8.4	5.2	4.3	4.7	3.3	2.6	-6.2	5.7
Myanmar	18.6	8.3	8.9	8.7	8.3	8.4	3.8*	-20.9*
Philippines	9.8	6.5	8.2	7.0	7.3	5.5	-13.1	8.5
Singapore[a,b]	23.9	-2.7	2.8	6.9	5.5	-1.0	-0.6	13.4
Thailand[a,c]	10.6	1.9	2.3	2.2	3.0	-0.1	-5.9	3.4*
Timor-Leste	7.9	22.2	7.6	-26.5	5.3	4.8	-28.5	...
Viet Nam	-9.9	9.6	7.6	8.0	8.9	8.9	4.0	4.1
The Pacific								
Cook Islands	-8.9	25.4	-13.5	19.1	7.0	10.5	-33.1*	-9.5*
Fiji	6.5	6.9	7.2	4.2	5.5	-0.9	-10.3	...
Kiribati	9.5	23.3	-2.3	-15.2	-13.9	-9.9	-1.6*	...
Marshall Islands	20.1	-12.9	-5.6	2.7	13.0	6.6	-4.7	-8.4
Micronesia, Federated States of	18.0	-6.1	5.1	4.0	-7.3	...	...	...
Nauru	39.4	-17.1	77.3	-26.8	-37.9	-21.0	-4.4*	1.5*
Niue	14.4	0.9	2.3	-4.7	90.4*	...	...	...
Palau	5.2	40.2	0.2	-5.8	2.3	0.1*	0.2*	...
Papua New Guinea	12.0	26.4	12.0	4.7	-7.5	7.5	-6.5	-2.7
Samoa	7.2	8.6	-2.6	-8.6	-4.8	10.8	-15.3	-3.2
Solomon Islands	13.2	-4.0	5.0	9.5	1.3	3.5	-3.8	...
Tonga	4.1	-0.6	12.7	9.7	-14.4	4.6	-2.9	...
Tuvalu	-41.6	36.7	...	9.5	-5.2	62.0	-26.6	2.7
Vanuatu	12.2	38.5	9.4	10.1	4.9	-8.3	...	...
Developed ADB Member Economies								
Australia[a]	...	...	...	...	...	...	...	...
Japan[a]	...	...	...	...	...	...	...	...
New Zealand[a]	...	...	...	...	...	...	...	...

... = data not available; -0.0 or 0.0 = magnitude is less than half of unit employed; * = provisional, preliminary, estimate; ADB = Asian Development Bank.

a National accounts are compiled using chain volume measures.

b Industry data refer to manufacturing, construction, and utilities comprising electricity, gas, steam, and air-conditioning supply; water supply; and sewerage, waste management, and remediation activities.

c Industry data refer to mining and quarrying; manufacturing; electricity, gas, steam, and air-conditioning supply; water supply; and sewerage, waste management, and remediation activities.

Source: Economies' official sources.

Table 2.2.15: Growth Rates of Services Real Value-Added
(%)

ADB Regional Member	2010	2015	2016	2017	2018	2019	2020	2021
Developing ADB Member Economies								
Central and West Asia								
Afghanistan	18.1	1.4	2.3	-0.7	1.9	-1.4	-5.9	...
Armenia	4.7	1.0	3.4	10.4	9.2	9.8	-8.7	6.9
Azerbaijan	8.8	4.4	-0.8	3.2	3.8	3.8	-4.4	7.9
Georgia[a]	8.2	3.8	2.8	6.4	5.8	6.1	-7.4	16.2
Kazakhstan	6.0	3.1	0.9	6.4	3.9	4.4	-5.3	4.0*
Kyrgyz Republic	-1.3	3.5	3.2	3.3	2.9	3.3	-8.9	6.2*
Pakistan	3.2	4.4	5.7	5.6	6.0	5.0	-1.2	6.0
Tajikistan	7.3	1.9	-1.5	6.2	4.5	7.3	-1.8	...
Turkmenistan	19.4	-13.2 (2014)	...	...	...	...	...	...
Uzbekistan	9.6	7.6	5.9	6.0	5.2	6.0	0.7	9.2*
East Asia								
China, People's Republic of	9.7	8.8	8.1	8.3	8.0	7.2	1.9	8.2*
Hong Kong, China[a,b]	6.9	1.7	2.3	3.5	3.1	-0.7	-6.7	5.8
Korea, Republic of[a]	5.1	3.1	2.9	2.6	3.8	3.4	-0.8	3.8
Mongolia	17.8 (2011)	0.6	2.7	7.1	5.1	6.4	-6.5	3.9
Taipei,China[a]	6.4	1.2	1.3	2.9	3.0	3.6	1.2	3.0
South Asia								
Bangladesh	5.5	5.8	6.3	6.4	6.6	6.9	3.9	5.7
Bhutan	15.2	5.6	10.3	7.1	10.3	9.8	-10.7	...
India	7.8	9.4	8.5	6.3	7.2*	6.3*	-7.8*	8.4*
Maldives	7.3	2.4	6.7	6.2	7.3	8.6	-34.3	39.0*
Nepal	5.8	5.4	1.2	8.4	9.3	6.8	-4.0	4.4
Sri Lanka	8.0	5.3	4.7	3.6	4.3	2.9	-1.9	3.3
Southeast Asia								
Brunei Darussalam	4.9 (2011)	-1.1	-1.7	1.1	0.8	3.4	-2.1	1.8
Cambodia	3.3	7.1	6.8	7.0	6.7	6.2	-6.3	-1.9
Indonesia	8.4	5.5	5.7	5.7	5.8	6.4	-1.5	3.6
Lao People's Democratic Republic	7.6	8.0	4.7	4.5	6.8	6.9	-1.2	1.4
Malaysia	7.4	5.3	5.7	6.5	7.0	6.2	-5.7	1.9
Myanmar	9.5	8.7	8.1	8.1	8.7	8.3	3.4*	-26.3*
Philippines	7.6	7.4	8.2	7.4	6.7	7.2	-9.1	5.4
Singapore[a,c]	10.9	4.2	3.0	3.8	3.4	1.9	-5.0	5.3
Thailand[a,d]	7.0	5.9	5.0	5.4	5.0	4.2	-6.9	0.8*
Timor-Leste	10.2	4.6	5.7	2.7	-2.1	1.2	-7.1	...
Viet Nam	-7.7	6.3	7.0	7.4	7.0	7.3	2.3	1.2
The Pacific								
Cook Islands	-5.8	2.4	12.3	6.6	5.1	6.4	-21.8*	-18.5*
Fiji	2.9	3.0	0.1	3.6	1.7	0.0	-17.1	...
Kiribati	-0.4	8.3	5.7	4.8	2.0	3.4	2.0*	...
Marshall Islands	3.2	3.7	2.2	5.0	2.6	1.6	-2.2	-0.1
Micronesia, Federated States of	2.4	3.0	2.8	2.9	0.9	...	...	...
Nauru	4.2	11.6	-7.0	3.1	13.4	-3.3	0.2*	1.5*
Niue	0.4	4.6	4.2	2.4	4.7*	...	...	...
Palau	-0.3	8.9	-0.7	-2.8	9.3	-0.0*	-0.1*	...
Papua New Guinea	12.4	-2.3	2.3	1.4	5.1	2.5	-0.6	3.0
Samoa	2.9	7.3	4.7	1.4	5.4	1.4	-6.4	-4.1
Solomon Islands	5.1	2.5	7.3	1.2	4.8	2.0	-3.0	...
Tonga	0.7	1.4	5.5	1.8	3.3	0.8	0.9	...
Tuvalu	2.3	7.1	...	2.1	3.7	5.4	1.7	1.7
Vanuatu	2.7	-2.5	4.5	4.6	0.8	6.1	...	...
Developed ADB Member Economies								
Australia[a]	...	...	...	...	...	...	...	...
Japan[a]	...	...	...	...	...	...	...	...
New Zealand[a]	...	...	...	...	...	...	...	...

... = data not available; * = provisional, preliminary, estimate; ADB = Asian Development Bank.

a National accounts are compiled using chain volume measures.
b Services data refer to import, export, wholesale, and retail trades; accommodation and food services; transportation, storage, postal, and courier services; information and communications; financing and insurance; real estate, professional, and business services; public administration, social services, and personal services; and ownership of premises.
c Services data refer to services-producing industries, including ownership of dwellings.
d Services data include construction.

Source: Economies' official sources.

Table 2.2.16: Growth Rates of Real Household Final Consumption
(%)

ADB Regional Member	2010	2015	2016	2017	2018	2019	2020	2021
Developing ADB Member Economies								
Central and West Asia								
Afghanistan	...	...	...	-6.2	26.2	11.3	0.0	...
Armenia[a]	3.9	-7.5	-2.1	14.0	4.8	11.5	-14.0	3.4
Azerbaijan[a]	10.8	10.3	1.7	0.8	4.6	5.9	-8.7	...
Georgia[a]	9.0 (2011)	3.8	-5.7	7.4	5.8	7.2	8.8	9.6*
Kazakhstan[a]	11.5	1.8	1.2	1.5	6.1	6.1	-3.7	5.0*
Kyrgyz Republic[a]	2.7	-0.9	-0.6	6.3	5.0	0.8	-8.3	...
Pakistan[a]	2.2	2.9	7.6	6.9	7.2	5.6	-2.9	9.4
Tajikistan[a]	10.5	-15.1	13.2	4.6	4.0	5.0	3.1	...
Turkmenistan[a]	-61.4	...	...	...	...	...	...	...
Uzbekistan[a]	10.3	11.8	8.3	4.2	7.0	5.3	-0.0	11.5*
East Asia								
China, People's Republic of	...	...	...	...	...	...	...	...
Hong Kong, China[a]	6.1	4.8	2.0	5.5	5.3	-0.8	-10.5	5.4
Korea, Republic of	4.6	2.2	2.3	2.8	3.1	2.1	-4.7	3.7
Mongolia[a]	15.8 (2011)	8.1	1.7	4.2	11.7	5.9	2.3	-6.6
Taipei,China	3.7	3.1	2.7	2.7	1.7	2.5	-2.5	...
South Asia								
Bangladesh	4.6	5.8	3.0	6.3	9.4	4.9	3.0	8.0
Bhutan[a]	5.7	10.0	-1.8	5.9	13.4	7.5	-8.0	...
India[a]	6.7	7.9	8.1	6.2	7.1*	5.2*	-6.0*	7.9*
Maldives	...	22.1	12.9	13.1	10.6	4.4	-27.2	...
Nepal[a]	6.2	2.6	4.2	0.8	6.2	8.1	3.6	...
Sri Lanka	9.9 (2011)	7.5	7.4	3.6	4.0	3.0	-3.0	4.4
Southeast Asia								
Brunei Darussalam[a]	5.4 (2011)	5.2	-1.3	4.7	2.2	6.1	5.2	9.4
Cambodia[a]	8.8	6.0	6.8	4.6	4.6	5.6	-1.9	-3.6
Indonesia[a]	4.7	5.0	5.0	4.9	5.1	5.0	-2.6	2.0
Lao People's Democratic Republic	...	...	...	...	...	...	...	...
Malaysia[a]	6.9	6.0	5.9	6.9	8.0	7.7	-4.3	1.9
Myanmar[b]	2.6	4.7	2.2	4.1	4.5	1.5	...	...
Philippines[a]	3.6	6.4	7.1	6.0	5.8	5.9	-8.0	4.2
Singapore	4.4	5.2	3.2	3.2	4.0	3.2	-12.9	4.5
Thailand[a]	5.5	2.6	2.9	3.1	4.6	4.0	-1.0	0.3*
Timor-Leste	5.2	1.7	3.0	6.5	2.0	3.7	-2.4	...
Viet Nam	8.2	9.3	7.3	7.3	7.3	7.4	0.5	2.0
The Pacific								
Cook Islands	...	...	...	...	...	...	...	...
Fiji	...	...	...	...	...	...	...	...
Kiribati	-2.0	11.5	5.2	4.2	-7.0	10.3	0.4*	...
Marshall Islands	-0.4	-1.2	3.1	10.5	-0.8	8.2	-19.4	15.4
Micronesia, Federated States of	...	...	...	...	...	...	...	...
Nauru	...	...	...	...	...	...	...	...
Niue	...	...	...	...	...	...	...	...
Palau	-3.1	4.2	6.0	-0.5	5.2	-2.9*	...	...
Papua New Guinea[a]	9.8 (2005)	...	...	...	...	...	...	...
Samoa	1.6	3.2	7.7	0.6	-3.7	5.6	6.9	5.3
Solomon Islands	8.7	2.5	3.5	0.0	7.7	2.3	-14.6	...
Tonga	2.3	8.2	6.5	1.0	4.2	0.5	-4.8	...
Tuvalu	...	...	...	...	...	...	...	...
Vanuatu	2.7	1.0	8.9	-1.9	3.4	0.4	...	...
Developed ADB Member Economies								
Australia	3.4	2.5	2.6	2.4	2.7	1.5	-3.1	1.0
Japan	2.3	-0.3	-0.6	1.0	0.4	-0.7	-5.9	1.1
New Zealand	2.5	4.3	6.5	4.9	4.7	2.5	0.5	...

... = data not available; 0.0 = magnitude is less than half of unit employed; * = provisional, preliminary, estimate; ADB = Asian Development Bank.

a Includes expenditure of nonprofit institutions serving households.
b Data refers to total final consumption expenditure.

Source: Economies' official sources.

Table 2.2.17: Growth Rates of Real Government Consumption Expenditure
(%)

ADB Regional Member	2010	2015	2016	2017	2018	2019	2020	2021
Developing ADB Member Economies								
Central and West Asia								
Afghanistan	...	...	...	-6.4	-5.6	28.4	-13.0	...
Armenia	3.9	4.7	-2.4	-2.1	-3.0	12.9	9.2	8.4
Azerbaijan	3.4	1.4	6.8	1.1	-3.9	2.2	3.4	...
Georgia	-3.3 (2011)	4.4	10.9	1.1	1.6	5.7	7.1	7.9*
Kazakhstan	2.7	2.4	2.3	2.1	-14.1	15.5	12.8	-1.1*
Kyrgyz Republic	-1.1	0.9	1.5	1.3	1.3	0.5	0.9	...
Pakistan	-0.6	8.1	8.2	4.5	5.5	-1.6	8.5	1.8
Tajikistan	0.9	3.3	1.7	10.9	4.5	0.7	2.3	...
Turkmenistan	3.7	...	...	...	...	...	...	...
Uzbekistan	7.0	6.7	2.7	1.5	4.8	5.7	1.4	3.4*
East Asia								
China, People's Republic of	...	...	...	...	...	...	...	...
Hong Kong, China	3.4	3.4	3.4	2.8	4.2	5.1	7.9	4.6
Korea, Republic of	5.6	3.8	4.4	3.9	5.3	6.4	5.1	5.6
Mongolia	15.3 (2011)	-4.7	13.3	-2.4	1.1	12.3	14.6	5.7
Taipei,China	1.2	-0.1	3.7	-0.4	4.0	0.6	2.6	3.8
South Asia								
Bangladesh	6.8	8.8	8.4	7.2	5.3	13.4	2.0	6.9
Bhutan	7.5	10.8	4.2	4.4	3.1	10.8	4.1	...
India	5.2	7.5	6.1	11.9	6.7*	3.4*	3.6*	2.6*
Maldives	...	3.7	3.3	-10.2	8.9	-4.3	5.4	...
Nepal	1.3	11.5	-12.0	21.4	2.1	9.8	3.8	...
Sri Lanka	-2.1 (2011)	10.2	2.3	-6.0	-5.1	13.0	4.4	2.2
Southeast Asia								
Brunei Darussalam	5.3 (2011)	-3.6	-6.5	7.4	1.6	1.8	-9.6	-1.0
Cambodia	12.5	4.4	5.7	6.5	6.5	5.8	15.2	78.7
Indonesia	0.3	5.3	-0.1	2.1	4.8	3.3	2.0	4.2
Lao People's Democratic Republic	...	...	...	...	...	...	...	...
Malaysia	3.4	4.5	1.1	5.7	3.4	1.8	3.9	6.6
Myanmar[a]							...	...
Philippines	4.2	7.9	9.4	6.5	13.4	9.1	10.5	7.1
Singapore	10.2	8.9	3.7	3.4	3.0	3.4	13.3	4.5
Thailand	8.9	2.5	2.2	0.3	2.7	1.6	1.4	3.2*
Timor-Leste	2.1	3.6	-1.2	-5.8	-0.3	3.2	4.9	...
Viet Nam	12.3	7.0	7.5	7.4	6.3	5.8	6.2	2.9
The Pacific								
Cook Islands	...	...	...	...	...	...	...	...
Fiji	...	...	...	...	...	...	...	...
Kiribati	-6.6	0.7	14.1	-0.2	13.5	-0.9	-13.2*	...
Marshall Islands	-0.7	4.8	9.9	0.4	5.6	6.3	-12.3*	12.3
Micronesia, Federated States of	...	...	...	...	...	...	...	...
Nauru	...	...	...	...	...	...	...	...
Niue	...	...	...	...	...	...	...	...
Palau	-1.5	1.3	4.1	-0.9	4.4	0.3*	...	...
Papua New Guinea	1.1 (2005)	...	...	...	...	...	...	...
Samoa	17.9	-4.6	-14.6	8.3	20.9	5.5	0.5	1.8
Solomon Islands	10.0	4.9	4.2	-5.5	14.4	6.1	-13.3	...
Tonga	-8.3	3.1	-1.4	2.4	1.1	9.7	16.8	...
Tuvalu	...	...	...	...	...	...	...	...
Vanuatu	5.0	16.9	-1.4	19.5	4.5	2.6	...	...
Developed ADB Member Economies								
Australia	1.6	2.3	4.9	4.9	3.5	5.1	7.2	5.9
Japan	1.9	1.9	1.6	0.1	1.0	1.9	2.3	2.1
New Zealand	1.9	2.2	1.9	3.7	3.5	5.8	7.5	...

... = data not available; * = provisional, preliminary, estimate; ADB = Asian Development Bank.

a For 2000–2019, real government consumption expenditure data are included in real household consumption expenditure.

Source: Economies' official sources.

Table 2.2.18: Growth Rates of Real Gross Capital Formation
(%)

ADB Regional Member	2010	2015	2016	2017	2018	2019	2020	2021
Developing ADB Member Economies								
Central and West Asia								
Afghanistan[a]	...	...	...	8.2	14.7	-17.3	33.4	...
Armenia	0.5	-3.2	-8.7	10.3	34.5	-14.3	-0.5	7.9
Azerbaijan	2.0	-8.2	-19.0	1.2	-4.3	1.1	-7.3	...
Georgia	14.3 (2011)	7.5	13.3	-2.3	6.5	-5.9	-15.2	-12.9*
Kazakhstan	2.0	5.5	2.5	3.1	2.9	12.2		0.5*
Kyrgyz Republic	-5.2	-2.3	8.1	6.9	16.0	7.9	-29.2	...
Pakistan[b]	-6.5	14.6	7.3	7.4	9.9	-9.7	-6.1	4.7
Tajikistan[c]	7.5	25.2 |	-6.6	-12.0	25.5	8.9	-4.6	...
Turkmenistan	21.5	...	...	...	...	...	...	...
Uzbekistan	...	...	...	...	...	...	...	...
East Asia								
China, People's Republic of	...	...	...	...	...	...	...	...
Hong Kong, China	11.3	-8.1	4.0	5.4	1.8	-16.9	-1.8	0.5
Korea, Republic of	17.1	6.5	6.3	10.9	-1.3	-1.9	0.9	2.3
Mongolia	62.8 (2011)	-26.5	-1.8	31.6	52.1	0.2	-40.7	74.1
Taipei,China	35.6	2.6	1.7	-0.8	6.9	7.3	6.9	17.3
South Asia								
Bangladesh[d,e]	8.6	7.1	8.9	8.4	12.1	6.9	4.0	8.1
Bhutan	46.1	16.5	12.0	-2.2	-5.3	-16.5	-14.3	...
India[f]	20.1	7.0	9.8	14.5	6.2*	-5.2*	-13.8*	...
Maldives	...	13.8	0.1	10.9	9.2	-1.6	-30.6	...
Nepal	34.4	7.0	-7.6	55.2	12.2	11.1	-29.5	...
Sri Lanka	20.2 (2011)	3.8	5.0	6.7	3.6	-10.5	-10.1	1.5
Southeast Asia								
Brunei Darussalam	37.0 (2011)	6.6	-11.1	8.0	28.1	-4.4	-9.3	-15.5
Cambodia	-7.9	9.9	10.0	6.0	6.0	6.5	12.8	6.5
Indonesia	8.8	3.0	5.0	5.7	8.5	2.4	-6.9	4.1
Lao People's Democratic Republic	...	...	...	...	...	...	...	...
Malaysia	25.3	6.7	4.4	6.3	-1.6	-3.8	-12.0	7.4
Myanmar	34.6	16.1	4.3	8.1	-1.5	1.6	...	...
Philippines	30.5	13.4	20.8	10.9	11.3	3.5	-34.2	20.3
Singapore	22.5	-9.8	9.6	11.2	-3.5	-0.6	-14.7	17.5
Thailand	32.0	2.1	-3.8	11.0	16.3	-3.4	-5.1	...
Timor-Leste	2.8	-5.0	15.7	-13.6	-0.8	-14.7	-42.8	...
Viet Nam[g]	10.4	9.0	9.7	9.8	8.2	7.9	4.1	4.0
The Pacific								
Cook Islands	...	...	...	...	...	...	...	...
Fiji	...	...	...	...	...	...	...	...
Kiribati	-9.3	57.4	-15.6	-10.5	-17.5	-20.4	-3.7*	...
Marshall Islands	18.8	-12.2	20.8	30.6	3.3	130.4	-63.2	12.2
Micronesia, Federated States of	...	...	...	...	...	...	...	...
Nauru	...	...	...	...	...	...	...	...
Niue	...	...	...	...	...	...	...	...
Palau	3.3	0.3	9.8	12.0	-10.0	8.5*	...	...
Papua New Guinea	-9.8 (2005)	...	...	...	...	...	...	...
Samoa	54.7	3.8	10.8	-2.5	-3.1	17.4	-20.7	0.4
Solomon Islands[a]	85.2	19.9	4.9	19.3	6.5	20.0	-12.6	...
Tonga	4.7	11.1	9.6	18.9	-23.2	7.9	-4.1	...
Tuvalu	...	...	...	...	...	...	...	...
Vanuatu	-4.7	46.5	-23.7	28.1	14.9	-3.6	...	...
Developed ADB Member Economies								
Australia	...	...	...	...	...	...	...	...
Japan	2.9	3.3	0.7	2.1	1.0	0.5	-5.1	-2.1
New Zealand	7.4	2.0	2.8	8.1	4.2	1.6	-5.5	...

... = data not available, | = marks break in series; * = provisional, preliminary, estimate; ADB = Asian Development Bank.

a Refers to gross fixed capital formation.
b For 2016 onward, data are revised due to the rebasing of national accounts to the base year 2015/2016.
c Prior to 2016, figures are based on the 1993 System of National Accounts. For 2016 onward, figures are based on the 2008 System of National Accounts.
d Refers to gross fixed capital formation, which includes data on changes in inventories.
e For 2007–2016, data refer to previous growth rates calculated using the base year 2005/2006; and, for 2017–2021, using the base year 2015/2016.
f Refers to gross capital formation, which refers to the sum of gross fixed capital formation, valuables, increases in stocks, and errors and omissions.
g For 2021, gross domestic product data are based on a re-evaluated scale, where some 2008 System of National Accounts concepts are applied.

Source: Economies' official sources.

Table 2.2.19: Growth Rates of Real Exports of Goods and Services
(%)

ADB Regional Member	2010	2015	2016	2017	2018	2019	2020	2021
Developing ADB Member Economies								
Central and West Asia								
Afghanistan	...	...	...	46.5	-24.7	-21.5	-35.6	...
Armenia	26.5	4.9	21.3	19.3	5.0	16.0	-33.5	16.5
Azerbaijan	9.1	-0.2	-2.0	-2.2	0.5	-4.3	-11.5	...
Georgia	16.6 (2011)	4.2	8.7	11.7	10.1	9.8	-37.6	25.0*
Kazakhstan	3.1	-4.1	-4.5	8.0	9.6	2.0	-11.3	2.0*
Kyrgyz Republic	-11.7	-5.6	-3.8	6.1	-2.7	16.2	-27.3	...
Pakistan[a]	15.7	-6.3	-1.6	2.5	10.0	13.2	1.5	6.5
Tajikistan[b]	23.0	- |	15.1	6.8	-5.2	21.5	21.8	...
Turkmenistan	11.7	...	...	...	...	...	...	...
Uzbekistan	1.6	2.1	4.3	14.8	11.8	16.2	-20.0	12.7*
East Asia								
China, People's Republic of	...	...	...	...	...	...	...	...
Hong Kong, China[c]	17.6	-1.4	0.7	5.8	3.7	-6.1	-6.7	17.0
Korea, Republic of	13.0	0.2	2.4	2.5	4.0	0.2	-1.7	10.8
Mongolia	18.2 (2011)	0.1	15.5	3.7	6.1	12.0	-5.3	-14.5
Taipei,China	27.6	0.4	-0.9	4.5	0.2	0.7	1.2	17.0
South Asia								
Bangladesh[d]	0.9	-2.8	2.2	-1.8	6.1	11.5	-17.5	9.2
Bhutan	7.5	-3.2	-5.3	6.5	4.6	14.4	-20.2	...
India	19.5	-5.6	5.0	4.6	11.9*	-3.4*	-9.2*	24.3*
Maldives	...	-9.9	8.9	7.4	10.5	6.7	-51.4	...
Nepal	-10.4	2.3	-17.3	8.9	7.7	5.5	-15.9	...
Sri Lanka	10.2 (2011)	4.7	-0.7	7.6	0.5	7.2	-9.6	17.0
Southeast Asia								
Brunei Darussalam	-3.0 (2011)	-9.9	-3.2	-4.1	5.7	14.9	7.5	7.6
Cambodia	20.6	7.2	8.6	5.3	5.3	7.8	1.1	13.5
Indonesia	15.3	-2.1	-1.7	8.9	6.5	-0.5	-8.1	24.0
Lao People's Democratic Republic	...	...	...	...	...	...	...	...
Malaysia	11.1	0.3	1.3	8.7	1.9	-1.0	-8.9	15.9
Myanmar	10.9	15.1	-0.4	13.5	12.0	11.3	...	...
Philippines	20.3	10.0	9.2	17.4	11.8	2.6	-16.1	8.0
Singapore	17.8	5.0	0.0	7.4	7.6	0.3	-0.2	6.8
Thailand	14.0	1.0	3.0	5.0	3.0	-3.0	-20.0	10.0*
Timor-Leste	28.0	-28.3	8.5	-39.1	16.6	-17.2	-51.1	...
Viet Nam[e]	14.6	12.6	13.9	16.7	14.3	6.7	4.4	14.0
The Pacific								
Cook Islands	...	...	...	...	...	...	...	...
Fiji	...	...	...	...	...	...	...	...
Kiribati	-20.7	34.5	21.9	-25.0	-16.8	72.0	-33.6*	...
Marshall Islands	44.3	-2.9	-11.3	-2.3	8.6	8.3	-3.3	-26.4
Micronesia, Federated States of	...	...	...	...	...	...	...	...
Nauru	...	...	...	...	...	...	...	...
Niue	...	...	...	...	...	...	...	...
Palau	5.7	12.7	-3.9	-9.3	-5.4	-13.1*	...	...
Papua New Guinea	6.8 (2005)	...	...	...	...	...	...	...
Samoa	3.1	7.2	10.3	3.9	5.6	15.4	-61.1	-15.7
Solomon Islands	32.7	-6.5	10.7	5.2	6.2	-2.8	-21.8	...
Tonga	-9.4	7.9	27.2	-5.8	1.3	-3.3	-4.7	...
Tuvalu	...	...	...	...	...	...	...	...
Vanuatu	1.0	4.9	19.5	-1.1	3.5	-3.7	...	...
Developed ADB Member Economies								
Australia	4.7	6.9	6.4	5.5	4.1	4.0	-1.7	-8.3
Japan	24.9	3.2	1.6	6.6	3.8	-1.5	-11.8	11.6
New Zealand	2.8	6.5	2.0	3.8	3.5	0.3	-17.8	...

... = data not available, | = marks break in series, – = magnitude equals zero, * = provisional, preliminary, estimate, 0.0 = magnitude is less than half of unit employed, ADB = Asian Development Bank.

a For 2016 onward, data are revised due to the rebasing of national accounts to the base year 2015/2016.
b Prior to 2016, figures are based on the 1993 System of National Accounts (SNA). For 2016 onward, figures are based on the 2008 SNA.
c The statistics for trade in goods and services are compiled based on the change of ownership principle in recording goods sent abroad for processing and merchanting under the standards stipulated in the 2008 SNA.
d For 2007–2016, data refer to previous growth rates calculated using the base year 2005/2006; and, for 2017–2021, using the base year 2015/2016.
e For 2021, gross domestic product data are based on a re-evaluated scale, where some 2008 System of National Accounts concepts are applied.

Source: Economies' official sources.

Table 2.2.20: Growth Rates of Real Imports of Goods and Services
(%)

ADB Regional Member	2010	2015	2016	2017	2018	2019	2020	2021
Developing ADB Member Economies								
Central and West Asia								
Afghanistan	...	...	...	-0.5	40.3	16.5	-7.1	...
Armenia	12.8	-15.3	6.3	24.6	13.3	11.6	-31.5	11.5
Azerbaijan	12.4	8.4	-3.2	-0.8	-0.2	-3.2	-17.1	...
Georgia	15.6 (2011)	7.2	2.4	8.1	10.3	6.6	-16.6	8.5*
Kazakhstan	2.9	-0.1	-2.0	1.0	6.6	14.9	-9.0	-2.7*
Kyrgyz Republic	-6.9	-13.2	-1.1	7.4	7.4	6.1	-28.0	...
Pakistan	4.3	-1.6	16.0	19.0	15.7	7.6	-5.1	14.5
Tajikistan	8.0	–	-7.5	-6.5	9.3	6.4	-0.4	...
Turkmenistan	7.3	...	...	...	...	...	...	...
Uzbekistan	0.4	-10.6	-1.3	13.7	42.3	13.3	-15.0	23.1*
East Asia								
China, People's Republic of	...	...	...	...	...	...	...	...
Hong Kong, China[a]	18.2	-1.8	0.9	6.6	4.5	-7.2	-6.9	16.0
Korea, Republic of	17.5	2.1	5.2	8.9	1.7	-1.9	-3.1	10.1
Mongolia	49.5 (2011)	-11.4	17.5	11.5	32.7	8.6	-15.5	9.6
Taipei,China	30.1	1.3	-1.0	1.6	0.8	0.5	-3.6	17.9
South Asia								
Bangladesh	0.7	3.2	-7.1	5.2	23.9	0.5	-11.4	15.3
Bhutan	28.7	13.5	-6.6	-0.4	6.6	-6.2	-12.4	...
India	15.8	-5.9	4.4	17.4	8.8*	-0.8*	-13.8*	35.5*
Maldives	...	1.0	9.7	8.2	12.8	-0.3	-41.1	...
Nepal	28.3	9.6	3.2	28.2	19.0	5.8	-15.2	...
Sri Lanka	23.6 (2011)	10.6	7.9	7.1	1.8	-5.8	-11.4	11.5
Southeast Asia								
Brunei Darussalam	33.7 (2011)	-8.9	-10.8	1.3	28.1	13.8	-2.1	27.1
Cambodia	16.8	6.5	8.6	4.1	4.1	6.0	7.3	23.1
Indonesia	17.3	-6.2	-2.4	8.1	12.1	-7.1	-16.7	23.3
Lao People's Democratic Republic	...	...	...	...	...	...	...	...
Malaysia	15.6	0.8	1.4	10.2	1.5	-2.4	-8.4	18.5
Myanmar	51.9	21.6	-11.4	10.0	-2.2	-7.7	...	...
Philippines	20.7	15.0	18.8	15.1	14.6	2.3	-21.6	13.0
Singapore	16.3	3.4	0.2	8.1	7.2	0.1	-2.3	7.6
Thailand	23.0	–		6.2	8.3	-5.2	-14.1	17.9*
Timor-Leste	-1.8	-7.4	8.1	-8.8	2.9	-6.5	-8.5	...
Viet Nam	13.7	18.1	15.3	17.5	12.8	9.5	2.8	16.2
The Pacific								
Cook Islands	...	...	...	...	...	...	...	...
Fiji	...	...	...	...	...	...	...	...
Kiribati	-8.2	18.8	5.5	-3.8	-9.0	14.0	-18.1*	...
Marshall Islands	9.5	-0.9	0.5	10.9	3.1	37.3	-31.4	-7.4
Micronesia, Federated States of	...	...	...	...	...	...	...	...
Nauru	...	...	...	...	...	...	...	...
Niue	...	...	...	...	...	...	...	...
Palau	0.9	2.5	8.3	-1.5	-3.6	0.6*	...	...
Papua New Guinea	4.7 (2005)	...	...	...	...	...	...	...
Samoa	27.4	-5.6	5.7	4.3	7.1	12.0	-20.1	15.1
Solomon Islands	52.2	0.8	4.1	-2.9	18.3	8.1	-37.1	...
Tonga	3.0	22.6	16.9	3.5	-1.4	4.8	-7.6	...
Tuvalu	...	...	...	...	...	...	...	...
Vanuatu	1.2	26.2	2.3	3.3	10.4	-15.1	...	...
Developed ADB Member Economies								
Australia	6.9	1.5	-0.3	5.2	7.0	0.2	-7.7	-2.8
Japan	11.3	0.4	-1.2	3.3	3.8	1.0	-7.2	5.1
New Zealand	11.5	2.6	5.6	7.8	4.3	1.1	-16.1	...

... = data not available, | = marks break in series, – = magnitude equals zero, * = provisional, preliminary, estimate, ADB = Asian Development Bank.

a The statistics for trade in goods and services were compiled based on the change of ownership principle in recording goods sent abroad for processing and merchanting under the standards stipulated in the System of National Accounts 2008.

Source: Economies' official sources.

Table 2.2.21: Growth Rates of Agriculture Production Index
(%)

ADB Regional Member	2010	2015	2016	2017	2018	2019	2020	2021
Developing ADB Member Economies								
Central and West Asia								
Afghanistan	-0.7	-5.4	6.6	-1.9	-2.6	13.2	6.9	...
Armenia	-13.4	8.3	-10.1	-0.9	-12.1	-2.3	5.4	...
Azerbaijan	-2.1	6.5	3.7	5.8	5.5	7.9	1.3	...
Georgia	-4.5	1.9	-4.4	-8.7	17.3	0.6	10.0	...
Kazakhstan[a]	-21.8	2.4	1.9	-2.3	0.5	-3.5	5.8	-7.7
Kyrgyz Republic[b]	-1.7	8.0	2.3	1.4	2.0	2.0	0.5	...
Pakistan	-1.9	-4.8	2.6	11.5	5.8	-13.4	1.1	...
Tajikistan	5.0	6.6	0.3	34.6	7.5	6.5	-14.5	...
Turkmenistan	4.6	2.2	-3.2	-1.9	-1.0	1.0	-0.8	...
Uzbekistan	...	-0.1	0.1	-5.0	-0.8	3.1	-0.6	0.9
East Asia								
China, People's Republic of	2.7	2.8	-0.4	1.7	0.7	-0.6	1.5	...
Hong Kong, China	–	–	–	6.3	5.9	–	–	–
Korea, Republic of	-4.5	-2.4	-1.0	-1.1	1.9	0.9	-1.9	...
Mongolia	-21.8	30.7	-4.3	1.3	17.5	7.5	27.1	...
Taipei,China[c]	2.1	-3.4	-3.7	5.8	2.5	-3.7	0.3	-3.1
South Asia								
Bangladesh	6.1	2.5	-0.6	7.6	-0.1	0.9	2.1	...
Bhutan	4.0	0.5	8.7	0.5	-9.5	3.7	2.8	...
India	8.7	-1.6	4.2	6.1	4.7	1.0	0.8	...
Maldives	-4.0	1.4	2.3	-0.8	-0.7	4.1	0.8	...
Nepal	1.0	–	2.4	4.5	0.6	5.4	3.1	2.6
Sri Lanka	13.7	12.8	-1.5	-16.4	18.5	2.4	13.9	...
Southeast Asia								
Brunei Darussalam	4.7	-2.2	6.4	-3.5	0.9	-1.5	6.8	...
Cambodia	7.7	4.1	6.9	6.3	4.8	2.3	...	...
Indonesia	-22.0	2.5	2.9	-2.4	22.5	8.1	...	...
Lao People's Democratic Republic	9.6	15.8	1.3	-6.4	0.4	1.8	6.1	...
Malaysia	1.7	6.3	-6.0	8.3	-3.4	-0.8	-1.9	...
Myanmar[d]	-3.5 (2011)	2.3	-0.8	-2.8	-3.9	-3.3	...	...
Philippines	-1.1	-0.1	-2.2	3.5	-0.5	-0.3	-0.6	...
Singapore	3.2	4.2	6.3	28.5	-16.5	9.7	29.0	...
Thailand	0.9	-2.7	-0.4	6.4	7.7	-1.4	-4.2	1.6
Timor-Leste	-0.2	1.5	-7.8	-1.9	6.8	2.3	-1.5	...
Viet Nam	2.1	1.7	0.5	1.7	3.4	-0.7	2.0	...
The Pacific								
Cook Islands	-2.0	-1.9	-9.7	-7.5	-5.3	-2.4	...	...
Fiji	-19.6	1.7	-24.2	35.6	4.5	-3.1	...	...
Kiribati	0.7	0.7	-0.3	0.5	-9.0	2.0	1.2	...
Marshall Islands	-5.0	8.0	40.7	–	-36.8	-6.4	...	...
Micronesia, Federated States of	-1.0	0.5	1.1	0.7	-0.1	0.3	-2.0	...
Nauru	0.9	0.6	0.6	-0.9	0.3	0.6	...	...
Niue	-0.6	-4.5	3.2	-1.2	-0.7	1.3	0.2	...
Palau	...	...	...	...	...	...	...	...
Papua New Guinea	-1.7	0.9	0.8	–	0.5	-0.2	0.5	...
Samoa	1.7	1.0	-4.3	-1.6	1.6	-12.2	10.4	...
Solomon Islands	-25.4	1.4	0.1	2.4	0.5	2.7	-1.3	...
Tonga	-0.8	-1.9	-5.3	0.1	-1.6	-0.1	–	...
Tuvalu	-1.4	1.5	0.7	0.1	0.3	0.2	0.2	...
Vanuatu	28.5	-6.8	-0.2	-0.9	-1.2	-0.3	-5.6	...
Developed ADB Member Economies								
Australia	-0.2	-1.2	-0.7	6.0	-8.1	-8.1	...	...
Japan	-2.3	-1.1	-0.3	0.4	-0.3	0.8	-1.3	...
New Zealand	–	2.1	-1.0	-1.8	4.0	-0.4	1.1	...

... = data not available, – = magnitude equals zero, ADB = Asian Development Bank.

Note: Data refer to the gross production index (2014–2016 = 100), except for Hong Kong, China; Indonesia; Kazakhstan; the Kyrgyz Republic; Myanmar; Pakistan; Taipei,China; Thailand; and Uzbekistan.

a Refers to the index of physical volume of the gross production (services) of agriculture.
b Refers to volume indices of agriculture, hunting, and forestry.
c Refers to the index of agricultural, forestry, and fishery production.
d For 2010–2015, fiscal year is April–March. For 2016 onward, fiscal year is October–September.

Sources: Food and Agriculture Organization of the United Nations. FAOSTAT Database. http://www.fao.org/faostat/en/#home (accessed 9 July 2022).
For Hong Kong, China; Indonesia; Kazakhstan; the Kyrgyz Republic; Myanmar; Pakistan; Taipei,China; Thailand; and Uzbekistan: Economies' official sources.

Table 2.2.22: Growth Rates of Manufacturing Production Index
(%)

ADB Regional Member	2010	2015	2016	2017	2018	2019	2020	2021
Developing ADB Member Economies								
Central and West Asia								
Afghanistan	...	...	...	...	...	...	...	...
Armenia	...	...	...	...	...	...	...	...
Azerbaijan	18.5	4.7	-5.6	-3.0	10.2	3.2	-1.0	8.5
Georgia	-73.8	-12.6	3.7	1.5	4.8	0.8	-6.1	9.7
Kazakhstan	17.3	-0.9	0.4	5.0	-1.0	1.2	-1.6	1.3
Kyrgyz Republic	19.4	-4.9	14.3	2.1	-2.4	3.2	-14.3	15.3
Pakistan	0.5	3.4	3.1	5.8	5.2	-2.3	-9.9	15.0
Tajikistan	673.7	4.8	-0.5	-1.6	-0.2	0.2	2.2	0.3
Turkmenistan	...	...	...	...	...	...	...	...
Uzbekistan	3.6	-1.9	0.8	-2.3	3.6	-1.2	1.2	0.3
East Asia								
China, People's Republic of[a]	16.6	7.0	6.8	7.2	6.5	6.0	3.4	9.8
Hong Kong, China[b]	3.5	-1.6	-0.4	0.4	1.3	0.4	-5.8	5.4
Korea, Republic of	16.7	-0.3	2.3	2.3	1.3	0.5	-0.2	7.6
Mongolia	...	...	...	...	...	...	...	...
Taipei,China	29.7	-1.2	1.9	5.3	3.9	-0.4	7.6	14.3
South Asia								
Bangladesh	-67.5	10.7	13.5	11.2	15.0	14.7	1.4	12.3
Bhutan	...	...	...	...	...	...	...	...
India[c]	9.0	3.0	4.1	4.6	3.9	-1.4	-9.6	11.7
Maldives	...	...	...	...	...	...	...	...
Nepal	-3.6	0.3	-27.5	17.1	10.0	7.2	-1.0	6.7
Sri Lanka	...	...	...	...	...	...	...	...
Southeast Asia								
Brunei Darussalam	...	...	...	...	...	...	...	...
Cambodia	...	...	...	...	...	...	...	...
Indonesia	-22.4	4.8	4.0	4.7	4.0	4.1	-10.1	...
Lao People's Democratic Republic	...	...	...	...	...	...	...	...
Malaysia	11.1	4.8	-19.2	4.4	3.1	2.4	-4.4	7.4
Myanmar[d]	10.1 (2011)	10.2 |	9.1	-34.8	9.7	7.3	...	...
Philippines	23.2	0.5	13.1	11.3	-28.7	-8.9	-40.5	50.4
Singapore[e]	29.7	-5.1	3.7	10.4	7.0	-1.5	7.5	13.3
Thailand	14.2	0.1	1.4	1.7	3.8	-3.4	-9.5	5.9
Timor-Leste	...	...	...	...	...	...	...	...
Viet Nam	...	1.6	0.8	2.9	-2.0	-1.6	-5.1	1.2
The Pacific								
Cook Islands	...	...	...	...	...	...	...	...
Fiji	7.6	-17.2	2.1	1.5	3.6	-4.6	-6.6	...
Kiribati	...	...	...	...	...	...	...	...
Marshall Islands	...	...	...	...	...	...	...	...
Micronesia, Federated States of	...	...	...	...	...	...	...	...
Nauru	...	...	...	...	...	...	...	...
Niue	...	...	...	...	...	...	...	...
Palau	...	...	...	...	...	...	...	...
Papua New Guinea	...	...	...	...	...	...	...	...
Samoa[e]	15.2	...	...	...	...	...	...	...
Solomon Islands	...	...	...	...	...	...	...	...
Tonga	...	...	...	...	...	...	...	...
Tuvalu	...	...	...	...	...	...	...	...
Vanuatu	...	...	...	...	...	...	...	...
Developed ADB Member Economies								
Australia	0.5	-1.5	-2.0	-0.6	2.2	-0.9	-1.4	1.5
Japan	15.6	-1.1	–	3.1	1.1	-3.0	-10.4	5.8
New Zealand	4.6	1.8	3.1	1.9	1.9	0.7	-3.5	3.9

... = data not available, – = magnitude equals zero, ADB = Asian Development Bank.

a Data include only industrial enterprises above a designated size (annual revenue from principal business of over 20 million yuan).

b Starting from the reference year 2008, the index of industrial production and producer price index for manufacturing industries are compiled based on the Standard Industrial Classification Version 2.0 of Hong Kong, China, which adopts the basic framework and principles of the International Standard Industrial Classification of All Economic Activities Revision 4.

c For the fiscal year beginning 1 April.

d For 2010–2015, fiscal year is April–March. For 2016 onward, fiscal year is October–September.

e Refers to volume indices of industrial production.

Source: Economies' official sources.

Data Issues and Comparability

Indicators in this theme were derived from national accounts statistics compiled in accordance with the UN System of National Accounts. As national statistical offices gradually adopt the latest 2008 System of National Accounts framework with regard to data compilation and methodologies, these indicators will become more consistent across economies. Currently, economies in the region have varying reference periods (e.g., calendar year versus fiscal year) and price valuation methods. Due to a lack of reliable data and limited technical and financial resources dedicated for national accounts compilation, some economies with small statistical offices are not able to provide timely estimates, while some are dependent upon the estimates of external institutions.

Table 2.3.1: Growth Rates of Consumer Price Index
(%)

ADB Regional Member	2010	2015	2016	2017	2018	2019	2020	2021
Developing ADB Member Economies								
Central and West Asia								
Afghanistan	4.9	-0.7	4.4	5.0	0.6	2.3	5.6	5.1
Armenia	8.2	3.7	-1.4	1.0	2.5	1.4	1.2	7.2
Azerbaijan	5.7	4.0	12.4	12.9	2.3	2.6	2.8	6.7
Georgia	7.1	4.0	2.1	6.0	2.6	4.9	5.2	9.6
Kazakhstan	7.1	6.6	14.6	7.4	6.0	5.3	6.8	8.0
Kyrgyz Republic	8.0	6.5	0.4	3.2	1.5	1.1	6.3	11.9
Pakistan	10.1	4.5	2.9	4.8	4.7	6.8	10.7	8.9
Tajikistan	9.8	5.1	6.1	6.7	5.4	8.0	9.4	8.0
Turkmenistan	4.4	7.4	3.6	8.0	13.2	13.0	10.0	12.5
Uzbekistan[a]	7.6	5.5	5.6	9.5	17.5	14.5	12.9	10.8
East Asia								
China, People's Republic of	3.3	1.4	2.0	1.6	2.1	2.9	2.5	0.9
Hong Kong, China	2.4	3.0	2.4	1.5	2.4	2.9	0.3	1.6
Korea, Republic of	2.9	0.7	1.0	1.9	1.5	0.4	0.5	2.5
Mongolia	12.9	1.0	1.3	6.3	8.2	5.2	2.3	13.4
Taipei,China	1.0	-0.3	1.4	0.6	1.4	0.6	-0.2	2.0
South Asia								
Bangladesh	6.8	6.4	5.9	5.4	5.8	5.5	5.7	5.6
Bhutan	7.0	4.5	3.2	5.0	2.7	2.7	5.6	7.3
India	10.4	4.9	4.6	3.7	3.4	4.8	6.5	5.1
Maldives	6.1	1.0	0.5	2.8	-0.1	0.2	-1.4	0.5
Nepal	9.6	7.2	9.9	4.5	4.2	4.6	6.2	3.6
Sri Lanka[b]	6.2	2.2	4.0	6.5	4.3	4.4	4.5	6.0
Southeast Asia								
Brunei Darussalam	0.4	-0.5	-0.3	-1.3	1.0	-0.4	1.9	1.7
Cambodia[b]	4.0	1.2	3.0	2.9	2.5	1.9	2.9	3.5
Indonesia[c]	5.1	6.4	3.5	3.8	3.2	2.8	2.0	1.6
Lao People's Democratic Republic	6.0	1.3	1.6	0.8	2.0	3.3	5.1	3.8
Malaysia	1.7	2.1	2.1	3.7	1.0	0.6	-1.1	2.5
Myanmar	7.7	9.5	6.9	4.6	6.8	8.9	3.8	...
Philippines	3.8	0.7	1.3	2.9	5.2	2.4	2.4	3.9
Singapore	2.8	-0.5	-0.5	0.6	0.4	0.6	-0.2	2.3
Thailand	3.3	-0.9	0.2	0.7	1.1	0.7	-0.9	1.2
Timor-Leste	5.2	0.6	-1.5	0.5	2.3	0.9	0.5	3.8
Viet Nam	9.2	0.6	2.7	3.5	3.5	2.8	3.2	1.8
The Pacific								
Cook Islands	1.5	1.1	-0.4	-0.3	0.1	0.4	1.0	3.1
Fiji	3.7	1.4	3.9	3.3	4.1	1.8	-2.6	0.2
Kiribati[b]	-3.0	0.6	1.9	0.4	0.6	-1.8	2.5	2.2
Marshall Islands[b]	1.8	-2.2	-1.5	0.1	0.8	-0.1	-0.7	2.7
Micronesia, Federated States of	3.6	0.0	-1.0	...	1.6	1.9	0.5	...
Nauru	-3.1	9.8	8.2	5.1	0.5	4.3	0.9	1.2
Niue	5.3	1.8	1.3	5.0	9.6	2.4	2.6	...
Palau	1.4	0.9	-1.0	0.7	2.1	0.2	0.2	2.7
Papua New Guinea	4.4 (2011)	6.0	6.7	5.4	4.4	3.9	4.9	4.5
Samoa	0.8	0.7	1.3	1.8	4.2	1.0	-1.6	3.1
Solomon Islands[b]	0.9	-0.6	0.5	0.5	3.5	1.6	3.0	-0.1
Tonga	3.5	-1.1	2.6	7.5	6.1	1.2	-0.3	5.7
Tuvalu	-1.9	3.1	3.5	4.1	2.1	3.5	1.6	6.7
Vanuatu	3.1	2.5	3.9	3.1	2.3	2.8	5.3	2.3
Developed ADB Member Economies								
Australia	2.3	1.7	1.4	1.7	1.9	1.6	1.3	1.6
Japan	-0.7	0.8	-0.1	0.5	1.0	0.5	-0.0	-0.2
New Zealand	2.3	0.3	0.6	1.9	1.6	1.6	1.7	3.9

... = data not available, -0.0 or 0.0 = magnitude is less than half of unit employed, ADB = Asian Development Bank.

Note: Data refer to the whole of each economy, unless otherwise indicated. In general, the consumer price index (CPI) data of economies are grouped according to the Classification of Individual Consumption According to Purpose (COICOP) adopted by the United Nations Statistical Commission in 1999. Other economies have switched to the most recent version, COICOP 2018. For more information on COICOP versions, please refer to United Nations' Classification of Economic Statistics available at https://unstats.un.org/unsd/classifications/econ/.

a Prior to 2016, values were calculated based on variable weights. From 2016 onward, values were calculated based on fixed weights.

b Data refer to capital city.

c For 2010, data refer to the CPI for 66 cities; for 2015–2018, 82 cities; and for 2019–2021, 90 cities. For 2019–2021, the CPI commodity grouping also changed based on COICOP 2018.

Source: Economies' official sources.

Table 2.3.2: Growth Rates of Food and Nonalcoholic Beverages Consumer Price Index
(%)

ADB Regional Member	2010	2015	2016	2017	2018	2019	2020	2021
Developing ADB Member Economies								
Central and West Asia								
Afghanistan	3.5	-0.8	5.7	6.9	-1.1	3.8	10.0	5.5
Armenia	9.4	3.1	-3.3	4.1	2.3	1.9	0.3	11.2
Azerbaijan	7.5	4.8	13.7	17.2	2.0	3.3	4.6	8.2
Georgia	11.7	4.2	1.6	6.8	2.2	8.1	10.5	10.8
Kazakhstan	5.9	5.7	12.9	8.5	4.7	8.1	10.5	10.8
Kyrgyz Republic	6.5	3.7	-6.5	2.5	-2.2	1.3	11.7	18.0
Pakistan[a]	12.6	3.5	-0.4	10.2	6.7	-4.6	15.5	13.2
Tajikistan	...	3.8	6.5	7.8	4.9	11.4	13.6	7.3
Turkmenistan	...	...	...	...	...	...	...	...
Uzbekistan	4.9	2.7	7.9	18.1	20.1	17.0	17.5	14.4
East Asia								
China, People's Republic of[b]	7.2	2.3	4.6	-1.4	1.8	9.2	10.6	-1.4
Hong Kong, China	3.5	3.4	3.6	1.1	4.3	9.9	7.7	1.4
Korea, Republic of	6.4	1.6	2.3	3.4	2.8	0.0	4.4	5.9
Mongolia	18.6	-5.9	1.7	7.3	9.1	8.4	8.5	12.9
Taipei,China	1.1	3.9	7.9	-1.8	0.6	2.2	0.4	3.6
South Asia								
Bangladesh[c]	7.7 (2012)	6.7	4.9	6.0	7.1	5.5	5.5	5.7
Bhutan	9.4	3.3	4.0	7.5	4.9	3.6	11.4	8.9
India	...	4.7	4.4	1.9	0.4	6.6	8.0	3.7
Maldives[d]	7.5	0.5	0.6	5.6	-1.1	-0.8	2.7	1.8
Nepal[e]	15.5	9.6	10.9	1.9	2.7	3.1	8.2	5.0
Sri Lanka[f]	6.9	5.5	6.1	9.3	3.4	0.8	11.4	11.7
Southeast Asia								
Brunei Darussalam	-0.0 (2011)	1.0	-0.5	0.3	1.9	-0.7	2.5	2.4
Cambodia[f]	4.3	4.0	5.6	3.4	2.5	2.1	4.6	3.4
Indonesia[g]	9.4	7.2	7.2	2.1	4.2	3.0	3.6	3.1
Lao People's Democratic Republic	5.6 (2012)	4.5	4.3	-0.1	1.2	4.7	8.6	3.0
Malaysia	2.5	3.6	3.8	3.9	1.7	1.6	1.3	1.7
Myanmar	7.4	13.1	9.2	4.4	6.6	9.0	2.8	...
Philippines	4.0	1.9	1.6	3.1	6.8	1.6	2.9	4.2
Singapore	2.3	1.2	2.3	1.3	1.3	1.1	2.9	1.6
Thailand	5.4	1.1	1.6	–	0.4	2.3	1.2	-0.1
Timor-Leste	6.4	0.3	-2.1	0.9	1.7	0.9	0.9	5.8
Viet Nam	10.7	1.5	2.4	-1.1	3.2	4.1	10.0	0.7
The Pacific								
Cook Islands[f,h]	2.6	0.1	1.0	0.6	0.6	1.3	2.7	4.2
Fiji	4.1	4.7	6.0	-2.1	3.4	4.9	-2.4	6.4
Kiribati[i]	-4.6	-0.6	1.7	1.8	-1.1	-2.0	1.2	3.9
Marshall Islands[f,j]	-1.5	2.3	-1.4	-0.5	1.3	0.5	-0.7	3.3
Micronesia, Federated States of	2.2	0.8	-1.2	...	-0.9	1.2	0.7	...
Nauru	-0.4	0.6 (2013)	...	...	...	...	...	...
Niue[k]	8.2	2.7	-0.2	3.4	0.6	5.1	5.2	...
Palau	1.8	1.7	-3.0	1.6	4.0	0.6	2.2	4.2
Papua New Guinea	-1.0 (2011)	4.9	5.1	2.8	0.8	3.0	2.2	4.4
Samoa	-6.6	3.3	5.9	1.4	5.6	1.0	-1.5	3.4
Solomon Islands[f,l]	-2.9	-3.0	0.5	-0.9	1.9	-0.4	1.3	-3.1
Tonga	3.0	1.8	1.3	8.5	6.7	1.7	1.9	7.2
Tuvalu	-5.9	4.0	3.5	4.5	3.3	3.6	0.6	5.8
Vanuatu	4.5	3.6	2.3	6.8	4.1	5.4	11.4	4.6
Developed ADB Member Economies								
Australia[m]	1.6	2.1	0.1	1.8	-0.0	2.0	3.1	1.8
Japan	-0.3	3.6	2.1	0.7	1.6	0.2	1.2	-0.0
New Zealand	1.0	-0.1	-0.6	2.2	-0.2	1.1	3.2	1.8

... = data not available, – = magnitude equals zero, 0.0 = magnitude is less than half of unit employed, ADB = Asian Development Bank.

Note: Data refer to the whole of each economy, unless otherwise indicated.

a For 2010 onward, growth rates were calculated using price indexes with base year 2007/2008 = 100 (for 2010–2019) and base year 2015/2016 = 100 (for 2020 and 2021) for food and nonalcoholic beverages only.
b For 2016 onward, excludes nonalcoholic beverages.
c Refers to food, nonalcoholic and alcoholic beverages, and tobacco.
d Refers to food (including fish) and nonalcoholic beverages. Data prior to 2004, featured in the Key Indicators Database, also include tobacco and narcotics.
e Includes alcoholic beverages, tobacco, and narcotics; and restaurants and hotels.
f Refers to capital city.
g For 2010–2018, data refer to Indonesia's consumer price index group "Foodstuff" consisting of cereals, cassava, and related products; meat and related products; fresh fish; preserved fish; eggs, milk, and related products; vegetables; beans and nuts; fruits; spices; fats and oils; and other food items. The group does not include alcoholic and nonalcoholic beverages. For 2019–2021, data refer to food, beverages, and tobacco. Both alcoholic and nonalcoholic beverages are included in this group.
h Refers to fruits and vegetables; meat, poultry, and fish; cereal products; soft drink and sweets; farm products; fats and oils; other food; and prepared food.
i Refers to the Tarawa Retail Price Index, which is based on data for South Tarawa, to represent all of Kiribati. Data refer to the weighted average of food and nonalcoholic drinks price indexes.
j Refers to food.
k For 2010, refers to food.
l For 2010–2017, excludes nonalcoholic beverages.
m Includes restaurants and hotels.

Source: Economies' official sources.

Table 2.3.3: Growth Rates of Wholesale and/or Producer Price Indexes
(%)

ADB Regional Member	2010	2015	2016	2017	2018	2019	2020	2021
Developing ADB Member Economies								
Central and West Asia								
Afghanistan	...	...	...	...	...	...	...	...
Armenia	22.6	-0.8	1.5	3.9	1.6	0.5	2.4	9.9
Azerbaijan	30.5	-30.6	27.5	36.8	26.0	3.2	-24.8	69.6
Georgia	11.3	7.5	-0.1	11.0	6.1	7.2	11.8	16.7
Kazakhstan	25.2	-20.5	16.8	15.3	19.0	5.1	-8.0	32.5
Kyrgyz Republic	22.8	8.8	6.4	1.7	1.5	4.3	21.3	11.5
Pakistan	13.8	-0.3	-1.1	4.5	5.3	16.0	10.2	9.4
Tajikistan	27.2	3.0	14.7	1.6	1.8	1.1	5.4	5.9
Turkmenistan	...	...	...	...	...	...	...	...
Uzbekistan	15.6	13.5	14.8	17.5	31.8	43.2	14.9	9.3
East Asia								
China, People's Republic of	5.5	-5.2	-1.4	6.3	3.5	-0.3	-1.8	8.1
Hong Kong, China	6.0	-2.7	1.3	3.8	2.0	1.0	2.3	1.2
Korea, Republic of	3.8	-4.0	-1.8	3.5	1.9	0.0	-0.5	6.4
Mongolia	...	...	-1.7	13.3	14.0	-1.4	-9.6	25.0
Taipei,China	5.5	-8.9	-3.0	0.9	3.6	-2.3	-7.8	9.5
South Asia								
Bangladesh[a]	8.9 (2006)	...	...	...	...	...	...	...
Bhutan	5.8 (2012)	0.6	1.2	5.8	4.7	-3.7	2.3	8.9
India	9.6	-3.7	1.7	2.9	4.3	1.7	1.3	13.0
Maldives	3.9	-2.4	...	...	...	...	...	...
Nepal	12.2	6.1	6.3	2.7	1.7	6.2	6.9	7.6
Sri Lanka	2.6	1.0	4.2	7.4	3.4	3.4	5.4	...
Southeast Asia								
Brunei Darussalam	...	...	...	...	...	...	...	...
Cambodia	...	...	...	...	...	...	...	...
Indonesia	4.9	4.4	7.9	4.6	5.5	0.9	1.3	2.6
Lao People's Democratic Republic	...	...	...	...	...	...	...	...
Malaysia	12.3 (2011)	-7.4	-1.1	6.7	-1.1	-1.4	-2.7	9.5
Myanmar	...	...	...	...	...	...	...	...
Philippines	5.9	1.6	0.9	1.9	1.9	1.6	2.5	3.1
Singapore	4.7	-15.3	-6.9	7.0	6.4	-3.3	-8.7	15.2
Thailand	9.4	-4.1	-1.2	0.7	0.5	-0.7	-1.6	4.7
Timor-Leste	...	...	...	...	...	...	...	...
Viet Nam	12.6	-0.6	-0.6	2.8	3.1	1.3	-0.6	2.9
The Pacific								
Cook Islands	...	...	...	...	...	...	...	...
Fiji	...	...	...	...	...	...	...	...
Kiribati	...	...	...	...	...	...	...	...
Marshall Islands	...	...	...	...	...	...	...	...
Micronesia, Federated States of	...	...	...	...	...	...	...	...
Nauru	...	...	...	...	...	...	...	...
Niue	...	...	...	...	...	...	...	...
Palau	...	...	...	...	...	...	...	...
Papua New Guinea	...	...	...	...	...	...	...	...
Samoa	...	...	...	...	...	...	...	...
Solomon Islands	...	...	...	...	...	...	...	...
Tonga	...	...	...	...	...	...	...	...
Tuvalu	...	...	...	...	...	...	...	...
Vanuatu	...	...	...	...	...	...	...	...
Developed ADB Member Economies								
Australia	-0.1	1.0	1.5	1.0	1.6	2.0	1.0	0.5
Japan	-0.1	-3.0	-3.5	2.3	2.6	-0.2	-2.3	4.8
New Zealand	2.3	-1.3	0.8	4.8	3.4	2.1	1.0	4.6

... = data not available, 0.0 = magnitude is less than half of unit employed, ADB = Asian Development Bank.

a For agricultural and industrial products only.

Source: Economies' official sources.

Table 2.3.4: Growth Rates of Gross Domestic Product Deflator
(%)

ADB Regional Member	2010	2015	2016	2017	2018	2019	2020	2021
Developing ADB Member Economies								
Central and West Asia								
Afghanistan	14.3	5.1	...	2.4	2.1	6.5	7.8	...
Armenia[a]	7.8	1.2	0.3	2.1	2.8	1.0	1.8	6.9
Azerbaijan	13.6	-8.9	14.7	16.2	12.2	-0.2	-7.6	21.2
Georgia	8.5	5.8	2.6	8.5	4.4	5.2	7.3	10.8
Kazakhstan	19.6	1.9	13.6	8.4	9.2	7.6	4.2	10.6
Kyrgyz Republic	10.0	3.4	6.1	6.3	3.4	-0.8	5.8	16.0
Pakistan	10.9	4.1	0.4	4.0	3.8	9.0	9.9	10.2
Tajikistan	12.4	5.5 (2014)	...	...	2.5	3.6	1.7	...
Turkmenistan	-2.5	-4.9	...	...	...	...	...	...
Uzbekistan	19.9	10.5	8.9	19.1	27.0	17.9	11.6	13.6
East Asia								
China, People's Republic of	6.9	0.1	1.4	4.2	3.5	1.3	0.5	4.4
Hong Kong, China	0.3	3.6	1.6	2.9	3.7	2.0	0.6	0.9
Korea, Republic of	2.7	3.2	2.0	2.2	0.5	-0.8	1.6	2.5
Mongolia	15.1 (2011)	7.4 (2014)	3.0	10.8	8.0	10.0	3.7	13.3
Taipei,China	-1.3	3.4	0.8	-0.8	-0.6	-0.2	1.3	3.0
South Asia								
Bangladesh	7.1	5.9	6.7	5.0	5.8	3.7	3.8	4.1
Bhutan	6.1	3.6	4.4	5.1	1.8	0.9	6.9	...
India	10.5	2.3	3.2	4.0	3.9	2.4	5.6	9.7
Maldives[b]	2.9	7.9	0.2	1.4	5.3	-2.6	-0.2	...
Nepal	14.4	4.5	7.1	7.0	3.1	4.3	5.6	3.9
Sri Lanka	7.3	3.0	5.4	5.5	4.3	3.9	3.1	8.1
Southeast Asia								
Brunei Darussalam	5.3	-17.6	-9.2	5.0	9.2	-3.3	-10.9	15.4
Cambodia	3.1	1.7	3.4	3.3	3.1	3.4	-0.7	1.3
Indonesia	7.3	4.0	2.4	4.3	3.8	1.6	-0.4	6.0
Lao People's Democratic Republic	3.1	2.3	3.0	1.9	1.9	1.2	2.8	3.6
Malaysia	5.4 (2011)	-0.4	1.7	3.8	0.6	0.1	-0.8	5.7
Myanmar	7.0	4.1	...	5.4	5.4	6.3	...	...
Philippines	4.4	-0.7	1.3	2.3	3.7	0.7	1.6	2.3
Singapore	1.1	3.1	0.4	2.8	3.5	-0.4	-3.0	4.0
Thailand	3.9	0.2	2.4	1.8	1.3	0.5	-1.2	1.9
Timor-Leste	11.0	7.2	0.1	1.0	-1.3	4.7	-19.3	...
Viet Nam	12.1	-0.2	1.1	4.1	3.4	1.8	1.3	2.8
The Pacific								
Cook Islands	1.9	6.4	-2.1	-0.2	2.0	-1.5	8.2	31.8
Fiji	2.5	2.5	2.6	1.7	1.4	2.4	...	...
Kiribati	0.8	4.6	6.4	2.5	1.6	-2.0	3.3	...
Marshall Islands	-0.7	-1.6	7.2	2.0	0.3	2.8	4.3	2.8
Micronesia, Federated States of	3.6	-5.3	4.0	7.5	9.4	1.5	0.5	...
Nauru	-18.1	-8.3	10.5	11.8	4.2	2.5	2.2	3.1
Niue	7.6	-0.3	0.5	1.9	11.2	...	...	...
Palau	-0.1	8.9	6.9	-1.1	-6.2	0.1	...	...
Papua New Guinea	10.0	-1.4	2.3	7.7	10.0	1.1	5.7	7.7
Samoa	4.1	4.4	1.1	1.4	-0.2	1.6	1.6	1.5
Solomon Islands	1.7	3.4	0.3	2.6	7.9	1.2	-1.3	...
Tonga	7.8	5.3	3.1	5.6	5.1	7.7	-3.6	...
Tuvalu	2.5	4.6	...	3.0	7.3	6.4	0.9	4.7
Vanuatu	1.5	5.9	1.6	5.4	3.2	3.3	...	...
Developed ADB Member Economies								
Australia	1.2	-0.6	-0.6	3.7	1.8	3.4	1.8	2.9
Japan	-1.9	2.1	0.4	-0.1	-0.0	0.6	0.9	-0.9
New Zealand	3.7	0.8	2.4	2.7	1.3	3.0	1.3	...

... = data not available, 0.0 = magnitude is less than half of unit employed, ADB = Asian Development Bank.

a For 2010, estimates are based on the 1993 System of National Accounts. For 2015 onward, estimates are based on the 2008 System of National Accounts.
b For 2010 onward, the gross domestic product (GDP) at current prices includes some product taxes that were not included in the calculation of GDP at constant prices, hence, the implicit GDP deflators may be overestimated.

Source: Economies' official sources.

Table 2.3.5: Growth Rates of Money Supply
(%)

ADB Regional Member	2010	2015	2016	2017	2018	2019	2020	2021
Developing ADB Member Economies								
Central and West Asia								
Afghanistan	39.3	3.7	9.7	4.1	2.6	5.7	12.1	...
Armenia	11.8	10.8	17.5	18.5	7.4	11.2	9.0	13.1
Azerbaijan[a]	24.3	-1.3	-1.9	9.0	5.7	20.0	1.1	18.7
Georgia[a]	30.1	17.3	21.1	14.6	13.9	17.6	24.6	11.4
Kazakhstan	23.1	8.0	46.2	7.5	7.1	11.0	19.2	24.1
Kyrgyz Republic	21.1	14.9	14.6	17.9	5.5	12.8	23.9	19.1
Pakistan	13.0	12.8	14.5	13.9	9.5	10.8	18.3	14.7
Tajikistan	18.6	18.7	37.1	21.8	5.1	17.0	18.4	8.2
Turkmenistan[a]	74.2	18.0	9.4	11.4	8.4	12.9	11.8	18.1
Uzbekistan	52.4	24.3	23.6	41.0	13.2	13.8	17.9	30.3
East Asia								
China, People's Republic of	18.9	13.3	11.3	9.0	8.1	8.7	10.1	9.0
Hong Kong, China	8.1	5.5	7.7	10.0	4.3	2.8	5.8	4.3
Korea, Republic of	6.0	8.2	7.1	5.1	6.7	7.9	9.8	12.9
Mongolia	62.5	-5.5	21.0	30.5	22.8	8.2	16.2	13.8
Taipei,China	5.5	5.8	3.6	3.6	2.7	4.5	9.4	7.4
South Asia								
Bangladesh	22.4	12.4	16.4	10.9	9.2	9.9	12.6	13.6
Bhutan	16.5	3.8	23.0	17.4	6.5	13.1	27.7	13.1
India[a]	16.1	10.1	10.1	9.2	10.5	8.9	12.2	8.8
Maldives	14.6	12.1	-0.2	5.2	3.4	9.5	14.2	26.7
Nepal	14.1	19.9	19.5	15.5	19.4	15.8	18.1	21.8
Sri Lanka	18.0	17.2	18.9	17.5	13.5	7.6	22.9	13.5
Southeast Asia								
Brunei Darussalam	4.8	-1.8	1.5	-0.4	2.8	4.3	-0.4	2.7
Cambodia	21.3	17.0	21.0	23.1	26.6	18.2	15.3	16.4
Indonesia	15.4	9.0	10.0	8.3	6.3	6.5	12.5	13.9
Lao People's Democratic Republic	39.5	14.7	10.9	12.2	8.4	18.9	16.3	24.0
Malaysia[a]	6.8	3.0	3.2	4.9	9.1	3.9	3.7	6.4
Myanmar	42.5	30.7	17.4	20.5	14.6	15.5	18.2	6.0
Philippines[a]	10.0	9.4	12.8	11.9	9.5	11.5	9.6	7.9
Singapore	8.6	1.5	8.0	3.2	3.9	5.0	13.2	...
Thailand	10.9	4.4	4.2	5.0	4.7	3.6	10.2	4.8
Timor-Leste	18.2	7.1	14.3	12.1	3.1	-7.1	10.2	28.7
Viet Nam	33.3	16.2	18.4	15.0	12.4	14.8	14.5	10.7
The Pacific								
Cook Islands	0.1	9.5	0.1	6.4	9.9	7.9	17.1	...
Fiji[a]	3.5	13.9	4.8	8.3	2.8	2.7	1.2	11.3
Kiribati	...	...	...	...	...	...	...	...
Marshall Islands	9.4	28.6	19.9	23.9	-3.3	-4.9	21.8	11.7
Micronesia, Federated States of	...	...	...	...	...	...	...	...
Nauru	...	...	...	...	...	...	...	...
Niue	...	...	...	...	...	...	...	...
Palau	12.0 (2011)	30.9	17.4	0.3	0.3	-3.2	10.3	...
Papua New Guinea[a]	11.4	8.0	10.9	-0.7	-4.0	4.4	7.0	11.7
Samoa	6.4	6.0	9.2	15.2	8.8	4.6	5.4	1.7
Solomon Islands[a]	13.3	15.5	13.4	3.5	6.8	-3.1	6.6	0.6
Tonga	5.1	9.3	16.7	13.7	7.6	4.4	1.1	26.0
Tuvalu	...	...	...	...	...	...	...	...
Vanuatu	1.3	11.4	10.6	9.3	13.1	7.0	-0.7	8.9
Developed ADB Member Economies								
Australia[a]	4.5	6.7	5.8	7.8	1.9	4.0	8.5	7.8
Japan[a]	1.9	2.5	3.2	2.9	2.2	2.0	7.7	3.3
New Zealand[b]	3.2	8.1	7.7	7.3	6.4	4.7	12.2	7.1

... = data not available, ADB = Asian Development Bank.

Note: Data are based on money supply M2 (M2), unless otherwise stated.

a Refers to money supply M3 (M3).
b Refers to money supply M3 (M3), except for 2016–2021 (M2).

Source: Economies' official sources.

Table 2.3.6: Money Supply
(% of GDP)

ADB Regional Member	2010	2015	2016	2017	2018	2019	2020	2021
Developing ADB Member Economies								
Central and West Asia								
Afghanistan	30.3	29.7	37.2	36.9	36.6	35.0	37.9	...
Armenia	26.3	36.8	43.0	46.4	46.1	47.2	54.4	54.5
Azerbaijan[a]	24.8	39.1	34.6	32.4	30.0	35.2	40.3	37.3
Georgia[a]	28.4	38.7	44.3	44.7	46.5	49.5	61.5	...
Kazakhstan	30.1	21.0	26.8	24.9	23.4	23.1	27.1	28.9
Kyrgyz Republic	31.4	33.3	34.4	36.5	35.8	37.2	47.4	47.0
Pakistan	37.7	40.2	38.6	40.5	40.2	39.8	43.4	42.4
Tajikistan	18.0	21.2	27.0	28.0	26.7	28.0	31.3	28.7
Turkmenistan[a]	17.3	48.2	...	...	...	...	...	...
Uzbekistan	17.7	18.4	19.7	22.3	18.9	17.2	17.9	19.1
East Asia								
China, People's Republic of	176.1	202.1	207.7	203.1	198.7	201.4	215.8	208.4
Hong Kong, China	401.7	484.4	502.2	517.2	506.0	518.3	583.3	567.1
Korea, Republic of	125.5	135.5	138.3	137.8	142.3	151.4	164.9	174.4
Mongolia	48.0	43.9	50.8	56.6	59.8	55.7	65.4	64.8
Taipei,China	220.2	233.9	235.3	237.8	238.9	242.7	253.5	248.2
South Asia								
Bangladesh	45.5	52.0	44.2	43.7	42.1	41.3	43.3	44.2
Bhutan	72.2	59.2	64.6	68.9	70.0	74.2	98.6	111.5
India[a]	85.2	84.4	83.1	81.7	81.7	83.7	95.2	87.5
Maldives	47.9	48.3	45.2	43.9	40.4	41.8	71.9	68.1
Nepal	60.3	77.5	86.1	84.2	89.5	92.8	108.1	120.8
Sri Lanka	27.3	35.1	37.6	39.4	41.9	43.4	53.6	54.5
Southeast Asia								
Brunei Darussalam	67.3	80.8	92.6	86.7	81.6	84.7	93.6	84.8
Cambodia	41.6	72.4	79.2	88.2	100.7	107.7	128.9	143.8
Indonesia	36.0	39.5	40.4	39.9	38.8	38.8	44.7	46.4
Lao People's Democratic Republic	38.0	51.2	51.5	53.1	53.1	59.1	64.8	75.0
Malaysia[a]	132.2	136.3	132.5	126.5	130.9	130.1	144.1	140.6
Myanmar	23.6	46.4	53.4	57.7	58.9	60.0	...	...
Philippines[a]	47.7	60.5	62.8	64.2	63.7	66.5	79.3	79.1
Singapore	123.3	122.9	127.6	122.4	118.5	123.5	150.3	137.7
Thailand	109.0	127.7	125.4	124.0	122.8	123.4	146.7	148.7
Timor-Leste[b]	33.5	40.3	44.5	50.9	53.6	38.5	39.9	...
Viet Nam	129.3	143.6	158.3	163.7	166.2	175.1	192.4	159.6
The Pacific								
Cook Islands	83.1	59.3	57.7	56.2	57.3	59.9	86.8	...
Fiji[a]	67.6	73.3	73.0	73.8	72.1	72.8	89.9	103.9
Kiribati	...	...	...	...	...	...	...	...
Marshall Islands	63.0	82.8	91.4	106.7	99.3	87.2	104.1	110.6
Micronesia, Federated States of	...	...	...	...	...	...	...	...
Nauru	...	...	...	...	...	...	...	...
Niue	...	...	...	...	...	...	...	...
Palau	46.2	72.2	79.7	82.4	83.4	82.1	102.0	...
Papua New Guinea[a]	34.0	33.6	34.5	30.7	26.9	26.5	29.3	28.6
Samoa	43.8	41.1	42.5	48.5	51.3	51.4	59.3	60.8
Solomon Islands[a]	28.6	40.4	43.2	42.3	40.8	38.4	42.9	43.0
Tonga	41.2	47.5	50.5	52.6	53.6	51.6	53.8	...
Tuvalu	...	...	...	...	...	...	...	...
Vanuatu	87.0	81.7	85.0	82.9	88.3	88.6	91.3	...
Developed ADB Member Economies								
Australia[a]	94.3	109.5	113.4	115.2	112.1	110.3	117.7	121.4
Japan[a]	216.6	232.5	237.1	240.2	244.0	248.0	277.1	284.2
New Zealand[c]	111.6	121.6	102.3	102.2	102.9	101.9	112.9	115.6

... = data not available, ADB = Asian Development Bank, GDP = gross domestic product.

Note: Data are based on money supply M2 (M2), unless otherwise stated.

a Refers to money supply M3 (M3).
b From September 2019, oil revenue from the Joint Petroleum Development Area is now included in GDP based on the new Timor-Leste Australia Maritime Boundary Treaty.
c Refers to money supply M3 (M3), except for 2016–2021 (M2).

Source: Economies' official sources.

Table 2.3.7: Interest Rates on Savings and Time Deposits
(% per annum, period averages)

ADB Regional Member	Savings Deposits								Time Deposits[a]							
	2010	2015	2016	2017	2018	2019	2020	2021	2010	2015	2016	2017	2018	2019	2020	2021
Developing ADB Member Economies																
Central and West Asia																
Afghanistan	5.4	3.1	1.6	1.3	1.6	1.5	0.8	...	8.2	5.2	4.4	3.1	2.3	3.4	2.4	...
Armenia	...	...	...	...	...	...	...	...	10.7	15.4	12.5	9.6	9.4	9.3	9.2	9.2
Azerbaijan	...	...	...	...	...	...	...	...	11.0	8.2	5.5	12.1	9.8	9.4	8.6	8.8
Georgia[b]	8.7	5.3	4.5	4.0	4.3	4.7	5.2	4.9	11.6	7.0	6.7	6.1	5.8	5.7	6.6	6.6
Kazakhstan[c]	...	...	...	...	...	...	...	...	9.8	7.5	11.4	11.2	10.5	9.1	8.6	8.3
Kyrgyz Republic	...	...	...	...	...	...	...	...	11.5	14.5	13.3	10.8	10.3	9.5	9.8	11.0
Pakistan	5.0	4.7	3.7	3.5	4.1	8.6	5.9	5.0	7.2	5.9	4.7	4.3	4.6	8.0	6.2	5.2
Tajikistan	3.8	0.9	1.2	1.4	1.1	0.6	1.0	0.9	17.8	15.6	16.4	14.6	12.8	11.6	10.7	11.5
Turkmenistan	...	...	...	...	...	...	...	...	11.3 (2004)	...	...	...	...	...	...	...
Uzbekistan[d]	...	16.5	18.1	18.0	15.9	18.3	18.6	19.4	...	18.3	18.7	18.5	16.4	18.6	19.2	18.7
East Asia																
China, People's Republic of	0.4	0.4	0.4	0.4	0.4	0.4	0.4	0.4	2.3	2.1	1.5	1.5	1.5	1.5	1.5	1.5
Hong Kong, China	0.0	0.0	0.0	0.0	0.0	0.1	0.0	0.0	0.2	0.1	0.1	0.2	0.2	0.3	0.2	0.1
Korea, Republic of[e]	3.2	1.7	1.5	1.5	1.8	1.7	1.0	1.1	3.9	1.8	1.6	1.7	2.0	1.9	1.2	1.2
Mongolia[f]	10.7	13.0	12.4	13.0	11.2	10.5	8.4	5.8	...	...	...	9.8	10.2	10.9	8.8	6.2
Taipei,China	0.2	0.3	0.3	0.2	0.2	0.2	0.1	0.1	1.0	1.3	1.1	1.1	1.1	1.1	0.8	0.8
South Asia																
Bangladesh[g]	4.9	4.5	3.6	3.2	3.3	3.3	2.8	2.2	9.0	9.0	7.3	6.4	7.4	8.2	6.5	5.7
Bhutan[h]	4.8	5.3	5.3	5.5	5.3	5.4	5.4	5.3	6.8	6.8	7.0	7.0	7.8	7.8	7.6	7.8
India	3.5	4.0	4.0	...	...	...	...	...	7.5	6.2	5.5	...	...	...	...	...
Maldives[i]	2.3	2.2	1.7	1.5	1.5	1.5	1.5	1.5	4.3	4.0	3.4	3.5	3.7	3.3	3.8	3.6
Nepal	7.0	2.9	2.2	4.0	4.6	5.0	4.2	3.0	8.1	6.5	5.8	10.4	10.4	9.8	9.0	7.3
Sri Lanka	5.0	5.0	4.3	4.0	4.0	4.0	3.5	3.5	8.5	7.3	11.0	11.0	10.5	9.8	5.3	5.5
Southeast Asia																
Brunei Darussalam	0.4	0.3	0.3	0.3	0.3	0.3	0.1	0.1	0.7	0.8	0.7	0.7	0.8	0.8	0.3	0.2
Cambodia	1.2	1.2	1.5	1.2	0.6	0.6	0.6	1.0	6.6	7.4	7.4	6.4	6.2	6.3	6.3	6.2
Indonesia	3.9	1.7	1.5	1.5	1.3	1.1	0.8	0.7	7.9	8.5	7.3	6.8	6.5	6.8	5.7	3.8
Lao People's Democratic Republic	3.4	2.6	1.8	1.7	1.8	1.8	1.7	1.7	9.1	7.6	5.6	5.4	5.4	5.4	5.4	5.3
Malaysia	0.9	1.1	1.0	1.0	1.0	1.0	0.6	0.5	2.8	3.3	3.2	3.1	3.3	3.2	2.1	1.7
Myanmar	...	...	...	10.0	10.0	10.0	6.2	5.0	...	...	...	8.0	8.0	8.0	5.8	5.0
Philippines[j]	1.6	0.7	0.7	0.7	0.9	1.2	...	...	2.1	3.1	3.0	2.8	3.5	4.6	...	...
Singapore	0.1	0.1	0.1	0.2	0.2	0.2	0.1	0.2	0.5	0.3	0.4	0.3	0.5	0.6	0.3	0.3
Thailand	0.5	0.5	0.5	0.5	0.5	0.5	0.3	0.3	1.6	1.4	1.4	1.4	1.4	1.3	0.5	0.5
Timor-Leste	0.8	0.8	0.8	0.4	0.4	0.5	0.5	...	1.3	1.3	1.2	0.7	0.7	0.7	0.6	...
Viet Nam[k]	3.0	0.7	0.6	0.6	0.5	0.5	0.2	0.1	11.5	6.3	6.8	6.9	7.1	7.3	6.8	5.5
The Pacific																
Cook Islands	...	...	...	...	...	...	...	...	...	...	...	...	...	...	...	...
Fiji	1.0	0.9	0.9	1.2	1.3	1.1	0.9	0.5	5.6	2.6	2.9	3.2	3.4	4.6	3.3	2.3
Kiribati	...	...	...	...	...	...	...	...	...	...	...	...	...	...	...	...
Marshall Islands	0.5	0.3	0.2	0.2	0.2	0.2	0.2	0.1	3.5	1.5	1.5	1.3	1.1	0.9	0.8	0.7
Micronesia, Federated States of	...	...	...	...	...	...	...	...	...	...	...	...	...	...	...	...
Nauru	...	...	...	...	...	...	...	...	...	...	...	...	...	...	...	...
Niue	...	...	...	...	...	...	...	...	...	...	...	...	...	...	...	...
Palau	0.9	0.1	0.1	0.1	0.1	0.1	...	...	0.8	0.2	0.2	0.2	0.4	0.4	...	...
Papua New Guinea	1.0	0.4	0.6	0.5	0.7	1.0	0.9	0.3	4.8	2.1	2.0	2.0	2.0	1.3	0.1	1.5
Samoa	1.0	1.0	1.0	1.0	1.0	1.0	1.0	1.0	2.9	2.9	2.9	2.9	2.9	2.9	2.9	2.9
Solomon Islands	0.3	0.3	0.3	0.3	0.4	0.6	0.5	0.3	5.0	0.7	0.9	1.0	1.3	1.5	1.6	1.2
Tonga	1.5	2.5	2.5	2.4	2.4	2.5	2.6	...	3.0	4.9	5.3	5.4	5.2	4.8	4.8	...
Tuvalu	...	...	...	...	...	...	...	...	...	...	...	...	...	...	...	...
Vanuatu	...	...	...	...	...	...	...	...	...	...	...	...	...	...	...	...
Developed ADB Member Economies																
Australia[l]	4.5	2.0	1.6	1.7	1.0	0.6	0.2	0.1	6.0	2.5	2.4	2.3	2.2	1.8	0.8	0.3
Japan[m]	0.0	0.0	0.0	0.0	0.0	0.0	0.0	0.0	0.1	0.1	0.0	0.0	0.0	0.0	0.0	0.0
New Zealand[n]	...	...	...	...	...	...	...	...	4.7	3.3	3.3	3.3	3.3	2.6	0.8	1.5

... = data not available, 0.0 = magnitude is less than half of unit employed, ADB = Asian Development Bank.

a Refers to interest rate on time deposits of 12 months, unless otherwise indicated.
b Refers to deposits allocated with maturity of more than 1 year.
c Refers to interest rates on deposits of more than 12 months.
d Refers to weighted average interest rate on all time household savings deposits and time deposits from 181 to 365 days.
e Refers to weighted averages of interest rates on newly extended time and savings deposits of commercial and specialized banks.
f Rates for savings deposits include both demand and time deposits. Rates for time deposits refer to the time deposit rate.
g Refers to savings bank accounts with checking facilities.
h For savings deposits, actual range of rates for 2015–2016 is 5.0%–7.0%; for 2017, 5.0%–6.0%; for 2019 and 2020, 5.0%–5.75%; and for 2021, from 5.0% to 5.6%. For time deposits, rate refers to fixed deposits of 1 year to less than 2 years for 2010 and actual range of rates is 4.5%–6.5%; for 2015–2017, 6.5%–7.5%; for 2018 and 2019, 6.0%–9.5%; for 2020, 6.0%–9.1%; and for 2021, 6.5%–9.1%.
i Refers to time deposits of 6 months to 1 year (local currency). Figures represent a weighted average.
j Rates for savings deposits refer to the annual percentage equivalent of commercial banks' actual monthly interest expenses on peso-savings deposits to the total outstanding levels of these deposits. Rates for time deposits refer to rates charged on interest-bearing deposits with maturities of over 1 year.
k For 2010, the rate for time deposit refers to maximum interest per annum for state enterprise deposits.
l Refers to interest rates of online savings deposits.
m Refers to savings deposits of at least ¥0.3 million, calculated as the arithmetic average of weekly figures. Refers to time deposits from 12 months to less than 2 years, calculated as the arithmetic average of the monthly figures.
n Refers to interest rate on time deposits of 6 months.

Sources: Economies' official sources. For the People's Republic of China: CEIC Database. https://www.ceicdata.com/en (accessed 8 July 2022).

Table 2.3.8: Yield on Short-Term Treasury Bills and Lending Interest Rates
(% per annum, period averages)

ADB Regional Member	Yield on Short-Term Treasury Bills[a]				Lending Interest Rates			
	2010	2015	2020	2021	2010	2015	2020	2021
Developing ADB Member Economies								
Central and West Asia								
Afghanistan	...	...	...	...	15.6	15.0	...	...
Armenia[b]	10.6	12.9	5.8	7.8	19.2	17.6	11.6	11.8
Azerbaijan	1.8	13.0 (2016)	...	...	20.7	17.5	17.2	16.4
Georgia	9.6	8.8	8.6	8.9	15.8	12.5	11.8	12.5
Kazakhstan[c]	3.2	4.0	10.7	9.6	...	...	...	...
Kyrgyz Republic	10.4	12.8	5.9	7.1	23.7	23.6	17.0	16.6
Pakistan[d]	12.5	7.1	8.6	7.6	14.0	10.2	10.8	8.7
Tajikistan[e]	6.7	0.8	...	...	23.4	25.8	23.5 (2019)	...
Turkmenistan	...	...	...	...	...	...	...	...
Uzbekistan	...	...	13.9	13.3	...	13.8	22.3	21.4
East Asia								
China, People's Republic of[f]	2.6	4.8 (2014)	...	...	5.8	4.4	4.4	4.4
Hong Kong, China[g]	0.2	0.0	0.4	0.0	5.0	5.0	5.0	5.0
Korea, Republic of[h]	2.7	1.8	0.9	0.9	5.5	3.5	2.8	2.9
Mongolia[i]	12.9 (2012)	14.5	...	...	20.1	19.6	16.9	...
Taipei,China[j]	0.3	0.4	0.3	0.2	2.7	2.8	2.4	2.4
South Asia								
Bangladesh[e]	4.5	5.8	4.8	1.3	12.2	11.7	8.3	7.3
Bhutan[e]	2.0	0.1	2.8	0.4	13.9	14.9	14.0	14.0
India[e,k]	6.2	7.4	3.3	3.5	8.3	10.0	9.2	8.7
Maldives[l]	4.9	6.8	3.5	3.5	10.4	11.1	11.6	11.6
Nepal[e]	6.9	0.7	1.9	3.1	...	...	...	...
Sri Lanka[m]	8.6	6.7	9.1 (2019)	...	10.2	7.0	11.2 (2019)	...
Southeast Asia								
Brunei Darussalam	...	...	...	...	5.5	5.5	5.5	5.5
Cambodia	...	...	...	...	...	...	...	...
Indonesia	7.0	8.3	5.5	3.7	13.3	12.7	9.5	8.9
Lao People's Democratic Republic[n]	8.0	...	...	...	22.6	...	...	...
Malaysia	2.6	3.1	2.0	1.8	5.0	4.6	3.9	3.4
Myanmar	...	...	...	...	20.9	16.0	14.8	...
Philippines[e]	3.5	1.7	2.0	1.1	7.7	5.6	7.1 (2019)	...
Singapore	0.3	0.3 (2013)	...	...	5.4	5.4	5.3	5.3
Thailand[e]	1.4	1.6	0.6	0.4	4.3	4.7	3.3	3.1
Timor-Leste	...	...	...	...	11.0 (2011)	13.5	14.1	11.2
Viet Nam[o]	11.1	4.2	...	...	13.1	7.1	7.6	7.8
The Pacific								
Cook Islands	...	...	...	...	...	...	...	...
Fiji[e]	3.4	1.2	1.8	0.6	7.5	5.8	6.2	5.9
Kiribati	...	...	...	...	...	...	...	...
Marshall Islands	...	...	...	...	...	...	...	...
Micronesia, Federated States of	...	...	...	...	15.1	15.7	14.5	...
Nauru	...	...	...	...	...	...	...	...
Niue	...	...	...	...	...	...	...	...
Palau	...	...	...	...	...	...	...	...
Papua New Guinea[p]	4.6	5.3	6.1 (2019)	...	10.4	8.7	8.7 (2019)	...
Samoa	...	...	...	...	10.7	9.5	8.7	8.5
Solomon Islands[e]	3.7	0.5	0.5	0.5	14.4	10.5	10.7	5.2
Tonga	...	...	...	...	9.9 (2012)	8.2	7.8	7.8
Tuvalu	...	...	...	...	...	...	...	...
Vanuatu	...	...	...	...	5.5	3.6	2.1	...
Developed ADB Member Economies								
Australia[q]	4.7	2.3	0.3	0.0	7.3	5.6	5.1 (2019)	...
Japan	0.4	0.2	-0.0	-0.1	1.6	1.1	...	...
New Zealand	2.8	3.0	0.4	0.4	6.3	5.8	– (2018)	...

... = data not available, – = magnitude equals zero, 0.0 = magnitude is less than half of unit employed, ADB = Asian Development Bank.

a Refers to 3-month Treasury bills, unless otherwise indicated.
b Refers to average yield on 9-month to 12-month Treasury bills since March 2001.
c Refers to short-term Treasury bills with maturities of 3, 6, 9, and 12 months.
d Refers to weighted average yield on 6-month Treasury securities.
e Refers to 91-day Treasury bills.
f Refers to 3-month Treasury bonds trading rate.
g Refers to annualized yields on 91-day Exchange Fund bills.
h Refers to 91-day certificates of deposit.
i Refers to weighted average rate on Treasury bills of all maturities. From December 2012 onward, refers to yield on 12-week Treasury bills.
j Refers to prime lending rates.
k Figures are for fiscal year ending March.
l Refers to rate on 28-day Treasury bills.
m Refers to weighted average rate on the last monthly issuance of 364-day Treasury bills since December 2001.
n Refers to weighted average auction rate for 12-month Treasury bills.
o Refers to average monthly yield on 360-day Treasury bills sold at auction.
p Refers to rate on 182-day Treasury bills.
q Refers to estimated closing yield in the secondary market on 13-week Treasury notes.

Sources: International Monetary Fund. International Financial Statistics. http://data.imf.org/ (accessed 6 July 2022); and Organisation for Economic Co-operation and Development. Main Economic Indicators. https://stats.oecd.org/ (accessed 6 July 2022). For Bhutan; India; Kazakhstan; and Taipei,China: Economies' official sources. For Malaysia for 2017–2021: Bank Negara Malaysia. Monthly Highlights and Statistics. https://www.bnm.gov.my/-/monthly-highlights-statistics-in-may-2022 (accessed 6 July 2022).

Table 2.3.9: Domestic Credit Provided by Banking Sector, and Bank Nonperforming Loans

ADB Regional Member	Domestic Credit Provided by Banking Sector[a] (% of GDP)					Bank Nonperforming Loans[b] (% of total gross loans)					
	2010	2015	2018	2019	2020	2010	2015	2018	2019	2020	2021
Developing ADB Member Economies											
Central and West Asia											
Afghanistan	...	...	...	...	...	49.9	12.1	8.9	...	...	...
Armenia	27.8	48.3	62.4	65.4	83.4	3.0	7.9	4.8	5.5	6.6	...
Azerbaijan	...	28.1 (2016)	13.1	14.6	15.4	...	...	...	...	...	...
Georgia	33.8	53.8	66.3	70.9	83.3	5.9	2.7	2.7	1.9	2.3	1.9
Kazakhstan	...	45.7	36.3	35.0	40.2	20.9	8.0	7.4	8.1	6.9	...
Kyrgyz Republic	...	...	...	...	...	14.8	6.7	7.3	7.7	10.1	10.8
Pakistan	...	...	...	...	...	14.7	11.4	8.0	8.6	9.2	7.9
Tajikistan	7.6	19.7	15.3	15.5	13.6	6.1	26.3	31.1	27.0	23.8	13.7
Turkmenistan	...	...	...	...	...	...	...	...	...	...	...
Uzbekistan	...	...	...	...	...	1.0	1.5	1.3	1.5	2.1	5.1
East Asia											
China, People's Republic of	...	...	...	...	...	1.1	1.7	1.8	1.9	1.8	...
Hong Kong, China	...	...	...	...	...	0.8	0.7	0.5	0.6	0.9	...
Korea, Republic of	...	...	...	...	...	0.6	0.5	0.3	0.3	0.2	...
Mongolia	...	...	...	...	...	...	...	...	...	...	...
Taipei,China	0.9	...	...	...	...	0.6	0.2	0.2	0.2	0.2	0.2
South Asia											
Bangladesh	...	...	...	...	...	1.9 (2011)	8.4	9.9	8.9	7.7	...
Bhutan	...	...	...	...	...	5.2	6.6	7.0	8.4	...	...
India	...	...	...	...	...	2.7 (2011)	5.9	9.5	9.2	7.9	...
Maldives	76.9	61.3	64.7	64.9	124.9	20.9 (2012)	14.1	8.9	9.4	8.3	...
Nepal	...	...	...	...	...	...	1.7 (2016)	1.6	1.7	1.7	...
Sri Lanka	...	...	...	...	...	3.8 (2011)	3.2	3.4	4.7	4.9	...
Southeast Asia											
Brunei Darussalam	22.7	40.0	27.7	29.5	66.1	6.9	4.0	3.9	3.9	3.9	3.1
Cambodia	...	...	...	...	...	3.1	1.6	2.0	1.6	1.8	1.7
Indonesia	34.2	46.8	47.2	46.5	53.7	2.3	2.3	2.2	2.3	2.6	2.6
Lao People's Democratic Republic	...	...	...	...	...	...	...	...	...	...	...
Malaysia	...	...	...	...	...	3.4	1.6	1.5	1.5	1.6	1.4
Myanmar	...	...	...	...	...	...	...	...	...	...	...
Philippines	...	82.3 (2017)	82.9	86.5	100.3	3.3	1.9	1.7	2.0	3.5	...
Singapore	...	...	...	...	...	1.4	0.9	1.3	1.3	...	...
Thailand	133.4	171.2	166.4	169.0	194.8	3.9	2.7	3.1	3.1	3.2	...
Timor-Leste	...	...	...	...	...	...	...	...	...	...	...
Viet Nam	...	...	...	...	...	2.1	2.8	2.1	1.8	1.9	...
The Pacific											
Cook Islands	...	...	...	...	...	...	...	...	...	...	...
Fiji	131.7	111.4	124.7	135.3	169.5	4.4	1.4	3.1	3.8	6.2	...
Kiribati	...	...	...	...	...	...	...	...	...	...	...
Marshall Islands	...	...	...	...	...	...	...	...	...	...	...
Micronesia, Federated States of	...	...	...	...	...	...	0.2	0.3	0.3	0.1	...
Nauru	...	...	...	...	...	...	...	...	...	...	...
Niue	...	...	...	...	...	...	...	...	...	...	...
Palau	...	...	...	...	...	...	...	...	...	...	...
Papua New Guinea	23.7	40.5	36.5	37.3	40.3	1.9	3.1	3.7	3.8	5.3	6.2
Samoa	61.5	75.8	80.3	82.5	82.3	...	3.7 (2016)	3.6	4.0	3.8	...
Solomon Islands	21.5	21.5	25.0	26.4	27.3	9.3	4.1	7.1	10.4	10.8	...
Tonga	...	...	...	...	...	14.4 (2012)	7.7	3.6	3.2	3.7	...
Tuvalu	...	...	...	...	...	...	...	...	...	...	...
Vanuatu	...	...	...	...	...	4.8	12.3	15.0 (2017)	...	...	...
Developed ADB Member Economies											
Australia	...	...	...	...	...	2.1	0.9	0.9	1.0	1.1	0.9
Japan	311.5	339.3	348.4	359.7	390.6	...	...	...	...	...	...
New Zealand	...	160.1	163.5	167.5	185.7	...	...	...	...	...	...

... = data not available, ADB = Asian Development Bank, GDP = gross domestic product.

a Domestic credit provided by the financial sector includes all credit to various sectors on a gross basis, with the exception of credit to the central government, which is net. The financial sector includes monetary authorities and deposit money banks, as well as other financial corporations where data are available (including corporations that do not accept transferable deposits, but do incur such liabilities as time and savings deposits). Examples of other financial corporations are finance and leasing companies, money lenders, insurance corporations, pension funds, and foreign exchange companies.

b Bank nonperforming loans to total gross loans are the value of nonperforming loans divided by the total value of the loan portfolio (including nonperforming loans before the deduction of specific loan-loss provisions). The loan amount recorded as nonperforming should be the gross value of the loan as recorded on the balance sheet, not just the amount that is overdue.

Sources: World Bank. World Development Indicators. https://databank.worldbank.org/source/world-development-indicators (accessed 7 July 2022). For Taipei,China: Central bank of Taipei,China. http://www.cbc.gov.tw (accessed 7 July 2022).

Table 2.3.10: Growth Rates of Stock Market Price Index
(%)

ADB Regional Member	2010	2015	2016	2017	2018	2019	2020	2021
Developing ADB Member Economies								
Central and West Asia								
Afghanistan	...	...	...	...	...	...	...	...
Armenia	...	...	...	...	...	...	...	...
Azerbaijan	...	...	...	...	...	...	...	...
Georgia	...	...	...	...	...	...	...	...
Kazakhstan	...	...	...	...	...	...	...	...
Kyrgyz Republic	...	...	...	...	...	...	...	...
Pakistan[a]	28.2	2.1	45.7	...	...	...	...	...
Tajikistan	...	...	...	...	...	...	...	...
Turkmenistan	...	...	...	...	...	...	...	...
Uzbekistan	...	...	...	-0.5	0.7	-42.7	8.6	40.0
East Asia								
China, People's Republic of	3.4	66.0	-19.0	6.7	...	...	...	...
Hong Kong, China	19.3	4.8	-12.0	22.3	10.2	-4.3	-8.4	7.3
Korea, Republic of	23.6	1.4	-1.2	16.5	0.5	-9.4	5.4	40.1
Mongolia	88.7	-14.6	-14.0	33.5	30.5	-0.8	-13.0	...
Taipei,China	23.1	-0.4	-2.2	16.5	4.0	1.6	11.9	40.3
South Asia								
Bangladesh[a]	82.8	-4.8	8.8	24.0	-13.8	-17.3	21.3	25.1
Bhutan	...	...	...	...	...	...	...	...
India	29.8	10.9	-3.6	8.6	...	...	...	...
Maldives	-20.4	8.9	4.8	7.4	6.8	5.2	7.7	0.0
Nepal	...	...	...	...	...	...	...	...
Sri Lanka[a]	96.0	-5.5	-9.7	2.3	-5.0	1.3	...	...
Southeast Asia								
Brunei Darussalam	...	...	...	...	...	...	...	...
Cambodia	...	...	...	...	...	...	...	...
Indonesia[a]	46.1	-12.1	15.3	20.0	-2.5	1.7	-5.1	10.1
Lao People's Democratic Republic	...	...	...	...	...	...	...	...
Malaysia	27.1	-6.1	-3.8	5.0	2.2	-8.4	-7.3	3.3
Myanmar	...	...	...	...	...	...	...	...
Philippines	43.1	5.5	0.9	8.0	0.1	2.8	-21.1	8.5
Singapore	30.3	-2.5	-11.6	10.3	...	...	...	...
Thailand	45.6	0.2	-2.1	12.7	6.6	-4.7	-18.1	17.6
Timor-Leste	...	...	...	...	...	...	...	...
Viet Nam[a]	12.2	6.1	14.8	...	...	...	...	...
The Pacific								
Cook Islands	...	...	...	...	...	...	...	...
Fiji	-11.1	22.0	26.4	22.4	57.6	45.0	1.5	-11.2
Kiribati	...	...	...	...	...	...	...	...
Marshall Islands	...	...	...	...	...	...	...	...
Micronesia, Federated States of	...	...	...	...	...	...	...	...
Nauru	...	...	...	...	...	...	...	...
Niue	...	...	...	...	...	...	...	...
Palau	...	...	...	...	...	...	...	...
Papua New Guinea	26.2	-6.3	...	...	7.5	-2.9	...	...
Samoa	...	...	...	...	...	...	...	...
Solomon Islands	...	...	...	...	...	...	...	...
Tonga	...	...	...	...	...	...	...	...
Tuvalu	...	...	...	...	...	...	...	...
Vanuatu	...	...	...	...	...	...	...	...
Developed ADB Member Economies								
Australia[a]	-2.6	-2.1	7.0	7.0	-6.9	...	...	...
Japan	2.0	22.7	-12.6	...	...	...	...	...
New Zealand	9.7	12.7	17.4	11.1	14.8	18.0	12.3	10.8

... = data not available, 0.0 = magnitude is less than half of unit employed, ADB = Asian Development Bank.

Note: All data in the table refer to growth rates of stock market prices (period average), unless otherwise indicated.
a Refers to growth rates of end-of-period stock market prices.

Sources: Asian Development Bank estimates using data from the International Monetary Fund's International Financial Statistics. http://data.imf.org/IFS (accessed 8 July 2022). For Taipei,China: Annual statistics from the stock exchange corporation in Taipei,China. http://www.twse.com.tw/en/statistics/ (accessed 8 July 2022).

Table 2.3.11: Stock Market Capitalization

ADB Regional Member	Stock Market Capitalization ($ million)							Stock Market Capitalization (% of GDP)						
	2010	2015	2016	2017	2018	2019	2020	2010	2015	2016	2017	2018	2019	2020
Developing ADB Member Economies														
Central and West Asia														
Afghanistan	...	...	...	...	...	...	...	...	...	...	...	...	...	...
Armenia	...	...	...	...	...	...	...	...	...	...	...	...	...	...
Azerbaijan	...	...	...	...	...	...	...	...	...	...	...	...	...	...
Georgia	...	...	...	...	...	...	...	...	...	...	...	...	...	...
Kazakhstan	26,672.7	34,891.9	40,161.2	45,558.3	37,005.3	44,972.4	45,202.4	18.0	18.9	29.3	27.3	20.6	24.8	26.4
Kyrgyz Republic	...	...	...	...	...	...	...	...	...	...	...	...	...	...
Pakistan	38,007.2	...	...	...	...	...	...	21.5	...	...	...	...	...	...
Tajikistan	...	...	...	...	...	...	...	...	...	...	...	...	...	...
Turkmenistan	...	...	...	...	...	...	...	...	...	...	...	...	...	...
Uzbekistan	...	...	...	...	...	...	...	...	...	...	...	...	...	...
East Asia														
China, People's Republic of	4,027,840.3	8,188,019.3	7,320,738.4	8,711,267.2	6,324,879.8	8,515,504.4	12,214,465.6	66.2	74.0	65.2	70.8	45.5	59.6	83.2
Hong Kong, China	2,711,316.2	3,184,874.2	3,193,235.5	4,350,514.6	3,819,215.4	4,899,234.6	6,130,420.4	1,185.9	1,029.4	995.2	1,274.8	1,055.8	1,349.5	1,777.5
Korea, Republic of	1,091,911.5	1,231,199.8	1,254,541.2	1,771,767.9	1,413,716.5	1,484,840.3	2,176,189.5	95.4	84.0	83.6	109.1	82.0	89.9	132.9
Mongolia	...	...	...	...	...	...	...	...	...	...	...	...	...	...
Taipei,China	752,520.1	768,179.4	843,120.6	1,045,758.6	972,241.3	1,177,469.7	1,518,132.7	169.4	143.7	155.2	177.0	159.6	192.6	226.8
South Asia														
Bangladesh	41,616.9	65,484.9	70,419.4	86,178.8	77,390.5	64,416.5	89,773.7	36.1	33.6	26.5	29.3	24.1	18.3	24.0
Bhutan	219.0	374.0	338.5	392.8	515.1	730.1	640.4	14.1	18.7	15.7	16.0	21.1	28.8	27.7
India	1,762,461.9	1,745,169.2	1,746,297.4	2,555,988.8	2,282,310.5	2,286,924.5	2,595,465.6	105.2	83.0	76.1	96.4	84.4	80.8	97.3
Maldives	...	...	...	...	...	...	...	...	...	...	...	...	...	...
Nepal	...	...	...	...	...	...	...	...	...	...	...	...	...	...
Sri Lanka	19,923.9	20,804.1	18,678.8	18,959.5	15,575.0	15,720.5	15,981.9	35.1	25.8	22.7	21.7	17.7	18.7	19.7
Southeast Asia														
Brunei Darussalam	...	...	...	...	...	...	...	...	...	...	...	...	...	...
Cambodia	...	...	...	...	...	...	...	...	...	...	...	...	...	...
Indonesia	360,388.1	353,271.0	425,767.8	520,686.7	486,765.9	523,321.9	496,086.1	47.7	41.0	45.7	51.3	46.7	46.8	46.9
Lao People's Democratic Republic	...	...	...	...	...	...	...	...	...	...	...	...	...	...
Malaysia	408,689.1	382,976.7	359,788.3	455,772.5	398,018.7	403,957.4	436,537.9	160.3	127.1	119.4	142.8	110.9	110.6	129.5
Myanmar	...	...	...	...	...	...	...	...	...	...	...	...	...	...
Philippines	157,320.5	238,819.9	239,738.0	290,401.4	258,155.7	275,302.2	272,790.3	75.5	77.9	75.2	88.4	74.4	73.1	75.4
Singapore	647,226.4	639,955.9	640,427.5	787,255.3	687,257.2	697,271.3	652,614.7	269.9	207.8	200.9	229.4	182.3	185.7	189.0
Thailand	277,731.7	348,798.0	432,956.2	548,795.4	500,741.0	569,228.3	543,164.6	81.4	86.9	104.7	120.3	98.8	104.6	108.7
Timor-Leste	...	...	...	...	...	...	...	...	...	...	...	...	...	...
Viet Nam	36,855.0	58,734.0	73,222.2	125,310.0	132,653.0	149,817.3	186,008.5	25.0	24.5	28.5	44.5	43.0	45.3	54.2
The Pacific														
Cook Islands	...	...	...	...	...	...	...	...	...	...	...	...	...	...
Fiji	...	...	...	...	...	...	...	...	...	...	...	...	...	...
Kiribati	...	...	...	...	...	...	...	...	...	...	...	...	...	...
Marshall Islands	...	...	...	...	...	...	...	...	...	...	...	...	...	...
Micronesia, Federated States of	...	...	...	...	...	...	...	...	...	...	...	...	...	...
Nauru	...	...	...	...	...	...	...	...	...	...	...	...	...	...
Niue	...	...	...	...	...	...	...	...	...	...	...	...	...	...
Palau	...	...	...	...	...	...	...	...	...	...	...	...	...	...
Papua New Guinea	11,027.3	1,718.9	1,643.1	1,681.6	...	...	...	77.4	7.9	7.9	7.4	...	...	...
Samoa	...	...	...	...	...	...	...	...	...	...	...	...	...	...
Solomon Islands	...	...	...	...	...	...	...	...	...	...	...	...	...	...
Tonga	...	...	...	...	...	...	...	...	...	...	...	...	...	...
Tuvalu	...	...	...	...	...	...	...	...	...	...	...	...	...	...
Vanuatu	...	...	...	...	...	...	...	...	...	...	...	...	...	...
Developed ADB Member Economies														
Australia	1,454,490.6	1,187,083.5	1,268,493.5	1,508,462.8	1,262,800.3	1,487,598.5	1,720,556.2	126.7	87.9	105.1	113.7	88.4	106.9	129.6
Japan	3,827,774.2	4,894,919.1	4,955,299.7	6,222,825.2	5,296,811.1	6,191,073.3	6,718,219.6	66.5	110.1	99.0	126.2	105.1	120.8	133.3
New Zealand	35,506.9 (2009)	74,350.5	80,048.5	94,691.3	86,132.6	107,879.8	132,198.5	29.3 (2009)	41.8	42.4	45.8	40.6	50.5	62.4

... = data not available, $ = United States dollars, ADB = Asian Development Bank, GDP = gross domestic product.

Sources: World Bank. World Development Indicators. https://databank.worldbank.org/source/world-development-indicators (accessed 9 July 2022). For Bhutan and Taipei,China: Asian Development Bank estimates using data from economies' official sources.

Table 2.3.12: Official Exchange Rates
(local currency units per $, period averages)

ADB Regional Member	2010	2015	2016	2017	2018	2019	2020	2021
Developing ADB Member Economies								
Central and West Asia								
Afghanistan	46.5	61.1	67.9	68.0	72.1	77.7	76.8	83.6
Armenia	373.7	477.9	480.5	482.7	483.0	480.4	489.0	503.8
Azerbaijan	0.8	1.0	1.6	1.7	1.7	1.7	1.7	1.7
Georgia	1.8	2.3	2.4	2.5	2.5	2.8	3.1	3.2
Kazakhstan	147.4	221.7	342.2	326.0	344.7	382.7	413.0	425.9
Kyrgyz Republic	46.0	64.5	69.9	68.9	68.8	69.8	77.3	84.6
Pakistan	85.2	102.8	104.8	105.5	121.8	150.0	161.8	162.9
Tajikistan	4.4	6.2	7.8	8.5	9.2	9.5	10.3	11.3
Turkmenistan	2.9	3.5	3.5	3.5	3.5	3.5	3.5	3.5
Uzbekistan[a]	1,578.4	2,568.0	2,965.3	5,113.9	8,069.6	8,836.8	10,054.3	10,609.5
East Asia								
China, People's Republic of	6.8	6.2	6.6	6.8	6.6	6.9	6.9	6.4
Hong Kong, China	7.8	7.8	7.8	7.8	7.8	7.8	7.8	7.8
Korea, Republic of	1,156.5	1,131.0	1,160.8	1,131.0	1,100.2	1,165.4	1,180.3	1,144.0
Mongolia	1,357.1	1,970.3	2,140.3	2,439.8	2,472.5	2,663.5	2,813.3	2,849.3
Taipei,China	31.6	31.9	32.3	30.4	30.2	30.9	29.6	28.0
South Asia								
Bangladesh	69.6	77.9	78.5	80.4	83.5	84.5	84.9	85.1
Bhutan	45.7	64.2	67.2	65.1	68.4	70.4	74.1	73.9
India	45.7	64.2	67.2	65.1	68.4	70.4	74.1	73.9
Maldives	12.8	15.4	15.4	15.4	15.4	15.4	15.4	15.4
Nepal	73.3	102.4	107.4	104.5	108.9	112.6	118.3	118.1
Sri Lanka	113.1	135.9	145.6	152.4	162.5	178.7	185.6	200.2
Southeast Asia								
Brunei Darussalam	1.4	1.4	1.4	1.4	1.3	1.4	1.4	1.3
Cambodia	4,184.9	4,067.8	4,058.7	4,050.6	4,051.2	4,061.1	4,092.8	4,098.7
Indonesia	9,090.4	13,389.4	13,308.3	13,380.8	14,236.9	14,147.7	14,582.2	14,308.1
Lao People's Democratic Republic	8,254.2	8,127.6	8,124.4	8,244.8	8,401.3	8,679.4	9,045.8	9,697.9
Malaysia	3.2	3.9	4.1	4.3	4.0	4.1	4.2	4.1
Myanmar[b]	5.6	1,162.6	1,234.9	1,360.4	1,429.8	1,518.3	1,381.6	1,615.7
Philippines	45.1	45.5	47.5	50.4	52.7	51.8	49.6	49.3
Singapore	1.4	1.4	1.4	1.4	1.3	1.4	1.4	1.3
Thailand	31.7	34.2	35.3	33.9	32.3	31.0	31.3	32.0
Timor-Leste[c]	1.0	1.0	1.0	1.0	1.0	1.0	1.0	1.0
Viet Nam	18,612.9	21,697.6	21,935.0	22,370.1	22,602.1	23,050.2	23,208.4	23,159.8
The Pacific								
Cook Islands[d]	1.4	1.4	1.4	1.4	1.4	1.5	1.5	1.4
Fiji	1.9	2.1	2.1	2.1	2.1	2.2	2.2	2.1
Kiribati	1.1	1.3	1.3	1.3	1.3	1.4	1.5	1.3
Marshall Islands[c]	1.0	1.0	1.0	1.0	1.0	1.0	1.0	1.0
Micronesia, Federated States of[c]	1.0	1.0	1.0	1.0	1.0	1.0	1.0	1.0
Nauru	1.1	1.3	1.3	1.3	1.3	1.4	1.5	1.3
Niue[d]	1.4	1.4	1.4	1.4	1.4	1.5	1.5	1.4
Palau[c]	1.0	1.0	1.0	1.0	1.0	1.0	1.0	1.0
Papua New Guinea	2.7	2.8	3.1	3.2	3.3	3.4	3.5	3.5
Samoa	2.5	2.6	2.6	2.6	2.6	2.6	2.7	2.6
Solomon Islands	8.1	7.9	7.9	7.9	8.0	8.2	8.2	8.0
Tonga	1.9	2.1	2.2	2.2	2.2	2.3	2.3	2.3
Tuvalu[e]	1.1	1.3	1.3	1.3	1.3	1.4	1.5	1.3
Vanuatu	96.9	109.0	108.5	107.8	110.2	114.7	115.4	109.5
Developed ADB Member Economies								
Australia	1.1	1.3	1.3	1.3	1.3	1.4	1.5	1.3
Japan	87.8	121.0	108.8	112.2	110.4	109.0	106.8	109.8
New Zealand	1.4	1.4	1.4	1.4	1.4	1.5	1.5	1.4

$ = United States (US) dollars, ADB = Asian Development Bank.

a Data show weighted averages of the official, bank, and parallel market rates.
b Beginning 1 April 2012, the Central Bank of Myanmar adopted the managed float exchange rate regime for kyat vis-à-vis the US dollar.
c Unit of currency is the US dollar.
d Unit of currency is the New Zealand dollar.
e Unit of currency is the Australian dollar.

Source: International Monetary Fund. International Financial Statistics. http://data.imf.org/ (accessed 28 June 2022). For Afghanistan for 2021: Asian Development Bank. *Asian Development Outlook 2022*. https://www.adb.org/publications/series/asian-development-outlook (accessed 28 June 2022). For the Republic of the Marshall Islands: Economic Policy, Planning and Statistics Office. Official communication, 6 April 2022. For Sri Lanka for 2021: Central Bank of Sri Lanka. https://www.cbsl.gov.lk/en/rates-and-indicators/exchange-rates (accessed 20 May 2022). For Taipei,China: Central bank of Taipei,China. Official communication, 17 June 2022. For Turkmenistan for 2000–2009: United Nations Statistics Division. UN National Accounts Main Aggregates Database. https://unstats.un.org/unsd/snaama/countryprofile (accessed 1 May 2022), and for 2010–2021: Interstate Statistical Committee of the Commonwealth of Independent States. http://www.cisstat.org/eng/index.htm (accessed 1 May 2022). For Uzbekistan for 2000–2012: United Nations Statistics Division. UN National Accounts Main Aggregates Database. https://unstats.un.org/unsd/snaama/countryprofile (accessed 4 May 2022), and for 2013–2021: Central Bank of Uzbekistan. https://cbu.uz/en/statistics/e-gdds/data/111573/ (accessed 4 May 2022).

Table 2.3.13: Purchasing Power Parity Conversion Factor
(local currency units per $, period averages)

ADB Regional Member	2010	2011	2015	2016	2017	2018	2019	2020	2021
Developing ADB Member Economies									
Central and West Asia									
Afghanistan	14.55	16.61	17.02	17.45	17.21	17.15	17.95	19.12	...
Armenia	160.19	163.65	172.92	161.23	155.97	156.58	155.47	156.72	160.80
Azerbaijan	0.32	0.38	0.38	0.43	0.51	0.55	0.54	0.50	0.58
Georgia	0.76	0.81	0.75	0.75	0.80	0.82	0.85	0.90	0.96
Kazakhstan	69.52	82.09	100.35	110.82	121.25	129.33	136.75	140.81	149.54
Kyrgyz Republic	13.11	15.73	17.15	16.74	16.96	17.13	17.50	18.35	20.43
Pakistan	21.30	24.96	31.47	32.38	33.59	34.07	36.49	39.65	41.92
Tajikistan	1.41	1.56	1.91	2.03	2.23	2.23	2.27	2.28	2.37
Turkmenistan	1.29	1.43	1.64	1.61	1.62	1.60	1.65	...	...
Uzbekistan	505.24	602.00	1,058.68	1,179.96	1,432.91	1,777.09	2,058.55	2,270.92	2,475.95
East Asia									
China, People's Republic of	3.33	3.52	3.87	3.99	4.18	4.23	4.21	4.18	4.19
Hong Kong, China	5.14	5.23	5.83	5.93	6.01	6.09	6.10	6.06	5.85
Korea, Republic of	840.99	854.59	857.48	858.81	872.62	854.87	864.63	824.60	847.46
Mongolia	473.09	533.53	717.07	729.22	791.44	834.50	901.59	923.88	1,004.55
Taipei,China	15.81	15.15	15.48	15.78	15.73	15.27	14.98	14.99	14.83
South Asia									
Bangladesh	22.15	23.41	27.28	28.50	29.74	30.73	31.29	32.11	32.10
Bhutan	15.42	16.40	18.59	18.83	19.21	19.09	18.92	19.98	...
India	14.60	15.55	19.24	19.90	20.65	20.95	21.07	21.99	23.14
Maldives	7.12	7.86	8.28	8.13	8.16	8.22	7.99	7.92	7.58
Nepal	20.40	25.25	29.94	32.00	31.23	31.83	32.74	33.39	33.83
Sri Lanka	38.63	39.29	45.18	46.28	49.39	50.08	50.46	51.83	53.70
Southeast Asia									
Brunei Darussalam	0.60	0.71	0.69	0.67	0.65	0.69	0.66	0.58	0.64
Cambodia	1,354.17	1,371.24	1,395.92	1,402.13	1,428.35	1,438.44	1,458.88	1,431.82	1,392.46
Indonesia	3,336.63	3,512.75	4,353.33	4,518.10	4,695.66	4,761.21	4,752.31	4,675.22	4,758.70
Lao People's Democratic Republic	2,463.99	2,666.53	2,819.73	2,759.43	2,789.11	2,776.33	2,760.20	2,864.64	2,852.48
Malaysia	1.42	1.47	1.57	1.59	1.65	1.63	1.60	1.57	1.59
Myanmar	245.89	261.78	318.98	347.07	366.71	377.66	394.27	404.55	407.06
Philippines	17.78	18.10	19.00	18.95	19.39	19.64	19.43	19.52	19.17
Singapore	0.85	0.85	0.88	0.88	0.89	0.90	0.88	0.84	0.84
Thailand	12.19	12.39	12.64	12.73	12.84	12.72	12.63	12.31	12.04
Timor-Leste	0.42	0.45	0.46	0.43	0.41	0.39	0.42	0.35	0.33
Viet Nam	5,813.73	6,915.34	7,413.46	7,315.61	7,395.34	7,469.26	7,474.85	7,505.11	7,405.19
The Pacific									
Cook Islands	...	...	...	...	...	...	...	...	...
Fiji	0.89	0.95	0.91	0.94	0.94	0.93	0.94	0.91	0.87
Kiribati	0.97	0.96	0.98	1.03	1.04	1.03	0.99	1.01	...
Marshall Islands	0.89	0.94	0.92	0.98	0.99	0.97	0.97	1.00	1.00
Micronesia, Federated States of	0.88	0.88	0.87	0.89	0.94	1.01	1.00	1.00	0.98
Nauru	0.90	1.00	0.76	0.96	1.06	1.07	1.09	1.10	1.09
Niue	...	...	...	...	...	...	...	...	...
Palau	0.77	0.75	0.89	0.93	0.90	0.88	0.85	0.87	...
Papua New Guinea	1.82	1.86	1.87	1.90	2.01	2.15	2.14	2.23	2.30
Samoa	1.69	1.66	1.70	1.70	1.66	1.64	1.64	1.62	1.58
Solomon Islands	5.94	6.37	7.01	6.94	6.91	6.95	6.91	7.06	7.07
Tonga	1.48	1.45	1.46	1.49	1.54	1.58	1.68	1.60	...
Tuvalu	1.11	1.11	1.19	1.27	1.29	1.35	1.42	1.42	1.39
Vanuatu	99.82	100.51	103.72	104.31	107.86	108.72	110.31	110.96	109.91
Developed ADB Member Economies									
Australia	1.50	1.51	1.47	1.45	1.48	1.47	1.48	1.45	1.44
Japan	111.71	107.45	103.47	105.52	105.10	104.16	104.31	101.24	100.41
New Zealand	1.50	1.49	1.48	1.44	1.43	1.47	1.43	1.44	1.49

... = data not available, $ = United States dollars, ADB = Asian Development Bank.

Note: For 2011 and 2017, purchasing power parity (PPP) figures are based on results from the 2011 and 2017 benchmark cycles of the International Comparison Program (ICP). For 2010 (and years prior featured in the Key Indicators Database), PPPs are extrapolated from the revised 2011 ICP PPP estimates. For 2012–2016, figures are interpolated from the two ICP reference years 2011 and 2017. For 2017 onward, figures are extrapolated from the 2017 ICP PPPs or imputed based on a regression model.

Sources: World Bank. World Development Indicators. https://databank.worldbank.org/source/world-development-indicators (accessed 19 July 2022). For Taipei,China: for 2010 and 2018–2021, Asian Development Bank estimates using data from the economy's official sources and World Bank data; for 2011–2017, World Bank. DataBank: ICP 2017. https://databank.worldbank.org/source/icp-2017 (accessed 20 July 2022).

Table 2.3.14: Price Level Indexes
(PPPs to official exchange rates, period averages, United States = 100)

ADB Regional Member	2010	2011	2015	2016	2017	2018	2019	2020	2021
Developing ADB Member Economies									
Central and West Asia									
Afghanistan	31.8	34.8	26.6	25.8	25.1	23.3	23.0	24.9	...
Armenia	42.9	43.9	36.2	33.6	32.3	32.4	32.4	32.0	31.9
Azerbaijan	39.8	48.6	36.8	27.0	29.4	32.6	31.9	29.2	34.0
Georgia	42.7	48.1	33.2	31.6	32.1	32.4	30.1	28.9	29.7
Kazakhstan	47.2	56.0	45.3	32.4	37.2	37.5	35.7	34.1	35.1
Kyrgyz Republic	28.5	34.1	26.6	23.9	24.6	24.9	25.1	23.7	24.1
Pakistan	25.4	29.2	31.0	31.0	32.0	31.0	26.7	25.1	26.2
Tajikistan	32.2	33.9	31.1	25.9	26.1	24.4	23.9	22.1	20.9
Turkmenistan	45.2	50.0	47.0	46.1	46.4	45.8	47.0	...	...
Uzbekistan	31.9	35.1	41.2	39.8	28.0	22.0	23.3	22.6	23.3
East Asia									
China, People's Republic of	49.2	54.5	62.2	60.0	61.9	63.9	60.9	60.6	64.9
Hong Kong, China	66.2	67.2	75.2	76.4	77.1	77.6	77.9	78.2	75.3
Korea, Republic of	72.7	77.1	75.8	74.0	77.2	77.7	74.2	69.9	74.1
Mongolia	34.9	42.2	36.4	34.1	32.4	33.8	33.8	32.8	35.3
Taipei,China	50.0	51.4	48.5	48.8	51.7	50.6	48.4	50.7	52.9
South Asia									
Bangladesh	32.0	32.9	35.1	36.4	37.6	37.4	37.2	37.9	37.9
Bhutan	33.7	35.1	29.0	28.0	29.5	27.9	26.9	27.0	...
India	32.0	32.4	29.4	29.7	32.0	30.0	29.7	29.6	31.1
Maldives	55.7	53.8	53.9	52.9	53.0	53.4	51.9	51.5	49.3
Nepal	27.4	34.9	30.1	30.1	29.4	30.5	29.0	28.7	28.7
Sri Lanka	34.2	35.5	33.3	31.8	32.4	30.8	28.2	27.9	27.0
Southeast Asia									
Brunei Darussalam	43.9	56.1	49.8	48.2	46.8	51.2	48.0	41.8	47.6
Cambodia	32.4	33.8	34.3	34.5	35.3	35.5	35.9	35.0	34.0
Indonesia	36.7	40.1	32.5	33.9	35.1	33.4	33.6	32.1	33.3
Lao People's Democratic Republic	29.9	33.2	34.7	34.0	33.8	33.0	31.8	31.7	29.4
Malaysia	44.1	47.9	40.1	38.4	38.5	40.3	38.6	37.3	38.4
Myanmar	25.2	32.9	29.2	28.2	27.2	27.3	25.7	28.3	27.3
Philippines	39.4	41.8	41.8	39.9	38.5	37.3	37.5	39.3	38.9
Singapore	62.7	67.3	64.0	63.6	64.2	66.4	64.3	60.9	62.5
Thailand	38.5	40.6	36.9	36.1	37.8	39.4	40.7	39.3	37.7
Timor-Leste	41.6	45.5	45.8	43.2	40.9	39.4	41.9	34.8	33.0
Viet Nam	31.2	33.7	34.2	33.4	33.1	33.0	32.4	32.3	32.0
The Pacific									
Cook Islands	...	...	...	...	...	...	...	...	...
Fiji	46.1	52.9	43.4	44.7	45.4	44.6	43.3	42.0	42.2
Kiribati	88.6	99.2	73.7	76.8	79.7	77.1	69.0	69.7	...
Marshall Islands	88.7	93.9	91.8	98.4	99.0	97.0	96.5	99.6	99.7
Micronesia, Federated States of	88.3	87.9	86.8	89.4	94.3	100.7	100.4	99.7	98.1
Nauru	79.6	98.5	63.4	69.8	79.7	83.2	78.2	73.8	81.1
Niue	...	...	...	...	...	...	...	...	...
Palau	77.0	74.9	89.1	92.9	90.2	88.0	84.8	87.3	...
Papua New Guinea	66.9	78.4	67.5	60.6	62.9	65.3	63.0	64.3	65.6
Samoa	66.5	69.6	70.0	65.0	65.7	64.1	62.6	60.1	61.4
Solomon Islands	73.7	83.4	88.6	87.4	87.6	87.3	84.5	86.0	88.0
Tonga	76.5	79.3	75.1	67.1	69.8	72.2	73.8	69.1	...
Tuvalu	102.2	114.5	89.4	94.7	99.2	100.7	98.6	97.4	104.1
Vanuatu	103.0	112.3	95.2	96.2	100.0	98.7	96.1	96.2	100.7
Developed ADB Member Economies									
Australia	132.4	149.0	122.6	105.6	111.4	114.0	106.0	96.9	107.4
Japan	127.3	134.6	85.5	97.0	93.7	94.3	95.7	94.8	91.5
New Zealand	107.9	117.4	103.1	100.3	101.7	101.7	94.1	93.1	105.1

... = data not available, ADB = Asian Development Bank, PPP = purchasing power parity.

Sources: World Bank. World Development Indicators. https://databank.worldbank.org/source/world-development-indicators (accessed 21 July 2022)
For Taipei,China: Asian Development Bank estimates using data from the economy's official sources and the World Bank's DataBank: ICP 2017. https://databank.worldbank.org/source/icp-2017 (accessed 20 July 2022).

Data Issues and Comparability

Not all reporting economies meet the standards and classifications of the International Monetary Fund (IMF) on the compilation of monetary and financial statistics available on the fund's Dissemination Standards Bulletin Board.[4]

Consumer price index coverage differs across economies. Most economies try to follow the Classification of Individual Consumption by Purpose guidelines, but the implementation varies across economies. In some instances, the basket of goods and services in the index is outdated or represents only urban areas (or the capital city). Other price measurements, such as the wholesale price index and the producer price index, are not available in Pacific economies.

Broad money supply in most economies relates to M2, which includes cash, checking deposits, savings deposits, money market securities, mutual funds, and other time deposits. However, 11 of the 44 economies with available data reported M3, thereby posing limits to comparability as M3 also includes less liquid financial assets. Not all economies publish the same types of aggregates, and even when aggregates have the same name (i.e., M1, M2, M3, etc.), their asset composition often differs significantly. For example, the definition of M2 in one economy may include time deposits with maturities of 1 year or less, whereas another economy's M2 definition may include time deposits with maturities of 2 years or less.

Finally, some economies use the central bank policy rate, while others use commercial bank rates in measuring banks' average deposit and lending rates.

4 For more information on the IMF's standards and classifications on the compilation of monetary and financial statistics, go to http://dsbb.imf.org/Pages/SDDS/StatMethod.aspx.

Table 2.4.1: Trade in Goods Balance
(% of GDP)

ADB Regional Member	2010	2015	2017	2018	2019	2020	2021
Developing ADB Member Economies							
Central and West Asia							
Afghanistan	-27.3	-32.4	-31.4	-31.2	-28.0	-25.3	...
Armenia	-22.3	-11.2	-12.2	-13.8	-12.6	-10.7	...
Azerbaijan	37.3	11.0	15.0	20.9	17.7	5.9	20.6
Georgia	-21.5	-26.4	-23.4	-23.4	-21.4	-19.8	-20.1*
Kazakhstan	19.3	6.3	10.0	14.3	10.0	6.0	10.7*
Kyrgyz Republic	-27.8	-33.8	-31.3	-36.2	-29.6	-18.5	-27.5*
Pakistan	-6.5	-6.4	-7.7	-8.7	-8.6	-7.0	-8.1
Tajikistan	-43.9	-27.7	-20.1	-24.3	-23.1	-17.8	-19.5*
Turkmenistan	9.9	-5.3	...	...	...	...	...
Uzbekistan	1.8	-2.4	-3.6	-13.0	-12.2	-10.4	-12.9*
East Asia							
China, People's Republic of	3.9	5.2	3.9	2.7	2.8	3.5*	3.2*
Hong Kong, China	1.4	-7.4	-6.7	-8.9	-4.2	-1.5	0.7
Korea, Republic of	4.2	8.2	7.0	6.4	4.8	4.9	4.2
Mongolia	-2.4	4.8	13.0	5.1	8.2	13.2	8.6
Taipei,China	8.3	13.7	13.8	11.0	9.4	11.2	11.4
South Asia							
Bangladesh	-4.5	-3.6	-3.2	-5.7	-4.5	-5.0	-5.7*
Bhutan	-20.5	-22.3	-21.6	-17.5	-16.9	-9.8	-17.3*
India	-7.6	-6.2	-6.0	-6.7	-5.6	-3.8*	-6.0*
Maldives[a]	-40.9 |	-40.4	-40.2	-45.8	-42.8	-38.9	-42.2*
Nepal[b]	-25.5	-27.4	-29.1	-32.9	-33.3	-27.1	-31.8
Sri Lanka[a]	-8.2 |	-9.9	-10.2	-10.9	-9.0	-7.0	-9.2
Southeast Asia							
Brunei Darussalam	45.3	22.4	19.8	17.4	16.4	11.5	...
Cambodia	-23.9	-21.9	-19.3	-23.8	-26.8	-9.8	-41.8
Indonesia	4.1	1.6	1.9	-0.0	0.3	2.7	3.7
Lao People's Democratic Republic[a]	-4.7 |	-14.0	-4.7	-5.0	-2.5	3.9	7.2
Malaysia	15.1	9.3	8.5	7.9	8.2	9.8	11.1
Myanmar[a]	0.1 |	-6.1	-9.5	-6.3	...	...	...
Philippines	-8.1	-7.6	-12.2	-14.7	-13.1	-9.3*	-13.7*
Singapore	26.4	30.1	29.4	27.6	26.1	30.0	29.8
Thailand	7.8	6.5	7.1	4.4	4.9	8.2*	7.9*
Timor-Leste[a,c]	-31.8 |	-39.9	-38.1	-37.2	-11.1	6.2	...
Viet Nam[a]	-4.4 |	3.8	4.8	6.7	8.1*	11.3	...
The Pacific							
Cook Islands	-25.2	-30.2	-32.9	-30.2	-32.3	...	...
Fiji	-23.5	-19.5	-20.4	-24.4	-25.4	-14.8	...
Kiribati	-41.1	-52.6	-52.2	-46.8	-53.0	-53.9*	...
Marshall Islands	-49.4	-28.6	-25.6	-28.6	-54.8	-22.2	-28.6
Micronesia, Federated States of	-43.2	-40.4	-32.8	-32.0	...	...	...
Nauru	33.6 (2012)	-47.9	-30.8	-46.0	-45.7	-57.9*	-57.7*
Niue	-60.3	-40.2	-43.6	-41.4*	...	...	...
Palau	-45.7	-49.1	-48.5	-48.4	-51.7*	-0.0*	...
Papua New Guinea	15.5	27.0	30.3	29.0	30.2	24.3	27.9*
Samoa	-36.7	-32.0	-32.2	-32.5	-33.6	-29.8	-36.0
Solomon Islands	-15.2	-1.3	0.4	0.3	-2.3	-1.7	-6.2
Tonga[c]	-53.0 |	-70.4	-74.5	-80.5	-83.5	-81.3	...
Tuvalu[c]	-54.3 |	-88.5	-42.8	-40.7	-61.6	-52.2	-44.0
Vanuatu	-28.3	-37.0	-29.1	-26.2	-29.5	...	...
Developed ADB Member Economies							
Australia	-0.7	-0.8	0.8	0.7	2.7	3.6	3.7
Japan	1.9	-0.2	0.9	0.2	0.0	0.5	0.3
New Zealand	1.4	-1.0	-1.0	-1.5	-0.9	0.5	...

... = data not available, | = marks break in series due to change in compilation methodology, -0.0 or 0.0 = magnitude is less than half of unit employed, * = provisional or preliminary, ADB = Asian Development Bank, GDP = gross domestic product.

a Change in compilation methodology from the International Monetary Fund's Balance of Payments Manual (fifth edition) [BPM5] to the International Monetary Fund's Balance of Payments and International Investment Position Manual (sixth edition) [BPM6].
b Based on BPM5.
c From September 2019, oil revenue from the Joint Petroleum Development Area is now included in GDP based on the new Timor-Leste Australia Maritime Boundary Treaty.
d Change in compilation methodology from BPM4 to BPM6.

Source: Economies' official sources.

Table 2.4.2: Trade in Services Balance
(% of GDP)

ADB Regional Member	2010	2015	2017	2018	2019	2020	2021
Developing ADB Member Economies							
Central and West Asia							
Afghanistan	6.0	-1.8	-4.6	-3.4	-3.0	-2.0	...
Armenia	-2.8	-0.9	1.4	0.2	-0.5	0.8	...
Azerbaijan	-3.3	-8.0	-8.3	-4.4	-5.4	-6.7	-3.9
Georgia	4.5	9.4	12.5	12.7	12.4	0.8	3.9*
Kazakhstan	-4.9	-2.6	-2.1	-2.6	-2.0	-1.8	-1.0*
Kyrgyz Republic	-4.2	-3.3	-1.2	-1.6	0.7	-2.3	-2.6*
Pakistan	-1.0	-1.1	-1.4	-1.8	-1.5	-1.1	-0.6
Tajikistan	-0.5	-2.5	-1.6	-2.8	-3.0	-3.3	-4.4*
Turkmenistan	...	...	...	...	...	...	...
Uzbekistan	-2.5	-0.9	-3.0	-4.6	-3.8	-3.0	-3.6*
East Asia							
China, People's Republic of	-0.2	-2.0	-2.1	-2.1	-1.8	-1.0*	-0.6*
Hong Kong, China	4.4	9.8	7.7	8.7	5.8	3.5	4.1
Korea, Republic of	-1.2	-1.0	-2.3	-1.7	-1.6	-0.9	-0.2
Mongolia	-4.2	-6.2	-10.6	-15.0	-14.0	-10.9	-9.1
Taipei,China	-2.5	-2.0	-1.5	-1.1	-0.8	0.6	1.6
South Asia							
Bangladesh	-1.1	-1.6	-1.1	-1.3	-0.9	-0.7	-0.7*
Bhutan	-4.6	-3.5	-2.2	-1.6	-2.0	-2.9	-3.9*
India	2.6	3.3	2.9	3.0	3.0	3.3*	3.4*
Maldives[a]	34.8 |	49.6	36.4	36.1	36.5	21.1	51.2*
Nepal[b]	-1.3	1.1	0.1	0.0	-0.4	-0.0	-1.7
Sri Lanka[a]	1.2 |	2.7	3.5	4.0	3.2	1.0	1.8
Southeast Asia							
Brunei Darussalam	-5.9	-7.8	-5.7	-7.4	-8.8	-7.1	...
Cambodia	9.0	9.5	8.4	9.7	10.4	-1.0	-5.4
Indonesia	-1.3	-1.0	-0.7	-0.6	-0.7	-0.9	-1.2
Lao People's Democratic Republic[a]	2.4 |	-1.6	-2.0	-1.5	-0.4	-0.5	-0.5
Malaysia	0.8	-1.8	-1.7	-1.2	-0.7	-3.3	-4.0
Myanmar[a]	-0.0 |	2.2	1.5	1.8	...	...	...
Philippines	2.8	1.8	2.6	3.3	3.5	3.8*	3.6*
Singapore	-0.1	-2.8	-3.0	1.2	2.6	1.7	1.6
Thailand	-2.1	3.9	5.3	4.4	4.5	-2.9*	-7.9*
Timor-Leste[a,c]	-107.7 |	-36.5	-21.2	-22.1	-20.8	-20.8	...
Viet Nam[a]	-2.1 |	-2.5	-1.8	-1.6	-0.6	-3.8	...
The Pacific							
Cook Islands	41.4	54.2	67.0	65.3	62.7	...	...
Fiji	17.1	16.0	15.4	16.6	14.9	-1.9	...
Kiribati	-25.6	-39.6	-35.5	-30.1	-28.4	-16.2*	...
Marshall Islands	-19.9	-18.0	-19.0	-17.2	-18.2	-12.3	-11.9
Micronesia, Federated States of	-15.2	-10.8	-8.3	2.1	...	...	...
Nauru	-13.5 (2012)	-15.9	8.4	13.1	8.7	5.8*	-7.9*
Niue	-40.5	13.0	16.5	21.1*	...	...	...
Palau	19.1	32.5	21.4	19.8	16.5*	-0.9*	...
Papua New Guinea	-17.2	-5.5	-5.7	-5.1	-5.2	-4.3	-4.4*
Samoa	14.3	15.1	17.2	19.2	20.5	-1.5	-2.6
Solomon Islands	-10.7	-5.8	-6.2	-4.6	-7.7	-6.6	-7.2
Tonga[c]	-2.1 |	1.2	5.8	6.7	6.3	3.8	...
Tuvalu[c]	-4.1 |	-82.3	-49.3	-38.8	-40.0	-40.0	-36.6
Vanuatu	22.3	13.5	19.0	23.1	20.8	...	...
Developed ADB Member Economies							
Australia	-0.2	-0.7	-0.3	-0.3	-0.3	0.3	0.7
Japan	-0.5	-0.4	-0.1	-0.2	-0.2	-0.7	-0.8
New Zealand	0.9	1.9	1.9	1.4	1.2	-0.9	...

... = data not available, | = marks break in series due to change in compilation methodology, -0.0 or 0.0 = magnitude is less than half of unit employed, * = provisional or preliminary, ADB = Asian Development Bank, GDP = gross domestic product.

a Change in compilation methodology from the International Monetary Fund's Balance of Payments Manual (fifth edition) [BPM5] to the International Monetary Fund's Balance of Payments and International Investment Position Manual (sixth edition) [BPM6].

b Based on BPM5.

c From September 2019, oil revenue from the Joint Petroleum Development Area is now included in GDP based on the new Timor-Leste Australia Maritime Boundary Treaty.

d Change in compilation methodology from BPM4 to BPM6.

Source: Economies' official sources.

Table 2.4.3: Current Account Balance
(% of GDP)

ADB Regional Member	2010	2015	2017	2018	2019	2020	2021
Developing ADB Member Economies							
Central and West Asia							
Afghanistan	-4.7	-20.3	-18.8	-21.2	-20.1	-15.5	...
Armenia	-13.6	-2.7	-1.5	-7.0	-7.3	-3.8	...
Azerbaijan	28.4	-0.4	4.1	12.8	9.1	-0.5	15.2
Georgia	-9.8	-11.8	-8.0	-6.8	-5.5	-12.4	-9.8*
Kazakhstan	0.9	-3.3	-3.1	-0.1	-4.0	-3.8	-3.0*
Kyrgyz Republic	-9.8	-16.2	-7.0	-11.6	-12.0	4.8	-8.7*
Pakistan	-2.2	-1.0	-3.6	-5.4	-4.2	-1.5	-0.6
Tajikistan	-10.3	-5.8	2.1	-4.9	-2.2	4.3	8.5*
Turkmenistan	-9.0	-17.3	...	...	...	...	0.6
Uzbekistan	5.0	1.0	2.4	-6.8	-5.6	-5.0	-6.9*
East Asia							
China, People's Republic of	3.9	2.6	1.5	0.2	0.7	1.7*	1.8*
Hong Kong, China	7.0	3.3	4.6	3.7	5.8	7.0	11.3
Korea, Republic of	2.4	7.2	4.6	4.5	3.6	4.6	4.9
Mongolia	-12.3	-8.2	-10.1	-16.7	-15.2	-5.1	-13.0
Taipei,China	8.3	13.6	14.1	11.6	10.6	14.2	14.8
South Asia							
Bangladesh	3.2	1.8	-0.5	-3.0	-1.3	-1.5	-1.1*
Bhutan	-24.3	-28.6	-25.1	-19.5	-21.2	-12.2	-22.0*
India	-2.9	-1.1	-1.8	-2.1	-0.9	0.9*	-1.2*
Maldives[a]	-13.8 |	-7.4	-21.6	-28.4	-26.6	-35.6	-9.2*
Nepal[b]	-2.3	4.5	-0.3	-7.1	-6.9	-0.9	-7.8
Sri Lanka[a]	-1.8 |	-2.2	-2.4	-3.0	-2.1	-1.4	-3.8
Southeast Asia							
Brunei Darussalam	36.5	16.6	16.4	6.9	6.6	4.5	...
Cambodia	-8.7	-8.9	-8.1	-11.8	-15.0	-8.5	-45.7
Indonesia	0.7	-2.0	-1.6	-2.9	-2.7	-0.4	0.3
Lao People's Democratic Republic[a]	0.4 |	-15.7	-7.4	-9.1	-7.0	-0.6	2.8
Malaysia	10.1	3.0	2.8	2.2	3.5	4.2	3.5
Myanmar[a]	0.0 |	-4.9	-7.9	-3.6	0.4*	-2.5*	-1.1*
Philippines	3.4	2.4	-0.7	-2.6	-0.8	3.2*	-1.8*
Singapore	22.9	18.7	17.3	15.2	14.5	16.8	18.1
Thailand	3.4	6.9	9.6	5.6	7.0	4.2	-2.2*
Timor-Leste[a,c]	180.2 |	12.8	-17.5	-12.1	3.9	-2.6	...
Viet Nam[a]	-3.7 |	-1.1	-0.7	2.4	4.6	5.6	...
The Pacific							
Cook Islands	15.5	31.1	40.3	38.2	35.1	...	...
Fiji	-7.1	-3.5	-6.7	-8.4	-12.6	-12.9	...
Kiribati	0.1	33.0	37.4	39.3	48.7	39.1*	...
Marshall Islands	-14.8	17.2	7.5	6.5	-24.4	20.5	5.8
Micronesia, Federated States of	-17.5	4.5	10.3	21.0	...	...	...
Nauru	38.1 (2012)	-18.5	12.3	8.0	4.9	2.8*	4.1*
Niue	-53.9	11.1	14.9	15.7*	...	...	...
Palau	-9.3	-8.8	-19.0	-15.5	-26.9*	-48.3*	...
Papua New Guinea	-4.4	20.2	23.5	22.9	22.1	20.2	21.1*
Samoa	-4.8	-1.5	-1.0	2.7	3.7	-9.5	-13.3
Solomon Islands	-16.0	-2.7	-4.3	-3.0	-9.5	-1.6	-5.6
Tonga[c]	-8.7 |	-9.0	7.0	4.4	-0.5	10.9	...
Tuvalu[c]	-3.8 |	-48.7	8.4	66.2	-11.2	17.4	34.6
Vanuatu	-5.6	0.3	-4.4	12.2	13.6	...	...
Developed ADB Member Economies							
Australia	-5.0	-3.7	-2.3	-2.8	-0.7	1.8	3.3
Japan	3.8	3.1	4.1	3.5	3.4	2.9	2.9
New Zealand	-2.8	-2.5	-2.9	-3.7	-2.3	-2.5	...

... = data not available, | = marks break in series due to change in compilation methodology, -0.0 or 0.0 = magnitude is less than half of unit employed, * = provisional or preliminary, ADB = Asian Development Bank, GDP = gross domestic product.

a Change in compilation methodology from the International Monetary Fund's Balance of Payments Manual (fifth edition) [BPM5] to the International Monetary Fund's Balance of Payments and International Investment Position Manual (sixth edition) [BPM6].

b Based on BPM5.

c From September 2019, oil revenue from the Joint Petroleum Development Area is now included in GDP based on the new Timor-Leste Australia Maritime Boundary Treaty.

d Change in compilation methodology from BPM4 to BPM6.

Source: Economies' official sources.

Table 2.4.4: Total Remittances, Inflows—Dollar Amounts
($ million)

ADB Regional Member	2010	2015	2016	2017	2018	2019	2020*
Developing ADB Member Economies							
Central and West Asia	**21,317**	**32,975**	**34,043**	**37,562**	**39,846**	**41,920**	**43,485**
Afghanistan	378	349	628	823	804	829	789
Armenia	1,669	1,491	1,382	1,539	1,488	1,528	1,327
Azerbaijan	1,410	1,270	643	1,133	1,226	1,275	1,403
Georgia	1,184	1,459	1,521	1,794	2,034	2,258	2,110
Kazakhstan	226	294	384	560	618	506	374
Kyrgyz Republic	1,266	1,688	1,995	2,486	2,689	2,411	2,200
Pakistan	9,690	19,306	19,819	19,856	21,193	22,245	26,105
Tajikistan	2,021	2,259	1,867	2,237	2,183	2,322	2,187
Turkmenistan	35	16	9	4	2	1	1
Uzbekistan	3,438	4,843	5,795	7,130	7,610	8,546	6,989
East Asia	**59,419**	**71,964**	**69,180**	**72,295**	**76,904**	**78,423**	**69,825**
China, People's Republic of	52,460	63,938	61,000	63,876	67,414	68,398	59,507
Hong Kong, China	340	387	399	437	425	451	458
Korea, Republic of	5,854	6,464	6,524	6,526	7,125	7,166	7,413
Mongolia	266	261	260	273	441	561	549
Taipei,China	500	915	997	1,183	1,500	1,846	1,960 (2021)
South Asia	**71,929**	**97,958**	**90,231**	**96,635**	**109,756**	**116,755**	**120,228**
Bangladesh	10,850	15,296	13,574	13,502	15,566	18,364	21,750
Bhutan	8	20	34	43	58	57	83
India	53,480	68,910	62,744	68,967	78,790	83,332	83,149
Maldives	3	4	4	4	4	4	4
Nepal	3,464	6,730	6,612	6,928	8,294	8,250	8,102
Sri Lanka	4,123	7,000	7,262	7,190	7,043	6,749	7,140
Southeast Asia	**43,120**	**63,438**	**65,738**	**69,364**	**74,784**	**77,977**	**75,227**
Brunei Darussalam	...	...	...	...	...	...	...
Cambodia	557	1,185	1,199	1,287	1,431	1,525	1,272
Indonesia	6,916	9,659	8,907	8,990	11,215	11,666	9,651
Lao People's Democratic Republic	42	189	189	243	240	297	265
Malaysia	1,103	1,644	1,604	1,649	1,686	1,638	1,454
Myanmar	115	2,005	2,346	2,578	2,840	2,421	2,250
Philippines	21,557	29,799	31,142	32,810	33,809	35,167	34,913
Singapore	...	...	...	...	...	...	...
Thailand	4,433	5,895	6,270	6,720	7,466	8,162	8,067
Timor-Leste	137	62	80	87	96	100	155
Viet Nam	8,260	13,000	14,000	15,000	16,000	17,000	17,200
The Pacific[a]	**479**	**705**	**699**	**689**	**752**	**804**	**837**
Cook Islands	...	...	...	...	...	...	...
Fiji	176	251	269	274	285	287	312
Kiribati	16	14	16	18	20	20	19
Marshall Islands	22	27	28	30	31	31	31
Micronesia, Federated States of	18	23	23	23	23	23	23
Nauru	...	...	...	...	...	...	...
Niue	...	...	...	...	...	...	...
Palau	2	2	2	2	2	2	2
Papua New Guinea	4	4	3	4	4	3	2
Samoa	139	130	130	136	147	147	150
Solomon Islands	14	19	20	16	20	25	28
Tonga	74	129	126	159	183	190	194
Tuvalu	4	4 (2013)	...	...	...	...	...
Vanuatu	12	105	81	26	35	75	76
Developed ADB Member Economies	**3,919**	**6,031**	**6,415**	**6,985**	**6,751**	**6,623**	**6,464**
Australia	1,864	2,175	2,057	2,002	1,861	1,752	1,192
Japan	1,684	3,325	3,830	4,443	4,369	4,374	4,875
New Zealand	371	532	528	540	520	497	397
DEVELOPING ADB MEMBER ECONOMIES[a]	**196,264**	**267,040**	**259,890**	**276,545**	**302,041**	**315,879**	**309,602**
ALL ADB REGIONAL MEMBERS[a]	**200,183**	**273,071**	**266,306**	**283,530**	**308,793**	**322,502**	**316,066**
WORLD[a]	**472,946**	**601,867**	**597,129**	**639,749**	**693,996**	**719,410**	**701,931**

... = data not available, * = provisional or preliminary, $ = United States dollars, ADB = Asian Development Bank.

Note: Figures are based on the International Monetary Fund's Balance of Payments and International Investment Position Manual (sixth edition).

a Includes only reporting economies with data corresponding to the year heading.

Source: World Bank. Migration and Remittances Data. https://www.worldbank.org/en/topic/migrationremittancesdiasporaissues/brief/migration-remittances-data (accessed 14 June 2022). For Taipei,China: Ministry of Finance R. O. C. Official communication, 7 July 2022; past communication.

Table 2.4.5: Total Remittances, Inflows—Proportion of Economic Activity
(% of GDP)

ADB Regional Member	2010	2015	2016	2017	2018	2019	2020*
Developing ADB Member Economies							
Central and West Asia[a]	**4.3**	**4.8**	**5.4**	**5.6**	**6.0**	**6.5**	**6.9**
Afghanistan	2.4	1.7	3.5	4.4	4.4	4.4	3.9
Armenia	18.0	14.1	13.1	13.3	11.9	11.2	10.5
Azerbaijan	2.7	2.4	1.7	2.8	2.6	2.6	3.3
Georgia	9.7	9.8	10.0	11.0	11.6	12.9	13.3
Kazakhstan	0.2	0.2	0.3	0.3	0.3	0.3	0.2
Kyrgyz Republic	26.4	25.3	29.3	32.3	32.5	27.2	28.3
Pakistan[b]	5.6	7.2 |	6.3	5.9	6.6	7.6	8.9
Tajikistan	35.8	27.3	26.7	29.7	28.1	28.0	26.9
Turkmenistan	0.2	0.0	...	...	...	...	...
Uzbekistan	6.9	5.6	6.7	11.5	14.5	14.3	11.7
East Asia	**0.8**	**0.5**	**0.5**	**0.5**	**0.5**	**0.5**	**0.4**
China, People's Republic of	0.9	0.6	0.5	0.5	0.5	0.5	0.4
Hong Kong, China	0.1	0.1	0.1	0.1	0.1	0.1	0.1
Korea, Republic of	0.5	0.4	0.4	0.4	0.4	0.4	0.5
Mongolia	3.7 |	2.2	2.3	2.4	3.3	3.9	4.1
Taipei,China	0.1	0.2	0.2	0.2	0.2	0.3	0.3 (2021)
South Asia[a]	**3.9**	**4.0**	**3.4**	**3.2**	**3.4**	**3.5**	**3.8**
Bangladesh	9.5	7.9	5.1	4.7	4.9	5.3	5.8
Bhutan	0.5	1.0	1.6	1.8	2.4	2.2	3.6
India	3.2	3.2	2.7	2.6	2.9	2.9	3.1
Maldives	0.1	0.1	0.1	0.1	0.1	0.1	0.1
Nepal	21.3	28.4	27.2	23.5	26.1	24.1	24.5
Sri Lanka	7.0	8.2	8.3	7.6	7.5	7.6	8.4
Southeast Asia[a]	**2.5**	**2.9**	**2.9**	**2.8**	**2.9**	**2.8**	**2.8**
Brunei Darussalam	...	...	...	...	...	...	...
Cambodia	5.0	6.6	6.0	5.8	5.8	5.6	4.9
Indonesia	0.9	1.1	1.0	0.9	1.1	1.0	0.9
Lao People's Democratic Republic	0.6	1.3	1.2	1.4	1.3	1.6	1.4
Malaysia	0.4	0.5	0.5	0.5	0.5	0.4	0.4
Myanmar	0.3 (2012)	3.2	3.9	4.2	4.4	3.5	...
Philippines	10.3	9.7	9.8	10.0	9.7	9.3	9.7
Singapore	...	...	...	...	...	...	...
Thailand	1.3	1.5	1.5	1.5	1.5	1.5	1.6
Timor-Leste	15.6	3.9	4.9	5.4	6.1	4.9	7.1
Viet Nam	7.1	6.7	6.8	6.7	6.5	6.5	6.3
The Pacific[a]	**2.3**	**2.3**	**2.3**	**2.1**	**2.2**	**2.2**	**2.3**
Cook Islands	...	...	...	...	...	...	...
Fiji	5.6	5.4	5.5	5.1	5.1	5.2	7.0
Kiribati	10.1	8.2	9.1	9.5	10.2	11.3	10.5
Marshall Islands	13.7	14.8	14.1	14.3	14.2	13.1	12.7
Micronesia, Federated States of	6.1	7.4	7.0	6.4	5.8	...	...
Nauru	...	...	...	...	...	...	...
Niue	...	...	...	...	...	...	...
Palau	0.9	0.8	0.8	0.8	0.8	0.8	0.8
Papua New Guinea	0.0	0.0	0.0	0.0	0.0	0.0	0.0
Samoa	19.8	15.8	14.9	15.4	16.5	16.1	18.1
Solomon Islands	1.6	1.4	1.5	1.1	1.2	1.6	1.8
Tonga	19.9	32.1	30.0	34.4	38.2	37.4	39.4
Tuvalu	12.5	10.9 (2013)	...	...	...	...	...
Vanuatu	1.8	14.3	10.3	3.0	3.8	8.0	...
Developed ADB Member Economies[a]	**0.1**	**0.1**	**0.1**	**0.1**	**0.1**	**0.1**	**0.1**
Australia	0.2	0.2	0.2	0.1	0.1	0.1	0.1
Japan	0.0	0.1	0.1	0.1	0.1	0.1	0.1
New Zealand	0.3	0.3	0.3	0.3	0.2	0.2	0.2
DEVELOPING ADB MEMBER ECONOMIES[a]	**1.6**	**1.4**	**1.4**	**1.3**	**1.3**	**1.3**	**1.3**
ALL ADB REGIONAL MEMBERS[a]	**1.0**	**1.1**	**1.0**	**1.0**	**1.0**	**1.1**	**1.0**

... = data not available, | = marks break in series, 0.0 = magnitude is less than half of unit employed, * = provisional or preliminary, ADB = Asian Development Bank, GDP = gross domestic product.

a Aggregate percentages calculated using only reporting economies with data available for both remittances and GDP in the years specified in the column headings.
b For 2016 onward, GDP data are revised due to the 2015/2016 rebasing of national accounts.

Sources: Economies' official sources; and World Bank. Migration and Remittances Data. https://www.worldbank.org/en/topic/migrationremittancesdiasporaissues/brief/migration-remittances-data (accessed 24 June 2022). For Taipei,China: Ministry of Finance R. O. C. Official communication, 7 July 2022; past communication.

Table 2.4.6: Foreign Direct Investment, Net Inflows—Dollar Amounts
($ million)

ADB Regional Member	2010	2015	2017	2018	2019	2020	2021
Developing ADB Member Economies							
Central and West Asia[a]	**20,334**	**20,069**	**16,307**	**8,137**	**14,022**	**12,955**	**...**
Afghanistan	191	169	52	119	23	13	...
Armenia	529	184	251	267	101	47	379
Azerbaijan	3,353	4,048	2,867	1,403	1,504	507	-1,708
Georgia	921	1,735	1,921	1,270	1,366	534	...
Kazakhstan	7,456	6,578	4,757	353	3,731	7,194	4,380
Kyrgyz Republic	473	1,144	-107	144	404	-402	...
Pakistan	2,022	1,673	2,496	1,737	2,234	2,057	2,102
Tajikistan	94	454	186	221	213	107	84
Turkmenistan	3,632	3,043	2,086	1,997	2,129	1,169	...
Uzbekistan	1,663	1,041	1,798	625	2,316	1,728	2,044
East Asia[a]	**340,093**	**430,126**	**314,609**	**353,649**	**265,787**	**387,085**	**366,744**
China, People's Republic of	243,703	242,489	166,084	235,365	187,170	253,096	212,477
Hong Kong, China	82,709	181,047	125,717	97,036	58,299	117,452	132,041
Korea, Republic of	9,497	4,104	17,913	12,183	9,634	8,765	16,820
Mongolia	1,691	94	1,494	1,952	2,443	1,719	...
Taipei,China	2,492	2,391	3,401	7,114	8,240	6,053	5,406
South Asia[a]	**29,486**	**47,877**	**43,787**	**46,800**	**54,422**	**66,886**	**46,737**
Bangladesh	1,232	2,831	1,810	2,422	1,908	1,525	1,389
Bhutan	75	6	-17	3	13	-3	...
India	27,397	44,009	39,966	42,117	50,611	64,362	44,708
Maldives	216	298	458	576	961	441	443
Nepal	88	52	196	68	186	127	196
Sri Lanka	478	680	1,373	1,614	743	434	...
Southeast Asia[a]	**108,413**	**132,976**	**171,491**	**153,933**	**181,812**	**123,080**	**...**
Brunei Darussalam	481	171	468	516	373	566	...
Cambodia	1,404	1,823	2,788	3,213	3,663	3,625	3,483
Indonesia	15,292	19,779	20,510	18,910	24,994	19,175	20,948
Lao People's Democratic Republic	279	1,078	1,693	1,358	756	968	...
Malaysia	10,886	9,857	9,368	8,304	9,155	4,313	17,582
Myanmar	901	4,084	4,804	1,768	1,736	1,834	...
Philippines	1,070	5,639	10,256	9,949	8,671	6,822	10,518
Singapore	55,322	69,775	99,210	81,181	111,480	74,751	105,491
Thailand	14,747	8,928	8,285	13,186	4,790	-4,845	11,422
Timor-Leste	30	43	7	48	75	72	...
Viet Nam	8,000	11,800	14,100	15,500	16,120	15,800	15,660
The Pacific[a]	**435**	**545**	**668**	**1,733**	**-493**	**-621**	**...**
Cook Islands	...	...	...	...	...	...	...
Fiji	178	205	388	469	322	239	404
Kiribati	-7	-1	1	-1	-1	3	...
Marshall Islands	-9	-5	6	10	4	7	...
Micronesia, Federated States of	0	1	...	...	...	...	...
Nauru	0	0	0	0	...	...	...
Niue	...	...	...	...	...	...	...
Palau	3	35	27	22	22	24	...
Papua New Guinea	36	214	161	1,135	-901	-935	...
Samoa	0	27	9	17	-2	4	9
Solomon Islands	166	32	43	25	33	9	...
Tonga	5	6	-6	20	2	4	0
Tuvalu	0	0	0	0	0	0	...
Vanuatu	63	31	38	38	27	24	...
Developed ADB Member Economies	**42,938**	**52,072**	**69,391**	**89,130**	**81,983**	**83,976**	**60,393**
Australia	35,211	46,893	48,199	61,325	39,101	18,404	29,155
Japan	7,441	5,252	18,802	25,289	39,961	61,515	27,322
New Zealand	286	-73	2,390	2,516	2,921	4,058	3,916
DEVELOPING ADB MEMBER ECONOMIES[a]	**498,761**	**631,593**	**546,861**	**564,252**	**515,549**	**589,385**	**606,281**
ALL ADB REGIONAL MEMBERS[a]	**541,699**	**683,665**	**616,252**	**653,383**	**597,532**	**673,362**	**666,673**
WORLD[a]	**1,927,819**	**2,721,473**	**2,199,485**	**936,221**	**1,506,375**	**1,256,907**	**...**

... = data not available, -0 or 0 = magnitude is less than half of unit employed, $ = United States dollars, ADB = Asian Development Bank.

Note: For any given year, a negative value for net inflows of foreign direct investment shows that the value of disinvestment by foreign investors was more than the value of capital newly invested in the reporting economy.

a Includes only reporting economies with data corresponding to the year heading.

Sources: World Bank. World Development Indicators. http://data.worldbank.org/indicator/BX.KLT.DINV.CD.WD?locations=MH (accessed 4 July 2022); and International Monetary Fund. Balance of Payments Analytic Presentation. https://data.imf.org/regular.aspx?key=62805741 (accessed 5 July 2022). For Taipei,China: Central bank of Taipei,China. https://www.cbc.gov.tw/ct.asp?xItem=1061&ctNode=535&mp=2 (accessed 4 July 2022).

Table 2.4.7: Foreign Direct Investment, Net Inflows—Proportion of Economic Activity
(% of GDP)

ADB Regional Member	2010	2015	2017	2018	2019	2020	2021
Developing ADB Member Economies							
Central and West Asia[a]	**4.1**	**2.9**	**2.1**	**0.9**	**1.8**	**1.9**	**...**
Afghanistan	1.2	0.8	0.3	0.6	0.1	0.1	...
Armenia	5.7	1.7	2.2	2.1	0.7	0.4	2.7
Azerbaijan	6.3	7.6	7.0	3.0	3.1	1.2	-3.1
Georgia	7.5	11.6	11.8	7.2	7.8	3.4	...
Kazakhstan	5.0	3.6	2.9	0.2	2.1	4.2	2.3
Kyrgyz Republic	9.9	17.1	-1.4	1.7	4.6	-5.2	...
Pakistan	1.2	0.6	0.7	0.5	0.8	0.7	0.6
Tajikistan	1.7	5.5	2.5	2.8	2.6	1.3	1.0
Turkmenistan	16.1	8.4	...	...	...	...	...
Uzbekistan	3.3	1.2	2.9	1.2	3.9	2.9	3.0
East Asia[a]	**4.3**	**3.2**	**2.1**	**2.1**	**1.6**	**2.2**	**1.8**
China, People's Republic of	4.0	2.2	1.3	1.7	1.3	1.7	1.2
Hong Kong, China	36.2	58.5	36.8	26.8	16.1	34.1	35.8
Korea, Republic of	0.8	0.3	1.1	0.7	0.6	0.5	0.9
Mongolia	23.5	0.8	13.0	14.8	17.2	12.9	...
Taipei,China	0.6	0.4	0.6	1.2	1.3	0.9	0.7
South Asia[a]	**1.6**	**1.9**	**1.4**	**1.5**	**1.6**	**2.1**	**1.3**
Bangladesh	1.1	1.5	0.6	0.8	0.5	0.4	0.3
Bhutan	4.9	0.3	-0.7	0.1	0.5	-0.1	...
India	1.6	2.1	1.5	1.5	1.8	2.4	1.4
Maldives	8.4	7.3	9.6	10.9	17.1	11.8	...
Nepal	0.5	0.2	0.7	0.2	0.5	0.4	0.5
Sri Lanka	0.8	0.8	1.5	1.7	0.8	0.5	...
Southeast Asia[a]	**5.5**	**5.4**	**6.1**	**5.1**	**5.7**	**4.1**	**...**
Brunei Darussalam	3.5	1.3	3.9	3.8	2.8	4.7	...
Cambodia	12.5	10.1	12.6	13.1	13.5	14.0	12.9
Indonesia	2.0	2.3	2.0	1.8	2.2	1.8	1.8
Lao People's Democratic Republic	4.1	7.5	9.9	7.5	4.0	5.1	...
Malaysia	4.3	3.3	2.9	2.3	2.5	1.3	4.7
Myanmar	...	6.5	7.9	2.7	2.5	...	...
Philippines	0.5	1.8	3.1	2.9	2.3	1.9	2.7
Singapore	23.1	22.7	28.9	21.5	29.7	21.6	26.6
Thailand	4.3	2.2	1.8	2.6	0.9	-1.0	2.3
Timor-Leste[b]	3.4	2.7	0.4	3.0	3.6	3.3	...
Viet Nam	6.9	6.1	6.3	6.3	6.2	5.8	4.3
The Pacific[a]	**2.1**	**1.8**	**2.0**	**5.0**	**-1.4**	**-2.0**	**...**
Cook Islands	...	...	...	...	...	...	...
Fiji	5.7	4.4	7.2	8.4	5.9	5.3	...
Kiribati	-4.3	-0.5	0.4	-0.6	-0.3	1.5	...
Marshall Islands	-5.8	-2.9	2.7	4.4	1.7	2.7	...
Micronesia, Federated States of	0.0	0.3	...	...	...	...	...
Nauru	0.0	0.0	0.0	0.0	...	...	...
Niue	...	...	...	...	...	...	...
Palau	1.5	12.4	9.6	7.5	8.0	9.3	...
Papua New Guinea	0.2	1.0	0.7	4.7	-3.6	-3.8	...
Samoa	0.0	3.3	1.0	1.9	-0.2	0.5	1.0
Solomon Islands	18.5	2.5	2.9	1.5	2.0	0.6	...
Tonga	1.3	1.6	-1.2	4.1	0.3	0.9	...
Tuvalu	1.4	0.9	0.7	0.6	0.6	0.2	...
Vanuatu	9.4	4.2	4.3	4.1	2.9	...	...
Developed ADB Member Economies[a]	**0.6**	**0.9**	**1.1**	**1.3**	**1.2**	**1.3**	**0.9**
Australia	2.9	3.8	3.6	4.5	2.9	1.4	1.9
Japan	0.1	0.1	0.4	0.5	0.8	1.2	0.6
New Zealand	0.2	-0.0	1.2	1.2	1.4	1.9	...
DEVELOPING ADB MEMBER ECONOMIES[a]	**4.1**	**3.3**	**2.5**	**2.4**	**2.1**	**2.4**	**2.1**
ALL ADB REGIONAL MEMBERS[a]	**2.8**	**2.7**	**2.2**	**2.2**	**1.9**	**2.2**	**1.9**

... = data not available, -0.0 or 0.0 = magnitude is less than half of the unit employed, ADB = Asian Development Bank, GDP = gross domestic product.

a Aggregate percentages calculated using only reporting economies with data available for both foreign direct investment and GDP in the years specified in the column headings.

b From September 2019, oil revenue from the Joint Petroleum Development Area is now included in GDP based on the new Timor-Leste Australia Maritime Boundary Treaty.

Sources: Economies' official sources; World Bank. World Development Indicators. http://data.worldbank.org/indicator/BX.KLT.DINV.CD.WD?locations=MH (accessed 4 July 2022); and International Monetary Fund. Balance of Payments Analytic Presentation. https://data.imf.org/regular.aspx?key=62805741 (accessed 5 July 2022). For Taipei,China: Central bank of Taipei,China. https://www.cbc.gov.tw/ct.asp?xItem=1061&ctNode=535&mp=2 (accessed 4 July 2022).

Table 2.4.8: Merchandise Exports
($ million)

ADB Regional Member	2010	2015	2017	2018	2019	2020	2021
Developing ADB Member Economies							
Central and West Asia[a]	**134,666**	**116,373**	**113,340**	**138,420**	**139,678**	**119,094**	**148,274**
Afghanistan	388	571	832	875	864	777	...
Armenia	1,041	1,485	2,238	2,412	2,649	2,537	3,022
Azerbaijan	26,374	15,586	15,152	20,794	19,868	12,588	21,692
Georgia	1,677	2,204	2,746	3,380	3,798	3,343	4,242*
Kazakhstan	60,271	45,956	48,503	61,111	58,066	47,541	60,340
Kyrgyz Republic	1,756	1,483	1,764	1,837	1,986	1,973	1,659
Pakistan	19,261	23,526	20,566	21,296	21,222	21,234	25,191
Tajikistan	1,195	891	1,198	1,073	1,174	1,407	2,149
Turkmenistan	9,679	12,164	7,788	11,651	12,592	...	...
Uzbekistan	13,023	12,508	12,554	13,991	17,459	15,102	16,611
East Asia	**2,713,944**	**3,552,563**	**3,656,154**	**3,962,930**	**3,887,604**	**3,961,133**	**5,101,919**
China, People's Republic of	1,577,754	2,273,468	2,263,345	2,486,682	2,499,482	2,589,952	3,363,959
Hong Kong, China	390,134	465,092	497,340	530,472	509,026	506,303	638,170
Korea, Republic of	466,384	526,757	573,694	604,860	542,233	512,498	644,400
Mongolia	2,909	4,669	6,201	7,012	7,620	7,576	9,247
Taipei,China	276,763	282,577	315,573	333,905	329,244	344,804	446,142
South Asia[a]	**274,793**	**310,212**	**346,850**	**386,691**	**368,409**	**335,220**	**476,955**
Bangladesh	16,099	30,588	33,462	35,691	39,404	32,087	36,783*
Bhutan	535	561	566	574	610	635	...
India	248,648	267,550	300,440	337,439	315,229	291,371	425,632
Maldives	62	144	318	339	361	286	285
Nepal	830	833	699	747	862	826	1,195
Sri Lanka	8,618	10,536	11,364	11,901	11,943	10,016	12,425
Southeast Asia[a]	**1,048,353**	**1,172,177**	**1,311,960**	**1,446,426**	**1,422,439**	**1,395,294**	**1,726,294**
Brunei Darussalam	8,887	6,338	5,585	6,577	7,247	6,611	11,054
Cambodia	3,903	9,336	11,224	12,963	14,986	18,522	19,469
Indonesia	157,779	150,366	168,828	180,013	167,683	163,192	231,523
Lao People's Democratic Republic	1,746	3,653	4,873	5,295	5,806	6,115	7,270
Malaysia	198,325	199,041	217,403	248,712	240,212	234,050	299,231
Myanmar	8,872	11,432	13,878	16,704	18,110	...	...
Philippines	51,498	58,827	68,713	69,307	70,927	65,215	74,653*
Singapore	352,553	357,730	372,939	411,957	390,361	373,725	457,081
Thailand	192,511	213,397	233,376	251,155	242,686	226,861*	270,977*
Timor-Leste	42	38	24	46	154	264	616
Viet Nam	72,237	162,017	215,119	243,697	264,267	282,629	336,311
The Pacific[a]	**7,012**	**10,067**	**11,703**	**12,321**	**13,170**	**10,749**	**11,937**
Cook Islands	5	14	20	17	18	19	15*
Fiji	837	982	987	1,007	1,027	826	893
Kiribati	4	10	15	8	12	9	9*
Marshall Islands	44	60	61	64	69	72	63
Micronesia, Federated States of	30	40	46	47	...	...	...
Nauru	32	14	19	12	4	4	5
Niue	1	1	2	2	2	1	1
Palau	16	18	14	14	11	7	2
Papua New Guinea	5,737	8,417	9,953	10,495	11,401	9,285	10,433*
Samoa	23	34	37	43	51	38	29
Solomon Islands	227	421	468	536	461	379	371
Tonga	8	18	19	13	20	15	...
Tuvalu	1	0	0	0	0	0	0
Vanuatu	48	39	61	63	48	46	54
Developed ADB Member Economies	**1,011,217**	**846,359**	**967,003**	**1,034,971**	**1,016,264**	**929,604**	**1,147,001**
Australia	212,027	187,525	230,950	257,480	271,069	250,138	345,153
Japan	767,826	624,681	697,951	737,877	705,733	640,594	757,081
New Zealand	31,365	34,152	38,102	39,613	39,463	38,872	44,767
DEVELOPING ADB MEMBER ECONOMIES[a]	**4,178,767**	**5,161,392**	**5,440,007**	**5,946,787**	**5,831,300**	**5,821,490**	**7,465,379**
ALL ADB REGIONAL MEMBERS[a]	**5,189,984**	**6,007,751**	**6,407,010**	**6,981,758**	**6,847,564**	**6,751,095**	**8,612,380**
WORLD[b]	**15,204,070**	**16,378,902**	**17,491,566**	**19,276,593**	**18,764,540**	**17,405,482**	**22,131,428**

... = data not available, 0 = magnitude is less than half of unit employed, * = provisional or preliminary, $ = United States dollars, ADB = Asian Development Bank.

a For estimating aggregates, imputation was done for economies with missing data by substituting available data from the nearest years.
b The world aggregate includes estimates derived from reports of partner economies for nonreporting and slow-reporting economies.

Sources: Economies' official sources; and International Monetary Fund. International Financial Statistics (IMF). http://data.imf.org/ (accessed 30 June 2022). For Nauru: for 2002–2015, Nauru Bureau of Statistics. 2016. Media Release on International Merchandise Trade Statistics (IMTS Release No. 01/2016), 3 November 2016; for 2016–2021, IMF. 2019 Article IV Staff Country Reports for the Republic of Nauru. For "World": IMF. Direction of Trade Statistics. http://data.imf.org/?sk=9D6028D4-F14A-464C-A2F2-59B2CD424B85 (accessed 30 June 2022).

Table 2.4.9: Growth Rates of Merchandise Exports
(%)

ADB Regional Member	2010	2015	2017	2018	2019	2020	2021
Developing ADB Member Economies							
Central and West Asia[a]	**25.3**	**-33.3**	**16.4**	**22.1**	**0.9**	**-14.7**	**24.5**
Afghanistan	-3.7	0.2	39.5	5.2	-1.3	-10.1	...
Armenia	46.6	-4.0	24.9	7.8	9.8	-4.2	19.1
Azerbaijan	25.3	-44.8	14.7	37.2	-4.5	-36.6	72.3
Georgia	48.0	-23.0	29.7	23.1	12.4	-12.0	26.9*
Kazakhstan	39.5	-42.2	32.0	26.0	-5.0	-18.1	26.9
Kyrgyz Republic	5.0	-21.3	12.1	4.1	8.1	-0.7	-15.9
Pakistan	12.0	-8.5	-1.4	3.6	-0.3	0.1	18.6
Tajikistan	18.3	-8.9	33.3	-10.4	9.5	19.8	52.7
Turkmenistan	3.8	-38.5	3.6	49.6	8.1	...	...
Uzbekistan	10.6	-7.7	3.8	11.4	24.8	-13.5	10.0
East Asia	29.8	-4.3	9.5	8.4	-1.9	1.9	28.8
China, People's Republic of	31.3	-2.9	7.9	9.9	0.5	3.6	29.9
Hong Kong, China	22.5	-1.8	7.6	6.7	-4.0	-0.5	26.0
Korea, Republic of	28.3	-8.0	15.8	5.4	-10.4	-5.5	25.7
Mongolia	54.3	-19.1	26.1	13.1	8.7	-0.6	22.1
Taipei,China	35.1	-11.2	13.4	5.8	-1.4	4.7	29.4
South Asia[a]	**38.2**	**-12.2**	**8.3**	**11.5**	**-4.7**	**-9.0**	**42.3**
Bangladesh	3.7	2.6	0.3	6.7	10.4	-18.6	14.6*
Bhutan	6.5	4.1	16.0	1.3	6.3	4.1	...
India	42.3	-13.9	9.2	12.3	-6.6	-7.6	46.1
Maldives	-63.6	-0.6	24.3	6.6	6.3	-20.8	-0.1
Nepal	-4.9	-11.6	7.0	6.9	15.5	-4.3	44.7
Sri Lanka	21.7	-5.3	10.2	4.7	0.4	-16.1	24.1
Southeast Asia[a]	**29.7**	**-9.7**	**13.9**	**10.2**	**-1.7**	**-1.9**	**23.7**
Brunei Darussalam	23.9	-40.2	13.6	17.8	10.2	-8.8	67.2
Cambodia	24.4	14.3	9.3	15.5	15.6	23.6	5.1
Indonesia	35.4	-14.6	16.3	6.6	-6.8	-2.7	41.9
Lao People's Democratic Republic	65.9	11.5	14.8	8.7	9.7	5.3	18.9
Malaysia	26.5	-14.9	14.6	14.4	-3.4	-2.6	27.8
Myanmar	32.4	-0.2	17.2	20.4	8.4	...	...
Philippines	34.0	-5.3	19.7	0.9	2.3	-8.1	14.5*
Singapore	30.5	-13.8	10.3	10.5	-5.2	-4.3	22.3
Thailand	27.2	-5.8	9.3	7.6	-3.4	-6.5*	19.4*
Timor-Leste	20.7	-1.7	-85.1	91.5	232.0	71.7	133.2
Viet Nam	26.5	7.9	21.8	13.3	8.4	6.9	19.0
The Pacific[a]	**30.4**	**-6.3**	**18.9**	**5.3**	**6.9**	**-18.4**	**11.1**
Cook Islands	88.0	-20.3	48.9	-14.3	0.7	10.8	-24.4*
Fiji	25.1	-19.5	7.0	2.1	2.0	-19.5	8.1
Kiribati	-38.0	-1.5	45.2	-46.3	49.3	-24.2	-1.6*
Marshall Islands	27.4	-13.9	16.0	4.9	8.1	3.6	-12.4
Micronesia, Federated States of	63.5	23.0	-5.6	1.7	...	...	...
Nauru	249.5	-39.4	-45.4	-38.7	-64.9	-1.0	9.2
Niue	1.0	-20.2	22.0	17.5	-7.7	-66.5	39.2
Palau	15.9	-5.3	5.5	-1.9	-18.5	-40.0	-71.1
Papua New Guinea	30.9	-4.2	21.3	5.4	8.6	-18.6	12.4*
Samoa	114.4	23.8	3.1	14.1	18.9	-24.3	-24.3
Solomon Islands	37.4	-7.6	8.3	14.5	-14.0	-17.7	-2.0
Tonga	7.1	-6.5	-12.1	-31.2	56.1	-24.0	...
Tuvalu	76.5	-12.0	-8.1	-11.3	51.6	-83.0	591.2
Vanuatu	-14.8	-38.0	22.1	2.9	-24.6	-3.2	17.3
Developed ADB Member Economies	**33.6**	**-12.9**	**11.2**	**7.0**	**-1.8**	**-8.5**	**23.4**
Australia	38.3	-21.8	20.2	11.5	5.3	-7.7	38.0
Japan	32.6	-9.5	8.4	5.7	-4.4	-9.2	18.2
New Zealand	26.6	-17.8	12.9	4.0	-0.4	-1.5	15.2
DEVELOPING ADB MEMBER ECONOMIES[a]	**30.2**	**-7.0**	**10.6**	**9.3**	**-1.9**	**-0.2**	**28.2**
ALL ADB REGIONAL MEMBERS[a]	**30.8**	**-7.9**	**10.7**	**9.0**	**-1.9**	**-1.4**	**27.6**
WORLD[b]	**22.7**	**-12.8**	**10.5**	**10.2**	**-2.7**	**-7.2**	**27.2**

... = data not available, * = provisional or preliminary, ADB = Asian Development Bank.

Note: Growth rates are based on the value of exports in United States dollars.

a For estimating aggregates, imputation was done for economies with missing data by substituting available data from the nearest years.
b The world aggregate includes estimates derived from reports of partner economies for nonreporting and slow-reporting economies.

Sources: Economies' official sources; and International Monetary Fund. International Financial Statistics. http://data.imf.org/ (accessed 30 June 2022).

Table 2.4.10: Merchandise Imports
($ million)

ADB Regional Member	2010	2015	2017	2018	2019	2020	2021
Developing ADB Member Economies							
Central and West Asia[a]	**109,356**	**138,059**	**142,796**	**154,749**	**160,784**	**145,092**	**169,399**
Afghanistan	5,154	7,723	7,793	7,407	6,777	6,538	...
Armenia	3,749	3,239	4,097	4,976	5,538	4,583	5,357
Azerbaijan	6,662	9,774	9,037	10,952	11,335	10,077	10,419
Georgia	5,236	7,304	8,057	9,362	9,519	8,053	10,084*
Kazakhstan	31,127	30,568	29,600	33,659	39,709	38,929	41,174
Kyrgyz Republic	3,223	4,154	4,495	5,292	4,989	3,719	5,570
Pakistan	34,169	45,394	52,742	55,189	49,869	43,483	55,181
Tajikistan	2,657	3,436	2,775	3,151	3,349	3,151	4,209
Turkmenistan	8,204	14,051	10,189	5,323	5,406	...	...
Uzbekistan	9,176	12,417	14,012	19,439	24,292	21,154	25,461
East Asia	**2,512,911**	**2,876,629**	**3,143,062**	**3,563,907**	**3,437,069**	**3,375,353**	**4,373,575**
China, People's Republic of	1,396,244	1,679,565	1,843,793	2,135,734	2,078,409	2,065,962	2,687,529
Hong Kong, China	433,102	522,001	559,074	602,335	563,487	550,421	682,828
Korea, Republic of	425,212	436,499	478,478	535,202	503,343	467,633	615,093
Mongolia	3,200	3,798	4,337	5,875	6,128	5,299	6,849
Taipei,China	255,153	234,768	257,380	284,761	285,702	286,039	381,276
South Asia[a]	**409,681**	**455,084**	**537,474**	**616,751**	**568,870**	**473,007**	**715,646**
Bangladesh	21,245	37,528	42,779	53,571	55,159	50,636	60,483*
Bhutan[b]	810	977	1,045	971	1,012	872	...
India	368,166	388,189	460,835	525,618	477,270	393,519	618,177
Maldives	909	1,890	2,360	2,960	2,888	1,838	2,574
Nepal	5,110	7,565	9,474	11,430	12,597	10,113	13,035
Sri Lanka	13,441	18,935	20,982	22,200	19,945	16,029	20,505
Southeast Asia[a]	**934,617**	**1,089,778**	**1,233,059**	**1,405,578**	**1,369,468**	**1,250,070**	**1,588,808**
Brunei Darussalam	2,536	3,235	3,083	4,168	5,100	5,319	10,749
Cambodia[b]	6,588	13,285	15,502	18,806	22,242	21,066	30,726
Indonesia	135,663	142,695	156,986	188,711	171,276	141,569	196,190
Lao People's Democratic Republic[b]	2,060	5,675 |	5,667	6,164	6,272	5,370	5,890
Malaysia	164,177	175,593	194,497	218,036	205,049	190,433	238,275
Myanmar	4,866	16,913	19,253	19,355	18,607	...	...
Philippines	54,933	71,067	96,093	112,841	111,593	89,812	117,879*
Singapore	312,669	307,968	327,390	370,832	358,985	328,661	406,318
Thailand	165,988	187,079	200,820	228,857	216,052	185,917*	231,066*
Timor-Leste	298	491	554	565	597	625	873
Viet Nam	84,839	165,776	213,215	237,242	253,697	262,691	332,235
The Pacific[a]	**7,058**	**6,961**	**7,719**	**8,582**	**9,127**	**7,071**	**7,453**
Cook Islands	91	110	135	135	136	105	83*
Fiji	1,806	2,268	2,406	2,729	2,781	1,731	2,166
Kiribati	73	103	108	103	112	109	146*
Marshall Islands	125	112	113	126	200	126	135
Micronesia, Federated States of	168	160	183	198	...	...	...
Nauru	13	93	54	61	58	58	64
Niue	9	13	15	18	14	12	14
Palau	103	156	174	171	171	149	156
Papua New Guinea[b]	3,522	2,551	3,060	3,512	3,933	3,284	3,024*
Samoa	280	298	321	333	357	285	338
Solomon Islands	405	485	516	593	553	452	526
Tonga	158	209	238	228	267	229	...
Tuvalu	22	37	27	25	33	34	34
Vanuatu	284	367	370	350	313	300	340
Developed ADB Member Economies	**915,836**	**885,006**	**933,113**	**1,020,015**	**977,235**	**875,951**	**1,068,515**
Australia	193,071	200,643	220,954	227,172	213,797	202,055	248,054
Japan	692,242	647,744	672,032	748,967	721,032	636,957	770,528
New Zealand	30,523	36,619	40,128	43,876	42,405	36,939	49,933
DEVELOPING ADB MEMBER ECONOMIES[a]	**3,973,622**	**4,566,512**	**5,064,111**	**5,749,566**	**5,545,319**	**5,250,593**	**6,854,881**
ALL ADB REGIONAL MEMBERS[a]	**4,889,458**	**5,451,517**	**5,997,224**	**6,769,581**	**6,522,554**	**6,126,544**	**7,923,396**
WORLD[c]	**15,469,170**	**16,566,724**	**17,724,764**	**19,532,428**	**19,028,243**	**17,526,156**	**22,141,001**

... = data not available, * = provisional or preliminary, $ = United States dollars, ADB = Asian Development Bank.

a For estimating aggregates, imputation was done for economies with missing data by substituting available data from the nearest years.
b The Key Indicators Database features a longer time series on trade in goods. The compilation methodology shifted from cost, insurance, and freight to free on board from 2004 onward for Bhutan; from 2005 onward for Cambodia; from 2017 onward for the Lao People's Democratic Republic; and from 2010 onward for Papua New Guinea.
c The world aggregate includes estimates derived from reports of partner economies for nonreporting and slow-reporting economies.

Sources: Economies' official sources; and International Monetary Fund (IMF). International Financial Statistics. http://data.imf.org/ (accessed 30 June 2022). For Nauru: for 2002–2015, Nauru Bureau of Statistics. 2016. Media Release on International Merchandise Trade Statistics (IMTS Release No. 01/2016), 3 November 2016; for 2016–2021, IMF. 2019 Article IV Staff Country Reports for the Republic of Nauru. For "World": IMF. Direction of Trade Statistics. http://data.imf.org/?sk=9D6028D4-F14A-464C-A2F2-59B2CD424B85 (accessed 30 June 2022).

Table 2.4.11: Growth Rates of Merchandise Imports
(%)

ADB Regional Member	2010	2015	2017	2018	2019	2020	2021
Developing ADB Member Economies							
Central and West Asia[a]	**6.0**	**-12.5**	**11.1**	**8.4**	**3.9**	**-9.8**	**16.8**
Afghanistan	54.5	-0.1	19.3	-5.0	-8.5	-3.5	...
Armenia	12.9	-26.8	25.2	21.4	11.3	-17.2	16.9
Azerbaijan	6.9	4.7	0.4	21.2	3.5	-11.1	3.4
Georgia	17.0	-15.1	9.7	16.2	1.7	-15.4	25.2*
Kazakhstan	9.6	-26.0	16.6	13.7	18.0	-2.0	5.8
Kyrgyz Republic	6.0	-27.6	12.4	17.7	-5.7	-25.5	49.8
Pakistan	2.5	-0.9	18.1	4.6	-9.6	-12.8	26.9
Tajikistan	3.4	-20.1	-8.4	13.6	6.3	-5.9	33.6
Turkmenistan	-8.8	-15.5	-22.7	-47.8	1.6	...	...
Uzbekistan	-2.8	-11.2	15.4	38.7	25.0	-12.9	20.4
East Asia	**35.5**	**-13.2**	**14.6**	**13.4**	**-3.6**	**-1.8**	**29.6**
China, People's Republic of	38.8	-14.3	16.1	15.8	-2.7	-0.6	30.1
Hong Kong, China	24.7	-4.1	8.3	7.7	-6.4	-2.3	24.1
Korea, Republic of	31.6	-16.9	17.8	11.9	-6.0	-7.1	31.5
Mongolia	49.7	-27.5	29.2	35.5	4.3	-13.5	29.2
Taipei,China	44.4	-16.2	12.6	10.6	0.3	0.1	33.3
South Asia[a]	**29.1**	**-11.6**	**18.7**	**14.7**	**-7.8**	**-16.9**	**51.3**
Bangladesh	5.1	2.5	7.5	25.2	3.0	-8.2	19.4*
Bhutan	40.7	4.5	2.8	-7.0	4.2	-13.9	...
India	30.7	-13.4	20.1	14.1	-9.2	-17.5	57.1
Maldives	-5.6	-4.9	11.1	25.4	-2.4	-36.4	40.1
Nepal	39.3	3.3	31.5	20.7	10.2	-19.7	28.9
Sri Lanka	31.8	-2.5	9.3	5.8	-10.2	-19.6	27.9
Southeast Asia[a]	**31.1**	**-11.0**	**15.1**	**14.0**	**-2.6**	**-8.7**	**27.1**
Brunei Darussalam	5.6	-10.0	15.4	35.2	22.3	4.3	102.1
Cambodia	35.0	10.5	9.8	21.3	18.3	-5.3	45.9
Indonesia	40.1	-19.9	15.7	20.2	-9.2	-17.3	38.6
Lao People's Democratic Republic	41.0	14.1	5.5	8.8	1.8	-14.4	9.7
Malaysia	33.1	-15.9	15.5	12.1	-6.0	-7.1	25.1
Myanmar	11.0	4.3	22.6	0.5	-3.9	...	...
Philippines	27.5	8.7	14.2	17.4	-1.1	-19.5	31.3*
Singapore	26.9	-18.5	12.1	13.3	-3.2	-8.4	23.6
Thailand	38.2	-10.7	13.0	14.0	-5.6	-13.9*	24.3*
Timor-Leste	1.0	-11.3	8.2	2.1	5.6	4.8	39.5
Viet Nam	21.3	12.1	21.9	11.3	6.9	3.5	26.5
The Pacific[a]	**18.9**	**-18.2**	**18.1**	**11.2**	**6.4**	**-22.5**	**5.4**
Cook Islands	11.2	-9.3	15.0	-0.2	1.2	-23.0	-21.3*
Fiji	17.0	-14.6	4.5	13.4	1.9	-37.8	25.2
Kiribati	5.4	-3.7	-3.0	-4.8	8.7	-2.4	34.4*
Marshall Islands	-21.2	-10.7	12.5	11.4	58.6	-37.2	7.5
Micronesia, Federated States of	-1.8	-0.3	-1.4	7.9	...	...	...
Nauru	-47.3	-18.0	-5.9	13.2	-4.1	-0.1	9.3
Niue	28.5	-15.4	13.1	17.8	-23.7	-13.9	18.3
Palau	9.3	4.4	2.7	-1.9	0.3	-12.7	4.4
Papua New Guinea	23.0	-30.2	47.8	14.8	12.0	-16.5	-7.9*
Samoa	36.6	-12.7	2.7	3.8	7.2	-20.1	18.4
Solomon Islands	51.2	-4.1	11.1	14.8	-6.7	-18.3	16.5
Tonga	10.3	-4.4	3.7	-4.0	17.2	-14.4	...
Tuvalu	59.2	66.4	13.1	-4.3	28.1	3.9	1.0
Vanuatu	-2.5	17.0	-3.1	-5.3	-10.6	-4.2	13.3
Developed ADB Member Economies	**25.1**	**-18.2**	**12.1**	**9.3**	**-4.2**	**-10.4**	**22.0**
Australia	23.4	-11.9	16.9	2.8	-5.9	-5.5	22.8
Japan	25.8	-20.1	10.7	11.4	-3.7	-11.7	21.0
New Zealand	21.5	-13.9	11.7	9.3	-3.4	-12.9	35.2
DEVELOPING ADB MEMBER ECONOMIES[a]	**32.7**	**-12.5**	**15.1**	**13.5**	**-3.6**	**-5.3**	**30.6**
ALL ADB REGIONAL MEMBERS[a]	**31.2**	**-13.5**	**14.6**	**12.9**	**-3.6**	**-6.1**	**29.3**
WORLD[b]	**21.6**	**-12.5**	**9.8**	**10.2**	**-2.6**	**-7.9**	**26.3**

... = data not available, * = provisional or preliminary, ADB = Asian Development Bank.e

Note: Growth rates are based on the value of imports in United States dollars.

a For estimating aggregates, imputation was done for economies with missing data by substituting available data from the nearest years.
b The world aggregate includes estimates derived from reports of partner economies for nonreporting and slow-reporting economies.

Sources: Economies' official sources; and International Monetary Fund. International Financial Statistics. http://data.imf.org/ (accessed 30 June 2022).

Table 2.4.12: Trade in Goods
(% of GDP)

ADB Regional Member	2010	2015	2017	2018	2019	2020	2021
Developing ADB Member Economies							
Central and West Asia[a]	**49.2**	**37.0**	**36.3**	**41.8**	**43.9**	**...**	**...**
Afghanistan	34.5	40.2	45.6	45.0	40.4	36.3	...
Armenia	51.7	44.8	55.0	59.3	60.1	56.3	60.4
Azerbaijan	62.4	47.8	59.2	67.4	64.8	53.1	58.8
Georgia	56.5	63.6	66.5	72.4	76.2	71.9	76.6
Kazakhstan	61.7	41.5	46.8	52.8	53.8	50.5	52.6
Kyrgyz Republic	103.8	84.4	81.3	86.2	78.6	73.2	84.6
Pakistan	30.6	25.8	21.7	23.8	24.4	22.0	23.5
Tajikistan	68.3	52.3	52.7	54.4	54.5	56.0	72.7
Turkmenistan	79.2	72.6	...	...	...	...	...
Uzbekistan	44.4	28.9	42.8	63.5	69.7	60.5	60.8
East Asia	**66.1**	**48.0**	**45.7**	**45.3**	**43.3**	**42.3**	**45.8**
China, People's Republic of	48.9	35.7	33.4	33.3	32.1	31.7	34.1
Hong Kong, China	360.1	319.0	309.6	313.2	295.4	306.4	357.8
Korea, Republic of	78.0	65.7	64.8	66.1	63.3	59.6	69.5
Mongolia	85.0	72.9	91.8	97.8	96.8	96.7	106.6
Taipei,China	119.7	96.8	97.0	101.5	100.6	94.2	106.8
South Asia[a]	**36.7**	**31.2**	**29.0**	**31.2**	**28.1**	**25.5**	**...**
Bangladesh	32.6	35.0	26.4	28.2	27.1	22.1	23.4
Bhutan[b]	86.9	76.7	65.7	63.1	64.0	65.1	...
India	36.9	30.5	29.0	31.2	27.8	25.6	32.6
Maldives	37.5	49.5	56.3	62.2	57.9	56.7	...
Nepal	36.5	35.5	34.6	38.4	39.3	33.1	39.4
Sri Lanka	37.6	34.6	34.3	36.1	35.8	30.5	37.3
Southeast Asia[a]	**99.7**	**91.2**	**90.9**	**95.1**	**88.0**	**...**	**...**
Brunei Darussalam	83.3	74.0	71.5	79.2	91.7	99.4	156.1
Cambodia[b]	93.3	125.3	120.5	129.3	137.4	153.0	186.2
Indonesia	38.9	34.0	32.1	35.4	30.3	28.8	36.1
Lao People's Democratic Republic[b]	56.4	64.7	61.7	63.2	64.4	60.2	69.0
Malaysia	142.1	124.3	129.1	130.1	121.9	126.0	144.2
Myanmar	...	45.3	54.5	55.6	53.0	...	...
Philippines	51.1	42.4	50.2	52.5	48.4	42.9	48.9
Singapore	277.4	216.1	204.1	207.6	199.6	203.4	217.5
Thailand	105.1	99.8	95.1	94.7	84.3	82.6	99.2
Timor-Leste[c]	38.5	33.2	35.8	38.6	36.6	40.9	...
Viet Nam	135.5	169.6	191.4	196.1	197.8	201.1	184.4
The Pacific[a]	**66.5**	**54.8**	**58.2**	**59.3**	**62.2**	**...**	**...**
Cook Islands	39.8	40.9	44.9	42.0	43.1	43.9	30.9
Fiji	84.2	69.4	63.4	66.9	69.5	57.1	...
Kiribati	49.6	66.5	65.4	56.5	69.6	65.3	...
Marshall Islands	103.8	93.0	81.9	86.0	112.5	80.7	77.9
Micronesia, Federated States of	66.6	63.1	62.6	60.9	...	...	...
Nauru	86.3	118.4	65.6	60.8	54.2	53.1	50.8
Niue	56.5	58.7	63.9	65.2	49.6	...	...
Palau	64.7	62.3	65.4	64.6	66.5	60.6	...
Papua New Guinea[b]	65.0	50.5	57.2	58.1	62.0	51.0	50.6
Samoa	43.3	40.2	40.6	42.0	44.7	39.0	42.8
Solomon Islands	70.4	69.2	66.9	69.9	62.6	54.1	...
Tonga	44.9	56.3	55.6	50.2	56.5	49.7	...
Tuvalu	72.7	105.7	59.1	53.3	60.7	65.5	57.3
Vanuatu	49.5	55.5	49.0	45.2	38.5	...	...
Developed ADB Member Economies[a]	**27.1**	**29.6**	**29.3**	**31.0**	**29.8**	**27.3**	**...**
Australia	33.9	31.8	33.5	35.2	35.8	33.2	38.2
Japan	25.4	28.6	27.8	29.5	27.8	25.3	30.9
New Zealand	42.2	39.7	37.9	39.4	38.4	35.8	...
DEVELOPING ADB MEMBER ECONOMIES[a]	**66.4**	**51.1**	**49.1**	**49.9**	**47.2**	**...**	**...**
ALL ADB REGIONAL MEMBERS[a]	**52.0**	**46.1**	**44.5**	**45.7**	**43.4**	**...**	**...**

... = data not available, ADB = Asian Development Bank, GDP = Gross Domestic Product.

Note: Trade in goods is calculated as the sum of merchandise exports and imports in United States dollars.

a For estimating aggregates, imputation was done for economies with missing data by substituting available data from the nearest years.

b The Key Indicators Database features a longer time series on trade in goods. The compilation methodology shifted from cost, insurance, and freight to free on board from 2004 onward for Bhutan; from 2005 onward for Cambodia; from 2017 onward for the Lao People's Democratic Republic; and from 2010 onward for Papua New Guinea.

c From September 2019, oil revenue from the Joint Petroleum Development Area is now included in GDP based on the new Timor-Leste Australia Maritime Boundary Treaty.

Sources: Economies' official sources; and International Monetary Fund. International Financial Statistics. http://data.imf.org/ (accessed 30 June 2022).

Table 2.4.13: Direction of Trade: Merchandise Exports
(% of total merchandise exports)

To / From / ADB Regional Member	Asia and the Pacific		Europe		North and Central America		Middle East		South America		Africa		Rest of the World	
	2010	2021	2010	2021	2010	2021	2010	2021	2010	2021	2010	2021	2010	2021
Developing ADB Member Economies														
Central and West Asia[a]	**28.2**	**32.5**	**53.1**	**51.3**	**8.6**	**5.5**	**8.1**	**4.0**	**0.3**	**0.4**	**1.2**	**1.7**	**0.4**	**4.6**
Afghanistan	63.7	77.9	21.6	9.6	1.1	1.4	13.6	11.1	0.0	0.0	0.0	0.1	0.0	0.0
Armenia	10.4	21.0	67.1	63.8	11.5	2.9	9.5	11.6	0.3	0.1	0.1	0.0	1.1	0.5
Azerbaijan	19.7	8.4	59.9	82.3	9.5	1.3	10.7	4.9	0.0	0.3	0.3	2.7	0.0	0.0
Georgia	33.8	40.1	42.0	50.5	18.6	5.0	4.6	3.0	0.4	0.9	0.6	0.5	0.0	0.0
Kazakhstan	24.2	36.1	64.5	59.8	6.0	1.7	4.5	1.9	0.1	0.1	0.1	0.3	0.7	0.0
Kyrgyz Republic	19.5	42.8	52.2	52.8	7.2	0.3	21.1	4.0	0.0	0.0	0.0	0.0	0.0	0.0
Pakistan	29.9	25.9	28.5	35.9	19.1	23.0	15.1	9.2	1.7	1.3	5.7	4.8	0.0	0.0
Tajikistan	44.9	54.1	42.6	36.3	0.0	0.0	8.6	2.4	0.0	0.0	3.9	7.1	0.0	0.0
Turkmenistan	52.0	82.4	38.4	15.2	1.9	0.2	7.1	1.1	0.0	1.1	0.7	0.0	0.0	0.0
Uzbekistan	60.8	30.0	32.1	24.9	0.0	0.2	7.0	1.6	0.1	0.0	0.0	1.3	0.0	42.1
East Asia[a]	**52.9**	**53.8**	**18.9**	**18.0**	**18.3**	**18.8**	**4.1**	**3.7**	**2.8**	**2.9**	**2.5**	**2.8**	**0.4**	**0.1**
China, People's Republic of	43.5	44.6	23.2	21.6	21.7	21.5	4.6	4.5	3.4	3.9	3.3	3.8	0.3	0.0
Hong Kong, China	72.2	78.9	12.6	10.0	12.4	7.3	1.4	2.3	0.9	0.8	0.5	0.7	0.1	0.0
Korea, Republic of	57.6	62.4	14.8	13.8	15.1	18.4	5.7	2.3	3.4	1.5	2.6	1.5	0.8	0.0
Mongolia	74.4	78.7	18.7	21.1	6.5	0.1	0.4	0.1	0.0	0.0	0.1	0.0	0.0	0.0
Taipei,China	71.1	72.0	10.6	8.6	13.0	16.4	2.3	1.3	1.3	0.7	0.8	0.5	1.0	0.5
South Asia[a]	**31.7**	**31.2**	**23.7**	**23.7**	**13.7**	**20.6**	**19.4**	**12.3**	**2.4**	**2.8**	**6.4**	**7.8**	**2.7**	**1.6**
Bangladesh	9.1	13.4	49.6	49.2	23.4	18.3	2.1	2.4	0.4	0.8	0.7	0.8	14.7	15.2
Bhutan	99.7	99.0	0.1	0.9	0.1	0.0	0.0	0.0	0.0	0.0	0.1	0.0	0.0	0.0
India	33.6	33.0	21.3	20.9	12.7	20.6	21.2	13.5	2.6	3.0	7.1	8.7	1.5	0.2
Maldives	59.7	61.2	35.9	30.7	0.7	4.0	3.1	0.5	0.0	0.5	0.6	3.1	0.0	0.0
Nepal	77.3	84.0	12.6	6.7	7.5	6.8	0.5	0.4	0.2	0.0	0.1	0.2	1.9	1.9
Sri Lanka	20.7	22.5	36.0	35.3	21.4	29.1	9.9	8.3	1.0	1.6	0.9	2.0	10.2	1.2
Southeast Asia[a]	**69.4**	**66.6**	**12.7**	**11.5**	**11.7**	**17.1**	**3.1**	**2.2**	**1.0**	**1.1**	**1.9**	**1.5**	**0.1**	**0.0**
Brunei Darussalam	99.6	99.6	0.2	0.1	0.2	0.1	0.0	0.2	0.0	0.0	0.0	0.0	0.0	0.0
Cambodia	41.6	32.1	17.6	22.0	39.7	44.2	0.3	0.4	0.4	0.5	0.1	0.4	0.2	0.3
Indonesia	70.9	70.2	12.5	10.6	10.2	12.6	3.2	3.0	1.5	1.3	1.7	2.3	0.0	0.0
Lao People's Democratic Republic	85.0	90.6	11.4	4.9	3.5	4.2	0.0	0.1	0.0	0.1	0.0	0.0	0.0	0.0
Malaysia	70.3	70.5	11.8	11.0	11.1	13.4	4.3	2.3	0.7	0.6	1.7	2.2	0.0	0.0
Myanmar	95.4	75.8	1.4	18.3	0.1	4.3	1.7	0.9	0.1	0.1	1.3	0.5	0.0	0.1
Philippines	67.3	68.4	14.8	12.4	16.0	17.6	1.1	0.8	0.5	0.6	0.4	0.3	0.0	0.0
Singapore	74.9	76.6	10.7	9.4	9.8	10.5	2.1	1.7	0.5	0.4	1.9	1.4	0.1	0.0
Thailand	62.9	64.5	14.6	10.9	12.1	17.4	5.0	3.2	2.1	1.8	3.0	2.0	0.3	0.2
Timor-Leste	58.1	64.8	23.6	31.7	0.2	1.6	6.2	0.0	0.1	1.7	11.8	0.2	0.0	0.0
Viet Nam	50.8	47.7	22.2	15.4	22.4	32.3	1.7	2.1	1.1	1.8	1.5	0.7	0.4	0.0
The Pacific[a]	**75.9**	**74.9**	**17.9**	**18.1**	**4.4**	**3.9**	**0.1**	**1.0**	**1.1**	**1.6**	**0.6**	**0.3**	**0.1**	**0.1**
Cook Islands	78.9	66.4	0.0	0.0	2.0	7.2	0.0	0.0	0.0	0.0	0.0	0.0	19.1	26.4
Fiji	71.8	72.2	7.5	3.0	18.7	24.3	0.3	0.3	0.0	0.0	0.8	0.2	0.8	0.0
Kiribati	97.8	93.2	2.2	0.0	0.0	6.8	0.0	0.0	0.0	0.0	0.0	0.0	0.0	0.0
Marshall Islands	0.3	24.6	95.5	70.1	4.2	1.2	0.0	3.8	0.0	0.1	0.0	0.3	0.0	0.0
Micronesia, Federated States of	88.2	96.7	2.6	0.1	9.2	3.1	0.0	0.0	0.0	0.1	0.1	0.0	0.0	0.0
Nauru	70.1	69.3	0.2	0.2	0.5	6.8	0.8	11.1	0.0	2.0	28.4	10.7	0.0	0.0
Niue	...	...	...	...	...	...	...	...	...	...	...	...	...	...
Palau	91.1	19.4	2.0	14.8	6.6	16.6	0.2	0.2	0.1	44.7	0.0	4.3	0.0	0.0
Papua New Guinea	80.8	83.1	17.0	13.1	2.0	1.6	0.0	0.0	0.0	2.1	0.2	0.0	0.0	0.1
Samoa	96.0	69.7	0.3	1.0	3.2	20.1	0.0	0.0	0.0	7.1	0.5	2.1	0.0	0.0
Solomon Islands	81.8	76.5	17.8	21.3	0.4	0.4	0.0	0.4	0.0	1.3	0.0	0.1	0.0	0.0
Tonga	96.2	83.8	0.0	0.0	3.8	16.1	0.0	0.0	0.0	0.0	0.0	0.0	0.0	0.0
Tuvalu	74.2	16.3	15.3	0.8	5.7	1.2	0.8	67.4	2.2	3.3	1.8	11.0	0.0	0.0
Vanuatu	31.6	67.5	1.8	3.6	20.5	6.9	0.4	18.1	45.3	2.6	0.4	1.3	0.0	0.0
Developed ADB Member Economies[a]	**63.5**	**68.4**	**12.8**	**10.4**	**16.9**	**15.9**	**3.4**	**2.5**	**1.6**	**1.1**	**1.4**	**1.0**	**0.3**	**0.8**
Australia	80.1	84.9	8.9	5.0	5.0	4.1	2.9	2.1	1.0	0.6	1.3	0.7	0.8	2.5
Japan	58.9	60.7	13.9	12.9	20.5	21.4	3.5	2.6	1.8	1.3	1.3	1.1	0.1	0.0
New Zealand	65.9	71.2	12.3	9.3	11.2	12.8	4.8	3.7	1.7	0.8	2.6	1.6	1.5	0.5
DEVELOPING ADB MEMBER ECONOMIES[a]	**55.2**	**54.9**	**18.6**	**17.5**	**16.1**	**18.2**	**4.9**	**3.8**	**2.3**	**2.4**	**2.5**	**2.8**	**0.5**	**0.2**
ALL ADB REGIONAL MEMBERS[a]	**56.8**	**56.7**	**17.5**	**16.6**	**16.2**	**17.9**	**4.6**	**3.7**	**2.1**	**2.3**	**2.3**	**2.6**	**0.5**	**0.3**
WORLD[a]	**31.0**	**34.2**	**40.3**	**37.7**	**17.3**	**18.2**	**4.6**	**3.8**	**2.9**	**2.5**	**2.7**	**2.6**	**1.3**	**1.0**

... = data not available, 0.0 = magnitude is less than half of unit employed, ADB = Asian Development Bank.

a Aggregates include estimates derived from reports of partner economies for nonreporting and slow-reporting economies.

Sources: International Monetary Fund. Direction of Trade Statistics. http://data.imf.org/?sk=9D6028D4-F14A-464C-A2F2-59B2CD424B85 (accessed 30 June 2022). For the Cook Islands and Taipei,China: Economies' official sources.

Table 2.4.14: Direction of Trade: Merchandise Imports
(% of total merchandise imports)

From / To / ADB Regional Member	Asia and the Pacific		Europe		North and Central America		Middle East		South America		Africa		Rest of the World	
	2010	2021	2010	2021	2010	2021	2010	2021	2010	2021	2010	2021	2010	2021
Developing ADB Member Economies														
Central and West Asia[a]	**36.6**	**43.0**	**41.6**	**36.8**	**4.6**	**4.3**	**14.3**	**11.6**	**1.5**	**1.7**	**1.3**	**2.3**	**0.0**	**0.3**
Afghanistan	70.7	69.5	15.6	6.6	2.2	0.7	10.6	22.9	0.5	0.1	0.4	0.1	0.0	0.1
Armenia	21.9	25.6	64.4	57.1	3.8	3.1	7.4	9.6	2.0	1.6	0.4	0.7	0.1	2.4
Azerbaijan	24.1	26.6	64.8	61.6	3.8	4.8	3.7	4.3	3.2	2.5	0.3	0.2	0.0	0.0
Georgia	26.4	28.4	62.6	58.4	3.9	6.7	4.6	3.2	1.9	3.1	0.6	0.2	0.0	0.0
Kazakhstan	27.2	36.6	62.7	57.5	7.0	3.6	1.2	0.8	1.4	0.4	0.4	0.4	0.0	0.8
Kyrgyz Republic	41.9	48.7	50.3	47.2	6.6	2.7	0.9	0.8	0.3	0.4	0.1	0.1	0.0	0.0
Pakistan	40.5	49.1	13.8	11.9	5.7	6.1	35.5	25.0	1.2	2.4	3.3	5.5	0.1	0.0
Tajikistan	48.4	52.6	39.6	43.3	3.5	0.8	7.3	2.1	1.1	1.0	0.0	0.0	0.0	0.3
Turkmenistan	24.7	22.1	73.4	73.5	1.1	2.2	0.7	0.5	0.1	1.6	0.0	0.0	0.0	0.0
Uzbekistan	41.3	47.9	49.6	47.0	1.6	1.3	5.0	1.7	2.4	1.7	0.2	0.4	0.0	0.0
East Asia[a]	**57.2**	**57.2**	**13.4**	**15.5**	**9.2**	**9.2**	**8.4**	**6.7**	**3.9**	**5.1**	**2.8**	**2.7**	**5.1**	**3.7**
China, People's Republic of	50.1	49.3	15.2	17.9	9.1	8.7	6.6	7.1	5.7	7.3	4.2	3.7	9.2	6.0
Hong Kong, China	82.4	84.6	9.2	7.4	6.1	4.9	1.4	1.9	0.6	0.7	0.3	0.5	0.0	0.0
Korea, Republic of	52.8	54.3	13.1	15.8	11.2	14.6	18.9	10.2	2.7	3.0	1.2	1.5	0.0	0.6
Mongolia	52.8	55.7	39.2	38.7	7.7	5.2	0.1	0.1	0.1	0.2	0.0	0.1	0.0	0.0
Taipei,China	60.8	66.7	10.5	12.4	11.5	11.7	12.3	6.6	2.2	1.6	2.7	1.0	0.0	0.0
South Asia[a]	**37.3**	**45.6**	**19.3**	**15.6**	**6.2**	**7.9**	**25.5**	**20.7**	**3.3**	**3.3**	**7.5**	**6.5**	**1.0**	**0.4**
Bangladesh	67.6	68.6	9.8	7.4	3.8	5.2	8.4	6.9	2.5	4.6	1.0	3.4	6.9	3.9
Bhutan	93.2	98.1	5.5	1.2	0.5	0.2	0.8	0.2	0.0	0.0	0.1	0.0	0.0	0.2
India	33.1	40.3	20.4	17.2	6.5	8.7	27.6	23.3	3.4	3.3	8.4	7.2	0.6	0.0
Maldives	59.7	57.5	9.7	10.7	8.9	3.6	19.9	27.0	0.6	0.8	1.2	0.6	0.0	0.0
Nepal	86.4	88.6	4.8	4.1	1.7	2.1	5.0	2.9	1.9	0.8	0.1	1.0	0.0	0.4
Sri Lanka	64.7	73.1	16.1	11.1	4.2	3.2	13.4	10.5	0.9	0.3	0.4	1.6	0.4	0.2
Southeast Asia[a]	**67.1**	**73.7**	**12.5**	**10.3**	**9.8**	**7.7**	**7.6**	**4.8**	**1.7**	**1.9**	**0.8**	**1.4**	**0.5**	**0.2**
Brunei Darussalam	77.8	55.8	10.8	22.9	10.2	2.1	0.5	16.0	0.1	1.3	0.1	1.8	0.6	0.0
Cambodia	90.0	93.5	6.7	4.3	2.7	1.3	0.2	0.4	0.2	0.4	0.1	0.0	0.0	0.0
Indonesia	72.6	75.3	9.4	8.0	8.0	6.9	6.0	4.2	2.3	2.6	1.7	3.0	0.1	0.0
Lao People's Democratic Republic	95.0	94.6	4.5	4.8	0.5	0.6	0.0	0.0	0.0	0.0	0.0	0.0	0.0	0.0
Malaysia	68.7	74.3	11.5	10.3	12.2	8.3	3.8	3.5	1.8	2.1	1.5	1.5	0.5	0.0
Myanmar	77.7	90.7	1.7	4.0	0.6	1.8	2.1	2.3	0.2	1.2	0.1	0.1	17.6	0.0
Philippines	69.4	80.2	8.9	7.8	11.6	7.2	8.5	3.1	1.4	1.4	0.2	0.2	0.0	0.0
Singapore	60.2	64.2	15.8	15.4	12.6	11.9	9.6	5.9	1.4	1.2	0.3	1.3	0.0	0.0
Thailand	65.2	69.7	12.8	10.6	6.7	6.3	11.6	8.6	1.6	1.8	0.9	1.9	1.3	1.1
Timor-Leste	95.9	95.7	3.0	1.9	0.6	0.7	0.1	0.1	0.0	1.6	0.4	0.0	0.0	0.0
Viet Nam	80.1	82.4	10.6	6.7	5.0	5.0	1.8	2.6	2.1	2.5	0.4	0.8	0.0	0.0
The Pacific[a]	**81.6**	**86.0**	**11.4**	**8.6**	**5.6**	**3.4**	**0.1**	**1.3**	**0.1**	**0.2**	**0.6**	**0.1**	**0.5**	**0.3**
Cook Islands	91.8	87.7	0.0	0.0	2.8	2.8	0.0	0.0	0.0	0.0	0.0	0.0	5.4	9.5
Fiji	91.4	85.3	2.6	3.5	3.9	10.3	0.3	0.5	0.2	0.2	0.5	0.1	1.2	0.1
Kiribati	83.0	91.6	4.6	6.9	11.7	1.4	0.0	0.0	0.3	0.0	0.4	0.0	0.0	0.0
Marshall Islands	0.1	83.3	99.7	12.6	0.0	1.9	0.0	2.1	0.0	0.0	0.1	0.0	0.0	0.0
Micronesia, Federated States of	48.1	54.0	1.2	0.6	38.1	23.5	0.1	0.0	0.0	7.3	0.3	0.3	12.1	14.3
Nauru	80.2	96.5	3.7	1.1	16.0	1.9	0.0	0.1	0.0	0.4	0.0	0.0	0.0	0.0
Niue	...	...	...	...	...	...	...	...	...	...	...	...	...	...
Palau	63.7	69.1	0.6	2.5	34.9	27.2	0.0	0.0	0.0	1.1	0.3	0.1	0.5	0.0
Papua New Guinea	88.3	95.7	5.6	2.7	5.1	1.1	0.0	0.0	0.2	0.1	0.8	0.3	0.0	0.0
Samoa	87.0	88.1	1.3	1.0	11.4	9.9	0.0	0.0	0.0	0.4	0.0	0.0	0.2	0.5
Solomon Islands	97.1	92.2	1.1	4.7	1.7	3.0	0.0	0.0	0.0	0.0	0.1	0.1	0.0	0.0
Tonga	84.3	86.8	1.9	1.7	13.2	10.6	0.1	0.0	0.2	0.8	0.1	0.0	0.2	0.0
Tuvalu	93.3	93.3	0.1	0.2	4.8	0.6	0.5	5.8	0.0	0.0	1.2	0.0	0.0	0.0
Vanuatu	91.7	92.2	5.0	5.4	2.3	1.8	0.1	0.1	0.1	0.4	0.8	0.1	0.1	0.0
Developed ADB Member Economies[a]	**54.4**	**58.0**	**14.9**	**16.8**	**12.3**	**13.1**	**13.5**	**7.7**	**2.6**	**2.4**	**1.6**	**1.6**	**0.7**	**0.4**
Australia	59.6	62.6	20.0	20.2	12.7	12.2	2.3	1.4	1.1	0.8	1.4	1.3	3.0	1.5
Japan	52.6	56.2	13.3	15.5	12.2	13.5	17.1	10.0	3.2	3.0	1.6	1.8	0.0	0.0
New Zealand	62.9	63.8	16.7	19.5	12.3	10.4	6.2	4.4	0.7	1.1	0.8	0.5	0.2	0.2
DEVELOPING ADB MEMBER ECONOMIES[a]	**57.1**	**59.7**	**14.6**	**14.8**	**8.9**	**8.6**	**10.0**	**7.7**	**3.3**	**4.0**	**2.8**	**2.7**	**3.4**	**2.5**
ALL ADB REGIONAL MEMBERS[a]	**56.6**	**59.5**	**14.6**	**15.1**	**9.6**	**9.2**	**10.7**	**7.7**	**3.1**	**3.8**	**2.5**	**2.6**	**2.9**	**2.2**
WORLD[a]	**33.5**	**37.8**	**39.1**	**37.6**	**13.1**	**12.9**	**6.0**	**4.5**	**3.5**	**3.1**	**2.9**	**2.6**	**2.0**	**1.5**

... = data not available, 0.0 = magnitude is less than half of unit employed, ADB = Asian Development Bank.

a Aggregates include estimates derived from reports of partner economies for nonreporting and slow-reporting economies.

Sources: International Monetary Fund. Direction of Trade Statistics. http://data.imf.org/?sk=9D6028D4-F14A-464C-A2F2-59B2CD424B85 (accessed 30 June 2022). For the Cook Islands and Taipei,China: Economies' official sources.

Table 2.4.15: International Reserves and Ratio to Imports

ADB Regional Member	International Reserves[a] ($ million)				Ratio to Imports[b] (months)			
	2010	2015	2020	2021	2010	2015	2020	2021
Developing ADB Member Economies								
Central and West Asia[c]	**77,894**	**93,691**	**117,745**	**...**	**9.4**	**9.4**	**10.6**	**...**
Afghanistan	5,147	6,990	9,741	...	12.9	11.6	19.9	...
Armenia	1,866	1,775	2,616	3,230	6.9	7.6	7.8	...
Azerbaijan	6,409	7,910	7,634	8,307	11.5	9.7	9.1	9.6
Georgia	2,264	2,521	3,913	4,271	5.4	4.3	6.3	5.5
Kazakhstan	28,275	27,871	35,638	34,378	10.3	10.1	11.6	10.4
Kyrgyz Republic	1,720	1,778	2,810	2,978	7.0	5.6	9.8	6.9
Pakistan	17,210	20,045	18,251	22,811	6.6	5.8	5.0	5.1
Tajikistan	403	494	2,238	2,499	1.7	2.1	9.9	8.1
Turkmenistan	...	...	...	...	...	...	...	...
Uzbekistan	14,600	24,307	34,904	35,139	18.0	25.2	22.0	18.3
East Asia	**3,825,691**	**4,564,136**	**4,830,581**	**4,944,234**	**20.0**	**19.7**	**17.8**	**13.9**
China, People's Republic of	2,875,894	3,405,385	3,357,028	3,427,045	27.8	26.1	20.2	15.5
Hong Kong, China	268,731	358,773	491,775	496,867	8.4	8.2	10.8	8.9
Korea, Republic of	291,571	367,944	441,907	461,964	8.4	10.4	12.1	9.7
Mongolia	2,288	1,323	4,542	4,374	8.9	4.1	10.4	7.6
Taipei,China	387,206	430,711	535,327	553,984	18.5	19.4	24.0	18.2
South Asia[c]	**320,411**	**395,960**	**648,455**	**...**	**9.0**	**10.3**	**16.3**	**...**
Bangladesh	11,178	27,493	43,164	46,154	6.3	8.8	10.2	9.1
Bhutan	1,002	1,103	1,510	...	15.1	13.1	20.4	...
India	297,746	351,551	586,045	633,761	9.3	10.6	17.6	12.3
Maldives	350	564	985	806	3.3	3.6	6.9	4.0
Nepal	2,939	7,945	11,085	9,204	7.2	12.5	13.1	8.7
Sri Lanka	7,196	7,304	5,666	...	6.4	4.6	4.2	...
Southeast Asia[c]	**688,196**	**731,611**	**1,104,611**	**...**	**9.3**	**8.5**	**...**	**...**
Brunei Darussalam	1,563	3,367	3,997	...	7.3	12.6	9.3	...
Cambodia	3,802	7,376	21,333	20,263	6.9	6.7	12.2	7.9
Indonesia	96,211	105,929	135,897	144,905	9.7	9.4	12.1	9.2
Lao People's Democratic Republic	817	1,072	1,425	1,476	4.8	2.3	3.2	3.0
Malaysia	106,525	95,287	107,636	116,890	8.6	7.8	8.5	7.2
Myanmar	5,729	4,599	7,670	...	16.0	4.0	4.5 (2018)	...
Philippines	62,373	80,667	110,117	108,794	14.0	14.6	16.1	12.1
Singapore	225,715	247,746	362,300	417,896	8.7	9.8	13.8	13.0
Thailand	172,129	156,514	258,128	245,985	12.4	10.0	16.6	12.8
Timor-Leste	406	438	657	935	15.9	8.0	12.1	14.0
Viet Nam	12,926	28,616	95,452	109,963	2.0	2.2	4.5	5.7
The Pacific[c]	**4,582**	**3,871**	**...**	**...**	**8.3**	**7.4**	**...**	**...**
Cook Islands	...	...	...	...	...	...	...	...
Fiji	721	919	1,081	1,518	5.6	5.9	8.8	...
Kiribati	8	7	8	...	1.3	0.7	0.6	...
Marshall Islands	...	...	...	...	...	...	...	...
Micronesia, Federated States of	56	135	452	497	4.2	9.7	13.9 (2018)	...
Nauru	...	...	...	...	...	...	...	...
Niue	...	...	...	...	...	...	...	...
Palau	...	...	...	...	...	...	...	...
Papua New Guinea	3,092	1,738	2,309 (2019)	...	10.5	8.2	7.0 (2019)	...
Samoa	173	112	277	295	7.4	4.5	11.7	10.5
Solomon Islands	266	534	661	695	8.9	14.6	19.6	17.8
Tonga	105	156	299	362	6.0	6.2	8.6	...
Tuvalu	...	...	...	...	...	...	...	...
Vanuatu	161	269	614	665	8.1	10.4	29.1	38.2
Developed ADB Member Economies[c]	**1,163,670**	**1,293,265**	**1,447,081**	**1,479,709**	**16.4**	**17.9**	**20.3**	**...**
Australia	42,268	45,412	42,538	57,846	2.6	2.7	2.4	2.9
Japan	1,104,680	1,233,153	1,390,809	1,405,749	21.2	23.5	27.6	23.0
New Zealand	16,723	14,700	13,733	16,114	6.5	5.1	4.3	...
DEVELOPING ADB MEMBER ECONOMIES[c]	**4,916,774**	**5,789,268**	**...**	**...**	**15.9**	**15.8**	**...**	**...**
ALL ADB REGIONAL MEMBERS[c]	**6,080,445**	**7,082,533**	**...**	**...**	**16.0**	**16.1**	**...**	**...**

... = data not available, $ = United States dollars, ADB = Asian Development Bank.

a Data refer to international reserves with gold at national valuation, unless otherwise specified, as of the end of the year. For Afghanistan (prior to 2008), Bhutan (2000–2018 and 2021), the Lao People's Democratic Republic (2021), Myanmar (2021), Nauru, Palau, Papua New Guinea (2020 and 2021), Samoa, Solomon Islands (prior to 2012), Sri Lanka (2021), Timor-Leste (prior to 2003), Tonga, Turkmenistan, Uzbekistan (2005–2012), and Vanuatu, data refer to international reserves without gold. For estimating regional aggregates, imputation was done for economies with missing data using available data from nearest years.

b Merchandise imports from the balance of payments were used in the calculations. The aggregate ratios were calculated using only reporting economies with data available for both reserves and imports in the years specified in the column headings.

c Aggregates include only reporting economies with data corresponding to the year heading.

Sources: For international reserves: International Monetary Fund (IMF). International Financial Statistics. http://data.imf.org/ (accessed 30 June 2022); for Hong Kong, China (2010): IMF. Official Communication, 11 May 2022; and for Taipei,China: economy's official source. For the reserves-to-imports ratio: Asian Development Bank estimates using data from the IMF's International Financial Statistics; official communications from the IMF; and economies' official sources.

Table 2.4.16: Net Official Development Assistance from All Sources to Developing Economies
($ million)

ADB Regional Member	2010	2016	2017	2018	2019	2020
Developing ADB Member Economies						
Central and West Asia[a]	**11,448**	**9,384**	**8,524**	**7,998**	**9,215**	**10,925**
Afghanistan	6,235	4,069	3,812	3,792	4,137	4,208
Armenia	320	326	258	142	417	134
Azerbaijan	156	79	124	87	119	123
Georgia	589	463	447	589	492	1,041
Kazakhstan	212	63	59	80	54	73
Kyrgyz Republic	372	519	465	439	443	485
Pakistan	2,933	2,961	2,364	1,387	2,013	2,592
Tajikistan	388	360	328	404	362	768
Turkmenistan	44	32	28	20	25	36
Uzbekistan	198	511	639	1,058	1,153	1,464
East Asia[a]	**959**	**-466**	**-224**	**-372**	**-298**	**129**
China, People's Republic of	672	-791	-990	-705	-609	-573
Hong Kong, China	...	...	...	...	...	...
Korea, Republic of	...	...	...	...	...	...
Mongolia	287	326	766	334	311	702
Taipei,China	...	...	...	...	...	...
South Asia[a]	**5,670**	**6,724**	**8,731**	**6,951**	**8,706**	**9,657**
Bangladesh	1,327	2,533	3,782	3,045	4,382	5,374
Bhutan	97	52	119	108	179	202
India	2,831	2,679	3,198	2,462	2,550	1,794
Maldives	88	23	46	131	71	311
Nepal	767	1,065	1,270	1,452	1,333	1,758
Sri Lanka	559	373	316	-247	192	218
Southeast Asia[a]	**6,365**	**6,146**	**6,180**	**5,992**	**4,814**	**9,075**
Brunei Darussalam	...	...	...	...	...	...
Cambodia	681	728	856	783	966	1,373
Indonesia	1,324	-108	280	963	-667	1,233
Lao People's Democratic Republic	389	399	480	589	622	529
Malaysia	-6	-52	-29	-35	-3	-5
Myanmar	355	1,537	1,542	1,712	2,044	2,870
Philippines	582	284	160	547	886	1,456
Singapore	...	...	...	...	...	...
Thailand	-20	228	250	-419	-352	198
Timor-Leste	290	224	232	208	230	250
Viet Nam	2,770	2,906	2,407	1,645	1,088	1,171
The Pacific[a]	**1,435**	**1,345**	**1,579**	**1,899**	**1,742**	**2,519**
Cook Islands	14	17	19	34	29	...
Fiji	76	117	146	121	129	194
Kiribati	24	61	77	80	57	58
Marshall Islands	25	13	73	54	66	183
Micronesia, Federated States of	64	51	98	99	93	172
Nauru	28	23	26	38	54	28
Niue	15	14	15	19	19	22
Palau	29	18	22	85	25	66
Papua New Guinea	514	532	533	790	649	1,055
Samoa	124	89	136	128	124	167
Solomon Islands	333	176	187	196	224	214
Tonga	66	83	87	97	108	163
Tuvalu	14	24	29	27	36	43
Vanuatu	109	129	133	131	131	154
DEVELOPING ADB MEMBER ECONOMIES[a]	**25,876**	**23,134**	**24,790**	**22,468**	**24,179**	**32,305**
DEVELOPING ECONOMIES WORLDWIDE[b]	**129,264**	**158,811**	**165,080**	**167,532**	**163,518**	**196,121**

... = data not available, $ = United States dollars, ADB = Asian Development Bank.

Note: Net official development assistance refers to concessional flows to developing economies and multilateral institutions provided by official agencies, including state and local governments, or by their executing agencies, administered with the objective of promoting the economic development and welfare of developing economies, and containing a grant element of at least 25%. Net flow takes into account principal repayments for loans, offsetting entries for forgiven debt, and recoveries made on grants.

a For reporting economies only.
b Includes data for all developing economies as reported in the Organisation for Economic Co-operation and Development's OECD.Stat database.

Source: Organisation for Economic Co-operation and Development. OECD.Stat Database. http://stats.oecd.org (accessed 20 July 2022).

Table 2.4.17: Net Other Official Flows from All Sources to Developing Economies
($ million)

ADB Regional Member	2010	2016	2017	2018	2019	2020
Developing ADB Member Economies						
Central and West Asia[a]	**4,070.1**	**5,540.1**	**2,663.7**	**1,869.2**	**3,028.3**	**5,598.8**
Afghanistan	71.2	97.2	56.1	0.2	14.8	-2.1
Armenia	288.3	197.2	157.6	156.7	225.3	82.1
Azerbaijan	179.9	1,114.7	1,738.5	490.7	343.6	-118.4
Georgia	250.2	486.6	262.1	218.9	411.9	851.3
Kazakhstan	2,247.2	441.4	-853.7	-586.6	-53.5	697.0
Kyrgyz Republic	18.3	-43.2	-6.0	51.2	33.4	15.3
Pakistan	345.3	1,102.3	378.2	-137.1	755.9	1,520.8
Tajikistan	6.4	13.6	15.6	48.2	75.4	62.5
Turkmenistan	647.4	926.1	532.3	127.6	-811.1	463.9
Uzbekistan	16.0	1,204.2	383.0	1,499.5	2,032.6	2,026.5
East Asia[a]	**3,355.5**	**896.3**	**1,036.2**	**818.7**	**1,086.2**	**1,273.9**
China, People's Republic of	3,196.3	139.9	1,227.3	645.4	664.0	854.0
Hong Kong, China	...	...	...	...	...	...
Korea, Republic of	...	...	...	...	...	...
Mongolia	159.3	756.4	-191.1	173.3	422.2	419.9
Taipei,China	...	...	...	...	...	...
South Asia[a]	**6,175.1**	**3,653.6**	**3,636.7**	**2,831.4**	**3,289.3**	**6,841.1**
Bangladesh	35.1	1,421.5	2,337.4	938.4	1,208.9	986.9
Bhutan	24.0	8.0	3.1	-5.2	6.4	5.3
India	5,967.5	1,935.6	1,190.1	1,650.9	1,899.4	5,310.5
Maldives	-33.9	-24.7	-23.8	18.0	-6.6	-17.3
Nepal	-6.9	0.7	-2.3	-0.2	51.2	3.1
Sri Lanka	189.3	312.6	132.3	229.5	130.0	552.6
Southeast Asia[a]	**3,916.6**	**3,110.3**	**60.5**	**4,789.0**	**5,858.8**	**8,703.3**
Brunei Darussalam	...	...	...	...	...	...
Cambodia	-5.0	-12.3	84.1	-24.8	86.5	-35.1
Indonesia	1,783.7	3,708.7	2,963.1	3,793.7	1,804.8	2,633.6
Lao People's Democratic Republic	-120.5	38.6	74.7	34.1	20.6	-12.1
Malaysia	159.2	-1,494.5	-739.8	-963.0	1,971.0	-164.1
Myanmar	30.9	100.6	96.4	16.3	130.4	290.1
Philippines	-680.3	203.1	-32.2	956.5	456.8	6,306.7
Singapore	...	...	...	...	...	...
Thailand	-71.5	-39.3	-1,051.6	-614.0	718.6	-104.9
Timor-Leste	4.6	24.8	11.8	26.5	38.3	8.6
Viet Nam	2,815.4	580.6	-1,345.9	1,563.7	631.8	-219.5
The Pacific[a]	**4,982.0**	**-144.7**	**-164.0**	**-2.7**	**62.5**	**744.5**
Cook Islands	9.7	-1.2	1.8	0.6	3.4	3.4 (2019)
Fiji	14.2	40.6	48.3	27.0	10.9	309.6
Kiribati	0.5	0.3	0.1	0.3	0.3	0.3 (2019)
Marshall Islands	-0.6	36.7	17.1	58.7	144.5	-30.4
Micronesia, Federated States of	0.8	2.3	1.5	0.2	0.1	-0.3
Nauru	0.3	62.5	19.4	0.4	0.1	0.1 (2019)
Niue	...	–	...	...	0.1	0.1 (2019)
Palau	6.4 (2011)	6.6	9.9	8.7	4.9	17.1
Papua New Guinea	4,892.3	-320.7	-267.2	-120.7	-181.4	451.5
Samoa	4.1	5.6	1.3	-0.2	0.7	-1.7
Solomon Islands	59.2	19.1	0.5	10.9	73.0	0.1
Tonga	0.3	2.5	1.2	2.3	2.0	–
Tuvalu	-0.1	0.2	0.1	0.2	0.2	–
Vanuatu	1.3	0.9	2.1	8.8	3.9	-1.4
DEVELOPING ADB MEMBER ECONOMIES[a]	**22,499.2**	**13,055.7**	**7,233.0**	**10,305.5**	**13,325.1**	**23,161.5**
DEVELOPING ECONOMIES WORLDWIDE[b]	**70,855.8**	**29,290.3**	**21,548.1**	**29,675.9**	**19,812.1**	**46,915.9**

... = data not available, – = magnitude equals zero, $ = United States dollars, ADB = Asian Development Bank.

Note: Net other official flows refer to official sector transactions with economies on the Development Assistance Committee List of Official Development Assistance Recipients, which do not meet the conditions for eligibility as official development assistance, either because they are not primarily aimed at development or because they have a grant element of less than 25%. The Development Assistance Committee List of Official Development Assistance Recipients is available at http://www.oecd.org/dac/financing-sustainable-development/development-finance-standards/daclist.htm. Net other official flows also include net export credits. Net flow takes into account principal repayments for loans, offsetting entries for forgiven debt, and recoveries made on grants.

a For reporting economies only.
b Includes data for all developing economies as reported in the Organisation for Economic Co-operation and Development's OECD.Stat database.

Source: Organisation for Economic Co-operation and Development. OECD.Stat Database. http://stats.oecd.org (accessed 16 July 2022).

Table 2.4.18: Net Private Flows from All Sources to Developing Economies
($ million)

ADB Regional Member	2010	2016	2017	2018	2019	2020
Developing ADB Member Economies						
Central and West Asia[a]	**-822**	**1,243**	**-1,184**	**-6,680**	**33**	**3,807**
Afghanistan	-21	-5	3	1	2	0
Armenia	-69	179	88	88	107	4
Azerbaijan	798	404	146	205	483	501
Georgia	22	190	361	334	224	343
Kazakhstan	-1,511	-86	-3,000	-7,575	-1,020	2,707
Kyrgyz Republic	23	-23	15	12	-1	-11
Pakistan	-75	192	703	-86	93	69
Tajikistan	18	-2	-42	43	-18	41
Turkmenistan	-46	285	107	-26	-230	-120
Uzbekistan	39	108	436	323	394	272
East Asia[a]	**46,322**	**42,731**	**38,835**	**31,500**	**42,949**	**10,822**
China, People's Republic of	46,301	42,145	38,767	31,290	42,360	12,032
Hong Kong, China	...	...	...	...	...	...
Korea, Republic of	...	...	...	...	...	...
Mongolia	22	586	68	210	589	-1,210
Taipei,China	...	...	...	...	...	...
South Asia[a]	**20,237**	**14,937**	**19,632**	**14,914**	**20,318**	**3,732**
Bangladesh	-3	-380	225	30	332	346
Bhutan	18	-0	-1	-7	0	1
India	19,976	14,812	18,961	13,980	19,550	3,759
Maldives	38	17	-1	148	148	-39
Nepal	-11	6	53	25	30	26
Sri Lanka	218	482	394	739	259	-361
Southeast Asia[a]	**21,463**	**23,520**	**25,424**	**21,095**	**69,611**	**8,594**
Brunei Darussalam	...	...	...	...	...	...
Cambodia	256	403	412	457	644	893
Indonesia	3,348	10,353	11,225	6,429	13,843	2,601
Lao People's Democratic Republic	172	44	72	27	97	4
Malaysia	6,573	2,133	2,961	79	9,102	502
Myanmar	260	356	452	415	559	715
Philippines	2,424	2,738	4,251	3,049	31,544	1,918
Singapore	...	...	...	...	...	...
Thailand	6,394	2,762	1,497	6,647	7,476	-1,127
Timor-Leste	-3	-42	15	4	8	-1
Viet Nam	2,038	4,772	4,537	3,989	6,337	3,089
The Pacific[a]	**978**	**925**	**1,211**	**-2,063**	**-1,091**	**-49**
Cook Islands	-0	-1	0	-18	-1	...
Fiji	-3	-15	45	40	9	21
Kiribati	-0	-9	-1	9	5	...
Marshall Islands	974	9	572	-515	30	-254
Micronesia, Federated States of	3	714	453	-1,641	-1,215	-6
Nauru	-0 (2011)	-0	0	-0	-0	-12
Niue	-0 (2012)	0	0	0	0	2
Palau	3	9	10	9	8	2
Papua New Guinea	-40	211	134	8	61	177
Samoa	17	8	6	54	-3	-1
Solomon Islands	3	-1	-8	-0	3	0
Tonga	-10	-0	0	0	4	0
Tuvalu	1 (2011)	0	0	...	...	0
Vanuatu	31	1	-1	-10	9	21
DEVELOPING ADB MEMBER ECONOMIES[a]	**88,177**	**83,357**	**83,916**	**58,766**	**131,819**	**26,907**
DEVELOPING ECONOMIES WORLDWIDE[b]	**324,145**	**128,540**	**235,112**	**96,427**	**216,914**	**-36,940**

... = data not available, -0 or 0 = magnitude is less than half of unit employed, $ = United States dollars, ADB = Asian Development Bank.

Note: Net private flows refer to the sum of direct investments and portfolio investments.

a For reporting economies only.
b Includes data for all developing economies as reported in the Organisation for Economic Co-operation and Development's OECD.Stat database.

Source: Organisation for Economic Co-operation and Development. OECD.Stat Database. http://stats.oecd.org (accessed 20 July 2022).

Table 2.4.19: Aggregate Net Resource Flows from All Sources to Developing Economies
($ million)

ADB Regional Member	2010	2016	2017	2018	2019	2020
Developing ADB Member Economies						
Central and West Asia[a]	**14,696**	**15,914**	**9,839**	**3,092**	**12,136**	**20,399**
Afghanistan	6,285	4,162	3,871	3,793	4,154	4,205
Armenia	539	663	487	368	735	239
Azerbaijan	1,135	1,598	2,005	783	945	391
Georgia	861	1,139	1,070	1,142	1,128	2,235
Kazakhstan	948	418	-3,794	-8,083	-1,021	3,709
Kyrgyz Republic	413	254	344	442	375	449
Pakistan	3,203	4,255	3,445	1,164	2,862	4,178
Tajikistan	413	357	286	483	405	855
Turkmenistan	645	1,244	667	122	-1,016	380
Uzbekistan	253	1,823	1,458	2,878	3,569	3,757
East Asia[a]	**50,636**	**43,162**	**39,645**	**31,945**	**43,734**	**10,742**
China, People's Republic of	50,169	41,494	39,004	31,230	42,415	10,843
Hong Kong, China	...	...	...	...	...	...
Korea, Republic of	...	...	...	...	...	...
Mongolia	468	1,668	641	715	1,319	-101
Taipei,China	...	...	...	...	...	...
South Asia[a]	**32,082**	**25,314**	**31,998**	**24,695**	**32,313**	**17,844**
Bangladesh	1,360	3,574	6,345	4,011	5,922	6,707
Bhutan	140	60	121	95	185	209
India	28,774	19,427	23,349	18,093	23,999	8,477
Maldives	93	15	22	297	212	255
Nepal	749	1,071	1,320	1,477	1,414	1,787
Sri Lanka	966	1,168	842	721	581	409
Southeast Asia[a]	**31,744**	**32,776**	**31,656**	**31,870**	**80,279**	**26,463**
Brunei Darussalam	...	...	...	...	...	...
Cambodia	932	1,119	1,352	1,215	1,697	2,230
Indonesia	6,456	13,953	14,468	11,185	14,980	6,541
Lao People's Democratic Republic	441	482	627	648	739	520
Malaysia	6,726	587	2,192	-918	11,071	394
Myanmar	646	1,993	2,090	2,143	2,732	3,868
Philippines	2,326	3,225	4,379	4,552	32,887	9,744
Singapore	...	...	...	...	...	...
Thailand	6,302	2,951	696	5,614	7,842	-1,141
Timor-Leste	292	207	259	238	276	258
Viet Nam	7,623	8,258	5,592	7,194	8,055	4,049
The Pacific[a]	**7,395**	**2,126**	**2,626**	**-167**	**713**	**3,169**
Cook Islands	23	15	21	17	31	...
Fiji	87	143	239	188	149	525
Kiribati	24	52	77	90	62	58
Marshall Islands	998	58	661	-402	240	-102
Micronesia, Federated States of	68	767	552	-1,542	-1,122	165
Nauru	28	85	45	38	54	17
Niue	15	14	15	19	19	24
Palau	32	33	42	102	37	85
Papua New Guinea	5,366	422	400	678	528	1,638
Samoa	145	103	143	182	121	164
Solomon Islands	395	194	179	206	300	215
Tonga	57	85	88	100	114	163
Tuvalu	14	25	29	28	37	43
Vanuatu	142	131	134	130	143	173
DEVELOPING ADB MEMBER ECONOMIES[a]	**136,553**	**119,292**	**115,765**	**91,435**	**169,176**	**78,617**
DEVELOPING ECONOMIES WORLDWIDE[b]	**523,963**	**315,874**	**421,016**	**293,035**	**399,365**	**200,133**

... = data not available, $ = United States dollars, ADB = Asian Development Bank.

Note: Aggregate net resource flows refer to the sum of net official development assistance, net other official flows, and net private flows.

a For reporting economies only.
b Includes data for all developing economies as reported in the Organisation for Economic Co-operation and Development's OECD.Stat database.

Source: Organisation for Economic Co-operation and Development. OECD.Stat Database. http://stats.oecd.org (accessed 16 July 2022).

Table 2.4.20: Total External Debt of Developing Economies—Dollar Amounts
($ million)

ADB Regional Member	Total External Debt			External Debt (Public and Publicly Guaranteed)		
	2010	2015	2020	2010	2015	2020
Developing ADB Member Economies						
Central and West Asia[a]	**224,376**	**294,713**	**384,816**	**68,355**	**107,668**	**163,234**
Afghanistan	2,436	2,597	3,036	1,976	1,990	1,958
Armenia	6,307	8,831	13,094	2,560	3,998	5,616
Azerbaijan	7,251	13,319	15,812	3,812	8,712	14,000
Georgia	8,790	14,875	20,089	3,274	5,721	7,967
Kazakhstan	119,151	153,180	162,974	3,845	20,114	25,430
Kyrgyz Republic	4,118	7,720	8,697	2,446	3,431	3,837
Pakistan	63,098	68,599	116,506	43,700	49,137	78,893
Tajikistan	3,561	5,144	6,798	1,806	2,093	3,125
Turkmenistan	1,682	7,004	5,636	1,513	6,869	5,342
Uzbekistan	7,981	13,445	32,174	3,423	5,605	17,064
East Asia[a]	**2,083,992**	**3,211,096**	**4,912,415**	**112,111**	**151,192**	**426,012**
China, People's Republic of	742,756	1,333,777	2,349,389	102,293	146,070	414,838
Hong Kong, China	879,034	1,300,348	1,878,975 (2021)	...	...	...
Korea, Republic of	354,693	396,064	632,394 (2021)	...	...	...
Mongolia	5,928	21,953	33,236	1,782	4,006	9,728
Taipei,China	101,581	158,954	213,592 (2021)	8,035	1,116	1,571 (2021)
South Asia[a]	**344,322**	**565,878**	**702,396**	**143,193**	**220,309**	**291,698**
Bangladesh	26,572	35,967	67,749	21,146	24,377	49,029
Bhutan	935	2,011	2,869	919	1,945	2,818
India	290,428	478,826	564,179	100,563	162,305	192,785
Maldives	917	1,006	3,352	628	685	2,843
Nepal	3,787	4,143	7,905	3,507	3,543	7,056
Sri Lanka	21,684	43,925	56,342	16,430	27,453	37,167
Southeast Asia[a]	**569,454**	**816,467**	**893,510**	**273,837**	**355,734**	**428,248**
Brunei Darussalam	...	...	...	...	...	...
Cambodia	4,010	9,436	17,562	3,060	5,638	8,758
Indonesia	198,278	307,749	417,532	102,748	159,571	248,419
Lao People's Democratic Republic	6,554	11,642	17,164	3,751	6,689	10,393
Malaysia	133,800	190,951	...	61,858	66,385	...
Myanmar	10,164	10,293	13,348	8,607	9,787	12,519
Philippines	65,350	76,261	98,480	45,086	38,855	56,220
Singapore	...	...	...	...	...	...
Thailand	106,358	132,186	204,147	15,929	22,396	39,540
Timor-Leste	76 (2012)	117	232	0 (2012)	46	220
Viet Nam	44,940	77,832	125,045	32,798	46,366	52,180
The Pacific[a]	**8,282**	**22,991**	**21,215**	**2,138**	**3,015**	**7,100**
Cook Islands	99	75	71 (2019)	...	...	...
Fiji	1,107	1,233	1,518	426	678	903
Kiribati	14	33	47 (2019)	...	...	...
Marshall Islands	105	95	67	...	...	...
Micronesia, Federated States of	...	...	...	...	...	...
Nauru	...	...	...	...	...	...
Niue	...	...	...	...	...	...
Palau	66	64	141	...	...	...
Papua New Guinea	5,987	20,387	17,971	1,042	1,501	5,112
Samoa	325	437	437	299	408	394
Solomon Islands	231	207	429	125	81	124
Tonga	154	184	194	144	175	185
Tuvalu	15	19	3	...	...	...
Vanuatu	178	257	456	103	172	383
DEVELOPING ADB MEMBER ECONOMIES[a]	**3,230,427**	**4,911,145**	**6,914,352**	**599,634**	**837,918**	**1,316,293**
DEVELOPING ECONOMIES WORLDWIDE[a,b]	**5,829,271**	**8,443,325**	**11,219,446**	**1,786,551**	**2,528,706**	**3,445,304 (2019)**

... = data not available, $ = United States dollars, ADB = Asian Development Bank.

Note: Refers to the sum of public and publicly guaranteed long-term debt, private nonguaranteed long-term debt, use of International Monetary Fund credit, and estimated short-term debt.

a Regional aggregates include only reporting economies with data corresponding to the year heading.
b Refers to all low- and middle-income economies as classified by the World Bank. For developing member economies not covered by the World Bank, data are from the economies' official sources.

Source: World Bank. International Debt Statistics. http://data.worldbank.org/data-catalog/international-debt-statistics (accessed 7 July 2022); and Asian Development Bank estimates using economies' official sources.

Table 2.4.21: Total External Debt of Developing ADB Member Economies—Proportion of Income
(% of GNI)

ADB Regional Member	Total External Debt			External Debt (Public and Publicly Guaranteed)		
	2010	2015	2020	2010	2015	2020
Developing ADB Member Economies						
Central and West Asia						
Afghanistan	15.3	13.5	15.0	12.4	10.3	9.6
Armenia	64.9	80.4	105.2	26.3	36.4	45.1
Azerbaijan	14.6	25.9	37.3	7.7	17.0	33.0
Georgia	73.1	101.8	133.0	27.2	39.1	52.7
Kazakhstan	92.6	88.7	104.4	3.0	11.6	16.3
Kyrgyz Republic	91.7	120.3	117.4	54.5	53.5	51.0
Pakistan	36.3	25.8	45.3	25.1	18.5	26.8
Tajikistan	51.1	52.5	71.1	25.9	21.4	32.8
Turkmenistan	8.1	20.8	15.0 (2019)	7.3	20.4	14.6 (2019)
Uzbekistan	15.8	15.3	53.9	6.8	6.4	28.6
East Asia						
China, People's Republic of	12.3	12.1	16.1	1.7	1.3	2.8
Hong Kong, China[a]	384.7	420.2	510.6 (2021)	...	...	...
Korea, Republic of	31.0	26.9	34.5 (2021)	...	...	...
Mongolia	89.7	206.1	275.8	27.0	37.6	80.7
Taipei,China[a,b]	22.9	29.7	27.6 (2021)	1.8	0.2	0.2 (2021)
South Asia						
Bangladesh	21.3	17.3	20.0	17.0	11.7	12.6
Bhutan	64.0	108.1	132.1	63.0	104.5	129.7
India	17.5	23.0	21.4	6.1	7.8	7.3
Maldives	40.3	26.6	96.9	27.6	18.1	82.7
Nepal	23.5	16.8	23.2	21.8	14.3	20.9
Sri Lanka	38.6	55.9	71.8	29.3	34.9	47.2
Southeast Asia						
Brunei Darussalam	...	...	...	...	...	...
Cambodia	37.4	55.7	70.8	28.5	33.3	35.2
Indonesia	27.0	37.0	40.5	14.0	19.2	24.1
Lao People's Democratic Republic	98.1	84.5	94.8	56.2	48.5	58.2
Malaysia[b]	54.2	66.3	...	24.3	22.0	...
Myanmar[b]	0.2	17.0	17.2	...	15.6	15.4 (2019)
Philippines	28.2	22.3	25.3	19.5	11.4	14.4
Singapore	...	...	...	...	...	...
Thailand	32.5	34.7	41.9	31.3	43.7	24.6
Timor-Leste	1.8 (2012)	4.2	9.7	0.0 (2012)	1.6	9.2
Viet Nam	40.3	43.0	48.9	23.0	20.4	15.9
The Pacific						
Cook Islands[a]	41.0	25.0	12.3 (2019)	...	...	...
Fiji	36.4	28.0	35.7	14.0	15.4	21.0
Kiribati[a]	8.5	20.0	23.0 (2019)	...	...	...
Marshall Islands[a]	62.7	52.2	28.0 (2019)	...	...	...
Micronesia, Federated States of[a]	28.9	25.6	...	...	...	...
Nauru	...	...	...	...	...	...
Niue	...	...	...	...	...	...
Palau[a]	36.2	23.1	31.1 (2019)	...	...	...
Papua New Guinea	45.4	95.6	73.7	7.9	7.0	21.0
Samoa	50.5	56.7	56.3	46.5	52.8	50.7
Solomon Islands	28.7	16.2	27.1	15.6	6.3	7.8
Tonga	40.6	41.8	36.7	37.9	1.5	1.1
Tuvalu[a]	49.1	53.5	5.5	...	...	...
Vanuatu	27.4	34.5	46.9	0.8	0.8	1.5

... = data not available, 0.0 = magnitude is less than half of unit employed, ADB = Asian Development Bank, GNI = gross national income.

a For total external debt as a percentage of GNI, gross domestic product is used in lieu of GNI.
b For public and publicly guaranteed external debt as a percentage of GNI, gross domestic product is used in lieu of GNI.

Sources: For total external debt (% of GNI): World Bank. International Debt Statistics. http://data.worldbank.org/data-catalog/international-debt-statistics (accessed 18 July 2022); and economies' official sources. For public and publicly guaranteed external debt (% of GNI): Asian Development Bank estimates using the World Bank's International Debt Statistics; and economies' official sources.

External Indebtedness

Table 2.4.22: Total External Debt of Developing ADB Member Economies—Proportion of Exports
(% of exports of goods, services, and primary income)

ADB Regional Member	2010	2015	2016	2017	2018	2019	2020
Developing ADB Member Economies							
Central and West Asia							
Afghanistan	88.7	152.4	188.7	189.5	141.1	142.4	176.9
Armenia	193.5	219.6	223.5	188.5	183.3	178.5	310.1
Azerbaijan	25.1	62.6	78.9	72.4	59.8	62.8	92.7
Georgia	191.5	213.9	230.1	189.0	170.2	171.8	291.6
Kazakhstan	174.7	287.6	373.0	282.6	225.0	232.3	299.6
Kyrgyz Republic	181.2	314.6	327.5	311.9	293.9	268.6	354.1
Pakistan	219.6	234.4	272.4	303.5	315.4	346.3	419.2
Tajikistan	158.4	200.6	230.3	208.1	228.8	230.3	230.5
Turkmenistan	...	...	...	...	...	...	...
Uzbekistan	60.5	97.0	121.4	111.2	102.3	112.3	199.7
East Asia							
China, People's Republic of	41.3	51.6	58.3	62.7	67.2	72.8	79.0
Hong Kong, China[a]	149.2	168.8	177.6	190.5	190.6	195.1	195.3 (2021)
Korea, Republic of[a]	62.4	59.5	60.3	58.9	57.7	67.1	77.2 (2021)
Mongolia	173.2	422.7	433.8	406.6	375.2	359.2	416.1
Taipei,China[a]	30.0	38.8	45.3	43.1	44.0	43.8	39.2 (2021)
South Asia							
Bangladesh	122.1	102.4	101.9	119.2	117.1	126.5	173.7
Bhutan	154.0	268.8	343.4	349.4	310.8	331.8	351.5
India	81.1	108.0	102.1	100.7	93.3	98.5	111.2
Maldives	45.6	31.9	38.7	45.5	64.9	71.2	186.8
Nepal	212.7	154.5	166.9	165.9	163.0	190.0	346.9
Sri Lanka	189.8	257.3	265.5	263.6	258.0	285.4	424.2
Southeast Asia							
Brunei Darussalam	...	...	...	...	...	...	...
Cambodia	65.8	69.2	68.5	70.2	71.2	70.3	83.8
Indonesia	117.6	176.7	185.6	177.0	171.6	193.8	227.6
Lao People's Democratic Republic	284.0	251.7	259.8	254.3	237.9	235.9	262.3
Malaysia[a]	57.3	86.1	94.2	...	...	...	...
Myanmar	129.5	70.7	72.4	72.8	62.7	58.9	...
Philippines	106.7	93.3	89.5	75.2	77.1	77.3	107.8
Singapore[a]	...	...	...	...	...	...	...
Thailand	45.7	47.8	49.1	51.6	51.1	53.7	75.3
Timor-Leste	1.9 (2012)	8.3	12.3	14.2	15.7	15.5	30.9
Viet Nam	56.1	44.8	45.2	45.5	41.1	41.5	42.9
The Pacific							
Cook Islands[a]	61.5	20.8	16.9	15.2	14.0	14.1	...
Fiji	58.7	52.5	54.6	49.9	45.5	49.7	117.4
Kiribati[a]	13.7	11.9	17.4	16.1	16.5	14.3	...
Marshall Islands[a]	94.1	57.2	55.5	47.7	42.7	38.1	35.5
Micronesia, Federated States of	...	...	...	...	...	...	...
Nauru	...	...	...	...	...	...	...
Niue	...	...	...	...	...	...	...
Palau[a]	62.8	35.1	43.1	48.7	55.8	60.3	163.1
Papua New Guinea	98.2	236.6	231.3	167.6	166.8	159.5	191.8
Samoa	154.0	182.6	162.7	155.8	139.4	118.9	347.0
Solomon Islands	68.9	35.9	44.2	59.3	44.7	54.7	88.4
Tonga	283.9	208.5	142.8	138.3	120.0	111.1	127.5
Tuvalu[a]	64.1	57.2	45.5	12.0	7.5	12.5	...
Vanuatu	48.9	71.7	71.2	92.8	81.1	90.5	172.2

... = data not available, 0.0 = magnitude is less than half of unit employed, ADB = Asian Development Bank.

a External debt as a percentage of exports of goods, services, and primary income was derived using balance-of-payments data.

Sources: World Bank. International Debt Statistics. http://data.worldbank.org/data-catalog/international-debt-statistics (accessed 7 July 2022); and Asian Development Bank estimates using economies' official sources.

Table 2.4.23: Total Debt Service Paid by Developing ADB Member Economies

ADB Regional Member	Debt Service Payment ($ million)				Debt Service Payment (% of exports of goods, services, and primary income)			
	2010	2015	2018	2020	2010	2015	2018	2020
Developing ADB Member Economies								
Central and West Asia[a]	**48,060**	**48,071**	**50,510**	**52,368**				**...**
Afghanistan	10	57	63	46	0.4	3.3	3.3	2.7
Armenia	969	1,546	1,667	1,472	29.7	38.4	28.5	34.9
Azerbaijan	414	1,907	2,682	1,836	1.4	9.0	9.9	10.8
Georgia	803	2,158	2,435	2,435	17.5	31.0	23.9	35.3
Kazakhstan	39,475	34,846	33,643	30,605	57.9	65.4	48.2	56.3
Kyrgyz Republic	557	413	564	629	24.5	16.8	20.3	25.6
Pakistan	4,319	4,109	6,026	9,000	15.0	14.0	19.1	32.4
Tajikistan	695	314	587	913	30.9	12.2	22.0	31.0
Turkmenistan	199	1,474	1,833	2,093	...	...	...	...
Uzbekistan	617	1,247	1,011	3,339	4.7	9.0	5.8	20.7
East Asia[a]	**58,805**	**134,639**	**257,935**	**284,566**				**...**
China, People's Republic of	52,104	126,687	240,940	273,800	2.9	4.9	8.3	9.2
Hong Kong, China	...	...	...	...	...	...	...	...
Korea, Republic of[b]	2,843	...	...	...	...	...	...	...
Mongolia	239	1,833	7,775	1,901	7.0	35.3	97.9	23.8
Taipei,China[b]	3,620	6,119	9,220	10,668 (2021)	1.1	1.6	2.3	2.1 (2021)
South Asia[a]	**27,284**	**55,341**	**74,684**	**85,948**				**...**
Bangladesh	1,106	1,634	2,869	3,867	5.1	4.7	6.4	9.9
Bhutan	87	129	87	58	14.4	17.2	10.6	7.1
India	24,413	49,662	63,647	76,239	6.8	11.2	11.4	15.0
Maldives	81	139	442	285	4.0	4.4	12.3	15.9
Nepal	188	226	244	275	10.6	8.4	7.2	12.1
Sri Lanka	1,408	3,551	7,396	5,223	12.3	20.8	36.1	39.3
Southeast Asia[a]	**62,061**	**111,229**	**104,080**	**136,067**				**...**
Brunei Darussalam	...	...	...	...	...	...	...	...
Cambodia	65	691	1,279	1,488	1.1	5.1	6.7	7.1
Indonesia	31,569	60,273	55,469	67,411	18.7	34.6	25.1	36.7
Lao People's Democratic Republic	302	421	869	1,034	13.1	9.1	13.4	15.8
Malaysia[b]	5,568	13,502	10,383 (2016)	...	2.4	6.1	4.9 (2016)	...
Myanmar	244	524	839	588	3.1	3.6	4.9	3.7 (2019)
Philippines	11,461	10,576	8,800	9,251	18.7	12.9	8.6	10.1
Singapore	...	...	...	...	...	...	...	...
Thailand	10,965	18,610	18,630	16,833	4.7	6.7	5.5	6.2
Timor-Leste	0 (2012)	1	3	8	–	0.1	0.3	1.1
Viet Nam	1,880	6,631	18,197	16,358	2.3	3.8	7.0	5.6
The Pacific[a]	**931**	**1,507**	**3,009**	**1,665**				**...**
Cook Islands[b,c]	3	5	6	4 (2019)	57.9	26.9	30.3	...
Fiji	59	340	108	275	3.1	14.5	3.9	21.3
Kiribati	1	1	1	2 (2019)	4.4	4.0	3.0	7.0 (2019)
Marshall Islands	9	8	7	7	11.7	8.5	9.6	8.1
Micronesia, Federated States of	5	7	6	...	13.5	8.1	3.6	...
Nauru	...	...	...	...	...	...	...	...
Niue	...	...	...	...	...	...	...	...
Palau	...	...	...	...	...	...	...	...
Papua New Guinea	812	1,098	2,779	1,326	13.3	12.7	26.1	14.1
Samoa	11	21	30	24	5.0	8.8	9.9	18.7
Solomon Islands	21	14	40	9	6.2	2.4	5.6	1.9
Tonga	5	6	10	6	9.3	7.3	6.6	3.9
Tuvalu	...	...	...	...	...	...	...	...
Vanuatu	6	7	20	19	1.6	1.9	4.1	7.3
DEVELOPING ADB MEMBER ECONOMIES[a]	**197,078**	**349,370**	**488,380**	**457,468**				**...**

... = data not available, 0 or 0.0 = magnitude is less than half of unit employed, $ = United States dollars, ADB = Asian Development Bank.

a Aggregates include only reporting economies with data corresponding to the year heading.
b Refers to principal repayments on long-term debt plus interest on short-term and long-term debt.
c Refers to debt service as a percentage of total exports, as reflected under "Direction of Trade" in the individual economy table available via the Key Indicators Database at https://kidb.adb.org.

Sources: World Bank. International Debt Statistics Online. http://data.worldbank.org/data-catalog/international-debt-statistics (accessed 5 July 2022); economies' official sources; and Asian Development Bank estimates using economies' official sources.

Tourism

Table 2.4.24: International Tourist Arrivals
('000)

ADB Regional Member	2010	2015	2016	2017	2018	2019	2020	2021
Developing ADB Member Economies								
Central and West Asia[a]	**9,288**	**12,458**	**12,825**	**15,707**	**22,370**	**25,095**	**...**	**...**
Afghanistan	...	...	...	...	...	...	...	...
Armenia	684	1,192	1,260	1,495	1,652	1,894	360*	870*
Azerbaijan	1,280	1,922	2,044	2,454	2,633	2,864	519*	...
Georgia	1,067	3,012	3,297	4,069	4,757	5,080	1,087*	1,577*
Kazakhstan	2,991	...	...	...	...	...	...	...
Kyrgyz Republic	1,224	4,000	3,853	4,568	6,947	8,508	...	...
Pakistan	907	...	...	...	...	...	...	...
Tajikistan	160	414	344	431	1,035	1,257	351*	...
Turkmenistan	...	...	...	...	...	...	...	...
Uzbekistan	975	1,918	2,027	2,690	5,346	6,749	1,504*	...
East Asia[a]	**90,570**	**107,630**	**114,159**	**113,169**	**119,106**	**119,396**	**13,282***	**...**
China, People's Republic of	55,664	56,886	59,270	60,740	62,900	65,700	7,967*	...
Hong Kong, China	20,085	26,686	26,553	27,884	29,263	23,752	1,359*	89*
Korea, Republic of	8,798	13,232	17,242	13,336	15,347	17,503	2,519*	967*
Mongolia	456	386	404	469	529	577	59*	33*
Taipei,China	5,567	10,440	10,690	10,740	11,067	11,864	1,378*	140*
South Asia[a]	**8,005**	**17,136**	**19,052**	**20,481**	**22,955**	**23,367**	**7,821***	**...**
Bangladesh	139	126	182	237	267	323	168*	...
Bhutan	41	155	210	255	274	316	30*	...
India	5,776	13,284	14,570	15,543	17,423	17,914	6,330*	...
Maldives	792	1,234	1,286	1,390	1,484	1,703	555*	1,322*
Nepal	603	539	753	940	1,173	1,197	230*	150*
Sri Lanka	654	1,798	2,051	2,116	2,334	1,914	508*	194*
Southeast Asia[a]	**70,471**	**104,243**	**110,771**	**120,569**	**128,620**	**138,592**	**25,451***	**...**
Brunei Darussalam	214	218	219	259	278	333	62*	...
Cambodia	2,508	4,775	5,012	5,602	6,201	6,611	1,306*	196*
Indonesia[b]	7,003 |	9,963	11,072	12,948	13,396	15,455	3,915*	...
Lao People's Democratic Republic	1,670	3,543	3,315	3,257	3,770	4,384	812*	...
Malaysia	24,577	25,721	26,757	25,948	25,832	26,101	4,333*	135*
Myanmar	792	4,681	2,907	3,443	3,551	4,364	903*	...
Philippines	3,520	5,361	5,967	6,621	7,168	8,261	1,483*	164*
Singapore	9,161	12,052	12,913	13,903	14,673	15,119	2,086*	...
Thailand	15,936	29,923	32,530	35,592	38,178	39,874	6,696*	428*
Timor-Leste	40	62	66	74	75	81	18*	...
Viet Nam	5,050	7,944	10,013	12,922	15,498	18,009	3,837*	157*
The Pacific[a]	**1,310**	**1,570**	**1,619**	**1,634**	**1,693**	**1,755**	**291***	**...**
Cook Islands	104	125	146	161	169	172	25*	26*
Fiji	632	755	792	843	870	894	147*	32*
Kiribati	5	4	6	6	7	8	1*	...
Marshall Islands	5	6	5	6	7	6	1*	...
Micronesia, Federated States of	45	31	30	...	19	18	...	...
Nauru	...	...	...	...	...	...	...	...
Niue	6	8	9	10	11	10	1*	...
Palau	85	162	138	123	106	94	18*	5*
Papua New Guinea	140	183	179	139	140	160	39*	...
Samoa	122	128	134	146	164	172	23*	...
Solomon Islands	21	22	23	26	28	29	4*	...
Tonga	47	54	59	63	54	67	9*	...
Tuvalu	2	2	3	3	3	4	1*	...
Vanuatu	97	90	95	109	116	121	22*	...
Developed ADB Member Economies[a]	**16,836**	**30,225**	**35,678**	**41,061**	**44,123**	**45,050**	**6,892***	**...**
Australia	5,790	7,449	8,269	8,815	9,246	9,466	1,828*	246*
Japan	8,611	19,737	24,039	28,691	31,191	31,882	4,116*	246*
New Zealand	2,435	3,039	3,370	3,555	3,686	3,702	948*	...
DEVELOPING ADB MEMBER ECONOMIES[a]	**179,644**	**243,037**	**258,425**	**271,560**	**294,744**	**309,462**	**...**	**...**
ALL ADB REGIONAL MEMBERS[a]	**196,480**	**273,262**	**294,104**	**312,621**	**338,867**	**353,255**	**...**	**...**
WORLD[c]	**955,675**	**1,197,427**	**1,240,866**	**1,332,972**	**1,413,000**	**1,466,000**	**405,000***	**427,000***

... = data not available, | = marks break in series, * = provisional or preliminary, ADB = Asian Development Bank.

Note: For Australia; Japan; the Kyrgyz Republic; the Republic of Korea; Taipei,China; Tajikistan; Uzbekistan: and Viet Nam: Data refer to international visitor arrivals at frontiers (including tourists and same-day visitors). For the rest of the economies: Data refer to international tourist arrivals at frontiers (overnight visitors only, i.e., excluding same-day visitors).

a Includes only reporting economies with data corresponding to the year heading.
b Prior to 2015, data refer to international tourist arrivals at frontiers (overnight visitors only, i.e., excluding same-day visitors). For 2015 onward, data refer to international visitor arrivals at frontiers (including tourists and same-day visitors).
c These aggregations were calculated by the World Tourism Organization, with approximations based on trends in the economies with data available.

Sources: United Nations World Tourism Organization. UNWTO.eLibrary. https://www.e-unwto.org (accessed 14 June 2022) and World Tourism Barometer and Statistical Annex, May 2022. https://www.e-unwto.org/doi/abs/10.18111/wtobarometereng.2022.20.1.3.

Table 2.4.25: International Tourism Receipts
($ million)

ADB Regional Member	2010	2015	2016	2017	2018	2019	2020	2021
Developing ADB Member Economies								
Central and West Asia[a]	**3,631**	**7,568**	**8,965**	**10,535**	**11,470**	**11,757**	**2,603***	**3,935***
Afghanistan	75	79	49	2	28	72	65*	...
Armenia	646	936	1,017	1,204	1,329	1,528	293*	720*
Azerbaijan	657	2,309	2,714	3,012	2,634	1,792	304*	313*
Georgia	659	1,868	2,111	2,704	3,222	3,269	542*	1,245*
Kazakhstan	1,005	1,632	1,858	2,135	2,255	2,463	459*	535*
Kyrgyz Republic	160	426	432	429	459	644	151*	...
Pakistan	305	317	322	352	390	494	438*	558*
Tajikistan	3	1	4	8	9	14	6*	11*
Turkmenistan	...	...	...	...	...	...	...	...
Uzbekistan	121	...	458	689	1,144	1,481	345*	553*
East Asia	**86,731**	**110,195**	**103,406**	**96,347**	**108,387**	**100,536**	**24,915***	**24,308***
China, People's Republic of	45,814	44,969	44,432	38,559	40,386	35,832	9,951*	11,328*
Hong Kong, China	21,689	35,795	31,398	31,709	35,268	28,913	2,859*	1,738*
Korea, Republic of	10,263	14,798	16,886	13,368	18,567	20,867	10,276*	10,457*
Mongolia	244	246	316	396	461	513	29*	...
Taipei,China	8,721	14,387	10,374	12,315	13,705	14,411	1,800*	785*
South Asia[a]	**17,244**	**27,290**	**29,203**	**35,117**	**37,074**	**38,697**	**15,611***	**13,935***
Bangladesh	81	150	214	341	353	388	217*	272*
Bhutan	40	94	92	103	103	120	84*	...
India	14,490	21,013	22,427	27,365	28,568	30,720	13,036*	13,036*
Maldives	1,713	2,569	2,506	2,744	3,028	3,157	1,398*	...
Nepal	344	483	446	639	641	705	194*	120*
Sri Lanka	576	2,981	3,518	3,925	4,381	3,607	682*	507*
Southeast Asia[a]	**68,484**	**105,091**	**112,990**	**126,174**	**138,235**	**146,910**	**30,632***	**10,182***
Brunei Darussalam	..	147	144	177	190	217	16*	...
Cambodia	1,519	3,137	3,212	3,639	4,362	4,769	1,015*	184*
Indonesia	6,958	10,761	11,206	13,139	16,426	16,911	3,382*	521*
Lao People's Democratic Republic	382	724	716	648	811	935	213*	...
Malaysia	18,152	17,666	18,085	18,385	19,608	19,829	2,988*	96*
Myanmar	72	2,120	2,197	1,969	1,652	2,483	...	...
Philippines	2,645	5,272	5,143	6,988	8,240	9,781	1,791*	600*
Singapore	14,178	16,617	18,943	19,890	20,422	20,313	5,176*	3,808*
Thailand	20,104	41,246	44,786	52,376	56,366	59,810	13,525*	4,812*
Timor-Leste	24	51	58	73	78	70	26*	12*
Viet Nam	4,450	7,350	8,500	8,890	10,080	11,792	2,500*	149*
The Pacific[a]	**1,256**	**1,640**	**1,746**	**1,865**	**1,842**	**...**	**...**	**...**
Cook Islands	111	173	202	230	234	228	...	...
Fiji	635	817	878	942	969	963	154*	35*
Kiribati	4	2	3	4	3	3	–	...
Marshall Islands	4	1	5	7	9	...	...	...
Micronesia, Federated States of	24	25	...	...	...	...	...	...
Nauru	1	2	3	4	2	...	...	...
Niue	...	...	7	8	...	...	...	...
Palau	73	149	141	116	...	...	...	...
Papua New Guinea	2	2	1	2	3	2	1*	...
Samoa	123	142	148	166	192	207	24*	...
Solomon Islands	44	51	59	67	81	71	...	...
Tonga	16	43	51	48	48	57	40*	...
Tuvalu	2	5	5	6	6	8	...	...
Vanuatu	217	228	243	265	295	278	62*	...
Developed ADB Member Economies[a]	**48,219**	**68,701**	**77,544**	**86,406**	**98,152**	**102,296**	**42,271***	**24,774***
Australia	28,472	34,269	37,019	41,747	45,098	45,709	25,820*	16,988*
Japan	13,224	24,968	30,752	34,065	42,093	46,054	10,700*	4,730*
New Zealand	6,523	9,464	9,773	10,594	10,961	10,533	5,751*	3,056*
DEVELOPING ADB MEMBER ECONOMIES[a]	**177,599**	**251,721**	**259,193**	**271,470**	**298,153**	**299,481**	**78,997***	**...**
ALL ADB REGIONAL MEMBERS[a]	**225,818**	**320,422**	**336,737**	**357,860**	**396,159**	**401,777**	**121,268***	**...**
WORLD[b]	**979,163**	**1,221,823**	**1,246,391**	**1,347,047**	**1,456,664**	**1,483,000**	**546,000***	**602,000***

... = data not available, * = provisional or preliminary, $ = United States dollars, ADB = Asian Development Bank.

a Includes only reporting economies with data corresponding to the year heading.
b Aggregations were calculated by the United Nations World Tourism Organization, with estimates made for nonreporting economies based on the previous year's values and the trend in neighboring economies.

Sources: United Nations World Tourism Organization. UNWTO.eLibrary. https://www.e-unwto.org (accessed 14 June 2022); and United Nations World Tourism Organization. 2022. *World Tourism Barometer, Statistical Annex*. Volume 20.

Data Issues and Comparability

Most of the data on international transactions presented in this section were taken from balance-of-payments statistics as reported by individual economies. IMF guidelines are followed by most governments in compiling these statistics. However, authorities have difficulty accurately recording nonofficial transactions such as migrant workers' remittances and private capital flows, which is one of the reasons that the IMF's Balance of Payments Manual (BPM) was updated to the sixth edition (BPM6) in 2009. All economies in the region have adopted BPM6 in recent years except two economies, which still rely on BPM5. However, there is not a single framework for an extended time series available for all economies. There are 20 economies reporting a mix of BPM5 and BPM6, and three economies reporting a mix of BPM4 and BPM6. This therefore affects the comparability of data across economies.

The World Trade Organization and other international agencies closely monitor international trade statistics. Common definitions are used by all economies, with the larger economies throughout Asia and the Pacific using standard forms and procedures for data processing.

Data on official development assistance, other official flows, and private direct investment and other private capital are compiled by the Organisation for Economic Co-operation and Development's Development Assistance Committee. These data are standardized on a calendar-year basis for all donors, but may have discrepancies for some economies owing to the fiscal-year data available in budget documents. Commitments from donors do not necessarily translate to actual disbursements to recipient economies of official development assistance.

Table 2.5.1: Road Indicators—Total Network, Passenger Kilometers Travel, Freight Kilometers Travel

ADB Regional Member	Road Indicators Network, Total (km)			Road Passenger Travel[a] (p-km million)			Road Freight Kilometers Travel[b] (t-km million)		
	2010	2015	2020	2010	2015	2020	2010	2015	2020
Developing ADB Member Economies									
Central and West Asia									
Afghanistan	19,138 (2011)	37,090	...	...	...	...	6,796.0 (2011)	4,423.0	...
Armenia	9,125	10,368	11,274	2,344.3	2,395.9	707.0	235.8	479.4	899.0
Azerbaijan	18,977	19,016	19,228	16,633.0	23,825.0	16,974.0	11,728.0	16,038.0	8,801.0
Georgia	19,040	20,553	21,110	...	...	...	619.7	664.3	712.1
Kazakhstan	96,018	96,529	95,768	...	...	...	80,300.0	161,864.0	185,197.3 (2018)
Kyrgyz Republic	...	...	...	7,209.5	9,005.6	7,980.3 (2021)	1,281.5	1,401.7	1,375.4 (2021)
Pakistan	260,040	263,942	270,972 (2019)	...	...	...	...	...	...
Tajikistan	...	...	...	...	510.1 (2017)	...	50,745.7	68,304.1	79,075.9
Turkmenistan	...	...	13,773	27,657.0	...	...	11,399.0	...	...
Uzbekistan	...	...	...	78,400.0	109,100.0	124,141.2 (2019)	24,464.2	12,800.0	15,879.3 (2019)
East Asia									
China, People's Republic of	4,008,200	4,577,300	5,198,100	1,502,080.0	1,074,270.0	464,100.0	4,338,970.0	5,795,570.0	6,017,180.0
Hong Kong, China	2,076	2,101	2,150	...	...	...	...	...	...
Korea, Republic of	...	99,024	104,828	104,671.0	385,018.1	...	103,898.0	132,382.0	...
Mongolia	...	109,567 (2017)	111,942	1,480.2	1,940.5	1,023.0 (2021)	1,834.0	2,374.0	2,314.0 (2021)
Taipei,China	40,335	41,952	42,138	...	...	...	29,631.6	37,805.3	44,550.3
South Asia									
Bangladesh	21,269	21,365	21,128 (2018)	...	...	...	...	...	...
Bhutan	4,661	11,177	18,265	...	...	...	...	...	...
India	4,582,439	5,472,144	6,386,297 (2019)	8,409,000.0	15,428,000.0	22,582,000.0 (2018)	1,287,300.0	2,027,400.0	2,697,000.0 (2018)
Maldives	...	...	...	...	...	...	...	...	...
Nepal	11,636 (2011)	12,898	11,179	...	...	...	...	...	...
Sri Lanka	29,119	31,280	31,144 (2018)	...	...	...	...	...	...
Southeast Asia									
Brunei Darussalam	3,127 (2011)	3,355	3,720	...	...	...	...	...	...
Cambodia	44,709 (2009)	...	61,534 (2019)	...	...	...	...	...	...
Indonesia	487,314	529,073	548,366	...	...	...	...	...	...
Lao People's Democratic Republic	47,491	56,332	58,264 (2019)	2,556.0	3,202.1	4,060.0	513.0	434.7	535.2
Malaysia	144,403	214,813	267,046	...	...	...	...	...	...
Myanmar	...	...	133,277 (2019)	...	40,840.0	28,581.8 (2019)	507.9	419.4	158.4 (2019)
Philippines	31,242	32,633	33,120	...	...	...	...	...	...
Singapore	8,895	9,246	9,530	...	...	...	...	...	...
Thailand	...	...	702,577 (2021)	452,040.0	663,561.0	735,051.0 (2019)	185.9	193.9	191.0 (2019)
Timor-Leste	...	8,701	8,811 (2018)	...	...	...	...	...	...
Viet Nam	...	309,969 (2016)	277,167 (2019)	69,197.4	105,382.2	144,061.2 (2019)	36,179.0	51,514.9	76,529.1 (2019)
The Pacific									
Cook Islands	...	...	...	...	...	...	...	...	...
Fiji	...	...	...	...	...	...	...	...	...
Kiribati	...	...	...	...	...	...	...	...	...
Marshall Islands	...	...	...	...	...	...	...	...	...
Micronesia, Federated States of	...	...	...	...	...	...	...	...	...
Nauru	...	...	...	...	...	...	...	...	...
Niue	...	...	...	...	...	...	...	...	...
Palau	...	...	...	...	...	...	...	...	...
Papua New Guinea	...	30,000 (2016)	...	...	...	...	...	...	...
Samoa	1,152 (2012)	...	...	...	...	...	...	...	...
Solomon Islands	...	...	...	...	...	...	...	...	...
Tonga	...	...	...	...	...	...	...	...	...
Tuvalu	...	120 (2017)	...	...	...	...	...	...	...
Vanuatu	1,776 (2012)	2,241 (2014)	2,048 (2018)	...	...	...	...	...	...
Developed ADB Member Economies									
Australia	872,292	874,143	877,651 (2018)	320,040.0	343,200.0	329,940.0 (2021)	186,100.0	207,300.0	230,100.0 (2021)
Japan	1,210,000	1,221,000	1,226,000 (2019)	77,677.0	71,443.5	65,556.0 (2019)	243,150.0	204,316.0	213,836.0 (2019)
New Zealand	94,126	94,822	96,963 (2021)	...	...	...	21,268.0	23,843.0	27,502.0

... = data not available, ADB = Asian Development Bank, km = kilometer, t = metric ton.

a A passenger-kilometer, abbreviated as p-km, is a unit of measurement representing the transport of 1 passenger by a defined mode of transport over 1 kilometer.

b A ton-kilometer, abbreviated as t-km, is a unit of measurement representing the transport of 1 metric ton of goods (including packaging and tare weights of intermodal transport units) by a defined mode of transport over 1 kilometer. Only the distance on the national territory of the reporting economy is taken into account for national, international and transit transport.

Source: Asian Development Bank. Asian Transport Outlook Database. https://data.adb.org/dataset/asian-transport-outlook-database (accessed 20 April 2022).

Transport

Table 2.5.2: Road Indicators—Registered Vehicles

ADB Regional Member	2010	2015	2016	2017	2018	2019	2020
Developing ADB Member Economies							
Central and West Asia							
Afghanistan	1,238,332 (2011)	1,887,263	1,906,938	1,936,686	1,951,428	1,980,033	...
Armenia	...	...	...	...	...	...	...
Azerbaijan	...	...	...	...	...	...	...
Georgia	702,700	1,081,400	1,167,200	1,228,100	1,289,100	1,339,300	1,404,400 (2021)
Kazakhstan	3,087,600	3,856,520	4,383,139	4,292,232	4,252,868	4,230,462	4,375,457
Kyrgyz Republic	...	...	...	...	...	...	...
Pakistan	7,853,002	17,826,048	21,057,912	23,812,676	26,566,167	29,106,354	...
Tajikistan	...	...	...	...	...	...	...
Turkmenistan	...	...	...	...	...	...	...
Uzbekistan	...	...	...	...	...	...	...
East Asia							
China, People's Republic of	77,216,700	161,614,900	184,501,300	208,083,900	231,232,300	252,571,200	272,088,300
Hong Kong, China	664,726	798,316	818,316	840,597	865,661	879,154	913,477
Korea, Republic of	...	23,151,659	23,984,039	24,724,770	25,410,979	25,914,261	26,019,150
Mongolia	608,274 (2012)	789,720	841,552	900,145	970,880	1,043,028	1,234,701 (2021)
Taipei,China	22,226,684	21,510,650	21,704,365	21,871,240	22,111,807	22,111,807	22,597,694 (2021)
South Asia							
Bangladesh	1,509,028	2,463,298	2,879,708	3,300,094	3,797,466	4,301,596	...
Bhutan	53,382	75,190	84,297	92,008	100,544	88,264	92,167
India	127,745,972	210,023,289	230,030,598	253,311,000	260,164,525	282,308,500	...
Maldives	46,028	77,776	87,126	97,213	108,532	...	...
Nepal	1,178,911	2,339,169	2,783,428	3,221,042	3,539,519	...	...
Sri Lanka	3,954,311	6,302,141	6,795,469	7,247,122	7,727,921	8,095,224	...
Southeast Asia							
Brunei Darussalam	165,849 (2009)	267,281	277,332	277,200	282,265	289,978	...
Cambodia	...	...	...	...	...	...	...
Indonesia	76,907,127	118,985,191	126,270,428	128,765,933	138,969,561	126,435,952	132,898,416
Lao People's Democratic Republic	1,008,788	1,717,144	1,850,020	1,979,606	2,105,207	2,233,685	2,343,240
Malaysia	20,188,565	26,301,952	27,613,259	26,350,246	29,277,453	30,497,054	31,642,275
Myanmar	2,147,404	5,077,699	5,541,361	6,337,002	6,853,995	7,092,843	...
Philippines	6,634,855	8,706,607	9,251,565	10,410,814	11,595,434	12,725,305	13,302,609 (2021)
Singapore	945,829	957,246	956,430	961,842	957,006	973,101	988,755 (2021)
Thailand	28,484,829	36,731,023	39,124,339	38,308,763	39,551,789	40,712,048	41,471,345
Timor-Leste	10,940	17,801	19,498	21,969	23,974	...	...
Viet Nam	1,274,000	2,107,000	2,516,000	2,902,000	3,148,400	...	...
The Pacific							
Cook Islands	...	...	...	...	...	...	...
Fiji	81,926	101,425	110,763	117,623	119,960	...	...
Kiribati	...	...	...	...	...	...	...
Marshall Islands	2,464 (2008)	...	...	...	...	...	...
Micronesia, Federated States of	7,662	8,509	9,160	8,584	9,777	11,807	...
Nauru	1,737 (2011)	...	...	...	...	...	...
Niue	926 (2011)	1,785 (2014)	...	...	...	...	...
Palau	5,643	5,832 (2014)	...	...	...	...	...
Papua New Guinea	...	...	...	...	...	...	...
Samoa	16,394 (2011)	17,449 (2013)	...	...	...	...	...
Solomon Islands	...	...	...	...	...	...	...
Tonga	19,432	...	...	...	...	...	...
Tuvalu	...	...	...	...	...	...	...
Vanuatu	5,368 (2009)	...	...	...	...	...	...
Developed ADB Member Economies							
Australia	16,061,100	18,007,600	18,387,200	18,781,100	19,173,300	19,505,100	19,933,313 (2021)
Japan	78,473,135	80,670,393	80,900,730	81,260,206	81,563,101	81,789,318	81,849,782
New Zealand	3,415,436	3,811,916	3,971,905	4,137,304	4,267,559	4,384,598	4,435,286

... = data not available, ADB = Asian Development Bank.

Source: Asian Development Bank. Asian Transport Outlook Database. https://data.adb.org/dataset/asian-transport-outlook-database (accessed 20 April 2022).

Table 2.5.3: Road Indicators—Safety

ADB Regional Member	Estimated Road Traffic Deaths, 2016		Road User Deaths, 2016[a] (%)				
	Total	Death Rate (per 100,000 people)	Four-Wheeled Vehicles	Two- and Three-Wheeled Vehicles	Cyclists	Pedestrians	Others
Developing ADB Member Economies							
Central and West Asia	**44,846**	**14.3**					
Afghanistan	5,230	15.1	...	...	...	...	...
Armenia	499	17.1	59.6	1.5	0.4	34.8	3.7
Azerbaijan	845	8.7	51.8	0.9	0.9	42.0	4.3
Georgia	599	15.3	44.9	0.5	0.7	26.5	27.4
Kazakhstan	3,158	17.6	59.8	4.3	1.7	30.9	3.3
Kyrgyz Republic	916	15.4	27.6	2.1	0.2	40.0	30.0
Pakistan	27,582	14.3	...	...	...	...	...
Tajikistan	1,577	18.1	57.4	...	2.3	40.3	–
Turkmenistan	823	14.5	...	...	...	...	...
Uzbekistan	3,617	11.5	...	...	...	...	...
East Asia[b]	**261,669**	**17.9**					
China, People's Republic of	256,180	18.2	...	...	...	...	...
Hong Kong, China	...	...	...	...	...	...	...
Korea, Republic of	4,990	9.8	...	20.5	5.9	39.9	33.7
Mongolia	499	16.5	39.3	18.6	1.2	28.7	12.2
Taipei,China	...	...	...	...	...	...	...
South Asia	**331,906**	**21.6**					
Bangladesh	24,954	15.3	...	...	...	...	...
Bhutan	139	17.4	...	...	...	...	...
India	299,091	22.6	17.9	39.6	1.7	10.4	30.4
Maldives	4	0.9	–	75.0	–	25.0	–
Nepal	4,622	15.9	...	...	...	...	...
Sri Lanka	3,096	14.9	6.2	50.8	8.1	29.2	5.7
Southeast Asia[b]	**114,030**	**17.8**					
Brunei Darussalam	...	...	...	...	...	...	...
Cambodia	2,803	17.8	6.2	73.5	2.3	9.6	8.4
Indonesia	31,726	12.2	4.9	73.6	3.2	15.5	2.7
Lao People's Democratic Republic	1,120	16.6	...	...	...	...	...
Malaysia	7,374	23.6	...	...	...	...	...
Myanmar	10,540	19.9	10.8	64.8	3.1	14.2	7.1
Philippines	12,690	12.3	0.3	4.7	0.1	1.0	93.9
Singapore	155	2.8	7.8	44.0	14.2	33.3	0.7
Thailand	22,491	32.7	12.3	74.4	3.5	7.6	2.3
Timor-Leste	161	12.7	...	...	...	...	...
Viet Nam	24,970	26.4	...	...	...	...	...
The Pacific[b]	**1,428**	**13.7**					
Cook Islands	3	17.3	20.0	80.0	–	–	–
Fiji	86	9.6	63.3	...	...	36.7	–
Kiribati	5	4.4	40.0	20.0	–	40.0	–
Marshall Islands	...	...	...	...	...	...	...
Micronesia, Federated States of	2	1.9	50.0	–	–	50.0	–
Nauru	...	...	...	...	...	...	...
Niue	...	...	...	...	...	...	...
Palau	...	...	...	...	...	...	–
Papua New Guinea	1,145	14.2	52.5	...	...	47.5	–
Samoa	22	11.3	41.2	–	5.9	47.1	5.9
Solomon Islands	104	17.4	...	...	...	...	...
Tonga	18	16.8	66.7	–	–	27.8	5.6
Tuvalu	...	...	...	...	...	...	...
Vanuatu	43	15.9	...	...	...	...	...
Developed ADB Member Economies	**6,939**	**4.4**					
Australia	1,351	5.6	60.9	19.3	2.2	14.0	3.5
Japan	5,224	4.1	32.4	17.2	15.1	35.0	1.0
New Zealand	364	7.8	68.5	15.9	1.5	7.6	6.4
DEVELOPING ADB MEMBER ECONOMIES[b]	**753,879**	**19.0**					
ALL ADB REGIONAL MEMBERS[b]	**760,818**	**18.4**					

... = data not available, – = magnitude equals zero, ADB = Asian Development Bank.

a Nature of road user deaths might not add up to 100% due to rounding.
b Regional aggregates include reporting economies only.

Source: World Health Organization. 2018. Global Status Report on Road Safety 2018. Geneva.

Table 2.5.4: Rail Indicators—Total Route, Length per Land Area

ADB Regional Member	Rail Lines, Total Route (km)			Rail Network, Length per Land Area (km per km^2 '000)		
	2010	2015	2020	2010	2015	2020
Developing ADB Member Economies						
Central and West Asia						
Afghanistan	106.0 (2011)	106.0	...	0.2 (2011)	0.2	...
Armenia	871.1	823.6	782.1	30.6	28.9	27.5
Azerbaijan	2,792.0	2,446.0	2,499.0	33.8	29.6	30.2
Georgia	1,566.0	1,576.0	1,576.0	22.5	22.7	22.7
Kazakhstan	15,016.1	15,341.1	16,636.7 (2019)	5.6	5.7	6.2 (2019)
Kyrgyz Republic	...	...	...	...	...	...
Pakistan	7,791.0	7,791.0	7,791.0 (2019)	10.1	10.1	10.1 (2019)
Tajikistan	...	...	...	...	...	...
Turkmenistan	...	...	...	...	...	...
Uzbekistan	4,227.2	4,238.0	...	9.9	9.6	...
East Asia						
China, People's Republic of	91,200.0	121,000.0	146,300.0	9.7	12.8	15.5
Hong Kong, China	...	...	...	...	...	...
Korea, Republic of	...	...	...	...	...	...
Mongolia	...	1,810.0 (2016)	1,100.0 (2019)	...	1.2 (2016)	0.7 (2019)
Taipei,China	1,085.0	1,065.0	1,065.0	30.0	29.4	29.4
South Asia						
Bangladesh	2,460.0	2,877.0	2,956.0 (2018)	18.9	22.1	22.7 (2018)
Bhutan	...	...	...	...	...	...
India	64,460.0	66,252.0	67,956.0 (2019)	21.7	22.3	22.9 (2019)
Maldives	...	...	...	...	...	...
Nepal	...	...	...	...	...	...
Sri Lanka	1,263.0	1,568.0	...	20.1	25.3	...
Southeast Asia						
Brunei Darussalam	...	...	...	...	...	...
Cambodia[a]	604.0	257.0	652.0 (2019)	3.4	1.5	3.7 (2019)
Indonesia	4,816.4	5,286.0	6,325.9	2.7	2.9	3.4
Lao People's Democratic Republic	...	...	...	...	...	...
Malaysia	1,792.0	1,775.0	1,775.0 (2018)	5.5	5.4	5.4 (2018)
Myanmar	5,487.8	6,107.4	6,112.3 (2019)	8.4	9.4	9.4 (2019)
Philippines	452.0	452.0	452.0	1.5	1.5	1.5
Singapore	...	...	...	...	...	...
Thailand	4,507.9	4,507.9	4,801.3	8.8	8.8	9.4
Timor-Leste	...	...	...	...	...	...
Viet Nam	2,577.0	3,147.0	3,163.0 (2018)	8.3	10.1	10.2 (2018)
The Pacific						
Cook Islands	...	...	...	...	...	...
Fiji	...	590.0 (2014)	...	...	32.3 (2014)	...
Kiribati	...	...	...	...	...	...
Marshall Islands	...	...	...	...	...	...
Micronesia, Federated States of	...	...	...	...	...	...
Nauru	...	...	...	...	...	...
Niue	...	...	...	...	...	...
Palau	...	...	...	...	...	...
Papua New Guinea	...	...	...	...	...	...
Samoa	...	...	...	...	...	...
Solomon Islands	...	...	...	...	...	...
Tonga	...	...	...	...	...	...
Tuvalu	...	...	...	...	...	...
Vanuatu	...	...	...	...	...	...
Developed ADB Member Economies						
Australia	...	33,343.0	32,894.0 (2019)	...	4.3	4.3 (2019)
Japan	...	...	...	...	...	...
New Zealand	...	...	3,700.0 (2019)	...	...	14.1 (2019)

... = data not available, ADB = Asian Development Bank, km = kilometer, km^2 = square kilometer.

a Data refers to railways rehabilitated and constructed.

Sources: For rail lines, total route: Asian Development Bank. Asian Transport Outlook Database. https://data.adb.org/dataset/asian-transport-outlook-database (accessed 20 April 2022). For rail network: Asian Development Bank estimates using land area data from World Bank. World Development Indicators. https://data.worldbank.org/indicator (accessed 5 May 2022).

Table 2.5.5: Railways—Passengers Carried and Goods Transported

ADB Regional Member	Passengers Carried[a] (p-km million)			Goods Transported[b] (t-km million)		
	2010	2015	2020	2010	2015	2020
Developing ADB Member Economies						
Central and West Asia						
Afghanistan	...	...	...	...	...	...
Armenia	125.6	104.3	68.0	743.2	640.3	842.0
Azerbaijan	2,747.0	2,945.0	996.0	8,331.0	6,269.0	4,861.0
Georgia	1,159.4	1,123.1	693.4	6,227.5	4,261.3	2,926.0
Kazakhstan	16,281.5	17,179.5	9,264.2	213,200.0	267,400.0	299,200.0
Kyrgyz Republic	98.7	40.8	21.0 (2021)	737.7	917.8	1,002.8 (2021)
Pakistan	20,619.0	21,201.0	29,595.0 (2019)	4,846.9	3,301.4	8,304.0 (2019)
Tajikistan	...	1.7 (2017)	...	10,445.6	6,125.6	6,305.3
Turkmenistan	1,685.0	...	...	9,715.0	...	...
Uzbekistan	3,500.0	4,180.5	4,983.3 (2019)	22,300.0	22,934.9	23,444.6 (2019)
East Asia						
China, People's Republic of	876,220.0	1,196,060.0	826,620.0	2,764,410.0	2,375,430.0	3,051,450.0
Hong Kong, China	...	...	...	...	...	...
Korea, Republic of	58,381.8	68,371.0	...	9,452.4	9,479.3	7,357.0 (2019)
Mongolia	1,220.0	996.7	95.7 (2021)	10,286.7	11,462.6	18,390.0 (2021)
Taipei,China	20,930.8	27,110.9	25,554.1	866.3	634.2	445.0 (2021)
South Asia						
Bangladesh	8,253.0 (2012)	8,711.0	...	693.0	694.0	...
Bhutan	...	...	...	...	...	...
India	978,508.0	1,149,835.0 (2016)	1,050,738.0 (2019)	...	...	...
Maldives	...	...	...	...	...	...
Nepal	...	...	...	...	...	...
Sri Lanka	4,568.0	7,407.0	7,709.5 (2018)	162.8	127.4	120.0 (2018)
Southeast Asia						
Brunei Darussalam	...	...	...	...	...	...
Cambodia	...	...	...	...	...	...
Indonesia	20,340.0	22,296.0	10,488.0	6,559.0	10,057.0	13,805.0
Lao People's Democratic Republic	...	0.1	0.0	...	...	...
Malaysia	1,532.2	426.1	200.9 (2019)	1,482.8	1,474.5	1,141.6 (2019)
Myanmar	5,371.4	3,416.2	1,444.2 (2019)	1,059.4	812.3	362.8 (2019)
Philippines	...	...	...	...	...	...
Singapore	7,880.0	9,391.0 (2014)	...	...	...	...
Thailand	846.0	6,133.4	5,906.5 (2018)	...	2,545.3	2,769.1 (2018)
Timor-Leste	...	...	...	...	...	...
Viet Nam	4,377.9	4,149.6	3,154.7 (2019)	3,960.9	4,035.5	3,739.5 (2019)
The Pacific						
Cook Islands	...	...	...	...	...	...
Fiji	...	...	...	...	...	...
Kiribati	...	...	...	...	...	...
Marshall Islands	...	...	...	...	...	...
Micronesia, Federated States of	...	...	...	...	...	...
Nauru	...	...	...	...	...	...
Niue	...	...	...	...	...	...
Palau	...	...	...	...	...	...
Papua New Guinea	...	...	...	...	...	...
Samoa	...	...	...	...	...	...
Solomon Islands	...	...	...	...	...	...
Tonga	...	...	...	...	...	...
Tuvalu	...	...	...	...	...	...
Vanuatu	...	...	...	...	...	...
Developed ADB Member Economies						
Australia	14,990.0	16,020.0	17,590.0 (2018)	258,600.0	401,600.0	...
Japan	393,466.0	427,486.2	435,063.0 (2019)	20,398.0	21,519.0	19,993.0
New Zealand	...	...	...	4,768.0 (2012)	4,348.0	4,443.0 (2021)

... = data not available, ADB = Asian Development Bank, km = kilometer, t = metric ton.

a A passenger-kilometer, abbreviated as p-km, is a unit of measurement representing the transport of 1 passenger by a defined mode of transport over 1 kilometer.
b A ton-kilometer, abbreviated as t-km, is a unit of measurement representing the transport of 1 metric ton of goods (including packaging and tare weights of intermodal transport units) by a defined mode of transport over 1 kilometer. Only the distance on the national territory of the reporting economy is taken into account for national, international and transit transport.

Source: Asian Development Bank. Asian Transport Outlook Database. https://data.adb.org/dataset/asian-transport-outlook-database (accessed 20 April 2022).

Transport

Table 2.5.6: Air Transport

ADB Regional Member	Aviation Total Passenger Kilometers[a] (p-km million)			Aviation Freight Transport[b] (t-km million)		
	2010	2015	2020	2010	2015	2020
Developing ADB Member Economies						
Central and West Asia						
Afghanistan	...	...	...	...	...	...
Armenia	1,278.6	27.4 (2016)	103.0	9.7	2.0 (2014)	0.7
Azerbaijan	1,613.0	3,338.0	984.0	139.0	582.0	2,302.0
Georgia	368.9	548.9	256.8	0.9	41.3	438.0
Kazakhstan	6,469.2	11,153.3	8,525.0	90.0	43.0	55.0
Kyrgyz Republic	814.2	1,966.1	1,086.0 (2021)	64.4	57.4	20.8 (2021)
Pakistan	16,209.0	13,751.0	14,938.0 (2019)	188.9	135.5	135.0 (2019)
Tajikistan	...	193.4 (2017)	...	2.2	2.1	0.7
Turkmenistan	2,712.0	...	...	29.0	...	...
Uzbekistan	5,800.0	6,786.0	10,998.1 (2019)	168.0	131.1	119.0 (2019)
East Asia						
China, People's Republic of	403,899.6	951,303.6 (2017)	631,130.0	17,890.0	20,807.0	24,020.0
Hong Kong, China	...	...	...	...	...	...
Korea, Republic of	135,770.8	198,443.4	...	145.0	112.0	...
Mongolia	907.2	1,993.5	449.0 (2021)	4.2	7.7	11.9 (2021)
Taipei,China	60,051.2	80,054.8	20,938.5	11,873.3	9,079.7	10,297.6
South Asia						
Bangladesh	5,027.0	6,645.0	7,072.0 (2018)	123.0	199.0	...
Bhutan	...	...	...	...	...	...
India	103,171.0	145,787.0	...	...	...	...
Maldives	...	...	...	...	...	...
Nepal	...	...	...	67.4	68.0	159.0 (2019)
Sri Lanka	9,399.6	12,737.3	16,180.0 (2018)	1,472.7	1,146.4	1,897.0 (2018)
Southeast Asia						
Brunei Darussalam	...	...	...	...	...	...
Cambodia	...	...	...	–	...	...
Indonesia	75,805.2	88,464.9	56,345.2	11,591.5	5,940.6	2,949.4
Lao People's Democratic Republic	82.8	846.1	560.0	1.2	0.4	1.0
Malaysia	66,719.0	87,210.0	25,018.0	...	...	...
Myanmar	566.1	1,452.2	1,639.9 (2019)	1.3	5.0	5.1 (2019)
Philippines	...	...	...	...	...	...
Singapore	...	...	...	...	...	...
Thailand	...	...	...	29,309.0	27,221.0	24,232.0 (2019)
Timor-Leste	...	...	...	...	...	...
Viet Nam	21,162.0	42,068.4	77,402.8 (2019)	426.8	599.5	922.5 (2019)
The Pacific						
Cook Islands	...	...	...	...	...	...
Fiji	...	...	...	...	...	...
Kiribati	...	...	...	...	...	...
Marshall Islands	...	...	...	...	...	...
Micronesia, Federated States of	...	...	...	...	...	...
Nauru	...	...	...	...	...	...
Niue	...	...	...	...	...	...
Palau	...	...	...	...	...	...
Papua New Guinea	...	...	...	...	...	...
Samoa	...	...	...	...	...	...
Solomon Islands	...	...	...	...	...	...
Tonga	...	...	...	...	...	...
Tuvalu	...	...	...	...	...	...
Vanuatu	...	...	...	...	...	...
Developed ADB Member Economies						
Australia	60,220.0	70,130.0	27,980.0 (2021)	300.0	300.0	300.0 (2018)
Japan	133,649.0	172,984.0	199,012.0 (2018)	7,339.1	8,766.4	925.0 (2019)
New Zealand	...	...	...	...	...	...

... = data not available, ADB = Asian Development Bank, km = kilometer, t = metric ton.

a A passenger-kilometer, abbreviated as p-km, is a unit of measurement representing the transport of 1 passenger by a defined mode of transport over 1 kilometer. For air transport, it includes both domestic and international flights.

b A ton-kilometer, abbreviated as t-km, is a unit of measurement representing the transport of 1 metric ton of goods (including packaging and tare weights of intermodal transport units) by a defined mode of transport over 1 kilometer. For air transport, it includes both domestic and international flights.

Source: Asian Development Bank. Asian Transport Outlook Database. https://data.adb.org/dataset/asian-transport-outlook-database (accessed 20 April 2022).

Table 2.5.7: Logistics

ADB Regional Member	Container Port Traffic (teu '000)			Liner Shipping Connectivity Index[a]			Logistics Performance Index[b]		
	2010	2015	2020	2010	2015	2019	2012	2016	2018
Developing ADB Member Economies									
Central and West Asia									
Afghanistan	...	...	...	...	...	...	2.3	2.1	1.9
Armenia	...	...	...	...	...	...	2.6	2.2	2.6
Azerbaijan	...	...	...	...	...	...	2.5	...	...
Georgia	210	222	260	5.3	5.7	6.8	...	2.4	2.4
Kazakhstan	...	...	...	...	...	...	2.7	2.8	2.8
Kyrgyz Republic	...	...	...	...	...	...	2.4	2.2	2.5
Pakistan	2,149	2,756	3,339	31.6	32.9	34.1	2.8	2.9	2.4
Tajikistan	...	...	...	...	...	...	2.3	2.1	2.3
Turkmenistan	...	...	...	...	...	...	...	2.2	2.4
Uzbekistan	...	...	...	...	...	...	2.5	2.4	2.6
East Asia									
China, People's Republic of	131,989	193,734	245,104	121.2	138.9	151.9	3.5	3.7	3.6
Hong Kong, China	23,600	20,114	17,969	91.0	94.2	89.5	4.1	4.1	3.9
Korea, Republic of	18,520	25,477	28,425	74.5	98.3	105.1	3.7	3.7	3.6
Mongolia	...	...	...	...	...	...	2.3	2.5	2.4
Taipei,China	12,497	14,492	14,594	...	...	...	3.7	3.7	3.6
South Asia									
Bangladesh	1,350	2,045	2,587	7.3	11.0	13.3	...	2.7	2.6
Bhutan	...	...	...	...	...	...	2.5	2.3	2.2
India	8,890	11,883	16,286	47.6	49.4	55.5	3.1	3.4	3.2
Maldives	50	84	89 (2018)	6.2	3.1	7.4	2.5	2.5	2.7
Nepal	...	...	...	...	...	...	2.0	2.4	2.5
Sri Lanka	4,100	5,185	6,850	37.5	49.2	62.1	2.8	...	2.6
Southeast Asia									
Brunei Darussalam	93	128	139 (2018)	5.1	4.9	7.7	...	2.9	2.7
Cambodia	286	474	764	6.1	7.6	8.0	2.6	2.8	2.6
Indonesia	9,010	12,032	14,025	33.0	35.7	44.4	2.9	3.0	3.2
Lao People's Democratic Republic	...	...	...	...	...	...	2.5	2.1	2.7
Malaysia	16,843	24,013	26,664	72.3	92.2	93.8	3.5	3.4	3.2
Myanmar	335	827	1,021	5.6	9.1	8.5	2.4	2.5	2.3
Philippines	5,589	7,210	7,505	21.2	22.4	30.6	3.0	2.9	2.9
Singapore	29,147	31,710	36,871	92.4	101.0	108.1	4.1	4.1	4.0
Thailand	6,819	9,463	10,214	40.5	42.5	52.9	3.2	3.3	3.4
Timor-Leste	...	...	...	1.6	5.8	2.9	...	...	...
Viet Nam	5,968	11,479	16,374 (2018)	41.2	48.4	66.5	3.0	3.0	3.3
The Pacific									
Cook Islands	...	...	...	...	...	...	...	...	...
Fiji	87	89	93 (2018)	12.8	12.7	11.2	2.4	2.3	2.4
Kiribati	...	...	...	...	...	...	...	...	...
Marshall Islands	...	...	...	3.8	5.7	4.9	...	...	...
Micronesia, Federated States of	...	...	...	...	...	...	...	...	...
Nauru	...	...	...	1.3 (2011)	2.5	2.2	...	...	...
Niue	...	...	...	...	...	...	...	...	...
Palau	...	...	...	3.9	3.9	3.4	...	...	...
Papua New Guinea	283	279	341 (2018)	8.5	12.7	12.6	...	2.5	2.2
Samoa	22	28	30 (2018)	...	...	...	...	...	...
Solomon Islands	...	...	...	6.3	11.2	10.7	...	2.4	2.6
Tonga	...	...	...	5.6	5.7	7.6	...	...	...
Tuvalu	...	...	...	1.0	3.0	2.0	...	...	...
Vanuatu	...	...	...	3.4	8.8	7.9	...	...	...
Developed ADB Member Economies									
Australia	6,372	7,621	8,657	30.8	32.5	34.3	3.7	...	3.8
Japan	18,966	20,138	21,386	72.4	74.8	71.2	3.9	4.0	4.0
New Zealand	2,331	3,119	3,174	21.3	23.4	31.9	3.4	3.4	3.9

... = data not available, ADB = Asian Development Bank, teu = twenty-foot equivalent unit.

a The Liner Shipping Connectivity Index captures how well economies are connected to global shipping networks. It is based on five components of the maritime transport sector: number of ships, their container-carrying capacity, maximum vessel size, number of services, and number of companies that deploy container ships in an economy's ports. The index generates a value of 100 for the economy with the highest average index in 2004.

b The index ranges from 1 to 5, with higher scores representing better performance.

Source: Asian Development Bank. Asian Transport Outlook Database. https://data.adb.org/dataset/asian-transport-outlook-database (accessed 20 April 2022).

Communications

Table 2.5.8: Access to Fixed Telephones, Mobile Phones, and Internet—Total Subscriptions
('000)

ADB Regional Member	Fixed Telephone Subscribers		Mobile Phone Subscribers		Fixed Broadband Subscribers	
	2010	2020	2010	2020	2010	2020
Developing ADB Member Economies						
Central and West Asia	**16,633.0**	**13,649.6**	**181,113.9**	**304,388.5**	**2,558.4**	**13,693.0**
Afghanistan	16.6	145.8	10,215.8	22,678.0	1.5	26.6
Armenia	592.3	427.5	3,865.4	3,488.8	93.6	430.4
Azerbaijan	1,506.6	1,652.7	9,100.1	10,344.3	475.3	1,995.5
Georgia	1,111.9	387.7	3,978.2	5,100.1	182.4	972.2
Kazakhstan	4,057.6	3,091.0	19,402.6	24,293.9	869.6	2,620.4
Kyrgyz Republic	489.1	299.0	5,275.5	8,511.0	23.1	289.0
Pakistan	6,079.1	2,876.8	99,185.8	175,624.4	789.5	2,523.0
Tajikistan	367.7	502.0	5,940.8	11,584.0	4.7	6.0
Turkmenistan	520.0	717.0	3,197.6	9,377.0	0.7	10.0
Uzbekistan	1,892.2	3,550.1	20,952.0	33,387.0	118.0	4,820.0
East Asia	**343,914.6**	**222,577.4**	**953,914.0**	**1,844,505.0**	**151,087.3**	**515,119.3**
China, People's Republic of	294,383.0	181,908.0	859,003.0	1,718,411.0	126,337.0	483,549.5
Hong Kong, China	4,361.7	3,900.6	13,793.7	21,865.2	2,167.7	2,885.6
Korea, Republic of	28,543.2	23,858.2	50,767.2	70,513.7	17,194.3	22,327.2
Mongolia	193.2	160.2	2,510.5	4,363.9	76.8	307.2
Taipei,China	16,433.5	12,750.4	27,839.5	29,351.2	5,311.6	6,049.9
South Asia	**40,845.6**	**24,813.6**	**847,557.4**	**1,399,395.6**	**11,717.3**	**36,121.2**
Bangladesh	1,280.8	1,390.0	67,923.9	176,279.5	414.6	10,052.8
Bhutan	26.3	23.0	394.3	745.1	8.7	3.2
India	35,090.0	20,052.2	752,190.0	1,153,709.8	10,990.0	22,950.0
Maldives	28.4	14.5	494.4	717.7	15.6	63.7
Nepal	841.7	726.0	9,195.6	38,213.0	60.2	1,270.0
Sri Lanka	3,578.5	2,607.9	17,359.3	29,730.5	228.3	1,781.5
Southeast Asia[a]	**73,120.0**	**34,137.5**	**532,636.5**	**918,246.4**	**14,515.4**	**53,826.5**
Brunei Darussalam	79.9	103.9	435.1	536.6	21.7	71.1
Cambodia	358.9	55.6	8,150.8	21,086.8	35.7	233.8
Indonesia	40,931.1	9,662.1	211,290.2	355,620.4	2,280.3	11,722.2
Lao People's Democratic Republic	103.1	1,491.0	4,003.4	4,100.0	5.9	128.0
Malaysia	4,609.8	7,467.9	33,858.7	43,723.6	2,097.8	3,358.8
Myanmar	493.3	524.0	594.0	78,548.3	23.0	688.8
Philippines	3,335.4	4,731.2	83,150.1	149,579.4	1,791.0 (2011)	7,936.6
Singapore	1,996.1	1,891.0	7,384.6	8,444.8	1,338.4	1,509.7
Thailand	6,835.1	5,003.0	71,726.3	116,294.0	3,251.9	11,478.3
Timor-Leste	2.9	2.0	473.0	1,377.9	0.5	0.1
Viet Nam	14,374.4	3,205.8	111,570.2	138,934.6	3,669.3	16,699.2
The Pacific[a]	**338.8**	**263.0**	**3,105.0**	**6,813.4**	**38.6**	**64.7**
Cook Islands	7.2	7.0	7.8	17.0	1.7	3.0
Fiji	129.8	48.5	697.9	991.5	23.3	23.1
Kiribati	8.4	0.0	10.6	54.7	0.8	0.2
Marshall Islands	...	...	...	16.0	...	1.0
Micronesia, Federated States of	8.5	7.0	27.5	22.0	1.0	6.0
Nauru	...	...	6.2	10.0	1.0	...
Niue	1.0	1.0	...	...	...	...
Palau	7.0	8.0	14.5	24.0	0.2	...
Papua New Guinea	121.2	166.0	1,909.1	4,818.0	6.1	21.0
Samoa	8.0	6.0	90.0	69.0	0.2	1.7
Solomon Islands	8.4	7.0	115.5	474.0	2.5	1.0
Tonga	31.0	7.0	54.3	62.0	1.1	5.0
Tuvalu	1.2	2.0	1.6	9.0	0.2	...
Vanuatu	7.1	3.5	169.9	246.2	0.5	2.8
Developed ADB Member Economies[a]	**78,123.7**	**69,036.6**	**150,497.1**	**228,655.9**	**40,703.8**	**54,865.4**
Australia	10,625.0	6,200.0	22,500.0	27,453.0	5,510.0	9,099.6
Japan	65,618.7	61,978.6	123,287.1	195,054.9	34,101.8	44,000.8
New Zealand	1,880.0	858.0	4,710.0	6,148.0	1,092.0	1,765.0
DEVELOPING ADB MEMBER ECONOMIES[a]	**474,856.2**	**295,445.3**	**2,518,342.9**	**4,473,349.5**	**179,918.3**	**618,827.5**
ALL ADB REGIONAL MEMBERS[a]	**552,980.0**	**364,481.9**	**2,668,840.0**	**4,702,005.4**	**220,622.1**	**673,692.9**

... = data not available, 0.0 = magnitude is less than half of unit employed, – = magnitude equals zero, ADB = Asian Development Bank.

a Regional aggregates are calculated as the sum of the reporting economies. Imputation was done for economies with missing data by substituting available data from the nearest years.

Source: International Telecommunication Union. World Telecommunication/ICT Indicators Database. http://www.itu.int/en/ITU-D/Statistics/Pages/stat/default.aspx (accessed 2 May 2022).

Click on the indicator name in the table header to access the time series in the Key Indicators Database

Table 2.5.9: Access to Fixed Telephones, Mobile Phones, and Internet—Subscriptions per 100 People

ADB Regional Member	Fixed Telephone			Mobile Cellular			Fixed Broadband			Internet Users		
	2010	2015	2020	2010	2015	2020	2010	2015	2020	2010	2015	2020
Developing ADB Member Economies												
Central and West Asia[a]	**5.8**	**4.8**	**3.9**	**63.0**	**74.4**	**86.7**	**0.9**	**2.8**	**3.9**			
Afghanistan	0.1	0.3	0.4	35.0	57.3	58.3	0.0	0.0	0.1	4.0	8.3	18.4
Armenia	20.6	18.8	14.4	134.3	118.4	117.7	3.3	9.8	14.5	25.0	59.1	76.5
Azerbaijan	16.7	18.7	16.3	100.7	111.2	102.0	5.3	19.7	19.7	46.0	77.0	84.6
Georgia	27.1	23.6	9.7	97.1	137.9	127.8	4.5	15.8	24.4	26.9	47.6	72.5
Kazakhstan	25.0	23.6	16.5	119.4	149.7	129.4	5.4	13.1	14.0	31.6	70.8	85.9
Kyrgyz Republic[b]	9.0	6.8	4.6	97.3	127.2	130.5	0.4	3.5	4.4	16.3	30.2	51.0
Pakistan	3.4	1.8	1.3	55.3	63.1	79.5	0.4	0.9	1.1	8.0	11.0	25.0
Tajikistan	4.9	5.4	5.3	78.9	100.4	121.5	0.1	0.1	0.1	11.6	19.0	...
Turkmenistan	10.2	11.6	11.9	62.9	140.9	155.5	0.0	0.1	0.2	3.0	15.0	...
Uzbekistan	6.6	9.1	10.6	73.5	70.4	99.8	0.4	5.8	14.4	15.9	42.8	71.1
East Asia[a]	**23.7**	**18.7**	**14.6**	**65.7**	**93.9**	**120.9**	**10.4**	**20.5**	**33.8**			
China, People's Republic of	21.5	16.4	12.6	62.8	91.8	119.4	9.2	19.7	33.6	34.3	50.3	70.4
Hong Kong, China	62.6	60.3	52.0	198.0	232.7	291.7	31.1	32.7	38.5	72.0	84.9	92.4
Korea, Republic of	57.6	56.8	46.5	102.5	116.0	137.5	34.7	39.4	43.5	83.7	89.9	96.5
Mongolia	7.1	8.5	4.9	92.3	102.3	133.1	2.8	6.9	9.4	10.2	22.5	62.5
Taipei,China	70.9	59.1	53.5	120.1	126.0	123.2	22.9	24.0	25.4	71.5	78.0	89.0
South Asia[a]	**2.9**	**2.0**	**1.6**	**59.3**	**78.2**	**87.7**	**0.8**	**1.5**	**2.3**			
Bangladesh	0.9	0.6	0.8	46.0	84.1	107.0	0.3	3.1	6.1	3.7	12.9	24.8
Bhutan	3.8	3.0	3.0	57.5	92.8	96.6	1.3	3.8	0.4	13.6	39.8	53.5
India	2.8	1.9	1.5	60.9	76.4	83.6	0.9	1.3	1.7	7.5	14.9	43.0
Maldives	7.8	4.8	2.7	135.2	162.6	132.8	4.3	5.1	11.8	26.5	54.5	62.9
Nepal	3.1	3.1	2.5	34.0	101.9	131.2	0.2	1.1	4.4	7.9	17.6	37.7
Sri Lanka	17.7	15.7	12.2	85.7	114.3	138.8	1.1	3.0	8.3	...	12.1	35.0
Southeast Asia[a,c]	**12.2**	**5.4**	**5.1**	**89.2**	**126.1**	**137.3**	**2.5**	**4.0**	**8.1**			
Brunei Darussalam	20.6	18.3	23.7	112.0	111.7	122.7	5.6	8.3	16.2	53.0	71.2	95.0
Cambodia	2.5	1.7	0.3	56.9	134.3	126.1	0.2	0.5	1.4	1.3	18.0	...
Indonesia	16.9	4.0	3.5	87.4	131.2	130.0	0.9	1.5	4.3	10.9	22.1	53.7
Lao People's Democratic Republic	1.6	14.3	20.5	64.1	55.3	56.4	0.1	0.2	1.8	7.0	18.2	33.8
Malaysia	16.3	14.8	23.1	120.0	145.7	135.1	7.4	10.1	10.4	56.3	71.1	89.6
Myanmar	1.0	1.0	1.0	1.2	77.8	144.4	0.0	0.1	1.3	0.3	10.9	35.1
Philippines[d]	3.5	3.2	4.3	88.5	115.4	136.5	1.9	2.8	7.2	25.0	36.9	49.8
Singapore	38.9	36.1	32.3	143.9	147.2	144.3	26.1	26.6	25.8	71.0	83.2	92.0
Thailand	10.2	7.7	7.2	106.7	149.8	166.6	4.8	9.1	16.4	22.4	39.3	77.8
Timor-Leste	0.3	0.2	0.2	43.3	115.1	104.5	0.0	0.1	0.0	3.0	18.6	29.1
Viet Nam	16.3	7.9	3.3	126.8	129.8	142.7	4.2	8.3	17.2	30.7	45.0	70.3
The Pacific[a,c]	**3.6**	**2.7**	**2.3**	**32.7**	**52.0**	**59.3**	**0.4**	**0.4**	**0.6**			
Cook Islands[e]	39.3	37.1	39.9	42.4	79.0	96.8	9.1	15.1	17.1	35.7	51.0	...
Fiji[f]	15.1	8.4	5.4	81.2	111.2	110.6	2.7	1.5	2.6	20.0	42.5	68.9
Kiribati	8.2	1.3	0.0	10.3	37.0	45.8	0.8	0.1	0.2	9.1	14.9	38.0
Marshall Islands[g]	...	4.1	...	...	27.0	27.0	...	1.7	1.7	7.0	19.3	...
Micronesia, Federated States of	8.2	6.3	6.1	26.7	20.7	19.1	1.0	3.0	5.2	20.0	31.5	...
Nauru[h]	19.1	...	...	62.0	90.5	92.4	9.5	...	...	54.0	62.4	...
Niue	61.8	61.8	61.5	...	...	...	...	...	...	77.0	...	...
Palau	38.9	40.8	44.2	80.8	134.4	132.6	1.3	6.9	...	...	...	...
Papua New Guinea	1.7	1.9	1.9	26.1	43.9	53.9	0.1	0.2	0.2	1.3	7.9	...
Samoa	4.3	5.9	3.0	48.4	62.3	34.8	0.1	1.1	0.9	7.0	25.4	...
Solomon Islands	1.6	1.2	1.0	21.9	70.4	69.0	0.5	0.2	0.1	5.0	10.0	...
Tonga	29.8	13.1	6.6	52.2	72.9	58.7	1.1	2.4	4.7	16.0	38.7	...
Tuvalu	11.4	18.0	17.0	15.2	59.5	76.3	2.3	4.1	...	14.6	27.3	...
Vanuatu	3.0	1.8	1.1	71.9	64.5	80.2	0.2	1.6	0.9	8.0	22.4	...
Developed ADB Member Economies[a,c]	**50.4**	**47.3**	**44.0**	**97.1**	**122.6**	**145.8**	**26.2**	**30.1**	**35.0**			
Australia	48.0	35.5	24.3	101.6	107.7	107.7	24.9	28.5	35.7	76.0	84.6	89.6
Japan	51.0	49.8	49.0	95.9	125.5	154.2	26.5	30.4	34.8	78.2	91.1	90.2
New Zealand	43.0	40.1	17.8	107.8	121.4	127.5	25.0	31.4	36.6	80.5	85.2	91.5
DEVELOPING ADB MEMBER ECONOMIES[a,c]	**12.6**	**9.0**	**7.1**	**66.7**	**91.4**	**107.7**	**4.8**	**9.1**	**14.9**			
ALL ADB REGIONAL MEMBERS[a,c]	**14.1**	**10.5**	**8.5**	**67.9**	**92.6**	**109.1**	**5.7**	**9.9**	**15.6**			

... = data not available, 0.0 = magnitude is less than half of unit employed, ADB = Asian Development Bank.

a Regional aggregates are derived from table 2.5.8 regional aggregate levels and population data from the United Nations' World Population Prospects 2019.
b For internet users, data for 2020 refers to 2019.
c Regional aggregates are calculated as the sum of the reporting economies. Imputation was done for economies with missing data by substituting available data from the nearest years.
d For fixed broadband, data for 2010 refers to 2011.
e For fixed telephone and mobile cellular, data for 2015 refers to 2016. For fixed broadband, data for 2015 refers to 2013.
f For internet users, data for 2020 refers to 2018.
g For fixed telephone, data for 2015 refers to 2014.
h For fixed telephone, data for 2010 refers to 2009. For internet users, data for 2010 refers to 2011 and data for 2015 refers to 2017.

Sources: International Telecommunication Union. World Telecommunication/ICT Indicators Database. http://www.itu.int/en/ITU-D/Statistics/Pages/stat/default.aspx (accessed 2 May 2022); and United Nations. World Population Prospects 2019. https://population.un.org/wpp/Download/Standard/Population/ (accessed 2 May 2022).

Data Issues and Comparability

Issues with data organization, collection, compilation, and dissemination affect the availability, quality, and timeliness of road statistics. Some regions, especially the Pacific, have incomplete or no data.

Most data on telephone and internet subscriptions came from questionnaires sent by the International Telecommunication Union to participating economies. Other information and reports were sourced from national ministries in charge of telecommunications and from staff estimates.

Table 2.6.1: Electricity Production and Sources

ADB Regional Member	Total Electricity Production (kWh billion)		Sources of Electricity (% of total): Combustible Fuels[a]		Hydropower		Solar		Others[b]	
	2010	2019	2010	2019	2010	2019	2010	2019	2010	2019
Developing ADB Member Economies										
Central and West Asia[c]	**310.1**	**411.9**	**67.7**	**72.2**	**30.4**	**23.4**	**0.0**	**0.4**	**1.9**	**4.0**
Afghanistan	0.9	1.3 (2020)	14.0	9.3 (2020)	86.0	88.3 (2020)	–	2.4 (2020)	–	– (2020)
Armenia	6.5	7.7	22.2	39.7	39.4	30.9	–	0.8	38.5	28.7
Azerbaijan	18.7	26.1	81.6	93.4	18.4	6.0	–	0.2	–	0.4
Georgia	10.1	11.2 (2020)	6.8	25.3 (2020)	93.2	73.9 (2020)	–	– (2020)	–	0.8 (2020)
Kazakhstan	82.7	106.9	90.3	89.2	9.7	9.4	0.0	0.8	–	0.7
Kyrgyz Republic[d]	12.1	15.1	8.2	8.3	91.8	91.7	–	–	–	–
Pakistan	94.4	134.8 (2020)	62.7	60.8 (2020)	33.7	28.8 (2020)	–	0.5 (2020)	3.6	9.9 (2020)
Tajikistan	16.4	19.7 (2020)	0.2	8.2 (2020)	99.8	91.8 (2020)	–	– (2020)	–	– (2020)
Turkmenistan	16.7	22.5	100.0	100.0	–	0.0	–	–	–	–
Uzbekistan[d]	51.7	63.0	79.0	89.7	21.0	10.3	–	0.0	–	0.0
East Asia[c]	**4,996.4**	**8,403.0**	**78.3**	**69.8**	**15.3**	**16.1**	**0.0**	**2.9**	**6.4**	**11.1**
China, People's Republic of	4,207.2	7,503.5	79.2	69.6	17.2	17.4	–	3.0	3.6	10.1
Hong Kong, China	38.3	35.2 (2020)	100.0	100.0 (2020)	–	– (2020)	–	– (2020)	–	– (2020)
Korea, Republic of	499.5	581.5	68.6	70.6	1.3	1.1	0.2	2.2	30.0	26.0
Mongolia	4.4	7.1 (2020)	98.9	93.2 (2020)	0.8	1.2 (2020)	0.2	0.8 (2020)	0.0	4.8 (2020)
Taipei,China	247.1	290.9 (2021)	...	...	...	...	...	...	...	...
South Asia[c]	**1,017.1**	**1,693.9**	**82.6**	**79.6**	**12.9**	**10.4**	**0.0**	**3.0**	**4.4**	**6.9**
Bangladesh	40.8	84.6	98.1	98.6	1.9	0.9	–	0.4	–	0.0
Bhutan	7.3	8.9	0.0	0.0	100.0	100.0	0.0	0.0	–	0.0
India	954.5	1,576.7	83.3	79.5	12.0	9.9	–	3.2	4.7	7.4
Maldives	0.4	0.8	99.2	97.2	–	–	0.2	2.5	0.6	0.4
Nepal	3.2	6.2	0.1	0.0	99.9	99.9	–	0.0	–	0.1
Sri Lanka	10.8	16.7	47.2	67.1	52.3	28.7	0.1	2.1	0.5	2.1
Southeast Asia[c]	**676.5**	**1,124.9**	**85.3**	**80.9**	**11.8**	**15.9**	**0.0**	**0.7**	**2.9**	**2.6**
Brunei Darussalam	3.8	4.9	100.0	100.0	–	–	–	0.0	–	–
Cambodia	1.0	8.7	96.5	52.5	3.2	46.4	0.3	1.1	–	–
Indonesia	169.6	299.6	84.2	89.0	10.3	6.6	0.0	0.0	5.5	4.4
Lao People's Democratic Republic	8.4	31.1	–	39.2	100.0	60.7	–	0.1	–	–
Malaysia	116.8	175.8	94.6	84.3	5.4	15.2	0.0	0.5	–	–
Myanmar	8.6	23.8	28.2	60.3	71.8	39.4	–	0.3	–	–
Philippines	67.8	103.2 (2020)	73.7	80.3 (2020)	11.5	7.0 (2020)	0.0	1.3 (2020)	14.7	11.4 (2020)
Singapore	45.4	53.7 (2020)	100.0	98.8 (2020)	–	– (2020)	0.0	1.2 (2020)	–	– (2020)
Thailand	159.5	190.7	96.5	92.0	3.5	3.4	0.0	2.7	0.0	1.9
Timor-Leste[d]	0.1	0.5	98.9	99.5	1.1	0.3	–	0.2	–	–
Viet Nam	95.4	227.7	70.5	62.4	29.4	37.4	–	0.0	0.1	0.1
The Pacific[c]	**5.1**	**6.7**	**63.9**	**69.1**	**27.6**	**22.9**	**0.0**	**1.2**	**8.4**	**6.8**
Cook Islands	0.0	0.0 (2020)	100.0	73.7 (2020)	–	– (2020)	–	26.3 (2020)	–	– (2020)
Fiji	0.9	1.0 (2020)	50.9	42.2 (2020)	48.4	56.4 (2020)	–	1.3 (2020)	0.8	0.1 (2020)
Kiribati	0.0	0.0 (2020)	97.1	84.2 (2020)	–	– (2020)	2.9	15.8 (2020)	–	– (2020)
Marshall Islands	0.1	0.1	100.0	97.8	–	–	–	2.2	–	–
Micronesia, Federated States of	0.1	0.1 (2020)	98.8	93.9 (2020)	–	0.2 (2020)	1.2	4.4 (2020)	–	1.6 (2020)
Nauru	0.0	0.0 (2020)	99.8	97.3 (2020)	–	– (2020)	0.2	2.7 (2020)	–	– (2020)
Niue	0.0	0.0 (2020)	97.9	87.7 (2020)	–	– (2020)	2.1	12.3 (2020)	–	– (2020)
Palau	0.1	0.1 (2020)	100.0	97.9 (2020)	–	– (2020)	–	2.1 (2020)	–	– (2020)
Papua New Guinea	3.6	4.7 (2020)	62.0	71.9 (2020)	26.4	19.0 (2020)	0.0	0.0 (2020)	11.6	9.0 (2020)
Samoa	0.1	0.2 (2020)	64.1	61.9 (2020)	35.9	24.0 (2020)	0.0	14.0 (2020)	–	0.1 (2020)
Solomon Islands	0.1	0.1 (2020)	99.4	95.3 (2020)	0.6	0.9 (2020)	–	3.7 (2020)	–	– (2020)
Tonga	0.1	0.1 (2020)	100.0	87.2 (2020)	–	– (2020)	–	9.2 (2020)	–	3.6 (2020)
Tuvalu	0.0	0.0 (2020)	98.8	71.3 (2020)	–	– (2020)	1.2	28.7 (2020)	–	– (2020)
Vanuatu	0.1	0.1	80.9	76.5	11.6	9.4	–	6.6	7.5	7.5
Developed ADB Member Economies	**1,468.5**	**1,353.8**	**68.6**	**75.3**	**8.8**	**9.5**	**0.3**	**6.2**	**22.4**	**9.0**
Australia	252.7	264.0	92.5	81.6	5.4	6.0	0.2	5.6	2.0	6.7
Japan	1,170.9	1,045.0	65.0	76.1	7.7	8.3	0.3	6.6	27.0	8.9
New Zealand	44.9	44.8	28.0	19.6	55.1	57.1	0.0	0.3	16.9	23.1
DEVELOPING ADB MEMBER ECONOMIES[c]	**7,005.2**	**11,640.3**	**79.1**	**72.5**	**15.3**	**15.5**	**0.0**	**2.6**	**5.5**	**9.4**
ALL ADB REGIONAL MEMBERS[c]	**8,473.6**	**12,994.2**	**77.3**	**72.8**	**14.2**	**14.9**	**0.1**	**3.0**	**8.5**	**9.4**

... = data not available, 0.0 = magnitude is less than half of unit employed, – = magnitude equals zero, ADB = Asian Development Bank, kWh = kilowatt-hour.

a Electricity from combustible fuels refers to the production of electricity from the combustion of fuels that are capable of igniting or burning, which would include coal, natural gas, oil, and other combustible fuels.
b Includes chemical heat, geothermal, nuclear, tide, other marine electricity, wind, wave, and other sources of energy.
c Includes only reporting economies with data corresponding to the year heading.
d Partial 2020 energy data are available from the United Nations' Energy Statistics Database. However, 2019 figures were reflected in this table to ensure comparability of data.

Sources: United Nations. Energy Statistics Database. http://data.un.org/Data.aspx?d=EDATA&f=cmID%3aEL (accessed 02 June 2022). For Taipei,China: Government of Taipei,China; Directorate-General of Budget, Accounting and Statistics; Official communication, 25 May 2022.

Electricity

Table 2.6.2: Electric Power Consumption
(kWh per capita)

ADB Regional Member	2010	2015	2017	2018	2019
Developing ADB Member Economies					
Central and West Asia[a]	**851.4**	**917.2**	**949.5**	**1,012.5**	**971.7**
Afghanistan	83.3	131.9	147.6	149.4	148.0 (2020)
Armenia	1,622.0	1,836.2	1,909.5	1,830.3	1,974.2
Azerbaijan	1,485.6	2,138.0	2,030.1	2,091.0	2,154.6
Georgia	1,869.7	2,465.3	2,799.8	2,985.3	3,023.8
Kazakhstan	3,877.4	4,348.2	4,398.9	5,202.6	4,348.0
Kyrgyz Republic	1,313.3	1,789.4	1,807.8	1,898.0	1,939.3
Pakistan	429.7	453.4	496.7	515.8	524.3
Tajikistan	1,881.1	1,479.9	1,558.7	1,526.2	1,569.0 (2020)
Turkmenistan	2,134.6	2,647.7	2,559.7	2,518.9	2,480.3
Uzbekistan	1,552.8	1,530.9	1,575.4	1,647.8	1,642.6
East Asia[a]	**3,015.0**	**3,937.6**	**4,395.5**	**4,714.8**	**4,901.5**
China, People's Republic of	2,648.1	3,595.7	4,055.0	4,386.3	4,591.5
Hong Kong, China	6,009.3	6,110.8	5,999.2	6,010.1	5,895.8 (2020)
Korea, Republic of[b]	9,253.5	9,968.8	10,536.6	10,659.9	10,507.5
Mongolia	1,241.1	1,762.1	1,910.4	2,034.5	2,079.4 (2020)
Taipei,China	10,654.8	10,958.0	11,415.5	11,613.4	12,196.1 (2021)
South Asia[a]	**519.6**	**728.7**	**790.0**	**804.0**	**886.0**
Bangladesh	233.9	331.2	412.4	436.3	483.9
Bhutan	2,814.9	2,826.2	2,931.7	2,897.3	2,987.0
India	562.6	789.5	848.1	860.5	949.3
Maldives	926.9	1,279.4	1,377.9	1,415.5	1,512.4
Nepal	101.4	143.1	206.6	231.4	230.0
Sri Lanka	454.5	561.5	638.4	665.1	691.2
Southeast Asia[a]	**1,013.5**	**1,268.9**	**1,403.4**	**1,456.5**	**1,504.6**
Brunei Darussalam	8,401.2	9,006.7	8,334.9	8,585.9	9,932.8
Cambodia	157.6	335.7	424.2	532.5	619.8
Indonesia	609.1	823.5	924.4	940.7	953.7
Lao People's Democratic Republic	390.6	628.8	714.3	767.1	919.9
Malaysia	3,929.8	4,367.2	4,710.5	4,848.6	4,967.3
Myanmar	124.7	254.3	296.7	333.6	345.7
Philippines	588.1	664.0	739.7	774.6	759.6 (2020)
Singapore	8,234.3	8,496.5	8,696.1	8,760.4	8,676.5 (2020)
Thailand	2,222.2	2,533.0	2,678.4	2,708.5	2,774.5
Timor-Leste	93.1	212.6	258.3	264.6	159.5 (2020)
Viet Nam	973.9	1,550.4	1,846.2	2,016.8	2,146.4
The Pacific[a]	**475.9**	**505.2**	**511.3**	**529.8**	**543.4**
Cook Islands	1,832.3	1,860.0	2,096.5	2,363.1	1,930.1 (2020)
Fiji	888.9	950.9	1,028.3	1,047.0	975.0 (2020)
Kiribati	192.4	203.7	219.0	219.3	218.5 (2020)
Marshall Islands	1,437.2	1,309.1	1,336.7	1,335.3	1,330.1
Micronesia, Federated States of	510.9	423.4	409.1	407.5	399.9 (2020)
Nauru	1,548.6	1,868.1	2,430.7	2,631.6	2,898.3 (2020)
Niue	1,712.7	1,858.4	1,898.3	2,049.7	2,181.7 (2020)
Palau	4,021.4	4,132.5	4,553.9	4,466.5	4,311.3 (2020)
Papua New Guinea	441.0	478.8	473.8	497.3	487.7 (2020)
Samoa	500.2	596.6	708.4	705.7	790.3 (2020)
Solomon Islands	142.1	137.1	141.8	134.1	128.4 (2020)
Tonga	410.0	487.9	576.5	561.1	601.0
Tuvalu	512.3	509.4	585.0	686.7	644.5 (2020)
Vanuatu	258.5	226.2	252.3	246.0	234.4 (2020)
Developed ADB Member Economies	**8,457.7**	**7,849.5**	**7,964.2**	**7,863.2**	**7,768.3**
Australia	9,966.3	9,384.3	9,350.4	9,379.7	9,401.0
Japan	8,169.5	7,529.5	7,679.7	7,547.4	7,421.9
New Zealand	9,285.7	8,766.7	8,429.1	8,370.7	8,352.9
DEVELOPING ADB MEMBER ECONOMIES[a]	**1,582.1**	**2,034.8**	**2,243.0**	**2,374.8**	**2,473.2**
ALL ADB REGIONAL MEMBERS[a]	**1,853.3**	**2,255.4**	**2,456.4**	**2,577.8**	**2,667.4**

... = data not available, ADB = Asian Development Bank, kWh = kilowatt-hour.

a Includes only reporting economies with data corresponding to the year heading.
b Partial 2020 energy data are available from the United Nations' Energy Statistics Database. However, to ensure comparability of data, 2019 figures are reflected in this table .

Sources: For electric power consumption: United Nations Statistics Division. Energy Statistics Database. http://data.un.org/Data.aspx?d=EDATA&f=cmID%3aEL (accessed 02 June 2022). For total population: United Nations. World Population Prospects 2019. https://population.un.org/wpp/Download/Standard/Population/ (accessed 05 April 2022). For Taipei,China: Asian Development Bank estimates using economy source.

Table 2.6.3: Use of Energy

ADB Regional Member	Energy Use (PJ)			GDP per Unit Use of Energy (constant 2017 $ million PPP per PJ)		
	2010	2015	2019	2010	2015	2019
Developing ADB Member Economies						
Central and West Asia	**10,359.0**	**10,829.7**	**11,617.1**	**154.6**	**185.4**	**203.6**
Afghanistan	140.6	168.9	189.0	406.2	421.3	415.6
Armenia	106.2	134.7	141.2	251.7	245.9	286.1
Azerbaijan	485.9	605.0	663.7	262.4	236.9	218.1
Georgia	139.8	197.8	215.0	263.8	237.4	259.4
Kazakhstan	3,363.4	3,180.4	3,002.8	100.7	134.0	162.5
Kyrgyz Republic	115.5	167.2	158.6	195.3	171.2	214.1
Pakistan	3,092.2	3,314.4	3,849.0	255.2	289.8	299.2
Tajikistan	143.4	166.6	207.7	125.4	151.5	160.7
Turkmenistan	951.4	1,159.8	1,191.3	46.1	62.3	77.5
Uzbekistan	1,820.6	1,734.8	1,998.8	77.7	115.5	123.4
East Asia[a]	**112,823.6**	**132,601.4**	**149,466.6**	**123.8**	**149.6**	**168.6**
China, People's Republic of	101,618.2	120,324.1	136,602.4	117.0	144.6	164.7
Hong Kong, China	544.0	575.9	584.6	663.2	724.3	765.2
Korea, Republic of	10,497.6	11,428.3	11,738.3	162.4	173.3	188.6
Mongolia	163.9	273.0	541.4	124.0	120.9	74.4
Taipei,China	...	...	...	...	...	...
South Asia	**29,778.9**	**37,943.3**	**43,787.2**	**201.5**	**216.1**	**239.0**
Bangladesh	1,493.3	1,803.3	2,067.7	337.4	379.6	437.6
Bhutan	56.8	63.8	71.5	98.9	115.0	126.7
India	27,409.7	35,122.8	40,565.6	190.7	203.8	225.3
Maldives	13.4	18.8	27.9	444.9	417.4	371.6
Nepal	445.6	501.6	597.4	163.5	179.4	189.3
Sri Lanka	360.1	432.9	457.2	513.5	576.0	623.8
Southeast Asia	**22,190.3**	**25,768.2**	**30,308.7**	**238.6**	**263.9**	**274.1**
Brunei Darussalam	135.7	113.8	168.9	194.1	230.2	159.3
Cambodia	196.4	252.3	338.3	198.0	217.9	213.9
Indonesia	8,072.8	8,708.7	11,145.8	248.2	301.1	286.8
Lao People's Democratic Republic	100.3	168.8	246.0	302.2	261.4	229.8
Malaysia	2,965.0	3,423.8	3,896.2	195.4	219.2	233.1
Myanmar	659.8	847.5	964.9	211.9	227.7	265.5
Philippines	1,706.3	2,143.0	2,520.2	325.9	347.9	382.4
Singapore	1,085.2	1,166.3	822.6	365.4	423.1	681.5
Thailand	4,930.8	5,668.4	5,795.3	196.2	197.4	221.5
Timor-Leste	4.4	6.9	9.8	722.7	568.1	479.5
Viet Nam	2,333.6	3,268.8	4,400.7	236.9	228.2	222.1
The Pacific[a]	**187.6**	**230.6**	**257.5**	**207.8**	**215.4**	**218.3**
Cook Islands	0.9	1.0	1.2	...	...	...
Fiji	20.8	25.2	26.1	436.3	434.1	466.0
Kiribati	1.3	1.4	1.6	146.7	171.6	156.2
Marshall Islands	2.0	2.0	2.0	101.3	103.0	119.0
Micronesia, Federated States of	1.5	2.1	2.2	243.8	176.9	181.1
Nauru	0.6	0.8	0.7	114.7	185.7	197.5
Niue	0.1	0.1	0.1	...	...	...
Palau	2.9	2.8	3.0	94.7	116.2	101.7
Papua New Guinea	140.9	178.0	201.5	176.8	185.9	186.9
Samoa	4.2	5.0	5.7	266.6	232.3	229.3
Solomon Islands	8.0	7.6	7.6	161.6	200.2	234.4
Tonga	1.7	1.6	2.3	322.1	367.2	292.2
Tuvalu	0.1	0.1	0.1	259.7	385.7	407.3
Vanuatu	2.7	2.9	3.3	270.4	277.3	282.9
Developed ADB Member Economies	**27,245.1**	**24,413.7**	**23,820.6**	**221.3**	**264.6**	**283.2**
Australia	5,396.3	5,330.4	5,424.5	183.4	212.5	230.6
Japan	21,009.5	18,125.8	17,436.5	232.1	283.4	302.8
New Zealand	839.3	957.5	959.6	194.8	197.5	223.7
DEVELOPING ADB MEMBER ECONOMIES[a]	**175,339.4**	**207,373.2**	**235,437.1**	**153.5**	**177.9**	**197.0**
ALL ADB REGIONAL MEMBERS[a]	**202,584.5**	**231,787.0**	**259,257.7**	**162.6**	**187.0**	**204.9**
WORLD[a]	**511,392.7**	**544,778.5**	**579,939.4**	**179.5**	**199.9**	**214.4**

... = data not available, – = magnitude equals zero, $ = United States dollars, ADB = Asian Development Bank, GDP = gross domestic product, PJ = petajoule, PPP = purchasing power parity.

a Aggregates include only reporting economies with data corresponding to the year heading.

Sources: For Energy Use: United Nations. Energy Statistics Database. https://data.un.org/SdmxBrowser/start (accessed 04 July 2022). For GDP per Unit Use of Energy: Asian Development Bank estimates using data from World Bank's World Development Indicators Database. https://databank.worldbank.org/source/world-development-indicators# (accessed on 4 July 2022); and United Nation's Energy Statistics Database. https://data.un.org/SdmxBrowser/start (accessed 04 July 2022).

Table 2.6.4: Energy Production and Imports

ADB Regional Member	Energy Production (PJ)			Energy Imports, Net (% of total energy use)		
	2010	2015	2019	2010	2015	2019
Developing ADB Member Economies						
Central and West Asia	**16,391.7**	**17,420.5**	**17,945.1**	**-58.2**	**-60.9**	**-54.5**
Afghanistan	41.4	61.0	82.4	70.5	63.9	56.4
Armenia	38.9	44.5	37.7	63.4	67.0	73.3
Azerbaijan	2,758.9	2,473.7	2,474.8	-467.8	-308.8	-272.9
Georgia	57.5	55.1	45.7	58.8	72.1	78.7
Kazakhstan	6,769.9	6,812.2	6,983.5	-101.3	-114.2	-132.6
Kyrgyz Republic	53.1	75.3	100.1	54.1	55.0	36.9
Pakistan	2,251.6	2,302.5	2,366.1	27.2	30.5	38.5
Tajikistan	114.7	131.3	169.9	20.0	21.2	18.2
Turkmenistan	1,981.9	3,407.3	3,399.1	-108.3	-193.8	-185.3
Uzbekistan	2,323.7	2,057.7	2,285.9	-27.6	-18.6	-14.4
East Asia[a]	**91,160.2**	**103,742.6**	**113,146.0**	**18.8**	**21.4**	**24.0**
China, People's Republic of	88,642.0	100,962.7	109,744.5	12.8	16.1	19.7
Hong Kong, China	...	...	...	...	...	...
Korea, Republic of	1,863.1	2,124.8	1,992.0	82.3	81.4	83.0
Mongolia	655.0	655.1	1,409.4	-299.8	-139.9	-160.3
Taipei,China	...	...	...	...	...	...
South Asia	**23,050.3**	**24,066.0**	**26,310.7**	**22.6**	**36.6**	**39.9**
Bangladesh	1,304.1	1,509.6	1,560.5	12.7	16.3	24.5
Bhutan	72.9	76.8	84.9	-28.4	-20.3	-18.8
India	21,104.5	21,875.0	24,030.0	23.0	37.7	40.8
Maldives	0.2	0.2	0.2	98.9	99.1	99.1
Nepal	384.4	423.6	457.2	13.7	15.5	23.5
Sri Lanka	184.3	180.8	177.8	48.8	58.2	61.1
Southeast Asia	**29,108.3**	**30,896.2**	**35,067.2**	**-31.2**	**-19.9**	**-15.7**
Brunei Darussalam	775.2	672.8	637.5	-471.3	-491.2	-277.3
Cambodia	124.4	143.0	162.4	36.6	43.3	52.0
Indonesia	16,605.0	17,364.0	21,266.8	-105.7	-99.4	-90.8
Lao People's Democratic Republic	97.7	162.1	275.7	2.6	4.0	-12.1
Malaysia	3,450.0	3,748.0	4,085.1	-16.4	-9.5	-4.9
Myanmar	966.5	1,177.4	1,213.6	-46.5	-38.9	-25.8
Philippines	998.9	1,091.9	1,273.9	41.5	49.0	49.5
Singapore	24.9	26.3	26.9	97.7	97.7	96.7
Thailand	2,951.7	3,130.9	3,125.0	40.1	44.8	46.1
Timor-Leste	366.8	345.2	224.4	-8,170.0	-4,875.1	-2,194.6
Viet Nam	2,747.2	3,034.7	2,775.8	-17.7	7.2	36.9
The Pacific[a]	**106.8**	**253.7**	**253.7**	**41.3**	**-12.4**	**0.7**
Cook Islands	...	0.0	0.0	...	98.8	97.0
Fiji	5.2	7.4	6.7	75.1	70.5	74.5
Kiribati	0.5	0.5	0.6	62.3	60.8	64.4
Marshall Islands	–	–	–	100.0	100.0	100.0
Micronesia, Federated States of	0.0	0.0	0.0	98.4	98.7	98.2
Nauru	0.0	0.0	0.0	100.0	99.9	99.5
Niue	0.0	0.0	0.0	80.3	83.7	82.9
Palau	...	0.0 (2016)	0.0	...	100.0 (2016)	99.8
Papua New Guinea	95.4	239.8	240.3	32.3	-34.7	-19.3
Samoa	1.5	1.6	1.7	63.3	67.6	69.6
Solomon Islands	3.2	3.3	3.3	59.6	56.4	56.2
Tonga	0.0	0.0	0.0	98.8	98.1	98.2
Tuvalu	0.0	0.0	0.0	99.8	97.4	94.4
Vanuatu	0.9	0.9	0.9	67.2	67.9	72.5
Developed ADB Member Economies	**18,626.4**	**18,138.9**	**21,446.5**	**31.6**	**25.7**	**10.0**
Australia	13,646.0	16,032.9	18,622.8	-152.9	-200.8	-243.3
Japan	4,205.5	1,321.9	2,079.3	80.0	92.7	88.1
New Zealand	775.0	784.0	744.4	7.7	18.1	22.4
DEVELOPING ADB MEMBER ECONOMIES[a]	**159,817.2**	**176,379.0**	**192,722.6**	**8.6**	**14.7**	**17.9**
ALL ADB REGIONAL MEMBERS[a]	**178,443.6**	**194,517.9**	**214,169.1**	**11.7**	**15.9**	**17.2**
WORLD[a]	**527,977.2**	**569,721.8**	**612,492.9**	**-3.4**	**-4.7**	**-5.7**

... = data not available, – = magnitude equals zero, ADB = Asian Development Bank, PJ = petajoule.

a The aggregates for energy production include only economies with available data corresponding to the year heading. The aggregates for net energy imports include only economies with available data corresponding to the year heading for both energy use and energy production. Net energy imports are calculated as the difference between total energy use and total energy production divided by total energy use.

Sources: For Energy Production: United Nations. Energy Statistics Database. https://data.un.org/SdmxBrowser/start (accessed 04 July 2022). For Net Energy Imports: Asian Development Bank estimates using data from United Nations' Energy Statistics Database. https://data.un.org/SdmxBrowser/start (accessed 04 July 2022).

Table 2.6.5: Retail Prices of Fuel Energy
($/L)

ADB Regional Member	Gasoline (Premium)			Diesel		
	2010	2015	2021	2010	2015	2021
Developing ADB Member Economies						
Central and West Asia						
Afghanistan	...	...	...	...	...	...
Armenia	1.01	0.90	0.90	0.92	0.89	0.86
Azerbaijan	...	...	...	...	...	...
Georgia	1.03	0.82	0.87	1.00	0.82	0.87
Kazakhstan	0.58	0.56	0.38 (2019)	0.53	0.44	0.50 (2019)
Kyrgyz Republic	...	...	...	...	...	...
Pakistan	0.80	0.68	0.71 (2019)	0.83	0.78	0.81 (2019)
Tajikistan	...	...	...	...	...	...
Turkmenistan	...	...	...	...	...	...
Uzbekistan	...	...	...	...	...	...
East Asia						
China, People's Republic of	...	...	...	...	...	...
Hong Kong, China	1.75	1.77	2.15	1.25	1.41	2.14
Korea, Republic of	1.48	1.34	1.39	1.30	1.15	1.22
Mongolia	1.01	0.79	0.77	0.96	0.91	0.82
Taipei,China	0.94	0.75	0.98	0.82	0.68	0.89
South Asia						
Bangladesh	...	...	...	...	...	...
Bhutan	...	...	...	...	...	...
India	1.05	1.18 (2014)	...	0.83	0.91 (2014)	...
Maldives	...	...	...	...	...	...
Nepal	1.22	1.22	0.97	0.95	0.97	0.83
Sri Lanka	1.02	0.86	0.88	0.65	0.70	0.60
Southeast Asia						
Brunei Darussalam	...	...	...	...	...	...
Cambodia	...	...	...	...	...	...
Indonesia	0.50	0.66	0.69 (2019)	0.50	0.64	0.55 (2019)
Lao People's Democratic Republic	...	...	...	...	...	...
Malaysia	0.67	0.63	0.47 (2020)	0.57	0.49	0.43 (2020)
Myanmar	150.50	0.76	0.59 (2019)	1.54 (2012)	0.80	0.65 (2019)
Philippines	0.96	0.90	1.09	0.76	0.60	0.86
Singapore	1.35	1.59	2.08	0.89	0.85	1.34
Thailand	1.02	0.81	0.89	0.91	0.72	0.88
Timor-Leste	...	...	...	...	...	...
Viet Nam	1.42 (2011)	1.12	1.42	0.93 (2011)	0.68	0.67
The Pacific						
Cook Islands	...	...	...	...	...	...
Fiji	...	...	...	...	...	...
Kiribati	...	...	...	...	...	...
Marshall Islands	...	...	...	...	...	...
Micronesia, Federated States of	...	...	...	...	...	...
Nauru	...	...	...	...	...	...
Niue	...	...	...	...	...	...
Palau	...	...	...	...	...	...
Papua New Guinea	...	...	...	...	...	...
Samoa	...	...	...	...	...	...
Solomon Islands	1.14	1.11	1.11	1.15	1.07	1.08
Tonga	...	...	...	...	...	...
Tuvalu	...	...	...	...	...	...
Vanuatu	1.50	1.36	1.44	...	...	...
Developed ADB Member Economies						
Australia	1.09	0.89	1.00	1.09	0.87	0.98
Japan	1.64	1.23	1.51	1.28	0.97	1.23
New Zealand	1.34	1.41	1.70	0.85	0.80	1.05

... = data not available, $ = United States dollars, ADB = Asian Development Bank, L = liter.

Source: Economies' official sources.

Click on the indicator name in the table header to access the time series in the Key Indicators Database

Data Issues and Comparability

Energy data are compiled by the United Nations Statistics Division (UNSD) using standard procedures that follow the definitions of the United Nations International Recommendations for Energy Statistics.[5] The UNSD Annual Questionnaire on Energy Statistics to the UN member economies is the primary source of information for the UNSD energy database. The UNSD sometimes prepares estimates where official data are incomplete or inconsistent. For the indicator on GDP per unit use of energy, the energy statistics adopt the territory principle, while national accounts are being compiled on the residency principle, which could be a potential source of inconsistency, although in practice differences are not huge (UN 2016).

For data on access to electricity, the Sustainable Energy for All (SE4ALL) database from the SE4ALL Global Tracking Framework—led jointly by the Energy Sector Management Assistance Program, the International Energy Agency, and the World Bank—provides recent updates on the proportion of access for an entire economy, as well as in rural and urban areas. The data for this indicator are a combination of economy-reported data and modeled estimates by the World Bank.

5 The full definitions can be found at https://unstats.un.org/UNSD/energy/ires/.

Table 2.7.1: Agriculture Land Use
(% of total land area)

ADB Regional Member	Agricultural Land			Arable Land			Permanent Cropland		
	2010	2015	2019	2010	2015	2019	2010	2015	2019
Developing ADB Member Economies									
Central and West Asia[a]	**67.5**	**67.4**	**67.1**	**13.8**	**14.2**	**14.2**	**0.4**	**0.4**	**0.4**
Afghanistan	58.1	58.1	58.3	11.9	11.9	11.9	0.2	0.2	0.3
Armenia	60.9	58.9	58.9	15.8	15.7	15.6	1.9	2.0	2.1
Azerbaijan	57.7	57.7	57.8	22.8	23.4	25.4	2.8	2.9	3.1
Georgia	35.4	34.8	34.1	5.7	5.3	4.4	1.8	1.6	1.7
Kazakhstan	80.4	80.1	79.4	10.6	11.0	11.1	0.0	0.0	0.0
Kyrgyz Republic	55.3	55.0	54.1	6.7	6.7	6.7	0.4	0.4	0.4
Pakistan	45.7	47.0	47.1	38.1	39.4	39.6	1.1	1.0	1.0
Tajikistan	34.0	34.1	34.1	5.3	5.2	5.0	1.0	1.0	1.1
Turkmenistan	72.4	72.0	72.0	4.1	4.1	4.1	0.1	0.1	0.1
Uzbekistan	58.7	58.0	58.0	9.6	9.2	9.2	0.8	0.9	0.9
East Asia[a]	**58.2**	**58.1**	**58.1**	**11.2**	**11.0**	**11.0**	**1.3**	**1.5**	**1.5**
China, People's Republic of	56.3	56.2	56.2	12.9	12.7	12.7	1.5	1.7	1.7
Hong Kong, China	5.2	4.9	4.8	3.3	3.0	2.9	1.0	1.0	1.0
Korea, Republic of	18.2	17.8	16.8	15.5	15.0	14.0	2.1	2.2	2.2
Mongolia	73.3	73.0	72.8	0.8	0.9	0.9	0.0	0.0	0.0
Taipei,China	23.0	22.5	22.3	16.9	16.7	16.7	6.1	5.8	5.6
South Asia[a]	**58.6**	**58.6**	**58.7**	**50.3**	**50.1**	**50.1**	**4.2**	**4.5**	**4.6**
Bangladesh	71.0	70.4	72.2	59.9	59.4	61.2	6.5	6.4	6.4
Bhutan	13.6	13.8	13.5	2.6	2.6	2.5	0.3	0.3	0.2
India	60.4	60.4	60.4	52.8	52.6	52.5	4.1	4.4	4.5
Maldives	23.0	21.3	21.3	13.0	13.0	13.0	6.7	5.0	5.0
Nepal	28.8	28.7	28.7	15.2	14.7	14.7	1.1	1.5	1.5
Sri Lanka	41.8	44.3	45.4	19.1	21.0	22.2	15.6	16.2	16.2
Southeast Asia[a]	**28.9**	**30.3**	**31.5**	**15.4**	**16.0**	**16.5**	**9.6**	**10.5**	**11.2**
Brunei Darussalam	2.5	2.5	2.5	0.8	0.8	0.8	1.1	1.1	1.1
Cambodia	30.9	31.5	31.5	21.5	22.0	22.0	0.9	1.1	1.1
Indonesia	29.6	30.5	33.2	12.6	12.7	14.0	11.2	12.0	13.3
Lao People's Democratic Republic	9.6	10.8	10.4	6.1	7.1	6.7	0.6	0.7	0.7
Malaysia	22.5	26.1	26.1	2.6	2.5	2.5	19.0	22.7	22.7
Myanmar	19.2	19.5	19.6	16.5	16.7	16.8	2.2	2.3	2.3
Philippines	40.6	41.7	41.7	17.8	18.7	18.7	17.8	17.9	17.9
Singapore	1.1	0.9	0.9	0.9	0.8	0.8	0.1	0.1	..
Thailand	41.2	43.3	43.3	30.8	32.9	32.9	8.8	8.8	8.8
Timor-Leste	25.0	25.6	25.6	10.1	10.4	10.4	4.8	5.0	5.0
Viet Nam	34.3	38.8	39.5	20.5	22.3	21.6	11.7	14.4	15.8
The Pacific[a]	**4.0**	**4.1**	**4.1**	**1.0**	**1.1**	**1.1**	**2.1**	**2.1**	**2.1**
Cook Islands	5.6	6.3	6.3	2.9	4.2	4.2	2.7	2.1	2.1
Fiji	23.3	23.3	23.3	9.0	9.0	9.0	4.7	4.7	4.7
Kiribati	42.0	42.0	42.0	2.5	2.5	2.5	39.5	39.5	39.5
Marshall Islands	72.2	47.8	47.8	11.1	11.1	11.1	44.4	36.1	36.1
Micronesia, Federated States of	31.4	31.4	31.4	2.9	2.9	2.9	24.3	24.3	24.3
Nauru	20.0	20.0	20.0	..	..	..	20.0	20.0	20.0
Niue	19.2	19.2	19.2	3.8	3.8	3.8	11.5	11.5	11.5
Palau	9.3	9.3	9.3	0.7	0.7	0.7	4.3	4.3	4.3
Papua New Guinea	2.6	2.6	2.6	0.7	0.7	0.7	1.5	1.5	1.5
Samoa	14.7	26.7	26.7	4.2	11.5	11.5	8.3	11.0	11.0
Solomon Islands	3.8	4.0	4.2	0.7	0.7	0.7	2.9	3.0	3.2
Tonga	44.4	48.6	48.6	23.6	27.8	27.8	15.3	15.3	15.3
Tuvalu	60.0	60.0	60.0	..	..	..	60.0	60.0	60.0
Vanuatu	15.3	15.3	15.3	1.6	1.6	1.6	10.3	10.3	10.3
Developed ADB Member Economies[a]	**47.2**	**43.7**	**45.3**	**3.6**	**4.3**	**4.2**	**0.1**	**0.1**	**0.1**
Australia	49.0	45.3	47.1	3.3	4.0	4.0	0.1	0.0	0.0
Japan	12.6	12.3	12.1	11.7	11.5	11.3	0.9	0.8	0.7
New Zealand	43.3	40.7	39.3	1.9	1.8	2.1	0.3	0.3	0.3
DEVELOPING ADB MEMBER ECONOMIES[a]	**54.0**	**54.2**	**54.3**	**17.6**	**17.7**	**17.8**	**3.0**	**3.3**	**3.4**
ALL ADB REGIONAL MEMBERS[a]	**52.3**	**51.6**	**52.1**	**14.1**	**14.3**	**14.4**	**2.3**	**2.5**	**2.6**
WORLD[a]	**36.8**	**36.4**	**36.5**	**10.5**	**10.6**	**10.6**	**1.2**	**1.3**	**1.3**

0.0 = magnitude is less than half of unit employed, ADB = Asian Development Bank.

a Aggregates are weighted averages estimated using total land area for the respective year headings.

Source: Food and Agriculture Organization of the United Nations. FAOSTAT Database. http://www.fao.org/faostat/en/#data/RL (accessed 8 July 2022)

Pollution

Table 2.7.2: Deforestation and Pollution

ADB Regional Member	Deforestation Rate[a,b] (average % change)			Carbon Dioxide Emissions[c] (t '000)			Nitrous Oxide Emissions (t '000 CO_2 equivalent)		
	2010	2015	2019	2010	2015	2019	2010	2015	2019
Developing ADB Member Economies									
Central and West Asia	**-0.02**	**-0.31**	**-0.20**	**605,620**	**594,860**	**669,600**	**94,790**	**103,720**	**115,800**
Afghanistan	0.00	0.00	0.00	7,110	5,950	6,080	4,580	4,620	5,010
Armenia	0.06	0.06	0.06	4,340	5,340	6,170	770	1,090	1,270
Azerbaijan	-0.44	-0.85	-1.04	24,310	31,770	35,510	3,360	4,100	4,130
Georgia	-0.22	0.00	0.00	5,320	9,200	10,110	1,830	2,270	2,160
Kazakhstan	0.24	-1.39	-0.86	229,700	190,730	212,110	11,050	10,890	12,170
Kyrgyz Republic	-0.40	-0.35	-1.43	6,350	10,270	10,050	1,640	1,800	1,920
Pakistan	1.01	0.81	1.09	140,620	164,130	190,570	53,510	58,250	66,670
Tajikistan	0.00	-0.56	-0.24	2,450	4,900	9,420	1,570	1,940	2,030
Turkmenistan	0.00	0.00	0.00	59,180	73,400	72,870	3,470	3,500	3,670
Uzbekistan	-1.17	-1.14	-0.71	126,240	99,170	116,710	13,010	15,260	16,770
East Asia	**-1.07**	**-0.84**	**-0.79**	**9,334,598**	**10,762,065**	**11,341,080**	**511,016**	**575,981**	**576,280**
China, People's Republic of[e]	-1.19	-0.93	-0.87	8,474,920	9,861,100	10,707,220	488,160	549,330	552,060
Hong Kong, China[e]	...	...	...	...	...	...	...	...	...
Korea, Republic of	0.14	0.16	0.16	575,220	607,830	610,790	9,260	9,870	10,330
Mongolia	0.06	0.01	0.01	14,310	17,300	23,070	8,640	12,250	13,890
Taipei,China[e]	...	...	...	270,148	275,835	282,842 (2018)	4,956	4,531	5,029 (2018)
South Asia	**-0.26**	**-0.33**	**-0.31**	**1,729,630**	**2,259,900**	**2,587,430**	**273,840**	**290,530**	**298,780**
Bangladesh	0.17	0.05	0.00	50,580	72,190	90,740	26,150	28,360	28,920
Bhutan	-0.37	-0.07	-0.07	400	770	1,050	110	100	110
India	-0.27	-0.38	-0.37	1,659,980	2,158,020	2,456,300	239,140	252,300	260,170
Maldives	–	–	–	960	1,370	2,110	10	10	10
Nepal	-0.30	0.00	0.00	4,640	7,190	13,450	5,670	6,540	7,120
Sri Lanka	0.30	-0.24	0.15	13,070	20,360	23,780	2,760	3,220	2,450
Southeast Asia	**0.29**	**0.73**	**0.58**	**1,149,430**	**1,409,450**	**1,748,710**	**181,950**	**194,400**	**213,530**
Brunei Darussalam	0.45	0.00	0.00	7,170	6,400	6,990	140	140	150
Cambodia	0.18	3.79	1.86	5,140	8,430	16,180	4,320	4,580	4,720
Indonesia	0.16	0.97	0.65	415,520	488,550	619,840	80,480	86,970	98,090
Lao People's Democratic Republic	0.29	0.21	0.21	2,880	8,880	18,710	2,510	2,720	2,860
Malaysia	0.39	-0.53	0.26	200,220	236,540	253,270	12,960	13,220	13,020
Myanmar	1.08	0.96	0.99	8,130	19,040	36,720	17,290	20,110	23,480
Philippines	0.68	-0.50	-0.49	81,930	111,010	145,420	12,760	12,610	14,070
Singapore	-0.41	1.52	1.13	42,410	45,430	47,380	6,750	8,390	9,940
Thailand	-0.54	0.01	0.18	234,380	264,000	267,090	22,620	19,820	21,580
Timor-Leste	0.15	0.15	0.15	240	520	620	220	270	260
Viet Nam	-1.21	-0.97	-0.52	151,410	220,650	336,490	21,900	25,570	25,360
The Pacific	**0.01**	**0.06**	**0.07**	**7,520**	**9,340**	**11,010**	**4,200**	**4,220**	**4,190**
Cook Islands	-0.01	0.00	0.00	...	...	...	...	...	...
Fiji	-0.63	-0.61	-0.59	1,160	1,380	1,630	330	180	210
Kiribati	0.00	0.00	0.00	50	60	90	–	–	10
Marshall Islands	0.00	0.00	0.00	140	150	180	–	–	–
Micronesia, Federated States of	-0.04	-0.04	-0.05	110	150	180	20	30	30
Nauru	...	...	...	40	60	60	–	–	–
Niue	0.03	-0.05	-0.05	...	...	...	...	...	...
Palau	-0.24	-0.21	-0.19	210	210	250	...	...	...
Papua New Guinea	0.03	0.09	0.09	5,020	6,510	7,580	3,600	3,740	3,660
Samoa	0.29	0.29	0.30	190	240	300	50	60	60
Solomon Islands	0.03	0.03	0.03	340	310	360	20	20	20
Tonga	0.00	0.00	0.00	120	120	160	50	50	50
Tuvalu	0.00	0.00	0.00	10	10	10	–	–	–
Vanuatu	0.00	0.00	0.00	130	140	210	130	140	150
Developed ADB Member Economies	**0.13**	**-0.42**	**-0.01**	**1,575,070**	**1,589,520**	**1,502,110**	**88,540**	**105,710**	**94,640**
Australia	0.17	-0.54	0.00	387,540	377,800	386,530	54,100	71,810	60,870
Japan	-0.04	0.02	0.00	1,156,480	1,179,440	1,081,570	20,080	18,720	18,700
New Zealand	0.00	0.00	-0.11	31,050	32,280	34,010	14,360	15,180	15,070
DEVELOPING ADB MEMBER ECONOMIES	**-0.34**	**-0.14**	**-0.17**	**12,826,798**	**15,035,615**	**16,357,830**	**1,065,796**	**1,168,851**	**1,208,580**
ALL ADB REGIONAL MEMBERS	**-0.24**	**-0.20**	**-0.14**	**14,401,868**	**16,625,135**	**17,859,940**	**1,154,336**	**1,274,561**	**1,303,220**

continued on next page

Table 2.7.2: Deforestation and Pollution *(continued)*

ADB Regional Member	Methane Emissions (t '000 CO_2 equivalent)			Other Greenhouse Gases[d] (t '000 CO_2 equivalent)		
	2010	2015	2019	2010	2015	2016
Developing ADB Member Economies						
Central and West Asia	**320,080**	**364,460**	**395,120**	**-12,708**	**-21,786**	**-2,334**
Afghanistan	15,200	15,960	16,370	2,582	-691	-1,800
Armenia	2,200	2,470	2,320	469	1,149	722
Azerbaijan	14,020	14,230	14,670	-54	-1,163	-514
Georgia	5,750	5,510	5,190	-248	1,005	1,190
Kazakhstan	48,590	47,350	48,890	-20,146	-20,260	-7,610
Kyrgyz Republic	3,890	4,370	4,800	1,569	3,669	2,918
Pakistan	125,460	146,050	162,760	-8,720	6,550	10,236
Tajikistan	4,330	5,230	5,660	-759	-753	260
Turkmenistan	53,740	77,780	80,480	-3,962	-6,292	-6,869
Uzbekistan	46,900	45,510	53,980	16,562	-4,999	-867
East Asia	**1,111,905**	**1,203,091**	**1,217,630**	**-261,624**	**-329,144**	**-304,445**
China, People's Republic of[e]	1,072,780	1,159,610	1,176,140	-285,418	-382,872	-364,711
Hong Kong, China[e]	...	...	...	...	...	...
Korea, Republic of	24,270	23,220	22,700	17,515	48,128	56,606
Mongolia	8,940	15,750	18,790	1,320	1,711	-224
Taipei,China[e]	5,915	4,511	4,315 (2018)	4,959	3,890	3,885
South Asia	**739,780**	**760,690**	**781,670**	**-176,304**	**-248,524**	**-325,548**
Bangladesh	85,580	89,830	92,650	-8,226	2,224	1,514
Bhutan	540	490	470	-676	-595	-422
India	623,370	638,820	656,650	-166,579	-254,017	-333,368
Maldives	90	110	130	213	360	737
Nepal	21,600	22,490	23,550	-124	-605	1,576
Sri Lanka	8,600	8,950	8,220	-911	4,110	4,415
Southeast Asia	**628,570**	**628,890**	**642,820**	**-1,686**	**37,794**	**15,648**
Brunei Darussalam	1,800	1,570	1,590	-301	-1,160	-902
Cambodia	18,190	17,660	18,200	963	3,006	3,983
Indonesia	270,500	271,360	280,950	-4,542	-4,638	-32,216
Lao People's Democratic Republic	6,950	7,590	7,560	88	4,531	10,919
Malaysia	31,790	36,250	36,810	-1,220	-9,767	-29,432
Myanmar	65,150	66,530	73,050	-123	3,206	5,188
Philippines	60,890	63,670	64,730	191	5,719	4,267
Singapore	3,160	3,860	4,250	411	3,025	2,728
Thailand	81,190	70,880	70,190	5,664	26,494	28,220
Timor-Leste	6,570	5,990	5,010	-28	146	204
Viet Nam	82,380	83,530	80,480	-2,789	7,232	22,688
The Pacific	**8,230**	**12,550**	**12,760**	**-752**	**-1,662**	**-715**
Cook Islands	...	...	...	...	...	...
Fiji	760	370	450	36	-18	107
Kiribati	20	20	20	25	21	17
Marshall Islands	30	30	30	...	...	...
Micronesia, Federated States of	40	50	50	...	...	...
Nauru	–	–	–	49	...	...
Niue	...	...	...	...	...	...
Palau	20	20	20	...	191	228
Papua New Guinea	6,200	10,790	10,860	-1,062	-1,905	-1,267
Samoa	270	300	310	75	91	130
Solomon Islands	340	380	410	143	61	108
Tonga	90	90	90	-66	-115	-91
Tuvalu	10	10	10	9	...	...
Vanuatu	450	490	510	40	12	52
Developed ADB Member Economies	**178,850**	**196,110**	**185,970**	**-62,498**	**-59,251**	**-39,327**
Australia	114,900	134,160	126,070	-21,765	-29,898	-17,269
Japan	30,520	28,850	27,380	-39,416	-29,850	-21,412
New Zealand	33,430	33,100	32,520	-1,317	497	-646
DEVELOPING ADB MEMBER ECONOMIES	**2,808,565**	**2,969,681**	**3,050,000**	**-453,073**	**-563,321**	**-617,394**
ALL ADB REGIONAL MEMBERS	**2,987,415**	**3,165,791**	**3,235,970**	**-515,571**	**-622,571**	**-656,721**

... = data not available, – = magnitude equals zero, 0.00 = magnitude is less than half of unit employed, ADB = Asian Development Bank, CO_2 = carbon dioxide, t = metric ton.

a Rate refers to percentage change over previous year. A negative value indicates that the deforestation rate is decreasing (i.e., reforestation).
b Aggregates are calculated as the percentage change of the sum of forest land area of the reporting economies.
c Data from the World Bank are expressed in kiloton (kt), while data provided in the table are expressed in thousands of metric tons (t), using a conversion factor of 1 kt = 1,000 metric tons.
d Other greenhouse gas emissions refer to hydrofluorocarbons, perfluorocarbons, and sulphur hexafluoride.
e For estimates for Hong Kong, China; the People's Republic of China; and Taipei,China, please refer directly to the FAOSTAT notes.

Sources: Food and Agriculture Organization of the United Nations. FAOSTAT Database. http://www.fao.org/faostat/en/#data/RL (accessed 8 July 2022); and World Bank. World Development Indicators. https://databank.worldbank.org/source/world-development-indicators# (accessed 11 July 2022). For Taipei,China: Directorate General of Budget, Accounting and Statistics. Statistical Yearbook 2020, https://eng.dgbas.gov.tw/lp.asp?CtNode=2351&CtUnit=1072&BaseDSD=36&mp=2 (accessed 11 July 2022).

Table 2.7.3: Freshwater Resources

ADB Regional Member	Internal Renewable Freshwater Resources (m^3 billion per year) 2018[b]	Internal Renewable Freshwater Resources (m^3 per inhabitant per year) 2018[c]	Annual Freshwater Withdrawals (m^3 billion) 2017	Water Productivity[a] (constant 2015 $ per m^3) 2017
Developing ADB Member Economies				
Central and West Asia	**370**	**1,087**	...	...
Afghanistan	47	1,268	20	1.0
Armenia	7	2,324	3	4.0
Azerbaijan	8	816	13	4.0
Georgia	58	15,599	2	8.9
Kazakhstan	64	3,521	22	8.6
Kyrgyz Republic	49	7,739	8	0.9
Pakistan	55	259	200	1.5
Tajikistan	63	6,973	10	0.9
Turkmenistan	1	240	28	1.5
Uzbekistan	16	496	59	1.5
East Asia[d]	**2,913**	**1,957**	...	...
China, People's Republic of	2,813	2,005	592	21.4
Hong Kong, China	...	...	...	...
Korea, Republic of	65	1,257	29	53.3
Mongolia	35	10,977	0	27.1
Taipei,China	...	...	...	...
South Asia	**1,880**	**1,202**	...	...
Bangladesh	105	651	36	6.2
Bhutan	78	103,394	0	6.7
India	1,446	1,069	648	3.8
Maldives	0	58	0	996.8
Nepal	198	7,054	9	2.8
Sri Lanka	53	2,437	13	6.7
Southeast Asia	**4,993**	**7,637**	...	...
Brunei Darussalam	9	19,815	0	138.9
Cambodia	121	7,422	2	9.4
Indonesia	2,019	7,542	223	4.3
Lao People's Democratic Republic	190	26,963	7	2.2
Malaysia	580	18,396	7	49.7
Myanmar	1,003	18,671	33	2.0
Philippines	479	4,491	93	3.8
Singapore	1	106	0	676.0
Thailand	225	3,234	57	7.5
Timor-Leste	8	6,479	1	1.3
Viet Nam	359	3,762	82	2.7
The Pacific[d]	**884**	**80,368**	...	...
Cook Islands	...	...	...	...
Fiji	29	32,315	0	59.5
Kiribati	...	...	...	...
Marshall Islands	...	...	...	...
Micronesia, Federated States of	...	...	...	...
Nauru	0	937	...	...
Niue	...	...	...	...
Palau	...	...	...	...
Papua New Guinea	801	93,071	0	60.5
Samoa	...	...	...	...
Solomon Islands	45	68,468	...	...
Tonga	...	...	...	...
Tuvalu	...	...	...	...
Vanuatu	10	34,168	...	...
Developed ADB Member Economies	**1,249**	**7,979**	...	...
Australia	492	19,694	16	89.1
Japan	430	3,391	81	56.1
New Zealand	327	66,727	10	19.4
DEVELOPING ADB MEMBER ECONOMIES[d]	**11,039**	**2,737**	...	...
ALL ADB REGIONAL MEMBERS[d]	**12,288**	**2,933**	...	...

... = data not available, 0 = magnitude is less than half of unit employed, $ = United States dollars, ADB = Asian Development Bank, m^3 = cubic meter.

a Gross domestic product in 2015 United States dollars per cubic meter of total freshwater withdrawal.
b Regional aggregates are calculated as the sum of the economies.
c Regional aggregates are weighted averages estimated using population.
d For reporting economies only.

Sources: Food and Agriculture Organization of the United Nations. AQUASTAT Database. http://www.fao.org/nr/water/aquastat/data/query/index.html (accessed 11 July 2022); and World Bank. World Development Indicators. http://data.worldbank.org/indicator (accessed 11 July 2022).

Data Issues and Comparability

Data on greenhouse gases (GHGs) have been compiled from the Emissions Database for Global Atmospheric Research, a joint project of the European Commission Joint Research Centre and the Netherlands Environmental Assessment Agency. This database applies a technology-based emissions factor approach consistently for all economies. It utilizes a consistent set of activity data for calculating various substances, GHGs, and air pollutants; and relies on the spatial allocation of emissions on a 0.1-degree by 0.1-degree grid.

There may be substantial uncertainty in economy-level data—especially for methane, nitrous oxide, and other GHGs—due to the limited accuracy of international activity data and the emission factors selected for calculating emissions on an economy level. However, since Intergovernmental Panel on Climate Change methodologies are consistently used, and data are based on international information sources, there is sound basis for comparability.[6]

The Food and Agricultural Organization of the United Nations monitors land use and forestry data using its own expert sources, country reports, satellite imagery, and official data reported on through questionnaires conducted by the organization.

6 For more information on the methodologies of the Emissions Database for Global Atmospheric Research, go to https://edgar.jrc.ec.europa.eu/methodology.

Government Finance

Table 2.8.1: Government Net Lending/Net Borrowing
(% of GDP)

ADB Regional Member	2010	2015	2016	2017	2018	2019	2020	2021
Developing ADB Member Economies								
Central and West Asia								
Afghanistan[a]	2.4	-1.4	0.2	-0.4	0.8	-1.7	-4.4	...
Armenia	-5.0	-4.8	-5.5	-4.8	-1.6	-0.8	-5.1*	-4.6
Azerbaijan	15.4	-2.8	2.4	1.9	9.5	6.2	-2.8	...
Georgia	-4.3	-1.0	-1.2	-0.1	-0.8	-1.6	-9.0	-5.9
Kazakhstan	5.0	-2.2	-2.8	-3.0	1.4	-0.5	-6.9	...
Kyrgyz Republic[b]	-4.9	-1.4	-4.4	-3.1	-1.1	-0.1	-3.3	-0.2
Pakistan[c]	-6.0	-5.2	-4.0	-5.2	-5.7	-7.8	-7.0	-6.0
Tajikistan[d]	-9.2 |	-7.4	-10.1	-11.8	-10.6	-7.8	0.3*	0.2
Turkmenistan	2.0	-0.7	...	...	...	...	...	...
Uzbekistan	...	3.3	4.0	1.5	3.2	0.5	-1.5	...
East Asia								
China, People's Republic of	-1.6	-3.4	-3.8	-3.7	-4.1	-4.9	-6.2	-3.8
Hong Kong, China	4.1	1.4	4.7	6.3	3.5	1.9	-8.9	...
Korea, Republic of	1.1 (2012)	1.2	2.5	2.6	3.1	0.8	-2.7	...
Mongolia	-3.2	-10.9	-23.0	-11.1	-4.1	-9.0	-20.4	-14.3
Taipei,China	-2.6	0.2	-0.3	-0.1	0.1	0.5	-0.3	...
South Asia								
Bangladesh[c]	-1.7	-2.2	-2.7	-3.0	-1.9	-4.6	-4.3	-3.2
Bhutan[c]	1.5	1.5	-1.1	-3.5	-0.3	-2.3	-2.4	-6.7
India[e]	-4.9	-3.9	-3.5	-3.5	-3.4	-4.7	-9.2*	-6.7
Maldives[f]	-12.9	-6.5	-10.0	-3.1	-5.3	-6.7	-23.5*	-16.6
Nepal[g]	-1.4	0.9	1.2	-2.4	-4.8	-4.8	-4.9	...
Sri Lanka	-6.1	-7.2	-5.0	-5.0	-5.0	-6.4	-12.7	-11.6
Southeast Asia								
Brunei Darussalam[h]	15.1	-14.8	-16.7	-13.2	0.2	-5.6	-19.3	...
Cambodia	-4.5	-0.9	-0.4	-0.8	0.4	2.2	-3.7*	-7.3
Indonesia	-0.6	-3.0	-1.9	-2.0	-1.7	-2.1	-6.1	-4.6
Lao People's Democratic Republic[i]	-0.9	-3.7	-4.9	-5.3	-4.2	-2.6	-4.9	...
Malaysia	-5.0	-3.1	-3.0	-2.9	-3.6	-3.4	-6.1	...
Myanmar[j]	-4.4 (2012)	-4.4	-3.3	-3.7	-5.9 |	-4.0	...	...
Philippines	-3.3	-1.3	-2.2	-2.1	-3.1	-3.3	-7.5	-8.3
Singapore[e]	7.5	4.2	5.0	7.6	4.8	7.4	-7.5	...
Thailand[i]	-0.7	0.2	0.4	-0.4	0.1	0.4	-4.5	-6.9
Timor-Leste	...	7.3	-10.4	8.4	5.0	-4.0	...	...
Viet Nam[k]	0.1	-4.4	-2.2	-1.2	-0.1	0.4*	-3.2*	-3.4
The Pacific								
Cook Islands[c]	2.9	-7.8	1.4	8.7*	5.2*	5.7*	-10.3	...
Fiji[l]	-2.6	-2.2	-0.8	-0.9	-4.6	...	...	...
Kiribati	-6.9 (2011)	56.1	21.6	16.8	51.9*	19.0*	30.8	...
Marshall Islands[i]	3.5	2.8	3.9	4.4	2.5	-1.8	5.0*	0.7
Micronesia, Federated States of[i]	0.5	10.3	7.3	14.2	24.2	...	...	...
Nauru[c]	0.1	10.5	21.4	20.1	33.6*	29.9*	35.7*	43.8
Niue	...	...	...	...	...	...	...	...
Palau[i]	-1.0	5.2	3.6	4.8	6.2	0.3*	...	...
Papua New Guinea	...	...	...	-2.4	-2.6	-5.0*	-8.6*	-7.1
Samoa	-8.1 (2012)	-3.7	0.7	-0.6	1.3	4.6	7.6	...
Solomon Islands	5.7	0.8	-3.2	-2.3	1.5	-1.5	-2.4	-5.1
Tonga[c]	...	...	1.5	3.6	2.9	3.1	0.9	...
Tuvalu	11.5 (2012)	40.0	4.6	...	...	...	...	...
Vanuatu	-1.7 (2012)	7.2	-0.3	2.2	8.4	7.0	...	...
Developed ADB Member Economies								
Australia[c]	-5.5	-2.9	-2.6	-2.2	-1.3	-1.2	-7.6	-9.3
Japan[e]	-8.8	-3.6	-3.5	-2.9	-2.4	-3.1	-10.0	...
New Zealand[c]	-3.5	0.1	0.5	1.3	1.3	1.2	-6.1	-1.9

... = data not available; | = marks break in series; * = preliminary, provisional, estimate; ADB = Asian Development Bank; GDP = gross domestic product.

Note: In general, economies follow the guidelines of the International Monetary Fund on Government Finance Statistics (GFS). Some economies still use the 1986 version of the GFS guidelines, while others have switched to the 2001 or 2014 guidelines. The comparability of the data in this table is limited by variations in the concepts and definitions used in different versions of the GFS framework. Data refer to government net lending/net borrowing as classified in the GFS 2001 or GFS 2014 framework, except for Bhutan; Brunei Darussalam; India; the Kyrgyz Republic; Maldives; Nauru; Pakistan; the People's Republic of China; Taipei,China; Tajikistan; Turkmenistan; and Viet Nam, where data refer to overall budgetary surplus/deficit as classified in the GFS 1986 framework. Data refer to general government, except for Bangladesh; Bhutan; Brunei Darussalam; Cambodia; the Federated States of Micronesia; Fiji; India; the Lao People's Democratic Republic; Malaysia; Maldives; the Marshall Islands; Nauru; Nepal; Palau; the Philippines; Solomon Islands; Sri Lanka; Taipei,China; Timor-Leste; Tonga; Tuvalu; Vanuatu; and Viet Nam, where data refer to central government. For Azerbaijan: Data for 2000–2007 (featured in the Key Indicators Database) are based on the state budget. For Cambodia: Data refer to central government excluding extra budgetary central government. For Pakistan: Data refer to the consolidated federal and provincial governments. For the People's Republic of China: Data refer to consolidated central and local governments. For Turkmenistan: Data prior to 2011 refer to central government.

a The longer time series featured in the Key Indicators Database refers to GFS data for 2005–2011 based on fiscal year beginning 21 March. For 2012, data cover 9 months from 21 March to 20 December. For 2013 onward, GFS data are based on fiscal year ending 20 December. For 2005–2015, national accounts data are based on fiscal year beginning 21 March. For 2016 onward, national accounts data are based on fiscal year ending 20 December.
b For 2007 onward, data are calculated excluding net lending.
c Data are based on fiscal year ending 30 June.
d National accounts data prior to 2015 are based on the 1993 System of National Accounts while figures for 2015 onward are based on the 2008 System of National Accounts.
e Data are based on fiscal year beginning 1 April.
f For 2013 onward, data are calculated excluding net lending.
g Data are based on fiscal year ending 15 July.
h The longer time series featured in the Key Indicators Database refers to data for 2003 onward based on fiscal year beginning 1 April. Data are derived as excess of revenue over expenditure (ordinary plus charged) less the sum of contribution to a development fund, contribution to a government trust fund, and capital and currency adjustments.
i Data are based on fiscal year ending 30 September.
j The longer time series featured in the Key Indicators Database refers to GFS data for 2012–2018 based on fiscal year beginning 1 April. For 2019, GFS data are based on fiscal year beginning 1 October.
k Includes local government budget.
l The longer time series featured in the Key Indicators Database refers to GFS data for 2000–2014 based on fiscal year ending 31 December. For 2015 onward, GFS data are based on fiscal year ending 31 July.

Sources: Economies' official sources. For Timor-Leste: International Monetary Fund. Government Finance Statistics. https://data.imf.org/ (accessed 13 May 2022). For Nauru (2012–2020): International Monetary Fund. Staff Country Reports. Republic of Nauru: 2021 Article IV. https://www.imf.org/en/Publications/CR/Issues/2022/02/07/Republic-of-Nauru-2021-Article-IV-Consultation-Press-Release-Staff-Report-and-Statement-by-512874 (accessed 28 April 2022).

Click on the indicator name in the table header to access the time series in the Key Indicators Database

Table 2.8.2: Government Taxes
(% of GDP)

ADB Regional Member	2010	2015	2017	2018	2019	2020	2021
Developing ADB Member Economies							
Central and West Asia							
Afghanistan[a]	8.8	7.1	8.7	9.5	8.4	7.5	...
Armenia	17.7	21.3	21.0	21.1	22.6	22.5	22.7
Azerbaijan	12.3	15.7	13.3	13.1	14.3	17.3	...
Georgia	22.3	23.6	24.3	23.4	24.1	22.2	22.5
Kazakhstan	19.6	13.6	13.8	15.1	15.1	12.4	...
Kyrgyz Republic	17.9	19.7	19.5	20.5	19.6	17.8	20.9
Pakistan[b]	10.0	11.0	11.2	11.4	10.2	10.0	9.5
Tajikistan[c]	18.0	20.8	20.3	20.5	20.4	18.3	19.9
Turkmenistan	17.5 (2011)	15.6	...	...	...	...	...
Uzbekistan	...	20.3	17.3	19.8	19.4	19.6	...
East Asia							
China, People's Republic of	17.8	18.1	17.4	17.0	16.0	15.2	15.1
Hong Kong, China[d]	13.5	14.4	14.3	13.8	13.3	14.0	...
Korea, Republic of	18.0 (2012)	17.6	19.0	20.1	20.0	20.2	...
Mongolia	24.2	17.7	17.9	20.3	20.9	18.7	20.9
Taipei,China	7.7	8.6	8.6	8.9	9.0	8.1	...
South Asia							
Bangladesh[b]	10.2	8.9	9.1	7.4	8.9	7.7	8.5
Bhutan[b]	13.3	15.0	14.2	16.6	15.7	13.0	11.7
India[d]	7.5	6.9	7.3	7.0	6.8	7.2	7.5
Maldives	8.8	19.4	20.2	19.4	19.2	19.0	18.1
Nepal[e]	13.4	14.7	18.0	19.1	19.8	15.7	...
Sri Lanka	10.9	11.7	11.6	11.2	10.9	7.7	7.3
Southeast Asia							
Brunei Darussalam[f]	...	...	...	...	...	...	...
Cambodia	7.3	14.6	15.8	17.1	19.7	17.9	16.2
Indonesia	12.1	12.0	11.2	11.5	11.1	9.5	10.2
Lao People's Democratic Republic[g]	13.8	13.5	12.2	11.7	11.5	9.4	...
Malaysia	13.3	14.1	12.9	12.0	11.9	10.9	...
Myanmar[h]	6.6 (2012)	7.5	7.9	7.4	7.0	...	...
Philippines	11.6	13.0	13.6	14.0	14.5	14.0	14.1
Singapore[d]	12.8	13.1	14.0	13.0	13.2	12.9	...
Thailand[g]	16.1	17.6	16.3	16.5	16.1	15.7	15.6
Timor-Leste	...	7.8	8.6	8.4	6.2	...	...
Viet Nam[i]	22.4	18.0	18.3	18.4	18.6	16.8	14.1
The Pacific							
Cook Islands[b]	27.0	23.5	26.0	27.0	29.5	34.0	...
Fiji	...	...	...	...	...	...	...
Kiribati[b]	18.3 (2011)	22.7	22.6	21.7	24.9	26.6	...
Marshall Islands[g]	15.8	14.0	14.3	14.5	14.6	13.9	14.1
Micronesia, Federated States of[g]	12.0	12.3	17.5	32.2	...	...	...
Nauru[b]	8.1 (2012)	21.7	21.2	29.6	36.1	48.4	48.4
Niue	...	...	...	...	...	...	...
Palau[g]	17.0	20.3	19.8	21.2	20.0	19.6	...
Papua New Guinea	...	...	12.3	13.2	13.0	11.5	11.6
Samoa[b]	20.9 (2012)	23.6	25.0	25.5	26.2	24.4	...
Solomon Islands	22.0	25.7	24.8	25.5	22.2	21.1	19.7
Tonga[b]	...	...	21.0	21.9	20.9	22.8	...
Tuvalu	28.5 (2012)	33.1	...	...	...	...	...
Vanuatu	17.3 (2012)	16.9	17.1	17.8	17.5	...	...
Developed ADB Member Economies							
Australia[b]	25.6	27.3	27.6	28.6	28.7	27.8	28.7
Japan[d]	15.6	18.6	18.7	19.1	18.8	20.0	...
New Zealand[b]	29.2	30.7	31.0	30.6	31.7	30.4	32.6

... = data not available, ADB = Asian Development Bank; GDP = gross domestic product.

Note: In general, economies follow the guidelines of the International Monetary Fund on Government Finance Statistics (GFS). Some economies still use the 1986 version of the GFS guidelines, while others have switched to the 2001 or 2014 guidelines. The comparability of the data in this table is limited by variations in the concepts and definitions used in different versions of the GFS framework. Data refer to government taxes as classified in the GFS 2001 or GFS 2014 framework, except for Bhutan; Brunei Darussalam; India; the Kyrgyz Republic; Maldives; Nauru; Pakistan; the People's Republic of China; Taipei,China; Tajikistan; Turkmenistan; and Viet Nam, where data refer to tax revenue as classified in the GFS 1986 framework. Data refer to general government, except for Bangladesh; Bhutan; Brunei Darussalam; Cambodia; the Federated States of Micronesia; Fiji; India; the Lao People's Democratic Republic; Malaysia; Maldives; the Marshall Islands; Nauru; Nepal; Palau; the Philippines; Solomon Islands; Sri Lanka; Taipei,China; Timor-Leste; Tonga; Tuvalu; Vanuatu; and Viet Nam, where data refer to central government. For Armenia: Data prior to 2010 (featured in the Key Indicators Database) refer to central government. For Azerbaijan: Data for 2000–2007 (featured in the Key Indicators Database) are based on the state budget. For Cambodia: Data refer to central government excluding extra budgetary central government. For Pakistan: Data refer to the consolidated federal and provincial governments. For the People's Republic of China: Data refer to consolidated central and local governments. For Turkmenistan: Data prior to 2011 refer to central government. For Viet Nam: Data include local government.

a The longer time series featured in the Key Indicators Database refers to GFS data for 2005–2011 based on fiscal year beginning 21 March. For 2012, GFS data cover 9 months from 21 March to 20 December. For 2013 onward, GFS data are based on fiscal year ending 20 December. For 2005–2015, national accounts data are based on fiscal year beginning 21 March. For 2016 onward, national accounts data are based on fiscal year ending 20 December.
b Data are based on fiscal year ending 30 June.
c National accounts data prior to 2015 are based on the 1993 System of National Accounts while figures for 2015 onward are based on the 2008 System of National Accounts.
d Data are based on fiscal year beginning 1 April.
e Data are based on fiscal year ending 15 July.
f The longer time series featured in the Key Indicators Database refers to data for 2003 onward based on fiscal year beginning 1 April.
g Data are based on fiscal year ending 30 September.
h For 2012–2018, GFS data are based on fiscal year beginning 1 April. For 2019, GFS data are based on fiscal year beginning 1 October. For 2012–2015, national accounts data are based on fiscal year beginning 1 April. For 2016 onward, national accounts data are based on fiscal year beginning 1 October.
i Taxes include local government taxes.

Sources: Economies' official sources. For Hong Kong, China; Nepal; and Timor-Leste: International Monetary Fund (IMF). Government Finance Statistics. https://data.imf.org/ (accessed April–June 2022). For Nauru (2015–2016): IMF. Staff Country Reports. Republic of Nauru: 2019 Article IV. https://www.imf.org/en/Publications/CR/Issues/2020/01/29/Republic-of-Nauru-2019-Article-IV-Consultation-Press-Release-Staff-Report-and-Statement-by-49001 (accessed 9 May 2021). For Nauru (2017–2021): IMF. Staff Country Reports. Republic of Nauru: 2021 Article IV. https://www.imf.org/en/Publications/CR/Issues/2022/02/07/Republic-of-Nauru-2021-Article-IV-Consultation-Press-Release-Staff-Report-and-Statement-by-512874 (accessed 28 April 2022).

Government Finance

Table 2.8.3: Government Revenue
(% of GDP)

ADB Regional Member	2010	2015	2017	2018	2019	2020	2021
Developing ADB Member Economies							
Central and West Asia							
Afghanistan[a]	23.0	23.9	27.3	29.8	26.9	24.1	...
Armenia	23.2	23.8	22.9	23.0	24.7	26.0	25.0
Azerbaijan	47.0	34.4	35.3	39.7	43.0	37.9	...
Georgia	26.9	30.4	31.0	28.6	29.2	27.2	27.3
Kazakhstan	25.5	17.6	19.9	19.6	19.1	17.4	...
Kyrgyz Republic	23.1	27.7	25.2	25.0	24.9	23.3	27.1
Pakistan[b]	14.2	14.4	13.9	13.3	11.2	13.2	12.4
Tajikistan[c]	19.3	23.7	22.5	23.3	23.0	21.9	29.8
Turkmenistan[d]	15.8	16.6	...	...	...	...	...
Uzbekistan	...	27.6	24.3	27.9	27.9	27.1	...
East Asia							
China, People's Republic of	20.2	22.1	20.7	19.9	19.3	18.0	17.7
Hong Kong, China[e]	22.3	21.7	25.8	23.8	23.3	23.3	...
Korea, Republic of	33.3 (2012)	32.2	33.2	33.4	34.1	34.3	...
Mongolia	32.0	25.8	26.1	28.5	29.3	25.5	29.5
Taipei,China	10.7	11.4	10.8	11.1	11.1	11.0	...
South Asia							
Bangladesh[b]	13.0	10.6	10.5	8.3	10.4	9.6	10.7
Bhutan[b]	27.4	21.4	19.5	22.8	18.2	21.8	25.4
India[e]	10.8	9.1	9.1	8.8	8.7	8.5	9.2
Maldives	19.3	26.4	27.2	26.2	25.6	24.8	24.1
Nepal[f]	18.1	18.6	21.3	23.2	23.2	20.0	...
Sri Lanka	12.6	12.6	12.8	12.6	11.9	8.7	8.3
Southeast Asia							
Brunei Darussalam[g]	49.0	20.9	23.1	32.9	26.4	12.2	...
Cambodia	13.8	18.5	20.4	22.1	24.8	21.9	18.9
Indonesia	16.6	15.1	14.1	14.8	14.3	12.3	13.4
Lao People's Democratic Republic[h]	21.7	20.3	16.3	16.2	15.6	12.6	...
Malaysia	19.4	18.6	16.1	16.1	17.5	15.9	...
Myanmar[i]	9.8 (2012)	11.8	11.8	10.9	10.2	...	...
Philippines	12.9	14.7	14.9	15.5	16.1	15.9	15.5
Singapore[e]	16.8	18.0	20.2	18.2	21.0	18.3	...
Thailand[h]	20.6	22.2	20.8	21.2	20.9	20.7	20.0
Timor-Leste	...	91.1	80.6	85.0	64.4	...	...
Viet Nam[j]	26.7	23.5	25.7	25.7	25.6	23.9	18.6
The Pacific							
Cook Islands[b]	38.3	39.7	38.8	42.3	43.0	50.2	...
Fiji[k]	25.5	28.5	26.4	28.5	26.8	25.1	22.1
Kiribati[b]	64.4 (2011)	127.8	103.4	131.0	121.3	130.0	...
Marshall Islands[h]	62.3	58.8	68.3	62.6	61.9	70.1	68.6
Micronesia, Federated States of[h]	67.7	66.0	78.2	79.7	...	...	...
Nauru[b]	39.2	74.5	100.6	108.5	136.0	151.4	137.0
Niue	...	...	...	...	...	...	...
Palau[h]	46.7	41.2	40.0	44.4	43.5	49.0	...
Papua New Guinea	...	...	15.5	17.7	16.3	14.2	14.7
Samoa[b]	30.2 (2012)	32.0	34.0	36.0	37.7	40.2	...
Solomon Islands	28.2	35.1	30.9	31.7	27.4	30.1	25.6
Tonga[b]	...	...	43.2	42.6	41.7	51.2	...
Tuvalu	105.3 (2012)	184.0	...	...	...	...	...
Vanuatu	22.8 (2012)	32.3	31.3	38.6	37.5	...	...
Developed ADB Member Economies							
Australia[b]	32.3	34.2	34.6	35.6	35.7	34.5	35.3
Japan[e]	29.9	35.0	34.9	35.5	35.3	36.8	...
New Zealand[b]	36.7	37.7	37.4	36.8	37.8	36.1	37.7

... = data not available, ADB = Asian Development Bank, GDP = gross domestic product.

Note: In general, economies follow the guidelines of the International Monetary Fund on Government Finance Statistics (GFS). Some economies still use the 1986 version of the GFS guidelines, while others have switched to the 2001 or 2014 guidelines. The comparability of the data in this table is limited by variations in the concepts and definitions used in different versions of the GFS framework. Data refer to government revenue as classified in the GFS 2001 or GFS 2014 framework, except for Bhutan; Brunei Darussalam; India; the Kyrgyz Republic; Maldives; Nauru; Pakistan; the People's Republic of China; Taipei,China; Tajikistan; Turkmenistan; and Viet Nam, where data refer to total government revenue as classified in the GFS 1986 framework. Data refer to general government, except for Bangladesh; Bhutan; Brunei Darussalam; Cambodia; the Federated States of Micronesia; Fiji; India; the Lao People's Democratic Republic; Malaysia; Maldives; the Marshall Islands; Nauru; Nepal; Palau; the Philippines; Solomon Islands; Sri Lanka; Taipei,China; Timor-Leste; Tonga; Tuvalu; Vanuatu; and Viet Nam, where data refer to central government. For Cambodia: Data refer to central government excluding extra budgetary central government. For Pakistan: Data refer to the consolidated federal and provincial governments. For the People's Republic of China: Data refer to consolidated central and local governments. For Turkmenistan: Data prior to 2011 refer to central government. For Viet Nam: Tax revenue includes local government taxes.

a The longer time series featured in the Key Indicators Database refers to GFS data for 2005–2011 based on fiscal year beginning 21 March. For 2012, GFS data cover 9 months from 21 March to 20 December. For 2013 onward, GFS data are based on fiscal year ending 20 December. For 2005–2015, national accounts data are based on fiscal year beginning 21 March. For 2016 onward, national accounts data are based on fiscal year ending 20 December.
b Data are based on fiscal year ending 30 June.
c National accounts data prior to 2015 are based on the 1993 System of National Accounts while figures for 2015 onward are based on the 2008 System of National Accounts.
d For 2010, data refer to central government revenue. For 2015 onward, data refer to general government revenue.
e Data are based on fiscal year beginning 1 April.
f Data are based on fiscal year ending 15 July.
g The longer time series featured in the Key Indicators Database refers to data for 2003 onward, based on fiscal year beginning 1 April.
h Data are based on fiscal year ending 30 September.
i For 2012–2018, GFS data are based on fiscal year beginning 1 April. For 2019, GFS data are based on fiscal year beginning 1 October. For 2012–2015, national accounts data are based on fiscal year beginning 1 April. For 2016 onward, national accounts data are based on fiscal year beginning 1 October.
j Taxes include local government taxes.
k The longer time series featured in the Key Indicators Database refers to GFS data for 2000–2014 based on fiscal year ending 31 December. For 2015 onward, GFS data are based on fiscal year ending 31 July. National accounts data are based on calendar year.

Sources: Economies' official sources. For Hong Kong, China; Nepal; and Timor-Leste: International Monetary Fund (IMF). Government Finance Statistics. https://data.imf.org/ (accessed April–June 2022). For Nauru (2015 and 2016): IMF. Staff Country Reports. Republic of Nauru: 2019 Article IV. https://www.imf.org/en/Publications/CR/Issues/2020/01/29/Republic-of-Nauru-2019-Article-IV-Consultation-Press-Release-Staff-Report-and-Statement-by-49001 (accessed 9 May 2021). For Nauru (2017–2021): IMF. Staff Country Reports. Republic of Nauru: 2021 Article IV. https://www.imf.org/en/Publications/CR/Issues/2022/02/07/Republic-of-Nauru-2021-Article-IV-Consultation-Press-Release-Staff-Report-and-Statement-by-512874 (accessed 28 April 2022).

Table 2.8.4: Government Expenditure
(% of GDP)

ADB Regional Member	2010	2015	2016	2017	2018	2019	2020	2021
Developing ADB Member Economies								
Central and West Asia								
Afghanistan[a]	20.6	25.2	29.0	27.7	29.0	28.6	28.5	...
Armenia	28.2	28.6	29.3	27.7	24.6	25.5	31.1	29.5
Azerbaijan	31.6	37.2	32.8	33.5	30.2	36.8	40.7	...
Georgia	31.2	31.4	32.3	31.2	29.4	30.9	36.2	33.2
Kazakhstan	20.4	19.8	20.5	22.9	18.2	17.2	24.3	...
Kyrgyz Republic	31.2	31.3	31.8	31.3	27.7	27.1	28.6	29.3
Pakistan[b]	20.4	20.2	18.3	19.4	19.0	18.9	20.4	18.5
Tajikistan[c]	27.2	31.9	33.4	34.6	34.0	30.8	29.6	29.6
Turkmenistan	13.8	17.3	...	...	...	...	...	...
Uzbekistan	...	24.3	23.6	22.8	24.7	27.4	28.5	...
East Asia								
China, People's Republic of	21.8	25.5	25.2	24.4	24.0	24.2	24.2	21.5
Hong Kong, China[d]	18.1	20.3	19.9	19.5	20.3	21.4	32.2	...
Korea, Republic of	32.2 (2012)	31.1	30.2	30.7	30.3	33.2	37.0	...
Mongolia	35.2	36.8	47.3	37.1	32.6	38.3	45.9	36.7
Taipei,China	13.4	11.2	11.2	10.9	11.1	10.6	11.3	...
South Asia								
Bangladesh[b]	14.8	12.7	12.9	13.4	10.2	15.0	13.9	13.9
Bhutan[b]	35.6	29.8	32.6	32.8	34.5	25.5	32.9	40.3
India[d]	15.7	13.0	12.8	12.5	12.2	13.4	17.7	15.9
Maldives	33.2	34.0	37.6	30.8	32.5	33.6	49.9	42.2
Nepal[e]	19.5	17.6	18.9	23.6	28.0	28.0	24.9	...
Sri Lanka	18.7	19.8	18.2	17.8	17.6	18.4	21.3	19.9
Southeast Asia								
Brunei Darussalam[f]	34.0	35.7	39.7	36.3	32.8	32.0	31.5	...
Cambodia	18.3	19.4	20.2	21.2	21.7	22.6	25.6	26.1
Indonesia	17.2	17.8	16.9	16.5	16.5	16.4	18.5	18.0
Lao People's Democratic Republic[g]	22.7	24.1	21.1	21.5	20.4	18.2	17.5	...
Malaysia	24.4	21.7	20.0	18.9	19.7	20.8	22.0	...
Myanmar[h]	14.2 (2012)	16.2	15.8	15.5	16.8	14.2	...	...
Philippines	16.2	16.0	16.7	17.0	18.6	19.4	23.4	23.8
Singapore[d]	9.3	13.8	13.4	12.6	13.4	13.5	25.7	...
Thailand[g]	21.3	22.0	21.0	21.2	21.1	20.5	25.3	26.9
Timor-Leste	...	83.7	98.6	72.2	80.0	68.4	...	...
Viet Nam[i]	27.2	28.2	26.8	27.1	25.9	25.3	27.2	22.1
The Pacific								
Cook Islands[b]	35.5	47.5	37.8	30.1	37.1	37.3	60.5	...
Fiji[j]	30.7	34.4	33.4	27.9	34.1	30.8	31.0	32.9
Kiribati[b]	71.3 (2011)	71.7	78.3	86.6	79.2	102.3	99.2	...
Marshall Islands[g]	58.8	56.0	57.1	64.0	60.1	63.7	65.1	67.9
Micronesia, Federated States of[g]	67.2	55.7	61.7	64.0	55.5	...	...	...
Nauru[b]	83.6	83.1	93.4	101.7	95.6	118.9	134.5	135.5
Niue	...	...	...	...	...	...	...	...
Palau[g]	25.8	26.4	27.1	29.3	33.5	34.3	54.0	...
Papua New Guinea	...	...	...	17.9	20.3	21.3	22.7	21.7
Samoa[b]	38.3 (2012)	35.7	31.9	34.7	34.7	33.1	32.6	...
Solomon Islands	22.6	34.3	34.0	33.1	30.2	29.0	32.6	30.7
Tonga[b]	...	...	37.2	39.6	39.7	38.6	50.3	...
Tuvalu	93.8 (2012)	144.0	150.0	...	...	...	...	...
Vanuatu	24.5 (2012)	25.1	25.9	29.1	30.2	30.5	...	...
Developed ADB Member Economies								
Australia[b]	37.8	37.1	37.4	36.8	36.8	36.9	42.1	44.7
Japan[d]	38.7	38.6	38.2	37.9	37.9	38.4	46.8	...
New Zealand[b]	40.3	37.6	36.8	36.1	35.5	36.6	42.2	39.6

... = data not available, ADB = Asian Development Bank, GDP = gross domestic product.

Note: In general, economies follow the guidelines of the International Monetary Fund on Government Finance Statistics (GFS). Some economies still use the 1986 version of the GFS guidelines, while others have switched to the 2001 or 2014 guidelines. The comparability of the data in this table is limited by variations in the concepts and definitions used in different versions of the GFS framework. Data refer to government expenditure as classified in the GFS 2001 or GFS 2014 framework, except for Bhutan; Brunei Darussalam; India; the Kyrgyz Republic; Maldives; Nauru; Pakistan; the People's Republic of China; Taipei,China; Tajikistan; Turkmenistan; and Viet Nam, where data refer to total government expenditure as classified in the GFS 1986 framework. Data refer to general government, except for Bangladesh; Bhutan; Brunei Darussalam; Cambodia; the Federated States of Micronesia; Fiji; India; the Lao People's Democratic Republic; Malaysia; Maldives; the Marshall Islands; Nauru; Nepal; Palau; the Philippines; Solomon Islands; Sri Lanka; Taipei,China; Timor-Leste; Tonga; Tuvalu; Vanuatu; and Viet Nam, where data refer to central government. For Cambodia: Data refer to central government excluding extra budgetary central government. For Pakistan: Data refer to the consolidated federal and provincial governments. For the People's Republic of China: Data refer to consolidated central and local governments. For Turkmenistan: Data prior to 2011 refer to central government.

a The longer time series featured in the Key Indicators Database refers to GFS data for 2005–2011 based on fiscal year beginning 21 March. For 2012, GFS data cover 9 months from 21 March to 20 December. For 2013 onward, GFS data are based on fiscal year ending 20 December. For 2005–2015, national accounts data are based on fiscal year beginning 21 March. For 2016 onward, national accounts data are based on fiscal year ending 20 December.
b Data are based on fiscal year ending 30 June.
c Prior to 2015, national accounts data are based on the 1993 System of National Accounts; and, for 2015 onward, are based on the 2008 System of National Accounts.
d Data are based on fiscal year beginning 1 April.
e Data are based on fiscal year ending 15 July.
f The longer time series featured in the Key Indicators Database showing Brunei Darussalam's government expenditure for 2003 onward are based on fiscal year beginning 1 April.
g Data are based on fiscal year ending 30 September.
h For 2012–2018, GFS data are based on fiscal year beginning 1 April. For 2019, data are based on fiscal year beginning 1 October. For 2012–2015, national accounts data are based on fiscal year beginning 1 April. For 2016 onward, national accounts data are based on fiscal year beginning 1 October.
i Includes local government expenditure.
j The longer time series featured in the Key Indicators Database refers to GFS data for 2000–2014 based on fiscal year ending 31 December. For 2015 onward, GFS data are based on fiscal year ending 31 July. National accounts data are based on calendar year.

Sources: Economies' official sources. For Timor-Leste: International Monetary Fund. Government Finance Statistics. https://data.imf.org/ (accessed 13 May 2022). For Nauru (2012–2021): International Monetary Fund. Staff Country Reports. Republic of Nauru: 2021 Article IV. https://www.imf.org/en/Publications/CR/Issues/2022/02/07/Republic-of-Nauru-2021-Article-IV-Consultation-Press-Release-Staff-Report-and-Statement-by-512874 (accessed 28 April 2022).

Click on the indicator name in the table header to access the time series in the Key Indicators Database

Table 2.8.5: Government Expenditure by Economic Activity
(% of GDP)

ADB Regional Member	Health				Education				Social Protection			
	2010	2015	2020	2021	2010	2015	2020	2021	2010	2015	2020	2021
Developing ADB Member Economies												
Central and West Asia												
Afghanistan[a]	0.9	1.2	1.8	...	3.6	3.6	2.1	...	0.5	1.4	1.1	...
Armenia	1.6	1.7	2.4	2.3	3.2	2.9	2.8	2.7	7.1	7.7	8.9	8.9
Azerbaijan	1.0	1.3	2.3	...	2.9	3.1	4.0	...	6.8	6.8	11.4	...
Georgia	2.1	2.7	3.7	4.3	2.8	4.4	4.4	4.1	6.5	7.3	9.5	7.8
Kazakhstan	2.5	2.1	2.8	...	3.5	3.3	4.8	...	4.5	4.5	6.5	...
Kyrgyz Republic	2.9	3.0	2.9	2.9	5.4	5.9	6.6	6.1	5.0	5.8	5.7	5.1
Pakistan	...	...	...	...	...	...	...	...	...	...	...	...
Tajikistan[b]	1.4	2.0	3.1	2.9	4.0	5.0	5.1	5.4	3.5	5.2	4.6	4.2
Turkmenistan	...	...	...	...	...	...	...	...	...	...	...	...
Uzbekistan	...	2.5	3.3	...	...	6.0	6.3	...	...	7.4	9.3	...
East Asia												
China, People's Republic of	1.2	1.7	1.9	1.7	3.0	3.8	3.6	3.3	2.2	2.8	3.2	3.0
Hong Kong, China[c]	2.4	3.2	3.9	...	3.5	3.4	4.1	...	2.4	2.9	4.2	...
Korea, Republic of	0.2	0.3	0.4	...	2.8	3.0	3.6	...	4.3	5.3	8.1	...
Mongolia	2.5	2.5	4.5	5.7	5.1	3.0	3.4	3.3	11.1	7.6	10.7	12.6
Taipei,China	0.2	0.1	0.1	...	1.7	1.4	1.5	...	3.1	3.3	3.3	...
South Asia												
Bangladesh[d]	0.8	0.7	0.6	0.7	2.0	2.0	2.3	2.3	0.9	0.7	1.2	1.2
Bhutan[d]	3.0	2.8	3.7	3.7	6.7	6.0	7.3	6.5	3.1	3.2	3.4	3.3
India[c,e]	1.0 (2011)	1.2	1.6	...	4.4 (2011)	4.4	4.9	...	1.4 (2011)	1.8	2.3	...
Maldives[f]	2.9	4.0	7.5	6.2	5.3	4.6	5.7	4.9	1.7	5.1	5.9	4.6
Nepal[g]	1.5	1.2	1.0	...	3.9	3.3	1.0	...	0.8	0.6	1.7	...
Sri Lanka	1.1	1.5	1.5 (2019)	2.2	1.6	1.9	1.8 (2019)	1.8	1.6	4.8	...	...
Southeast Asia												
Brunei Darussalam[h]	1.8	2.3	2.3	...	3.6	4.1	4.1	...	0.8	0.8	0.7	...
Cambodia	1.3	1.3	1.7	3.3	1.6	2.0	2.9	2.5	0.5	0.8	1.2	1.1
Indonesia	1.0	1.1	1.7	1.9	3.4	3.3	3.0	2.0	0.1	0.3	2.0	1.7
Lao People's Democratic Republic	...	...	...	...	...	...	...	...	...	...	...	...
Malaysia	2.0	2.0	2.2	...	6.1	4.8	4.5	...	...	...	...	...
Myanmar[i]	0.7 (2012)	1.0	0.8 (2019)	...	1.5 (2012)	2.1	2.0 (2019)	...	0.4 (2012)	0.8	0.9 (2019)	...
Philippines[j,k]	0.3	0.8	1.4	1.1	2.4	2.8	3.7	3.9	1.6	1.3	3.6	2.4
Singapore[c]	1.2	2.1	3.3	...	3.0	2.9	3.1	...	1.1	1.8	7.9	...
Thailand[l]	...	1.1	1.4	2.0	...	3.8	3.1	3.1	...	2.5	5.6	5.2
Timor-Leste	4.0	3.7	3.3 (2018)	...	7.8	6.5	4.7 (2018)	...	16.3	11.7	8.5 (2018)	...
Viet Nam	...	...	...	...	...	...	...	...	...	...	...	...
The Pacific												
Cook Islands[d]	3.9	3.0	3.2	...	4.0	3.5	3.3	...	3.9	4.2	5.0	...
Fiji	...	...	...	...	...	...	...	...	...	...	...	...
Kiribati[d]	...	9.9	11.0	...	...	9.9	12.2	...	...	1.4	1.1	...
Marshall Islands[l]	7.8	7.5	8.9	...	19.6	16.4	12.7	...	–	–	2.3	...
Micronesia, Federated States of	...	...	...	...	...	...	...	...	...	...	...	...
Nauru	...	...	...	...	...	...	...	...	...	...	...	...
Niue	...	...	...	...	...	...	...	...	...	...	...	...
Palau	...	...	...	...	...	...	...	...	...	...	...	...
Papua New Guinea	...	...	...	...	...	...	...	...	...	...	...	...
Samoa[d]	3.6	5.4	4.9	5.9	5.8	4.5	4.6	5.9	1.1	2.1	1.1	1.7
Solomon Islands	...	...	...	...	...	...	...	...	...	...	...	...
Tonga	...	...	...	...	...	...	...	...	...	...	...	...
Tuvalu	8.5 (2012)	9.4	...	...	16.0 (2012)	23.2	...	...	6.1 (2012)	18.3	...	...
Vanuatu	3.0 (2011)	2.5	2.7 (2018)	...	6.4 (2011)	5.6	6.7 (2018)	...	0.0 (2011)	0.1	0.0 (2018)	...
Developed ADB Member Economies												
Australia[d]	6.7	6.8	7.4	7.8	5.9	5.4	5.7	5.6	9.9	10.4	11.0	11.8
Japan[c]	6.8	7.3	7.8	...	2.8	2.6	2.7	...	2.1	2.5	2.8	...
New Zealand[d]	7.0	6.8	7.1	7.5	6.8	6.2	6.3	5.7	12.5	11.5	11.0	11.8

... = data not available, – = magnitude equals zero, ADB = Asian Development Bank, GDP = gross domestic product.

Note: In general, economies follow the guidelines of the International Monetary Fund on Government Finance Statistics (GFS). Some economies still use the 1986 version of the GFS guidelines, while others have switched to the 2001 or 2014 guidelines. The comparability of the data in this table is limited by variations in the concepts and definitions used in different versions of the GFS framework. The table refers to government expenditure by economic activity as classified in the GFS 2001 or GFS 2014 framework, except for Bhutan; Brunei Darussalam; India; the Kyrgyz Republic; the People's Republic of China; and Taipei,China, where data refer to health, education, and social security and welfare, as classified in the GFS 1986 framework. For Maldives, data prior to 2017 are classified in the GFS 1986 framework, while data for 2017 onward follow the GFS 2014 framework. Data refer to general government, except for Bangladesh; Bhutan; Brunei Darussalam; Cambodia; India; Malaysia; Maldives; the Marshall Islands; Nepal; the Philippines; Samoa; Sri Lanka; Taipei,China; Timor-Leste; Tuvalu; and Vanuatu, where data refer to central government. For Cambodia: Data refer to central government excluding extra budgetary central government. For the People's Republic of China: Data refer to consolidated central and local governments.

a The longer time series featured in the Key Indicators Database refers to GFS data for 2005–2011 based on fiscal year beginning 21 March. For 2012, GFS data cover 9 months from 21 March to 20 December. For 2013 onward, GFS data are based on fiscal year ending 20 December. For 2005–2015, national accounts data are based on fiscal year beginning 21 March. For 2016 onward, national accounts data are based on fiscal year ending 20 December.
b National accounts data prior to 2015 are based on the 1993 System of National Accounts, while data for 2015 onward are based on the 2008 System of National Accounts.
c Data are based on fiscal year beginning 1 April.
d Data are based on fiscal year ending 30 June.
e Data exclude local bodies.
f Prior to 2012, refers to total expenditure. For 2012 onward, refers to total budget. For 2020, GDP estimates used are projections available as of 15 March 2021 from the Government of Maldives' Ministry of Finance.
g Data are based on fiscal year ending 15 July.
h For 2003 onward, data are based on fiscal year beginning 1 April.
i For 2012–2018, GFS data are based on fiscal year beginning 1 April. For 2019, GFS data are based on fiscal year beginning 1 October. For 2012–2015, national accounts data are based on fiscal year beginning 1 April. For 2016 onward, national accounts data are based on fiscal year beginning 1 October.
j For 2000–2013, data on education include expenditure on recreation, culture, and religion.
k For 2000–2018, data refer to obligation basis. For 2019–2021, data refer to cash basis.
l Data are based on fiscal year ending 30 September.

Sources: Economies' official sources. For Hong Kong, China and Nepal: Asian Development Bank estimates using data from the International Monetary Fund's Government Finance Statistics. https://data.imf.org/ (accessed April–June 2022). For Sri Lanka: Asian Development Bank estimates using data from the Central Bank of Sri Lanka, official communication, 5 May 2022.

Table 2.8.6: Corruption Perceptions Index

ADB Regional Member	2012	2015	2017	2018	2019	2020	2021	Rank in 2020[a]	Rank in 2021[a]
Developing ADB Member Economies									
Central and West Asia									
Afghanistan	8.0	11.0	15.0	16.0	16.0	19.0	16.0	165	174
Armenia	34.0	35.0	35.0	35.0	42.0	49.0	49.0	60	58
Azerbaijan	27.0	29.0	31.0	25.0	30.0	30.0	30.0	129	128
Georgia	52.0	52.0	56.0	58.0	56.0	56.0	55.0	45	45
Kazakhstan	28.0	28.0	31.0	31.0	34.0	38.0	37.0	94	102
Kyrgyz Republic	24.0	28.0	29.0	29.0	30.0	31.0	27.0	124	144
Pakistan	27.0	30.0	32.0	33.0	32.0	31.0	28.0	124	140
Tajikistan	22.0	26.0	21.0	25.0	25.0	25.0	25.0	149	150
Turkmenistan	17.0	18.0	19.0	20.0	19.0	19.0	19.0	165	169
Uzbekistan	17.0	19.0	22.0	23.0	25.0	26.0	28.0	146	140
East Asia									
China, People's Republic of	39.0	37.0	41.0	39.0	41.0	42.0	45.0	78	66
Hong Kong, China	77.0	75.0	77.0	76.0	76.0	77.0	76.0	11	12
Korea, Republic of	56.0	54.0	54.0	57.0	59.0	61.0	62.0	33	32
Mongolia	36.0	39.0	36.0	37.0	35.0	35.0	35.0	111	110
Taipei,China	61.0	62.0	63.0	63.0	65.0	65.0	68.0	28	25
South Asia									
Bangladesh	26.0	25.0	28.0	26.0	26.0	26.0	26.0	146	147
Bhutan	63.0	65.0	67.0	68.0	68.0	68.0	68.0	24	25
India	36.0	38.0	40.0	41.0	41.0	40.0	40.0	86	85
Maldives	...	...	33.0	31.0	29.0	43.0	40.0	75	85
Nepal	27.0	27.0	31.0	31.0	34.0	33.0	33.0	117	117
Sri Lanka	40.0	37.0	38.0	38.0	38.0	38.0	37.0	94	102
Southeast Asia									
Brunei Darussalam	55.0	...	62.0	63.0	60.0	60.0	...	35	...
Cambodia	22.0	21.0	21.0	20.0	20.0	21.0	23.0	160	157
Indonesia	32.0	36.0	37.0	38.0	40.0	37.0	38.0	102	96
Lao People's Democratic Republic	21.0	25.0	29.0	29.0	29.0	29.0	30.0	134	128
Malaysia	49.0	50.0	47.0	47.0	53.0	51.0	48.0	57	62
Myanmar	15.0	22.0	30.0	29.0	29.0	28.0	28.0	137	140
Philippines	34.0	35.0	34.0	36.0	34.0	34.0	33.0	115	117
Singapore	87.0	85.0	84.0	85.0	85.0	85.0	85.0	3	4
Thailand	37.0	38.0	37.0	36.0	36.0	36.0	35.0	104	110
Timor-Leste	33.0	28.0	38.0	35.0	38.0	40.0	41.0	86	82
Viet Nam	31.0	31.0	35.0	33.0	37.0	36.0	39.0	104	87
The Pacific									
Cook Islands	...	...	...	...	...	...	...	...	...
Fiji	...	...	...	...	...	...	55.0	...	45
Kiribati	...	...	...	...	...	...	...	...	...
Marshall Islands	...	...	...	...	...	...	...	...	...
Micronesia, Federated States of	...	...	...	...	...	...	...	...	...
Nauru	...	...	...	...	...	...	...	...	...
Niue	...	...	...	...	...	...	...	...	...
Palau	...	...	...	...	...	...	...	...	...
Papua New Guinea	25.0	25.0	29.0	28.0	28.0	27.0	31.0	142	124
Samoa	...	...	...	...	...	...	...	...	...
Solomon Islands	...	...	39.0	44.0	42.0	42.0	43.0	78	73
Tonga	...	...	...	...	...	...	...	...	...
Tuvalu	...	...	...	...	...	...	...	...	...
Vanuatu	...	...	43.0	46.0	46.0	43.0	45.0	75	66
Developed ADB Member Economies									
Australia	85.0	79.0	77.0	77.0	77.0	77.0	73.0	11	18
Japan	74.0	75.0	73.0	73.0	73.0	74.0	73.0	19	18
New Zealand	90.0	91.0	89.0	87.0	87.0	88.0	88.0	1	1

... = data not available, ADB = Asian Development Bank.

Note: The Key Indicators Database features a longer time series of scores on the Corruption Perceptions Index. This includes scores for 2000–2011, which refer to perceptions of the degree of corruption as seen by business people and analysts. Those scores range from 0 (highly corrupt) to 10 (very clean) and are not comparable over time. From 2012 onward, an updated methodology was used to calculate scores, and these are presented on a scale from 0 (highly corrupt) to 100 (very clean). Due to the differences in methodology, scores prior to 2012 should not be compared with scores for 2012 onward.

a Based on Transparency International's methodology, an economy's rank indicates its position relative to the Corruption Perceptions Index of other economies of the world; 2020 and 2021 rankings compare 180 economies.

Source: Transparency International. Corruption Perceptions Index. https://www.transparency.org/ (accessed 19 April 2022).

Data Issues and Comparability

Most economies generally follow the IMF's Government Finance Statistics (GFS) guidelines: some still use the 1986 version, while others have switched to the 2001 or 2014 versions. The comparability of the data is limited by variations in the concepts and definitions used in different versions of the GFS framework. Furthermore, there is no single framework for an extended time series available in most economies that are using the 2014 guidelines, with most economies recording their transactions on a cash basis (and a few on an accrual basis).

Data on government expenditures and revenue are derived from economy sources and are therefore not standard throughout Asia and the Pacific. Data refer to general government for some economies, and central government for other economies.

Statistics on perceived corruption are taken from nonofficial sources. Common procedures are used in all economies and the researchers producing these data have refined their procedures over several surveys. However, because of the subjective nature of many of the data, they can only be used to give a broad idea of trends, levels, and rankings, so small changes from one year to the next should be interpreted with caution.

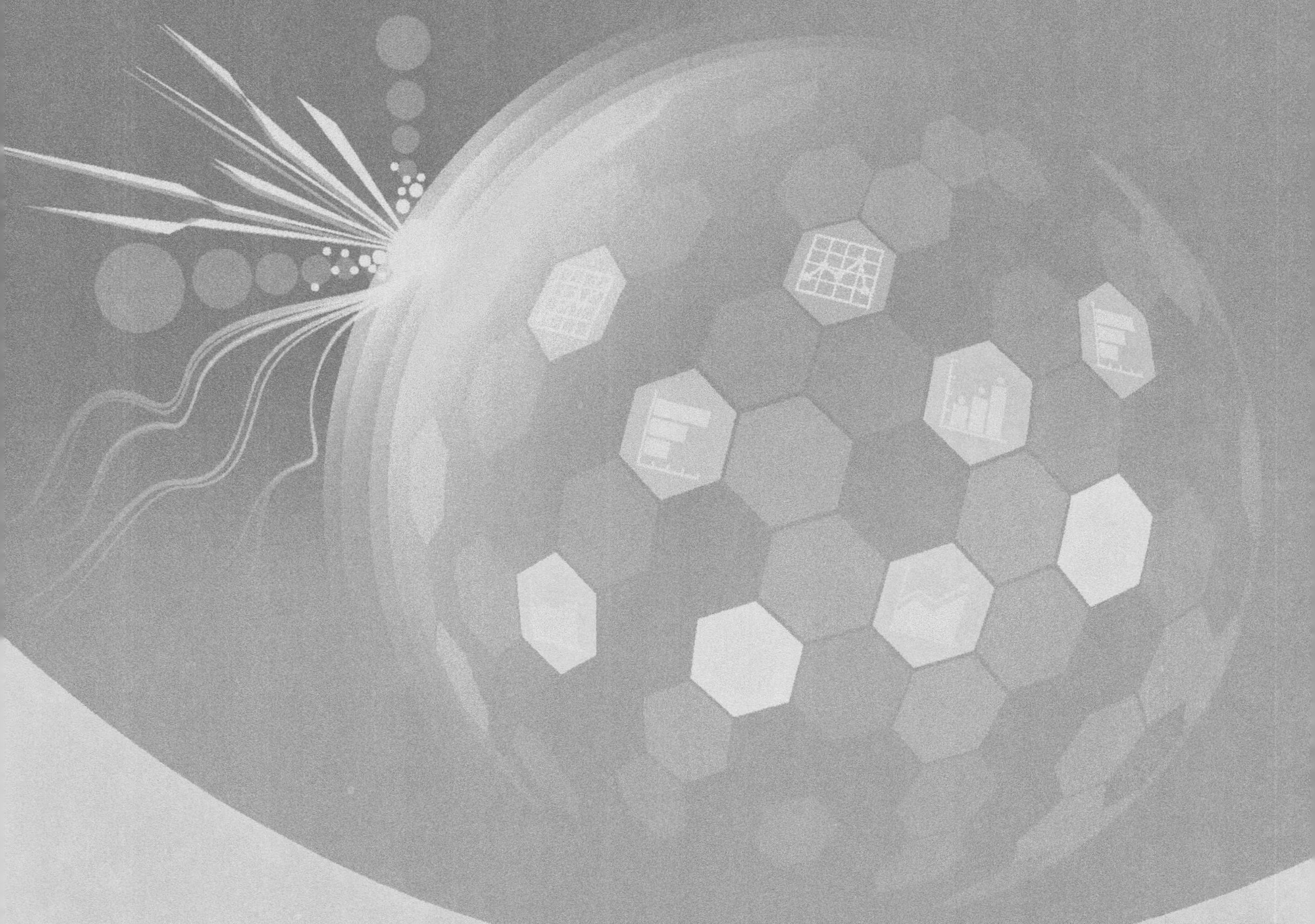

PART III
Global Value Chains

The Implications of the Global Chip Shortage in Asia

Semiconductors or microchips play an important role in the modern world. They are an essential input to many of today's electronics, including personal computers and handheld devices, medical equipment, robotics, transport technologies, and advanced manufacturing machinery. In a 2022 report, Asian Development Bank (ADB) estimates suggest that about 65% of total world exports rely, either directly or indirectly, on semiconductors (ADB 2022a).

However, global events—including trade conflicts, geopolitical tensions, and the coronavirus disease (COVID-19) pandemic—have threatened the world supply of semiconductors. At the same time that there has been a surge in demand for electronic products, cloud computing, and other new technologies during the pandemic, associated lockdowns and quarantining of manufacturing enterprises in the People's Republic of China (PRC) and other Asian economies have placed further strain on the limited capacity of semiconductor manufacturers. Climate change and natural disasters also continue to hamper semiconductor production, with typhoons, floods, and earthquakes disrupting logistics and supply networks and posing various other challenges to producers.

In 2022, Part III of *Key Indicators for Asia and the Pacific* focuses on analyzing the global chip shortage and its implications for 26 economies in the region, focusing on the electrical and optical equipment sector. It makes use of data for 2000 to 2020 from the Observatory of Economic Complexity (OEC) and for 2000 to 2021 from ADB's Multiregional Input-Output Tables (MRIOTs) to understand the changes that have taken place in the international trade for semiconductors and the subsequent effects of these changes on economies in the region.[1]

For the purposes of this analysis, the 26 economies assessed are Australia; Bangladesh; Bhutan; Brunei Darussalam; Cambodia; Fiji; Hong Kong, China; India; Indonesia; Japan; Kazakhstan; the Kyrgyz Republic; the Lao People's Democratic Republic; Malaysia; Maldives; Mongolia; Nepal; Pakistan; the PRC; the Philippines; the Republic of Korea; Singapore; Sri Lanka; Taipei,China; Thailand; and Viet Nam.

Part III demonstrates that the impacts of the semiconductor shortage on the selected economies can depend on several things, including their participation in global value chains (GVCs), their competitive advantage in the electrical and optical equipment sector, and the level of diversity of their exports. A clear assessment of these indicators is important in mitigating the consequences of the global chip shortage and helping with economic recovery.

1 Product exports data from the OEC are based on the BACI dataset, which reconciles data from the United Nations Statistical Division's Comtrade dataset. As of the time of writing, data available from the OEC are only up to 2020.

Chips are integral to servers. An IT specialist at ADB's Tajikistan Resident Mission ensures the bank's mainframes can cater for the rise in digitalization and cloud computing (photo by Nozim Kalandarov/ADB).

Asia's Role in Semiconductor Production and Electrical and Optical Equipment Exports

Among the most complex GVCs is the chain for semiconductors. Many economies participate in various stages of semiconductor production; from research and development to design, manufacturing, assembly, testing, and packaging. Ultimately, these chips are used as inputs in electronic devices and transport equipment for final consumption in the modern world. This significant role of semiconductors in international trade has allowed economies to participate in, and reap the benefits of integrating into, GVCs.

The Asia and Pacific region plays a significant role in the GVC for semiconductors in general and the electrical and optical equipment sector in particular (Figure 3.1). Estimates from the OEC show that, in 2016–2020, the 26 reporting economies of the region contributed 83.7% of the world's total exports of integrated circuits, up from only 60.4% in 2000.

Among these 26 economies, the five biggest contributors were Taipei,China, which contributed 22.7% of the region's exports of integrated circuits in 2016–2020, followed by the PRC (18.7%), the Republic of Korea (18.0%), Singapore (13.3%), and Malaysia (11.0%). Following these five were Japan (6.0%), the Philippines (4.7%), Viet Nam (2.6%), Thailand (1.9%), and Hong Kong, China (1.0%). These economies have specialized tasks within the GVCs for integrated circuits. For instance, Taipei,China is considered a leader in wafer foundry; the Republic of Korea specializes in the manufacture of advanced chips; and the Philippines focuses on product testing and packaging.

Figure 3.1: Exports of Integrated Circuits and Electrical and Optical Equipment

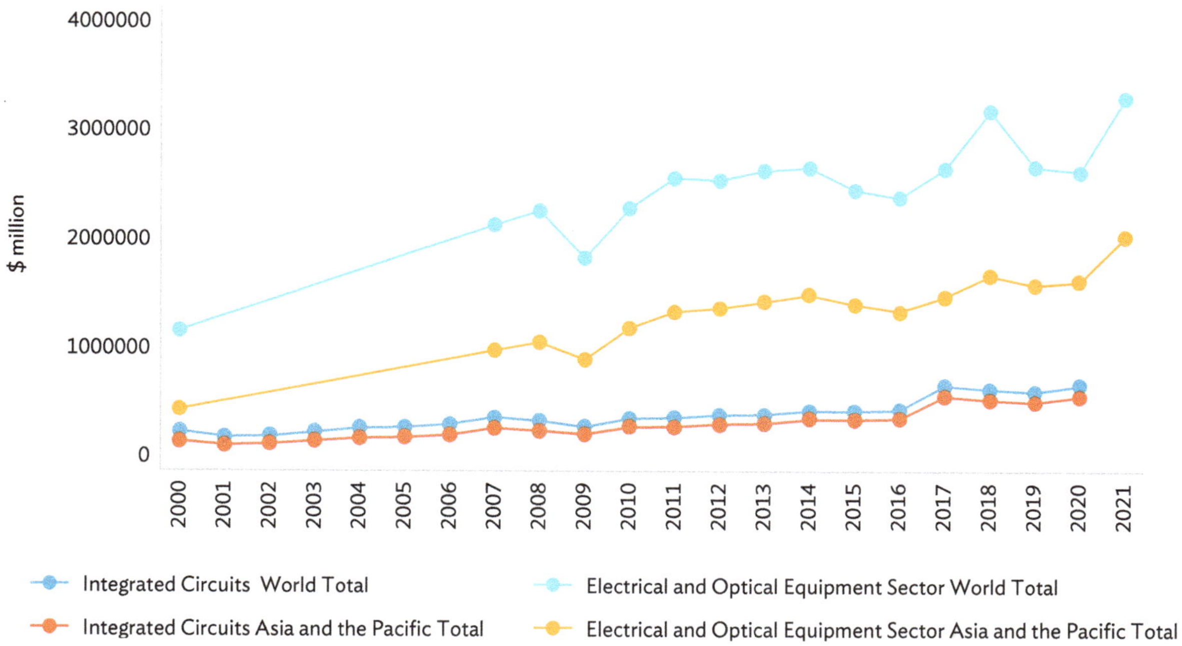

Note: The graphic covers 26 economies of Asia and the Pacific: Australia; Bangladesh; Bhutan; Brunei Darussalam; Cambodia; Fiji; Hong Kong, China; India; Indonesia; Japan; Kazakhstan; the Kyrgyz Republic; the Lao People's Democratic Republic; Malaysia; Maldives; Mongolia; Nepal; Pakistan; the People's Republic of China; the Philippines; the Republic of Korea; Singapore; Sri Lanka; Taipei,China; Thailand; and Viet Nam. All products under HS Rev. 92 ID 8542 from the Observatory of Economic Complexity were considered in calculating for integrated circuits exports. Electrical and optical equipment sector exports were derived from the Asian Development Bank's Multiregional Input-Output Tables. Data from the Observatory of Economic Complexity are available only up to 2020.

Source: Asian Development Bank calculations using estimates from the Observatory of Economic Complexity and the Asian Development Bank Multiregional Input-Output Tables.

Click here for figure data

The importance of integrated circuits in electronics manufacturing for a given economy can be indicated by the proportion of integrated circuits (HS4 Rev. 92 ID 8542) in total electrical equipment and machineries (HS2 Rev. 92 ID 85) exports (Figure 3.2). In 2016–2020, Singapore had the highest share of integrated circuits in total electrical equipment and machinery exports at 69.6%, followed by Taipei,China at 68.8%. Over half of electrical equipment and machinery exports are integrated circuits in the Philippines (57.9%), Malaysia (57.4%), and the Republic of Korea (55.4%).

As with the exporting of integrated circuits, Asia and the Pacific also claims an increasing share of the world's exports in the electrical and optical equipment sector. Data from the MRIOTs show that, in 2000, the region made up only 37.5% of the total world exports in the sector. By 2021, that share had increased to 61.5%.

Figure 3.2: Share of Integrated Circuits in Electrical Equipment and Machinery Exports, 2016–2020

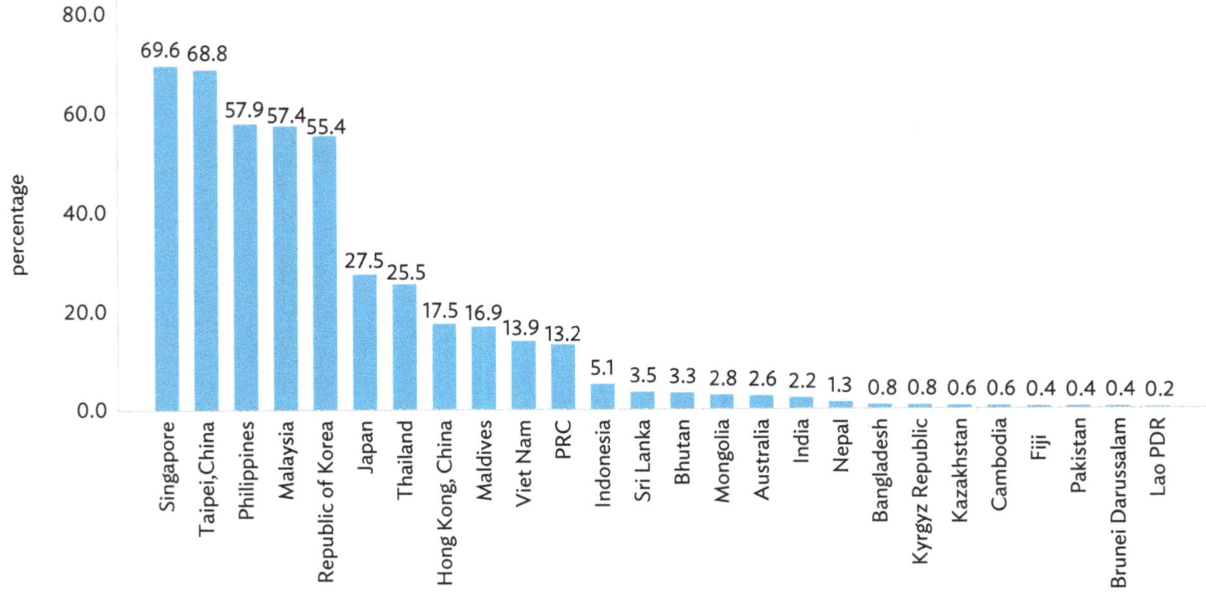

Lao PDR = Lao People's Democratic Republic, PRC = People's Republic of China.

Note: All products under HS Rev. 92 ID 8542 from the Observatory of Economic Complexity were considered in calculating for integrated circuits exports, while all products under HS Rev. 92 ID 85 were considered in calculating for electrical equipment and machinery exports.

Source: Asian Development Bank calculations using estimates from the Observatory of Economic Complexity.

Click here for figure data

Focusing on GVCs, the role of Asia and the Pacific in the electrical and optical equipment sector has increased since the start of the millennium. An increasing portion of value-added in GVC intermediates has increasingly originated from the region, up from only 37.1% in 2000 to 56.3% in 2021. Meanwhile, within the region, there has also been an evolution in the roles that economies play in the trade of electrical and optical intermediates.

In 2000, the United States exported the most value-added in GVC intermediates in the electrical and optical sector, accounting for over 27.0% of the world total (Figure 3.3.a). Its biggest exports to Asia and the Pacific went to Taipei,China, followed by the Republic of Korea, Malaysia, Japan, and Singapore. Within the region, the biggest player in 2000 was Japan, which contributed about 16.8% of total world domestic value-added exports in GVC intermediates in the electrical and optical equipment sector. Japan's biggest ties were with other Asian economies, namely Taipei,China and the Republic of Korea.

By 2021, the landscape of electrical and optical equipment GVCs had changed. The PRC was by then the biggest contributor to total world domestic value-added in GVC intermediates in the sector, with a share of 16.6% (Figure 3.3.b). The shares of the Republic of Korea and Taipei,China also grew, from less than 6% each to 12.5% and 11.3%, respectively. On the other hand, Japan's share had fallen to 8.3% by 2021. GVC ties within Asia and the Pacific were also more prominent in 2021 compared to 2000.

Figure 3.3: Exports of Domestic Value-Added in Global Value Chain Intermediates in the Electrical and Optical Equipment Sector

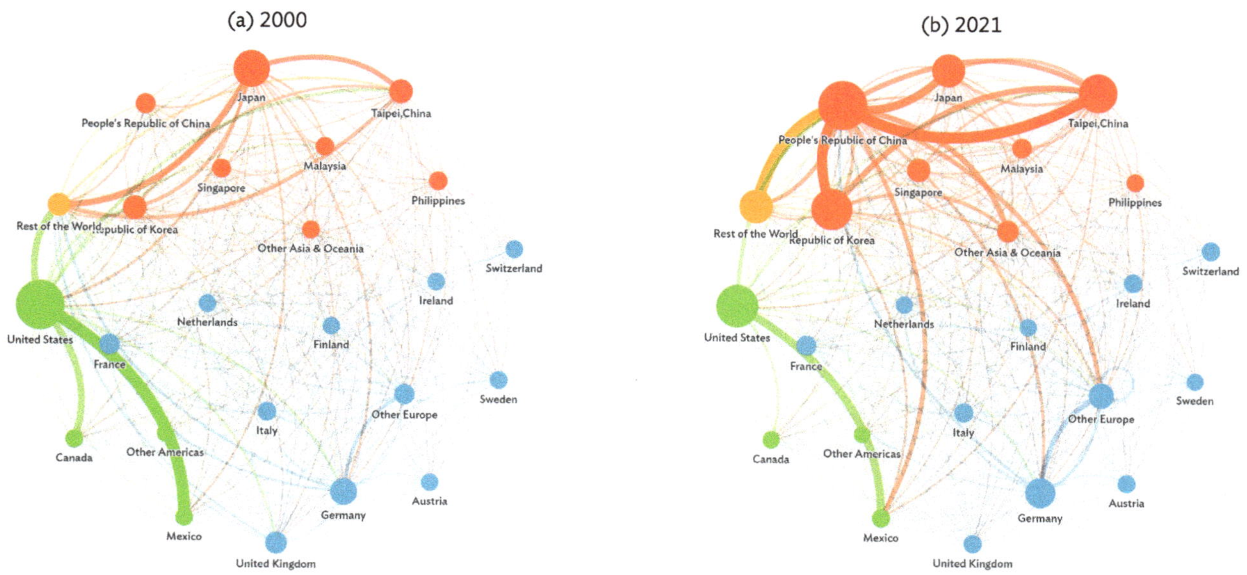

Note: Nodes and edges are determined using the REX and REF components of the Borin and Mancini (2019) exports decomposition framework by origin sector. REX refers to domestic value-added re-exported by a second economy *r* and eventually reabsorbed by *r* or a third economy. REF refers to domestic value-added re-exported by a second economy *r* and eventually reabsorbed by the economy of origin.

Source: Asian Development Bank (ADB) calculations using the ADB Global Value Chain Indicators and the ADB Multiregional Input-Output Tables.

Click here for figure data

Compared to the whole world, Asia and the Pacific saw a larger year-on-year increase in integrated circuit exports in 2017 (60.4%), but the region experienced slightly sharper declines in 2018 (-5.5%) and 2019 (-4.7%) as shown in Figure 3.4.a. This was partly due to interregional and intraregional trade conflicts and slower demand for electronic goods. A stronger rebound in integrated circuit exports can be seen in the region compared to the world in 2020, as demand for electronics, particularly personal computers and handheld devices, increased during COVID-19 lockdowns. This faster rebound in Asia and the Pacific's exports of integrated circuits led to an overall increase of 4.9 percentage points in the region's share of global exports from 2016 to 2020.

The pattern of growth in the electrical and optical equipment sector in 2016–2021 is different (Figure 3.4.b). Growth from 2016 to 2017 was only 1.0 percentage point slower in Asia and the Pacific compared to the world (at 10.1% and 11.1%, respectively). From 2017 to 2018, there was a more significant increase in electrical and optical equipment sector exports for both Asia and the Pacific and the world, although this growth was 7.1 percentage points higher for the world as a whole. Conversely, from 2018 to 2019, Asia and the Pacific experienced a relatively milder decline of 5.2%, while the world decline was 16.1%. The region also enjoyed a stronger rebound from 2019 to 2020, with electrical and optical equipment sector exports growing by 2.1%, while the world total shrank by 1.4%. In 2021, the region's exports from the electrical and optical equipment sector continued to grow by 25.6%, less than 0.1 percentage point slower than world average growth.

Figure 3.4: Year-on-Year Growth in Exports of Integrated Circuits and Electrical and Optical Equipment

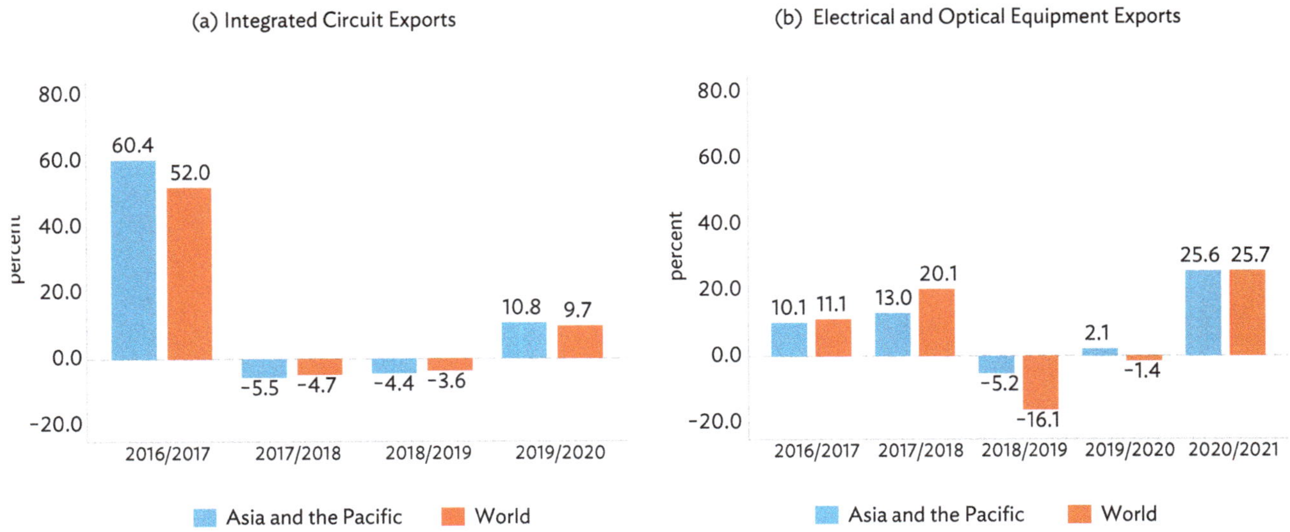

Note: The graphic covers 26 economies of Asia and the Pacific: Australia; Bangladesh; Bhutan; Brunei Darussalam; Cambodia; Fiji; Hong Kong, China; India; Indonesia; Japan; Kazakhstan; the Kyrgyz Republic; the Lao People's Democratic Republic; Malaysia; Maldives; Mongolia; Nepal; Pakistan; the People's Republic of China; the Philippines; the Republic of Korea; Singapore; Sri Lanka; Taipei,China; Thailand; and Viet Nam. All products under HS Rev. 92 ID 8542 were considered in calculating for integrated circuits exports.

Source: Asian Development Bank calculations using estimates from the Observatory of Economic Complexity and the Asian Development Bank Multiregional Input-Output Tables.

Click here for figure data

The two growth patterns shown in Figure 3.4.a and 3.4.b suggest that, despite COVID-19 lockdowns in 2020, electronics exports continued to surge for economies in Asia and the Pacific. This suggests that demand-side factors played a significant role as the lockdowns placed strong emphasis on, and drove the adoption of, digital technologies for remote connectivity, leading to stronger demand for chips and other electronics. This growth continued through 2021. Furthermore, Burkacky et al. (2022) show that, throughout 2020 and 2021, forecast demand for most electronics exceeded pre-pandemic forecasts for most industries. After declining trends in 2020, the import price index for semiconductor and other electronics manufacturing also continuously increased in the United States, indicating rising demand as well as supply constraints in 2021 (Figure 3.5).

In general, exports of integrated chips partially move in line with exports from the electrical and optical equipment sector, although integrated chips exports show less volatility and a slower upward momentum (Figure 3.1). Chips also act as inputs to the production of other electrical and optical equipment sector goods, so a shortage in the supply of chips can have an impact on the output of this sector.

Among the 26 economies assessed in the MRIOTs, there were eight economies where the shares of their electrical and optical equipment sectors made up over 14.0% of their total economy exports in 2019–2021. These economies included Taipei,China (48.9%), the Republic of Korea (31.4%), the PRC (30.3%), the Philippines (26.4%), Malaysia (23.7%), Singapore (21.0%), Japan (19.5%), and Viet Nam (14.2%).

Figure 3.5: United States Import Price Indices for Integrated Circuits and Electrical Machinery and Equipment

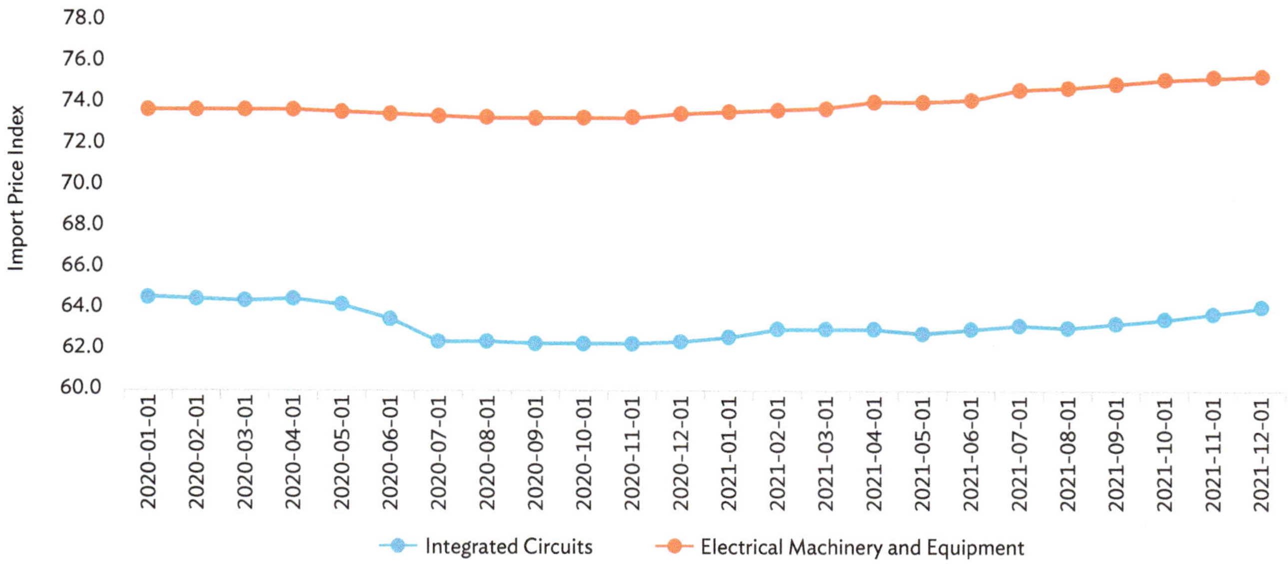

Note: Integrated circuits fall under HS4 Rev. 92 ID 8542, while electrical machinery and equipment fall under HS2 Rev. 92 ID 85. Index = 100 for the year 2000.

Sources: Federal Reserve Bank of St. Louis. Import Price Index (Harmonized System): Electronic Integrated Circuits; Parts Thereof. https://fred.stlouisfed.org/series/IP8542 (accessed 24 June 2022); and Import Price Index (Harmonized System): Electrical Machinery and Equipment and Parts Thereof; Sound Recorders and Reproducers, Television Image and Sound Recorders and Reproducers, and Parts and Accessories of Such Articles. https://fred.stlouisfed.org/series/IP85 (accessed 24 June 2022).

Click here for figure data

How Exposed are Asia and the Pacific's Economies to Semiconductor Supply Shortages?

While GVC participation offers the chance to create greater economic activity, it can also create vulnerabilities for economies whenever shocks are experienced throughout the chain. With GVCs, economies perform specialized tasks within production chains, making them reliant on both upstream suppliers and downstream customers. Thus, disruption in any part of the chain can have impacts on other segments of the chain. From a backward perspective, constraints from suppliers can lead to production delays. From a forward perspective, economic downturns in recipient economies can create production limitations or shutdowns.

How vulnerable economies of the Asia and Pacific region are to the global chip shortage can be explored using GVC indicators. First, GVC participation indices can indicate what proportion of exports rely on backward and forward linkages (Figure 3.6). Backward participation in GVCs tells us what proportion of a sector's exports rely on foreign value-added, while forward participation in GVCs tell us what proportion of a sector's exports is domestic value-added in intermediates that undergo more than two border crossings. The Borin and Mancini (2019) trade decomposition framework allows us to calculate trade-based participation indices for the 26 economies assessed in the MRIOTs for 2019–2021 (Figure 3.6).

Figure 3.6: Trade-Based Global Value Chain Participation Rates

(a) Backward Participation in GVCs of the Electrical and Optical Equipment Sector

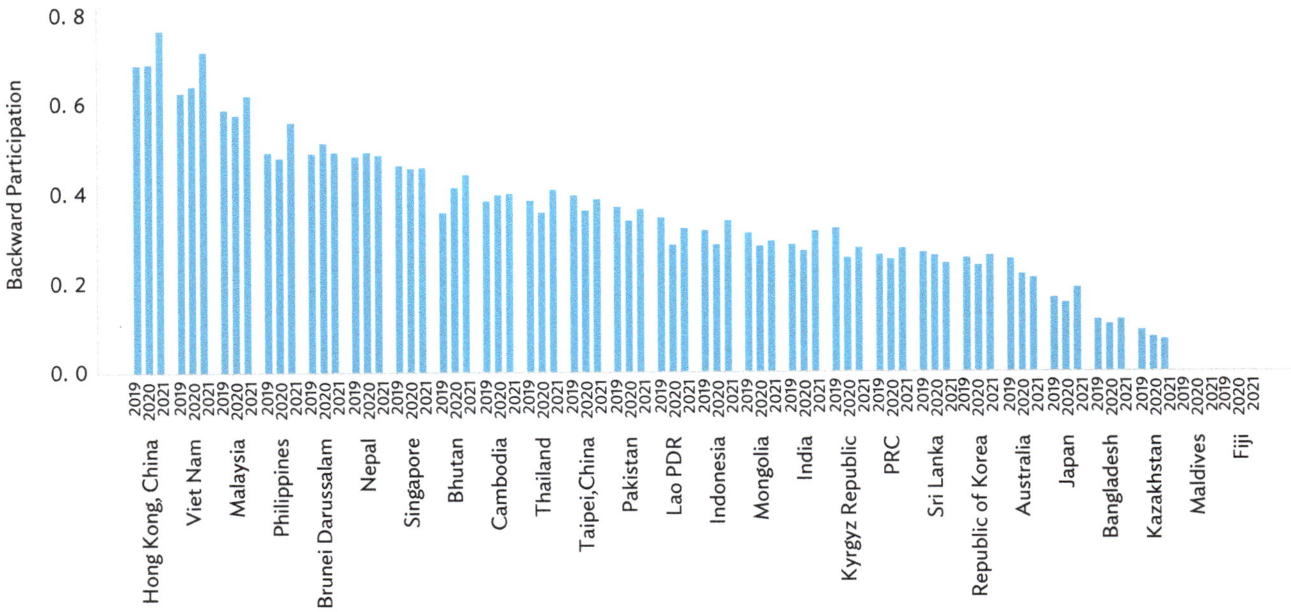

(b) Forward Participation in GVCs of the Electrical and Optical Equipment Sector

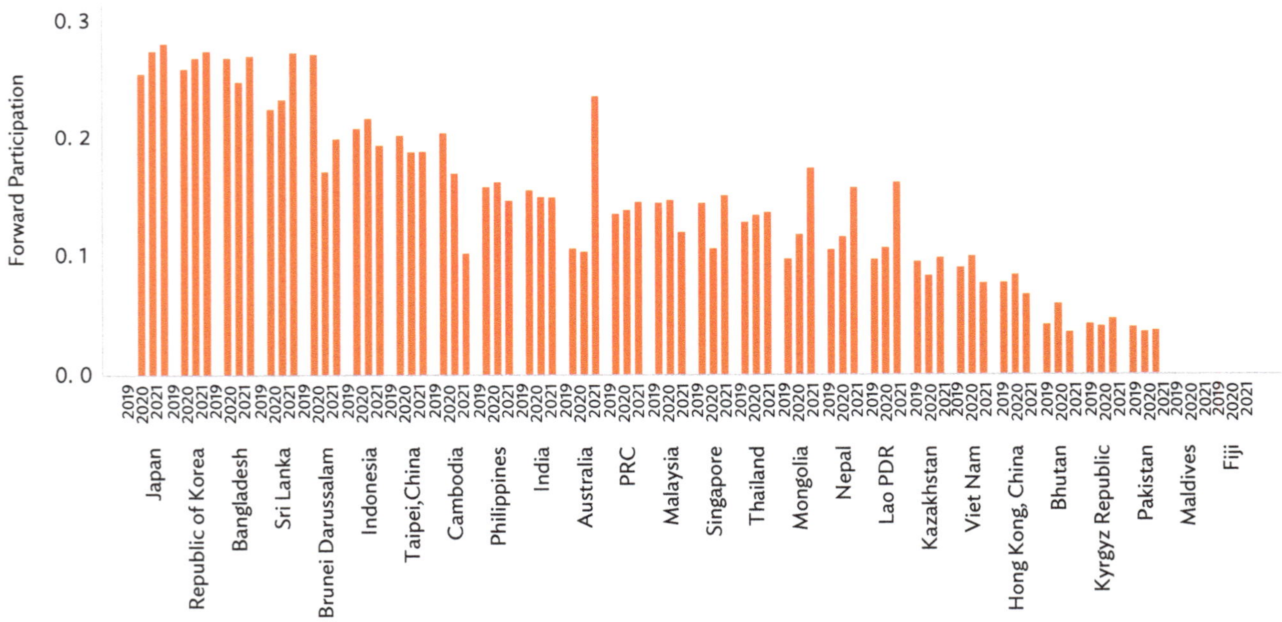

GVC = global value chain, Lao PDR = Lao People's Democratic Republic, PRC = People's Republic of China.
Note: Participation rates are calculated based on the Borin and Mancini (2019) trade decomposition by exporting sector.
Source: Asian Development Bank (ADB) calculations using the ADB Global Value Chain Indicators and the ADB Multiregional Input-Output Tables.

Click here for figure data

Among the economies of the region where the share of the electrical and optical equipment sector in total exports was over 14.0% for 2019–2021, Viet Nam showed the highest backward participation at over 66.0%. Viet Nam is known for the assembly of electronics that are closer to finished products, such as mobile phones, household appliances, and computers. Thus, it can be expected that Viet Nam's electrical and optical equipment sector exports will have a high share of foreign value-added content, making it vulnerable to the chip supply shortage.[2] At the other end of the spectrum is Japan, an established semiconductor chip producer, where backward participation for 2019–2021 was at just over 16.8% of exports. Compared to Viet Nam, a significant portion of Japan's electronics exports are semiconductor chips, explaining why backward participation is relatively low for the economy.[3] It is also interesting to note that, for many of the 26 reporting economies, backward participation in the electrical and optical equipment sector declined from 2019 to 2020, but many reporting economies also saw strong rebounds in backward participation in 2021.

Among the eight Asian economies with 14.0%+ shares of exports contributed by the electrical and optical equipment sector, Japan showed the highest forward GVC participation for 2019–2021 (at 25.5% to 28.0%), followed by the Republic of Korea (at 25.9% to 27.4%), implying relatively high content of domestic value-added in GVC intermediates in the total sector exports of the two economies. These economies are known producers of semiconductor chips and other electronic parts that are used as inputs in downstream production. On the other hand, Viet Nam, which showed the highest backward participation, registered the lowest forward participation among the eight economies, posting less than 9.8% for 2019–2021.

Economies with high forward GVC participation in the electrical and optical equipment sector and large contributions of semiconductor chips to their total exports may benefit from the global chip shortage if the price of semiconductor chips rises, holding all else equal. However, production bottlenecks within these economies can cause a ripple effect that will impact upstream suppliers and economies further downstream that rely on their production of semiconductor chips.

Another indicator that can be used to assess vulnerability is revealed comparative advantage (RCA) and its indices as represented in Figure 3.7. RCA tells us whether an economy is competitive in a given sector, but it can also inform us if an economy relies more heavily on a sector for exports (compared to the world average). For economies where RCA is greater than 1 in the electrical and optical equipment sector, the contribution of the sector to total exports and to total domestic value-added generation in these economies is larger compared to the world average.

Using both gross exports and domestic value-added to calculate for RCA shows that the same eight economies that rely heavily on electrical and optical equipment sector exports have RCA in that sector. Moreover, data from the OEC reveal that these eight

2 Data from the OEC show that, among products classified using HS4, integrated circuits made up the largest share of imports in Viet Nam.

3 Japan's vulnerability to the chip shortage is exacerbated by its transport equipment industry, which also relies on semiconductor chips.

Figure 3.7: Revealed Comparative Advantage in the Electrical and Optical Equipment Sector

(a) Revealed Comparative Advantage Based on Exports

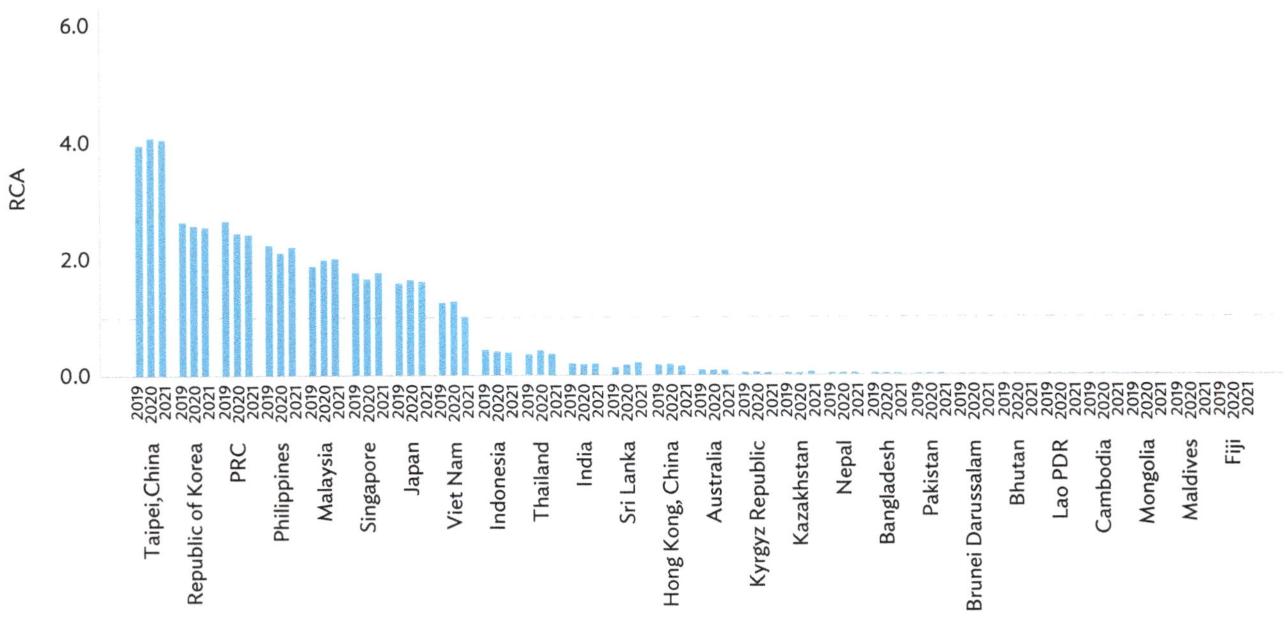

(b) Revealed Comparative Advantage Based on Value-Added

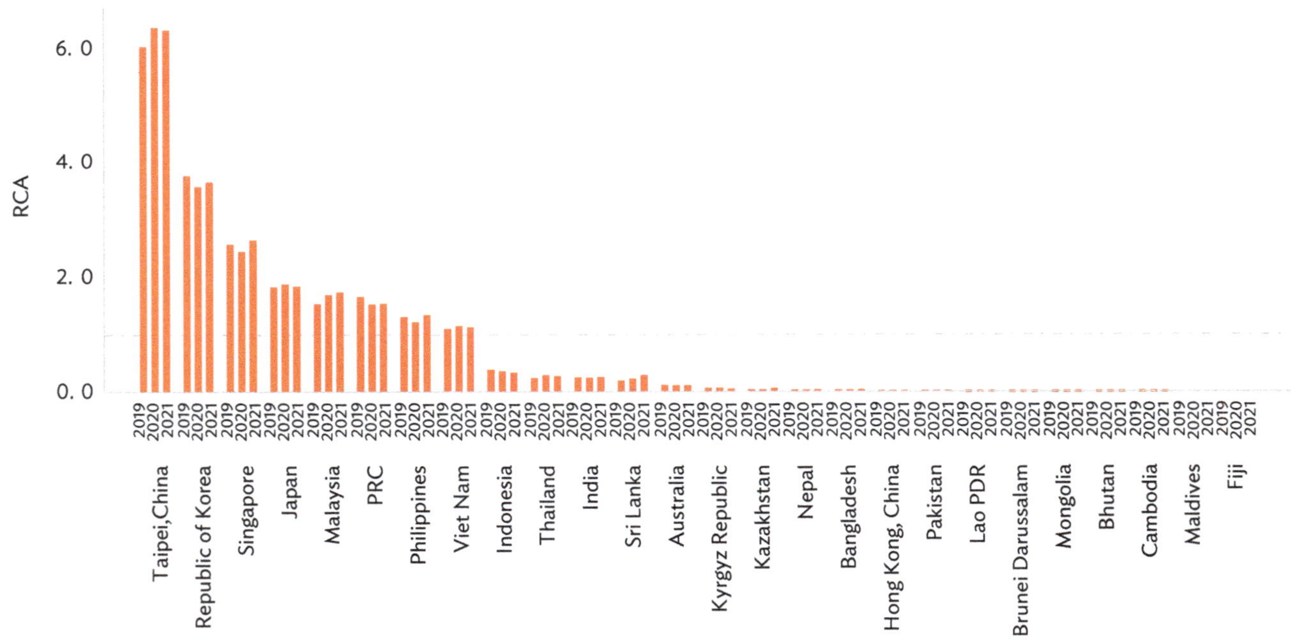

Lao PDR = Lao People's Democratic Republic, PRC = People's Republic of China, RCA = revealed comparative advantage.

Note: Revealed comparative advantage based on value-added is calculated using the Borin and Mancini (2019) exports decomposition by origin sector.

Source: Asian Development Bank (ADB) calculations using the ADB Global Value Chain Indicators and the ADB Multiregional Input-Output Tables.

Click here for figure data

economies were in the top 10 exporters of integrated circuits in 2020, making up 81.9% of total exports for the product category. For some of these economies, integrated circuits also made up a large portion of electrical equipment and machineries exports.

Across the 26 economies assessed for 2019–2021, Taipei,China showed the highest RCA using both gross exports and domestic value-added exports. Estimates from the OEC show that, in 2020, 20.7% of integrated circuit exports came from Taipei,China, highlighting the large and direct role of Taipei,China in the production of chips. Moreover, the OEC shows that integrated circuits made up 36.9% of Taipei,China's product exports and 71.1% of their electrical machinery and equipment exports.[4] In turn, electrical machinery and equipment made up some 51.8% of Taipei,China's product exports. The large role of semiconductors and the electrical and optical equipment sector in Taipei,China makes it vulnerable to disruptions in chip production. However, the economy also stands to benefit from an increased demand for semiconductor chips if it can meet this demand.

While the eight economies with 14.0%+ shares of total exports coming from the electrical and optical equipment sector appear to have a strong footing in the exporting of integrated circuits and for RCA in the sector, it is important to know where the bottlenecks in chip production are. It is also important to consider whether the electrical and optical equipment sector relies heavily on semiconductor chips production and assembly or on downstream sectors that make use of these chips, such as in the production of smartphones, computers, and other electronic devices.

For economies where RCA is driven by chip production, an economy may benefit in the short to medium run on the increased prices of semiconductors, if that economy is readily able to address bottlenecks in production and external sources of delay while meeting the growing demand for chips. Meanwhile, economies where RCA in the electrical and optical equipment sector is driven by the production of electronics that make use of chips may be negatively hit by the supply crunch.

A final measure of vulnerability in this assessment is the use of diversification indices. These can tell us whether economies' exports and production are too dependent on the electrical and optical equipment sector, implying a higher vulnerability to the global chip shortage. Figure 3.8 highlights the eight economies that have over 14.0% of total exports coming from the electrical and optical equipment sector and shows their average Hirschman Herfindahl Indices (HHIs) for 2019–2021. Note that a higher HHI value implies higher specialization or concentration, while a lower HHI value implies greater diversification.

Among the eight economies, Taipei,China showed the highest HHI values for both gross exports and domestic value-added for 2019–2021, implying that it was the least diversified. This high reliance on electrical and optical equipment using both gross exports and domestic value-added exports indicates that a shortage affecting Taipei,China's electrical and optical equipment sector can have large impacts on the economy. A large part of Taipei,China's domestic value-added was exported through

4 The share of integrated circuits in electrical machinery and equipment exports is calculated by dividing the value of integrated circuits (HS4 ID 8542) from the value of electrical machinery and equipment (HS2 ID 85) exports.

Figure 3.8: Average Hirschman Herfindahl Indices on Exports Diversification, 2019–2021

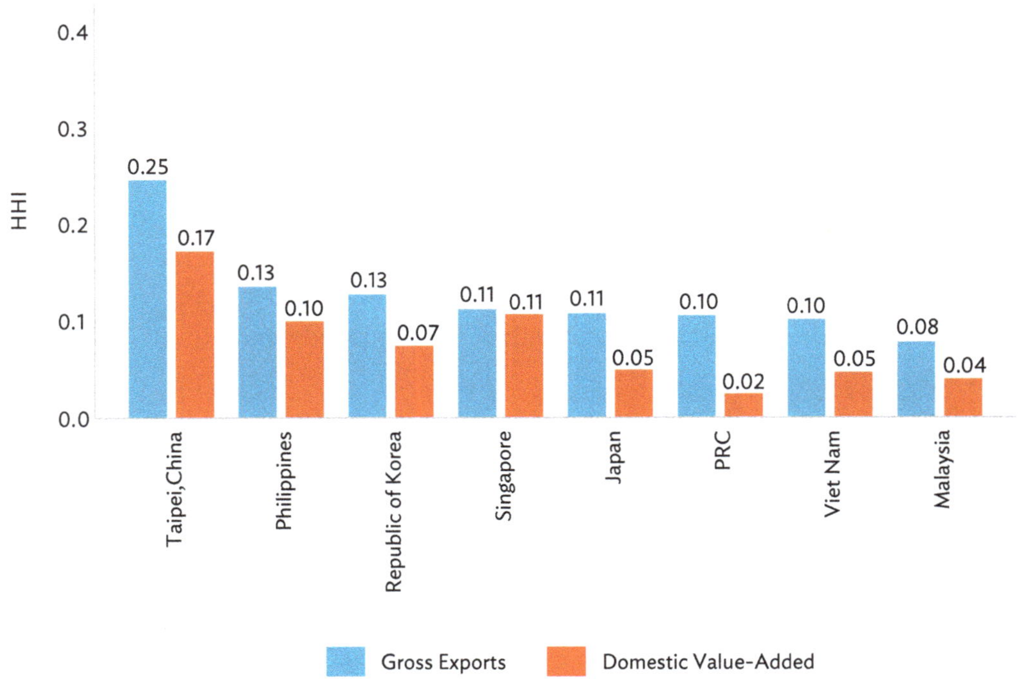

HHI = Hirschman Herfindahl Index, PRC = People's Republic of China.

Note: Hirschman Herfindahl Index based on value-added is calculated using the Borin and Mancini (2019) exports decomposition by origin sector.

Source: Asian Development Bank (ADB) calculations using the ADB Global Value Chain Indicators and the ADB Multiregional Input-Output Tables.

Click here for figure data

its gross exports in the electrical and optical equipment sector, which means that bottlenecks in its electronics exports may negatively impact economic activity within its other domestic sectors. The lower HHI when using domestic value-added implies that many domestic sectors were actually contributing to support Taipei,China's exports in the electrical and optical equipment sector. On the other hand, the increase in demand for integrated circuits could benefit Taipei,China in the short run through increased revenues, holding all things equal, and these short-run benefits have the potential to spill over to the other domestic sectors linked to the electrical and optical equipment sector.

Meanwhile, Japan showed a relatively more diverse economy both in terms of gross exports and domestic value-added for 2019–2021. Japan's gross exports were dominated by their electrical and optical equipment sector and their transport equipment sector, but the economy also had large contributions from other manufacturing sectors. It must be noted, however, that while Japan showed a relatively diverse economy, with different sectors participating more equally to exports and production, the two largest sectors rely on semiconductor chips, lending the economy a certain degree of vulnerability to the global chip shortage. The higher prices in semiconductors and the lower supply available to the automotive sector, given competing demand from electronics manufacturing, could cause a slowdown in Japan's economic growth despite higher prices and stronger demand for chips and chip-dependent products.

Malaysia and Viet Nam had the lowest HHIs in terms of gross exports and relatively low HHIs in terms of domestic value-added. While exports in the electrical and optical equipment sector of the two economies made up a sizeable share of total gross and value-added exports, other sectors also contributed significant shares to total gross and value-added exports. How much impact a shortage in semiconductor chips may have on the two economies will depend on several things, including the role of chips in the electrical and optical equipment sector and on the ability of other sectors to absorb or compensate for a supply crunch in the electrical and optical equipment sector and other chip-dependent sectors. With over half of Malaysia's electronics exports coming from integrated circuits, the economy may partly benefit from the chip shortage through increased prices, but, at the same time, may suffer from a shortage in supply for its other electronic products. In Viet Nam, integrated circuits exports play a smaller role, as the economy's electrical and optical equipment sector is known mostly for near-final goods production, which is highly dependent on the supply of chips. Thus, the impact of a shortage on Viet Nam's electrical and optical equipment sector may be larger. However, for these two economies, other sectors with sizeable shares appear to be less dependent on chip production, creating a buffer against the global shortage. The higher diversification in these two economies can reduce the negative impacts of the chip shortage because their economies are not highly dependent on any one sector.

Conclusion

The Asia and the Pacific region has been playing an increasingly large role in the GVCs for the electrical and optical equipment sector and in the exporting of semiconductor chips and electronic products. Most economies in East Asia and several in Southeast Asia show greater participation in the GVCs and exports of integrated circuits and electrical and optical equipment sector, making them vulnerable to the global shortage in chips. However, depending on which segment of the chain these economies are in, they can also benefit from the shortage in the immediate term.

Given the region's participation in the GVCs for semiconductors and the electrical and optical equipment sector, addressing the global chip shortage could benefit many economies in Asia and the Pacific. Policies to address such supply shortages in the face of excess demand should create resilient supply chains, especially in light of production bottlenecks induced by natural disasters, increased political instability across the world, and ever-growing scarcity of resources.

References

Asian Development Bank (ADB). 2022a. *Asian Economic Integration Report 2022: Advancing Digital Services Trade in Asia and the Pacific.* https://www.adb.org/publications/asian-economic-integration-report-2022

——. 2022b. Multiregional Input-Output Tables, 2000, 2007–2021. Retrieved 5 July 2022. https://mrio.adbx.online

——. 2022c. Global Value Chain Indicators, 2000, 2007–2021. Retrieved 5 July 2022. https://mrio.adbx.online

P. Bajaj, K. Baris, P.G. Gonzales, C.R. Jabagat, J.E. Lazatin, and E. Tan. 2022. A Case for Value-Added Exports in the Estimation of Export Diversification in Asia and the Pacific. *ADB Economics Working Paper* no. 650. https://www.adb.org/sites/default/files/publication/778261/ewp-650-value-added-exports-estimation-export-diversification.pdf

A. Borin and M. Mancini. 2019. Measuring What Matters in Global Value Chains and Value-Added Trade. *Policy Research Working Paper* No. 8804. https://openknowledge.worldbank.org/handle/10986/31533

O. Burkacky, J. Deichmann, P. Pfingstag, and J. Werra. 2022. Semiconductor Shortage: How the Automotive Industry Can Succeed. *McKinsey & Company*. 10 June. https://www.mckinsey.com/industries/semiconductors/our-insights/semiconductor-shortage-how-the-automotive-industry-can-succeed

Federal Reserve Bank of St. Louis. Import Price Index (Harmonized System): Electrical Machinery and Equipment and Parts Thereof; Sound Recorders and Reproducers, Television Image and Sound Recorders and Reproducers, and Parts and Accessories of Such Articles. https://fred.stlouisfed.org/series/IP85 (accessed 24 June 2022).

Federal Reserve Bank of St. Louis. Import Price Index (Harmonized System): Electronic Integrated Circuits; Parts Thereof. https://fred.stlouisfed.org/series/IP8542 (accessed 24 June 2022).

Observatory of Economic Complexity (OEC). Harmonized System (HS) Products. https://oec.world/en/product-landing/hs (accessed 10 June 2022).

Global Value Chain Tables for Economies of Asia and the Pacific

Table 3.1.1: Value-Added Decomposition of Exports

ADB Regional Member	Exports ($ million)	DAVAX	REX	REF	FVA	PDC
		(% share in exports)				
Australia						
2010	274,868.26	60.89	25.55	0.70	12.69	0.17
2019	327,004.59	65.38	21.74	0.75	11.93	0.20
2020	326,951.25	66.81	21.27	0.67	11.08	0.17
2021	344,536.72	64.81	24.40	0.64	10.00	0.15
Bangladesh						
2010	18,348.86	73.96	11.49	0.04	14.50	0.02
2019	45,530.63	74.11	3.64	0.02	22.23	0.01
2020	38,764.93	75.67	4.21	0.02	20.10	0.01
2021	43,979.86	74.48	4.27	0.02	21.23	0.01
Bhutan						
2010	520.74	66.13	17.75	0.01	16.11	0.00
2019	860.58	71.15	7.71	0.01	21.13	0.00
2020	689.69	74.21	6.82	0.01	18.97	0.00
2021	866.85	64.20	15.35	0.02	20.43	0.00
Brunei Darussalam						
2010	9,239.73	47.21	42.90	0.09	9.77	0.03
2019	7,804.89	52.24	26.05	0.03	21.68	0.01
2020	6,886.06	54.37	24.35	0.02	21.26	0.01
2021	6,382.65	54.57	25.47	0.02	19.97	0.00
Cambodia						
2010	4,040.54	61.64	11.11	0.01	27.23	0.00
2019	16,549.26	54.58	12.74	0.08	32.56	0.03
2020	15,793.23	52.89	12.88	0.10	34.09	0.04
2021	17,417.33	48.36	15.41	0.07	36.14	0.03
Fiji						
2010	1,159.77	58.88	12.69	0.01	28.42	0.00
2019	2,645.44	63.25	11.64	0.00	25.10	0.00
2020	1,235.39	62.60	14.58	0.01	26.52	0.00
2021	1,350.03	61.20	14.12	0.00	28.49	0.00
Hong Kong, China						
2010	143,433.66	57.46	12.06	0.13	30.16	0.20
2019	142,570.39	63.51	12.68	0.14	23.60	0.07
2020	119,725.93	64.92	12.63	0.14	22.26	0.06
2021	141,542.59	62.57	13.89	0.13	23.35	0.06
India						
2010	315,327.88	63.00	17.31	0.66	18.88	0.16
2019	532,827.28	66.45	13.73	0.48	19.21	0.12
2020	499,939.89	68.60	13.53	0.47	17.29	0.12
2021	665,757.86	65.39	13.81	0.52	20.14	0.15
Indonesia						
2010	183,521.00	59.89	24.41	0.65	14.89	0.16
2019	208,057.76	64.12	20.06	0.41	15.32	0.09
2020	182,850.63	65.72	20.24	0.36	13.61	0.07
2021	255,731.34	63.33	21.01	0.35	15.22	0.09

continued on next page

Table 3.1.1: continued

Table 3.1.1: Value-Added Decomposition of Exports						
ADB Regional Member	Exports ($ million)	DAVAX	REX	REF	FVA	PDC
		(% share in exports)				
Japan						
2010	835,356.24	63.21	19.84	1.25	15.29	0.41
2019	893,209.12	63.66	18.01	0.93	17.13	0.27
2020	784,375.78	64.09	19.36	1.04	15.25	0.27
2021	909,153.13	61.18	19.25	0.92	18.34	0.30
Kazakhstan						
2010	64,075.60	55.85	33.94	0.16	10.02	0.04
2019	63,749.95	55.80	32.18	0.19	11.78	0.05
2020	51,786.61	60.17	28.86	0.19	10.74	0.04
2021	65,583.88	56.07	33.93	0.18	9.78	0.04
Kyrgyz Republic						
2010	2,289.01	54.68	12.54	0.01	32.76	0.00
2019	3,125.60	51.51	21.79	0.03	26.66	0.01
2020	2,435.84	53.04	22.04	0.01	24.90	0.01
2021	3,661.41	49.84	22.78	0.02	27.36	0.01
Lao People's Democratic Republic						
2010	2,307.70	68.55	18.21	0.07	13.16	0.01
2019	6,474.52	61.21	25.61	0.11	13.05	0.02
2020	5,887.62	63.74	26.70	0.11	9.44	0.01
2021	8,049.97	60.91	27.99	0.10	10.98	0.02
Malaysia						
2010	221,762.42	43.87	17.56	0.35	37.63	0.58
2019	238,379.77	49.64	16.15	0.26	33.68	0.27
2020	207,035.98	48.08	17.36	0.26	34.05	0.25
2021	256,784.35	46.12	16.42	0.22	36.95	0.29
Maldives						
2010	1,790.11	54.89	14.29	0.00	30.81	0.00
2019	3,894.41	57.25	15.08	0.01	27.66	0.00
2020	1,786.51	61.91	14.08	0.00	24.00	0.00
2021	3,443.18	58.58	15.09	0.00	26.41	0.00
Mongolia						
2010	2,954.96	55.63	20.14	0.01	24.21	0.00
2019	8,047.16	55.54	16.53	0.01	27.91	0.01
2020	7,656.53	56.11	17.00	0.01	26.87	0.01
2021	9,019.02	54.35	17.54	0.01	28.09	0.01
Nepal						
2010	1,560.12	65.68	11.19	0.03	23.10	0.00
2019	2,666.05	58.37	13.11	0.05	28.47	0.00
2020	2,236.15	60.00	13.23	0.05	26.72	0.00
2021	1,834.54	61.14	12.77	0.05	26.03	0.00
Pakistan						
2010	23,586.96	73.89	15.83	0.05	10.24	0.00
2019	25,609.98	77.92	11.76	0.04	10.28	0.00
2020	25,758.77	79.41	11.22	0.04	9.34	0.00
2021	29,058.04	77.76	12.17	0.04	10.03	0.00
People's Republic of China						
2010	1,697,752.15	65.47	13.07	1.91	18.56	0.99
2019	2,641,283.02	66.51	13.65	2.52	16.47	0.85
2020	2,723,263.84	67.14	13.61	2.68	15.69	0.88
2021	3,553,522.92	64.96	13.90	2.88	17.16	1.10

continued on next page

Table 3.1.1: continued

Table 3.1.1: Value-Added Decomposition of Exports

ADB Regional Member	Exports ($ million)	DAVAX	REX	REF	FVA	PDC
		(% share in exports)				
Philippines						
2010	52,542.26	56.50	22.13	0.16	21.11	0.10
2019	82,157.70	58.48	17.96	0.17	23.34	0.06
2020	70,004.95	59.06	18.52	0.13	22.24	0.05
2021	78,018.17	55.96	17.03	0.13	26.82	0.06
Republic of Korea						
2010	518,902.44	49.09	14.91	0.36	35.17	0.47
2019	648,610.58	50.23	18.06	0.57	30.75	0.39
2020	596,945.09	53.11	18.86	0.58	27.10	0.35
2021	750,439.11	48.82	19.37	0.57	30.82	0.41
Singapore						
2010	304,907.06	36.67	13.24	0.20	49.06	0.84
2019	452,197.06	40.16	12.27	0.14	46.90	0.54
2020	423,639.04	41.31	10.98	0.12	47.08	0.51
2021	484,268.17	40.03	12.57	0.11	46.76	0.54
Sri Lanka						
2010	11,091.20	65.35	14.18	0.03	20.44	0.01
2019	19,426.21	65.82	10.80	0.02	23.36	0.01
2020	13,031.63	68.07	10.63	0.01	21.28	0.00
2021	15,370.75	67.02	9.87	0.01	23.09	0.00
Taipei,China						
2010	315,573.89	38.77	17.39	0.23	43.01	0.60
2019	385,509.36	42.45	17.49	0.26	39.29	0.51
2020	388,430.01	46.62	17.41	0.28	35.21	0.48
2021	513,719.17	44.05	17.60	0.31	37.42	0.62
Thailand						
2010	152,231.46	50.98	15.19	0.27	33.37	0.20
2019	323,768.89	57.15	11.89	0.18	30.63	0.15
2020	257,700.84	55.88	12.51	0.19	31.26	0.15
2021	294,554.35	52.25	12.72	0.20	34.67	0.16
Viet Nam						
2010	83,473.61	45.34	9.94	0.08	44.54	0.10
2019	279,720.22	44.58	6.55	0.10	48.57	0.20
2020	286,206.89	43.77	6.45	0.11	49.43	0.23
2021	335,869.10	38.80	5.91	0.09	54.97	0.23

$ = United States dollars, ADB = Asian Development Bank, DAVAX = domestic value-added immediately absorbed by direct importer, FVA = foreign value-added, PDC = pure double-counted terms, REF = re-exported domestic value-added absorbed by home economy, REX = re-exported domestic value-added absorbed abroad.

Source: Asian Development Bank. Multiregional Input-Output Tables. https://mrio.adbx.online/ (accessed 05 July 2022)

Table 3.2.1: Value-Added Decomposition of Exports—Primary Sector								
ADB Regional Member	By Export Sectors				By Origin Sectors			
	Total	DAVAX	REX+REF	FVA+PDC	Total	DAVAX	REX+REF	FVA+PDC
	($ million)	(% share in total)			($ million)	(% share in total)		
Australia								
2010	138,753.90	58.00	31.80	10.21	113,373.83	59.81	31.02	9.17
2019	169,411.19	64.31	26.25	9.44	135,242.77	67.49	27.00	5.51
2020	167,570.63	66.37	25.29	8.34	136,886.50	69.31	26.31	4.38
2021	182,245.51	63.90	28.59	7.51	154,522.38	66.12	29.27	4.61
Bangladesh								
2010	483.48	78.31	15.71	5.98	3,258.73	67.19	11.35	21.46
2019	320.92	67.12	22.74	10.14	6,074.09	62.13	2.54	35.33
2020	182.74	70.90	19.86	9.23	5,048.88	61.89	2.41	35.70
2021	208.84	72.89	17.25	9.86	5,832.67	58.52	2.44	39.04
Bhutan								
2010	72.77	81.23	12.49	6.27	86.44	73.06	11.21	15.74
2019	121.85	87.38	4.69	7.93	146.69	79.05	5.76	15.19
2020	64.86	89.42	7.69	2.89	84.15	74.85	6.44	18.71
2021	80.04	91.06	5.84	3.10	107.68	72.45	5.08	22.47
Brunei Darussalam								
2010	4,888.53	62.68	30.51	6.82	5,970.73	56.16	41.91	1.93
2019	4,212.97	49.02	31.03	19.95	4,349.70	58.90	33.31	7.80
2020	3,369.61	53.80	25.67	20.53	3,608.15	62.11	28.86	9.03
2021	2,931.77	52.42	27.42	20.16	3,489.88	60.79	30.03	9.18
Cambodia								
2010	221.32	55.22	34.86	9.92	703.53	54.94	18.46	26.60
2019	3,476.50	48.06	36.91	15.04	4,246.31	46.55	29.58	23.87
2020	4,015.44	50.97	33.03	16.01	4,543.37	49.50	28.45	22.05
2021	4,563.76	40.85	42.66	16.49	5,160.62	39.34	36.40	24.26
Fiji								
2010	85.34	64.27	8.29	27.44	194.25	45.02	6.58	48.40
2019	260.43	72.07	10.27	17.66	374.06	67.89	8.32	23.79
2020	155.47	68.52	12.59	19.04	194.52	71.09	10.90	18.01
2021	174.00	65.50	13.41	21.24	222.94	66.58	10.64	22.77
Hong Kong, China								
2010	87.98	33.49	16.10	50.41	3,526.13	0.69	0.30	99.01
2019	245.40	66.03	3.07	30.90	3,105.87	3.88	0.20	95.92
2020	204.09	71.97	4.20	23.83	2,465.13	4.79	0.30	94.91
2021	259.24	68.13	5.99	25.88	3,590.20	4.06	0.37	95.57
India								
2010	24,905.40	73.08	22.05	4.87	59,791.32	50.52	14.90	34.58
2019	34,691.53	72.90	20.95	6.15	91,901.89	52.11	11.88	36.01
2020	35,552.48	77.16	17.07	5.77	79,557.98	60.24	11.67	28.10
2021	49,950.41	73.49	19.85	6.65	117,726.93	53.63	12.12	34.25
Indonesia								
2010	48,635.33	54.93	38.45	6.62	70,190.64	58.61	32.98	8.41
2019	44,359.60	69.03	26.80	4.17	65,470.64	67.69	24.23	8.09
2020	36,970.10	70.09	26.35	3.56	56,117.22	69.38	23.91	6.71
2021	64,204.12	67.91	27.87	4.22	90,182.37	66.74	25.52	7.73
Japan								
2010	2,588.34	48.40	19.29	32.31	47,082.04	9.48	3.65	86.87
2019	3,199.94	53.09	20.69	26.21	49,708.39	10.37	3.30	86.32
2020	3,115.34	54.26	21.51	24.22	32,987.68	14.41	4.79	80.80
2021	3,473.51	50.62	20.48	28.90	47,713.87	11.27	3.92	84.81

continued on next page

Table 3.2.1: continued

Table 3.2.1: Value-Added Decomposition of Exports—Primary Sector

ADB Regional Member	By Export Sectors				By Origin Sectors			
	Total	DAVAX	REX+REF	FVA+PDC	Total	DAVAX	REX+REF	FVA+PDC
	($ million)	(% share in total)			($ million)	(% share in total)		
Kazakhstan								
2010	36,138.31	50.61	38.94	10.45	30,318.58	53.85	40.20	5.95
2019	38,608.56	48.53	39.07	12.40	27,308.24	54.34	41.51	4.15
2020	28,560.23	52.83	35.81	11.37	21,360.57	58.91	37.90	3.19
2021	35,852.82	49.63	40.34	10.03	28,170.15	54.76	41.88	3.36
Kyrgyz Republic								
2010	968.93	55.99	10.27	33.75	841.84	52.94	9.70	37.37
2019	613.66	61.83	13.74	24.43	483.59	60.44	12.52	27.04
2020	380.80	62.90	14.91	22.19	313.23	63.23	12.17	24.60
2021	681.51	61.58	12.89	25.54	571.64	61.47	11.59	26.93
Lao People's Democratic Republic								
2010	1,149.98	67.36	22.24	10.40	1,183.56	72.06	22.85	5.09
2019	2,210.04	62.14	27.20	10.66	2,405.28	63.86	27.21	8.93
2020	1,954.92	63.73	28.72	7.55	2,126.94	65.07	29.13	5.80
2021	2,991.35	61.43	29.80	8.77	3,180.16	62.36	30.10	7.54
Malaysia								
2010	22,272.41	60.72	29.27	10.01	52,089.38	47.21	21.11	31.68
2019	20,607.44	63.86	27.98	8.15	44,069.78	54.58	19.66	25.76
2020	15,098.26	64.37	27.31	8.31	34,884.12	54.54	20.72	24.74
2021	21,768.83	62.34	28.67	8.99	48,517.52	51.65	20.04	28.31
Maldives								
2010	19.66	47.16	7.79	45.05	169.66	43.07	10.66	46.28
2019	21.21	77.14	0.02	22.84	347.98	37.05	8.23	54.72
2020	38.09	79.30	0.27	20.43	204.57	52.23	8.30	39.47
2021	46.29	75.47	0.37	24.21	370.05	45.54	8.98	45.48
Mongolia								
2010	2,098.21	54.18	20.89	24.93	1,551.90	62.62	23.55	13.82
2019	6,567.25	55.96	16.40	27.64	4,224.72	72.96	21.32	5.72
2020	6,296.59	56.48	16.74	26.78	3,831.16	72.98	21.48	5.54
2021	7,526.61	54.76	17.18	28.07	4,578.95	71.27	22.22	6.51
Nepal								
2010	164.81	89.12	3.64	7.24	327.48	65.13	4.79	30.08
2019	132.97	87.00	5.07	7.93	440.60	45.85	4.21	49.94
2020	138.96	86.73	5.76	7.51	386.87	57.02	5.60	37.37
2021	141.17	86.08	6.68	7.23	359.76	59.11	6.35	34.54
Pakistan								
2010	1,066.91	84.14	11.85	4.01	7,372.38	72.98	14.63	12.38
2019	1,688.74	83.99	11.73	4.29	8,559.21	79.88	10.43	9.69
2020	1,134.73	78.29	18.12	3.59	8,629.70	80.90	11.01	8.09
2021	1,207.01	77.40	18.56	4.04	9,940.05	79.54	11.31	9.15
People's Republic of China								
2010	22,608.99	69.27	21.09	9.64	264,218.87	58.05	12.74	29.21
2019	24,485.76	73.59	19.23	7.18	322,381.54	57.97	13.47	28.55
2020	26,498.21	75.70	17.61	6.69	333,229.24	60.36	13.64	26.00
2021	33,242.98	73.35	19.13	7.51	472,387.18	57.28	14.08	28.64
Philippines								
2010	1,265.16	67.75	24.10	8.15	7,284.04	55.59	14.21	30.20
2019	1,535.24	78.41	13.23	8.36	7,292.35	44.67	9.13	46.20
2020	1,668.54	79.97	12.46	7.57	6,563.32	53.99	10.25	35.76
2021	1,994.51	76.80	13.93	9.26	8,430.16	46.53	9.94	43.54

continued on next page

Table 3.2.1: continued

Table 3.2.1: Value-Added Decomposition of Exports—Primary Sector

ADB Regional Member	By Export Sectors				By Origin Sectors			
	Total	DAVAX	REX+REF	FVA+PDC	Total	DAVAX	REX+REF	FVA+PDC
	($ million)	(% share in total)			($ million)	(% share in total)		
Republic of Korea								
2010	775.91	72.51	10.84	16.65	60,832.49	6.23	1.55	92.22
2019	754.04	73.06	10.86	16.07	52,453.99	5.87	1.36	92.77
2020	780.83	73.76	11.63	14.62	35,635.42	9.21	2.06	88.73
2021	927.48	71.05	12.99	15.96	59,973.34	6.12	1.52	92.36
Singapore								
2010	85.90	59.40	14.67	25.93	25,490.07	0.19	0.05	99.76
2019	115.41	54.27	15.68	30.06	19,606.93	0.30	0.08	99.63
2020	110.27	55.14	15.28	29.59	12,180.07	0.44	0.11	99.45
2021	126.29	57.50	12.81	29.69	16,549.85	0.38	0.09	99.53
Sri Lanka								
2010	392.44	65.83	22.53	11.64	1,504.86	48.46	11.51	40.03
2019	417.91	73.32	15.42	11.25	2,194.96	43.96	7.12	48.93
2020	404.87	75.56	14.87	9.57	1,519.26	54.10	8.05	37.84
2021	557.13	75.41	15.55	9.04	2,072.12	50.79	8.63	40.58
Taipei,China								
2010	1,651.57	65.71	8.71	25.58	33,449.08	4.54	1.03	94.43
2019	890.85	68.15	12.17	19.68	28,964.18	6.40	1.41	92.19
2020	896.46	69.13	13.07	17.80	21,402.86	8.66	1.84	89.50
2021	1,067.25	67.05	13.70	19.25	32,618.98	6.69	1.52	91.79
Thailand								
2010	4,913.82	55.63	31.24	13.14	20,197.43	37.45	12.07	50.47
2019	19,370.52	70.61	14.20	15.19	50,430.46	44.91	7.06	48.03
2020	18,416.62	72.17	14.75	13.08	40,332.42	51.46	8.42	40.12
2021	18,950.09	67.76	17.32	14.92	48,791.42	44.32	8.52	47.16
Viet Nam								
2010	13,065.86	48.47	15.57	35.97	20,224.43	47.69	11.12	41.19
2019	16,357.87	49.75	12.52	37.74	51,258.46	44.88	5.86	49.27
2020	16,230.36	51.71	10.97	37.32	51,156.60	46.37	5.13	48.50
2021	21,633.81	48.75	11.29	39.96	67,440.08	40.86	4.53	54.61

$ = United States dollars, ADB = Asian Development Bank, DAVAX = domestic value-added immediately absorbed by direct importer, FVA = foreign value-added, PDC = pure double-counted terms, REF = re-exported domestic value-added absorbed by home economy, REX = re-exported domestic value-added absorbed abroad.

Source: Asian Development Bank. Multiregional Input-Output Tables. https://mrio.adbx.online/ (accessed 05 July 2022).

Table 3.2.2: Value-Added Decomposition of Exports—Low-Technology Manufacturing Sector

ADB Regional Member	By Export Sectors				By Origin Sectors			
	Total	DAVAX	REX+REF	FVA+PDC	Total	DAVAX	REX+REF	FVA+PDC
	($ million)	(% share in total)			($ million)	(% share in total)		
Australia								
2010	25,502.55	76.17	10.43	13.40	25,958.53	66.40	19.69	13.91
2019	30,097.25	77.26	7.82	14.92	28,790.67	68.83	16.41	14.76
2020	31,435.15	78.10	7.00	14.89	28,908.93	70.26	15.75	13.99
2021	31,921.58	76.57	9.59	13.84	29,292.26	67.33	18.30	14.38
Bangladesh								
2010	15,825.13	73.09	11.20	15.71	7,188.26	78.48	11.98	9.55
2019	38,756.14	74.26	1.14	24.60	19,478.85	86.10	1.51	12.39
2020	32,402.15	75.99	1.59	22.42	16,294.98	86.45	2.08	11.47
2021	36,978.84	74.62	1.80	23.59	18,379.83	85.21	2.31	12.49
Bhutan								
2010	210.42	60.18	27.96	11.86	228.70	65.24	25.21	9.55
2019	350.84	73.76	0.79	25.44	294.48	82.45	2.15	15.40
2020	345.00	80.79	0.49	18.72	305.23	90.33	1.57	8.10
2021	430.97	65.93	13.94	20.12	372.02	76.31	16.12	7.57
Brunei Darussalam								
2010	29.64	46.54	6.65	46.81	126.92	20.76	15.54	63.71
2019	94.73	43.44	4.21	52.35	264.39	18.92	4.05	77.03
2020	99.38	41.71	3.61	54.69	241.35	22.69	4.93	72.39
2021	81.13	42.80	4.49	52.72	206.15	17.45	3.10	79.45
Cambodia								
2010	2,124.18	59.96	4.05	35.98	1,467.60	73.16	5.16	21.67
2019	7,198.29	50.88	1.65	47.47	4,833.95	67.88	2.69	29.43
2020	7,200.42	48.59	2.03	49.37	4,636.70	65.53	3.15	31.32
2021	8,784.63	47.20	2.21	50.60	5,346.16	66.48	3.36	30.16
Fiji								
2010	207.66	66.37	9.80	23.83	164.94	67.24	10.97	21.78
2019	497.50	69.72	6.36	23.92	351.11	71.49	8.26	20.25
2020	238.49	70.59	7.65	21.91	165.13	69.84	9.82	20.34
2021	294.79	67.07	6.99	26.11	192.02	68.70	9.32	21.98
Hong Kong, China								
2010	10,503.80	43.74	8.65	47.61	8,498.59	43.65	8.89	47.45
2019	6,989.62	44.90	8.84	46.25	7,398.83	36.40	6.77	56.82
2020	4,982.97	48.25	7.48	44.27	6,047.14	36.99	5.98	57.03
2021	6,024.46	42.32	7.34	50.34	7,634.08	33.40	6.04	60.56
India								
2010	50,210.11	68.88	12.55	18.57	30,064.99	65.87	15.38	18.75
2019	83,816.13	74.67	10.19	15.14	57,353.42	68.72	12.87	18.41
2020	75,581.76	75.22	10.40	14.38	51,463.27	69.76	13.08	17.16
2021	103,519.55	72.57	10.47	16.95	69,849.31	65.99	12.78	21.23
Indonesia								
2010	61,583.24	65.93	18.04	16.03	33,623.86	70.32	19.02	10.65
2019	74,722.45	66.43	13.30	20.27	42,711.83	73.34	15.04	11.61
2020	67,958.20	68.58	13.85	17.58	38,627.92	74.40	15.43	10.17
2021	86,070.29	65.25	14.32	20.43	48,883.88	71.80	15.89	12.31
Japan								
2010	48,927.35	59.78	26.99	13.23	80,192.82	62.71	24.11	13.18
2019	48,371.14	63.79	23.33	12.88	83,517.81	63.78	20.53	15.69
2020	45,271.44	65.09	23.26	11.65	74,256.27	64.27	21.57	14.16
2021	51,256.85	62.89	22.81	14.30	88,887.46	61.43	21.39	17.17

continued on next page

Table 3.2.2: continued

Table 3.2.2: Value-Added Decomposition of Exports—Low-Technology Manufacturing Sector								
ADB Regional Member	By Export Sectors				By Origin Sectors			
	Total ($ million)	DAVAX (% share in total)	REX+REF	FVA+PDC	Total ($ million)	DAVAX (% share in total)	REX+REF	FVA+PDC
Kazakhstan								
2010	993.75	64.31	20.72	14.97	1,872.96	48.34	21.71	29.95
2019	1,932.26	72.01	11.79	16.21	2,597.37	54.88	18.29	26.84
2020	1,824.75	74.81	11.27	13.92	2,140.55	60.31	15.63	24.06
2021	3,202.07	72.89	14.27	12.83	3,107.36	62.28	18.42	19.29
Kyrgyz Republic								
2010	221.19	46.65	6.39	46.96	170.74	45.30	6.76	47.94
2019	406.05	65.24	4.52	30.24	296.66	64.15	7.43	28.42
2020	332.95	68.69	3.63	27.68	252.42	69.13	7.74	23.14
2021	438.88	64.81	4.71	30.48	357.27	60.36	10.13	29.51
Lao People's Democratic Republic								
2010	600.65	76.36	8.82	14.82	407.57	84.37	7.85	7.78
2019	3,111.61	60.49	26.41	13.10	2,384.01	64.93	30.09	4.98
2020	3,049.61	62.45	27.62	9.93	2,431.46	66.64	30.10	3.26
2021	3,874.05	59.53	28.76	11.71	2,944.74	64.17	31.99	3.84
Malaysia								
2010	65,036.85	43.95	15.76	40.29	23,776.93	48.14	16.20	35.66
2019	56,413.69	53.57	14.07	32.36	27,308.22	55.61	15.83	28.56
2020	53,808.97	51.95	16.94	31.12	24,524.78	54.57	18.50	26.93
2021	70,243.43	50.42	15.82	33.76	31,750.67	52.63	17.42	29.94
Maldives								
2010	30.89	47.04	9.27	43.69	168.36	38.06	9.25	52.69
2019	71.19	61.99	4.02	33.99	282.44	28.55	6.55	64.90
2020	77.76	66.72	3.33	29.94	123.13	34.93	5.88	59.18
2021	107.61	62.98	2.65	34.92	234.64	26.97	5.18	67.85
Mongolia								
2010	125.72	64.95	11.82	23.23	184.29	48.46	14.86	36.68
2019	231.15	57.62	9.41	32.97	509.87	42.59	11.08	46.32
2020	234.32	60.77	9.35	29.88	613.10	49.31	13.62	37.07
2021	250.89	58.83	10.30	30.87	617.39	42.18	12.10	45.72
Nepal								
2010	343.28	63.21	9.15	27.64	226.21	66.18	10.77	23.04
2019	541.67	71.24	7.30	21.46	303.59	61.18	7.68	31.14
2020	481.98	72.24	7.46	20.30	264.44	63.17	8.11	28.72
2021	503.51	71.83	8.56	19.61	248.35	66.00	9.19	24.81
Pakistan								
2010	12,497.72	74.13	16.06	9.82	4,436.24	76.64	16.31	7.06
2019	15,131.69	79.59	10.09	10.32	5,218.75	82.71	10.41	6.88
2020	16,157.32	80.64	9.81	9.56	5,549.73	83.66	10.03	6.31
2021	18,707.51	79.82	10.14	10.04	6,294.19	82.91	10.49	6.60
People's Republic of China								
2010	373,984.43	78.05	8.54	13.41	272,183.27	76.19	11.90	11.91
2019	606,343.82	77.61	10.96	11.43	419,932.90	75.31	13.57	11.11
2020	623,086.55	77.83	11.33	10.84	428,346.91	75.16	13.77	11.08
2021	816,803.96	75.70	12.31	11.99	574,982.29	73.23	14.70	12.07
Philippines								
2010	10,611.31	72.61	13.35	14.04	8,516.89	68.52	17.13	14.34
2019	11,052.85	73.03	11.96	15.02	9,452.76	66.64	13.76	19.60
2020	10,963.88	74.57	11.84	13.59	8,615.42	68.14	14.01	17.85
2021	12,328.52	70.37	13.38	16.26	9,448.67	64.03	14.39	21.57

continued on next page

Table 3.2.2: continued

Table 3.2.2: Value-Added Decomposition of Exports—Low-Technology Manufacturing Sector

ADB Regional Member	By Export Sectors				By Origin Sectors			
	Total	DAVAX	REX+REF	FVA+PDC	Total	DAVAX	REX+REF	FVA+PDC
	($ million)	(% share in total)			($ million)	(% share in total)		
Republic of Korea								
2010	36,177.69	52.46	18.94	28.60	47,340.91	46.51	15.84	37.66
2019	39,193.22	51.16	22.65	26.20	61,348.48	49.22	19.50	31.28
2020	39,388.03	54.35	21.41	24.24	60,174.76	53.09	20.01	26.90
2021	43,488.92	52.04	21.68	26.29	72,584.83	48.13	19.90	31.97
Singapore								
2010	11,793.32	39.25	6.51	54.24	18,218.36	34.43	9.95	55.63
2019	13,638.42	49.36	7.90	42.73	23,935.39	33.16	7.36	59.48
2020	11,538.27	49.68	7.15	43.18	20,694.97	33.17	6.76	60.07
2021	12,309.97	48.35	8.90	42.75	23,687.69	30.18	7.45	62.37
Sri Lanka								
2010	5,779.00	69.47	8.89	21.65	3,778.44	77.14	10.80	12.07
2019	8,054.06	66.15	5.76	28.10	5,620.56	76.16	6.94	16.90
2020	6,707.38	69.84	5.24	24.92	4,291.30	79.47	6.29	14.24
2021	10,000.37	69.54	5.80	24.65	6,199.24	79.92	6.43	13.65
Taipei,China								
2010	22,044.54	41.44	16.00	42.56	25,438.91	37.02	15.21	47.77
2019	30,841.91	45.57	19.23	35.20	33,128.62	42.12	17.55	40.33
2020	29,755.56	49.61	19.49	30.90	33,675.11	45.58	17.64	36.78
2021	39,216.44	46.97	20.20	32.83	43,600.99	42.02	17.71	40.27
Thailand								
2010	32,265.52	59.72	14.16	26.11	23,438.04	62.75	17.92	19.32
2019	81,048.40	63.63	9.95	26.41	48,785.07	66.08	12.74	21.18
2020	75,259.22	66.04	9.98	23.98	41,869.92	66.62	13.23	20.15
2021	82,075.46	61.25	10.51	28.24	46,428.39	62.87	13.66	23.47
Viet Nam								
2010	42,158.30	46.48	5.63	47.89	20,082.67	65.55	8.59	25.86
2019	161,943.33	49.99	3.34	46.67	70,923.50	65.94	5.64	28.42
2020	161,108.28	49.61	3.17	47.23	70,677.81	64.26	5.41	30.33
2021	190,188.97	43.73	2.64	53.62	81,356.28	59.54	5.04	35.42

$ = United States dollars, ADB = Asian Development Bank, DAVAX = domestic value-added immediately absorbed by direct importer, FVA = foreign value-added, PDC = pure double-counted terms, REF = re-exported domestic value-added absorbed by home economy, REX = re-exported domestic value-added absorbed abroad.

Source: Asian Development Bank. Multiregional Input-Output Tables. https://mrio.adbx.online/ (accessed 05 July 2022).

Table 3.2.3: Value-Added Decomposition of Exports—Medium- and High-Technology Manufacturing Sector

ADB Regional Member	By Export Sectors				By Origin Sectors			
	Total	DAVAX	REX+REF	FVA+PDC	Total	DAVAX	REX+REF	FVA+PDC
	($ million)	(% share in total)			($ million)	(% share in total)		
Australia								
2010	53,320.57	52.65	23.70	23.65	30,418.37	50.06	21.27	28.67
2019	50,831.01	52.68	23.43	23.89	29,251.65	44.75	17.16	38.09
2020	52,404.01	53.68	24.90	21.42	28,497.25	46.48	17.76	35.76
2021	53,351.24	51.39	28.35	20.27	28,676.49	44.35	20.97	34.67
Bangladesh								
2010	428.51	76.47	8.74	14.79	1,033.21	47.14	6.41	46.45
2019	783.29	67.81	16.90	15.29	3,151.38	33.32	3.31	63.37
2020	723.04	69.59	15.73	14.68	2,628.21	40.01	3.89	56.10
2021	890.78	67.58	16.27	16.15	3,198.75	41.89	4.16	53.95
Bhutan								
2010	103.79	75.02	3.79	21.19	52.60	63.30	4.57	32.13
2019	84.52	58.92	15.67	25.41	77.63	44.02	9.76	46.22
2020	65.48	57.32	11.05	31.64	61.65	41.52	6.83	51.65
2021	82.84	49.70	10.10	40.20	73.36	37.92	7.80	54.29
Brunei Darussalam								
2010	3,613.84	25.87	65.18	8.95	1,939.41	29.20	61.19	9.61
2019	2,879.38	58.97	21.45	19.57	1,767.71	59.37	22.63	18.00
2020	3,073.38	56.53	24.22	19.24	1,792.68	59.88	25.95	14.16
2021	2,959.42	58.13	25.06	16.81	1,780.69	59.10	25.98	14.92
Cambodia								
2010	26.33	52.27	11.56	36.16	224.95	10.62	2.26	87.11
2019	263.07	52.41	7.61	39.98	1,085.59	15.44	2.79	81.76
2020	327.02	49.70	8.28	42.02	1,139.99	17.66	3.34	79.00
2021	413.55	49.87	7.23	42.89	1,252.04	19.67	3.89	76.44
Fiji								
2010	24.77	54.92	7.52	37.57	94.98	18.66	2.96	78.38
2019	63.28	49.12	16.35	34.54	153.62	23.51	6.28	70.22
2020	27.18	55.09	11.85	33.49	77.50	24.00	5.43	70.57
2021	35.96	50.07	11.91	38.47	90.31	22.95	5.65	71.40
Hong Kong, China								
2010	11,308.48	15.25	7.12	77.63	7,809.99	5.21	2.59	92.19
2019	9,815.22	22.39	6.37	71.24	6,301.25	5.77	1.72	92.51
2020	9,725.61	22.41	7.62	69.97	5,768.64	5.62	1.99	92.39
2021	10,068.82	16.33	6.35	77.33	6,782.72	4.66	1.88	93.46
India								
2010	100,793.88	47.35	18.04	34.61	53,860.37	57.79	20.48	21.73
2019	190,637.85	49.45	15.65	34.90	100,170.07	62.48	19.28	18.23
2020	175,502.68	52.35	15.80	31.86	102,019.84	64.66	19.06	16.28
2021	240,257.49	47.72	15.05	37.23	138,862.26	62.09	19.24	18.67
Indonesia								
2010	58,384.31	55.38	22.53	22.09	38,255.53	55.73	21.87	22.40
2019	60,063.35	56.28	23.55	20.17	39,596.00	55.69	21.22	23.09
2020	52,934.48	57.81	23.94	18.24	34,996.49	56.84	21.79	21.36
2021	72,752.02	55.30	23.29	21.41	47,682.29	54.39	21.30	24.31
Japan								
2010	591,965.90	61.07	20.77	18.16	353,505.53	67.67	22.34	9.99
2019	648,406.01	60.46	18.68	20.86	375,103.85	68.71	21.42	9.87
2020	586,971.46	61.59	20.18	18.22	350,653.46	68.06	22.49	9.45
2021	671,104.46	57.38	20.49	22.14	384,955.00	64.70	23.32	11.98

continued on next page

Table 3.2.3: continued

Table 3.2.3: Value-Added Decomposition of Exports—Medium- and High-Technology Manufacturing Sector

ADB Regional Member	By Export Sectors				By Origin Sectors			
	Total	DAVAX	REX+REF	FVA+PDC	Total	DAVAX	REX+REF	FVA+PDC
	($ million)	(% share in total)			($ million)	(% share in total)		
Kazakhstan								
2010	12,807.45	53.66	35.90	10.44	10,023.65	49.09	32.60	18.31
2019	12,012.13	61.80	27.26	10.94	10,042.19	49.80	24.17	26.03
2020	11,272.12	64.15	25.34	10.51	9,381.50	55.03	23.31	21.66
2021	20,676.72	59.85	30.72	9.43	13,786.75	54.40	28.41	17.19
Kyrgyz Republic								
2010	791.22	55.58	15.57	28.84	711.58	60.45	16.95	22.60
2019	1,377.96	34.42	34.51	31.07	1,184.63	36.27	37.31	26.42
2020	1,107.99	36.07	34.87	29.06	970.21	38.27	38.08	23.65
2021	1,597.71	32.01	36.91	31.08	1,299.55	32.53	38.65	28.82
Lao People's Democratic Republic								
2010	8.85	42.28	22.38	35.34	113.78	10.26	3.51	86.22
2019	20.43	38.35	29.53	32.12	231.01	12.19	5.20	82.62
2020	26.17	43.12	31.65	25.23	183.48	16.43	7.38	76.19
2021	36.89	39.66	31.48	28.86	286.52	16.27	7.83	75.90
Malaysia								
2010	74,578.51	28.19	16.72	55.08	62,320.88	33.63	17.23	49.15
2019	85,362.59	32.15	14.83	53.01	66,181.95	37.16	15.69	47.15
2020	80,544.49	32.80	14.91	52.29	61,257.73	37.11	16.01	46.88
2021	101,519.96	30.79	13.01	56.20	77,932.84	35.77	14.48	49.75
Maldives								
2010	0.78	57.50	3.77	38.74	61.02	4.52	1.03	94.45
2019	1.64	57.37	14.55	28.08	125.04	2.99	0.74	96.27
2020	2.05	57.03	18.14	24.83	57.38	4.45	1.04	94.51
2021	3.29	63.43	8.67	27.99	114.14	3.98	0.76	95.26
Mongolia								
2010	57.57	48.13	17.24	34.63	284.85	11.64	4.22	84.13
2019	206.47	36.83	35.29	27.89	732.94	8.61	6.85	84.54
2020	209.97	35.74	38.30	25.96	705.65	10.24	8.10	81.66
2021	236.23	33.84	39.98	26.18	860.28	8.45	7.71	83.84
Nepal								
2010	172.75	47.61	9.43	42.95	140.45	36.20	6.93	56.86
2019	336.40	49.07	7.38	43.55	275.39	40.55	6.31	53.14
2020	294.09	49.78	6.78	43.44	241.90	40.20	5.81	54.00
2021	298.43	47.89	9.94	42.17	224.19	41.62	8.57	49.81
Pakistan								
2010	1,470.11	56.22	17.06	26.72	1,503.73	53.39	13.55	33.06
2019	1,428.13	60.80	14.07	25.13	1,612.63	54.54	10.70	34.76
2020	973.02	62.55	14.61	22.84	1,345.88	51.05	9.55	39.40
2021	1,128.75	57.46	16.50	26.03	1,576.32	49.21	10.78	40.01
People's Republic of China								
2010	1,012,324.70	59.87	15.34	24.79	592,153.63	65.35	16.01	18.64
2019	1,638,989.82	61.59	16.62	21.79	893,998.95	65.72	17.32	16.96
2020	1,696,018.20	62.52	16.56	20.92	926,718.42	66.18	17.17	16.65
2021	2,224,310.53	59.76	17.29	22.95	1,204,862.19	63.93	18.06	18.01
Philippines								
2010	21,597.88	36.60	26.40	37.00	12,460.43	38.78	26.54	34.68
2019	30,927.51	38.73	15.36	45.91	17,740.23	40.94	15.78	43.28
2020	26,739.00	40.19	15.57	44.24	15,066.17	40.94	15.65	43.40
2021	31,085.86	34.39	13.81	51.80	18,264.58	36.88	14.72	48.40

continued on next page

Table 3.2.3: continued

Table 3.2.3: Value-Added Decomposition of Exports—Medium- and High-Technology Manufacturing Sector

ADB Regional Member	By Export Sectors				By Origin Sectors			
	Total	DAVAX	REX+REF	FVA+PDC	Total	DAVAX	REX+REF	FVA+PDC
	($ million)	(% share in total)			($ million)	(% share in total)		
Republic of Korea								
2010	427,862.23	47.31	14.37	38.31	246,379.44	59.62	18.26	22.12
2019	513,811.10	47.91	18.49	33.60	298,744.48	58.41	22.82	18.77
2020	467,004.12	50.92	19.42	29.66	281,440.83	59.32	22.92	17.75
2021	596,758.50	46.23	19.92	33.85	347,620.52	56.32	24.60	19.08
Singapore								
2010	146,471.99	27.13	12.86	60.01	76,898.67	37.20	17.54	45.25
2019	158,867.13	36.21	13.30	50.49	94,420.12	46.43	16.85	36.71
2020	151,450.02	39.46	11.53	49.00	88,274.20	50.68	14.58	34.74
2021	181,192.83	36.87	14.26	48.87	106,502.08	47.56	18.18	34.26
Sri Lanka								
2010	928.69	49.20	9.63	41.17	978.90	47.45	9.51	43.04
2019	1,672.66	46.74	10.36	42.90	1,768.83	44.65	9.28	46.07
2020	1,333.90	50.10	12.25	37.65	1,217.78	48.55	11.13	40.31
2021	1,918.50	48.07	13.72	38.21	1,672.43	48.05	12.78	39.16
Taipei,China								
2010	240,938.23	34.37	17.15	48.48	150,968.93	45.49	23.02	31.49
2019	309,890.91	39.48	17.28	43.25	200,247.38	48.66	21.70	29.64
2020	321,583.58	44.34	17.09	38.58	217,483.09	52.74	20.62	26.64
2021	422,257.77	41.64	17.23	41.13	280,234.33	49.98	20.93	29.09
Thailand								
2010	79,185.74	41.23	14.37	44.39	44,066.27	47.68	16.00	36.31
2019	116,188.81	42.27	11.62	46.11	70,728.33	52.29	12.36	35.35
2020	118,116.06	44.17	12.36	43.47	68,513.73	52.51	13.12	34.37
2021	121,989.04	38.95	10.85	50.20	69,133.62	49.77	12.37	37.86
Viet Nam								
2010	17,018.58	33.51	13.47	53.02	17,618.47	29.94	10.89	59.16
2019	86,088.15	31.30	9.98	58.72	73,335.44	30.00	8.24	61.76
2020	93,849.60	30.23	9.80	59.97	79,894.04	29.20	8.36	62.44
2021	104,954.36	24.99	8.79	66.23	92,888.97	26.10	8.36	65.54

$ = United States dollars, ADB = Asian Development Bank, DAVAX = domestic value-added immediately absorbed by direct importer, FVA = foreign value-added, PDC = pure double-counted terms, REF = re-exported domestic value-added absorbed by home economy, REX = re-exported domestic value-added absorbed abroad.

Source: Asian Development Bank. Multiregional Input-Output Tables. https://mrio.adbx.online/ (accessed 05 July 2022).

Table 3.2.4: Value-Added Decomposition of Exports—Business Services Sector

ADB Regional Member	By Export Sectors				By Origin Sectors			
	Total	DAVAX	REX+REF	FVA+PDC	Total	DAVAX	REX+REF	FVA+PDC
	($ million)	(% share in total)			($ million)	(% share in total)		
Australia								
2010	50,135.67	67.10	23.56	9.34	93,297.07	62.90	24.57	12.53
2019	61,681.68	69.09	21.59	9.31	117,890.45	65.53	21.23	13.24
2020	60,535.27	69.56	20.92	9.52	116,926.49	66.29	20.49	13.22
2021	61,819.37	68.62	23.16	8.22	116,400.99	65.62	23.42	10.96
Bangladesh								
2010	1,427.57	80.16	14.48	5.36	5,076.26	73.69	11.68	14.62
2019	5,199.41	74.55	17.57	7.87	13,917.22	69.25	6.66	24.09
2020	4,897.75	74.42	17.97	7.61	12,014.56	72.18	7.39	20.43
2021	5,293.40	74.66	17.44	7.90	13,477.37	71.89	7.21	20.90
Bhutan								
2010	123.96	59.70	15.25	25.05	141.37	64.16	14.89	20.96
2019	274.41	64.14	14.71	21.15	317.51	63.80	12.85	23.35
2020	186.23	62.51	15.54	21.95	213.58	60.79	13.68	25.53
2021	240.71	55.66	23.03	21.31	283.36	51.63	20.60	27.77
Brunei Darussalam								
2010	676.52	48.70	17.54	33.75	1,054.08	32.57	20.05	47.37
2019	525.52	42.19	17.39	40.42	1,307.23	27.52	11.99	60.49
2020	293.47	42.09	19.54	38.37	1,121.32	27.72	12.00	60.28
2021	350.35	44.70	19.27	36.41	839.29	28.80	11.89	59.30
Cambodia								
2010	1,597.60	64.97	16.84	18.19	1,556.98	61.14	14.40	24.46
2019	5,463.60	63.38	12.56	24.06	6,099.05	56.61	11.10	32.29
2020	4,161.52	62.11	13.05	24.84	5,244.97	52.52	10.54	36.94
2021	3,580.07	60.22	14.46	25.32	5,432.61	46.15	10.48	43.37
Fiji								
2010	824.07	56.17	14.12	29.71	674.51	66.35	16.43	17.23
2019	1,760.47	59.96	13.30	26.74	1,642.29	63.58	13.82	22.60
2020	785.46	58.45	17.49	29.79	779.49	58.39	16.95	24.66
2021	808.55	57.66	17.31	31.28	825.74	57.53	16.59	25.88
Hong Kong, China								
2010	120,938.90	62.58	12.91	24.51	118,546.96	63.72	13.42	22.86
2019	122,121.25	67.44	13.66	18.90	119,557.17	69.47	14.17	16.36
2020	102,812.77	69.43	13.60	16.97	100,803.69	71.12	14.15	14.73
2021	121,280.56	66.85	15.19	17.96	117,494.74	69.08	15.77	15.15
India								
2010	128,576.96	68.55	20.61	10.84	155,362.83	67.42	19.88	12.70
2019	210,943.32	76.10	13.94	9.97	262,481.79	71.87	13.82	14.31
2020	204,234.53	77.67	13.64	8.69	251,354.89	72.39	13.23	14.38
2021	258,799.71	76.17	14.56	9.27	317,851.23	70.67	13.73	15.60
Indonesia								
2010	12,909.05	67.52	21.36	11.12	38,109.33	56.99	19.75	23.26
2019	23,739.19	65.21	23.70	11.09	54,208.30	58.39	19.82	21.79
2020	20,218.72	65.42	25.41	9.17	47,720.74	60.16	20.46	19.38
2021	26,562.69	65.32	23.80	10.88	62,159.49	58.12	19.94	21.93
Japan								
2010	188,197.35	70.70	20.71	8.59	333,935.56	66.26	21.51	12.23
2019	188,759.93	74.27	18.92	6.81	361,303.29	65.50	18.22	16.28
2020	145,556.12	73.54	20.62	5.84	307,282.55	64.69	19.49	15.82
2021	179,208.37	74.60	18.53	6.87	364,452.70	63.70	18.76	17.54

continued on next page

Table 3.2.4: continued

Table 3.2.4: Value-Added Decomposition of Exports—Business Services Sector

ADB Regional Member	By Export Sectors				By Origin Sectors			
	Total	DAVAX	REX+REF	FVA+PDC	Total	DAVAX	REX+REF	FVA+PDC
	($ million)	(% share in total)			($ million)	(% share in total)		
Kazakhstan								
2010	13,483.76	70.18	21.61	8.21	21,103.99	62.37	27.70	9.92
2019	10,781.67	71.28	18.63	10.10	23,184.85	60.27	27.29	12.44
2020	9,867.48	73.51	17.62	8.87	18,486.74	64.33	23.76	11.91
2021	5,718.63	72.74	18.95	8.31	20,145.81	58.32	29.95	11.72
Kyrgyz Republic								
2010	239.78	52.40	16.05	31.55	509.30	51.93	12.50	35.57
2019	428.40	61.74	14.75	23.51	897.40	54.96	13.39	31.65
2020	331.21	60.70	14.10	25.20	648.13	53.87	12.03	34.10
2021	558.71	55.26	16.15	28.58	1,092.92	51.57	17.08	31.35
Lao People's Democratic Republic								
2010	525.67	62.52	20.60	16.88	581.67	61.91	19.42	18.67
2019	1,127.86	61.70	20.94	17.36	1,434.72	59.00	19.59	21.41
2020	855.55	68.96	19.42	11.62	1,132.84	63.22	18.79	17.98
2021	1,145.85	64.86	21.28	13.86	1,619.44	60.53	20.93	18.55
Malaysia								
2010	58,382.07	56.35	17.92	25.73	78,512.67	49.44	17.76	32.80
2019	73,524.06	62.03	17.07	20.90	95,202.01	55.31	16.24	28.46
2020	55,200.86	60.93	19.91	19.15	81,919.94	52.07	17.81	30.12
2021	60,926.03	59.81	19.60	20.59	93,310.59	50.48	17.03	32.49
Maldives								
2010	1,707.68	55.10	14.41	30.49	1,348.60	60.81	15.95	23.24
2019	3,734.00	56.62	15.45	27.93	2,968.53	64.02	17.34	18.64
2020	1,617.11	60.68	15.05	24.27	1,283.15	67.29	16.35	16.36
2021	3,196.73	57.58	15.86	26.63	2,537.91	64.72	17.57	17.71
Mongolia								
2010	667.77	58.91	19.77	21.32	886.62	59.10	20.56	20.34
2019	996.89	55.77	15.50	28.74	2,436.78	43.32	12.81	43.87
2020	875.41	56.53	16.25	27.21	2,370.07	45.18	13.76	41.07
2021	960.96	54.48	17.20	28.32	2,783.12	44.15	14.56	41.29
Nepal								
2010	780.53	64.42	13.56	22.02	795.84	70.07	14.42	15.51
2019	1,581.83	52.71	17.08	30.21	1,547.41	63.76	17.88	18.37
2020	1,250.95	53.79	17.91	28.31	1,252.74	63.12	18.01	18.88
2021	846.12	54.54	17.33	28.13	934.96	64.46	17.06	18.47
Pakistan								
2010	7,061.63	72.65	17.80	9.55	8,965.98	74.74	18.29	6.96
2019	5,710.26	75.12	15.30	9.58	8,631.63	76.92	13.89	9.20
2020	5,875.76	76.87	14.30	8.83	8,687.86	78.34	13.04	8.62
2021	6,247.73	73.48	16.91	9.60	9,566.85	76.20	14.76	9.04
People's Republic of China								
2010	276,698.17	68.17	21.96	9.87	535,048.38	63.96	16.56	19.49
2019	352,710.76	69.46	22.80	7.74	934,087.72	66.22	17.11	16.67
2020	360,192.19	69.18	23.68	7.14	965,398.59	66.76	17.46	15.79
2021	457,902.75	69.81	22.33	7.86	1,215,439.69	64.95	17.56	17.49
Philippines								
2010	18,372.71	69.22	22.66	8.12	23,204.98	61.75	24.62	13.63
2019	37,111.56	69.09	22.63	8.28	45,462.94	65.57	21.50	12.93
2020	29,571.50	68.55	24.48	6.97	38,138.56	64.86	22.44	12.70
2021	31,491.78	69.62	22.24	8.14	40,184.00	64.50	20.51	14.99

continued on next page

Table 3.2.4: continued

Table 3.2.4: Value-Added Decomposition of Exports—Business Services Sector

ADB Regional Member	By Export Sectors				By Origin Sectors			
	Total	DAVAX	REX+REF	FVA+PDC	Total	DAVAX	REX+REF	FVA+PDC
	($ million)	(% share in total)			($ million)	(% share in total)		
Republic of Korea								
2010	50,284.70	60.01	20.16	19.83	150,065.83	49.36	15.57	35.07
2019	92,356.55	61.77	18.06	20.17	224,077.09	50.31	17.15	32.54
2020	87,439.12	63.35	19.03	17.62	208,936.07	52.52	17.83	29.65
2021	106,591.01	61.09	19.69	19.22	257,451.07	49.16	18.27	32.57
Singapore								
2010	139,924.89	45.09	14.55	40.35	175,221.79	41.47	14.04	44.48
2019	269,657.60	41.01	12.08	46.91	299,552.12	41.05	12.33	46.62
2020	251,400.60	41.07	10.98	47.95	289,801.94	40.58	10.92	48.51
2021	280,685.06	40.74	11.80	47.46	322,990.05	40.12	12.03	47.85
Sri Lanka								
2010	3,968.35	63.06	22.16	14.78	4,584.15	65.20	18.72	16.09
2019	9,066.18	68.46	15.20	16.34	9,295.70	68.70	14.26	17.04
2020	4,562.05	70.03	17.73	12.24	5,755.95	67.64	14.45	17.91
2021	2,891.76	69.27	20.35	10.38	5,188.23	64.58	13.65	21.76
Taipei,China								
2010	49,626.00	57.07	21.18	21.75	98,920.64	40.38	15.88	43.74
2019	43,539.94	60.62	20.21	19.16	115,904.33	41.11	15.22	43.67
2020	35,898.02	63.76	21.71	14.53	109,153.54	42.53	15.10	42.37
2021	50,817.10	61.17	21.88	16.94	148,697.66	42.00	16.01	41.99
Thailand								
2010	31,849.89	62.70	17.68	19.63	59,903.56	52.52	15.53	31.95
2019	92,144.07	65.02	13.65	21.33	139,939.95	59.80	13.20	26.99
2020	44,870.43	62.58	17.30	20.12	102,571.26	55.90	13.91	30.19
2021	66,019.87	59.67	18.27	22.06	122,218.40	52.51	14.59	32.90
Viet Nam								
2010	10,830.04	54.78	15.13	30.09	24,398.53	38.59	9.90	51.51
2019	14,227.31	55.66	17.48	26.87	80,049.31	39.59	6.72	53.69
2020	13,796.31	56.44	19.13	24.43	80,367.04	39.26	6.83	53.91
2021	17,009.40	53.22	19.84	26.95	89,156.93	32.11	5.71	62.18

$ = United States dollars, ADB = Asian Development Bank, DAVAX = domestic value-added immediately absorbed by direct importer, FVA = foreign value-added, PDC = pure double-counted terms, REF = re-exported domestic value-added absorbed by home economy, REX = re-exported domestic value-added absorbed abroad.

Source: Asian Development Bank. Multiregional Input-Output Tables. https://mrio.adbx.online/ (accessed 05 July 2022).

Table 3.2.5: Value-Added Decomposition of Exports—Personal and Public Services Sector

ADB Regional Member	By Export Sectors				By Origin Sectors			
	Total	DAVAX	REX+REF	FVA+PDC	Total	DAVAX	REX+REF	FVA+PDC
	($ million)	(% share in total)			($ million)	(% share in total)		
Australia								
2010	7,155.56	80.39	13.16	6.45	11,820.46	71.14	21.11	7.75
2019	14,983.46	81.44	9.97	8.59	15,829.07	78.10	14.29	7.61
2020	15,006.19	82.85	9.59	7.56	15,733.35	79.51	13.65	6.84
2021	15,199.03	82.64	11.01	6.35	15,645.33	78.65	15.44	5.91
Bangladesh								
2010	184.17	83.02	11.99	4.99	1,792.40	84.33	12.56	3.11
2019	470.87	71.81	22.27	5.93	2,909.09	86.18	6.48	7.34
2020	559.25	77.81	16.81	5.38	2,778.33	86.35	6.75	6.91
2021	608.00	75.03	19.27	5.70	3,091.26	85.76	6.97	7.27
Bhutan								
2010	9.81	68.85	17.61	13.54	11.64	68.97	14.45	16.58
2019	28.96	73.36	14.93	11.72	24.27	69.27	13.43	17.30
2020	28.12	75.06	14.91	10.02	25.09	70.43	13.59	15.98
2021	32.29	75.31	14.35	10.34	30.42	67.38	12.09	20.53
Brunei Darussalam								
2010	31.20	63.03	16.95	20.02	148.59	48.92	35.38	15.70
2019	92.30	55.57	15.93	28.51	115.86	48.65	16.14	35.21
2020	50.21	56.96	15.19	27.85	122.56	52.23	20.18	27.59
2021	59.97	56.98	16.28	26.76	68.18	45.84	14.17	40.00
Cambodia								
2010	71.12	60.50	19.68	19.82	87.48	62.37	16.49	21.14
2019	147.80	67.13	9.25	23.62	284.36	54.40	9.95	35.65
2020	88.83	67.68	8.33	23.99	228.21	47.86	9.08	43.06
2021	75.31	67.47	9.58	22.96	225.93	37.70	8.67	53.64
Fiji								
2010	17.93	76.23	9.37	14.40	31.10	61.94	9.01	29.05
2019	63.76	81.54	8.27	10.19	124.38	70.82	9.15	20.03
2020	28.79	84.68	6.24	9.26	64.60	71.26	10.08	18.65
2021	36.73	82.48	6.89	10.82	70.52	71.02	9.88	19.10
Hong Kong, China								
2010	594.50	64.56	21.68	13.76	5,051.99	54.07	11.77	34.16
2019	3,398.91	79.29	10.17	10.54	6,207.29	69.58	11.59	18.83
2020	2,000.49	80.83	8.69	10.48	4,641.59	72.28	11.56	16.16
2021	3,909.51	79.67	8.45	11.88	6,041.12	72.54	11.89	15.57
India								
2010	10,841.53	92.44	1.57	5.99	16,248.37	78.66	7.39	13.94
2019	12,738.45	89.68	5.39	4.93	20,920.13	74.38	8.77	16.84
2020	9,068.43	89.92	5.08	5.00	15,544.58	71.96	8.15	19.89
2021	13,230.70	88.56	5.66	5.78	21,468.91	70.98	8.38	20.64
Indonesia								
2010	2,009.07	76.45	13.98	9.57	3,341.63	62.29	16.94	20.77
2019	5,173.18	74.53	19.55	5.92	6,071.01	66.70	19.40	13.90
2020	4,769.13	80.14	14.59	5.26	5,388.40	72.19	16.50	11.31
2021	6,142.22	75.14	18.65	6.21	6,823.47	67.44	18.93	13.62
Japan								
2010	3,677.31	79.65	15.28	5.08	20,640.29	61.84	21.04	17.12
2019	4,472.10	84.66	9.32	6.03	23,575.86	66.91	17.91	15.18
2020	3,461.42	85.91	8.66	5.42	19,198.00	66.59	19.01	14.40
2021	4,109.95	84.40	8.84	6.76	23,146.67	64.92	19.17	15.91

continued on next page

Table 3.2.5: continued

Table 3.2.5: Value-Added Decomposition of Exports—Personal and Public Services Sector								
ADB Regional Member	By Export Sectors				By Origin Sectors			
	Total	DAVAX	REX+REF	FVA+PDC	Total	DAVAX	REX+REF	FVA+PDC
	($ million)	(% share in total)			($ million)	(% share in total)		
Kazakhstan								
2010	652.33	79.94	8.46	11.60	756.43	62.15	18.24	19.61
2019	415.33	80.10	10.81	9.09	617.29	53.73	12.28	33.98
2020	262.02	84.16	7.78	8.06	417.27	54.37	9.43	36.20
2021	133.63	83.27	9.09	7.64	373.83	43.46	12.21	44.33
Kyrgyz Republic								
2010	67.89	59.84	17.74	22.42	55.55	61.46	17.80	20.73
2019	299.53	75.78	13.53	10.69	263.31	77.76	14.11	8.13
2020	282.89	78.85	12.47	8.68	251.84	79.03	12.74	8.23
2021	384.60	78.11	12.01	9.88	340.05	79.81	12.69	7.50
Lao People's Democratic Republic								
2010	22.55	71.78	12.58	15.64	21.12	63.48	11.25	25.26
2019	4.58	88.24	4.66	7.10	19.50	24.29	3.05	72.67
2020	1.37	87.17	6.81	6.02	12.90	17.70	3.62	78.68
2021	1.84	81.87	10.79	7.33	19.10	18.03	4.88	77.09
Malaysia								
2010	1,492.57	84.17	1.55	14.28	5,062.56	29.22	3.92	66.86
2019	2,471.98	77.19	8.26	14.55	5,617.83	33.10	5.15	61.75
2020	2,383.40	76.32	10.00	13.68	4,449.69	39.19	7.17	53.64
2021	2,326.11	75.62	9.05	15.33	5,272.98	32.00	5.48	62.52
Maldives								
2010	31.09	56.00	17.44	26.55	42.46	53.39	15.17	31.44
2019	66.37	81.11	11.15	7.74	170.42	67.95	14.37	17.69
2020	51.50	80.58	10.10	9.33	118.28	76.23	14.44	9.33
2021	89.26	80.22	10.50	9.34	189.40	73.00	14.54	12.45
Mongolia								
2010	5.69	77.78	7.06	15.16	47.31	54.31	17.38	28.31
2019	45.40	64.38	11.15	24.47	142.85	35.56	8.46	55.98
2020	40.24	67.50	9.79	22.71	136.56	39.90	9.67	50.44
2021	44.34	65.67	10.47	23.85	179.29	42.49	10.76	46.76
Nepal								
2010	98.74	76.71	15.68	7.61	70.15	75.87	14.93	9.21
2019	73.18	76.21	12.91	10.88	99.06	70.89	15.01	14.10
2020	70.17	76.46	12.89	10.65	90.20	73.21	15.75	11.03
2021	45.31	75.15	13.99	10.85	67.28	72.90	16.05	11.05
Pakistan								
2010	1,490.58	87.80	6.96	5.24	1,308.63	87.31	7.50	5.19
2019	1,651.16	80.92	13.39	5.69	1,587.76	80.86	13.47	5.68
2020	1,617.95	87.22	7.84	4.93	1,545.60	86.48	8.47	5.06
2021	1,767.04	84.29	10.39	5.32	1,680.63	83.66	10.80	5.53
People's Republic of China								
2010	12,135.87	76.58	12.75	10.68	34,148.00	63.32	14.16	22.51
2019	18,752.86	73.77	16.62	9.61	70,882.04	67.20	16.94	15.86
2020	17,468.68	79.59	12.50	7.91	69,575.83	68.50	16.43	15.07
2021	21,262.69	78.43	12.83	8.74	85,857.52	66.33	16.73	16.93
Philippines								
2010	695.20	72.68	18.20	9.12	1,075.92	59.72	18.40	21.87
2019	1,530.55	75.03	14.42	10.55	2,209.43	63.92	15.99	20.09
2020	1,062.03	76.87	14.17	8.96	1,621.56	63.21	16.09	20.70
2021	1,117.50	74.96	14.63	10.42	1,690.84	61.15	15.39	23.46

continued on next page

Table 3.2.5: continued

Table 3.2.5: Value-Added Decomposition of Exports—Personal and Public Services Sector

ADB Regional Member	By Export Sectors				By Origin Sectors			
	Total	DAVAX	REX+REF	FVA+PDC	Total	DAVAX	REX+REF	FVA+PDC
	($ million)	(% share in total)			($ million)	(% share in total)		
Republic of Korea								
2010	3,801.91	67.78	17.32	14.90	14,283.77	55.71	17.06	27.23
2019	2,495.66	77.76	8.74	13.50	11,986.63	43.93	13.02	43.05
2020	2,333.00	78.92	8.88	12.20	10,759.78	47.43	13.96	38.61
2021	2,673.21	78.13	8.81	13.06	12,811.25	42.65	13.59	43.76
Singapore								
2010	6,630.96	64.78	14.74	20.48	9,078.18	46.32	11.48	42.20
2019	9,918.50	67.48	12.89	19.63	14,682.91	46.39	9.90	43.71
2020	9,139.87	67.83	12.12	20.05	12,694.51	45.38	8.71	45.90
2021	9,954.02	66.79	13.38	19.83	14,543.32	43.88	9.56	46.56
Sri Lanka								
2010	22.73	68.52	21.66	9.83	244.85	61.50	17.80	20.70
2019	215.40	75.97	9.80	14.23	546.17	66.71	11.88	21.41
2020	23.43	75.16	15.20	9.65	247.36	62.19	11.23	26.58
2021	2.99	75.31	13.10	11.59	238.77	58.99	8.34	32.67
Taipei,China								
2010	1,313.56	76.94	7.36	15.70	6,796.34	41.30	13.61	45.09
2019	345.74	73.25	15.94	10.81	7,264.86	37.92	15.34	46.74
2020	296.39	75.49	15.53	8.97	6,715.83	40.99	15.36	43.65
2021	360.61	74.71	15.77	9.52	8,567.73	38.52	15.55	45.93
Thailand								
2010	4,016.49	74.13	10.31	15.56	4,626.16	61.72	11.57	26.71
2019	15,017.09	71.66	14.52	13.82	13,885.12	68.30	14.98	16.72
2020	1,038.51	72.79	14.42	12.79	4,414.46	46.26	12.26	41.48
2021	5,519.87	70.46	15.19	14.36	7,984.10	56.54	14.53	28.93
Viet Nam								
2010	400.82	70.11	5.11	24.78	1,149.50	30.17	4.07	65.76
2019	1,103.56	66.58	6.08	27.35	4,153.54	29.60	4.16	66.24
2020	1,222.35	66.38	5.57	28.05	4,111.93	30.75	4.10	65.15
2021	2,082.57	62.61	4.69	32.70	5,027.45	28.42	2.91	68.67

$ = United States dollars, ADB = Asian Development Bank, DAVAX = domestic value-added immediately absorbed by direct importer, FVA = foreign value-added, PDC = pure double-counted terms, REF = re-exported domestic value-added absorbed by home economy, REX = re-exported domestic value-added absorbed abroad.

Source: Asian Development Bank. Multiregional Input-Output Tables. https://mrio.adbx.online/ (accessed 05 July 2022).

Table 3.3.1: Global Value Chain Participation Rates

ADB Regional Member	Trade-Based (%) (export-sector breakdown)				Production-Based (%) (origin sector breakdown)			
	2010	2019	2020	2021	2010	2019	2020	2021
Australia								
Aggregate	39.11	34.62	33.19	35.19	16.55	18.63	18.61	17.71
Primary	42.00	35.69	33.63	36.10	63.35	74.12	73.66	68.36
Low-technology manufacturing	23.83	22.74	21.90	23.43	8.30	9.64	9.80	9.14
Medium- to high-technology manufacturing	47.35	47.32	46.32	48.61	30.35	32.55	31.90	29.91
Business services	32.90	30.91	30.44	31.38	10.90	12.14	12.02	11.09
Personal and public services	19.61	18.56	17.15	17.36	3.46	3.39	3.23	2.85
Bangladesh								
Aggregate	26.04	25.89	24.33	25.52	4.61	1.93	1.79	1.89
Primary	21.69	32.88	29.10	27.11	4.67	1.19	0.92	1.06
Low-technology manufacturing	26.91	25.74	24.01	25.38	9.31	1.40	1.55	1.82
Medium- to high-technology manufacturing	23.53	32.19	30.41	32.42	2.95	1.65	1.58	1.70
Business services	19.84	25.45	25.58	25.34	3.54	3.07	2.79	2.83
Personal and public services	16.98	28.19	22.19	24.97	2.39	1.15	1.05	1.05
Bhutan								
Aggregate	33.87	28.85	25.79	35.80	20.24	12.29	8.30	19.74
Primary	18.77	12.62	10.58	8.94	16.21	13.94	4.74	4.32
Low-technology manufacturing	39.82	26.24	19.21	34.07	31.79	4.94	3.38	36.72
Medium- to high-technology manufacturing	24.98	41.08	42.68	50.30	12.51	26.97	26.13	33.86
Business services	40.30	35.86	37.49	44.34	18.24	18.69	16.17	19.38
Personal and public services	31.15	26.64	24.94	24.69	2.67	3.67	3.29	3.52
Brunei Darussalam								
Aggregate	52.79	47.76	45.63	45.43	57.10	36.94	40.45	34.36
Primary	37.32	50.98	46.20	47.58	79.66	58.00	63.86	53.94
Low-technology manufacturing	53.46	56.56	58.29	57.20	8.39	5.23	6.47	3.19
Medium- to high-technology manufacturing	74.13	41.03	43.47	41.87	80.07	50.80	70.67	56.20
Business services	51.30	57.81	57.91	55.30	20.65	14.22	13.68	9.42
Personal and public services	36.97	44.43	43.04	43.02	5.04	2.23	3.24	1.26
Cambodia								
Aggregate	38.36	45.42	47.11	51.64	10.85	18.67	17.07	17.68
Primary	44.78	51.94	49.03	59.15	7.42	36.85	31.51	34.99
Low-technology manufacturing	40.04	49.12	51.41	52.80	8.66	4.79	4.66	4.94
Medium- to high-technology manufacturing	47.73	47.59	50.30	50.13	7.03	14.59	14.40	15.29
Business services	35.03	36.62	37.89	39.78	19.18	23.80	22.30	21.45
Personal and public services	39.50	32.87	32.32	32.53	3.88	3.99	2.84	2.17
Fiji								
Aggregate	41.12	36.75	41.11	42.61	16.78	24.01	15.67	16.03
Primary	35.73	27.93	31.63	34.65	14.47	17.23	13.60	13.41
Low-technology manufacturing	33.63	30.28	29.56	33.10	13.78	18.35	12.70	12.74
Medium- to high-technology manufacturing	45.08	50.88	45.35	50.38	13.83	34.37	20.25	22.02
Business services	43.83	40.04	47.28	48.58	22.44	36.28	24.73	25.52
Personal and public services	23.77	18.46	15.50	17.71	2.22	5.49	3.34	3.53
Hong Kong, China								
Aggregate	42.54	36.49	35.08	37.43	24.04	17.52	15.61	17.25
Primary	66.51	33.97	28.03	31.87	19.95	8.44	7.89	12.66
Low-technology manufacturing	56.26	55.10	51.75	57.68	15.50	9.13	7.37	8.33
Medium- to high-technology manufacturing	84.75	77.61	77.59	83.67	67.59	58.71	57.91	62.60
Business services	37.42	32.56	30.57	33.15	29.03	21.67	19.62	21.43
Personal and public services	35.44	20.71	19.17	20.33	4.58	4.22	3.17	3.95

continued on next page

Table 3.3.1: continued

Table 3.3.1: Global Value Chain Participation Rates

ADB Regional Member	Trade-Based (%) (export-sector breakdown)				Production-Based (%) (origin sector breakdown)			
	2010	2019	2020	2021	2010	2019	2020	2021
India								
Aggregate	37.00	33.55	31.40	34.61	9.60	8.41	8.79	9.32
Primary	26.92	27.10	22.84	26.51	8.14	6.42	6.14	7.62
Low-technology manufacturing	31.12	25.33	24.78	27.43	5.00	4.93	5.29	5.11
Medium- to high-technology manufacturing	52.65	50.55	47.65	52.28	14.38	16.39	17.91	18.25
Business services	31.45	23.90	22.33	23.83	13.92	10.87	11.56	12.06
Personal and public services	7.56	10.32	10.08	11.44	1.31	1.71	1.32	1.47
Indonesia								
Aggregate	40.11	35.88	34.28	36.67	16.08	11.43	10.88	13.90
Primary	45.07	30.97	29.91	32.09	31.14	22.66	20.40	26.94
Low-technology manufacturing	34.07	33.57	31.42	34.75	11.47	8.14	7.92	9.50
Medium- to high-technology manufacturing	44.62	43.72	42.19	44.70	24.62	19.85	20.85	24.43
Business services	32.48	34.79	34.58	34.68	8.68	7.45	7.34	8.64
Personal and public services	23.55	25.47	19.86	24.86	2.41	2.99	2.69	3.20
Japan								
Aggregate	36.79	36.34	35.91	38.82	7.55	8.05	7.78	8.91
Primary	51.60	46.91	45.74	49.38	5.03	6.07	5.86	6.93
Low-technology manufacturing	40.22	36.21	34.91	37.11	5.89	5.84	5.38	6.06
Medium- to high-technology manufacturing	38.93	39.54	38.41	42.62	24.03	28.16	29.33	34.53
Business services	29.30	25.73	26.46	25.40	6.62	6.74	6.27	7.25
Personal and public services	20.35	15.34	14.09	15.60	0.84	0.94	0.82	0.99
Kazakhstan								
Aggregate	44.15	44.20	39.83	43.93	38.49	30.64	25.84	30.64
Primary	49.39	51.47	47.17	50.37	72.42	69.87	64.07	71.98
Low-technology manufacturing	35.69	27.99	25.19	27.11	6.71	9.07	7.28	11.17
Medium- to high-technology manufacturing	46.34	38.20	35.85	40.15	63.91	53.99	48.12	67.44
Business services	29.82	28.72	26.49	27.26	26.92	19.47	15.97	17.22
Personal and public services	20.06	19.90	15.84	16.73	3.67	1.77	0.87	0.75
Kyrgyz Republic								
Aggregate	45.32	48.49	46.96	50.16	19.10	19.89	18.06	21.69
Primary	44.01	38.17	37.10	38.42	27.36	14.36	10.74	11.32
Low-technology manufacturing	53.35	34.76	31.31	35.19	6.35	6.05	5.59	7.71
Medium- to high-technology manufacturing	44.42	65.58	63.93	67.99	48.37	82.09	81.46	89.54
Business services	47.60	38.26	39.30	44.74	13.43	11.21	9.66	14.67
Personal and public services	40.16	24.22	21.15	21.89	4.21	11.20	10.59	13.73
Lao People's Democratic Republic								
Aggregate	31.45	38.79	36.26	39.09	21.26	25.21	23.26	32.07
Primary	32.64	37.86	36.27	38.57	38.17	48.61	43.55	65.30
Low-technology manufacturing	23.64	39.51	37.55	40.47	8.80	33.55	31.63	37.71
Medium- to high-technology manufacturing	57.72	61.65	56.88	60.34	7.46	8.97	8.01	12.66
Business services	37.48	38.30	31.04	35.14	15.20	12.94	11.56	17.30
Personal and public services	28.22	11.76	12.83	18.13	1.08	0.08	0.05	0.09
Malaysia								
Aggregate	56.13	50.36	51.92	53.88	41.35	29.40	28.72	31.76
Primary	39.28	36.14	35.63	37.66	59.70	45.34	44.14	46.35
Low-technology manufacturing	56.05	46.43	48.05	49.58	38.51	25.87	27.34	32.22
Medium- to high-technology manufacturing	71.81	67.85	67.20	69.21	52.34	43.42	44.59	45.14
Business services	43.65	37.97	39.07	40.19	40.07	27.73	26.63	28.71
Personal and public services	15.83	22.81	23.68	24.38	1.85	2.44	2.39	2.42

continued on next page

Table 3.3.1: continued

Table 3.3.1: Global Value Chain Participation Rates

ADB Regional Member	Trade-Based (%) (export-sector breakdown)				Production-Based (%) (origin sector breakdown)			
	2010	2019	2020	2021	2010	2019	2020	2021
Maldives								
Aggregate	45.11	42.75	38.09	41.42	30.29	27.88	18.92	28.73
Primary	52.84	22.86	20.70	24.53	36.26	29.64	16.03	31.11
Low-technology manufacturing	52.96	38.01	33.28	37.02	19.34	8.28	5.82	9.54
Medium- to high-technology manufacturing	42.50	42.63	42.97	36.57	14.74	9.63	8.41	7.93
Business services	44.90	43.38	39.32	42.42	39.37	36.05	26.55	36.93
Personal and public services	44.00	18.89	19.42	19.78	3.99	7.25	6.37	8.36
Mongolia								
Aggregate	44.37	44.46	43.89	45.65	28.82	40.88	41.96	43.20
Primary	45.82	44.04	43.52	45.24	47.34	72.30	71.46	71.54
Low-technology manufacturing	35.05	42.38	39.23	41.17	11.20	12.10	18.09	14.61
Medium- to high-technology manufacturing	51.87	63.17	64.26	66.16	32.34	50.38	57.46	55.10
Business services	41.09	44.23	43.47	45.52	23.95	28.31	32.53	34.38
Personal and public services	22.22	35.62	32.50	34.33	3.39	2.84	2.98	4.07
Nepal								
Aggregate	34.32	41.63	40.00	38.86	4.44	4.14	3.63	2.97
Primary	10.88	13.00	13.27	13.92	1.36	1.57	1.95	1.91
Low-technology manufacturing	36.79	28.76	27.76	28.17	5.02	3.55	3.48	3.56
Medium- to high-technology manufacturing	52.39	50.93	50.22	52.11	14.12	10.24	9.89	12.05
Business services	35.58	47.29	46.21	45.46	7.42	6.49	5.58	3.91
Personal and public services	23.29	23.79	23.54	24.85	2.18	1.09	0.91	0.69
Pakistan								
Aggregate	26.11	22.08	20.59	22.24	6.09	3.63	3.74	3.60
Primary	15.86	16.01	21.71	22.60	5.59	3.55	3.90	3.61
Low-technology manufacturing	25.87	20.41	19.36	20.18	7.05	3.85	4.33	4.32
Medium- to high-technology manufacturing	43.78	39.20	37.45	42.54	6.31	4.15	3.81	3.63
Business services	27.35	24.88	23.13	26.52	6.54	3.75	3.82	3.67
Personal and public services	12.20	19.08	12.78	15.71	3.44	2.82	2.41	2.48
People's Republic of China								
Aggregate	34.53	33.49	32.86	35.04	10.56	7.04	7.34	7.91
Primary	30.73	26.41	24.30	26.65	9.44	7.30	7.42	8.75
Low-technology manufacturing	21.95	22.39	22.17	24.30	7.49	5.89	6.21	6.90
Medium- to high-technology manufacturing	40.13	38.41	37.48	40.24	16.01	12.82	13.62	14.07
Business services	31.83	30.54	30.82	30.19	11.83	7.21	7.52	7.87
Personal and public services	23.42	26.23	20.41	21.57	2.04	1.21	1.17	1.23
Philippines								
Aggregate	43.50	41.52	40.94	44.04	14.29	11.17	10.22	10.07
Primary	32.25	21.59	20.03	23.20	10.54	5.92	5.90	6.59
Low-technology manufacturing	27.39	26.97	25.43	29.63	8.77	4.40	4.67	4.74
Medium- to high-technology manufacturing	63.40	61.27	59.81	65.61	34.30	23.86	24.86	25.62
Business services	30.78	30.91	31.45	30.38	17.48	15.72	13.88	13.39
Personal and public services	27.32	24.97	23.13	25.04	2.77	2.46	1.87	1.71
Republic of Korea								
Aggregate	50.91	49.77	46.89	51.18	17.63	18.76	17.82	20.44
Primary	27.49	26.94	26.24	28.95	9.38	6.79	6.37	6.97
Low-technology manufacturing	47.54	48.84	45.65	47.96	13.75	13.13	12.79	14.58
Medium- to high-technology manufacturing	52.69	52.09	49.08	53.77	35.66	42.91	40.99	46.53
Business services	39.99	38.23	36.65	38.91	14.65	15.95	15.48	17.27
Personal and public services	32.22	22.24	21.08	21.87	2.82	1.37	1.30	1.36

continued on next page

Table 3.3.1: continued

Table 3.3.1: Global Value Chain Participation Rates

ADB Regional Member	Trade-Based (%) (export-sector breakdown)				Production-Based (%) (origin sector breakdown)			
	2010	2019	2020	2021	2010	2019	2020	2021
Singapore								
Aggregate	63.33	59.84	58.69	59.97	50.14	43.42	43.88	45.27
Primary	40.60	45.73	44.86	42.50	46.40	40.69	39.46	37.98
Low-technology manufacturing	60.75	50.64	50.32	51.65	24.07	21.83	23.54	23.37
Medium- to high-technology manufacturing	72.87	63.79	60.54	63.13	63.89	52.18	44.35	50.91
Business services	54.91	58.99	58.93	59.26	55.61	48.91	51.27	51.26
Personal and public services	35.22	32.52	32.17	33.21	15.10	12.26	11.47	11.96
Sri Lanka								
Aggregate	34.65	34.18	31.93	32.98	7.90	8.41	5.52	5.30
Primary	34.17	26.68	24.44	24.59	7.16	5.66	4.35	5.47
Low-technology manufacturing	30.53	33.85	30.16	30.46	8.13	6.15	4.73	5.93
Medium- to high-technology manufacturing	50.80	53.26	49.90	51.93	9.96	17.21	14.88	17.79
Business services	36.94	31.54	29.97	30.73	11.54	13.49	8.22	6.30
Personal and public services								
Taipei,China	31.48	24.03	24.84	24.69	1.04	1.27	0.50	0.34
Aggregate	61.23	57.55	53.38	55.95	28.38	27.90	25.54	28.96
Primary	34.29	31.85	30.87	32.95	11.41	10.58	10.12	11.33
Low-technology manufacturing	58.56	54.43	50.39	53.03	24.08	26.65	24.61	26.05
Medium- to high-technology manufacturing	65.63	60.52	55.66	58.36	59.82	63.13	56.09	60.71
Business services	42.93	39.38	36.24	38.83	20.89	16.81	15.09	18.24
Personal and public services	23.06	26.75	24.51	25.29	2.74	2.68	2.39	2.77
Thailand								
Aggregate	49.02	42.85	44.12	47.75	20.14	22.40	20.07	22.19
Primary	44.37	29.39	27.83	32.24	18.52	31.53	29.22	32.44
Low-technology manufacturing	40.28	36.37	33.96	38.75	19.36	25.90	24.42	26.51
Medium- to high-technology manufacturing	58.77	57.73	55.83	61.05	32.79	30.59	35.36	32.61
Business services	37.30	34.98	37.42	40.33	20.82	21.28	18.52	21.80
Personal and public services	25.87	28.34	27.21	29.54	4.42	9.53	2.13	4.71
Viet Nam								
Aggregate	54.66	55.42	56.23	61.20	21.88	22.83	23.92	23.39
Primary	51.53	50.25	48.29	51.25	33.62	29.00	27.67	27.20
Low-technology manufacturing	53.52	50.01	50.39	56.27	15.24	17.46	18.10	16.84
Medium- to high-technology manufacturing	66.49	68.70	69.77	75.01	33.25	44.50	48.33	54.01
Business services	45.22	44.34	43.56	46.78	21.27	23.64	25.22	23.82
Personal and public services	29.89	33.42	33.62	37.39	1.57	2.00	2.06	1.70

ADB = Asian Development Bank.
Note: Export sector breakdown accounts the value added to the exporting sector where it is embedded. Origin sector breakdown accounts the value added to the sector where it originated from.
Source: Asian Development Bank. Multiregional Input-Output Tables. https://mrio.adbx.online/ (accessed 05 July 2022).

Table 3.4.1: Revealed Comparative Advantage Indices—Primary Sector						
ADB Regional Member	Gross		Value-Added			
			By Export Sectors		By Origin Sectors	
	Exports	RCA	VAX	RCA	VAX	RCA
	($ million)	(ratio)	($ million)	(ratio)	($ million)	(ratio)
Australia						
2010	138,753.90	4.71	123,426.13	4.18	102,032.40	2.78
2019	169,411.19	5.59	151,607.74	4.90	126,377.97	3.60
2020	167,570.63	5.80	152,095.29	5.15	129,661.62	3.98
2021	182,245.51	5.35	167,041.24	4.71	146,122.44	3.71
Bangladesh						
2010	483.48	0.25	454.14	0.23	2,558.01	1.06
2019	320.92	0.08	288.02	0.07	3,927.34	0.90
2020	182.74	0.05	165.66	0.05	3,245.89	0.93
2021	208.84	0.05	188.05	0.05	3,554.73	0.80
Bhutan						
2010	72.77	1.30	68.19	1.26	72.82	1.08
2019	121.85	1.53	112.17	1.52	124.39	1.49
2020	64.86	1.06	62.98	1.10	68.40	1.08
2021	80.04	0.93	77.55	0.98	83.48	0.94
Brunei Darussalam						
2010	4,888.53	4.94	4,554.92	4.41	5,851.12	4.55
2019	4,212.97	5.82	3,371.35	5.08	4,009.27	5.33
2020	3,369.61	5.54	2,677.04	4.81	3,281.58	5.35
2021	2,931.77	4.65	2,340.25	3.97	3,168.83	4.84
Cambodia						
2010	221.32	0.51	198.98	0.55	516.03	1.14
2019	3,476.50	2.27	2,941.00	2.43	3,220.62	2.35
2020	4,015.44	2.88	3,357.37	3.15	3,527.15	3.00
2021	4,563.76	2.65	3,800.56	2.97	3,898.46	2.74
Fiji						
2010	85.34	0.69	61.91	0.60	100.22	0.78
2019	260.43	1.06	214.44	1.00	285.06	1.17
2020	155.47	1.42	126.11	1.29	159.48	1.48
2021	174.00	1.30	137.29	1.17	172.17	1.32
Hong Kong, China						
2010	87.98	0.01	43.51	0.00	34.95	0.00
2019	245.40	0.02	169.50	0.01	126.57	0.01
2020	204.09	0.02	155.39	0.02	125.39	0.01
2021	259.24	0.02	192.06	0.02	158.92	0.01
India						
2010	24,905.40	0.74	23,532.81	0.75	38,838.20	0.99
2019	34,691.53	0.70	32,294.41	0.70	58,419.42	1.11
2020	35,552.48	0.80	33,324.83	0.79	56,911.08	1.22
2021	49,950.41	0.76	46,189.98	0.76	76,819.52	1.14
Indonesia						
2010	48,635.33	2.47	44,857.21	2.33	63,636.04	2.67
2019	44,359.60	2.30	42,257.99	2.22	59,854.76	2.77
2020	36,970.10	2.29	35,486.81	2.20	52,132.60	2.93
2021	64,204.12	2.54	61,191.31	2.46	82,830.04	2.99

continued on next page

Table 3.4.1: continued

Table 3.4.1: Revealed Comparative Advantage Indices—Primary Sector

ADB Regional Member	Gross		Value-Added			
			By Export Sectors		By Origin Sectors	
	Exports ($ million)	RCA (ratio)	VAX ($ million)	RCA (ratio)	VAX ($ million)	RCA (ratio)
Japan						
2010	2,588.34	0.03	1,710.37	0.02	6,070.07	0.06
2019	3,199.94	0.04	2,314.19	0.03	6,698.91	0.07
2020	3,115.34	0.04	2,317.13	0.03	6,243.52	0.08
2021	3,473.51	0.04	2,425.52	0.03	7,148.13	0.08
Kazakhstan						
2010	36,138.31	5.27	32,320.15	4.52	28,472.88	3.21
2019	38,608.56	6.53	33,777.18	5.55	26,135.37	3.78
2020	28,560.23	6.24	25,278.63	5.35	20,647.06	3.95
2021	35,852.82	5.53	32,209.99	4.73	27,181.57	3.59
Kyrgyz Republic						
2010	968.93	3.95	641.79	3.36	527.15	2.22
2019	613.66	2.12	463.47	1.86	352.67	1.25
2020	380.80	1.77	296.16	1.58	236.07	1.14
2021	681.51	1.88	507.31	1.65	417.55	1.22
Lao People's Democratic Republic						
2010	1,149.98	4.65	1,029.18	4.14	1,121.99	3.63
2019	2,210.04	3.68	1,971.93	3.23	2,187.78	3.16
2020	1,954.92	3.76	1,805.93	3.31	2,002.00	3.32
2021	2,991.35	3.76	2,726.55	3.30	2,937.75	3.20
Malaysia						
2010	22,272.41	0.94	19,923.28	1.18	35,365.70	1.68
2019	20,607.44	0.93	18,804.09	1.10	32,548.87	1.68
2020	15,098.26	0.82	13,769.08	0.99	26,140.75	1.70
2021	21,768.83	0.86	19,711.64	1.06	34,637.16	1.68
Maldives						
2010	19.66	0.10	10.80	0.07	91.14	0.48
2019	21.21	0.06	16.37	0.05	157.56	0.45
2020	38.09	0.24	30.31	0.22	123.82	0.81
2021	46.29	0.14	35.11	0.12	201.74	0.62
Mongolia						
2010	2,098.21	6.63	1,574.82	5.66	1,337.16	3.87
2019	6,567.25	8.80	4,751.24	7.54	3,982.24	5.58
2020	6,296.59	9.30	4,609.72	8.03	3,618.31	5.71
2021	7,526.61	8.44	5,413.31	7.24	4,280.26	5.15
Nepal						
2010	164.81	0.99	152.82	1.03	228.89	1.24
2019	132.97	0.54	122.38	0.59	220.41	0.94
2020	138.96	0.70	128.46	0.76	242.10	1.31
2021	141.17	0.78	130.90	0.84	235.33	1.35
Pakistan						
2010	1,066.91	0.42	1,023.68	0.39	6,456.74	1.98
2019	1,688.74	0.71	1,615.48	0.65	7,727.46	2.73
2020	1,134.73	0.50	1,092.88	0.46	7,929.22	3.00
2021	1,207.01	0.42	1,157.28	0.38	9,027.70	2.69

continued on next page

Table 3.4.1: continued

Table 3.4.1: Revealed Comparative Advantage Indices—Primary Sector

ADB Regional Member	Gross		Value-Added			
			By Export Sectors		By Origin Sectors	
	Exports	RCA	VAX	RCA	VAX	RCA
	($ million)	(ratio)	($ million)	(ratio)	($ million)	(ratio)
People's Republic of China						
2010	22,608.99	0.12	19,875.40	0.12	182,923.21	0.89
2019	24,485.76	0.10	22,021.25	0.10	223,751.23	0.86
2020	26,498.21	0.11	23,937.65	0.11	239,238.76	0.96
2021	33,242.98	0.09	29,678.67	0.09	325,979.35	0.91
Philippines						
2010	1,265.16	0.22	1,158.21	0.23	5,076.06	0.80
2019	1,535.24	0.20	1,403.34	0.21	3,915.04	0.51
2020	1,668.54	0.27	1,539.02	0.28	4,208.67	0.68
2021	1,994.51	0.26	1,805.56	0.27	4,750.62	0.65
Republic of Korea						
2010	775.91	0.01	644.31	0.02	4,709.97	0.09
2019	754.04	0.01	629.20	0.01	3,772.11	0.07
2020	780.83	0.01	663.58	0.02	3,994.80	0.08
2021	927.48	0.01	775.34	0.01	4,557.46	0.07
Singapore						
2010	85.90	0.00	63.42	0.00	61.25	0.00
2019	115.41	0.00	80.64	0.00	73.00	0.00
2020	110.27	0.00	77.58	0.00	67.34	0.00
2021	126.29	0.00	88.73	0.00	77.49	0.00
Sri Lanka						
2010	392.44	0.33	346.46	0.32	902.08	0.66
2019	417.91	0.23	370.70	0.23	1,120.62	0.61
2020	404.87	0.35	366.04	0.35	944.13	0.81
2021	557.13	0.37	506.62	0.37	1,230.94	0.81
Taipei,China						
2010	1,651.57	0.05	1,227.21	0.06	1,858.19	0.07
2019	890.85	0.02	713.98	0.03	2,255.83	0.08
2020	896.46	0.03	735.32	0.03	2,242.03	0.08
2021	1,067.25	0.02	860.07	0.02	2,671.37	0.07
Thailand						
2010	4,913.82	0.30	4,240.02	0.34	9,957.91	0.64
2019	19,370.52	0.65	16,388.46	0.68	26,153.48	0.95
2020	18,416.62	0.81	15,969.55	0.88	24,101.72	1.21
2021	18,950.09	0.65	16,078.09	0.73	25,720.51	1.05
Viet Nam						
2010	13,065.86	1.46	8,340.60	1.46	11,869.25	1.67
2019	16,357.87	0.63	10,152.40	0.65	25,951.40	1.47
2020	16,230.36	0.64	10,138.18	0.69	26,287.52	1.61
2021	21,633.81	0.65	12,937.26	0.75	30,543.21	1.59

0.00 = magnitude is less than half of unit employed, $ = United States dollars, ADB = Asian Development Bank, RCA = revealed comparative advantage, VAX = value-added exports.

Source: Asian Development Bank. Multiregional Input-Output Tables. https://mrio.adbx.online/ (accessed 05 July 2022).

Table 3.4.2: Revealed Comparative Advantage Indices—Low-Technology Manufacturing Sector

ADB Regional Member	Gross		Value-Added			
			By Export Sectors		By Origin Sectors	
	Exports	RCA	VAX	RCA	VAX	RCA
	($ million)	(ratio)	($ million)	(ratio)	($ million)	(ratio)
Australia						
2010	25,502.55	0.60	22,011.44	0.59	22,209.42	0.73
2019	30,097.25	0.57	25,552.29	0.54	24,398.12	0.65
2020	31,435.15	0.57	26,703.53	0.55	24,738.27	0.64
2021	31,921.58	0.56	27,440.71	0.53	24,953.82	0.59
Bangladesh						
2010	15,825.13	5.55	13,334.32	5.39	6,499.59	3.22
2019	38,756.14	5.23	29,221.76	4.99	17,064.74	3.66
2020	32,402.15	5.00	25,133.72	4.78	14,424.37	3.45
2021	36,978.85	5.07	28,254.48	4.84	16,082.97	3.36
Bhutan						
2010	210.42	2.60	185.46	2.69	206.86	3.68
2019	350.84	2.50	261.57	2.33	249.13	2.79
2020	345.00	2.99	280.43	2.95	280.49	3.71
2021	430.97	3.00	344.12	2.96	343.72	3.61
Brunei Darussalam						
2010	29.64	0.02	15.76	0.01	46.02	0.04
2019	94.73	0.07	45.14	0.04	60.71	0.08
2020	99.38	0.09	45.03	0.05	66.63	0.09
2021	81.13	0.08	38.36	0.04	42.35	0.06
Cambodia						
2010	2,124.18	3.38	1,359.82	2.93	1,149.51	3.04
2019	7,198.29	2.67	3,780.95	2.05	3,411.14	2.32
2020	7,200.42	2.72	3,644.91	2.07	3,184.15	2.27
2021	8,784.63	3.04	4,339.37	2.32	3,733.55	2.43
Fiji						
2010	207.66	1.15	158.17	1.21	129.01	1.21
2019	497.50	1.16	378.49	1.16	279.98	1.07
2020	238.49	1.15	186.60	1.15	131.54	1.02
2021	294.79	1.32	218.30	1.27	149.81	1.07
Hong Kong, China						
2010	10,503.80	0.47	5,496.72	0.35	4,459.81	0.35
2019	6,989.62	0.30	3,753.66	0.21	3,190.68	0.22
2020	4,982.97	0.25	2,775.07	0.18	2,595.81	0.21
2021	6,024.46	0.26	2,989.95	0.16	3,007.62	0.20
India						
2010	50,210.11	1.02	40,690.30	1.02	24,271.99	0.75
2019	83,816.13	0.97	70,889.85	1.00	46,563.42	0.83
2020	75,581.76	0.90	64,496.13	0.92	42,427.47	0.76
2021	103,519.55	0.94	85,676.68	0.96	54,739.01	0.75
Indonesia						
2010	61,583.24	2.16	51,510.62	2.11	29,917.31	1.50
2019	74,722.45	2.21	59,417.24	2.05	37,640.27	1.63
2020	67,958.20	2.22	55,885.26	2.09	34,612.53	1.63
2021	86,070.29	2.03	68,321.30	1.88	42,757.87	1.44

continued on next page

Table 3.4.2: continued

Table 3.4.2: Revealed Comparative Advantage Indices—Low-Technology Manufacturing Sector						
ADB Regional Member	Gross		Value-Added			
			By Export Sectors		By Origin Sectors	
	Exports	RCA	VAX	RCA	VAX	RCA
	($ million)	(ratio)	($ million)	(ratio)	($ million)	(ratio)
Japan						
2010	48,927.35	0.38	41,664.08	0.38	68,471.52	0.77
2019	48,371.14	0.33	41,514.10	0.34	69,543.01	0.72
2020	45,271.44	0.34	39,400.97	0.35	62,892.71	0.71
2021	51,256.85	0.34	43,340.40	0.35	72,721.91	0.72
Kazakhstan						
2010	993.75	0.10	842.65	0.09	1,309.16	0.18
2019	1,932.26	0.19	1,609.96	0.17	1,892.65	0.26
2020	1,824.75	0.21	1,565.07	0.20	1,620.50	0.26
2021	3,202.07	0.29	2,781.68	0.28	2,500.15	0.31
Kyrgyz Republic						
2010	221.19	0.62	117.28	0.48	88.86	0.45
2019	406.05	0.80	283.11	0.75	212.21	0.70
2020	332.95	0.82	240.72	0.77	193.96	0.78
2021	438.88	0.72	305.02	0.68	251.78	0.69
Lao People's Democratic Republic						
2010	600.65	1.67	511.22	1.62	375.63	1.46
2019	3,111.61	2.95	2,699.32	2.90	2,260.91	3.05
2020	3,049.61	3.10	2,742.01	3.03	2,347.62	3.26
2021	3,874.05	2.90	3,415.20	2.83	2,826.80	2.86
Malaysia						
2010	65,036.85	1.89	38,670.08	1.80	15,229.59	0.87
2019	56,413.69	1.45	38,043.53	1.47	19,448.58	0.94
2020	53,808.97	1.55	36,969.71	1.61	17,867.24	0.98
2021	70,243.43	1.65	46,413.51	1.72	22,184.50	1.00
Maldives						
2010	30.89	0.11	17.39	0.09	79.65	0.50
2019	71.19	0.11	46.99	0.10	99.14	0.27
2020	77.76	0.26	54.48	0.24	50.26	0.27
2021	107.61	0.19	70.62	0.17	75.44	0.22
Mongolia						
2010	125.72	0.27	96.51	0.27	116.67	0.41
2019	231.15	0.18	154.92	0.16	273.62	0.36
2020	234.32	0.18	164.28	0.17	385.75	0.51
2021	250.89	0.17	173.42	0.16	335.08	0.37
Nepal						
2010	343.28	1.41	248.25	1.31	173.97	1.13
2019	541.67	1.25	424.94	1.35	208.83	0.83
2020	481.98	1.29	383.74	1.38	188.34	0.85
2021	503.51	1.65	404.41	1.77	186.58	1.00
Pakistan						
2010	12,497.72	3.41	11,266.14	3.38	4,121.50	1.51
2019	15,131.69	3.63	13,568.35	3.57	4,858.58	1.61
2020	16,157.32	3.75	14,611.02	3.68	5,198.87	1.65
2021	18,707.51	3.88	16,827.03	3.82	5,877.47	1.63

continued on next page

Table 3.4.2: continued

Table 3.4.2: Revealed Comparative Advantage Indices—Low-Technology Manufacturing Sector

ADB Regional Member	Gross		Value-Added			
			By Export Sectors		By Origin Sectors	
	Exports	RCA	VAX	RCA	VAX	RCA
	($ million)	(ratio)	($ million)	(ratio)	($ million)	(ratio)
People's Republic of China						
2010	373,984.43	1.42	321,120.04	1.53	236,159.18	1.38
2019	606,343.82	1.41	528,781.94	1.51	365,098.46	1.31
2020	623,086.55	1.37	546,670.74	1.46	372,058.06	1.25
2021	816,803.96	1.38	705,363.82	1.49	492,319.30	1.27
Philippines						
2010	10,611.31	1.30	9,113.57	1.40	7,285.98	1.37
2019	11,052.85	0.83	9,380.62	0.90	7,587.82	0.92
2020	10,963.88	0.94	9,461.41	1.03	7,067.46	0.96
2021	12,328.52	0.95	10,310.56	1.07	7,399.21	0.94
Republic of Korea						
2010	36,177.69	0.45	25,681.53	0.49	29,343.44	0.69
2019	39,193.22	0.37	28,616.86	0.39	41,776.30	0.72
2020	39,388.03	0.39	29,551.87	0.40	43,610.24	0.75
2021	43,488.92	0.35	31,755.22	0.37	48,957.32	0.69
Singapore						
2010	11,793.32	0.25	5,379.57	0.22	8,048.09	0.41
2019	13,638.42	0.19	7,793.54	0.20	9,675.86	0.31
2020	11,538.27	0.16	6,545.97	0.17	8,247.09	0.28
2021	12,309.97	0.15	7,034.10	0.16	8,894.64	0.25
Sri Lanka						
2010	5,779.00	3.35	4,527.29	3.26	3,321.88	2.93
2019	8,054.06	2.55	5,789.72	2.35	4,669.70	2.38
2020	6,707.38	3.08	5,034.97	2.89	3,679.78	2.65
2021	10,000.37	3.92	7,533.75	3.78	5,352.06	3.28
Taipei,China						
2010	22,044.54	0.45	12,628.21	0.45	13,243.52	0.58
2019	30,841.91	0.49	19,924.46	0.52	19,699.54	0.65
2020	29,755.56	0.46	20,499.36	0.49	21,217.22	0.63
2021	39,216.44	0.46	26,258.70	0.49	25,946.78	0.59
Thailand						
2010	32,265.52	1.36	23,781.76	1.50	18,846.74	1.46
2019	81,048.40	1.54	59,530.63	1.61	38,367.27	1.30
2020	75,259.22	1.75	57,120.59	1.91	33,359.44	1.40
2021	82,075.46	1.68	58,788.73	1.82	35,448.16	1.34
Viet Nam						
2010	42,158.30	3.25	21,957.91	3.02	14,880.44	2.51
2019	161,943.33	3.56	86,302.61	3.65	50,721.04	2.69
2020	161,108.28	3.36	84,948.53	3.48	49,185.84	2.53
2021	190,188.97	3.41	88,131.11	3.48	52,490.24	2.53

$ = United States dollars, ADB = Asian Development Bank, RCA = revealed comparative advantage, VAX = value-added exports.
Source: Asian Development Bank. Multiregional Input-Output Tables. https://mrio.adbx.online/ (accessed 05 July 2022).

Table 3.4.3: Revealed Comparative Advantage Indices—Medium- and High-Technology Manufacturing Sector						
	Gross		Value-Added			
			By Export Sectors		By Origin Sectors	
ADB Regional Member	Exports	RCA	VAX	RCA	VAX	RCA
	($ million)	(ratio)	($ million)	(ratio)	($ million)	(ratio)
Australia						
2010	53,320.57	0.41	40,327.13	0.41	21,509.39	0.33
2019	50,831.01	0.34	38,446.92	0.33	17,995.58	0.24
2020	52,404.01	0.35	40,902.92	0.35	18,190.80	0.24
2021	53,351.24	0.34	42,245.03	0.34	18,612.33	0.23
Bangladesh						
2010	428.51	0.05	364.91	0.06	553.03	0.13
2019	783.29	0.04	662.82	0.05	1,153.67	0.12
2020	723.04	0.04	616.28	0.05	1,153.31	0.14
2021	890.78	0.04	746.02	0.05	1,472.41	0.16
Bhutan						
2010	103.79	0.43	81.78	0.45	35.69	0.30
2019	84.52	0.22	63.00	0.23	41.72	0.24
2020	65.48	0.21	44.75	0.20	29.80	0.20
2021	82.84	0.21	49.53	0.18	33.53	0.18
Brunei Darussalam						
2010	3,613.84	0.84	3,282.12	0.95	1,749.17	0.77
2019	2,879.38	0.81	2,314.72	0.93	1,448.83	0.91
2020	3,073.38	0.98	2,481.63	1.12	1,538.54	1.06
2021	2,959.42	1.01	2,461.74	1.18	1,514.78	1.12
Cambodia						
2010	26.33	0.01	16.79	0.01	28.97	0.04
2019	263.07	0.03	157.83	0.03	197.84	0.07
2020	327.02	0.05	189.47	0.04	239.19	0.09
2021	413.55	0.05	236.09	0.05	294.75	0.10
Fiji						
2010	24.77	0.05	15.46	0.05	20.53	0.09
2019	63.28	0.05	41.41	0.05	45.75	0.09
2020	27.18	0.05	18.19	0.05	22.81	0.09
2021	35.96	0.06	22.29	0.05	25.83	0.10
Hong Kong, China						
2010	11,308.48	0.17	2,516.69	0.06	606.36	0.02
2019	9,815.22	0.15	2,819.80	0.06	471.20	0.02
2020	9,725.61	0.18	2,917.21	0.08	438.27	0.02
2021	10,068.82	0.15	2,280.47	0.05	442.94	0.02
India						
2010	100,793.88	0.68	65,298.43	0.62	41,780.11	0.60
2019	190,637.85	0.79	123,122.38	0.71	81,280.32	0.73
2020	175,502.68	0.77	118,685.68	0.71	84,782.25	0.77
2021	240,257.49	0.79	149,541.12	0.70	112,004.77	0.80
Indonesia						
2010	58,384.31	0.68	45,117.23	0.70	29,456.49	0.70
2019	60,063.35	0.63	47,637.01	0.67	30,270.59	0.66
2020	52,934.48	0.63	43,038.63	0.67	27,376.85	0.65
2021	72,752.02	0.62	56,876.92	0.65	35,914.39	0.63

continued on next page

Table 3.4.3: continued

Table 3.4.3: Revealed Comparative Advantage Indices—Medium- and High-Technology Manufacturing Sector

ADB Regional Member	Gross		Value-Added			
			By Export Sectors		By Origin Sectors	
	Exports	RCA	VAX	RCA	VAX	RCA
	($ million)	(ratio)	($ million)	(ratio)	($ million)	(ratio)
Japan						
2010	591,965.90	1.51	477,271.86	1.66	313,572.19	1.66
2019	648,406.01	1.59	507,331.77	1.71	334,186.84	1.75
2020	586,971.46	1.64	473,976.28	1.77	313,485.68	1.79
2021	671,104.46	1.61	516,251.28	1.73	334,695.91	1.72
Kazakhstan						
2010	12,807.45	0.43	11,440.49	0.48	8,168.47	0.52
2019	12,012.13	0.41	10,660.89	0.47	7,404.94	0.51
2020	11,272.12	0.48	10,055.21	0.53	7,327.76	0.60
2021	20,676.72	0.69	18,677.52	0.78	11,387.75	0.73
Kyrgyz Republic						
2010	791.22	0.74	562.96	0.88	550.72	1.31
2019	1,377.96	0.97	949.62	1.02	871.39	1.46
2020	1,107.99	1.00	785.91	1.05	740.68	1.52
2021	1,597.71	0.95	1,100.92	1.02	924.83	1.31
Lao People's Democratic Republic						
2010	8.85	0.01	5.72	0.01	15.66	0.03
2019	20.43	0.01	13.83	0.01	40.10	0.03
2020	26.17	0.01	19.52	0.01	43.63	0.03
2021	36.89	0.01	26.16	0.01	68.96	0.04
Malaysia						
2010	74,578.51	0.72	33,145.76	0.59	31,433.37	0.85
2019	85,362.59	0.79	39,944.23	0.62	34,842.77	0.85
2020	80,544.49	0.85	38,252.75	0.69	32,397.80	0.90
2021	101,519.96	0.86	44,283.83	0.68	39,013.28	0.91
Maldives						
2010	0.78	0.00	0.48	0.00	3.39	0.01
2019	1.64	0.00	1.18	0.00	4.66	0.01
2020	2.05	0.00	1.54	0.00	3.15	0.01
2021	3.29	0.00	2.37	0.00	5.41	0.01
Mongolia						
2010	57.57	0.04	37.62	0.04	45.19	0.07
2019	206.47	0.06	148.87	0.06	113.28	0.07
2020	209.97	0.06	155.46	0.07	129.37	0.09
2021	236.23	0.06	174.35	0.07	139.01	0.08
Nepal						
2010	172.75	0.24	98.39	0.20	60.49	0.18
2019	336.40	0.28	189.65	0.24	128.89	0.26
2020	294.09	0.29	166.18	0.25	111.18	0.25
2021	298.43	0.35	172.33	0.31	112.37	0.31
Pakistan						
2010	1,470.11	0.13	1,076.05	0.12	1,005.70	0.17
2019	1,428.13	0.12	1,068.33	0.11	1,051.38	0.18
2020	973.02	0.08	750.36	0.08	815.23	0.13
2021	1,128.75	0.08	834.41	0.08	945.09	0.14

continued on next page

Table 3.4.3: continued

Table 3.4.3: Revealed Comparative Advantage Indices—Medium- and High-Technology Manufacturing Sector						
ADB Regional Member	Gross		Value-Added			
			By Export Sectors		By Origin Sectors	
	Exports	RCA	VAX	RCA	VAX	RCA
	($ million)	(ratio)	($ million)	(ratio)	($ million)	(ratio)
People's Republic of China						
2010	1,012,324.70	1.27	739,513.05	1.34	468,859.25	1.29
2019	1,638,989.82	1.36	1,237,381.91	1.43	717,580.23	1.30
2020	1,696,018.20	1.36	1,290,664.80	1.43	744,514.06	1.27
2021	2,224,310.53	1.36	1,643,270.53	1.44	948,713.38	1.27
Philippines						
2010	21,597.88	0.88	13,557.42	0.79	8,110.54	0.72
2019	30,927.51	0.83	16,681.18	0.65	10,034.70	0.61
2020	26,739.00	0.84	14,879.93	0.67	8,510.35	0.59
2021	31,085.86	0.87	14,947.15	0.64	9,400.89	0.62
Republic of Korea						
2010	427,862.23	1.76	262,496.81	1.91	190,826.80	2.11
2019	513,811.10	1.74	338,192.90	1.87	240,523.76	2.08
2020	467,004.12	1.71	325,698.40	1.85	229,487.47	2.00
2021	596,758.50	1.73	391,326.42	1.88	278,783.99	2.05
Singapore						
2010	146,471.99	1.03	58,180.87	0.92	41,824.35	1.01
2019	158,867.13	0.77	78,450.84	0.81	59,594.26	0.96
2020	151,450.02	0.78	77,084.63	0.85	57,493.34	0.97
2021	181,192.83	0.81	92,433.76	0.89	69,854.76	1.03
Sri Lanka						
2010	928.69	0.18	546.12	0.15	557.38	0.23
2019	1,672.66	0.19	954.75	0.16	953.56	0.25
2020	1,333.90	0.22	831.37	0.20	726.59	0.27
2021	1,918.50	0.27	1,184.99	0.25	1,017.11	0.32
Taipei,China						
2010	240,938.23	1.63	123,596.47	1.68	102,984.98	2.13
2019	309,890.91	1.77	175,047.63	1.86	140,207.26	2.32
2020	321,583.58	1.81	196,608.39	1.93	158,784.42	2.39
2021	422,257.77	1.79	247,234.68	1.91	197,600.29	2.35
Thailand						
2010	79,185.74	1.11	43,791.19	1.05	27,920.15	1.02
2019	116,188.81	0.79	62,371.68	0.68	45,563.05	0.78
2020	118,116.06	1.00	66,522.67	0.92	44,805.97	0.95
2021	121,989.04	0.90	60,517.46	0.78	42,805.09	0.84
Viet Nam						
2010	17,018.58	0.44	7,978.87	0.42	7,181.28	0.57
2019	86,088.15	0.68	35,378.49	0.61	27,940.64	0.75
2020	93,849.60	0.72	37,376.00	0.64	29,876.75	0.78
2021	104,954.36	0.68	35,276.81	0.58	31,875.68	0.80

0.00 = magnitude is less than half of unit employed, $ = United States dollars, ADB = Asian Development Bank, RCA = revealed comparative advantage, VAX = value-added exports.

Source: Asian Development Bank. Multiregional Input-Output Tables. https://mrio.adbx.online/ (accessed 05 July 2022).

Table 3.4.4: Revealed Comparative Advantage Indices—Business Services Sector

ADB Regional Member	Gross		Value-Added			
			By Export Sectors		By Origin Sectors	
	Exports	RCA	VAX	RCA	VAX	RCA
	($ million)	(ratio)	($ million)	(ratio)	($ million)	(ratio)
Australia						
2010	50,135.67	0.73	45,163.80	0.68	81,009.26	0.84
2019	61,681.68	0.70	55,619.98	0.67	101,554.43	0.80
2020	60,535.27	0.69	54,460.49	0.64	100,807.90	0.78
2021	61,819.37	0.70	56,444.97	0.64	103,016.96	0.77
Bangladesh						
2010	1,427.57	0.31	1,350.36	0.31	4,332.05	0.68
2019	5,199.41	0.43	4,785.36	0.46	10,560.08	0.67
2020	4,897.75	0.47	4,520.67	0.50	9,555.96	0.69
2021	5,293.40	0.47	4,870.50	0.49	10,656.06	0.71
Bhutan						
2010	123.96	0.95	92.91	0.76	111.74	0.63
2019	274.41	1.19	216.35	1.09	243.34	0.81
2020	186.23	1.01	145.34	0.88	159.04	0.64
2021	240.71	1.09	189.41	0.96	204.65	0.69
Brunei Darussalam						
2010	676.52	0.29	448.11	0.19	554.40	0.16
2019	525.52	0.25	313.00	0.17	516.30	0.19
2020	293.47	0.16	180.80	0.11	445.23	0.18
2021	350.35	0.21	224.05	0.15	341.45	0.15
Cambodia						
2010	1,597.60	1.58	1,306.92	1.58	1,176.03	0.98
2019	5,463.60	1.23	4,148.55	1.27	4,128.71	0.83
2020	4,161.52	0.99	3,127.40	1.02	3,306.32	0.71
2021	3,580.07	0.80	2,673.07	0.84	3,075.65	0.64
Fiji						
2010	824.07	2.84	579.17	2.48	558.25	1.65
2019	1,760.47	2.48	1,289.67	2.22	1,271.02	1.44
2020	785.46	2.38	596.49	2.13	587.19	1.37
2021	808.55	2.34	606.13	2.09	611.98	1.39
Hong Kong, China						
2010	120,938.90	3.37	91,139.00	3.25	91,285.98	2.25
2019	122,121.25	3.20	98,839.70	3.11	99,800.38	2.07
2020	102,812.77	3.21	85,209.46	3.12	85,800.12	2.06
2021	121,280.56	3.35	99,314.40	3.22	99,515.28	2.13
India						
2010	128,576.96	1.63	113,542.13	1.59	134,419.06	1.30
2019	210,943.32	1.48	188,855.12	1.51	223,650.02	1.18
2020	204,234.53	1.53	185,474.76	1.54	214,049.15	1.16
2021	258,799.71	1.52	233,384.66	1.55	266,692.94	1.17
Indonesia						
2010	12,909.05	0.28	11,412.31	0.26	29,064.09	0.46
2019	23,739.19	0.43	20,985.10	0.41	42,174.78	0.54
2020	20,218.72	0.41	18,257.57	0.40	38,289.66	0.54
2021	26,562.69	0.41	23,556.90	0.38	48,313.63	0.52

continued on next page

Table 3.4.4: continued

Table 3.4.4: Revealed Comparative Advantage Indices—Business Services Sector

ADB Regional Member	Gross		Value-Added			
			By Export Sectors		By Origin Sectors	
	Exports	RCA	VAX	RCA	VAX	RCA
	($ million)	(ratio)	($ million)	(ratio)	($ million)	(ratio)
Japan						
2010	188,197.35	0.90	169,661.72	0.87	288,806.57	1.02
2019	188,759.93	0.79	174,082.02	0.81	299,204.02	0.92
2020	145,556.12	0.69	135,598.69	0.70	255,681.13	0.87
2021	179,208.37	0.77	165,427.33	0.79	297,433.23	0.94
Kazakhstan						
2010	13,483.76	0.84	12,353.14	0.76	18,974.76	0.81
2019	10,781.67	0.63	9,662.48	0.59	20,248.06	0.81
2020	9,867.48	0.71	8,966.90	0.66	16,245.24	0.79
2021	5,718.63	0.34	5,232.05	0.31	17,747.44	0.70
Kyrgyz Republic						
2010	239.78	0.42	164.10	0.38	328.05	0.52
2019	428.40	0.51	327.56	0.49	613.09	0.60
2020	331.21	0.51	247.70	0.46	427.01	0.52
2021	558.71	0.60	398.95	0.53	750.12	0.65
Lao People's Democratic Republic						
2010	525.67	0.91	436.91	0.78	472.98	0.58
2019	1,127.86	0.65	932.03	0.57	1,127.25	0.45
2020	855.55	0.54	756.15	0.48	928.89	0.39
2021	1,145.85	0.56	987.00	0.48	1,318.72	0.43
Malaysia						
2010	58,382.07	1.05	43,222.71	1.13	52,537.58	0.95
2019	73,524.06	1.15	57,944.27	1.26	67,860.53	0.97
2020	55,200.86	1.00	44,431.80	1.12	57,013.19	0.94
2021	60,926.03	0.93	48,217.11	1.05	62,785.20	0.90
Maldives						
2010	1,707.68	3.81	1,186.96	3.41	1,035.18	2.05
2019	3,734.00	3.58	2,690.91	3.26	2,415.06	1.93
2020	1,617.11	3.39	1,224.63	3.07	1,073.17	1.76
2021	3,196.73	3.63	2,347.56	3.25	2,088.24	1.90
Mongolia						
2010	667.77	0.90	525.32	0.83	706.16	0.77
2019	996.89	0.46	710.30	0.42	1,367.61	0.53
2020	875.41	0.43	637.12	0.39	1,396.57	0.56
2021	960.96	0.42	688.75	0.37	1,633.79	0.58
Nepal						
2010	780.53	2.00	608.59	1.80	672.22	1.38
2019	1,581.83	2.21	1,103.42	1.98	1,262.42	1.49
2020	1,250.95	2.09	896.42	1.86	1,015.65	1.38
2021	846.12	1.80	607.84	1.57	761.78	1.30
Pakistan						
2010	7,061.63	1.20	6,382.50	1.07	8,336.12	0.97
2019	5,710.26	0.83	5,158.11	0.77	7,832.46	0.77
2020	5,875.76	0.85	5,351.35	0.78	7,932.98	0.76
2021	6,247.73	0.84	5,642.10	0.76	8,695.98	0.77

continued on next page

Table 3.4.4: continued

Table 3.4.4: Revealed Comparative Advantage Indices—Business Services Sector

ADB Regional Member	Gross		Value-Added			
			By Export Sectors		By Origin Sectors	
	Exports	RCA	VAX	RCA	VAX	RCA
	($ million)	(ratio)	($ million)	(ratio)	($ million)	(ratio)
People's Republic of China						
2010	276,698.17	0.65	242,214.67	0.65	419,618.86	0.77
2019	352,710.76	0.50	312,605.58	0.50	753,065.03	0.80
2020	360,192.19	0.49	321,960.64	0.50	785,957.84	0.80
2021	457,902.75	0.50	404,998.20	0.51	966,404.45	0.80
Philippines						
2010	18,372.71	1.40	16,857.37	1.45	20,005.63	1.19
2019	37,111.56	1.69	33,965.61	1.85	39,497.82	1.41
2020	29,571.50	1.58	27,464.85	1.72	33,240.33	1.37
2021	31,491.78	1.58	28,878.91	1.78	34,099.00	1.38
Republic of Korea						
2010	50,284.70	0.39	40,070.06	0.43	96,894.78	0.72
2019	92,356.55	0.53	73,343.04	0.57	150,082.93	0.76
2020	87,439.12	0.55	71,644.95	0.57	145,947.44	0.76
2021	106,591.01	0.56	85,619.06	0.59	172,338.54	0.78
Singapore						
2010	139,924.89	1.83	83,284.64	1.95	97,001.28	1.56
2019	269,657.60	2.23	142,808.25	2.06	159,494.48	1.51
2020	251,400.60	2.22	130,546.34	2.00	148,883.43	1.50
2021	280,685.06	2.27	147,171.55	2.03	168,106.70	1.53
Sri Lanka						
2010	3,968.35	1.43	3,380.29	1.36	3,845.21	1.07
2019	9,066.18	1.74	7,583.05	1.74	7,709.97	1.16
2020	4,562.05	1.31	4,002.84	1.33	4,724.33	1.03
2021	2,891.76	0.74	2,591.14	0.77	4,058.31	0.79
Taipei,China						
2010	49,626.00	0.63	38,687.26	0.78	55,438.56	0.77
2019	43,539.94	0.42	35,082.49	0.52	65,058.73	0.63
2020	35,898.02	0.35	30,571.41	0.42	62,669.93	0.56
2021	50,817.10	0.39	42,054.99	0.47	85,902.92	0.63
Thailand						
2010	31,849.89	0.84	25,523.02	0.90	40,614.88	0.99
2019	92,144.07	1.06	72,313.25	1.10	101,899.67	1.03
2020	44,870.43	0.65	35,729.99	0.69	71,403.75	0.90
2021	66,019.87	0.88	51,276.72	0.94	81,745.17	0.99
Viet Nam						
2010	10,830.04	0.52	7,562.53	0.58	11,817.05	0.63
2019	14,227.31	0.19	10,387.13	0.25	37,009.07	0.58
2020	13,796.31	0.18	10,406.57	0.25	36,967.72	0.57
2021	17,009.40	0.20	12,399.11	0.29	33,662.56	0.52

$ = United States dollars, ADB = Asian Development Bank, RCA = revealed comparative advantage, VAX = value-added exports.

Source: Asian Development Bank. Multiregional Input-Output Tables. https://mrio.adbx.online/ (accessed 05 July 2022).

Table 3.4.5: Revealed Comparative Advantage Indices—Personal and Public Services Sector						
ADB Regional Member	Gross		Value-Added			
	Exports	RCA	By Export Sectors		By Origin Sectors	
			VAX	RCA	VAX	RCA
	($ million)	(ratio)	($ million)	(ratio)	($ million)	(ratio)
Australia						
2010	7,155.56	1.36	6,675.38	1.22	10,843.40	1.24
2019	14,983.46	2.13	13,662.71	1.89	14,563.54	1.30
2020	15,006.19	2.25	13,838.19	1.99	14,601.82	1.38
2021	15,199.03	2.25	14,203.66	1.97	14,670.06	1.34
Bangladesh						
2010	184.17	0.52	174.92	0.49	1,735.98	3.01
2019	470.87	0.48	442.35	0.49	2,694.49	1.94
2020	559.25	0.71	528.69	0.71	2,585.50	2.28
2021	608.00	0.71	572.58	0.71	2,865.45	2.32
Bhutan						
2010	9.81	0.98	8.48	0.85	9.71	0.60
2019	28.96	1.57	25.57	1.49	20.07	0.75
2020	28.12	2.00	25.30	1.87	21.08	1.03
2021	32.29	1.90	28.95	1.79	24.18	0.98
Brunei Darussalam						
2010	31.20	0.18	24.95	0.13	125.15	0.41
2019	92.30	0.55	65.97	0.43	75.05	0.31
2020	50.21	0.36	36.20	0.28	88.71	0.45
2021	59.97	0.48	43.89	0.37	40.88	0.22
Cambodia						
2010	71.12	0.92	57.02	0.84	68.98	0.64
2019	147.80	0.42	112.89	0.40	182.90	0.42
2020	88.83	0.28	67.52	0.27	129.86	0.34
2021	75.31	0.22	58.02	0.22	104.69	0.26
Fiji						
2010	17.93	0.81	15.35	0.80	22.06	0.72
2019	63.76	1.12	57.26	1.14	99.46	1.28
2020	28.79	1.14	26.17	1.13	52.54	1.50
2021	36.73	1.39	32.83	1.38	57.04	1.58
Hong Kong, China						
2010	594.50	0.22	511.10	0.22	3,319.91	0.91
2019	3,398.91	1.11	3,036.93	1.10	5,030.75	1.18
2020	2,000.49	0.82	1,789.36	0.80	3,886.88	1.14
2021	3,909.51	1.41	3,442.07	1.36	5,094.17	1.32
India						
2010	10,841.53	1.79	10,186.39	1.75	13,940.71	1.50
2019	12,738.45	1.11	12,082.98	1.12	17,331.57	1.03
2020	9,068.43	0.89	8,596.06	0.86	12,407.50	0.82
2021	13,230.70	1.02	12,436.60	1.01	16,972.79	0.90
Indonesia						
2010	2,009.07	0.57	1,811.70	0.51	2,635.13	0.46
2019	5,173.18	1.16	4,845.16	1.09	5,202.10	0.76
2020	4,769.13	1.28	4,508.65	1.19	4,765.27	0.83
2021	6,142.22	1.23	5,742.39	1.14	5,872.90	0.76

continued on next page

Table 3.4.5: continued

ADB Regional Member	Gross		Value-Added			
			By Export Sectors		By Origin Sectors	
	Exports	RCA	VAX	RCA	VAX	RCA
	($ million)	(ratio)	($ million)	(ratio)	($ million)	(ratio)
Japan						
2010	3,677.31	0.23	3,466.89	0.22	16,854.58	0.66
2019	4,472.10	0.23	4,182.64	0.23	19,791.95	0.69
2020	3,461.42	0.22	3,259.22	0.21	16,249.26	0.68
2021	4,109.95	0.23	3,815.97	0.22	19,261.34	0.74
Kazakhstan						
2010	652.33	0.53	576.38	0.44	607.54	0.29
2019	415.33	0.30	377.41	0.27	406.90	0.18
2020	262.02	0.25	240.10	0.22	265.36	0.16
2021	133.63	0.10	123.33	0.09	207.67	0.10
Kyrgyz Republic						
2010	67.89	1.54	52.66	1.49	44.03	0.78
2019	299.53	4.46	267.47	4.61	241.87	2.69
2020	282.89	5.69	258.33	5.84	231.10	3.44
2021	384.60	5.37	346.61	5.56	314.53	3.32
Lao People's Democratic Republic						
2010	22.55	0.51	19.02	0.41	15.79	0.21
2019	4.58	0.03	4.26	0.03	5.33	0.02
2020	1.37	0.01	1.29	0.01	2.75	0.01
2021	1.84	0.01	1.71	0.01	4.38	0.02
Malaysia						
2010	1,492.57	0.35	1,278.72	0.41	1,674.29	0.33
2019	2,471.98	0.48	2,108.15	0.53	2,143.52	0.35
2020	2,383.40	0.56	2,053.44	0.63	2,057.81	0.41
2021	2,326.11	0.46	1,966.71	0.52	1,972.66	0.34
Maldives						
2010	31.09	0.90	22.84	0.80	29.11	0.64
2019	66.37	0.79	61.23	0.86	140.27	1.27
2020	51.50	1.41	46.69	1.42	107.25	2.15
2021	89.26	1.32	80.98	1.36	165.80	1.84
Mongolia						
2010	5.69	0.10	4.82	0.09	33.91	0.41
2019	45.40	0.26	34.29	0.23	62.87	0.28
2020	40.24	0.26	31.10	0.23	67.67	0.33
2021	44.34	0.25	33.76	0.22	95.44	0.41
Nepal						
2010	98.74	3.29	91.19	3.31	63.67	1.44
2019	73.18	1.28	65.21	1.35	85.06	1.14
2020	70.17	1.54	62.69	1.58	80.22	1.33
2021	45.31	1.26	40.39	1.27	59.82	1.24
Pakistan						
2010	1,490.58	3.29	1,412.05	2.90	1,240.37	1.59
2019	1,651.16	3.00	1,556.67	2.68	1,497.07	1.66
2020	1,617.95	3.08	1,537.64	2.72	1,466.95	1.71
2021	1,767.04	3.11	1,672.52	2.73	1,587.10	1.71

Table 3.4.5: Revealed Comparative Advantage Indices—Personal and Public Services Sector

continued on next page

Table 3.4.5: continued

Table 3.4.5: Revealed Comparative Advantage Indices—Personal and Public Services Sector

ADB Regional Member	Gross		Value-Added			
			By Export Sectors		By Origin Sectors	
	Exports	RCA	VAX	RCA	VAX	RCA
	($ million)	(ratio)	($ million)	(ratio)	($ million)	(ratio)
People's Republic of China						
2010	12,135.87	0.37	10,725.06	0.35	25,887.71	0.53
2019	18,752.86	0.33	16,496.03	0.31	57,791.75	0.70
2020	17,468.68	0.31	15,790.91	0.30	57,256.03	0.71
2021	21,262.69	0.31	18,994.02	0.29	68,888.76	0.69
Philippines						
2010	695.20	0.69	631.25	0.66	839.61	0.55
2019	1,530.55	0.87	1,366.99	0.86	1,762.36	0.72
2020	1,062.03	0.74	965.70	0.73	1,284.10	0.64
2021	1,117.50	0.73	999.77	0.75	1,292.21	0.64
Republic of Korea						
2010	3,801.91	0.38	3,216.79	0.42	10,334.51	0.85
2019	2,495.66	0.18	2,153.46	0.19	6,780.36	0.39
2020	2,333.00	0.19	2,043.27	0.20	6,562.14	0.42
2021	2,673.21	0.18	2,318.59	0.19	7,157.33	0.39
Singapore						
2010	6,630.96	1.13	5,258.40	1.50	5,231.93	0.94
2019	9,918.50	1.02	7,940.58	1.32	8,236.26	0.89
2020	9,139.87	1.06	7,284.11	1.36	6,847.42	0.84
2021	9,954.02	1.05	7,956.20	1.33	7,750.75	0.85
Sri Lanka						
2010	22.73	0.11	20.49	0.10	194.10	0.60
2019	215.40	0.52	184.73	0.49	429.12	0.73
2020	23.43	0.09	21.17	0.09	181.57	0.48
2021	2.99	0.01	2.64	0.01	160.73	0.38
Taipei,China						
2010	1,313.56	0.22	1,105.97	0.27	3,719.86	0.57
2019	345.74	0.04	307.88	0.05	3,855.08	0.43
2020	296.39	0.04	269.37	0.04	3,770.27	0.41
2021	360.61	0.04	325.75	0.04	4,612.81	0.41
Thailand						
2010	4,016.49	1.37	3,386.41	1.46	3,382.71	0.91
2019	15,017.09	2.16	12,925.30	2.28	11,545.86	1.32
2020	1,038.51	0.20	904.30	0.21	2,576.21	0.40
2021	5,519.87	0.96	4,720.30	1.05	5,662.37	0.83
Viet Nam						
2010	400.82	0.25	301.37	0.28	393.26	0.23
2019	1,103.56	0.18	801.35	0.22	1,399.82	0.25
2020	1,222.35	0.21	878.97	0.25	1,430.42	0.27
2021	2,082.57	0.32	1,400.70	0.40	1,573.31	0.29

$ = United States dollars, ADB = Asian Development Bank, RCA = revealed comparative advantage, VAX = value-added exports.
Source: Asian Development Bank. Multiregional Input-Output Tables. https://mrio.adbx.online/ (accessed 05 July 2022).

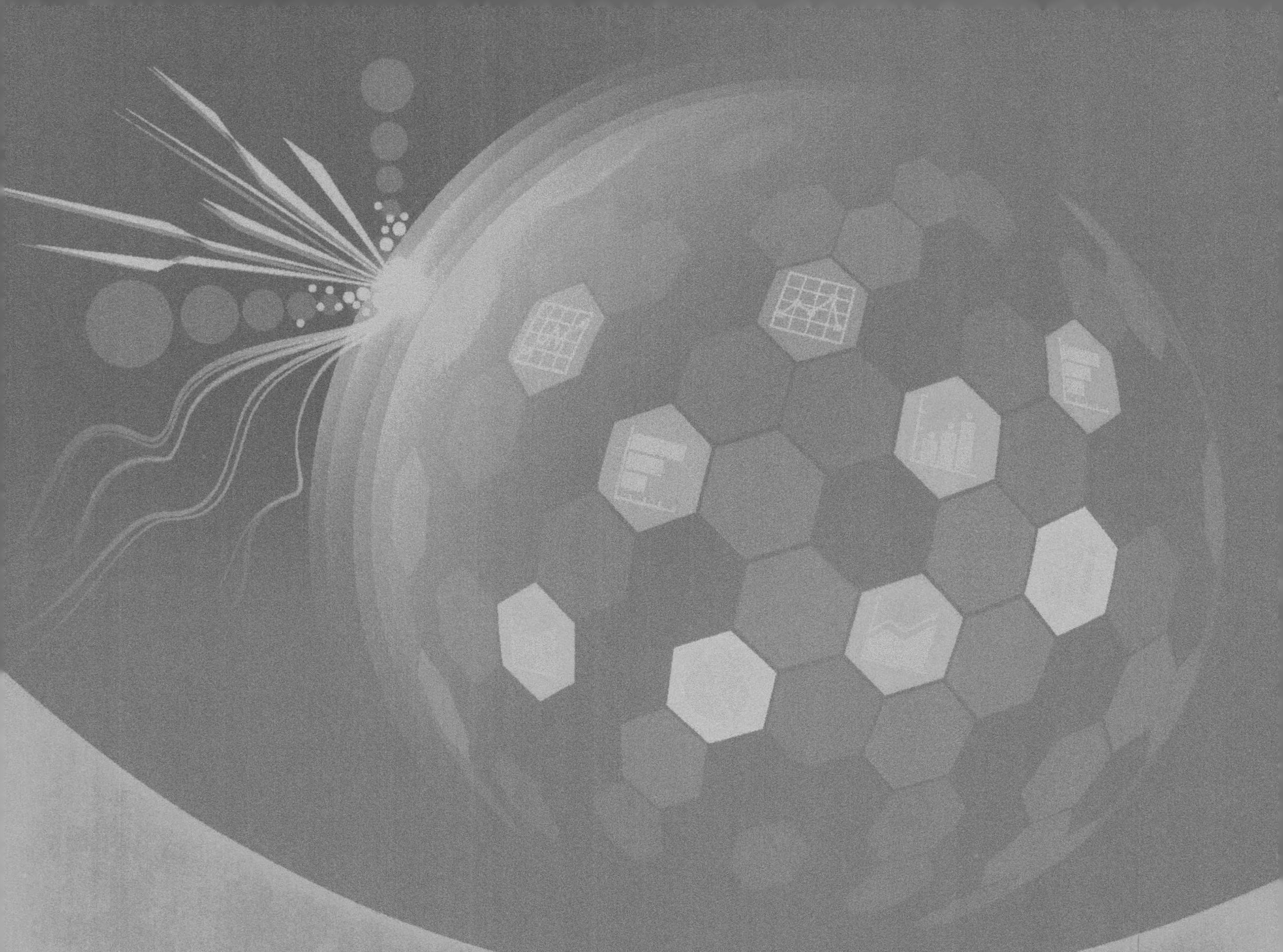

PART IV

Harnessing Administrative Data for a More Resilient Data and Statistical System

Overview

National statistical systems (NSSs) play a vital role in the production and dissemination of official statistics, which are an essential "public good". NSSs comprise national statistics offices (NSOs) and other public entities that are responsible for collecting, processing, and disseminating official statistics for policymaking. In developing economies, NSSs typically rely on more commonly used conventional methods, such as sample surveys and censuses, in compiling official statistics for a wide range of development themes, including population and demographic trends, economic performance, monetary and financial scenarios, work and employment, and poverty and living conditions, among others.

When the Millennium Development Agenda was adopted more than 2 decades ago, it ushered in greater appreciation of NSSs' critical role in promoting socioeconomic development. NSSs, in collaboration with the international statistics community, led the way in compiling data that served as a clear monitoring framework for assessing socioeconomic progress with respect to the specific, time-bound, and quantified targets of the Millennium Development Goals. The subsequent adoption of the 2030 Agenda for Sustainable Development, which has significantly more development targets under the Sustainable Development Goals (SDGs) than did the Millennium Development Goals, brought into focus expanding national and global data needs. For instance, the availability of disaggregated data by various geographical and demographic classes is more needed now than ever before to produce information that is important for decision-making. This has led to the calls for a "data revolution" wherein data from multiple sources can be integrated to provide more nuanced and meaningful information that can more efficiently meet the expanding and evolving data requirements of policymakers (UN 2013).

High-quality data facilitate actionable insights. Especially during pandemics or other periods of uncertainty, when scenarios may change rapidly, having timely and reliable data is crucial for governments and other policymakers to develop solutions to the issues at hand.

The coronavirus disease (COVID-19) pandemic disrupted operations of NSSs and made conducting conventional surveys and censuses—which are commonly used to compile development statistics, including SDG indicators—challenging, especially while lockdowns were in place. This is because such data collection activities typically require face-to-face interactions in the field.

To reconcile the need for timely and reliable statistics with disruptions in conventional ways of collecting data, it is important to discover ways to facilitate "data resilience". Data resilience, in this context, refers to the continuous flow of information amid challenges encountered in collecting, compiling, and analyzing data. As such, resilience hinges on the capacity to ensure data flows as efficiently as possible, which requires an understanding of what types of information are available from various sources of data. This includes understanding how data are collected and, in case of disruption where particular types of data cannot be accessed through conventional methods, how other sources of data can contribute. The need to promote resilience and improve the efficiency of statistical production processes underscores the importance of exploring other sources of data that have long existed but have not been maximized in terms of their use for statistical purposes.[1]

Administrative records, though typically built for regulatory purposes or to supplement administration of various government programs, are a potentially rich source of information that can be triangulated with survey, census, and other types of data to provide more nuanced, timely, and granular development indicators. Though administrative data may not be originally collected for statistical purposes, there is an increasing recognition of their rich statistical potential as they can produce statistics through data integration. Gross domestic product (GDP) estimates, for instance, are a product of integration of various administrative data, particularly on production values, sales, exports, and imports. Administrative data can also produce full population coverage, such as the generation of local-level statistics, and can enhance the frequency of releasing statistics as in the case of statistical registers (UNESCAP 2022). Identifiers from administrative data can be used for matching records to link micro or macro data from various sources. In some economies, population registers supplemented by housing registers have even replaced conduct of population censuses.

If collected properly, the use of administrative data offers various advantages. While possibly enhancing statistical quality, using administrative data also saves costs if such data are routinely and properly collected. Nationally representative surveys such as household income and expenditure surveys (HIESs), which are typically collected by NSOs, entail substantial resources and cost on average about $1.7 million to conduct (UNSDSN 2015). However, some of the information (e.g., income) gathered during HIESs is also available in other administrative sources such as tax registers. In addition to HIESs, information collected from other surveys also overlap with administrative data. Therefore, by harnessing existing administrative data, the scope of such surveys could be streamlined to obtain data with a larger sample size at a lower cost (IPA 2016).

---

1 Principle 5 of the Fundamental Principles of Official Statistics gives guidance on the use of administrative data vis-à-vis other sources of data. It states that, "Data for statistical purposes may be drawn from all types of sources, be they administrative or statistical records. Statistical agencies are to choose the sources with regard to quality, timeliness, costs and burden on the respondents (UNSD 1994)." With the goal of quality and timeliness of data, collection should be cost-effective and reduce the burden on respondents. The conduct of some surveys and censuses may be avoided when administrative records are well-maintained, timely, and meet statistical standards on definitions, concepts, classifications, coverage, methods, and completeness (ADB 2010).

In addition, when conducting impact evaluation studies, use of administrative data can save hundreds of thousands of dollars over the cost of running surveys needed to collect data, which typically constitutes a major expenditure item for such studies (Rawlings 2013). A reduced cost in data collection is beneficial for resource-constrained settings such as during crises, when a considerable portion of government resources may have to be reallocated to cover socioeconomic assistance programs. Administrative data can also potentially cover a large segment of the economy and reduce the response burden that typically results from statistical inquiries such as censuses and surveys.

On the other hand, there are also challenges in using administrative data for the purpose of compiling development indicators, as such data are not originally designed for statistical objectives. Furthermore, the use of administrative data may be constrained by existing legal regulations on data confidentiality.

Table 4.1 lists some of the benefits and disadvantages of using administrative data.

Table 4.1: Advantages and Limitations of Administrative Data

Advantages	Limitations
(i) Simplicity, speed, and frequency of updating	(i) Concepts, definitions, classifications, and methods not suited for statistical purposes
(ii) Lower costs	(ii) Incomplete coverage and poor reporting
(iii) Wider coverage, completeness, and disaggregations	(iii) Coverage biases
(iv) Low-response burden	(iv) Less flexible

Source: Asian Development Bank. 2010. Administrative Data Sources for Compiling Millennium Development Goals and Related Indicators.

Some of these limitations of administrative data can be avoided by identifying needed information, reviewing existing forms and records, and minimally redesigning forms to meet statistical purposes without compromising administrative requirements (ADB 2010).

Given the rich potential of administrative data to facilitate more resilient statistical systems, the challenges surrounding its use, particularly in the context of developing economies, underscore the need to strengthen capacity in handling and integrating such data. Within the international statistical community, the United Nations Statistics Division and Global Partnership for Sustainable Development Data have established the Collaborative on the Use of Admin Data for Statistics or "Collab" for short. This initiative coordinates a multistakeholder collective of economies and regional and international agencies that aspire to strengthen the capacity to harness administrative data for compiling development statistics. The collaborative is a forum for exchanging resources, instruments, best practices, and knowledge, and for increasing understanding among the NSSs of the merits of sharing and integrating administrative data sources to strengthen the quality, timeliness, coverage, and granularity of statistics (UN DESA 2022).

In October 2021 to February 2022, the Economic Research and Regional Cooperation Department's Statistics and Data Innovation Unit (EROD-SDI) of the Asian Development Bank (ADB) conducted a survey on the use of administrative data for the compilation of employment-related indicators that complements the knowledge resources put together through the Collab initiative. This chapter provides insights from a statistical standpoint by examining the survey responses from 24 NSOs, 8 labor ministries, and 4 social welfare ministries of ADB's member economies in the Asia and Pacific region[2]. Although the labor and social welfare ministries that responded do not constitute a representative sample, they provided rich qualitative information about their objectives in compiling administrative data, issues encountered in using these data, policy uses, effects of the COVID-19 pandemic on their data collection activities, and plans to further harness administrative data as a complementary source of information for compiling development statistics.

What are the Common Uses of Administrative Data?

In Asia and the Pacific, administrative data collected by NSOs and labor and social welfare ministries serve a wide range of purposes.

Administrative data are usually collected by NSOs, labor ministries, social welfare agencies, social security institutions, offices that maintain administrative registers, and line ministries. Population registers are maintained by NSOs while business registers are either lodged in NSOs or trade and industry agencies. NSOs from economies with decentralized statistical systems, on the other hand, collate administrative data from line ministries. Several datasets on work, employment, housing, taxation, trade goods, and social protection are collected administratively. Labor ministries and relevant social welfare ministries keep data on insurance records, work-related injuries, labor inspection, and social security records (ADB 2021a).

As shown in Figure 4.1, a considerable number of survey respondents collected administrative data for statistical purposes. Other common reasons for data collection included registration of important events and inputs for delivery of services. Of the 24 responding NSOs, two thirds collected administrative data for statistical purposes and about one third collected data to keep a register of important events such as births and deaths. A few NSOs collected data for delivery of services and monitoring of important transactions, while only one collected data on other routine operations.

---

2 The EROD-SDI survey garnered responses from the NSOs of the following economies: Armenia; Azerbaijan; Bangladesh; Bhutan; Brunei Darussalam; Cambodia; the Cook Islands; Fiji; Georgia; Hong Kong, China; Indonesia; Kazakhstan; Malaysia; Mongolia; Nauru; Nepal; Pakistan; the Marshall Islands; the Philippines; Singapore; Thailand; Timor-Leste; Uzbekistan; and Viet Nam. Responses were also garnered from the labor ministries of the following economies: Armenia; Azerbaijan; Georgia; Hong Kong, China; Mongolia; the Philippines; Samoa; and Singapore; as well as from the social welfare ministries of Singapore; Sri Lanka; and Tonga.

Of the 12 responding labor and social welfare ministries, more than half reported using administrative data for delivery of services, but only one third of these respondents also cited using such data for statistical purposes.

Administrative data can feed into policy formulation, whether by ministries that collected such data or by other government offices. As Figure 4.2 shows, administrative data collected by NSOs were deemed useful for economic, labor, education, health, social protection, and finance policies. In Singapore, for example, administrative

Figure 4.1: Common Uses of Administrative Data, by Source of Data

Administrative data collected by NSOs and labor and social welfare ministries were used mostly for statistical purposes and/or delivery of services.

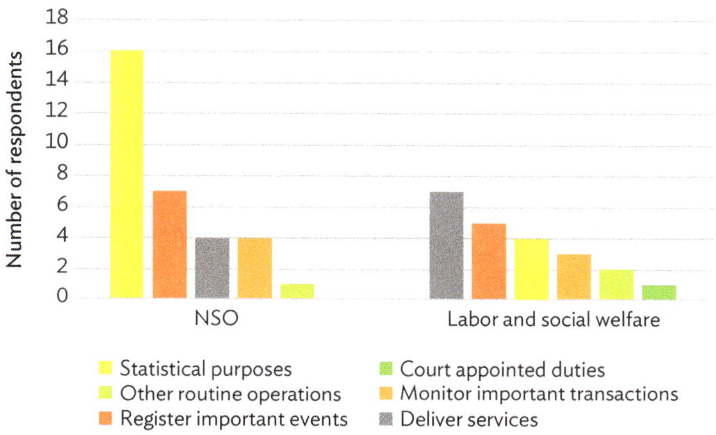

NSO = national statistics office.

Note: The Asian Development Bank survey garnered responses from 24 NSOs as well as 8 labor ministries and 4 social welfare ministries in the bank's member economies across Asia and the Pacific.

Source: Asian Development Bank. 2022. Survey on the Use of Administrative Data for the Compilation of Employment-Related Indicators.

Figure 4.2: Use of Administrative Data in Policy Formulation, by Source of Data

Information from administrative data fed into a wide range of socioeconomic policies.

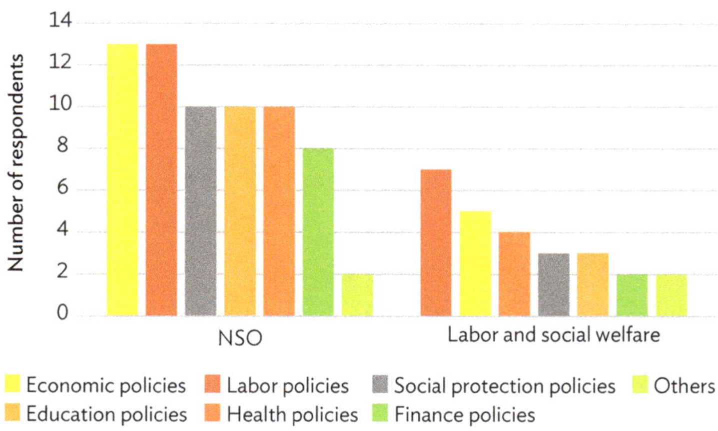

NSO = national statistics office.

Note: The Asian Development Bank survey garnered responses from 24 NSOs as well as 8 labor ministries and 4 social welfare ministries in the bank's member economies across Asia and the Pacific.

Source: Asian Development Bank. 2022. Survey on the Use of Administrative Data for the Compilation of Employment-Related Indicators.

data from the Accounting and Corporate Regulatory Authority were deemed useful for economic and finance policies. More than half of the responding labor and social welfare ministries used administrative data for policies on labor and more than a third applied such data to economic policies. Among these ministries, however, there appeared to be somewhat less emphasis on using administrative data for education, social protection, and finance policies.

How are Administrative Datasets Used in Different Economies?

In many developed economies, whether in Asia and the Pacific or elsewhere, administrative data are being used to serve a wide range of statistical objectives. One example is the use of administrative data to support more effective editing and imputation of missing survey responses and quality assessment or evaluation of survey-derived data. Since administrative data usually produce a complete count of units, these data sources are suitable for preparing, supplementing, or updating statistical registers and sampling frames. Furthermore, administrative data can be used for indirect estimation, as a source of auxiliary information for use in the estimation process.

Even before the COVID-19 pandemic, a number of economies also used administrative data for official statistics. For example, Nordic economies have been using administrative data as the foundation of their statistical systems for several years. Furthermore, at the height of the pandemic, readily available administrative datasets that listed segments of the population more likely to be severely affected by the pandemic proved useful in delivering social welfare transfers as efficiently as possible. In economies where such administrative data were not readily available, a listing of target recipients had to be compiled, which was not efficient given lockdowns and other containment measures.

For lower-income economies, however, there is much to be done in terms of harnessing administrative data, and this is particularly evident in the developing economies of Asia and the Pacific. Since the primary purpose and intent of collecting administrative data is for implementing administrative regulations, several challenges arise regarding its use for statistical purposes.

The content of administrative data is highly dependent on legislation that serves administrative objectives and may use concepts, definitions, classifications, and methods that may not be consistent with statistical standards. Moreover, changes in definitions across time to meet the requirements of administrative regulations may affect the continuity of the data. The scope and coverage of administrative data collected may not meet the need of the statistical users, given that the data may exclude or include certain units of interest by the legislation. In addition, administrative data

ministrative data in action. Although many administrative records are collected as products of a government ministry's core functions, they provide rich potential for nanced compilation of statistical outputs (photo by Eric Sales/ADB).

may only cater to units that have access to certain information or services and may disregard a significant portion of the population. Lastly, the procedures in collecting and managing administrative data may affect the reliability of the data. Given that administrative data are originally collected for record-keeping rather than statistical purposes, emphasis is not given to checks and balances, updates and corrections, and any other procedure that proves to be vital for statistical analysis.

Nevertheless, there is rich potential in integrating an administrative dataset with other administrative data or conventional sources of data used for compilation of development statistics. More than half (56%) of respondents who took part in the ADB survey reported that they could source from other government agencies administrative data that can be integrated with the data produced by NSOs and labor ministries.

Integrating administrative data managed by a specific government agency with other data sources managed elsewhere usually entails "record linkage", which refers to the identification and combination of records corresponding to the same entities, e.g., persons, enterprises, households, etc. (UNESCAP 2021). In this context, there are two types of record linkage: deterministic matching and probabilistic or statistical matching.

It is possible to conduct deterministic matching when unique identifiers exist that correspond to the same units from different data sources. For example, in Nordic economies, which have rich experience in producing statistics based on administrative sources, unit-level identifiers are present in almost all major administrative registers used for statistics compilation (UNECE 2021). Furthermore, statistics laws in many Nordic economies give their NSOs access to administrative data at unit level (with identifiers) and allow them to link these data with other administrative data sources for statistical purposes (UNECE 2021).

In general, limited availability and/or constraints in accessing unified identification systems across different data sources, which are common in a number of developing economies in Asia and the Pacific, render statistical use of administrative data records less straightforward. In such instances, governments resort to statistical matching by integrating based on a set of variables that are common across datasets and identifying similar records on a probabilistic basis (UNESCAP 2021).

In addition to availability of unified identification systems, there are other practical considerations that need to be taken into account when data from multiple administrative sources need to be combined. Such considerations include consistency of concepts, definitions, reference dates, coverage, and data quality standards adopted by each administrative source (UNESCAP 2021).

How Did the COVID-19 Pandemic Affect the Collection of Administrative Data?

The COVID-19 pandemic exposed some limitations and gaps in conventional data sources used to compile work and employment statistics in particular and development indicators in general. Conducting surveys and censuses, updating administrative datasets, and other data collection activities were all affected by the pandemic. Only one economy covered by the ADB survey reported no impact on data collection activities during the COVID-19 pandemic (Figure 4.3). More than half (53%) of lower middle-income economies, half (50%) of high-income economies, and a third (33%) of upper middle-income economies had to cancel, postpone, or reschedule these activities due to restrictions on the movement of people. About a quarter of high-income economies and a third of both upper middle- and lower middle-income economies cancelled their data collection activities to reallocate resources for COVID-19 response. For these government agencies, this meant shifting from face-to-face interviews and field data collection to phone-, web- or electronic-based methods and/or other hybrid approaches of data collection. In the wake of the pandemic, more than one third of high-income and upper middle-income economies and a third of lower middle-income economies opted to use administrative data (collected themselves or by government offices or nongovernment organizations) to supplement their typical sources of labor

Figure 4.3: Impacts of the COVID-19 Pandemic on Data Collection Activities, by Economy Income and Statistical Capacity

With conventional data collection disrupted, many economies employed alternative strategies, including increased use of administrative data, to meet the data demands of policymakers.

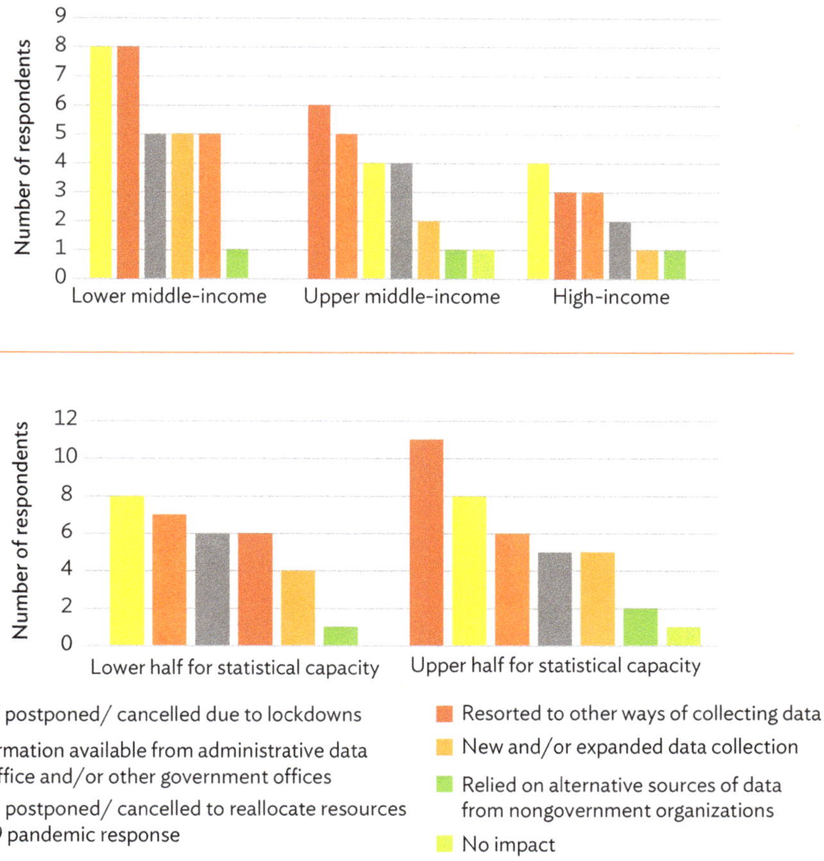

COVID-19 = coronavirus disease, NSO = national statistics office.

Notes: 1) The Asian Development Bank survey garnered responses from 24 NSOs as well as 8 labor ministries and 4 social welfare ministries in the bank's member economies across Asia and the Pacific.
2) Other ways of collecting data include shifting from face-to-face interviews and/or field data collection to phone-based, web-based, electronic-based and/or other hybrid approaches of data collection.
3) Using the overall averages of the World Bank's Statistical Capacity Index for the respondent economies, these economies were divided into a lower half and an upper half according to statistical capacity.

Source: Asian Development Bank. 2022. Survey on the Use of Administrative Data for the Compilation of Employment-Related Indicators.

and employment statistics. For policy design, administrative data from specific groups of workers and business sectors severely affected by the pandemic were collected by 3 upper middle-income and 3 lower middle-income economies.

When the 26 participating economies are divided into two groups (a lower half and an upper half) on the basis of statistical capacity[3], 8 agencies that belong to economies in the lower half had to reschedule, postpone, or cancel their data collection activities

3 The groups were determined on the basis of the World Bank's Statistical Capacity Index. However, the World Bank now compiles the Statistical Performance Indicator, which considers five pillars: data use, data services, data products, data sources, and data infrastructure. This indicator is set to be more comprehensive and forward-looking than the Statistical Capacity Index (World Bank 2021).

Complementing field data. National statistical systems typically collect data through censuses and surveys, but administrative data can provide rich information to complement these traditional data (photo by Ron Lester Durante/ADB).

due to lockdowns imposed during the pandemic; and 7 agencies in this group had to rely on information available from administrative data collected by their office or other government agencies. For agencies belonging to economies in the upper half for statistical capacity, 11 had to resort to other ways of collecting data; 8 had to reschedule, postpone, or cancel their data collection activities due to lockdowns; and 6 had to rely on information available from administrative data collected by their office or other government agencies.

While a substantial number of economies turned to administrative data to supplement statistical output during the pandemic, many also reported challenges and concerns surrounding the collection and use of such data. These challenges include constraints in access to, and the coverage and quality of, administrative data as well as limitations in collection and analysis because of operational disruptions caused by lockdowns and other mobility restrictions (Figure 4.4). The quality of data was the top concern of NSOs and labor and social welfare ministries across all economy income groupings. Unlike high-income economies, completeness of data coverage was a major concern for upper and lower middle-income economies. Other concerns included the inability to assess data due to disruptions in office operations, limited access due to office-level agreements, inadequate access to information technology infrastructure, data not consolidated in a database, and a lack of available personnel to compile the data.

Economies belonging to the upper half in terms of statistical capacity had issues mostly with quality and completeness of administrative data while those in the lower half were concerned mostly with quality, data not consolidated in a database, disruptions in office operations, and lack of human resources to compile data.

Figure 4.4: Issues Encountered in Collecting and Using Administrative Data, by Economy Income and Statistical Capacity

Suitability of administrative data for compilation of statistical outputs is a major concern for both NSOs and other government agencies across all economy income groupings.

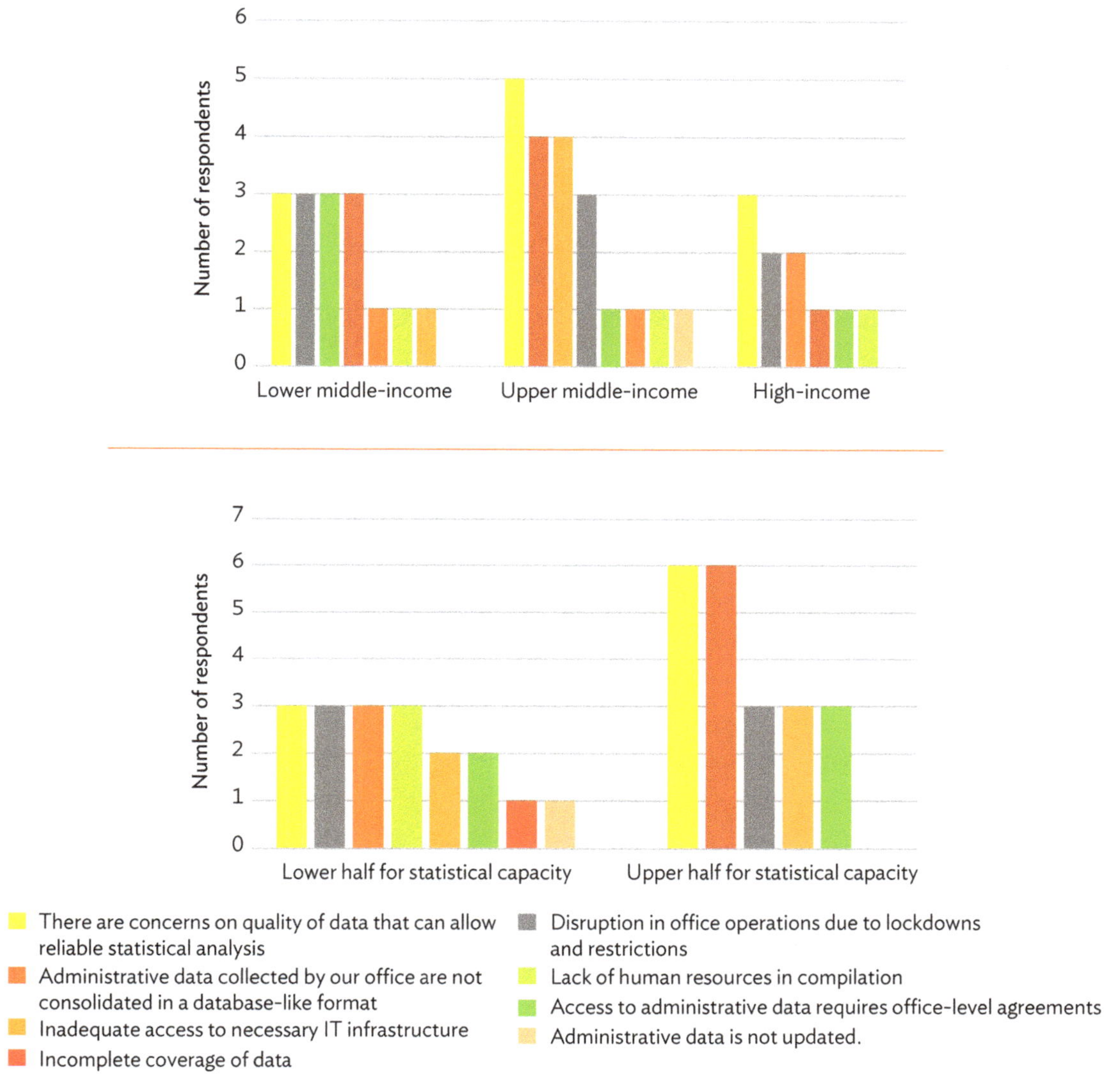

IT = information technology, NSO = national statistics office.

Notes: 1) The Asian Development Bank survey garnered responses from 24 NSOs as well as 8 labor ministries and 4 social welfare ministries in the bank's member economies across Asia and the Pacific.
2) Using the overall averages of the World Bank's Statistical Capacity Index for the respondent economies, these economies were divided into a lower half and an upper half according to statistical capacity.

Source: Asian Development Bank. 2022. Survey on the Use of Administrative Data for the Compilation of Employment-Related Indicators.

Initiatives to Promote the Use of Administrative Data in Asia and the Pacific

This section highlights the experiences of selected developing ADB member economies in harnessing administrative data. It covers a variety of initiatives implemented across the Asia and Pacific region, ranging from new legislation on official statistical compilation to some examples of administrative statistics used in measures ensuring equitable distribution of food support for vulnerable populations.

Armenia

In 2018, Armenia adopted the Law on Official Statistics, which introduced the National Statistical System (NSS) covering all producers of official statistics in the economy. The law identifies the Statistical Committee of the Republic of Armenia (Armstat) as the main producer of official statistics. Further, the law grants Armstat the right to access and utilize administrative records and registers to produce official statistics, and obligates line ministries and public institutions to grant access and make such records and registers available for official statistical purposes.

Armstat has been making use of important administrative data held by line ministries and public institutions. For instance, since 2018, it has been using information on number of payrolled employees, earnings (wages and/or salaries), and number of organizations from the Database of the Personal Income Tax and Social Tax (Payment) of the State Revenue Committee of the Republic of Armenia. The database includes information on all organizations with one or more paid employees.

The 2022 population census of Armenia will be conducted using a register-based, combined-census method. This census was originally planned for 2020 but was postponed due to the COVID-19 pandemic. Administrative data from the State Population Register will be used to obtain the minimum set of variables for the population census. This includes personal identification code, name, status (residence status or refugee status), registered address, citizenship, sex, date of birth, and birthplace. A sample survey will be conducted to collect all the variables defined by the census program.

To further increase the use of administrative data for statistical purposes in Armenia, the NSS recognizes the importance of coordination among statistical and other government agencies that produce administrative data, the need to improve the administrative registers and databases of line ministries, and increasing the number of staff and capacity development related to statistical analysis.

Bhutan

Administrative data provides a vital role for an economy with a sparse population, as is the case in Bhutan, because compiling such data is more practical than conducting regular surveys. Prior to the COVID-19 pandemic, the Statistics Division of the Ministry of Labour and Human Resources started the development of the Bhutan Labour Market Information System (BLMIS) to rationalize the collection and use of administrative data on the Bhutanese labor market. BLMIS is an online, real-time database system that collects employment data from all formal sectors of the economy. The system intends to provide employment statistics that are more accessible, more reliable, more frequent, and consistent with international standards and to serve as a mechanism to evaluate the statistics compiled by the National Statistics Bureau (NSB) through the annual conduct of the national Labour Force Survey. As a result of this initiative, the Ministry of Labour and Human Resources has been able to use the BLMIS datasets to design national-level employment policies and examine the employment situation in the formal economy. BLMIS has also improved partnerships with key stakeholders in terms of the production, use, and dissemination of official statistics on employment (Tenzin 2020).

To improve the collection and management of local-level data, the United Nations Population Fund, in cooperation with the NSB, established a database system at the *gewog* (a group of villages in a rural area) level. The project was initially undertaken in one *dzongkhag* (district) in 2014, then expanded to the remaining 205 *gewogs* of Bhutan. The NSB collected *gewog*-level data based on administrative records on population and households, basic household services, local businesses, communications, local disasters, and educational and health statistics, as well as detailed information on the livestock, forestry, and agriculture sectors (which make up a large proportion of employment in Bhutan). Moving forward, the NSB aims to expand the coverage of local-level data collection to urban areas (UN DESA 2021a).

To address the bias resulting from the consumer price index used to deflate exports and imports data for GDP estimations, the NSB utilized the data from administrative external trade registers, compiled by the Department of Revenue and Customs, as inputs to the methodology for estimating the Import and Export Price Index. This is considered a crucial step in improving the economic statistics of Bhutan, particularly in enhancing GDP data. As a way forward, there is a need to ascertain a reliable mechanism between the NSB and the Department of Revenue and Customs to ensure the timeliness and institutionalization of generating the Import and Export Price Index (UN DESA 2021b).

Mongolia

Even before the COVID-19 pandemic, the Government of Mongolia was already leveraging administrative sources for collecting employment-related data. The Ministry of Labour and Social Protection (MLSP) compiles data on registered unemployed, foreign workers with labor contract, employees working abroad on a contractual basis, and collective labor disputes. The General Agency for Specialized Inspection registers data on occupational accidents while the Civil Service Council records data on government employees.

The National Statistics Office of Mongolia oversees the dissemination of the registered unemployment statistics compiled by the MLSP. However, this practice was halted in April 2021 because of the ongoing enhancement of the registration system, although the other administrative data collection activities of other government entities were not impacted by the pandemic.

The Government of Mongolia uses a labor market information system, which creates a labor market database by registering and mediating information from employers or establishments and job seekers and unemployed people. The MLSP is preparing to integrate the labor market information system with other government databases and introduce an "e-job" electronic platform in 2022. The use of an electronic labor market platform has improved access to services for citizens and enterprises and reduced the burden on public services. As of 2022, there are 140 services in the platform, of which 53 services have been transferred to electronic form.

The General Office for Labor and Welfare Services under the MLSP also employs various administrative data sources in assessing the beneficiaries of Mongolia's Food Stamp Program (FSP). The FSP Database, Integrated Household Database, National Insurance Database as well as the Household Socio-Economic Surveys provide information on the characteristics of the beneficiaries. The assessment resulted in the removal of several FSP beneficiaries, which decreases inclusion errors and thus increases the program budget (ADB 2022). The National Statistics Office of Mongolia and selected government institutions of Mongolia have also reached an agreement to come up with an integrated database, which will include the (i) state registration data, i.e., civil and corporate data, of the General Authority for State Registration; (ii) social insurance data of the General Authority for Social Insurance; (iii) social welfare data of the General Authority for Labor and Social Welfare; (iv) education data of the Ministry of Education and Science; (v) tax data of the Mongolian Tax Authority; (vi) trade data of the Customs General Authority; (vii) price data of the Information Technology Center of Custom, Taxation, and Finance; and (viii) COVID-19 data of the National Center for Communicable Diseases.

Singapore

In the production of Singapore's demographic statistics, the statistical database with basic demographic information on Singapore's population and the statistical database on residential dwellings, both of which draw data from multiple administrative sources, have been enhanced continuously. These databases enable the compilation of annual data on basic register-based information such as age, gender, ethnicity, geographic location, and type of dwelling starting from the year 2000.

The COVID-19 pandemic caused unprecedented challenges for the conduct of Singapore's Census 2020. The Singapore Department of Statistics' strategy of integrating available information from other government agencies and using administrative data for consistency checks and validation of the census results reduced respondent burden by minimizing the need to recontact households after the initial enumeration. In addition, the department has implemented automated processes in coding selected data items to mitigate resource constraints in data processing.

The Manpower Research and Statistics Department integrates administrative data and labor force survey data as inputs to Singapore's official Labour Market Report. Employment data are compiled primarily from administrative records while the self-employed component—consisting of own-account workers, employers, or contributing family workers—is estimated from the Labour Force Survey. Data on the number of resident employees are compiled from the Central Provident Fund's administrative records of active contributors (defined as resident employees who have at least one fund contribution paid for them), while data on nonresidents working in Singapore are compiled from administrative records of relevant and valid work passes issued by the Ministry of Manpower.

Measures to Further Harness Administrative Data for More Resilient Statistical Systems

There are ongoing initiatives that promote the use of administrative data, but there is a need to scale up these initiatives.

ADB's survey revealed that little more than half of the responding NSOs and labor and social welfare ministries from upper middle-income economies that already collect administrative data plan to expand the collection of such data to supplement or enhance their current data portfolios (Figure 4.5). Particularly, 7 agencies each from upper and lower middle-income economies and 3 from high-income economies have plans to expand their collection activities for administrative data, while 14 NSOs and labor and social welfare ministries have no such plans. Further, none of the 5 agencies

Figure 4.5: Status of Programs for the Collection of Administrative Data, by Source of Data, Economy Income, and Statistical Capacity

Around the same number of NSOs and ministries planned to expand the collection of administrative data as those not considering such expansion.

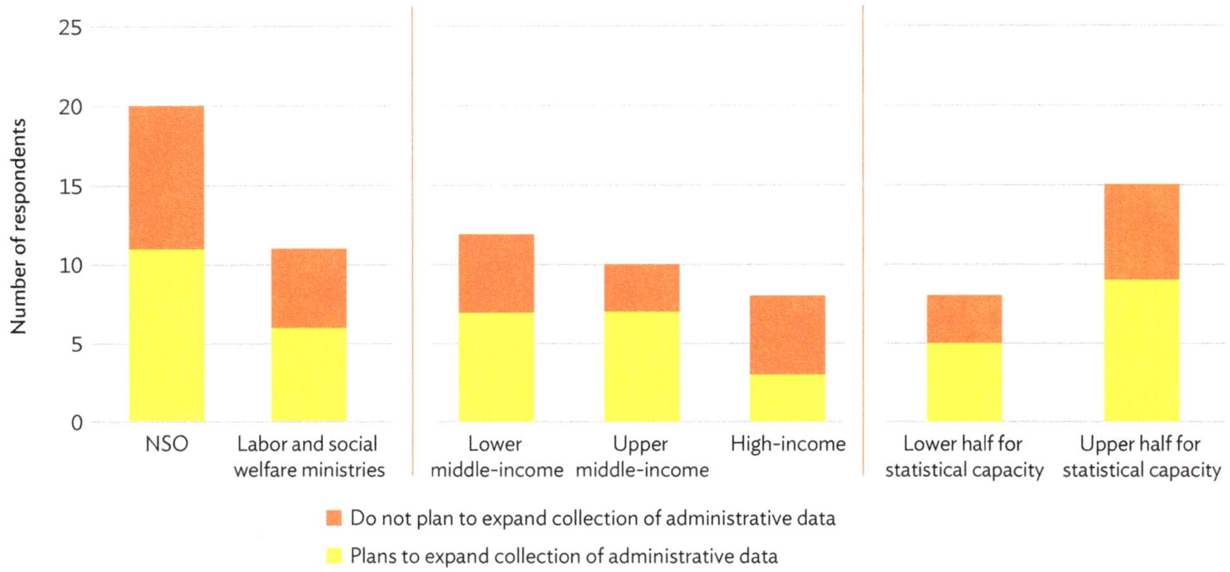

NSO = national statistics office.

Notes: 1) The Asian Development Bank survey garnered responses from 24 NSOs as well as 8 labor ministries and 4 social welfare ministries in the bank's member economies across Asia and the Pacific.
2) Using the overall averages of the World Bank's Statistical Capacity Index for the respondent economies, these economies were divided into a lower half and an upper half according to statistical capacity.

Source: Asian Development Bank. 2022. Survey on the Use of Administrative Data for the Compilation of Employment-Related Indicators.

that did not collect administrative data in upper and lower middle-income economies indicated any plans at the time of the survey to implement administrative data collection.

Within economies classified in the upper half for statistical capacity, all nine agencies that already collected administrative data had plans to expand their data collection activities, while five of the eight agencies in the lower half that already collected such data also had plans for expansion of these activities (Figure 4.5). By contrast, all six agencies in the upper half that already collect administrative data had no plans for expansion, while three of the eight agencies in the lower half also indicated no plans to expand their administrative data collection activities.

The results of the ADB survey indicate that there may be a need to boost initiatives on the use of administrative data across Asia and the Pacific. NSOs, which also manage volumes of administrative data, could take the lead in promoting the use of such data for the purposes of compiling development statistics. Strengthening appreciation among government agencies for the potential of using administrative data to refine statistical output should also be a priority to boost initiatives.

Access to administrative data needs to be expanded.

In some economies of Asia and the Pacific, legislation on statistical compilation allows NSOs full or partial access to administrative records in the public sector for statistical purposes. As privacy issues are impediments to data integration, some laws even provide NSOs access to private sector data. In some economies, however, the relevant data exist but either cannot be accessed by NSOs or can only be accessed for a fee.

Communication campaigns are needed to explain the value of statistical compilation from administrative data. Aside from a legal framework, it is important to have mechanisms that facilitate close collaboration and exchange of data and metadata among stakeholders. The Collab initiative's draft guidance and template for memoranda of understanding on such issues can help identify roles and responsibilities between the NSO and the administrative data owner.

Collaboration is essential to leverage the use of administrative data.

The owners of administrative data are mostly agencies other than NSOs. Thus, if NSOs are to take the lead in promoting the use of administrative data, they need to strengthen their working arrangements with government ministries and even with enterprises in the public sector.

A feedback system that helps the NSO and the data owner liaise on improvements to issues around administrative data (e.g., data quality) can significantly contribute to the strengthening of the administrative data system. This will consequently also strengthen the broader statistical system of any given economy. However, understanding the context under which the administrative data system was created is crucial. The administrative considerations that originally dictated the concepts, definitions, coverage, frequency, and timeliness of the administrative records may undergo changes and this can distort time series derived from the administrative data source.

The NSO needs to be the custodian of data quality—paying special attention to the consistency of concepts, definitions, and classifications as well as overall data integrity when there are multiple sources of administrative data. Each data item in the administrative records that is planned to be used for statistical purposes needs to be assessed to identify, understand, and correct sources of errors found in the system. It is possible that some of the items in the administrative records might be of very poor quality and therefore might not be useful.

An effective capacity building program is needed to promote and sustain the use of administrative data.

The NSOs may lead in initiating capacity building activities for other government agencies and enterprises from the private sector that are the owners of administrative data.

A united data effort. National statistical systems should invest in harnessing data to help address data gaps and limitations typical to censuses and surveys (photo by Lester Ledesma/ADB).

Long-term structural investments and genuine knowledge transfer are necessary to develop an enabling environment for the use of administrative data. The NSOs and other data owners will need their staff to develop new skill sets— both technical and soft skills that will enable them to harness new technologies, collaborate to understand legal and policy issues, and effectively communicate and negotiate with each other—as this is crucial for the use of administrative data to thrive.

In response to the growing demand to fill gaps in the data needed for accurate policy design and informed decision-making, the Collab initiative has developed a series of products and strategies useful in facilitating the use of administrative data (UN DESA 2022).

Guides and templates. A guide and template for improving coordination and cooperation within the NSS and for increasing access to administrative data for statistics production has been published. To institutionalize collaboration among relevant producers and users of administrative data, it is important to have formal agreements. A guide was published on December 2021 to guarantee and facilitate sustainable coordination and cooperation between the NSOs and other data owners. This publication provides a comprehensive introduction to memoranda of understanding and offers a variety of specific economy examples and a template that can be used as a basis for drafting them.

Expert clinics. These are organized by the Collab and its members. Each clinic particularly focuses on members' needs and serves as a forum to share experiences, inspire statistical innovation, and find solutions together. The experts that are invited to the exchange all belong to the statistics community and they do not receive remuneration for the services they provide to the clinics.

Self-assessment tool. This was designed to develop the understanding of how current statistical legislation facilitates the access and use of administrative data for the NSOs and their relevant NSS. The NSOs and other producers of official statistics are asked to complete an assessment and explore areas related to the governance of the NSS and the provisions of the statistical laws that directly or indirectly support the access and use of administrative data.

Inventory of resources. This initiative systematizes information on the use administrative of data for statistical purposes so that they become more readily available and easier to find. The inventory includes recommendations and practical examples; however, it should be noted that all materials may not fully conform with international guidelines.

ADB has likewise been promoting expanded integration of administrative data into national data and statistical ecosystems. For example, an ADB study released in 2021 offers insights on how labor statistics derived from administrative data can provide information to formulate and evaluate action plans on unemployment and work conditions and to gauge the prevalence of the working poor (ADB 2021a). It served as a supplement to ADB handbooks on the use of administrative data sources for compiling a wide range of development indicators (ADB 2010; ADB 2021b).

Furthermore, ADB has conducted a number of initiatives with components that aim to strengthen statistical capacity in using administrative data. The list of recently concluded and ongoing initiatives includes innovative data collection methods for agricultural and rural statistics (ADB 2018), improvement of statistical business registers (ADB 2019), strengthening economic statistics compilation systems (ADB 2020), development of and building capacity in new statistical resources and technologies (ADB 2021c), and use of multiple data sources to monitor progress towards the SDGs for Mongolia (ADB 2022).

Strengthening the use of administrative data calls for more action.

In the ADB survey on the use of administrative data, the government agencies that responded proposed specific actions that would drive and support the acceptance and use of such data. These actions are shown in Figure 4.6. Establishing a statistical database or register that is readily accessible to users was deemed important by 15 NSOs and 10 labor and social welfare ministries. Forming more partnerships with other government agencies was suggested by 16 NSOs and 9 labor and social welfare ministries. Other specific actions that were suggested to boost the use of administrative data are (in order of the level of agreement): ensuring regular updating of administrative data, conducting training on data analytics, improved coverage and granularity of data, improving data quality that can allow reliable statistical analysis, strengthening data confidentiality, simplifying data-sharing protocols, conducting research, and exploring innovative dissemination practices.

Figure 4.6: Proposed Initiatives to Strengthen the Use of Administrative Data

NSOs and government ministries from developing economies agreed a range of ways to stimulate the integration of administrative data in statistical compilation.

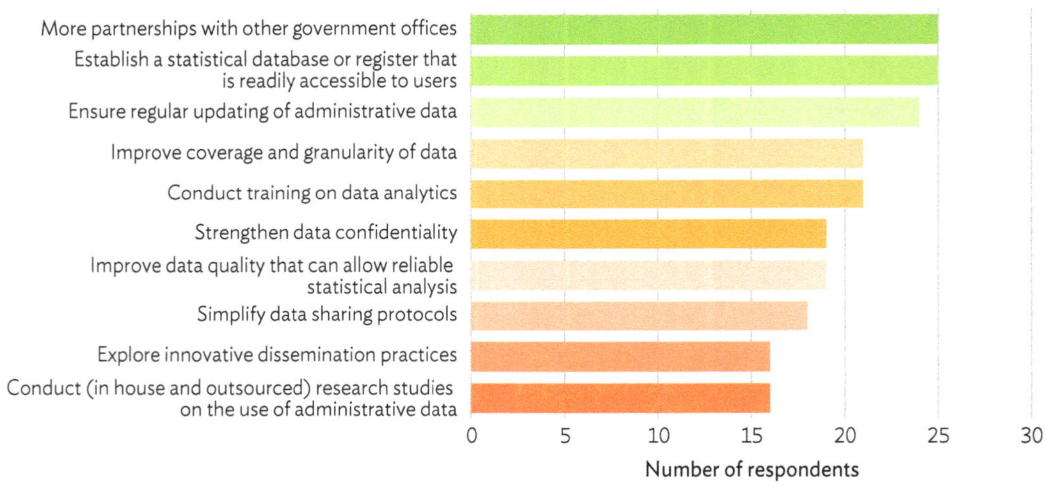

NSO = national statistics office.

Note: The Asian Development Bank survey garnered responses from 24 NSOs as well as 8 labor ministries and 4 social welfare ministries in the bank's member economies across Asia and the Pacific.

Source: Asian Development Bank. 2022. Survey on the Use of Administrative Data for the Compilation of Employment-Related Indicators.

Digitization of government services could produce a wealth of naturally occurring data, including administrative data.

The fast-moving developments in digital technology are leading governments to embrace digitization for delivering better services and assistance to citizens. Economies are shifting towards paperless, cashless solutions and platforms that make government services available to people through internet and mobile technologies. The COVID-19 pandemic has further highlighted the importance of digital ecosystems.

Many economies have looked into designing new applications and services to help in the fight against the novel coronavirus. Further, governments have mobilized digital innovations to reach out to vulnerable groups and respond to their needs. They have built online registration systems and leveraged digital financial services to efficiently disseminate relief and cash aids.

The digitization of government services is producing a wealth of naturally occurring administrative data. If used effectively, these datasets have the potential to contribute to closing data gaps and assisting in the development of relevant social policies.

References

Asian Development Bank (ADB). 2010. *Administrative Data Sources for Compiling Millennium Development Goals and Related Indicators.* Manila. https://www.adb.org/sites/default/files/publication/28297/sources-compiling-mdg.pdf.

ADB. 2018. *Technological Innovation for Agricultural Statistics. Key Indicators for Asia and the Pacific 2018 Special Supplement.* https://www.adb.org/sites/default/files/publication/446186/tech-innovation-agristats-ki2018.pdf.

ADB. 2019. *Statistical Business Registers for Improved Information on Small, Medium-Sized, and Large Enterprises.* https://www.adb.org/sites/default/files/project-documents/47108/47108-001-tcr-en.pdf.

ADB. 2020. *Strengthening Economic Statistics for Measuring Progress Toward Sustainable Development Goals.* https://www.adb.org/sites/default/files/project-documents/54260/54260-001-tar-en.pdf.

ADB. 2021a. *Preparing a Road Map on the Use of Administrative Data for Compiling Employment Statistics. ADB Briefs.* No. 179. https://www.adb.org/sites/default/files/publication/705846/adb-brief-179-administrative-data-employment-statistics.pdf.

ADB. 2021b. *Practical Guidebook on Data Disaggregation for the Sustainable Development Goals.* https://www.adb.org/sites/default/files/publication/698116/guidebook-data-disaggregation-sdgs.pdf.

ADB. 2021c. *Development of New Statistical Resources and Building Capacity in New Data Sources and Technologies.* https://www.adb.org/sites/default/files/project-documents/55242/55242-001-tar-en.pdf.

ADB. 2022. *Technical Assistance Consultant's Report Mongolia: Building Capacity for an Effective Social Welfare System Food Stamps and Employment Service.* Manila. https://www.adb.org/sites/default/files/project-documents/51387/51387-001-tacr-en_0.pdf.

D. Brackfield. 2007. *Administrative Data Framework.* Paper submitted to the Organisation for Economic Co-operation and Development Short-Term Economic Statistics Working Party. Paris. 25–27 June 2007. https://www.oecd.org/sdd/fin-stats/38486345.pdf.

Innovations for Poverty Action (IPA). 2016. Using Administrative Data for Monitoring and Evaluation. https://www.poverty-action.org/publication/goldilocks-deep-dive-using-administrative-data-monitoring-and-evaluation.

C. Jialin and T. Y. Lip. 2017. Challenges in the Development of Register-Based Population Statistics. *Statistics Singapore Newsletter.* Singapore Department of Statistics. March. https://www.singstat.gov.sg/-/media/files/publications/population/ssnmar17-pg1-7.pdf.

L. Rawlings. 2013. Who's Afraid of Administrative Data? Why Administrative Data can be Faster, Cheaper and Sometimes Better. 26 June 2013. https://blogs.worldbank.org/impactevaluations/whos-afraid-administrative-data-why-administrative-data-can-be-faster-cheaper-and-sometimes-better.

L. Rivas, J. Crowley, C.H. Dziobek, and P. Tumbarello. 2018. Using Administrative Data to Enhance Policymaking in Developing Countries: Tax Data and the National Accounts. *IMF eLIBRARY*. 2 August. https://www.elibrary.imf.org/view/journals/001/2018/175/article-A001-en.xml.

Singapore Department of Statistics. 2020. *Introduction to Population Census 2020.* https://www.singstat.gov.sg/-/media/files/publications/cop2020/admin/ch1.ashx.

Statistical Committee of the Republic of Armenia (Armstat). 2020. *The Use of Administrative Data in Producing Migration Statistics in Armenia*. UNECE Online Meeting on Migration Statistics. 27-29 October 2020. https://unece.org/fileadmin/DAM/stats/documents/ece/ces/ge.10/2020/mtg3/Armenia_engP.pdf.

Armstat. 2021. *Transforming from Traditional to Combined Population Census in Armenia*. https://getinthepicture.org/system/files/sites/default/files/4.%20Armenia%20Presentation.pdf.

Statistics Canada. 2016. Acquisition, Use and Management of Administrative Data and Alternative Data. *In Compendium of Management Practices for Statistical Organizations from Statistics Canada's International Statistical Fellowship Program*. p. 197. Ottawa. https://www150.statcan.gc.ca/n1/en/pub/11-634-x/11-634-x2016001-eng.pdf?st=i3M9fxpj.

U. Tenzin. 2020. *A New Approach Towards Utilizing Administrative Data Sources.* Paper presented for the 2020 Asia–Pacific Statistics Week. Bangkok, Thailand. 15-19 June 2020. https://www.unescap.org/sites/default/files/APS2020/72_A_New_Approach_Towards_Utilizing_Administrative_Data_Sources_Ugyen_Tenzin_Bhutan.pdf.

United Nations (UN). 2013. *A New Global Partnership: Eradicate Poverty and Transform Economies Through Sustainable Development: The Report of the High-Level Panel of Eminent Persons on the Post-2015 Development Agenda*. https://www.post2020hlp.org/wp-content/uploads/docs/UN-Report.pdf.

United Nations, Department of Economic and Social Affairs (UN DESA). 2021a. *Collaborative on the Use of Administrative Data for Statistics Case Study: Bhutan Gewog Data (Local Level Data)*. https://unstats.un.org/capacity-development/admin-data/DetailedView/60d9ed2b63e8753688667ce5.

UN DESA. 2021b. *Collaborative on the Use of Administrative Data for Statistics Case Study: Producing Export and Import Price Indices in Bhutan*. https://unstats.un.org/capacity-development/admin-data/DetailedView/60d9ed2b63e8753688667ce4.

UN DESA. 2022. *Collaborative on the Use of Administrative Data for Statistics.* https://unstats.un.org/capacity-development/admin-data/.

United Nations Economic Commission for Europe (UNECE). 2021. *Guidelines for Assessing the Quality of Administrative Sources for Use in Censuses*. https://unece.org/sites/default/files/2021-03/03_CensusAdminQuality_forConsultation_0.pdf.

United Nations Economic and Social Commission for Asia and the Pacific (UNESCAP). 2021. *Asia-Pacific Guidelines to Data Integration for Official Statistics*. https://www.unescap.org/sites/default/d8files/knowledge-products/Data_Integration_Guidelines_ESCAP.pdf.

UNESCAP. 2022. Innovation Meets Tradition: Administrative Data Shaping Censuses in Asia and the Pacific. Blogs. 22 April. https://www.unescap.org/blog/innovation-meets-tradition-administrative-data-shaping-censuses-asia-and-pacific.

United Nations Statistics Division (UNSD) and United Nations Department of Economic and Social Affairs (UN DESA). 2018. *Use of Administrative Data for Official Statistics: The Global Perspective*. Presented for the International Workshop on Sustainable Development Goal Indicators. Beijing, China. 26–29 June 2018. https://unstats.un.org/sdgs/files/meetings/sdg-inter-workshop-june-2018/Day2_Session3_Adm%20Data_UNSD.pdf.

United Nations Sustainable Development Solutions Network (UNSDSN). 2015. *Data for Development: A Needs Assessment for SDG Monitoring and Statistical Capacity Development*. https://sustainabledevelopment.un.org/content/documents/2017Data-for-Development-Full-Report.pdf.

M. Varghese and F. Elfayez. 2022. A Digital Philippines: Leveraging ID for a Digital Social Protection Delivery. *World Bank Blogs*. 31 March. https://blogs.worldbank.org/eastasiapacific/digital-philippines-leveraging-id-digital-social-protection-delivery.

World Bank. 2021. *Measuring the Statistical Performance of Countries: An Overview of Updates to the World Bank Statistical Capacity Index*. https://documents1.worldbank.org/curated/en/815721616086786412/pdf/Measuring-the-Statistical-Performance-of-Countries-An-Overview-of-Updates-to-the-World-Bank-Statistical-Capacity-Index.pdf.

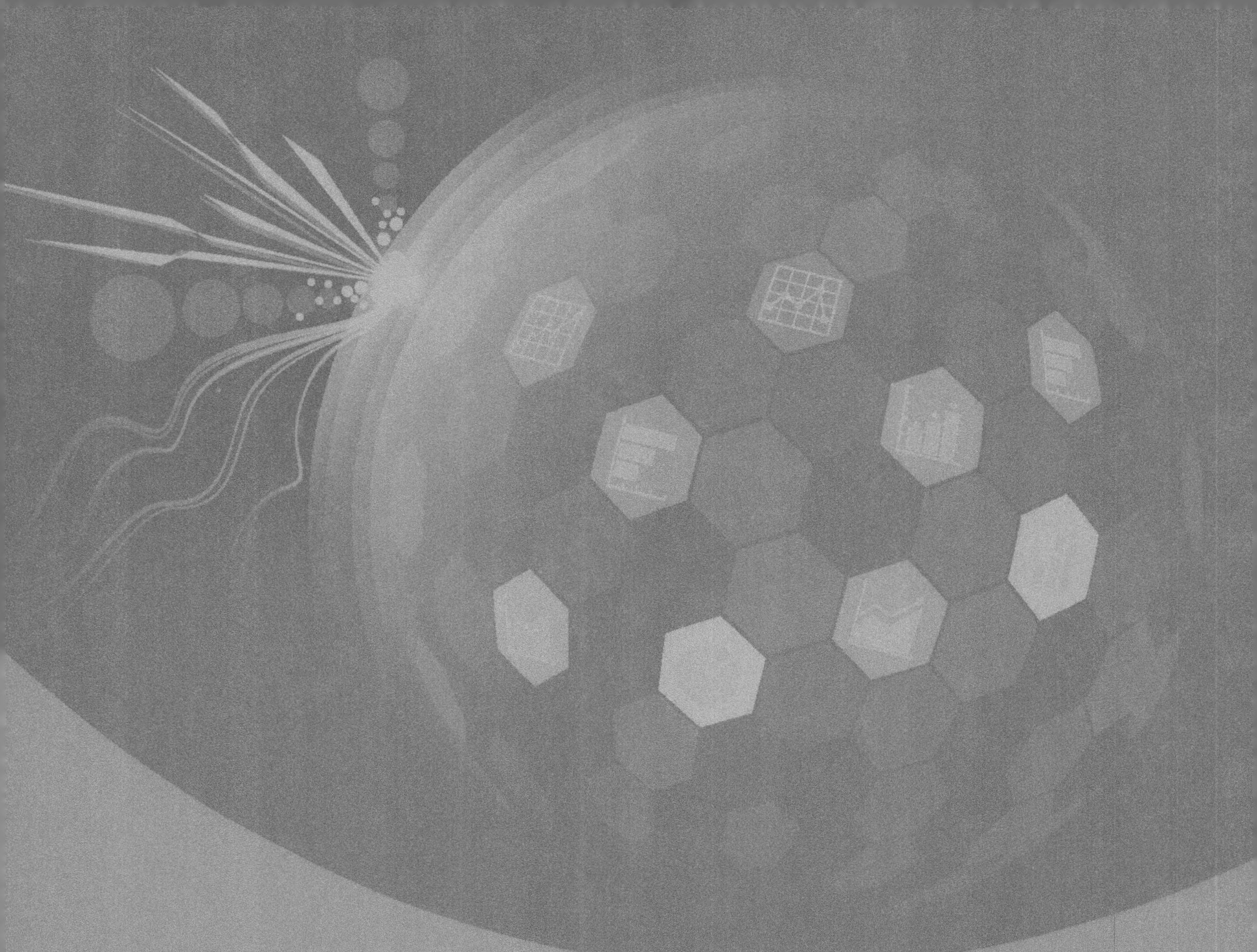

Definitions

Sustainable Development Goals

Goals and Targets	Statistical Indicators	Definition
Goal 1. End poverty in all its forms everywhere		
Target 1.1: By 2030, eradicate extreme poverty (currently measured as people living on less than $1.90 a day) for all people everywhere.	1.1.1.a: Proportion of the population living below the international poverty line, by sex, age, employment status, and geographical location (urban or rural)	Proportion of the population living on less than $1.90 a day, measured at 2011 international prices, adjusted for purchasing power parity (PPP). Note: The PPP conversion factor for private consumption is the number of units of an economy's currency required to buy the same amount of goods and/or services in the domestic market as a United States (US) dollar would buy in the US.
	1.1.1.b: Proportion of the employed population living below the international poverty line, by sex	Proportion of the employed population living in households with per capita consumption or income below the international poverty line of $1.90 a day. Note: The proportion of working poor in total employment (also known as the working poverty rate) combines data on household income or consumption with labor force framework variables measured at the individual level, and sheds light on the relationship between household poverty and employment. The numbers are International Labour Organization modeled estimates. Employed persons refer to all persons of working age who, during a short reference period such as a day or a week, performed work for others in exchange for pay or profit.
Target 1.2: By 2030, reduce at least by half the proportion of men, women, and children of all ages living in poverty in all its dimensions, according to national definitions.	1.2.1: Proportion of the population living below the national poverty line, by sex, age, and geographical location (urban or rural)	Percentage of the total population living below the national poverty line. Note: National poverty rates are defined at economy-specific poverty lines in local currencies, which are different in real terms across economies and different from the international poverty line of $1.90 a day. Thus, national poverty rates cannot be compared across economies or with the poverty rate of $1.90 a day.
Target 1.3: Implement nationally appropriate social protection systems and measures for all, including floors, and by 2030 achieve substantial coverage of the poor and the vulnerable	1.3.1: Proportion of population covered by social protection floors/systems, by sex, distinguishing children, unemployed persons, older persons, persons with disabilities, pregnant women, newborns, work-injury victims and the poor and the vulnerable.	Percentage of the population effectively covered by a social protection system, including social protection floors, which provide old age pensions, social security, and health insurance benefits. Effective coverage of social protection is measured by the number of people who are either actively contributing to a social insurance scheme or receiving benefits (contributory or noncontributory). Coverage is expressed as a share of the respective population. (i) Population covered by at least one social protection benefit (effective coverage): proportion of the total population receiving at least one contributory or noncontributory cash benefit, or actively contributing to at least one social security scheme. (ii) Older persons: ratio of persons above statutory retirement age receiving an old-age pension to the number of persons above statutory retirement age (including contributory and noncontributory). (iii) Poor persons covered by social assistance: ratio of social assistance recipients to the population living below the national poverty line. (iv) Vulnerable persons covered by social assistance: ratio of social assistance recipients to the total number of vulnerable persons (defined as all children plus adults not covered by contributory benefits and persons above retirement age not receiving contributory benefits, i.e., pensions). (v) Children: ratio of children or households receiving child or family cash benefits to the total number of children or households with children.

(continued on next page)

Goals and Targets	Statistical Indicators	Definition
Goal 2. End hunger, achieve food security and improved nutrition, and promote sustainable agriculture		
Target 2.1: By 2030, end hunger and ensure access by all people, in particular the poor and people in vulnerable situations, including infants, to safe, nutritious, and sufficient food all year round.	2.1.1: Prevalence of undernourishment	Proportion of the population whose habitual food consumption is insufficient to provide the dietary energy levels that are required to maintain a normal active and healthy life. Note: Undernourishment is defined as the condition by which a person has access, on a regular basis, to amounts of food that are insufficient to provide the energy required for conducting a normal, healthy, and active life, given his or her own dietary energy requirements.
Target 2.2: By 2030, end all forms of malnutrition, including achieving, by 2025, the internationally agreed targets on stunting and wasting in children under 5 years of age, and address the nutritional needs of adolescent girls, pregnant and lactating women, and older persons.	2.2.1: Prevalence of stunting—height for age <-2 standard deviation from the median of the World Health Organization (WHO) Child Growth Standards—among children under 5 years of age	Prevalence of stunting—height-for-age <-2 standard deviation from the median of WHO Child Growth Standards—among children under 5 years of age. Note: Child stunting refers to a child who is too short for his or her age as a result of chronic or recurrent malnutrition.
	2.2.2.a: Prevalence of malnutrition—weight for height >+2 standard deviation from the median of the WHO Child Growth Standards—among children under 5 years of age (overweight)	Prevalence of overweight—weight for height >+2 standard deviation from the median of WHO Child Growth Standards—among children under 5 years of age. Note: Child overweight refers to a child who is too heavy for his or her height.
	2.2.2.b: Prevalence of malnutrition—weight for height <-2 standard deviation from the median of the WHO Child Growth Standards—among children under 5 years of age (wasting)	Prevalence of wasting—weight for height <-2 standard deviation from the median of WHO Child Growth Standards—among children under 5 years of age. Note: Child wasting refers to a child who is too thin for his or her height as a result of recent rapid weight loss or the failure to gain weight.
Target 2.a: Increase investment, including through enhanced international cooperation, in rural infrastructure, agricultural research and extension services, technology development, and plant and livestock gene banks in order to enhance agricultural productive capacity in developing economies, in particular least developed economies.	2.a.1: The agriculture orientation index for government expenditures	The Agriculture Orientation Index for Government Expenditures is defined as the agriculture share of government expenditure, divided by the agriculture value-added share of gross domestic product (GDP), where "agriculture" refers to the agriculture, forestry, fishing, and hunting sector. The measure is a currency-free index, calculated as the ratio of these two shares. National governments are requested to compile government expenditures according to the Government Finance Statistics system and the Classification of Functions of Government, and agriculture value-added share of GDP according to the System of National Accounts. Note: Government Expenditure are all expenses and acquisition of nonfinancial assets associated with supporting a particular sector, as defined in the Government Finance Statistics Manual 2014 developed by the International Monetary Fund (IMF).
	2.a.2: Total official flows (official development assistance plus other official flows) to the agriculture sector	Gross disbursements of total official development assistance (ODA) and other official flows from all donors to the agriculture sector. Note: (i) The Development Assistance Committee defines ODA as those flows to economies and territories on the committee's List of ODA Recipients and to multilateral institutions which are: (ii) provided by official agencies, including state and local governments, or by their executive agencies; and

(continued on next page)

Goals and Targets	Statistical Indicators	Definition
		(iii) each transaction is administered with the promotion of the economic development and welfare of developing economies as its main objective; and is concessional in character and conveys a grant element of at least 25% (calculated at a rate of discount of 10%). Other Official Flows are defined as transactions by the official sector which do not meet the conditions for eligibility as ODA, either because they are not primarily aimed at development, or because they are not sufficiently concessional. They also exclude officially supported export credits.
Goal 3. Ensure healthy lives and promote well-being for all at all ages		
Target 3.1: By 2030, reduce the global maternal mortality ratio to less than 70 per 100,000 live births.	3.1.1: Maternal mortality ratio	Number of maternal deaths during a given time period per 100,000 live births during the same time period. It depicts the risk of maternal death relative to the number of live births and essentially captures the risk of death in a single pregnancy (proxied by a single live birth). Note: Maternal deaths refers to the death of a woman while pregnant or within 42 days of termination of pregnancy, irrespective of the duration and site of the pregnancy, from any cause related to or aggravated by the pregnancy or its management (from direct or indirect obstetric death), but not from unintentional or incidental causes.
	3.1.2: Proportion of births attended by skilled health personnel	Proportion of childbirths attended by professional health personnel (generally doctors, nurses, or midwives, but can refer to other health professionals providing childbirth care). These are competent maternal and newborn health professionals educated, trained, and regulated to national and international standards. They are competent to: (i) provide and promote evidence-based, human-rights based, quality, socioculturally sensitive, and dignified care to women and newborns; (ii) facilitate physiological processes during labor and delivery to ensure a clean and positive childbirth experience; and (iii) identify and manage or refer women and/or newborns with complications. Note: Having a skilled attendant at the time of delivery is an important lifesaving intervention for both mothers and babies. Not having access to this key assistance is detrimental to the health of women and newborns because it could cause the death of the women and/or the newborn or long-lasting morbidity. Achieving universal coverage for this indicator is therefore essential for reducing maternal and newborn mortality.
Target 3.2: By 2030, end preventable deaths of newborns and children under 5 years of age, with all economies aiming to reduce neonatal mortality to at least as low as 12 per 1,000 live births and under-5 mortality to at least as low as 25 per 1,000 live births.	3.2.1: Under-5 mortality rate	The probability of a child born in a specific year or period dying before reaching the age of 5 years, if subject to age specific mortality rates of that period, expressed per 1,000 live births. Note: The under-5 mortality rate as defined here is, strictly speaking, not a rate (i.e., the number of deaths divided by the number of population at risk during a certain period of time) but a probability of death derived from a life table and expressed as a rate per 1,000 live births.
	3.2.2: Neonatal mortality rate	Probability that a child born in a specific year or period will die during the first 28 completed days of life, if subject to age-specific mortality rates of that period, expressed per 1,000 live births. Note: Neonatal deaths (deaths among live births during the first 28 completed days of life) may be subdivided into early neonatal deaths, occurring during the first 7 days of life, and late neonatal deaths, occurring after the seventh day but before the 28th completed day of life.

(continued on next page)

Goals and Targets	Statistical Indicators	Definition
Target 3.3: By 2030, end the epidemics of AIDS, tuberculosis, malaria, and neglected tropical diseases; and combat hepatitis, water-borne diseases, and other communicable diseases.	3.3.1: Number of new HIV infections per 1,000 uninfected population, by sex, age, and key populations	Number of new HIV infections per 1,000 persons among the uninfected population.
	3.3.2: Tuberculosis incidence per 100,000 population	Estimated number of new and relapse tuberculosis cases (all forms of tuberculosis, including cases in people living with HIV) arising in a given year, expressed as a rate per 100,000 population.
	3.3.3: Malaria incidence per 1,000 population	The number of new cases of malaria per 1,000 people at risk each year.
Target 3.4: By 2030, reduce by one third premature mortality from noncommunicable diseases through prevention and treatment, and promote mental health and well-being.	3.4.1: Mortality rate attributed to cardiovascular disease, cancer, diabetes, or chronic respiratory disease	Probability of dying between the ages of 30 and 70 years from cardiovascular diseases, cancer, diabetes, or chronic respiratory diseases, defined as the percentage of 30-year-old people who would die before their 70th birthday from cardiovascular disease, cancer, diabetes, or chronic respiratory disease, assuming that s/he would experience current mortality rates at every age and s/he would not die from any other cause of death (e.g., injuries or HIV/AIDS). Note: Probability of dying refers to the likelihood that an individual would die between two ages given current mortality rates at each age, calculated using life table methods. The probability of death between two ages may be called a mortality rate.
	3.4.2: Suicide mortality rate	The number of suicide deaths in a year, divided by the population and multiplied by 100,000.
Target 3.6: By 2020, halve the number of global deaths and injuries from road traffic accidents.	3.6.1: Death rate due to road traffic injuries	Number of road traffic fatal injury deaths per 100,000 population.
Target 3.7: By 2030, ensure universal access to sexual and reproductive health care services, including for family planning, information and education, and the integration of reproductive health into national strategies and programme	3.7.1: Proportion of women of reproductive age (15–49 years) who have their need for family planning satisfied by modern methods	The percentage of women of reproductive age (15-49 years) currently using a modern method of contraception among those who desire either to have no (additional) children or to postpone the next pregnancy. The indicator is also referred to as the demand for family planning satisfied with modern methods.
	3.7.2: Adolescent birth rate (15–19 years) per 1,000 women in that age group	Annual number of births to females aged 15–19 years per 1,000 females in the respective age group.
Target 3.8: Achieve universal health coverage, including financial risk protection, access to quality essential healthcare services and access to safe, effective, quality and affordable essential medicines and vaccines for all	3.8.1 Coverage of essential health services (defined as the average coverage of essential services based on tracer interventions that include reproductive, maternal, newborn and child heath, infectious diseases, non-communicable diseases and service capacity and access, among the general and the most disadvantaged population)	Coverage of essential health services is defined as the average coverage of essential services based on tracer interventions that include reproductive, maternal, newborn and child health, infectious diseases, non-communicable diseases and service capacity and access, among the general and the most disadvantaged population. The indicator is an index reported on a unitless scale of 0 to 100, which is computed as the geometric mean of 14 tracer indicators of health service coverage. Note: The index of health service coverage is computed as the geometric means of tracer indicators. The tracer indicators are organized by four broad categories of service coverage: (i) reproductive, maternal, newborn, and child health; (ii) infectious diseases; (iii) noncommunicable diseases; and (iv) service capacity and access.

(continued on next page)

Goals and Targets	Statistical Indicators	Definition
Target 3.9: By 2030, substantially reduce the number of deaths and illnesses from hazardous chemicals and air, water, and soil pollution and contamination.	3.9.1: Mortality rate attributed to household and ambient air pollution	Expressed as the number of deaths and death rate. Death rates are calculated by dividing the number of deaths by the total population (or indicated if a different population group is used, e.g., children under 5 years). Note: Evidence from epidemiological studies has shown that exposure to air pollution is linked to, among others, the important diseases taken into account in this estimate: - acute respiratory infections i (estimated in all age groups); - cerebrovascular diseases (stroke) in adults (estimated above 25 years); - ischemic heart diseases (IHD) in adults (estimated above 25 years of); - chronic obstructive pulmonary disease (COPD) in adults (estimated above 25 years); and - lung cancer in adults (estimated above 25 years).
	3.9.2: Mortality rate attributed to unsafe water, unsafe sanitation, and lack of hygiene—exposure to unsafe water, sanitation, and hygiene for all (WASH) services	Number of deaths from unsafe water, unsafe sanitation, and lack of hygiene —exposure to unsafe water, sanitation and hygiene for all (WASH) services—in a year, divided by the population, and multiplied by 100,000.
Target 3.c: Substantially increase health financing and the recruitment, development, training, and retention of the health workforce in developing economies, especially in least developed economies and small island developing States	3.c.1: Health worker density and distribution	Density of medical doctors: The density of medical doctors is defined as the number of medical doctors, including generalists and specialist medical practitioners, per 10,000 population in a given national and/ or subnational area. The International Standard Classification of Occupations (ISCO) unit group codes included in this category are 221, 2211, and 2212 of ISCO-08. Density of nursing and midwifery personnel: The density of nursing and midwifery personnel is defined as the number of nursing and midwifery personnel per 10,000 population in a given national and/or subnational area. The ISCO-08 codes included in this category are 2221, 2222, 3221, and 3222.
Target 3.d: Strengthen the capacity of all economies, in particular developing economies, for early warning, risk reduction, and management of national and global health risks	3.d.1: International Health Regulations (IHR) capacity and health emergency preparedness	The revised International Health Regulations (IHR) were adopted in 2005 and entered into force in 2007. Under the IHR, States Parties are obliged to develop and maintain minimum core capacities for surveillance and response, including at points of entry, in order to early detect, assess, notify, and respond to any potential public health events of international concern. Article 54 of the IHR states that: States Parties and the Director-General shall report to the Health Assembly on the implementation of these Regulations as decided by the Health Assembly. The IHR self-assessment and reporting tool captures the level of self-assessed national capacities. They are essential public health capacities that States Parties are required to have in place throughout their territories pursuant to Articles 5 and 12, and Annex 1A of the IHR (2005) requirements.

(continued on next page)

Goals and Targets	Statistical Indicators	Definition
Goal 4. Ensure inclusive and equitable quality education and promote lifelong learning opportunities for all		
Target 4.1: By 2030, ensure that all girls and boys complete free, equitable, and quality primary and secondary education leading to relevant and effective learning outcomes	4.1.1.a: Proportion of children and young people in grades 2/3 achieving at least a minimum proficiency level 4.1.1.b: Proportion of children and young people at the end of primary achieving at least a minimum proficiency level 4.1.1.c: Proportion of children and young people at the end of lower secondary achieving at least a minimum proficiency level	Percentage of children and young people achieving at least a minimum proficiency level in (i) reading and (ii) mathematics during primary education (Grade 2 or 3), at the end of primary education, and at the end of lower secondary education. The minimum proficiency level will be measured relative to new common reading and mathematics scales currently in development. Note: This indicator is expressed as proportion of children and/or young people at the relevant stage of education in a given year achieving or exceeding the predefined proficiency level in a given subject.
	4.1.2: Completion rate (primary education, lower secondary education, upper secondary education)	Percentage of a cohort of children or young people aged 3–5 years above the intended age for the last grade of each level of education who have completed that grade. Note: A completion rate at or near 100% indicates that all or most children and adolescents have completed a level of education by the time they are 3 to 5 years older than the official age of entry into the last grade of that level of education. A low completion rate indicates low or delayed entry into a given level of education, high drop-out, high repetition, late completion, or a combination of these factors.
Target 4.2: By 2030, ensure that all girls and boys have access to quality early childhood development, care, and preprimary education, so that they are ready for primary education.	4.2.2: Participation rate in organized learning (1 year before the official primary entry age), by sex	Percentage of children in the given age range who participate in one or more organized learning programs, including programs which offer a combination of education and care. Participation in early childhood and in primary education are both included. The age range will vary by economy depending on the official age for entry to primary education. Note: An organized learning program is one that consists of a coherent set or sequence of educational activities designed with the intention of achieving predetermined learning outcomes or the accomplishment of a specific set of educational tasks. Early childhood and primary education programs are examples of organized learning programs. The official primary entry age is the age at which children are obliged to start primary education, according to national legislation or policies.
Target 4.c: By 2030, substantially increase the supply of qualified teachers, including through international cooperation for teacher training in developing economies, especially least developed economies and small island developing states.	4.c.1.a: Proportion of teachers in preprimary education who have received at least the minimum organized teacher training 4.c.1.b: Proportion of teachers in primary education who have received at least the minimum organized teacher training	Percentage of teachers by level of education taught (pre-primary, primary, lower secondary, and upper secondary education) who have received at least the minimum organized pedagogical teacher training pre-service and in-service required for teaching at the relevant level in a given economy. Note: Number of teachers in a given level of education who are trained is expressed as a percentage of all teachers in that level of education. A teacher is trained if they have received at least the minimum organized pedagogical teacher training pre-service and in-service required for teaching at the relevant level in each economy.

(continued on next page)

Goals and Targets	Statistical Indicators	Definition
	4.c.1.c: Proportion of teachers in lower secondary education who have received at least the minimum organized teacher training 4.c.1.d: Proportion of teachers in upper secondary education who have received at least the minimum organized teacher training	
Goal 5. Achieve gender equality and empower all women and girls		
Target 5.3: Eliminate all harmful practices, such as child, early, and forced marriage, and female genital mutilation.	5.3.1: Proportion of women aged 20–24 years who were married or in a union before age 15 and before age 18	Proportion of women aged 20–24 years who were married or in a union before age 15 years and before age 18 years. Note: Both formal (i.e., marriages) and informal unions are covered under this indicator. Informal unions are generally defined as those in which a couple lives together (i.e., cohabits) for some time, intends to have a lasting relationship, but for which there has been no formal civil or religious ceremony.
Target 5.5: Ensure women's full and effective participation in, and equal opportunities for leadership at, all levels of decision-making in political, economic, and public life.	5.5.1: Proportion of seats held by women in national parliaments	The proportion of seats held by women in national parliaments, as of 1 January of reporting year, is currently measured as the number of seats held by women members in single or lower chambers of national parliaments, expressed as a percentage of all occupied seats. Note: National parliaments can be bicameral or unicameral. This indicator covers the single chamber in unicameral parliaments and the lower chamber in bicameral parliaments. It does not cover the upper chamber of bicameral parliaments. Seats are usually won by members in general parliamentary elections. Seats may also be filled by nomination, appointment, indirect election, rotation of members, and by-election. Seats refer to the number of parliamentary mandates, or the number of members of parliament.
	5.5.2: Proportion of women in managerial positions	Proportion of females in the total number of persons employed in senior and middle management. Senior and middle management correspond to major group 1 in International Standard Classification of Occupations (ISCO)-08 and ISCO-88, minus category 14 in ISCO-08 (hospitality, retail, and other services managers) and minus category 13 in ISCO-88 (general managers), since these comprise mainly managers of small enterprises. Note: The indicator provides information on the proportion of women who are employed in decision-making and managerial roles in government, large enterprises, and institutions, thus providing some insight into women's power in decision-making and in the economy (especially compared to men's power in those areas).

(continued on next page)

Goals and Targets	Statistical Indicators	Definition
Goal 6. Ensure availability and sustainable management of water and sanitation for all		
Target 6.1: By 2030, achieve universal and equitable access to safe and affordable drinking water for all.	6.1.1: Proportion of population using safely managed drinking water services	Proportion of the population using safely managed drinking water services is currently being measured by the proportion of the population using an improved basic drinking water source that is located on premises, available when needed, and free of fecal (and priority chemical) contamination. Note: Improved drinking water sources include the following: piped water into a dwelling, yard, or plot; public taps or standpipes; boreholes or tubewells; protected dug wells; protected springs; packaged water; delivered water and rainwater. "Located on premises": a water source at the point of collection is within the dwelling, yard, or plot. "Available when needed": households are able to access sufficient quantities of water when needed. "Free from fecal (and priority chemical) contamination": water complies with relevant national or local standards. In the absence of such standards, reference is made to the WHO Guidelines for Drinking Water Quality https://www.who.int/teams/environment-climate-change-and-health/water-sanitation-and-health/water-safety-and-quality/drinking-water-quality-guidelines. E. coli or thermotolerant coliforms are the preferred indicator for microbiological quality, and arsenic and fluoride are the priority chemicals for global reporting. The WHO/UNICEF Joint Monitoring Programme (JMP) for Water Supply, Sanitation, and Hygiene estimates access to basic services for each economy, separately in urban and rural areas, by fitting a regression line to a series of data points from household surveys and censuses. This approach was used to report on use of 'improved water' sources for Millennium Development Goal monitoring. The JMP is evaluating the use of alternative statistical estimation methods as more data become available. The JMP 2017 update and SDG baselines report describes in more detail how data on availability and quality from different sources, can be combined with data on use of different types of supplies, as recorded in the current JMP database to compute the safely managed drinking water services indicator. https://washdata.org/report/jmp-2017-report-final.
Target 6.2: By 2030, achieve access to adequate and equitable sanitation and hygiene for all, and end open defecation, paying special attention to the needs of women and girls and those in vulnerable situations.	6.2.1.a: Proportion of population using safely managed sanitation services	The proportion of the population using a basic sanitation facility, including handwashing facility with soap and water, that is not shared with other households and where excreta is safely disposed in situ or treated off-site. Note: Improved sanitation facilities include flush or pour-flush toilets to sewer systems, septic tanks or pit latrines, ventilated improved pit latrines, pit latrines with a slab, and composting toilets. "Safely disposed in situ": when pit latrines and septic tanks are not emptied, the excreta may still remain isolated from human contact and can be considered safely managed. For example, with the new SDG indicator, households that use twin pit latrines or safely abandon full pit latrines and dig new facilities, a common practice in rural areas, would be counted as using safely managed sanitation services.

(continued on next page)

Goals and Targets	Statistical Indicators	Definition
		"Treated offsite": not all excreta from toilet facilities conveyed in sewers (as wastewater) or emptied from pit latrines and septic tanks (as faecal sludge) reaches a treatment site. For instance, a portion may leak from the sewer itself or, due to broken pumping installations, be discharged directly to the environment. Similarly, a portion of the faecal sludge emptied from containers may be discharged into open drains, to open ground or water bodies, rather than being transported to a treatment plant. And finally, even once the excreta reach a treatment plant a portion may remain untreated, due to dysfunctional treatment equipment or inadequate treatment capacity, and be discharged to the environment. For the purposes of SDG monitoring, adequacy of treatment will initially be assessed based on the reported level of treatment. "A handwashing facility with soap and water": a handwashing facility is a device to contain, transport or regulate the flow of water to facilitate handwashing.
Target 6.4: By 2030, substantially increase water-use efficiency across all sectors and ensure sustainable withdrawals and supply of freshwater to address water scarcity and substantially reduce the number of people suffering from water scarcity.	6.4.2: Level of water stress: freshwater withdrawal as a proportion of available freshwater resources	The level of water stress: freshwater withdrawal as a proportion of available freshwater resources is the ratio between total freshwater withdrawn by all major sectors and total renewable freshwater resources, after taking into account environmental water requirements. Note: Total freshwater withdrawal is the volume of freshwater extracted from its source (rivers, lakes, aquifers) for agriculture, industries, and municipalities. Freshwater withdrawal includes primary freshwater (not withdrawn before), secondary freshwater (previously withdrawn and returned to rivers and groundwater, such as discharged wastewater and agricultural drainage water) and fossil groundwater. Main sectors, as defined by International Standard Industrial Classification standards, include agriculture, forestry and fishing, manufacturing, electricity industry, and services. Environmental water requirements are the quantities of water required to sustain freshwater and estuarine ecosystems. This indicator is also known as water withdrawal intensity. Total renewable freshwater resources are expressed as the sum of internal and external renewable water resources. Internal renewable water resources are defined as the long-term average annual flow of rivers and recharge of groundwater, generated from endogenous precipitation, for a given economy. External renewable water resources refer to the flows of water entering the economy, taking into consideration the quantity of flows reserved to upstream and downstream economies through agreements or treaties.
Target 6.a: By 2030, expand international cooperation and capacity-building support to developing economies in water- and sanitation-related activities and programmes, including water harvesting, desalination, water efficiency, wastewater treatment, recycling, and reuse technologies.	6.a.1: Amount of water- and sanitation-related ODA that is part of a government-coordinated spending plan	Amount of water- and sanitation-related ODA that is part of a government-coordinated spending plan is defined as the proportion of total water- and sanitation-related ODA disbursements that are included in the government budget. Note: The amount of water- and sanitation-related ODA is a quantifiable measurement as a proxy for "international cooperation and capacity development support" in financial terms. A low value of this indicator (near 0%) would suggest that international donors are investing in water- and sanitation-related activities and programs in the economy, outside the purview of the national government. A high value (near 100%) would indicate that donors are aligned with the national government and national policies and plans for water and sanitation.

(continued on next page)

Goals and Targets	Statistical Indicators	Definition
Goal 7. Ensure access to affordable, reliable, sustainable, and modern energy for all		
Target 7.1: By 2030, ensure universal access to affordable, reliable, and modern energy services.	7.1.1: Proportion of population with access to electricity	Percentage of the population with access to electricity. Note: Access to electricity addresses major critical issues in all the dimensions of sustainable development. The target has a wide range of social and economic impacts, including facilitating development of household-based income-generating activities and lightening the burden of household tasks.
	7.1.2: Proportion of population with primary reliance on clean fuels and technology	Number of people using clean fuels and technologies for cooking, heating and lighting divided by total population reporting that any cooking, heating or lighting, expressed as percentage. “Clean” is defined by the emission rate targets and specific fuel recommendations (i.e. against unprocessed coal and kerosene) included in the normative guidance WHO guidelines for indoor air quality: household fuel combustion.
Target 7.2: By 2030, increase substantially the share of renewable energy in the global energy mix.	7.2.1: Renewable energy share in total final energy consumption	Percentage of final consumption of energy that is derived from renewable resources. Note: Renewable energy consumption includes consumption of energy derived from hydro, solid biofuels, wind, solar, liquid biofuels, biogas, geothermal, marine sources, and waste. Total final energy consumption is calculated from national balances and statistics as total final consumption minus nonenergy use.
Target 7.3: By 2030, double the global rate of improvement in energy efficiency.	7.3.1: Energy intensity measured in terms of primary energy and GDP	Energy supplied to the economy per unit value of economic output. Note: Total energy supply, as defined by the International Recommendations for Energy Statistics, is made up of production, plus net imports, minus international marine and aviation bunkers plus-stock changes. GDP is the measure of economic output. For international comparison purposes, GDP is measured in constant terms at PPP.
Goal 8. Promote sustained, inclusive, and sustainable economic growth, full and productive employment, and decent work for all		
Target 8.1: Sustain per-capita economic growth in accordance with national circumstances and, in particular, at least 7% GDP growth per annum in the least developed economies.	8.1.1: Annual growth rate of real GDP per capita	Percentage change in the real GDP per capita between 2 consecutive years. Note: Real GDP per capita is calculated by dividing GDP at constant prices by the population of an economy or area. The data for real GDP is measured in constant US dollars to facilitate the calculation of economy growth rates and aggregation of the economy data.
Target 8.2: Achieve higher levels of economic productivity through diversification, technological upgrading, and innovation, including through a focus on high-value-added and labor-intensive sectors.	8.2.1: Annual growth rate of real GDP per employed person	Annual percentage change in real GDP per employed person. Note: The real GDP per employed person being a measure of labor productivity, this indicator represents a measure of labor productivity growth, thus providing information on the evolution, efficiency and quality of human capital in the production process.

(continued on next page)

Goals and Targets	Statistical Indicators	Definition
Target 8.5: By 2030, achieve full and productive employment and decent work for all women and men, including for young people and persons with disabilities, and equal pay for work of equal value.	8.5.2: Unemployment rate, by sex, age, and persons with disabilities	Percentage of persons in the labor force who are unemployed. Note: Unemployed persons are defined as all those of working age (usually persons aged 15 and above) who were not in employment, carried out activities to seek employment during a specified recent period, and were currently available to take up employment given a job opportunity, where: (i) "not in employment" is assessed with respect to the short reference period for the measurement of employment; (ii) to "seek employment" refers to any activity when carried out, during a specified recent period comprising the past 4 weeks or 1 month, for the purpose of finding a job or setting up a business or agricultural undertaking; (iii) the point when the enterprise starts to exist should be used to distinguish between search activities aimed at setting up a business and the work activity itself, as evidenced by the enterprise's registration to operate or by when financial resources become available, the necessary infrastructure or materials are in place, or the first client or order is received, depending on the context; and (iv) "currently available" serves as a test of readiness to start a job in the present, assessed with respect to a short reference period comprising that used to measure employment (depending on national circumstances, the reference period may be extended to include a short subsequent period not exceeding 2 weeks in total, so as to ensure adequate coverage of unemployment situations among different population groups).
Target 8.6: By 2020, substantially reduce the proportion of youth not in employment, education, or training.	8.6.1: Proportion of youth (aged 15–24 years) not in education, employment, or training	Proportion of youth (aged 15–24 years) who are not in education, employment, or training, also known as "the NEET rate". It conveys the number of young persons not in education, employment, or training as a percentage of the total youth population.
Target 8.7: Take immediate and effective measures to eradicate forced labor, end modern slavery and human trafficking, and secure the prohibition and elimination of the worst forms of child labor, including recruitment and use of child soldiers, and, by 2025, end child labor in all its forms.	8.7.1: Proportion of children aged 5–17 years engaged in child labor	The number of children aged 5–17 years reported to be in child labor during the reference period (usually the week prior to the survey). The proportion of children in child labor is calculated as the number of children in child labor, divided by the total number of children in the population.
Target 8.10: Strengthen the capacity of domestic financial institutions to encourage and expand access to banking, insurance, and financial services for all.	8.10.1: Number of commercial bank branches and ATMs per 100,000 adults	The number of commercial bank branches per 100,000 adults refers to the number of commercial banks branches reported by the central bank or the main financial regulator of the economy every year. To make it comparable, this number is presented as a reference per 100,000 adults in the respective economy. The number of ATMs per 100,000 adults, refers to the number of ATMs in the economy for all types of institutions, such as commercial banks, non-deposit-taking microfinance institutions, deposit-taking microfinance institutions, credit unions, financial cooperatives, and others. This information is reported every year by the central bank or the main financial regulator of the economy. To make it comparable, this number is presented as a reference per 100,000 adults in the respective economy.

(continued on next page)

Goals and Targets	Statistical Indicators	Definition
	8.10.2: Proportion of adults (aged 15 years and older) with an account at a bank or other financial institution or with a mobile-money service provider	Percentage of adults (aged 15+) who report having an account (of their own or held with someone else) at a bank or another type of financial institution or have personally used a mobile-money service in the past 12 months.
Target 8.a: Increase Aid for Trade support for developing economies, in particular least developed economies, including through the Enhanced Integrated Framework for Trade-related Technical Assistance to Least Developed Economies	8.a.1 Aid for Trade commitments and disbursements	Aid for Trade commitments and disbursements is the gross disbursements and commitments of total Official Development Assistance (ODA) from all donors for aid for trade.
Goal 9. Build resilient infrastructure, promote inclusive and sustainable industrialization, and foster innovation		
Target 9.1: Develop quality, reliable, sustainable, and resilient infrastructure, including regional and transborder infrastructure, to support economic development and human well-being, with a focus on affordable and equitable access for all.	9.1.a: Passenger volume by road transport, measured in millions of passenger-kilometers	Passenger and freight volumes are the sums of the passenger and freight volumes reported for the road and rail carriers in terms of number of people and metric tons of cargo, respectively. Note: The International Transport Forum collects data on transport (rail and road) statistics on annual basis from all its member economies. Data are collected from transport ministries, statistical offices, and other institutions designated as official data sources. Although there are clear definitions for all the terms used in this survey, economies might have different methodologies to calculate passenger-kilometers and ton-kilometers. Methods could be based on traffic or mobility surveys, using very different sampling methods and estimating techniques, which could affect the comparability of the statistics.
	9.1.b: Freight volume by road transport, measured in millions of ton-kilometers	
	9.1.c: Passenger volume by rail transport, measured in millions of passenger-kilometers	
	9.1.d: Freight volume by rail transport, measured in millions of ton-kilometers	
Target 9.2: Promote inclusive and sustainable industrialization and, by 2030, significantly raise industry's share of employment and GDP, in line with national circumstances, and double its share in least developed economies.	9.2.1: Manufacturing value-added as a proportion of GDP and per capita	Manufacturing value-added (MVA) as a proportion of GDP is a ratio between MVA and GDP, both reported in constant 2015 US dollars. MVA per capita is calculated by dividing MVA in constant 2015 US dollars by the population of an economy or area.
	9.2.2: Manufacturing employment as a proportion of total employment	Share of manufacturing employment in total employment.

(continued on next page)

Goals and Targets	Statistical Indicators	Definition
Target 9.4: By 2030, upgrade infrastructure and retrofit industries to make them sustainable, with increased resource-use efficiency and greater adoption of clean and environmentally sound technologies and industrial processes, with all economies taking action in accordance with their respective capabilities.	9.4.1: Carbon dioxide (CO_2) emissions per unit of value-added	CO_2 emissions per unit of value-added is an indicator calculated as ratio between CO_2 emissions from fuel combustion and the value-added of associated economic activities. The indicator can be calculated for the whole economy (total CO_2 emissions to GDP) or for specific sectors, notably the manufacturing sector (CO_2 emissions from manufacturing industries per MVA). CO_2 emissions per unit of GDP are expressed in kilograms of CO_2 per constant 2010 US dollar PPP of GDP. CO_2 emissions from manufacturing industries per unit of MVA are measured in kilograms of CO_2 equivalent per unit of MVA in constant 2015 US dollars.
Target 9.5: Enhance scientific research and upgrade the technological capabilities of industrial sectors in all economies, in particular developing economies, including, by 2030, encouraging innovation and substantially increasing the number of research and development workers per 1 million people and public and private research and development spending.	9.5.1: Research and development expenditure as a proportion of GDP	Amount of research and development expenditure divided by the total output of the economy.
	9.5.2: Researchers (full-time equivalent) per million inhabitants	Number of research and development workers per 1 million people.
Target 9.a: Facilitate sustainable and resilient infrastructure development in developing economies through enhanced financial, technological, and technical support to African economies, least developed economies, landlocked developing economies, and small island developing States.	9.a.1: Total official international support (ODA plus other official flows) to infrastructure	Gross disbursements of total ODA and other official flows from all donors in support of infrastructure.
Target 9.b: Support domestic technology development, research, and innovation in developing economies, including by ensuring a conducive policy environment for, among other things, industrial diversification and value addition to commodities.	9.b.1: Proportion of medium- and high-tech industry value-added in total value-added	Ratio of the value-added by medium- and high-tech (MHT) industry to total MVA. Note: Industrial development generally entails a structural transition from resource-based and low-tech activities to MHT activities. A modern, highly complex production structure offers better opportunities for skills development and technological innovation. MHT activities are also the high-value addition industries of manufacturing with higher technological intensity and labor productivity. Increasing the share of MHT sectors also reflects the impact of innovation.
Target 9.c: Significantly increase access to information and communications technology and strive to provide universal and affordable access to the Internet in least developed economies by 2020.	9.c.1.a: Proportion of population covered by narrowband (2G) mobile networks 9.c.1.b: Proportion of population covered by 3G mobile networks	Proportion of the population covered by a mobile network, broken down by technology, refers to the percentage of inhabitants living within range of a mobile-cellular signal, irrespective of whether or not they are mobile-phone subscribers or users. This is calculated by dividing the number of inhabitants within range of a mobile-cellular signal by the total population and multiplying by 100. Note: Coverage refers to Long-Term Evolution (LTE), broadband (3G), and narrowband (2G) mobile-cellular technologies:

(continued on next page)

Goals and Targets	Statistical Indicators	Definition
	9.c.1.c: Proportion of population covered by LTE mobile networks	2G mobile population coverage refers to the percentage of inhabitants within range of a mobile networks with access to data communications (e.g. Internet) at downstream speeds below 256 Kbit/s. This includes mobile-cellular technologies such as general packet radio service (GPRS), code division multiple access (CDMA) 2000 1x and most enhanced data for GSM (global system for mobile communications) evolution (EDGE) implementations. 3G population coverage refers to the percentage of inhabitants that are within range of at least a 3G mobile-cellular signal, irrespective of whether or not they are subscribers. Long-term evolution (LTE) population coverage refers to the percentage of inhabitants that live within range of LTE/LTE-Advanced, mobile WiMAX/WirelessMAN or other more advanced mobile-cellular networks, irrespective of whether or not they are subscribers.
Goal 10. Reduce inequality within and among economies		
Target 10.1: By 2030, progressively achieve and sustain income growth of the bottom 40% of the population at a rate higher than the national average.	10.1.1.a: Growth rates of household expenditure or income per capita among the bottom 40% of the population	The growth rate in the welfare aggregate of the bottom 40% of the population is calculated as the annualized average growth rate in per capita real consumption or income of the bottom 40% of the income distribution in an economy from household surveys over a period of approximately 5 years.
	10.1.1.b: Growth rates of household expenditure or income per capita	The national average growth rate in the welfare aggregate is calculated as the annualized average growth rate in per capita real consumption or income of the total population in an economy from household surveys over a period of approximately 5years.
Goal 11. Make cities and human settlements inclusive, safe, resilient, and sustainable		
Target 11.1: By 2030, ensure access for all to adequate, safe, and affordable housing and basic services, and upgrade slums.	11.1.1: Proportion of the urban population living in slums, informal settlements, or inadequate housing	The proportion of the urban population that lives in slums or informal settlements as well as those living in inadequate housing. Note: Most of the criteria for defining slums, informal settlements, and inadequate housing overlap. The criteria for informal settlements are essentially captured in the definition of slums, which combines both slums and informal settlements as one entity. Slums and informal settlements are therefore combined into one component of the indicator, providing some continuity with what was captured under Millennium Development Goal 7. At a later stage, a composite index will be developed that will incorporate all measures (combining slums, informal settlements, and inadequate housing) to provide one estimate.
Target 11.5: By 2030, significantly reduce the number of deaths and the number of people affected, and substantially decrease the direct economic losses relative to global GDP caused by disasters, including water-related disasters, with a focus on protecting the poor and people in vulnerable situations	11.5.2: Direct economic loss in relation to global GDP, damage to critical infrastructure, and number of disruptions to basic services, attributed to disasters	Direct economic loss is the monetary value of total or partial destruction of physical assets existing in the affected area. Direct economic loss is nearly equivalent to physical damage. Note: The original national disaster loss databases usually register physical damage value (housing unit loss, infrastructure loss, etc.), which needs conversion to a monetary value according to the United Nations International Strategy for Disaster Reduction methodology. The converted global value is divided by global GDP (inflation adjusted, constant US dollars) calculated from the World Bank Development Indicators.

(continued on next page)

Goals and Targets	Statistical Indicators	Definition
Target 11.6: By 2030, reduce the adverse per capita environmental impact of cities, including by paying special attention to air quality and municipal and other waste management.	11.6.2: Annual mean levels of fine particulate matter (PM), e.g., PM2.5 and PM10, in cities, measured in total (population weighted) micrograms per cubic meter	The mean annual concentration of fine suspended particles of less than 2.5 microns in diameters (PM2.5) is a common measure of air pollution. Note: The mean is a population-weighted average for urban population in an economy and is expressed in micrograms per cubic meter.
Goal 12. Ensure sustainable consumption and production patterns		
Target 12.2: By 2030, achieve the sustainable management and efficient use of natural resources	12.2.1: Material footprint, material footprint per capita, and material footprint per GDP	Material footprint is the attribution of global material extraction to domestic final demand of an economy. The total material footprint is the sum of the material footprint for biomass, fossil fuels, metal ores, and nonmetal ores. This indicator is calculated as raw material equivalent of imports plus domestic extraction minus raw material equivalents of exports. For the attribution of the primary material needs of final demand, a global, multiregional input-output framework is employed.
	12.2.2: Domestic material consumption, domestic material consumption per capita, and domestic material consumption per GDP	Domestic material consumption (DMC) is a standard material flow accounting indicator and reports the apparent consumption of materials in a national economy. Note: DMC reports the amount of materials that are used in a national economy. DMC is a territorial (production side) indicator. DMC also presents the amount of material that needs to be handled within an economy, which is either added to material stocks of buildings and transport infrastructure or used to fuel the economy as material throughput. DMC describes the physical dimension of economic processes and interactions. It can also be interpreted as long-term waste equivalent. Per capita DMC describes the average level of material use in an economy – an environmental pressure indicator – and is also referred to as metabolic profile.
Goal 13. Take urgent action to combat climate change and its impacts		
Target 13.1: Strengthen resilience and adaptive capacity to climate-related hazards and natural disasters in all economies.	13.1.1.a: Number of persons affected by disasters	Number of people who were directly affected by disasters per 100,000 population. Note: Directly affected means people who have suffered injury, illness, or other health effects; who were evacuated, displaced, or relocated; or have suffered direct damage to their livelihoods, economic, physical, social, cultural, and/or environmental assets.
	13.1.1.b: Number of deaths due to disasters	The number of people who died during disaster, or directly after, as a direct result of the hazardous event.
	13.1.2: Number of economies that adopt and implement national disaster risk reduction strategies in line the Sendai Framework for Disaster Risk Reduction 2015–2030	Number of economies that adopt and implement local disaster risk reduction strategies in line with national disaster risk reduction strategies. Note: The score of adoption and implementation of national disaster risk reduction strategies in line with the Sendai Framework (Index) was developed to monitor progress and achievement against Indicator 13.1.2. The score of an economy indicates its compliance of alignment of national strategies with the Sendai Framework based on self-assessments of the economy using 10 criteria for monitoring the progress of national disaster risk reduction strategies.

(continued on next page)

Goals and Targets	Statistical Indicators	Definition
Goal 14. Conserve and sustainably use the oceans, seas, and marine resources for sustainable development		
Target 14.5: By 2020, conserve at least 10% of coastal and marine areas, consistent with national and international law and based on the best available scientific information.	14.5.1: Coverage of protected areas in relation to marine areas	The indicator shows trends over time in the mean percentage of each important site for marine biodiversity (i.e., those that contribute significantly to the global persistence of biodiversity) that is covered by designated protected areas and other effective area-based conservation measures. Note: The International Union for Conservation of Nature (IUCN) defines protected areas as clearly defined geographical spaces, recognized, dedicated, and managed through legal or other effective means, to achieve the long-term conservation of nature with associated ecosystem services and cultural values. Importantly, a variety of specific management objectives are recognized within this definition, spanning conservation, restoration, and sustainable use. The status "designated" is attributed to a protected area when the corresponding authority, according to national legislation or common practice (e.g., by means of an executive decree or the like), officially endorses a document of designation. The designation must be made for the purpose of biodiversity conservation, not de facto protection arising because of some other activity (e.g., military).
Goal 15. Protect, restore, and promote sustainable use of terrestrial ecosystems, sustainably manage forests, combat desertification, halt and reverse land degradation, and halt biodiversity loss		
Target 15.1: By 2020, ensure the conservation, restoration, and sustainable use of terrestrial and inland freshwater ecosystems and their services, in particular forests, wetlands, mountains, and drylands, in line with obligations under international agreements.	15.1.1: Forest area as a proportion of total land area	Size of forest cover in relation to land area. Note: Forest is defined as "land spanning more than 0.5 hectares with trees higher than 5 meters and a canopy cover of more than 10%, or trees able to reach these thresholds in situ. It does not include land that is predominantly under agricultural or urban land use". Land area is the area of an economy excluding area under inland waters and coastal waters.
	15.1.2: Proportion of important sites for terrestrial and freshwater biodiversity that are covered by protected areas, by ecosystem type	Proportion of important sites for terrestrial and freshwater biodiversity that are covered by protected areas shows temporal trends in the mean percentage of each important site for terrestrial and freshwater biodiversity (i.e., those that contribute significantly to the global persistence of biodiversity) that is covered by designated protected areas.
Target 15.4: By 2030, ensure the conservation of mountain ecosystems, including their biodiversity, in order to enhance their capacity to provide benefits that are essential for sustainable development	15.4.1: Coverage by protected areas of important sites for mountain biodiversity	Coverage by protected areas of important sites for mountain biodiversity shows temporal trends in the mean percentage of each important site for mountain biodiversity (i.e., those that contribute significantly to the global persistence of biodiversity) that is covered by designated protected areas. Note: Protected areas, as defined by the IUCN (IUCN; Dudley 2008), are clearly defined geographical spaces, recognized, dedicated, and managed, through legal or other effective means, to achieve the long-term conservation of nature with associated ecosystem services and cultural values. Importantly, a variety of specific management objectives are recognized within this definition, spanning conservation, restoration, and sustainable use: "(i) Category Ia: Strict nature reserve; (ii) Category Ib: Wilderness area; (iii) Category II: National park; (iv) Category III: Natural monument or feature; (v) Category IV: Habitat/species management area; (vi) Category V: Protected landscape/seascape; (vii) Category VI: Protected area with sustainable use of natural resources."

(continued on next page)

Goals and Targets	Statistical Indicators	Definition
Target 15.5: Take urgent and significant action to reduce the degradation of natural habitats, halt the loss of biodiversity and, by 2020, protect and prevent the extinction of threatened species.	15.5.1: Red List Index	The Red List Index measures changes in aggregate extinction risk across groups of species. It is based on genuine changes in the number of species in each category of extinction risk on the IUCN Red List of Threatened Species (IUCN 2015), which is expressed as changes in an index ranging from 0 to 1. Note: The Red List Index value ranges from 1 (all species are categorized as "Least Concern") to 0 (all species are categorized as "Extinct"), indicating how far the set of species has moved overall toward extinction. Threatened species are those listed on The IUCN Red List of Threatened Species in the categories Vulnerable, Endangered, or Critically Endangered (i.e., species that are facing a high, very high, or extremely high risk of extinction in the wild in the medium-term future).
Goal 16. Promote peaceful and inclusive societies for sustainable development; provide access to justice for all; and build effective, accountable, and inclusive institutions at all levels		
Target 16.1: Significantly reduce all forms of violence and related death rates everywhere.	16.1.1: Number of victims of intentional homicide per 100,000 population	Total count of victims of intentional homicide divided by the total population, expressed per 100,000 population. Intentional homicide is defined as the unlawful death inflicted upon a person with the intent to cause death or serious injury (International Classification of Crime for Statistical Purposes, ICCS 2015). Population refers to total resident population in a given economy in a given year. Note: This indicator is widely used at national and international levels to measure the most extreme form of violent crime, providing a direct indication of lack of security.
Target 16.3: Promote the rule of law at the national and international levels and ensure equal access to justice for all.	16.3.2: Unsentenced detainees as a proportion of the overall prison population	Total number of persons held in detention who have not yet been sentenced, as a percentage of the total number of persons held in detention, on a specified date.
Target 16.5: Substantially reduce corruption and bribery in all their forms.	16.5.2: Proportion of businesses that had at least one contact with a public official and that paid a bribe to a public official, or were asked for a bribe by those public officials during the previous 12 months	Proportion of firms that were asked for a gift or informal payment when meeting with tax officials. Note: This indicator aims to ascertain whether or not firms have been solicited for gifts or informal payments (i.e., bribes) when meeting with tax officials. Paying taxes are required of formal forms in most economies, and the rationale for this indicator is to measure the incidence of corruption during this routine interaction.
Target 16.9: By 2030, provide legal identity for all, including birth registration.	16.9.1: Proportion of children under 5 years of age whose births have been registered with a civil authority, by age	Proportion of children under 5 years of age whose births have been registered with a civil authority.
Goal 17. Strengthen the means of implementation and revitalize the Global Partnership for Sustainable Development		
Target 17.4: Assist developing economies in attaining long-term debt sustainability through coordinated policies aimed at fostering debt financing, debt relief, and debt restructuring, as appropriate, and address the external debt of highly indebted poor economies to reduce debt distress	17.4.1: Debt service as a proportion of exports of goods and services	Percentage of debt services (principle and interest payments) to the exports of goods and services. Debt services covered in this indicator refer only to public and publicly guaranteed debt. Note: Concepts of public and publicly guaranteed external debt and exports of goods and services data are in accordance with the sixth edition of the Balance of Payments and International Investment Position Manual (BPM6) methodology

(continued on next page)

Goals and Targets	Statistical Indicators	Definition
Target 17.9: Enhance international support for implementing effective and targeted capacity-building in developing economies to support national plans to implement all the Sustainable Development Goals, including through North-South, South-South, and triangular cooperation.	17.9.1: Dollar value of financial and technical assistance (including through North-South, South-South, and triangular cooperation) committed to developing economies	Gross disbursements of total ODA and other official flows from all donors for capacity-building and national planning. Note: ODA refers to "those flows to economies and territories on the Development Assistance Committee List of ODA Recipients and to multilateral institutions which are (i) provided by official agencies, including state and local governments, or by their executive agencies; and (ii) each transaction is administered with the promotion of the economic development and welfare of developing economies as its main objective; and is concessional in character and conveys a grant element of at least 25% (calculated at a rate of discount of 10%). Other official flows (excluding officially supported export credits) are defined as transactions by the official sector that do not meet the conditions for eligibility as ODA, either because they are not primarily aimed at development or because they are not sufficiently concessional.
Target 17.18: By 2020, enhance capacity-building support to developing economies, including for least developed economies and small island developing states, to increase significantly the availability of high-quality, timely, and reliable data disaggregated by income, gender, age, race, ethnicity, migratory status, disability, geographic location, and other characteristics relevant in national contexts.	17.18.3: Number of economies with a national statistical plan that is fully funded and under implementation, by source of funding	Count of economies that are either (i) implementing a strategy, (ii) designing a strategy, or (iii) awaiting adoption of a strategy in the current year. Note: The indicator is based on the annual Status Report on National Strategies for the Development of Statistics. In collaboration with its partners, PARIS21 reports on economy progress in designing and implementing national statistical plans. This indicator can be disaggregated by geographical area. Regional-level aggregates are based on the total count of national strategies.
Target 17.19: By 2030, build on existing initiatives to develop measurements of progress on sustainable development that complement GDP, and support statistical capacity-building in developing economies.	17.19.1: Dollar value of all resources made available to strengthen statistical capacity in developing economies	US dollar value of ongoing statistical support in developing economies. Note: The indictor is based on the Partner Report on Support to Statistics, which is designed and administered by PARIS21 to provide a snapshot of the US dollar value of ongoing statistical support in developing economies.
	17.19.2: Number of economies that have conducted at least one population and housing census in the past 10 years	Economies that have conducted at least one population and housing census in the past 10 years. This includes economies that compile their detailed population and housing statistics from population registers, administrative records, sample surveys, other sources, or a combination of those sources.

Regional Trends and Tables

Indicator	Definition
PEOPLE	
Population	
Midyear Population	Estimates of the midyear de facto population. De facto population includes all persons physically present in the economy during the census day, including foreign, military, and diplomatic personnel and their accompanying household members; and transient foreign visitors in the economy or in harbors. Note: Some economies have population data referenced to different period end points (e.g., 1 January for the Kyrgyz Republic, 31 December for the People's Republic of China, and 1 October for India).
Growth Rates in Population	Number of people added to (or subtracted from) a population over a given period of time because of natural increase and net migration, expressed as a percentage of the population at the given period of time.
Net International Migration Rate	Number of immigrants minus the number of emigrants over a period, divided by the person-years lived by the population of the receiving economy over that period. It is expressed as net number of migrants per 1,000 population.
Urban Population (as % of total population)	Population living in urban areas, defined in accordance with the national definition or as used in the most recent population census. Because of national differences in the characteristics that distinguish urban from rural areas, the distinction between urban and rural populations is not amenable to a single definition that would be applicable to all economies. National definitions are most commonly based on size of locality. Population that is not urban is considered rural. The estimated population living in urban areas at midyear as a percentage of the total midyear population in an economy.
Age Dependency Ratio	Ratio of the nonworking-age population to the working-age population. Since economies define working age differently, a straightforward application of the definition will lead to noncomparable data. The Asian Development Bank therefore uses the following United Nations definition that can be calculated directly from an age distribution: $\frac{\text{Population aged (0–14) + (65 and over) years}}{\text{Population aged (15–64) years}} \times 100$
Labor Force and Employment	
Labor Force Participation Rate	Percentage of the labor force to the working-age population. The labor force is the sum of those employed and unemployed but seeking work. The labor force participation rate measures the extent of the economically active working-age population in an economy. It provides an indication of the relative size of the supply of labor available for the production of goods and services in the economy. It must be noted that the definition of working-age population varies across economies. Note: Recommendations from the 19th International Conference of Labour Statisticians have been adopted by some economies, and hence these economies may not have comparable data across years. The conference provides the statistical concept of work for reference purposes; and the operational concepts, definitions, and guidelines for (i) three distinct subsets of work activities, referred to as forms of work, which include own-use production work, employment work, and volunteer work; (ii) related classifications of the population according to their labor force status and main work status; and (iii) measures of labor underutilization. The concept of employment has also been refined to refer to work for pay or profit.
Employment in Agriculture	Employment in agriculture, including forestry and fishing, that corresponds to division 1 (International Standard of Industrial Classification [ISIC] revision 2), tabulation categories A and B (ISIC revision 3), and category A of ISIC revision 4.

(continued on next page)

Indicator	Definition
Employment in Industry	Employment in industry includes mining and quarrying; manufacturing; electricity, gas, steam, and air-conditioning supply; water supply; sewage, waste management, and remediation activities; and construction.
Employment in Mining and Quarrying	Employment in mining and quarrying that corresponds to division 2 (ISIC revision 2), tabulation category C (ISIC revision 3), and category B of ISIC revision 4.
Employment in Manufacturing	Employment in manufacturing that corresponds to division 3 (ISIC revision 2), tabulation category D (ISIC revision 3), and category C of ISIC revision 4.
Employment in Electricity, Gas, Steam, and Air-Conditioning Supply; Water Supply; Sewerage, Waste Management and Remediation Activities	Employment in electricity, gas, steam, and air-conditioning supply; water supply; sewerage, waste management, and remediation activities that corresponds to division 4 (ISIC revision 2), tabulation category E (ISIC revision 3), and categories D and E of ISIC revision 4.
Employment in Construction	Employment in construction that corresponds to division 5 (ISIC revision 2), tabulation category F (ISIC revisions 3), and category F of ISIC revision 4.
Employment in Service	Employment in service includes wholesale and retail trade; repair of motor vehicles and motorcycles; accommodation and food service activities; transportation and storage; information and communication; financial and insurance activities; real estate activities; and other services.
Employment in Wholesale and Retail Trade; Repair of Motor Vehicles and Motorcycles	Employment in wholesale and retail trade; repair of motor vehicles and motorcycles that corresponds to division 6 (subdivisions 61 and 62, ISIC revision 2); tabulation category G (ISIC revision 3); and category G of ISIC revision 4.
Employment in Transportation and Storage	Employment in transport and storage that corresponds to division 7 (subdivision 71, ISIC revision 2); tabulation category I (subcategories 60–63, ISIC revision 3); and category H of ISIC revision 4.
Employment in Accommodation and Food Service Activities	Employment in accommodation and food service activities that corresponds to division 6 (subdivision 63, ISIC revision 2); tabulation category H (ISIC revision 3); and category I of ISIC revision 4.
Employment in Information and Communication	Employment in information and communication that corresponds to division 7 (subdivision 72, ISIC revision 2); tabulation category I (subcategory 64, ISIC revision 3); and category J of ISIC revision 4.
Employment in Financial and Insurance Activities	Employment in financial and insurance activities that corresponds to division 8 (subdivisions 81–82, ISIC revision 2), tabulation category J (ISIC revision 3), and category K of ISIC revision 4.
Employment in Real Estate Activities	Employment in real estate activities that corresponds to division 8 (subdivision 83, ISIC revision 2); tabulation category K (subcategory 70, ISIC revision 3); and category L of ISIC revision 4.
Employment in Other Services	Employment in other services that corresponds to divisions 9 and 0 (ISIC revision 2), tabulation categories L to Q (ISIC revision 3), and categories M to U of ISIC revision 4.
Underemployment	Persons in time-related underemployment comprise all persons in employment who satisfy the following three criteria during the reference period: a) are willing to work additional hours; b) are available to work additional hours i.e., are ready, within a specified subsequent period, to work additional hours given opportunities for additional work; and c) worked less than a threshold relating to working time (i.e., persons whose hours actually worked in all jobs during the reference period were below a threshold, to be chosen according to national circumstances). The time-related underemployment rate is calculated as follows: $\text{TRU (\%)} = \frac{\text{Persons in time-related underemployment}}{\text{Persons employed}} \times 100$
Poverty Indicators	
Proportion of Population below $1.90 a Day (2011 PPP)	Percentage of the population living on less than $1.90 a day at 2011 purchasing power parity (PPP).
Proportion of Population below $3.20 a Day (2011 PPP)	Percentage of the population living on less than $3.20 a day at 2011 PPP.

(continued on next page)

Indicator	Definition
Income Ratio of Highest 20% to Lowest 20%	Income or consumption share that accrues to the richest 20% of the population, divided by the income or consumption share of the lowest 20% of the population.
Gini Coefficient or Index	Measure of the degree to which an economy's income distribution diverges from perfect equal distribution. A value of zero (0) implies perfect equality while a value of one (1) implies perfect inequality.
Human Development Index	Composite index of long and healthy life (measured by life expectancy at birth), knowledge (measured by expected years of schooling and mean years of schooling), and decent standard of living (measured by gross national income per capita in United States [US] PPP dollars).
Social Indicators	
Life Expectancy at Birth	Number of years that a newborn is expected to live if prevailing patterns of mortality at the time of his or her birth are to stay the same throughout his or her life.
Crude Birth Rate	Ratio of the total number of live births in a given period to the midyear total population of the same period, expressed per 1,000 people.
Crude Death Rate	Ratio of the number of deaths occurring within a given period to the midyear total population of the same period, expressed per 1,000 people.
Total Fertility Rate	Number of children that would be born to a woman if she were to live to the end of her childbearing years and bear children in accordance with current age-specific fertility rates.
Primary Education Completion Rate	Total number of new entrants in the last grade of primary education, regardless of age, expressed as a percentage of the total population at the theoretical entrance age to the last grade of primary education. This indicator is also known as "gross intake ratio to the last grade of primary." The ratio can exceed 100% due to overaged and underaged children who enter primary school late, early, and/or repeat grades.
Adult Literacy Rate	The percentage of the population aged 15 years and older who can both read and write (with understanding) a short simple statement on his or her everyday life. Generally, literacy also encompasses numeracy, i.e., the ability to make simple arithmetic calculations.
Expected years of schooling, primary to tertiary	Number of years a person of school entrance age can expect to spend within the specified level of education (from primary to tertiary level).
Mean years of schooling	Average number of completed years of education of an economy's population aged 25 years and older, excluding years spent repeating individual grades.
Pupil to qualified teacher ratio	The total number of pupils and students in the relevant level in a given academic year expressed as a percentage of the number of qualified teachers in the same level in that academic year. A qualified teacher has the minimum academic qualifications necessary to teach at a specific level of education in a given economy. This is usually related to the subject(s) they teach. The higher the pupil to qualified teacher ratio, the lower the relative access of pupils to qualified teachers.
Pupil to trained teacher ratio	The total number of pupils and students in the relevant level in a given academic year expressed as a percentage of the number of trained teachers in the same level in that academic year. A trained teacher has fulfilled at least the minimum organized teacher-training requirements (pre-service or in-service) to teach a specific level of education according to the relevant national policy or law. These requirements usually include pedagogical knowledge (broad principles and strategies of classroom management and organization that transcend the subject matter being taught—typically approaches, methods, and techniques of teaching) and professional knowledge (knowledge of statutory instruments and other legal frameworks that govern the teaching profession). The higher the pupil to trained teacher ratio, the lower the relative access of pupils to trained teachers. Results can be compared with established national norms on the number of pupils per trained teacher for each level of education.
Physicians	Physicians, including general and specialist medical practitioners, expressed in terms of the number per 1,000 people.
Hospital Beds	In-patient beds for both acute and chronic care available in public, private, general, and specialized hospitals and rehabilitation centers expressed in terms of the number per 1,000 people.

(continued on next page)

Indicator	Definition
Number of Adults Living with HIV	All adults, defined as men and women aged 15 years and older, with HIV infection, whether or not they have developed symptoms of AIDS, estimated to be alive at the end of a specific year.
ECONOMY AND OUTPUT	
National Accounts	
Gross Domestic Product	Unduplicated market value of the total production activity of all resident producer units within the economic territory of an economy during a given period. It is calculated without making deductions for depreciation of fabricated assets or for depletion and degradation of natural resources. Transfer payments are excluded from the calculation of gross domestic product (GDP). GDP can be calculated using the production, expenditure, and income approaches. Production-based GDP is the sum of the gross value-added by all resident producers in the economy, plus any taxes and minus any subsidies not included in the value of the products. Gross value-added is the net output of an industry after adding up all outputs and subtracting intermediate inputs. Income-based GDP is the sum of the compensation of employees, mixed income, operating surplus, consumption of fixed capital, and taxes, less subsidies on production and imports. Expenditure-based GDP is the sum of final consumption expenditure of households, nonprofit institutions serving households, and the government; gross capital formation; and exports minus imports of goods and services. GDP can be measured at current prices (the prices of the current reporting period), and constant prices (obtained by expressing values in terms of a base period and chain volume measure).
GDP at PPP	Measures obtained by using PPP to convert the GDP into a common currency, and by valuing them at a uniform price level. They are the spatial equivalent of a time series of GDP for a single economy expressed at constant prices. At the level of GDP, they are used to compare the economic size of economies.
GDP at Current US Dollar	GDP at local currency units are obtained from the economy sources and are converted to US dollars using the official exchange rates from the International Monetary Fund (IMF). The exchange rates used are expressed as the average rate for a period of time (average of period), calculated as annual averages based on the monthly averages (local currency units relative to the US dollar).
GDP per Capita at PPP	GDP at PPP, divided by the midyear population.
GNI per Capita, Atlas Method	The gross national income (GNI) converted to US dollars using the World Bank Atlas method, divided by the midyear population. GNI is the sum of value-added by all resident producers, plus any product taxes (less subsidies) not included in the valuation of output, plus net receipts of primary income (compensation of employees and property income) from abroad. GNI, calculated in national currency, is usually converted to US dollars at official exchange rates for comparisons across economies, although an alternative rate is used when the official exchange rate is judged to diverge by an exceptionally large margin from the rate actually applied in international transactions. To smooth fluctuations in prices and exchange rates, a special Atlas method of conversion is used by the World Bank. This applies a conversion factor that averages the exchange rate for a given year and the 2 preceding years, adjusted for differences in rates of inflation between the economy, and through 2000, the G-5 economies (France, Germany, Japan, the United Kingdom, and the US). From 2001, these economies include the Euro area, Japan, the United Kingdom, and the US.
GDP per Capita at Current US Dollar	GDP at current US dollar value, divided by the midyear population.
Agriculture Value-Added	The gross output of the agriculture sector, less the corresponding value of intermediate consumption. The industrial origin of value-added is determined by ISIC revision 4, where agriculture corresponds to ISIC Section A and includes agriculture, forestry, and fishing.

(continued on next page)

Indicator	Definition
Industry Value-Added	The gross output of industry sectors, less the corresponding value of intermediate consumption. The industrial origin of value-added is determined by ISIC revision 4, where industry corresponds to ISIC Sections B-F and includes mining and quarrying (B); manufacturing (C); electricity, gas, steam, and air-conditioning supply (D); water supply; sewerage, waste management, and remediation activities (E); and construction (F).
Services Value-Added	The gross output of services sectors, less the corresponding value of intermediate consumption. The industrial origin of value-added is determined by ISIC revision 4, where services corresponds to ISIC Sections G-U and includes wholesale and retail trade; repair of motor vehicles and motorcycles (G); transport and storage (H); accommodation and food service activities (I); information and communication (J); financial and insurance activities (K); real estate activities (L); professional, scientific, and technical activities (M); administrative and support service activities (N); public administration and defense; compulsory social security (O); education (P); human health and social work activities (Q); arts, entertainment, and recreation (R); other service activities (S); activities of households as employers; undifferentiated goods- and services-producing activities of households for own use (T); and activities of extraterritorial organizations and bodies (U).
Household Consumption Expenditure	Market value of all goods and services, including durable products (such as cars, washing machines, and home computers), purchased or received as income in kind by households. It excludes purchases of dwellings but includes imputed rent for owner-occupied dwellings. It also includes payments and fees to governments to obtain permits and licenses. The expenditure of nonprofit institutions serving households is generally included for most economies.
Government Consumption Expenditure	Includes all current outlays on purchases of goods and services (including wages and salaries of government employees). It also includes most expenditure on national defense and security but excludes government military expenditures that are part of public investment.
Gross Capital Formation	Total value of gross fixed capital formation, changes in inventories, and acquisitions less disposals of valuables. Gross fixed capital formation is the total value of a producer's acquisitions, less disposals, of tangible goods (such as buildings) and intangible goods (such as computer software) that are intended for use in production during several accounting periods, plus certain specified expenditure on services that adds to the value of non-produced assets. Changes in inventories are changes in stocks of produced goods and goods for intermediate consumption, and the net increase in the value of work in progress. Valuables are goods (such as precious metals and works of art) that are not used up in production but are acquired as stores of value in the expectation that they will retain or increase their value over time.
Exports of Goods and Services	Consist of sales, bartering, or gifts or grants of goods and services from residents to nonresidents. The treatment of exports in the System of National Accounts is generally identical with that in the balance of payments accounts as described in the IMF's Balance of Payments Manual.
Imports of Goods and Services	Consist of purchases, bartering, or receipts of gifts or grants of goods and services by residents from nonresidents. The treatment of imports in the System of National Accounts is generally identical to that in the balance of payments accounts as described in the IMF's Balance of Payments Manual.
Gross Domestic Saving	Difference between GDP and final consumption expenditure, where final consumption expenditure is the sum of the final consumption of household, nonprofit institutions serving households, and the government.
Production	
Agriculture Production Index	Relative level of the aggregate volume of agricultural production for each year in comparison with the base period. It is based on the sum of price-weighted quantities of different agricultural commodities produced.
Manufacturing Production Index	An index covering production in manufacturing. The exact coverage, the weighting system, and the methods of calculation vary from economy to economy, but the divergences are less important than, for example, in the case of price and wage indexes.

(continued on next page)

Indicator	Definition
MONEY, FINANCE, AND PRICES	
Prices	
Consumer Price Index	An index that measures changes in prices against a reference period of a basket of goods and services purchased by households. Based on the purpose of the consumer price index, different baskets of goods and services can be selected. For macroeconomic purposes, a broad-based basket is used to represent the relative price movement of household final consumption expenditure.
Food and Nonalcoholic Beverages Price Index	An index that covers food and nonalcoholic beverages purchased by the household mainly for consumption or preparation at home including services for food processing for own consumption. The index corresponds to Classification of Individual Consumption by Purpose (COICOP) Version 1999 and 2018 division 01. Excluded are food and nonalcoholic beverages that are provided as part of a food-serving service under COICOP division 11: restaurants and hotels (COICOP Version 1999) or restaurants and accommodation services (COICOP Version 2018).
Alcoholic Beverages, Tobacco, and Narcotics Price Index	An index that covers the purchase of alcoholic beverages, tobacco, and narcotics, regardless of where these are consumed, but not provided as part of a food-and-beverage-serving service under hotels and restaurants. Services for the production of alcohol for own consumption are also included. The index corresponds to COICOP division 02. Excluded are alcoholic beverages purchased for immediate consumption in hotels, restaurants, cafes, bars, kiosks, street vendors, automatic vending machines, etc. classified under restaurants, cafes, and the like (COICOP Group 11.1.1).
Clothing and Footwear Price Index	An index that covers all clothing materials, garments, articles and accessories, footwear and related services, including cleaning, repair, and hire of clothing and footwear, and the purchase of secondhand clothing and footwear. The index corresponds to COICOP division 03.
Housing, Water, Electricity, Gas, and Other Fuels Price Index	An index that covers goods and services for the use of the house or dwelling and its maintenance and repair; the supply of water and miscellaneous services related to the dwelling; and energy used for heating or cooling. The index corresponds to COICOP division 04.
Furnishings, Household Equipment, and Routine Household Maintenance Price Index	An index that covers a wide range of products to equip the house or dwelling and the household durables, semidurables, and nondurables as well as some household services. Includes all kinds of furniture (including lightning equipment, household textiles, glassware, tableware and household utensils), major and smaller electric household appliances, tools and equipment for house and garden, and goods for routine household maintenance. The index also includes the repair, installation, and rental services of the goods. Domestic services by paid staff in private service, supplied by enterprises or self-employed persons, window-cleaning and disinfecting services, as well as dry-cleaning and laundering of household textiles and carpets, are also included. The index corresponds to COICOP division 05.
Health Price Index	An index that covers health services provided during an overnight stay, services that do not require an overnight stay, diagnostic imaging services, medical laboratory services, patient emergency transportation, and emergency rescue services. The index also includes medicines and health products, covering all products that are separately invoiced from health services, except when administered under the direct supervision of a health care professional during an overnight stay. The index corresponds to COICOP division 06.
Transport Price Index	An index that covers four main categories of goods and services for transportation: (i) purchase of vehicles covers motor cars, motor cycles, bicycles, and animal-drawn vehicles; (ii) goods and services for the operation of the personal transport equipment cover parts and accessories for personal transport equipment, fuels and lubricants, and the repair and maintenance of personal transport equipment including expenditures for parking spaces in garages or in public places, expenditures for tolls, and expenditures to acquire a driving certificate; (iii) transport services provided by the market, structured by the mode of transport; and (iv) transport services of goods covers postal and courier services, removal and storage

(continued on next page)

Indicator	Definition
	services, and the delivery of any kinds of goods when charged separately. The index corresponds to COICOP division 07. It excludes purchases of recreational vehicles such as camper vans, caravans, trailers, aeroplanes, and boats that are classified under the Recreation and Culture Price Index (COICOP Version 1999) or Recreation, Sport, and Culture (COICOP Version 2018).
Communication Price Index/Information and Communication Price Index	The index corresponds to division 08 in COICOP versions 1999 and 2018. In COICOP Version 1999, this index covers three main groups of goods and services: (i) information and communication equipment, including equipment for the capture, recording, and reproduction of sound and vision; software; and information and communication services; (ii) information and communication services, including telephones and other communication services; internet access services; television and radio licenses; fee and subscription services, including streaming services of films and music; and (iii) repair, maintenance, and rental of information and communication equipment. In COICOP Version 2018, this index covers three main groups and services: (i) information and communication equipment, including equipment for the reception, recording, and reproduction of sound and vision; (ii) software; and (iii) information and communication services, which include telephone and other communication services, internet access services, television and radio licences, fee and subscription services (including streaming services of films and music); and repair, maintenance, and hire of information and communication equipment.
Recreation and Culture Price Index/ Recreation, Sport, and Culture Price Index	An index that covers a wide range of goods and services for recreation, sport, and culture and is structured into eight groups: (i) recreation durables such as photographic equipment, other major durables for recreation, such as camper vans, boats, yachts, aeroplanes, and the like; (ii) nonmajor durable recreational goods such as games and toys, including video game computers, celebration articles, equipment for sport, camping, and open-air recreation; (iii) garden products and plants and flowers and purchases of pets and expenditures for pets, excluding veterinary services; (iv) recreational services cover rental, maintenance, and repair of goods, veterinary and other services for pets, recreational and leisure services, such as amusement parks, games of chance and expenditures for sporting services, both expenditures for practicing sports as well as expenditures for attendance of sport events; (v) cultural goods such as musical instruments and audio-visual media; (vi) cultural services such as cinemas, theatres, concerts, museums, and other cultural sites, and photographic services; (vii) newspapers, all kinds of books, stationery and drawing materials; and (viii) package holidays that include transportation, accommodation, food provision, or tour guide. The index corresponds to COICOP division 09.
Education Price Index/Education Services Price Index	An index that covers educational services only. It includes: (i) education by radio or television broadcasting as well as e-learning and correspondence courses; (ii) admission and registration fees as well as tuition fees; and (iii) other education-related fees such as camps and/or field trips, course fees, diploma fees, examination fees, graduation fees, laboratory fees, physical education fees, etc. The index corresponds to COICOP division 10. It excludes expenditures on other education-related goods and services such as school uniforms, education support services, such as health-care services, transport services (except in the case of excursions that are part of the normal school program), text books and academic journals, stationery, catering services, and accommodation services.
Restaurants and Hotels Price Index / Restaurants and Accommodation Service Price Index	An index that covers food and beverage services provided by restaurants, cafes, and similar facilities, either with full or limited- or self-service, or by canteens, cafeterias, or refectories at work or at school and other educational establishment's premises. It also includes catering services and accommodation services. Services for visitors and other travellers away from their principal or secondary residence are included. If not separately invoiced, it also includes food and beverage services and other serving services, such as housekeeping, parking, laundry, swimming pools and exercise rooms, recreational facilities, and conference and convention facilities. The index corresponds to COICOP division 11.

(continued on next page)

Indicator	Definition
Insurance and Financial Services Price Index	An index that covers insurance and financial services. Insurance and financial services are provided by financial corporations. Insurance services are subdivided by type of insurance. Financial services are subdivided by financial intermediation services indirectly measured and by other forms of actual and indirect charges and remittance fees for financial services. For the definition and measurement of insurance and financial services, specific national accounts concepts (under the 2008 System of National Accounts) do apply. The index corresponds to COICOP Version 2018 division 12.
Miscellaneous Goods and Services Price Index	An index that covers insurance and financial services. It also includes personal care, prostitution, personal effects not elsewhere classified, social protection, financial services not elsewhere classified, and other services not elsewhere classified. The index corresponds to COICOP Version 1999 division 12.
Personal Care, Social Protection, and Miscellaneous Goods and Services Price Index	An index that covers goods and services for personal care, jewelry and watches, services of social protection, and all other services for households, which are not elsewhere classified. Goods and services for personal care cover electric and nonelectric appliances for personal care as well as hairdressing services. Goods of personal effects cover jewelry and watches, celebratorial and devotional items, and travel goods and items. Social protection services cover childcare, nonmedical retirement homes for elderly persons and disabled persons, and services to maintain persons in their private homes and related services. This index also covers all the other services for households, which are not elsewhere classified, such as fees for legal and administrative services, fees for real estate agencies, charges for undertaking, and payments for various personal services. This index also includes religious services. The index corresponds to COICOP Version 2018 division 13.
Wholesale Price Index	A measure that reflects changes in the prices paid for goods at various stages of distribution up to the point of retail. It can include prices of raw materials for intermediate and final consumption, prices of intermediate or unfinished goods, and prices of finished goods. The goods are usually valued at purchasers' prices.
Producer Price Index	A measure of the change in the prices of goods and services, either as they leave their place of production or as they enter the production process. A measure of the change in the prices received by domestic producers for their outputs or of the change in the prices paid by domestic producers for their intermediate inputs.
GDP Deflator	A measure of the annual rate of price change in the economy as a whole for the period shown, obtained by dividing GDP at current prices by GDP at constant prices.
Money and Finance	
Money Supply	Refers to the total amount of money in circulation in a specific economy. Money supply can be measured in different ways: M1 (Narrow Money) is a measure of money supply that includes all coins and notes (M0) as well as personal money in current accounts. M2 (Intermediate Money) is the sum of M1 and personal money in deposit accounts. M3 (Broad Money) is the sum of M2 and government and other deposits. According to the Organization for Economic Co-operation and Development, M3 includes currency, deposits with an agreed maturity of up to 2 years, deposits redeemable at notice of up to 3 months and repurchase agreements, money market fund shares or units, and debt securities up to 2 years. Not all economies publish the same types of aggregates, and even when aggregates are the same name (e.g., M1, M2, M3, etc.), their asset composition often differs significantly. Cross-economy differences in national definitions of lowered-ordered aggregates also arise from differences in the maturity categories of nontransferable deposits included in a particular money aggregate. For example, the definition of M2 in one economy may include time deposits with maturities of 1 year or less, whereas another economy's M2 definition may include time deposits with maturities of 2 years or less.

(continued on next page)

Indicator	Definition
	When the monetary policy strategy consists of monetary aggregate targeting, the choice of the definition of the targeted aggregate is guided mainly by two considerations. The aggregate should be sufficiently sensitive to interest rate changes for the central bank to be able to control it and display a stable relationship over time to the movement of the overall price level. Liabilities excluded from broad money are the sum of all exclusions from broad money. They may include deposits; debt securities; loans; insurance, pension, and standardized guarantee schemes; financial derivatives and employee stock options; trade credit and advances; equity; or other items.
Interest Rate on Savings Deposits	Rate paid by commercial and similar banks for savings deposits.
Interest Rate on Time Deposits	Rate paid by commercial and similar banks for time deposits.
Lending Interest Rate	Bank rate that usually meets the short- and medium-term financing needs of the private sector. This rate is normally differentiated according to creditworthiness of borrowers and objectives of financing.
Yield on Short-Term Treasury Bills	Rate at which short-term securities are issued or traded in the market.
Domestic Credit Provided by Banking Sector	Includes all credits to various sectors on a gross basis, except credit to the central government, which is net. The banking sector includes monetary authorities, deposit money banks, and other banking institutions for which data are available (including institutions that do not accept transferable deposits but do incur such liabilities as time and savings deposits). Examples of other banking institutions are savings and mortgage loan institutions and building and loan associations.
Ratio of Bank Nonperforming Loans to Total Gross Loans	Value of nonperforming loans divided by the total value of the loan portfolio (including nonperforming loans before the deduction of loan loss provisions). The amount recorded as nonperforming should be the gross value of the loan as recorded in the balance sheet, not just the amount that is overdue.
Stock Market Price Index	Index that measures changes in the prices of stocks traded in the stock exchange. The price changes of the stocks are usually weighted by their market capitalization.
Stock Market Capitalization	The share price times the number of shares outstanding (including their several classes) for listed domestic companies. Investment funds, unit trusts, and companies whose only business goal is to hold shares of other listed companies are excluded. Data are end of year values converted to US dollars using corresponding year-end foreign exchange rates. Also known as market value.
Exchange Rates	
Official Exchange Rate	The exchange rate determined by national authorities or the rate determined in the legally sanctioned exchange market. It is calculated as an annual average based on the monthly averages (local currency units relative to the US dollar).
Purchasing Power Parity Conversion Factor	Number of units of economy B's currency that are needed in economy B to purchase the same quantity of an individual good or service, which one unit of economy A's currency can purchase in economy A.
Price Level Index	Ratio of the relevant PPP to the exchange rate. It is expressed as an index on a base of 100. A price level index (PLI) greater than 100 means that, when the national average prices are converted at exchange rates, the resulting prices tend to be higher on average than prices in the base economy (or economies) of the region (and vice versa). At the level of GDP, PLIs provide a measure of the differences in the general price levels of economies. PLIs are also referred to as comparative price levels.
GLOBALIZATION	
Balance of Payments	
Trade in Goods Balance	Difference between exports and imports of goods.
Trade in Services Balance	Difference between exports and imports of services.
Current Account Balance	Sum of net exports of goods, services, net income, and net current transfers.

(continued on next page)

Indicator	Definition
Total Remittances	Sum of personal remittances and social benefits. Personal remittances include personal transfers (part of current transfers); compensation of employees less taxes, social contributions, transport, and travel; and capital transfers between households. Social benefits include benefits payable under social security funds and pension funds: they may be in cash or in kind. Includes income from individuals working abroad for short periods, income from individuals residing abroad, and social benefits from abroad.
Foreign Direct Investment	Refers to net inflows of investment to acquire a lasting management interest (10% or more of voting stock) in an enterprise operating in an economy other than that of the investor. It is the sum of equity capital, reinvestment of earnings, other long-term capital, and short-term capital as shown in the balance of payments.
External Trade	
Merchandise Exports and Imports	Covering all movable goods, with a few specified exceptions, the ownership of which changes between a resident and a foreigner. For merchandise exports, it represents the value of the goods and related distributive services at the customs frontier of the exporting economy, i.e., the free on board (FOB) value. Merchandise imports, on the other hand, are reported in cost, insurance, and freight (CIF) values.
Trade in Goods	Sum of merchandise exports and merchandise imports.
Direction of Trade	
Direction of Trade: Merchandise Exports and Imports	The direction of trade represents the value of merchandise exports and imports disaggregated according to an economy's primary trading partners. Imports are reported on a CIF basis and exports are reported on a FOB basis, with the exception of a few economies for which imports are also available in FOB. Time series data includes estimates derived from reports of partner economies for nonreporting and slow-reporting economies.
International Reserves	
International Reserves	External assets that are readily available to, and controlled by, monetary authorities for meeting balance-of-payments financing needs, for intervention in exchange markets to affect the currency exchange rate, and for other related purposes (such as maintaining confidence in the currency and the economy and serving as a basis for foreign borrowing). Consist of monetary gold, special drawing rights holdings, reserve position in the IMF, currency and deposits, securities (including debt and equity securities), financial derivatives, and other claims (loans and other financial instruments).
Ratio of International Reserves to Imports	International reserves outstanding at the end of the year as a proportion of imports of goods from the balance of payments during the year, where imports of goods are expressed in terms of a monthly average. It is a useful measure for reserve needs of economies with limited access to capital markets.
Capital Flows	
Net Official Development Assistance	Concessional flows to developing economies and multilateral institutions provided by official agencies, including state and local governments, or by their executing agencies, administered with the objective of promoting the economic development and welfare of developing economies, and containing a grant element of at least 25%. Net flow takes into account principal repayments for loans, offsetting entries for forgiven debt, and recoveries made on grants.
Net Other Official Flows	Official sector transactions with economies on the Development Assistance Committee List of Official Development Assistance Recipients, which do not meet the conditions for eligibility as official development assistance, either because they are not primarily aimed at development, or because they have a grant element of less than 25%. The Development Assistance Committee list of recipients of official development assistance is available at http://www.oecd.org/dac/financing-sustainable-development/development-finance-standards/daclist.htm. Net flow takes into account principal repayments for loans, offsetting entries for forgiven debt, and recoveries made on grants.

(continued on next page)

Indicator	Definition
Net Private Flows	Sum of direct investment and portfolio investment. Direct investment is a category of international investment made by a resident entity in one economy (direct investor) with the objective of establishing a lasting interest in an enterprise that is resident in an economy other than that of the investor (direct investment enterprise). "Lasting interest" implies the existence of a long-term relationship between the direct investor and the enterprise and a significant degree of influence by the direct investor on the management of the direct investment enterprise. Direct investment involves both the initial transaction between the two entities and all subsequent capital transactions between them and among affiliated enterprises, both incorporated and unincorporated. Portfolio investment is the category of international investment that covers investment in equity and debt securities, excluding any such instruments that are classified as direct investment or reserve assets.
Aggregate Net Resource Flows	Sum of net official development assistance, net other official flows, and net private flows.
External Indebtedness	
Total External Debt	Debt owed to nonresidents repayable in currency, goods, or services. It is the sum of public, publicly guaranteed, and private nonguaranteed long-term debt, use of IMF credit, and short-term debt. Short-term debt includes all debt having an original maturity of 1 year or less and interest in arrears on long-term debt.
Public and Publicly Guaranteed Debt	Comprises long-term external obligations of public debtors, including the national government, political subdivisions (or an agency of either), and autonomous public bodies, and external obligations of private debtors that are guaranteed for repayment by a public entity.
External Debt as a Percentage of GNI	Total external debt as a percentage of GNI. GNI is the sum of value-added by all resident producers plus any product taxes (less subsidies) not included in the valuation of output, plus net receipts of primary income (compensation of employees and property income) from abroad.
External Debt as a Percentage of Exports of Goods and Services and Primary Income	Total external debt as a percentage of exports of goods, services, and primary income. Exports of goods, services, and primary income constitute the total value of exports of goods and services, receipts of compensation of nonresident workers, and investment income from abroad.
Total Debt Service Paid	The sum of principal repayments and interest actually paid in currency, goods, or services on long-term debt, interest paid on short-term debt, and repayments (repurchases and charges) to the IMF.
Total Debt Service Paid as a Percentage of Exports of Goods and Services and Primary Income	Total debt service paid as a percentage of exports of goods, services, and primary income.
Tourism	
International Tourist Arrivals	The number of tourists (overnight visitors) who travel to an economy other than that in which they usually reside, and outside their usual environment, for a period not exceeding 12 months, and whose main purpose of visit is other than the activity remunerated from within the economy visited. In some cases, data may also include same-day visitors when data on overnight visitors are not available separately. Data refer to the number of arrivals and not to the number of people.
International Tourism, Receipts	The receipts earned by a destination economy from inbound tourism and covering all tourism receipts resulting from expenditures made by visitors from abroad. These include lodging, food and drinks, fuel, transport in the economy, entertainment, shopping, etc. This concept includes receipts generated by overnight visits as well as by same-day trips. It does, however, exclude the receipts related to international transport by contracted residents of the other economies (for instance ticket receipts from foreigners travelling with a national company).

(continued on next page)

Indicator	Definition
TRANSPORT AND COMMUNICATIONS	
Transport	
Road Network	This includes both paved and unpaved roads. Paved roads are roads surfaced with crushed stone (macadam) with hydrocarbon binder or bituminized agents, with concrete, or with cobblestones. Unpaved roads are roads surfaced with a stabilized base, but not surfaced with crushed stone, hydrocarbon binder or bituminized agents, concrete, or cobblestones.
Passenger Kilometers Traveled	A passenger-kilometer is a unit of measurement representing the transport of 1 passenger by a defined mode of transport, e.g., road, over 1 kilometer.
Freight Kilometers Traveled	A ton-kilometer is a unit of measurement representing the transport of 1 metric ton of goods (including packaging and tare weights of intermodal transport units) by a defined mode of transport, e.g., road, over a distance of 1 kilometer. Only the distance on the national territory of the reporting economy is taken into account for national, international, and transit transport.
Registered Vehicles	Mode-specific vehicle registrations refer to the number of newly (first-time) registered vehicles recorded by the authorities. This publication reports cumulative number of vehicle registrations.
Road Traffic Deaths	Death caused by a road traffic crash and occurring within 24 hours (Kiribati, the Federated States of Micronesia, Solomon Islands, Timor-Leste, Tonga); 7 days (Azerbaijan, Bhutan, the People's Republic of China, Tajikistan, Turkmenistan, Viet Nam); 30 days (Armenia, Australia, Cambodia, Fiji, India, Indonesia, Japan, Kazakhstan, the Republic of Korea, Lao PDR , Malaysia, Mongolia, Myanmar[1], Nepal, New Zealand, Papua New Guinea, Singapore, Sri Lanka, Uzbekistan); unlimited time period (Afghanistan[2], the Cook Islands, Georgia, Maldives, the Philippines, Samoa, Thailand); within a year (the Kyrgyz Republic); no definition for other economies.
Rail Lines	Rail lines are the length of railway route available for train service, irrespective of the number of parallel tracks.
Rail Network	Length of rail lines divided by the land area.
Railways, Passengers Carried	Passengers carried by railway are the number of passengers transported by rail multiplied by kilometers traveled.
Railways, Goods Transported	Goods transported by railway are the volume of goods transported by railway, measured in metric tons multiplied by kilometers traveled.
Aviation Total Passenger Kilometers	The number of aviation passengers carried, including both domestic and international aircraft passengers of air carriers registered in a given economy, multiplied by kilometers traveled.
Aviation Freight Transport	The volume of aviation freight, express, and diplomatic bags carried on each flight stage (operation of an aircraft from takeoff to its next landing), measured in metric tons, multiplied by kilometers traveled.
Container Port Traffic	Measures the flow of containers from land to sea transport modes, and vice versa, in twenty-foot equivalent units (TEU), a standard-size container. Data refer to coastal shipping as well as international journeys. Transshipment traffic is counted as two lifts at the intermediate port (once to offload and again as an outbound lift) and includes empty units.

1 ADB placed on hold its assistance in Myanmar effective 1 February 2021 (https://www.adb.org/publications/myanmar-fact-sheet).

2 ADB placed on hold its assistance in Afghanistan effective 15 August 2021 (https://www.adb.org/news/adb-statement-afghanistan).

(continued on next page)

Indicator	Definition
Liner Shipping Connectivity Index (LSCI)	The current version of the LSCI is generated from the following six components: (i) the number of scheduled ship calls per week in the economy; (ii) deployed annual capacity in TEU: total deployed capacity offered at the economy; (iii) the number of regular liner shipping services from and to the economy; (iv) the number of liner shipping companies that provide services from and to the economy; (v) the average size in TEU of the ships deployed by the scheduled service with the largest average vessel size; and (vi) the number of other economies that are connected to the economy through direct liner shipping services.
Logistics Performance Index	An interactive benchmarking tool created by the World Bank to help economies identify the challenges and opportunities they face in their performance on trade logistics and what they can do to improve their performance.
Communications	
Telephone Subscribers	Fixed-telephone subscriptions refer to the sum of active number of analogue fixed telephone lines, voice-over-IP subscriptions, fixed wireless local loop subscriptions, ISDN voice-channel equivalents, and fixed public payphones.
Mobile Phone Subscribers	The proportion of individuals who used a mobile telephone in the 3 months prior to data collection. A mobile (cellular) telephone refers to a portable telephone subscribing to a public mobile telephone service using cellular technology, which provides access to the PSTN. This includes analogue and digital cellular systems and technologies such as IMT-2000 (3G) and IMT- Advanced. Users of both postpaid subscriptions and prepaid accounts are included.
Fixed-Broadband Subscribers	Fixed-broadband subscriptions refer to fixed subscriptions to high-speed access to the public internet (a TCP/IP connection), at downstream speeds equal to, or greater than, 256 kilobits per second. This includes cable modem, DSL, fiber-to-the-home/building, other fixed (wired)- broadband subscriptions, satellite broadband and terrestrial fixed wireless broadband. This total is measured irrespective of the method of payment. It excludes subscriptions that have access to data communications (including the Internet) via mobile-cellular networks. It should include fixed WiMAX and any other fixed wireless technologies. It includes both residential subscriptions and subscriptions for organizations.
Internet Users	The frequency of internet use by individuals who used the internet from any location in the 3 months prior to data collection. Internet can be used via a computer, mobile, phone, personal digital assistant, games machine, digital TV, etc.
ENERGY AND ELECTRICITY	
Energy	
GDP per Unit of Energy Use	The ratio of GDP to total energy use (measured per petajoule) with GDP converted to 2017 constant international dollars using PPP rates. An international dollar has the same purchasing power over GDP as a US dollar has in the US.
Energy Production	Primary energy production that is the capture or extraction of fuels or energy from natural energy flows, the biosphere, and natural reserves of fossil fuels within the national territory in a form suitable for use. Inert matter removed from the extracted fuels and quantities reinjected, flared, or vented are not included. The resulting products are referred to as primary products.
Energy Use	Energy production plus imports minus exports, minus international marine bunkers, minus international aviation bunkers, minus stock changes. Also referred to as energy supply.
Energy Imports, Net	Energy imports, net estimated as energy use less production, both measured in petajoules.

(continued on next page)

Indicator	Definition
Electricity	
Electricity Production	Gross production, which is the sum of the electrical energy production by all the generating units and/or installations concerned (including pumped storage), measured at the output terminals of the main generators. Also referred to as electricity generation.
Sources of Electricity	Refers to the different types of technology and/or processes for the generation or production of electricity, including: (i) electricity from combustible fuels, which refers to the production of electricity from the combustion of fuels that are capable of igniting or burning, i.e., reacting with oxygen to produce a significant rise in temperature; (ii) hydroelectricity, which refers to electricity produced from devices driven by flowing, or falling fresh water; (iii) nuclear electricity, which refers to electricity generated by nuclear plants; and (iv) other electricity, which includes solar, wind, wave, tidal, other marine electricity, geothermal, electricity generated from chemical heat, and electricity from other sources not elsewhere specified.
Electric Power Consumption Per Capita	Total electricity consumption divided by midyear population, where consumption refers to energy-industries-own-use and final consumption. Energy-industries-own-use refers to the consumption of electricity for the direct support of the production and preparation for use of fuels and energy. Final consumption refers to the consumption of electricity by manufacturing, construction and nonfuel mining, transport, and households and other consumers (nonenergy use being irrelevant for electricity).
ENVIRONMENT	
Land	
Agricultural Land or Area	Land area that is arable, under permanent crops, and/or under permanent meadows and pastures.
Arable Land	Land under temporary agricultural crops (double-cropped areas are counted only once), temporary meadows for mowing or pasture, land under market, and kitchen gardens and land temporarily fallow (less than 5 years). The abandoned land resulting from shifting cultivation is not included. Data for arable land are not meant to indicate the amount of land that are potentially cultivable.
Permanent Cropland	Land cultivated with long-term crops that do not have to be replanted for several years (such as cocoa and coffee); land under trees and shrubs producing flowers, such as roses and jasmine; and nurseries (except those for forest trees, which should be classified under "forestry"). Permanent meadows and pastures are excluded from land under permanent crops.
Deforestation Rate	Rate of permanent conversion of natural forest area into other uses, including shifting cultivation, permanent agriculture, ranching, settlements, and infrastructure development. Deforested areas do not include areas logged but intended for regeneration or areas degraded by fuelwood gathering, acid precipitation, or forest fires. A negative rate indicates reforestation or increase in forest area.
Pollution	
Carbon Dioxide Emissions	Carbon dioxide emissions, largely by-products of energy production and use, account for the largest share of greenhouse gases, which are associated with global warming. Anthropogenic carbon dioxide emissions result primarily from fossil fuel combustion and cement manufacturing. In combustion, different fossil fuels release different amounts of carbon dioxide for the same level of energy used: oil releases about 50% more carbon dioxide than natural gas, while coal releases about twice as much. Cement manufacturing releases about half a metric ton of carbon dioxide for each metric ton of cement produced. Data for carbon dioxide emissions include gases from the burning of fossil fuels and cement manufacture but excludes emissions from land use such as deforestation.
Nitrous Oxide Emissions	Nitrous oxide emissions are mainly from fossil fuel combustion, fertilizers, rainforest fires, and animal waste. Nitrous oxide is a powerful greenhouse gas, with an estimated atmospheric lifetime of 114 years, compared with 12 years for methane. The per-kilogram global warming potential of nitrous oxide is nearly 310 times that of carbon dioxide within 100 years.

(continued on next page)

Indicator	Definition
Methane Emissions	Methane emissions are those stemming from human activities including but not limited to agriculture and from industrial methane production. A kilogram of methane is 21 times as effective at trapping heat in the earth's atmosphere as a kilogram of carbon dioxide within 100 years.
Other Greenhouse Gases	By-product emissions of hydrofluorocarbons, perfluorocarbons, and sulfur hexafluoride. Although emissions of these artificial gases are small, they are more powerful greenhouse gases than carbon dioxide, with much higher atmospheric lifetimes and high global warming potential.
Freshwater	
Internal Renewable Water Resources	Internal renewable water resources (IRWR) refer to the long-term average annual flow of rivers and recharge of aquifers generated from endogenous precipitation. Double-counting of surface water and groundwater resources is avoided by deducting the overlap from the sum of the surface water and groundwater resources. IRWR in billion cubic meters per year refers to surface water produced internally, plus groundwater produced internally deducted by the overlap between surface water and groundwater. IRWR in cubic meters per inhabitant per year is calculated as total annual IRWR divided by total population.
Annual Freshwater Withdrawals	Sum of surface water withdrawal and groundwater withdrawal. Total water withdrawal summed by sector deducted by desalinated water produced, direct use of treated wastewater, and direct use of agricultural drainage water.
Water Productivity	Water productivity is the ratio of the net benefits from crop, forestry, fishery, livestock, and mixed agricultural systems to the amount of water used to produce those benefits. It is calculated as GDP in constant US dollar prices, divided by annual total water withdrawal.
GOVERNMENT AND GOVERNANCE	
Government Finance	
Government Net lending / Net borrowing	Net lending (+)/net borrowing (–) is a summary measure indicating the extent to which government is either putting financial resources at the disposal of other sectors in the economy or abroad, or utilizing the financial resources generated by other sectors in the economy or from abroad. It may be viewed as an indicator of the financial impact of government activity on the rest of the economy and the rest of the world. Net lending (+)/net borrowing (–) is a balancing item calculated as the net operating balance (revenue minus expense) minus the net investment in nonfinancial assets. Net lending/net borrowing is also equal to the net acquisition of all financial assets minus the net incurrence of all liabilities from transactions. For economies following the IMF's Government Finance Statistics 1986 framework, the indicator refers to the overall budgetary surplus/deficit measured as the difference between total revenue (including grants) and total expenditure (including net lending).
Government Taxes	Taxes are compulsory, unrequited amounts receivable by government units from institutional units. Certain compulsory receivables, such as fines, penalties, and most social security contributions are not considered taxes. For economies following the IMF's Government Finance Statistics 1986 framework, tax revenue are compulsory transfers to the central government for public purposes, which includes social security contributions.

Indicator	Definition
Government Revenue	Government revenue is an increase in net worth resulting from a transaction. Revenue transactions have counterpart entries either in an increase in assets or in a decrease in liabilities - thereby increasing net worth. General government units have four types of revenue: (i) compulsory levies in the form of taxes and certain types of social contributions; (ii) property income derived from the ownership of assets; (iii) sales of goods and services; and (iv) other transfers receivable from other units. For economies following the IMF's Government Finance Statistics 1986 framework, the total revenue (including grants) consists of current and capital revenues. Current revenue is the revenue accruing from taxes as well as all current nontax revenues, except transfers received from foreign governments and international institutions. Capital revenue constitutes the proceeds from the sale of nonfinancial capital assets.
Government Expenditure	Government expenditure is the sum of expense and the net investment in nonfinancial assets. Expense is a decrease in net worth resulting from a transaction. The major types of expense are compensation of employees, use of goods and services subsidies, grants, social benefits, and other expense. The acquisition of a nonfinancial asset by purchase or barter is not an expense because it has no effect on net worth. Similarly, amounts payable on loans extended and repayments on loans incurred are not classified as expense. Nonfinancial assets are economic assets other than financial assets. Nonfinancial assets are stores of value and provide benefits either through their use in the production of goods and services or in the form of property income and holding gains. These assets are classified as fixed assets, inventories, valuables, and nonproduced assets. For economies following the IMF's Government Finance Statistics 1986 framework, total expenditure (including net lending) consists of current and capital expenditures. Current expenditure comprises purchases of goods and services by the central government, transfers to noncentral government units and to households, subsidies to producers, and interest on public debt. Capital expenditure covers outlays for the acquisition or construction of capital assets and for the purchase of intangible assets, as well as capital transfers to domestic and foreign recipients. Loans and advances for capital purposes are also included.
Government Expenditure on Education	Government expenditure on education includes expenditure on services provided to individual pupils and students and expenditure on services provided on a collective basis. Expenditure on education is allocated to pre-primary and primary education, secondary education, post-secondary nontertiary education, tertiary education, subsidiary services to education, education not definable by level, and research and development (R&D) education. For economies following the IMF's Government Finance Statistics 1986 framework, the indicator refers to government expenditure on education affairs and services.
Government Expenditure on Health	Government expenditure on health includes expenditure on services provided to individual persons and services provided on a collective basis. Expenditure on health is allocated to medical products, appliances, and equipment; outpatient services; hospital services; public health services; R&D health; and health not elsewhere classified. For economies following the IMF's Government Finance Statistics 1986 framework, the indicator refers to government expenditure on health affairs and services.

(continued on next page)

Indicator	Definition
Government Expenditure on Social Protection	Government expenditure on social protection includes expenditure on services and transfers provided to individual persons and households and expenditure on services provided on a collective basis. Expenditure on social protection is allocated to sickness and disability, old age, survivors, family and children, unemployment, housing, social exclusion not elsewhere classified, and R&D social protection. For economies following the IMF's Government Finance Statistics 1986 framework, the indicator refers to government expenditure on social security and welfare affairs and services.
Governance	
Corruption Perceptions Index	Ranks economies and territories based on how corrupt or otherwise their public sector is perceived to be. It is a composite index—a combination of polls—drawing on corruption-related data collected by a variety of reputable institutions. The index reflects the views of observers from around the world, including experts living and working in the economies and territories evaluated. From 2000 to 2011, scores ranged from 10 (highly clean) to 0 (highly corrupt). From 2012 onward, calculation of the score has used an updated methodology and is now presented on a 100 (very clean) to 0 (highly corrupt) scale. Due to this difference in methodology, scores from years prior to and including 2011 should not be compared with scores from 2012 onward. An economy's rank indicates its position relative to the other economies or territories included in the index. It is important to keep in mind that an economy's rank can change simply because new economies enter the index or others drop out.

www.ingramcontent.com/pod-product-compliance
Lightning Source LLC
Chambersburg PA
CBHW060758240926
51847CB00020B/164
* 9 7 8 9 2 9 2 6 9 6 9 8 6 *